CompTIA®
IT Fundamentals
Study Guide

Quentin Docter

SYBEX®
A Wiley Brand

Senior Acquisitions Editor: Kenyon Brown
Development Editor: Kim Wimpsett
Technical Editors: Scott Johnson and Ian Seaton
Production Editor: Dassi Zeidel
Copy Editor: Linda Recktenwald
Editorial Manager: Mary Beth Wakefield
Production Manager: Kathleen Wisor
Associate Publisher: Jim Minatel
Supervising Producer: Rich Graves
Book Designers: Judy Fung and Bill Gibson
Proofreader: Josh Chase, Word One New York
Indexer: Ted Laux
Project Coordinator, Cover: Brent Savage
Cover Designer: Wiley
Cover Image: ©Getty Images Inc./Jeremy Woodhouse

In memory of grandpa Joe, who taught me the fundamentals of IT and so much more.

Acknowledgments

First and foremost, I need to thank my family. Without their support and patience, I would never be able to work on projects like this.

They say it takes a village to produce a book, and it always amazes me at the number of people who are involved. I have been fortunate to work with a great Sybex crew yet again. Kim Wimpsett was the development editor. Thanks, Kim, for keeping me on track, aware of the rules, and partially sane! Kenyon Brown is the acquisitions editor for this book—thank you, Kenyon, for asking me to take on this book.

In addition, Dassi Zeidel was an excellent production editor; I have had the pleasure of working with her before, and I appreciate her attention to detail. Scott Johnson was my technical editor—Scott, it was really good to get to work with you again. To Linda Recktenwald , the copy editor, thank you so much for dealing with my consistent grammar mistakes. I may not have the best grammar, but at least I am consistent about it!

About the Author

Quentin Docter started in the IT industry as a tech support agent for Packard Bell in 1994. Since then he has worked in tech support, network administration, consulting, training, web development, and project management. During his career, he has achieved certifications from CompTIA (including IT Fundamentals), Microsoft, Cisco, Novell, and Sun Microsystems. He is the author of several books, including the *CompTIA A+ Complete Study Guide* by Sybex, an imprint of Wiley.

Contents at a Glance

Contents

Appendixes   **579**

Table of Exercises

Becoming a CompTIA Certified IT Professional is Easy

It's also the best way to reach greater professional opportunities and rewards.

Why Get CompTIA Certified?

Growing Demand

Labor estimates predict some technology fields will experience growth of over 20% by the year 2020.* CompTIA certification qualifies the skills required to join this workforce.

Higher Salaries

IT professionals with certifications on their resume command better jobs, earn higher salaries and have more doors open to new multi-industry opportunities.***

Verified Strengths

91% of hiring managers indicate CompTIA certifications are valuable in validating IT expertise, making certification the best way to demonstrate your competency and knowledge to employers.**

Universal Skills

CompTIA certifications are vendor neutral—which means that certified professionals can proficiently work with an extensive variety of hardware and software found in most organizations.

 Learn > 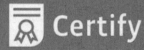 Certify >  Work

Learn more about what the exam covers by reviewing the following:

- Exam objectives for key study points.
- Sample questions for a general overview of what to expect on the exam and examples of question format.
- Visit online forums, like LinkedIn, to see what other IT professionals say about CompTIA exams.

Purchase a voucher at a Pearson VUE testing center or at CompTIAstore.com.

- Register for your exam at a Pearson VUE testing center.
- Visit pearsonvue.com/CompTIA to find the closest testing center to you.
- Schedule the exam online. You will be required to enter your voucher number or provide payment information at registration.
- Take your certification exam.

Congratulations on your CompTIA certification!

- Make sure to add your certification to your resume.
- Check out the CompTIA Certification Roadmap to plan your next career move.

Learn more: Certification.CompTIA.org/ITfundamentals

* Source: CompTIA 9th Annual Information Security Trends study: 500 U.S. IT and Business Executives Responsible for Security
** Source: CompTIA Employer Perceptions of IT Training and Certification
*** Source: 2013 IT Skills and Salary Report by CompTIA Authorized Partner

Introduction

If you're picking up this book, it means that it's likely that either you're thinking about getting into the IT industry or you are relatively new to it. Either way, you are probably getting advice from nearly everyone you meet. One of the common refrains you probably hear is "Get certified!" With so many certifications out there, you might wonder where to start—CompTIA IT Fundamentals is that place.

Certification is one of the best things you can do for your career if you are working in, or want to break into, the IT profession because it proves that you know what you're talking about regarding the subjects in which you're certified. It also powerfully endorses you as a professional in a way that's very similar to a physician being board certified in a certain area of expertise. It can add to your resume and make you more attractive to potential employers and more valuable as an employee. In these challenging economic times, keeping ahead of the competition—even standing out among your present colleagues—could make a big difference in whether you gain a promotion or possibly keep your job instead of being the one who gets laid off!

In this book, you'll find out what the IT Fundamentals exam is all about because each chapter covers a part of the exam. I've included some great review questions at the end of each chapter to help crystallize the information you learned and solidly prepare you to ace the exam.

A really cool thing about working in IT is that it's constantly evolving, so there are always new things to learn and fresh challenges to master. Once you obtain your IT Fundamentals certification and discover that you're interested in taking it further by getting into more complex topics (and making more money), the CompTIA A+ certification is definitely your next step.

What Is the CompTIA IT Fundamentals Certification?

IT Fundamentals is a certification developed by the Computing Technology Industry Association (CompTIA) that exists to provide resources and education for the computer and technology community. This is the same body that developed the A+ exam for PC technicians, Network+ for networking experts, and Security+ for security practitioners.

Way back in 1995, members of the organization got together to develop a new certification that tests skills for IT. To ensure industry-wide support, it was sponsored by many past and present IT industry leaders like these:

- Compaq Computers
- Digital Equipment Corporation (a part of Compaq)
- IBM
- Lotus
- Microsoft
- Novell
- TSS

- U.S. Robotics
- US West
- Wave Technologies

The IT Fundamentals exam was designed to test the skills of those with little to no experience in the field, but who want to show that they have a broad general understanding of core IT topics. It tests areas such as computer hardware, operating systems and applications, basic networking, security, and setting up and maintaining a computer.

Why Become IT Fundamentals Certified?

Because CompTIA is a well-respected developer of vendor-neutral industry certifications, becoming IT Fundamentals certified proves you have a base level of knowledge in the specific areas tested by the IT Fundamentals objectives.

Three major benefits are associated with becoming IT Fundamentals certified:

Proof of Professional Achievement   Computer professionals are pretty competitive when it comes to collecting more certifications than their peers. And because the IT Fundamentals certification broadly covers the entire field of computers, it's a great stepping-stone to prove that you have what it takes to succeed in this industry. Because it's rare to gain something that's worth a lot with little effort, I'll be honest—preparing for the IT Fundamentals exam isn't exactly a lazy day at the beach. But passing the test is worth it because it will get the attention of potential employers.

Opportunity for Advancement   We all like to get ahead in our careers—advancement results in more responsibility and prestige, and it usually means a fatter paycheck, greater opportunities, and added options. In the IT sector, a great way to make sure all that good stuff happens is by earning a lot of technology certifications, including IT Fundamentals.

Fulfillment of Training Requirements   IT Fundamentals, because of its wide-reaching industry support, is recognized as a baseline of computer knowledge. This can potentially fulfill IT-related training requirements set forth by your company.

Customer Confidence   As companies discover the CompTIA advantage, they will undoubtedly require qualified staff to achieve these certifications. Many companies outsource their work to consulting firms with experience working with security. Firms that have certified staff have a definite advantage over firms that don't.

How to Become IT Fundamentals Certified

As this book goes to press, Pearson VUE is the sole IT Fundamentals exam provider. The following are the necessary contact information and exam-specific details for registering. Exam pricing might vary by country or by CompTIA membership.

Vendor	Website	Phone Number
Pearson VUE	www.pearsonvue.com/comptia	U.S. and Canada: 877-551-PLUS (7587)

When you schedule the exam, you'll receive instructions regarding appointment and cancellation procedures, ID requirements, and information about the testing center location. In addition, you'll receive a registration and payment confirmation letter. Exams can be scheduled up to six weeks out or as late as the next day (or, in some cases, even the same day).

 Exam prices and codes may vary based on the country in which the exam is administered. For detailed pricing and exam registration procedures, refer to CompTIA's website at www.comptia.org.

After you've successfully passed your IT Fundamentals exam, CompTIA will award you a certification. Within four to six weeks of passing the exam, you'll receive your official CompTIA IT Fundamentals certificate and ID card. (If you don't receive these within eight weeks of taking the test, contact CompTIA directly using the information found in your registration packet.)

Tips for Taking the IT Fundamentals Exam

Here are some general tips for taking your exam successfully:

- Bring two forms of ID with you. One must be a photo ID, such as a driver's license. The other can be a major credit card or a passport. Both forms must include a signature.

- Arrive early at the exam center so you can relax and review your study materials, particularly tables and lists of exam-related information. Once you are ready to enter the testing room, you will need to leave everything outside; you won't be able to bring any materials into the testing area.

- Read the questions carefully. Don't be tempted to jump to an early conclusion. Make sure you know exactly what each question is asking.

- Don't leave any unanswered questions. Unanswered questions are scored against you. There will be questions with multiple correct responses. When there is more than one correct answer, a message at the bottom of the screen will prompt you to either "choose two" or "choose all that apply." Be sure to read the messages displayed to know how many correct answers you must choose.

- When answering multiple-choice questions you're not sure about, use a process of elimination to get rid of the obviously incorrect answers first. Doing so will improve your odds if you need to make an educated guess.

- On form-based tests (nonadaptive), because the hard questions will take the most time, save them for last. You can move forward and backward through the exam.

- For the latest pricing on the exams and updates to the registration procedures, visit CompTIA's website at www.comptia.org.

Who Should Read This Book?

You—if want to pass the IT Fundamentals exam and pass it confidently! This book is chock full of the exact information you need and directly maps to IT Fundamentals exam objectives (listed later in this introduction), so if you use it to study for the exam, your odds of passing shoot way up.

And in addition to including every bit of knowledge you need to learn to pass the exam, I've included some really great tips and solid wisdom to equip you even further to successfully work in the real IT world.

What Does This Book Cover?

This book covers everything you need to know to pass the CompTIA IT Fundamentals exam. But in addition to studying the book, it's a good idea to practice on actual computers if you can.

Here's a list of the 12 chapters in this book:

Chapter 1, "Core Hardware Components"   This chapter introduces you to the core insides of a computer, specifically motherboards, processors, memory, storage, expansion slots, power, and cooling systems.

Chapter 2, "Peripherals and Connectors"   While core hardware is important, users can truly customize their computer experience by adding peripheral hardware. To connect all of those toys to your system, you need to know which connectors to use, and this chapter teaches you all of that.

Chapter 3, "Operating Systems"   Without an operating system, computer hardware makes a pretty good doorstop. The operating system is the most critical piece of software on a computer, because it coordinates the efforts of the hardware and provides an interface for the user to interact with the machine.

Chapter 4, "Software Applications"   This chapter covers a variety of common application types that reside on computers, such as productivity software, collaboration software, antimalware utilities, and specialized software like games. It also teaches you the proper ways to install, uninstall, and manage applications.

Chapter 5, "Networking Technologies and Wireless Routers"   Who doesn't want to get on the Internet? Wireless routers are popular today as a method to get Internet connectivity. You'll learn about basic networking technologies and how to configure a wireless router in this chapter.

Chapter 6, "Network Sharing and Storage"   Building on the basic networking technologies in Chapter 5, this chapter shows you how to share resources on a network for other users to access, such as files and printers. It also introduces cloud computing and virtualization.

Chapter 7, "Mobile Devices"   It seems like mobile devices are everywhere, doesn't it? In this chapter, you will learn how to set up and configure mobile devices to participate on a network, as well as how to use devices from different platforms.

Chapter 8, "Security Threats"   The downside to computers is that it seems like hackers are everywhere. This chapter will introduce you to common threats posed by would-be attackers, so you know how to avoid them.

Chapter 9, "Security Best Practices"   This chapter builds on Chapter 8 by showing you how to set up your system to protect it against attacks. You will learn about concepts such as access control, device hardening, and safe web browsing and email use.

Chapter 10, "Buying and Configuring a Workstation"   Buying a new computer can be thrilling! Getting it home and having a tangled mess of wires can be a bit of a downer. In this chapter, you will understand what to look for in your ideal computer, as well as what to do when you get home to set it up so that it runs just as you want it to.

Chapter 11, "Computer Support and Backups"   Inevitably, computers will run into problems—it's the nature of electronic components. This chapter will show you how to troubleshoot any issues that pop up. Warning: after reading this chapter all of your family members will call on you for technical support (if they don't already)! This chapter also shows you how to back up your data so you don't have a catastrophic loss.

Chapter 12, "Environmental and Safety Concepts"   Working with computers isn't particularly dangerous, but there are some safety concepts to be aware of to protect yourself as well as your hardware from damage. And when you're ready to upgrade your gear, you should know how to safely dispose of old equipment.

What's Included in the Book

I've included several study learning tools throughout the book:

Assessment Test   At the end of this introduction is an Assessment Test that you can use to check your readiness for the exam. Take this test before you start reading the book; it will help you determine the areas you might need to brush up on. The answers to the Assessment Test questions appear on a separate page after the last question of the test. Each answer includes an explanation and a note telling you the chapter in which the material appears.

Objective Map and Opening List of Objectives   Just before the Assessment Test you'll find a detailed exam objective map, showing you where each of the exam objectives is covered in this book. In addition, each chapter opens with a list of the exam objectives it covers. Use these to see exactly where each of the exam topics is covered.

Exam Essentials   Each chapter, just after the summary, includes a number of exam essentials. These are the key topics you should take from the chapter in terms of areas to focus on when preparing for the exam.

Lab Exercises   Each chapter includes a hands-on lab to give you more experience. These exercises map to the exam objectives. Some ask specific questions, and the answers to these can be found in Appendix B.

Chapter Review Questions   To test your knowledge as you progress through the book, there are 20 review questions at the end of each chapter. As you finish each chapter, answer the review questions and then check your answers—the correct answers and explanations are in Appendix A. You can go back to reread the section that deals with each question you got wrong to ensure that you answer correctly the next time you're tested on the material.

Interactive Online Learning Environment and Test Bank

The interactive online learning environment that accompanies *CompTIA IT Fundamentals Study Guide: Exam FC0-U51* provides a test bank with study tools to help you prepare for the certification exam—and increase your chances of passing it the first time! The test bank includes the following:

Sample Tests   All of the questions in this book are provided, including the *Assessment Test*, which you'll find at the end of this introduction, and the *Chapter Tests*, which include the Review Questions at the end of each chapter. In addition, there are two *Practice Exams*. Use these questions to test your knowledge of the study guide material. The online test bank runs on multiple devices.

Flashcards   Questions are provided in digital flashcard format (a question followed by a single correct answer). You can use the flashcards to reinforce your learning and provide last-minute test prep before the exam.

Other Study Tools   A glossary of key terms from this book and their definitions is available as a fully searchable PDF.

Go to http://sybextestbanks.wiley.com to register and gain access to this interactive online learning environment and test bank with study tools.

How to Use This Book

If you want a solid foundation for the serious effort of preparing for the IT Fundamentals exam, then look no further because I've spent countless hours putting together this book with the sole intention of helping you to pass it!

This book is loaded with valuable information, and you will get the most out of your study time if you understand how I put the book together. Here's a list that describes how to approach studying:

1. Take the Assessment Test immediately following this introduction. (The answers are at the end of the test, but no peeking!) It's okay if you don't know any of the answers—that's what this book is for. Carefully read over the explanations for any question you get wrong, and make note of the chapters where that material is covered.

2. Study each chapter carefully, making sure you fully understand the information and the exam objectives listed at the beginning of each one. Again, pay extra-close attention to any chapter that includes material covered in questions you missed on the Assessment Test.

3. Complete the lab exercise at the end of each chapter. Do *not* skip these exercises. One reason is that they directly map to the CompTIA objectives and reinforce the material. Another reason is that it gives you hands-on experience, which is crucial.

4. Answer all the review questions related to each chapter. Specifically note any questions that confuse you, and study the corresponding sections of the book again. And don't just skim these questions—make sure you understand each answer completely.

5. Try your hand at the Practice Exams. The more questions you practice, the better you will be when you sit for the real exam.

6. Test yourself using all the electronic flashcards. This is a brand-new and updated flashcard program to help you prepare for the latest CompTIA IT Fundamentals exam, and it is a really great study tool.

Learning every bit of the material in this book is going to require applying yourself with a good measure of discipline. So try to set aside the same time period every day to study, and select a comfortable and quiet place to do so. If you work hard, you will be surprised at how quickly you learn this material.

If you follow the steps listed here and study with the Review Questions, Practice Exams, electronic flashcards, and all the written labs, you would almost have to try to fail the CompTIA IT Fundamentals exam. However, studying for the IT Fundamentals exam is like training for a marathon—if you don't go for a good run every day, you're not likely to finish very well.

Exam Objectives

Speaking of objectives, you're probably pretty curious about those, right? CompTIA asked groups of IT professionals to fill out a survey rating the skills they felt were important in their jobs, and the results were grouped into objectives for the exam and divided into five domains.

This table gives you the extent by percentage that each domain is represented with on the actual examination.

Domain	% of Examination
1.0 Software	21%
2.0 Hardware	18%
3.0 Security	21%
4.0 Networking	16%
5.0 Basic IT literacy	24%
Total	100%

Exam objectives are subject to change at any time without prior notice and at CompTIA's sole discretion. Please visit CompTIA's website (www.comptia.org) for the most current listing of exam objectives.

CompTIA IT Fundamentals Study Guide

FC0-U51 Exam Objectives

Exam specifications and content are subject to change at any time without prior notice and at CompTIA's sole discretion. Please visit CompTIA's website (www.comptia.org) for the most current information on the exam content.

Assessment Test

1. Which of the following optical discs will store the most data?
   A. CD-ROM
   B. DVD-ROM DL
   C. DVD-ROM DS
   D. RS-ROM

2. Which of the following devices are used to permanently store user data in a computer? Choose two.
   A. HDD
   B. RAM
   C. ROM
   D. SSD

3. Which of the following on your computer is considered firmware?
   A. RAM
   B. SSD
   C. CMOS
   D. BIOS

4. What was the first widely adopted video connector standard?
   A. CGA
   B. VGA
   C. XGA
   D. DVI

5. What type of removable storage is often used in digital cameras?
   A. Flash drive
   B. NAS
   C. Memory card
   D. Mobile media card

6. Which of the following devices is considered an input-only device?
   A. Scanner
   B. Printer
   C. Touchscreen
   D. Flash drive

7. Which operating system named its versions after large cats?

    A. iOS

    B. OS X

    C. Android

    D. Chrome OS

8. Your computer has a 64-bit CPU. Which statement is true regarding which operating systems you can install on it?

    A. 64-bit operating systems only.

    B. 64-bit or 32-bit operating systems.

    C. 32-bit operating systems only.

    D. It depends on how much RAM your system has.

9. What happens to a file when you move it from one directory to another in Windows on the same hard drive?

    A. It gets erased from the original location and re-created in the new location.

    B. It is maintained in the original location and re-created in the new location.

    C. Nothing happens to the file; the metadata gets changed pointing to the new directory.

    D. Nothing happens to the file.

10. A .flac file is an example of what type of file?

    A. Image

    B. Video

    C. Audio

    D. Compressed

11. You are configuring some Windows computers for an office, and the manager tells you that employees should not be able to play the games. What should you do?

    A. Uninstall the games from within Control Panel.

    B. Uninstall the games from within Windows Update.

    C. In the Start menu, right-click the Games folder and select Delete.

    D. Delete and reinstall Windows, and deselect the games upon reinstallation.

12. A common compression format file extension seen on UNIX and Linux computers is what?

    A. .rar

    B. .dmg

    C. .iso

    D. .gz

13. What type of software is used to create 3-D drawings for construction projects?

   A. CAD

   B. Graphic design

   C. PDF

   D. Specialized

14. You open your web browser and type in www.google.com, but your computer can't find the website. Your neighbor's computer finds it just fine. What is most likely the cause?

   A. Incorrect DNS configuration.

   B. Incorrect DHCP configuration.

   C. Incorrect WPA2 configuration.

   D. The website is down.

15. Your friend Marcos asks you which of the following is the most secure. What do you tell him?

   A. 802.11n

   B. Infrared

   C. Fiber-optic

   D. UTP

16. Your need to set up a wireless router for a friend. He wants to be sure that his network is secure. Which wireless security method should you implement?

   A. WPA2

   B. WPA

   C. NAT

   D. WEP

17. Which of the following types of networks features decentralized security and resource administration?

   A. LAN

   B. WAN

   C. Peer-to-peer

   D. Client-server

18. You need to install a local storage solution that multiple users can easily access and has its own file-management software. Which option should you choose?

   A. NAS

   B. DAS

   C. Network drive

   D. Cloud

19. Which of the following is an advantage of using a workgroup instead of a homegroup?

    A. It's more secure because it requires a password.

    B. It has guaranteed compatibility because all computers must be running Windows 7 or newer.

    C. It's more secure because all clients must be on the same local network.

    D. It's more flexible because multiple operating systems can join it.

20. Angela has an iPhone with a biometric scanner enabled. She powered the device off, and just turned it back on. What methods can she use to unlock her phone?

    A. Fingerprint only

    B. Passcode only

    C. Fingerprint or passcode

    D. Fingerprint, passcode, or iris scan

21. You are setting up a new Wi-Fi connection on your iPad. What is the first step in the process?

    A. Enter the wireless password.

    B. Verify the Internet connection.

    C. Verify wireless capabilities.

    D. Locate SSID.

    E. Turn on Wi-Fi.

22. What type of security is involved when pairing two Bluetooth devices together?

    A. SSL certificates are exchanged.

    B. A PIN is provided by the Bluetooth device.

    C. The Bluetooth security layer negotiates the security mechanism.

    D. There is no security involved.

23. Which of the following are considered physical security risks? (Choose two.)

    A. Dumpster diving

    B. Phishing

    C. Software theft

    D. Password cracking

24. What is the primary difference between a computer virus and a worm?

    A. A virus can replicate itself to infect another computer.

    B. A worm can replicate itself to infect another computer.

    C. Viruses only damage operating systems while worms damage software applications.

    D. Viruses can't cause total system crashes whereas worms can.

25. You are online and you see a link to a free virus-scanning program appear. You click it, and after a few minutes your computer starts behaving erratically. What happened?

    A. The virus scanner found a virus and is deleting it.

    B. The link is attempting to crack your password.

    C. The link was a phishing attempt.

    D. The link was a Trojan horse.

26. Which of the following are considered device hardening techniques? (Choose two.)

    A. Disabling Bluetooth

    B. Requiring complex passwords

    C. Enabling single sign-on

    D. Installing antispyware software

27. For security purposes, which of the following user accounts are disabled by default?

    A. Guest

    B. Users

    C. Power Users

    D. Administrator

28. You are browsing the Internet to purchase a gift for a friend. What two things should you look for to ensure it's safe to enter your credit card information? (Choose two.)

    A. Security seal of approval

    B. RSA Secure Access symbol

    C. A lock symbol

    D. `HTTPS://`

29. You are helping a friend choose the right laptop for their needs. Which of the following are criteria that should be important for choosing the laptop? (Choose two.)

    A. Display size

    B. Weight

    C. CPU speed

    D. Memory

30. Your office recently purchased five new workstations, and you are responsible for setting them up properly. After unpacking them, what is the next step you should perform?

    A. Configure the Internet connection.

    B. Configure localization settings.

    C. Power on the computer.

    D. Plug in the cables.

31. You are setting up a workstation for your neighbor. After following the operating system setup wizard, what is the next step to take in the setup process?

A. Configure peripherals.

B. Create user accounts.

C. Install security software.

D. Uninstall unneeded software.

32. You just installed a new HP printer on your Dell computer, and it's not printing. What is the first source to check for information on the problem?

A. Dell's website

B. HP's website

C. Google search

D. Internet technical community groups

33. When configuring a backup solution for your computer, you decide that speed is the most important factor. Which storage option should you choose?

A. Locally attached storage

B. Network attached storage

C. Cloud storage

D. Offline storage

34. You have just completed a backup of your PC onto an optical disc. What is the next step you need to take?

A. Store the backup in a secure location.

B. Burn the disc to ensure the data is saved.

C. Test the backup to verify it works.

D. Copy the backup data to a cloud.

35. You are conducting an ergonomic assessment of your working environment. What should be true of the monitor placement?

A. The bottom of the monitor should be level with your eyes.

B. The top of the monitor should be level with your eyes.

C. The center of the monitor should be level with your eyes.

D. Monitor position does not matter in ergonomic assessments.

36. At home, you are walking across a carpeted floor and touch a door handle. The handle shocks you and it stings a little. What caused this shock?

A. RoHS

B. EMI

C. ESD

D. UPS

37. You need to purchase a device for your desktop computer so that if you lose power in your house, the computer can still operate until you shut it down safely. What do you need?

   A. Surge suppressor

   B. Power replicator

   C. Power strip

   D. UPS

Answers to the Assessment Test

1. C. A double-sided DVD-ROM can store more data than a dual-layer DVD-ROM, and both can store much more than a CD-ROM. There is no RS-ROM. See Chapter 1 for more information.

2. A, D. Hard disk drives (HDD) are used to permanently store user data. Solid state drives (SSD) are one type of hard drive. See Chapter 1 for more information.

3. D. The Basic Input/Output System (BIOS) is firmware. It's stored on a flash memory chip (sometimes referred to as CMOS). See Chapter 1 for more information.

4. B. VGA was the first widely used video connector standard, and it was released in 1987. See Chapter 2 for more information.

5. C. Digital cameras use memory cards. The most popular form of memory card in the market today is the SD card. MMC (Multi Media Card) is a variant of SD cards but there is no such thing as a "Mobile Media Card." See Chapter 2 for more information.

6. A. Scanners are input devices. Printers produce output. Touchscreens and flash drives are both input and output devices. See Chapter 2 for more information.

7. B. Apple's OS X was named for large cats. Now versions are named after locations in California. See Chapter 3 for more information.

8. B. A 64-bit processor can handle 32-bit or 64-bit OSs. It is a waste of power to use a 32-bit OS on it, but it will work. See Chapter 3 for more information.

9. C. Moving a file is analogous to a cut and paste. It takes the file from one folder and places it in another within Windows. However, on the hard drive the only thing that happens is the file gets associated with a new folder. It does not physically move. See Chapter 3 for more information.

10. C. The `.flac` extension is for audio files. See Chapter 4 for more information.

11. A. Games and other software components can be added and removed from within Control Panel. See Chapter 4 for more information.

12. D. The `.gz` extension is used by gzip, which is a UNIX- and Linux-compatible compression utility. See Chapter 4 for more information.

13. A. Computer Aided Design (CAD) software is designed to create 2-D and 3-D drawings for construction projects. CAD is a type of specialized software. See Chapter 4 for more information.

14. A. DNS servers resolve host names to IP addresses. It's possible that your computer has the wrong address for the DNS server. DHCP automatically configures TCP/IP clients, and WPA2 is a security protocol. If the website was down, your neighbor would not be able to access it either. See Chapter 5 for more information.

15. C. Wired connections are more secure than wireless ones. Fiber-optic cable is also immune to wiretaps, which makes it more secure than UTP. See Chapter 5 for more information.

16. A. WPA2 is the most secure wireless security protocol in use today. See Chapter 5 for more information.

17. C. A peer-to-peer network is one where all computers are equals. Each one is responsible for setting its own security and resource sharing. See Chapter 6 for more information.

18. A. Network attached storage (NAS) is an external hard drive (or multiple hard drives) complete with its own file management and sharing software. See Chapter 6 for more information.

19. D. Homegroups require their clients to be running Windows 7 or newer, and they are more secure than workgroups because a password is needed to join. An advantage of a workgroup is that multiple client OSs can participate, such as OS X. See Chapter 6 for more information.

20. B. With biometrics enabled, you can use either the passcode or your fingerprint to access a locked device. However, if it was just powered off, the only option is to enter the passcode. See Chapter 7 for more information.

21. C. The proper steps in order are to verify wireless capabilities, turn on Wi-Fi, locate SSID, enter the wireless password, and verify the Internet connection. See Chapter 7 for more information.

22. B. When pairing two Bluetooth devices, you need to enter the PIN into your mobile device that allows it to connect to the Bluetooth device. See Chapter 7 for more information.

23. A, C. Examples of physical security risks include hardware damage and theft, software and license theft, shoulder surfing, and dumpster diving. See Chapter 8 for more information.

24. B. Viruses and worms are similar in the damage they do. The major difference is that while a virus needs a host to replicate and spread, a worm can replicate itself and spread without user intervention. See Chapter 8 for more information.

25. D. The link was most likely a Trojan horse, which pretends to be a beneficial program but then does damage to your computer. It most likely installed malware on your system. See Chapter 8 for more information.

26. A, D. Device hardening makes it harder for attackers to gain access to your system by reducing the potential areas of attack. Two examples of device hardening are disabling unused or unneeded services and installing antimalware. See Chapter 9 for more information.

27. A. The Guest account is disabled by default and should remain disabled if it is not being used. See Chapter 9 for more information.

28. C, D. Secure websites will start with HTTPS:// instead of HTTP://. In addition, there will be a lock symbol near the address in the address bar. See Chapter 9 for more information.

29. A, B. Processor speed and memory are important for all computers. The display size and weight are considerations that are more specifically related to laptops than desktop computers. See Chapter 10 for more information.

30. D. The first step in setting up a workstation is to plug in the cables. See Chapter 10 for more information.

31. C. After performing the initial setup of the operating system, the next step is to install security software. The security software is the second most important piece of software on the computer, so it should be taken care of immediately after the OS setup. See Chapter 10 for more information.

32. B. Always check the manufacturer's website first. Since it's an HP printer, check their site and not Dell's. See Chapter 11 for more information.

33. A. When choosing a backup solution, know that locally attached storage devices will always be faster than network storage or cloud-based solutions. See Chapter 11 for more information.

34. C. After completing a backup, you should verify that the backup is working properly. See Chapter 11 for more information.

35. B. When placing a computer monitor, the top of the monitor should be at or slightly below eye level for the user. See Chapter 12 for more information.

36. C. The shock is caused by static electricity, which is also known as electrostatic discharge (ESD). See Chapter 12 for more information.

37. D. An uninterruptable power supply contains batteries that allow your computer to operate even if there is no power coming to it. See Chapter 12 for more information.

Chapter

1

Core Hardware Components

THE FOLLOWING COMPTIA IT FUNDAMENTALS EXAM OBJECTIVES ARE COVERED IN THIS CHAPTER:

✓ **2.3 Identify the purpose of internal computer components**

- CPU
- Power Supply
- RAM
- Storage
  - Optical drive
  - Hard drive
  - Solid state drive
- Expansion cards
  - Video card
  - Audio card
  - Network card
  - Modem
- Motherboard/mainboard
- System cooling
  - Case fans
  - CPU fans
  - Liquid cooling

✓ **2.2 Compare and contrast common computer connector types**

- Power
  - AC/DC

What better way to kick off a book on IT fundamentals than to talk about the most fundamental components of all—core hardware. When you really break it down to the basics, computers are simply collections of specialized hardware devices that work together (with software) to provide you with the functionality you want. Sometimes the hardware is in your hands, and other times it's halfway around the world, but it's always necessary. Even soft and fluffy-sounding terms such as "the cloud" (which I will talk about in Chapter 6, "Network Sharing and Storage") rely on much of the same hardware that sits snugly within your tablet or smartphone case.

To begin our journey of understanding fundamental IT concepts, I will discuss components that are generally included inside the case. Some are absolutely critical while others just provide features that are nice to have, such as sound or a network connection. In this way, I'll start from the inside out so you understand what makes computers work the way they do.

Introducing Internal Components

In this section, I will talk about components that are generally inside the computer case. Some of them are exclusively found inside the case, such as the motherboard and the processor, whereas others can be internal or external. For example, internal hard drives (for storage) are standard in desktop and laptop computers, but you can also buy external hard drives for expanded storage. Network cards are another great example. Today, they are generally built into the computer, but you can easily find external ones as well. Regardless of the location of your hard drive or network card, it still provides the same functionality.

Most computer components are modular. That is, they can be removed and replaced by another piece of hardware that does the same thing, provided that it's compatible and it fits. For example, if the hard drive in your laptop fails, it can be removed and replaced by another hard drive. This isn't always the case, of course, and the general rule is that the smaller the device, the less modular it is. This is because to achieve the smaller size, manufacturers need to integrate more functionality onto the same component. It's usually quicker and just as cost-effective to replace a device such as a smartphone rather than repair it if a part fails. If a component is modular and can be replaced, you will sometimes hear it referred to as a *field replaceable unit (FRU)*.

Since I'm talking about components that are inside the case, it would be unfortunate to ignore the case itself. Cases are usually a combination of metal and plastic and serve two primary functions:

- Keeping all of the components securely in place
- Protecting the components from harm

Protecting the components is the key. Water and other liquids are obviously bad for electronic devices, and direct exposure to sunlight and dust can cause parts to overheat and fail. The case guards against all of those things. And in some cases (pun intended), it can make your device easily mobile as well.

Throughout this section, I will specifically talk about PC (desktop and laptop) hardware. Many of the principles here apply to smaller devices such as smartphones too.

Exploring Motherboards, Processors, and Memory

These three components—motherboards, processors, and memory—are the holy trinity of computers. Pretty much every personal computing device made today requires all three of these parts. So, without further ado, let's dive in.

Motherboards

The *motherboard* is the most important component in the computer because it connects all the other components together. Functionally, it acts much like the nervous system of the computer. You will also hear it called the system board or the mainboard. With this introduction, you might think this piece of hardware is complex, and you'd be right! Manufacturers and hardware resellers don't make it easy to understand what you're dealing with either. Here's the description for a motherboard for sale on an Internet hardware site:

> Asus P9X79 Intel X79 DDR3 LGA2011 ATX Motherboard w/ 3x PCI-Express X16, SATA 6G, 2x eSATA, GBLAN, USB 3.0, FireWire

What does that all mean? Is it even human language? Don't worry. By the end of this section on motherboards, you will understand what it all means.

The first thing to know about motherboards is that they are a printed circuit board (PCB)—a conductive series of pathways laminated to a nonconductive substrate—that lines the bottom of the computer. Most of the time they are green, but you will also see brown, blue, and red ones. Some of the most popular brands right now are Asus, Gigabyte, and MicroStar (MSI). Figure 1.1 shows a typical motherboard.

FIGURE 1.1   A motherboard

All other components are attached to this circuit board. Some are physically attached directly to the board and aren't intended to be removed, such as the underlying circuitry, the central processing unit (CPU) slot, random access memory (RAM) slots, expansion slots, and a variety of other chips. Components such as the CPU and the RAM get physically attached to the motherboard. Other devices such as hard drives and power supplies are attached via their own connectors.

Manufacturers can also integrate components such as the CPU, video card, network card, and others directly onto the motherboard as opposed to having slots for them to connect into. The smaller motherboards (for example, for laptops) are more likely to have integrated components.

Let's start breaking down the features and components typically associated with motherboards. The following list might look long, but breaking each one down separately will help you understand the importance of each one. Here are the topics coming up:

- Form factors
- Chipsets
- Processor sockets
- Memory slots
- Expansion slots
- Disk controllers
- Power connectors
- BIOS/firmware
- CMOS and CMOS battery
- Back-panel connectors
- Front-panel connectors

In the following sections, you will learn about some of the most common components of a motherboard and what they do. I'll show what each component looks like so you can identify it on most any motherboard you run across.

Form Factors

Motherboards are classified by their design, which is called a *form factor*. There are dozens of form factors in existence. Because motherboards mount to the system case, it's important to know what types of motherboards your case supports before replacing one. Desktop computer cases often support multiple sizes of motherboards, but laptops are another story. With laptops, you almost always need to replace an old motherboard with the same version.

The most common form factors used today are Advanced Technology Extended (ATX), micro ATX, and ITX.

> ITX is not one specific form factor but a collection of small form factor (SFF) boards.

The form factors differ in size and configuration of the components on the motherboard. In addition, they may have different power requirements. Micro ATX and ITX are specifically designed to be paired with low-wattage power supplies in order to reduce the amount of heat produced by the computer. Because these two are smaller, they also offer fewer options for adding expansion cards versus the ATX design.

Here's a quick history lesson. The XT form factor was developed by IBM in 1983 and is generally considered the first industry-standard PC form factor. In 1985, IBM released the Baby-AT, which because of its smaller size quickly became the most popular form factor in the market. The Baby-AT was the king until 1996 when Intel released the ATX standard. As of this writing, the ATX and micro ATX (which is similar in configuration to ATX, only smaller) are still the most popular computer form factors.

Table 1.1 gives you the dimensions of common form factors.

TABLE 1.1 Motherboard form factors

Form Factor	Release Year	Size
Baby-AT	1985	8.5 × 10–13 in. (216 × 254–330 mm)
ATX	1996	12 × 9.6 in. (305 × 244 mm)
Micro ATX	1996	9.6 × 9.66 in. (244 × 244 mm)
Mini-ITX	2001	6.7 × 6.7 in. (170 × 170 mm)
Nano-ITX	2003	4.7 × 4.7 in. (120 × 120 mm)
Pico-ITX	2007	3.9 × 2.8 in. (100 × 72 mm)
Mobile-ITX	2007	2.95 × 1.77 in. (75 × 45 mm)
Neo-ITX	2012	6.7 × 3.35 in. (170 × 85 mm)

With how quickly computer technology evolves, it is amazing that the form factors remain popular as long as they do. The advent of smaller devices such as tablets and smartphones has driven the most recent design changes.

Chipsets

The motherboard's *chipset* is a collection of chips or circuits that perform interface and peripheral functions for the processor. This collection of chips provides interfaces for memory, expansion cards, and onboard peripherals and generally dictates how a motherboard will communicate with the installed peripherals.

Chipsets are usually given a name and model number by the original manufacturer, for example, Intel's X79. What features make the X79 so great? I will be honest; I have no idea. There are so many chipsets out there that it's impossible to know the features of every one. But, if you need to know, having the manufacturer and model can help you look up the features of that particular chipset, such as the type of RAM supported, the type and brand of onboard video, and so on.

The functions of chipsets can be divided into two major functional groups, called Northbridge and Southbridge. It's unlikely that you'll be tested on these on the IT Fundamentals exam, but I want to introduce them just in case you hear the terms. Plus, I think it helps better explain exactly what the chipset does.

Northbridge   The Northbridge subset of a motherboard's chipset performs one important function: management of high-speed peripheral communications. The Northbridge is responsible primarily for communications with integrated video and processor-to-memory communications.

The communications between the CPU and memory occur over what is known as the *frontside bus (FSB)*, which is just a set of signal pathways connecting the CPU and main memory. The *backside bus (BSB)*, if present, is a set of signal pathways between the CPU and any external cache memory.

Southbridge   The Southbridge subset of the chipset is responsible for providing support to the onboard slower peripherals (PS/2, parallel ports, serial ports, Serial and Parallel ATA, and so on), managing their communications with the rest of the computer and the resources given to them. If you're thinking about any component other than the CPU, memory and cache, or integrated video, the Southbridge is in charge.

Figure 1.2 shows the chipset of a motherboard, with the heat sink of the Northbridge, at the top left, connected to the heat-spreading cover of the Southbridge, at the bottom right.

FIGURE 1.2   Northbridge and Southbridge

Real World Scenario

Who's Driving the Bus?

When talking about the Northbridge, I mentioned a bus (specifically a front-side bus), so now is a good time to talk about what a bus is and give you some historical context. You'll probably hear the term come up often when talking about computer hardware, in ways such as system bus, expansion bus, parallel bus, and serial bus.

A *bus* is a common collection of signal pathways over which related devices communicate within the computer system. It refers specifically to a data path, or the way the computer communicates over that path.

Take serial and parallel, for example. A serial bus communicates one bit of data at a time, whereas a parallel bus communicates in several parallel channels (eight, for example) at once. Based on this explanation, you might think that parallel is faster than serial. After all, eight lanes should move more data than one lane, right? Sometimes, but not always. It depends on how fast you can get each lane to move.

Serial was developed before parallel, because at its core it's an easier technology to implement. In the late 1980s parallel became much more popular for printers because it was a lot faster. The only downside to parallel was that the different streams of data needed to be carefully synchronized. This slowed down transmissions so they weren't exactly eight times faster than comparable serial connections.

By 1996, manufacturers had advanced the speed of serial technology enough that it was faster than parallel, and the world saw the introduction of Universal Serial Bus (USB). It was faster than parallel and had a lot of additional features as well such as the ability to hot plug devices (plug and unplug them without needing to shut the system down). Today, many of the fastest peripheral-connecting technologies in use such as USB, FireWire, and Serial ATA (SATA) are all serial.

So, while parallel was king for a day, you can now get faster transmissions via serial technology.

Processor Sockets

The *central processing unit (CPU)* is the "brain" of any computer. There are many different types of processors for computers, and the processor you have must fit into the socket on the motherboard. Typically, in today's computers, the processor is the easiest component to identify on the motherboard. It is usually the component that has either a large fan and/or a *heat sink* (usually both) attached to it.

CPU sockets are almost as varied as the processors they hold. Sockets are basically flat and have several columns and rows of holes or pins arranged in a square, as shown in

Figure 1.3. You'll hear terms like pin grid array (PGA) or land grid array (LGA) to describe the socket type. In Figure 1.3, the left socket is PGA, and the right one is an LGA 2011. PGA sockets have holes, and the processors have pins that fit into the holes. LGA sockets have contacts (often pins) built in to them, which connect with contacts on the CPU. Both sockets have locking mechanisms to hold the processor in place. PGA uses a simple lever, while LGA has a more complex locking harness (which is closed in Figure 1.3). LGA chips may also be soldered to their sockets.

FIGURE 1.3   CPU sockets

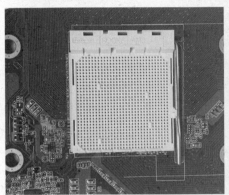

SOCKET 2011 IMGP3918 BY SMIAL (TALK) - OWN WORK. LICENSED UNDER FAL VIA WIKIMEDIA COMMONS - HTTP://COMMONS.WIKIMEDIA.ORG/
WIKI/FILE:SOCKET_2011_IMGP3918.JPG#/MEDIA/FILE:SOCKET_2011_IMGP3918.JPG

 In the motherboard-for-sale example, LGA 2011 is the socket on that board.

Memory Slots

Memory or random access memory (RAM) slots are for the modules that hold memory chips that make up primary memory that is used to store currently used data and instructions for the CPU. Many and varied types of memory are available for PCs today. Examples include DDR2 and DDR3. Memory for desktops comes on circuit boards called dual inline memory modules (DIMMs) and for laptops on small outline DIMMs (SODIMMs). (I will talk about what these acronyms mean later in this chapter, in the "Memory" section.)

Memory slots are easy to identify on a motherboard. First, they are long and slender and generally close to the CPU socket. Classic DIMM slots were usually black and, like all memory slots, were placed very close together. (Today manufacturers make memory slots of various colors.) Metal pins in the bottom make contact with the metallic pins on each memory module. Small metal or plastic tabs on each side of the slot keep the memory module securely in its slot. Figure 1.4 shows some memory slots on a desktop motherboard.

FIGURE 1.4   DIMM slots

Laptops are space constrained, so they user the smaller form factor SODIMM chips. SODIMM slots are configured so the chips lie nearly parallel to the motherboard, as shown in Figure 1.5.

FIGURE 1.5   SODIMM slots

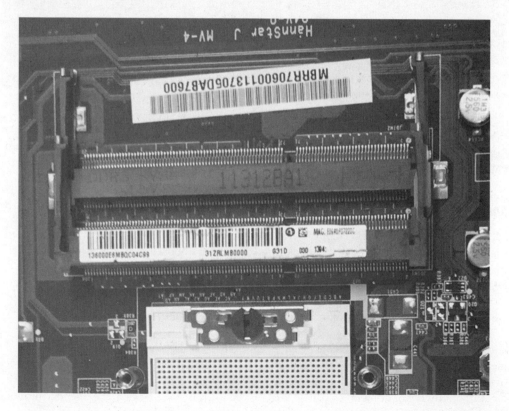

Motherboard designers can also speed up the system by adding *cache memory* between the CPU and RAM. Cache is a fast form of memory and improves system performance by predicting what the CPU will ask for next and prefetching this information before being asked. I will talk about cache more in the "Processors" section later in this chapter.

If there is cache on your motherboard, it is not likely to be a removable component. Therefore, it does not have a slot or connector like RAM does.

Expansion Slots

The most visible parts of any motherboard are the *expansion slots*. These are small plastic slots, usually from 1 to 6 inches long and approximately ½ inch wide. As their name suggests, these slots are used to install various devices in the computer to expand its capabilities. Some expansion devices that might be installed in these slots include video, network, sound, and disk interface cards.

If you look at the motherboard in your computer, you will more than likely see one of the main types of expansion slots used in computers today:

- PCI
- AGP
- PCIe

Each type differs in appearance and function. In the following sections, I will cover how to visually identify the different expansion slots on the motherboard.

PCI Expansion Slots

Some of the most common expansion slots for many years were the 32-bit *Peripheral Component Interconnect (PCI)* slots. They are easily recognizable because they are only around 3 inches long and classically white, although modern boards take liberties with the color. Although popularity has shifted from PCI to PCIe, the PCI slot's service to the industry cannot be ignored; it has been an incredibly prolific architecture for many years.

PCI expansion buses operate at 33 MHz or 66 MHz over a 32-bit (4-byte) channel, resulting in data rates of 133 MBps and 266 MBps, respectively, with 133 MBps being the most common. PCI is a shared-bus topology, which means that mixing 33 MHz and 66 MHz adapters in a 66 MHz system will slow all adapters to 33 MHz.

PCI slots and adapters are manufactured in 3.3 and 5V versions. Universal adapters are keyed to fit in slots based on either of the two voltages. The notch in the card edge of the common 5V slots and adapters is oriented toward the front of the motherboard and the notch in the 3.3V adapters toward the rear. Figure 1.6 shows several PCI expansion slots. Note the 5V 32-bit slot in the foreground and the 3.3V 64-bit slots. Also notice that a universal 32-bit card, which has notches in both positions, is inserted into and operates fine in the 64-bit 3.3V slot in the background.

FIGURE 1.6 PCI expansion slots

AGP Expansion Slots

Accelerated Graphics Port (AGP) slots are known mostly for legacy video card use and have been supplanted in new installations by PCI Express slots and their adapters. AGP slots were designed to be a direct connection between the video circuitry and the PC's memory. They are also easily recognizable because they are usually brown and are located right next to the PCI slots on the motherboard. AGP slots are slightly shorter than PCI slots and are pushed back from the rear of the motherboard in comparison with the position of the PCI slots. Figure 1.7 shows an example of an older AGP slot, along with a white PCI slot for comparison. Notice the difference in length between the two.

FIGURE 1.7 An AGP slot compared to a PCI slot

AGP performance is based on the original specification, known as AGP 1x. It uses a 32-bit (4-byte) channel and a 66 MHz clock, resulting in a data rate of 266 MBps. AGP 2x, 4x, and 8x specifications multiply the 66 MHz clock they receive to increase throughput linearly. For instance, AGP 8x uses the 66 MHz clock to produce an effective clock frequency of 533 MHz, resulting in throughput of 2133 MBps over the 4-byte channel. Note that this maximum throughput is only a fraction of the throughput of PCIe x16, which is covered in the following section.

PCIe Expansion Slots

One of the newest expansion slot architectures that is being used by motherboards is *PCI Express (PCIe)*. It was designed to be a replacement for AGP and PCI. PCIe has the advantage of being faster than AGP while maintaining the flexibility of PCI. PCIe has no plug compatibility with either AGP or PCI. As a result, modern PCIe motherboards still tend to have regular PCI slots for backward compatibility, but AGP slots typically are not included.

There are seven different speeds supported by PCIe, designated ×1 (pronounced "by 1"), ×2, ×4, ×8, ×12, ×16, and ×32, with ×1, ×4, and ×16 being the most common. A slot that supports a particular speed will be of a specific physical size because faster cards require more wires and therefore are longer. As a result, a ×8 slot is longer than a ×1 slot but shorter than a ×16 slot. Every PCIe slot has a 22-pin portion in common toward the rear of the motherboard, which you can see in Figure 1.8, in which the rear of the motherboard is to the left. These 22 pins comprise mostly voltage and ground leads. Figure 1.8 shows, from top to bottom, a ×16 slot, two ×1 slots, and a legacy PCI slot.

FIGURE 1.8   PCIe expansion slots

Compared to its predecessors, PCIe is fast. Even at the older PCIe 2.0 standard, a PCIe ×1 card will run at 500 MBps, which is comparable to the best that PCI can offer (533 MBps). Current PCIe standards (PCIe 3.0) let a ×16 card operate at a screaming 15.75 GBps.

NOTE   PCIe 4.0 is expected to be finalized in late 2016, and it doubles the speeds of PCIe 3.0.

Its high data rate makes PCIe the current choice of gaming aficionados. The only downside with PCIe (and with later AGP slots) is that any movement of these high-performance devices can result in temporary failure or poor performance. Consequently, both PCIe and AGP slots have a latch and tab that secure the adapters in place.

Disk Controllers

One of the endearing features of computers is that they store data and allow it to be retrieved at a later time. (It's true that they sometimes mysteriously lose our data too, but that's another story.) The long-term storage device is called a hard drive, and it plugs into the motherboard as well.

There are a few different hard drive standard connectors. The older one that you will run into is called *Integrated Drive Electronics (IDE)* or *Parallel ATA (PATA)*. The newer and much faster one is called *Serial ATA (SATA)*. Figure 1.9 shows the two IDE connectors (both the black and the white one are the same). Figure 1.10 shows four SATA connectors. Notice how they are conveniently labeled for you on the motherboard!

FIGURE 1.9 IDE hard drive connectors

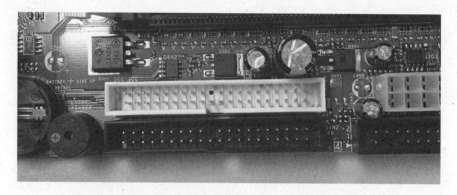

FIGURE 1.10 SATA hard drive connectors

Power Connectors

Computers are obviously electronics, and electronics, of course, require power. In addition to the other sockets and slots on the motherboard, a special connector (the 24-pin block connector shown in Figure 1.11) allows the motherboard to be connected to the power supply to receive power. This connector is where the ATX power adapter plugs in.

FIGURE 1.11   A 24-pin ATX power connector

BIOS/Firmware

Firmware is the name given to any software that is encoded in hardware, usually a read-only memory (ROM) chip, and can be run without extra instructions from the operating system. Most computers and large printers use firmware in some sense. The best example of firmware is a computer's *Basic Input/Output System (BIOS)* routine, which is burned into a flash memory chip located on the motherboard. Also, some expansion cards, such as video cards, use their own firmware utilities for setting up peripherals.

Aside from the processor, the most important chip on the motherboard is the BIOS chip. This special memory chip contains the BIOS system software that boots the system and initiates the memory and hard drive to allow the operating system to start.

The BIOS chip is easily identified: if you have a brand-name computer, this chip might have on it the name of the manufacturer and usually the word *BIOS*. For clones, the chip usually has a sticker or printing on it from one of the major BIOS manufacturers (AMI, Phoenix/Award, Winbond, and so on). Figure 1.12 gives you an idea of what a BIOS chip might look like. This one is made by Fintek.

FIGURE 1.12   A BIOS chip on a motherboard

When you power on your computer, the BIOS initializes and runs a system-checking routine called the *power-on self-test (POST)*. The POST routine does the following things:

- Verifies the integrity of the BIOS itself
- Verifies and confirms the size of primary memory
- Analyzes and catalogs other forms of hardware, such as buses and boot devices
- Offers the user a key sequence to enter the configuration screen
- Hands over control to the boot device (usually a hard drive) highest in the configured boot order to load the operating system

If all of its tests complete successfully, the POST process finishes. If there is an error, it can produce a beep code or displayed code that indicates there is an issue. Each BIOS publisher has its own series of codes that can be generated. Figure 1.13 shows a simplified POST display during the initial boot sequence of a computer.

FIGURE 1.13   An example of a BIOS boot screen

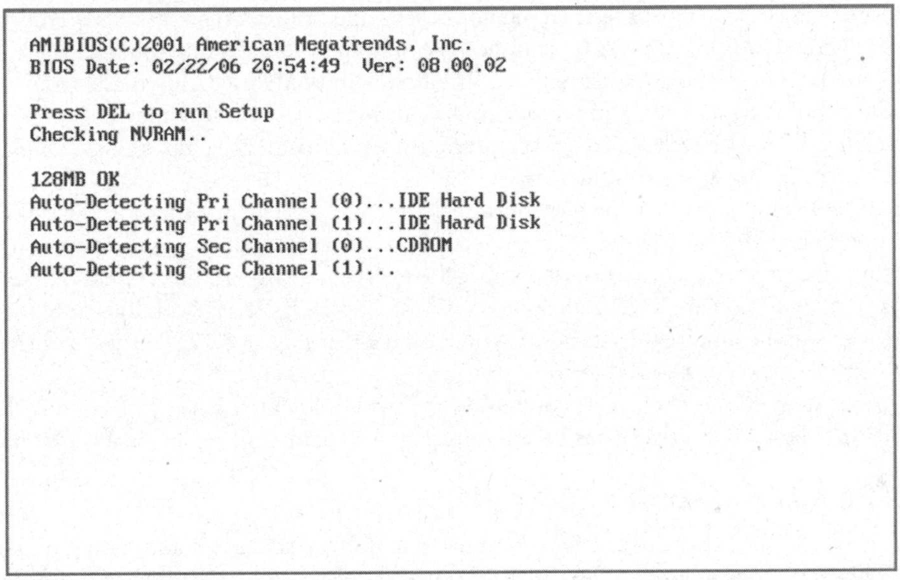

```
AMIBIOS(C)2001 American Megatrends, Inc.
BIOS Date: 02/22/06 20:54:49  Ver: 08.00.02

Press DEL to run Setup
Checking NVRAM..

128MB OK
Auto-Detecting Pri Channel (0)...IDE Hard Disk
Auto-Detecting Pri Channel (1)...IDE Hard Disk
Auto-Detecting Sec Channel (0)...CDROM
Auto-Detecting Sec Channel (1)...
```

As mentioned in the list, the POST routine offers the user a chance to enter the BIOS and change the configuration settings. This is usually done by pressing a key during the boot process, such as F2 or F12, or in the case of Figure 1.13 the Delete key. The computer will prompt you, but usually the prompt goes by quickly. If you get a screen showing that the operating system has started, you're too late.

Inside the BIOS, you can make system configuration selections (such as changing the system time or selecting a preferred boot device) and save the results. Also, many BIOSs offer diagnostic routines that you can use to have the BIOS analyze the state and quality of the same components it inspects during bootup, but at a much deeper level.

Flashing the BIOS

When you upgrade your system's hardware, the system BIOS typically recognizes it upon bootup. If you upgraded your hard drive, processor, or memory and it's not recognized, though, you might need to update your system BIOS. This is done through a process called *flashing the BIOS*.

To flash the BIOS, you will need to download the most current version from the manufacturer of your computer (or motherboard, if you built your own system) and follow the instructions.

CMOS and CMOS Battery

Your PC has to keep certain settings when it's turned off and its power cord is unplugged, such as the date and time, hard drive configuration, memory and CPU settings, boot sequence, and power management features.

These settings are kept in a special memory chip called the *complementary metal oxide semiconductor (CMOS)*. CMOS (pronounced *see-moss*) is actually a manufacturing technology for integrated circuits, but since the first commonly used chip made from CMOS technology was a BIOS memory chip, the terms have become somewhat interchangeable. To be technically correct, though, the name of the chip is the CMOS, and the BIOS settings are stored on the chip.

The CMOS chip must have power constantly or it will lose its information (just like RAM does when your computer is powered off). To prevent CMOS from losing its rather important information, motherboard manufacturers include a small battery called the *CMOS battery* to power the CMOS memory. Most CMOS batteries look like watch batteries or small cylindrical batteries. If you look back at Figure 1.12, you will see the CMOS battery next to the BIOS.

If your system does not retain its configuration information after it's been powered off, it's possible that the CMOS battery has failed. Replacing it is similar to replacing a watch battery.

Back-Panel Connectors

If you've ever looked at the back of a computer, you know that there's a lot going on back there. There could be a dozen or so different types of connectors, including ones for power, video, audio, a keyboard and mouse, networking (such as Gigabit Ethernet), and other devices. Generally speaking, all of these connectors are connected to one of two things: the motherboard or an expansion card that's attached to the motherboard. I will talk about all of these in Chapter 2, "Peripherals and Connectors." For now, I offer you Figure 1.14, showing several connectors on the back panel.

FIGURE 1.14 Computer back panel

Front-Panel Connectors

Even though the front panel of the computer isn't as chaotic as the back panel, there's still a lot happening. The front of your computer might have one or more memory card readers or optical drives such as a DVD-ROM. It's kind of old-school to have these devices accessible from the front of your system. Years ago you might have had 3½″ or 5¼″ floppy drives on the front of your system too. (Google them!)

With the obsolescence of floppy drives, a lot more real estate opened up on the front of your computer. Computer manufacturers realized that accessibility was a big deal and started moving connectors that used to be found only on the backs of systems to the front. Now, your system will likely have most if not all of the following types of connectors on the front panel. All of them get connected to the motherboard in some fashion.

Power Button   Having a *power button* in an easily accessible place seems kind of obvious, doesn't it? Well, they used to be on the back or side of computers too. Many times your power button will also double as a power light, letting you know that the system is on.

Reset Button   Reset buttons are hit-or-miss on computers today. The idea is that this button would reboot your computer from a cold startup without removing power from the components. The reset button is incredibly handy to have when a software application locks up your entire system. Because power is not completely lost, the reset button may not help if you had a memory issue.

Drive Activity Lights   These little lights often look like circular platters (like a hard drive) or have a hard drive icon next to them. They let you know that your hard drive is working.

Audio Ports   The front of most computers now has a port for headphones as well as a microphone. Long gone are the days where you had to put your computer in a certain spot on or under your desk, just so your short headphones cord could reach all the way to the back of the box.

Other Connectors   Trying to get to the back of your computer to plug in a flash drive is about as convenient as ripping out the back seat of your car to get stuff out of the trunk. It might actually be faster to just remove your hard drive and give it your friend so they can copy the files they need. (Okay, not really.) Fortunately, most new computers have one or more USB ports on the front of the box, in addition to FireWire, Thunderbolt, or external SATA (eSATA). I will cover these different connectors in Chapter 2.

 Real World Scenario

Motherboard, Revisited

At the beginning of this section, I gave you the description of a motherboard for sale.

Asus P9X79 Intel X79 DDR3 LGA2011 ATX Motherboard w/ 3x PCI-Express X16, SATA 6G, 2x eSATA, GBLAN, USB 3.0, FireWire

Now that you've learned about motherboards, let's translate the acronym string. Asus P9X79 is the manufacturer and model of the motherboard. It has the Intel X79 chipset, uses DDR3 memory, and has an LGA2011 CPU socket. It is ATX style and has three PCIe x16 slots, SATA hard drive connectors, and two eSATA ports, gigabyte networking (GBLAN), USB, and FireWire external connectors.

Armed with this information, you can now compare motherboards to each other to determine which one has some of the features you are looking for!

Processors

The processor is the most important component on the motherboard. The role of the CPU, or central processing unit, is to control and direct all the activities of the computer. Because of this role, the CPU often gets called the brain of the computer. The analogy isn't perfect, because the processor isn't capable of thinking independently. It just does what it's instructed to do, which is math. It just happens to do it quickly. Still, the analogy of the processor as the computer's brain is close enough.

Processors are a small silicon chips consisting of an array of *millions* of transistors. Intel and Advanced Micro Devices (AMD) are the two largest PC-compatible CPU manufacturers.

 The terms *processor* and *CPU* are interchangeable.

CPUs are generally square, with contacts arranged in rows of pins. Older CPU sockets were in a configuration called a pin grid array (PGA). The newer version uses a configuration called the land grid array (LGA). LGA is sturdier than PGA, because it has the pins in the socket versus on the processor, which results in less damage to processors from trying to incorrectly insert them into their sockets. Figure 1.15 shows an AMD processor.

FIGURE 1.15   AMD Athlon processor

For as powerful as processors are, they don't look that impressive from the outside. And, rarely will you see a processor without an accompanying heat-removal system. Your processor will have either a metal heat sink (it looks like rows of aluminum fins sticking up from it), a fan, or a combination of the two. Without a heat sink and/or fan, a modern processor would generate enough heat to destroy itself within a few seconds.

CPU Characteristics

The most important characteristic your processor can have is compatibility. Does it fit into your motherboard? Beyond this, there are literally dozens of different characteristics that CPUs have, such as hyperthreading and virtualization support. Most of those topics are beyond the scope of this book. Here, we'll focus on three key characteristics: architecture, speed, and cache.

Architecture

Processors you find today will be labeled as 32-bit or 64-bit. What this refers to is the set of data lines between the CPU and the primary memory of the system; they can be 32- or 64-bits wide, among other widths. The wider the bus, the more data that can be processed per unit of time, and hence, the more work that can be performed. For true 64-bit CPUs, which have 64-bit internal registers and can run x64 versions of Microsoft operating systems, the external system data bus will always be 64-bits wide or some larger multiple thereof.

Another term you will hear in terms of architecture is the number of cores a processor has. You might see something labeled dual-core or quad-core. To keep making better and faster processors every year, manufacturers constantly have to find ways to increase the number of instructions a processor can handle per second. Multicore means the CPU is actually made up of several processors working in unison, within the same package.

Speed

Hertz (Hz) are electrical cycles per second. Each time the internal clock of the processor completes a full cycle, a single Hz has passed. Back in 1981, IBM's first PC ran at 4.77 MHz (megahertz) which is 4.77 million cycles per second. Modern processors operate at billions (gigahertz, GHz) of cycles per second. For example, you might see a processor that runs at 3.5 GHz. Generally speaking, faster is better.

Moore's Law

There's a computer corollary called Moore's law, which states that the number of transistors in processors doubles about every two years. So far throughout the history of PCs, the law has held pretty true. And more transistors means faster processors.

Experts are predicting that based on current manufacturing technology, Moore's law will no longer be true by around 2017. You simply can't pack more silicon-based transistors into tiny spaces and make them work without generating too much heat. It will be interesting to see the progression of CPU speeds in the next few years. Will new technologies come along that allow us to keep pumping out faster computers? Or will we hit a lull where innovation stalls? Stay tuned....

To save power during times when it's not busy, many CPUs can throttle down their speed to reduce the amount of energy used. CPU throttling is very common in processors for mobile devices, where heat generation and system-battery drain are key issues of full power usage.

Cache

I already mentioned cache when I was talking about motherboards, but many of today's processors also include their own built-in cache. Cache is a very quick form of memory that greatly speeds up the performance of your computer.

You'll see three different cache designations. Level 1 cache (*L1 cache*) is the smallest and fastest, and it's on the processor die itself. In other words, it's an integrated part of the manufacturing pattern that's used to stamp the processor pathways into the silicon chip. You can't get any closer to the processor than that.

While the definition of *L1 cache* has not changed much over the years, the same is not true for other cache levels. *L2* and *L3 cache* used to be on the motherboard, but now have moved on-die in most processors as well. The biggest differences are the speed and whether they are shared. *L2 cache* is larger but a little slower than *L1 cache*. For processors with multiple cores, each core will generally have its own dedicated *L1* and *L2 caches*. A few processors share a common *L2 cache* among the cores. *L3 cache* is larger and slower than L1 or L2, and is usually shared among all processor cores.

The typical increasing order of capacity and distance from the processor die is L1 cache, L2 cache, L3 cache, and RAM. This is also the typical decreasing order of speed. The following list includes representative capacities of these memory types. The cache capacities are for each core of the original Intel Core i7 processor. The RAM capacity is simply a modern example.

- L1 cache: 64 KB (32 KB each for data and instructions)
- L2 cache: 256 KB
- L3 cache: 4 MB–12 MB
- RAM: 4 GB–64 GB

CPU Functionality

I've talked a lot about the features of processors, but what is it that they really do? (To quote the movie *Office Space*, perhaps the other components look at the processor and ask, "What would you say you *do* here?") The short answer is: "math."

Processors are made up of millions of transistors, which are electrical gates that let power through or don't depending on their current state. They're the basis of binary processing—that is, processing based on things being in one of two states: on or off, 1 or 0.

At their most basic level, all computers understand is 1s and 0s; it's the processor's job to do math on strings of 1s and 0s. The math that it performs is based on what's known as an instruction set—rules on how to do the math. It accepts numbers as input, performs calculations on them, and delivers other numbers as output. How many numbers the processor can accept at a time varies. Earlier I mentioned 32-bit versus 64-bit architecture.

Processors with 64-bit architecture can accept more data at once, and as you can imagine that can make them much faster than their 32-bit cousins.

Binary numbering is a bit unfamiliar to most people, because we're more accustomed to using the decimal numbering system (numbers 0–9). Exercise 1.1 will get you more familiar with the binary numbering system.

EXERCISE 1.1

Converting between Decimal and Other Numbering Systems

1. In Windows 7, open the Calculator application.

2. Choose View ➢ Programmer to switch to Programmer view, as shown here. Notice in Figure 1.16, on the left, that the Dec radio button is selected. Dec is short for Decimal.

FIGURE 1.16   Calculator in Programmer view

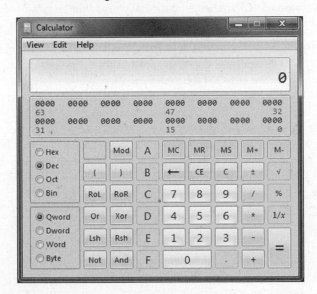

3. Enter the number **267**.

4. Click the Bin radio button. The number is converted to binary (100001011). You will also see that all of your number keys are grayed out except 0 and 1.

5. Click the Hex radio button. The number is converted to hexadecimal (10B). Now you can also use all of your number keys, as well as the letter keys A–F.

6. Click Dec again to return to Decimal.

7. Experiment with other numbers. What would your birthdate look like in binary or hex? Close the calculator when you are finished.

Memory

Memory, generically speaking, is data storage that uses on/off states on a chip to record patterns of binary data. (Remember, computers deal only with 1s and 0s!) Inside a memory chip is a grid of on/off switches. An on value represents 1, and an off value represents 0.

Memory can be either static or dynamic. *Static memory* (aka nonvolatile memory) doesn't require power to maintain its contents. *Dynamic memory* (aka volatile memory) has to be constantly powered on to retain its contents.

Broadly speaking, all memory can be divided into one of two types: ROM and RAM. *Read-only memory (ROM)* chips store data permanently; you can't make changes to their content at all. (It takes a special ROM-writing machine to write one.) This type of memory is always static. The BIOS on your motherboard is stored on a ROM chip.

> BIOS chips today are updatable, through a process I mentioned earlier called flashing the BIOS. BIOS chips are now stored on a newer, modified version of ROM called electronically erasable programmable ROM (EEPROM), which allows the ROM to be updated by using electronic pulses.

The programming on simple electronic devices that will never need to be user-updated, like the computer on an exercise treadmill that stores various fitness programs, will also be stored on ROM. The main advantage of ROM is its reliability. It can never be accidentally changed or deleted. The disadvantages of ROM are that it's slow compared to RAM and that you can't ever update it; you have to pull the chip out of the system and replace it. Because of these drawbacks, ROM isn't used as a PC's primary memory source; a PC has only a small amount of ROM.

Random access memory (RAM) can be written and rewritten on the device in which it's installed. It's called *random access* because the data is stored in whatever locations are available in it, and when reading data back from RAM, only the required data is read, not the entire contents.

> You can never have too much RAM.

RAM can be either static or dynamic. Static RAM (SRAM), also called flash RAM, is the type you use when you store files on a USB flash drive. Static RAM is nonvolatile; you can disconnect a flash RAM device and carry it with you, and the next time you connect it to a computer, the data will still be there. Most of the memory on a PC's motherboard is dynamic RAM (DRAM), so when someone refers to a computer's memory or RAM, you can generally assume that they mean the DRAM on the motherboard. Dynamic RAM is volatile; when you turn off your computer, its content is gone.

The motherboard's RAM functions as a work area when the computer is on. The OS is loaded into it, as are any applications you have open and any data associated with those applications. The more free RAM in the computer, the larger the available workspace, so the more applications and data files you'll be able to have open at once. If your system runs low on RAM, it can use slower virtual memory to compensate. Exercise 1.2 shows you how to configure your virtual memory.

🌐 Real World Scenario

Virtual Memory

Many OSs, including Microsoft Windows, use a tremendous amount of RAM as they operate, to the point that even a well-equipped PC might not have enough RAM to do everything that a user wants. To prevent the user from being denied an activity because of lack of available memory, these OSs employ virtual memory to take up the slack.

With virtual memory, a portion of the hard disk is set aside as a holding area for the contents of RAM. When there isn't enough space in RAM to hold the data that needs to be placed there, the OS's virtual memory management utility temporarily moves some of the least-recently used data in RAM onto the hard disk, making room for the new incoming data. Then, if an application calls for the data that was moved out, the virtual memory manager moves something else out and swaps the needed data back in again.

Because of all this data swapping, the reserved area on the hard disk for virtual memory is sometimes called a *swap file* or a *page file*.

The main drawback of virtual memory is its speed, which is limited to the speed at which the hard drive can store and retrieve data. Compared to the speed of the processor and memory, the hard disk is very slow. Therefore, the less physical RAM available in a system, and the more that system has to rely on virtual memory, the more slowly applications will run on that system. That's why adding more RAM to a system is often a worthwhile upgrade.

EXERCISE 1.2

Assessing Your Computer's RAM and Virtual Memory

1. In Windows 7, click Start and then right-click Computer and click Properties. (Alternatively, open Control Panel ➢ System And Security ➢ System.)

2. In the System section of the page that appears, note the amount of Installed Memory (RAM). This is the total physical amount of RAM.

3. In the bar at the left, click Advanced System Settings. The System Properties dialog box opens.

4. On the Advanced tab, in the Performance section, click Settings. The Performance Options dialog box opens.

5. Click the Advanced tab, and, in the Virtual Memory section, note the total paging file size for all drives, as shown in Figure 1.17. This is the amount of virtual memory set aside for the system's use.

FIGURE 1.17   Virtual memory

6. Click the Change button. The Virtual Memory dialog box opens.

7. Click Cancel to close the dialog box without making any changes. (It's usually best to leave this setting to be automatically managed by the system.)

8. Click Cancel to close the Performance Options dialog box.

9. Click Cancel to close the System Properties dialog box.

10. Under the System heading, find the Rating line, and click Windows Experience Index.

11. The Performance And Information Tools section of Control Panel opens.

12. Note the subscore next to Memory (RAM), as shown in Figure 1.18. If this number is the lowest of the subscores by a substantial amount, the computer's performance might be improved by adding more RAM. As shown here, the RAM has the highest score (7.5) of any component, so this system has adequate RAM.

FIGURE 1.18   System performance subscores

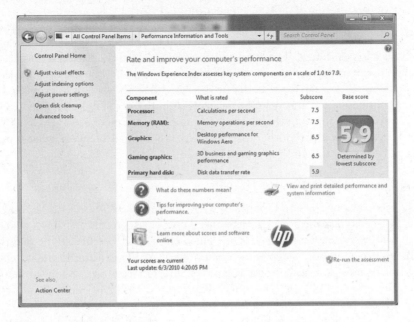

13. Close the Control Panel window.

Memory Bus Speeds

The pathway that delivers data to and from the memory is called a memory bus. Memory has a bus width that determines how many columns are in each row of storage. All the bits in a single row are read together as a single value, so the wider the memory bus width, the more data that can be read at once. For example, in memory with an 8-bit width, you might have a number like 01001100. In memory with a 32-bit width, you could have a number with up to 32 binary digits.

The memory bus also has a speed, which determines how quickly data will travel on its pathway. Memory on modern PCs is synchronized with the system bus, which in turn is controlled by the system timer on the motherboard. (Remember the Northbridge? It controls all of that.) The system timer determines the speed at which data enters the processor. Memory that operates at the same speed as the front-side bus is called single data rate (SDR) synchronous dynamic read-only memory (SDRAM).

The original successor to SDR SDRAM was double data rate (DDR) SDRAM, also sometimes called DDR1. It makes higher transfer rates achievable by strictly controlling the timing of the electrical data and clock signals so that data can be double-pumped into the RAM. The term *double data rate* is a reference to DDR's capability of achieving nearly twice the bandwidth of SDR.

After DDR1 came DDR2 SDRAM, which enables greater throughput and requires lower power by running the internal clock at half the speed of the data bus, in addition to double-pumping the bus. This effectively multiplies the DDR1-level performance by two, so that there are a total of four data transfers per internal clock cycle.

DDR3 goes even further, once again doubling the data rate, to a total of eight times the original SDR throughput. It also uses about 30 percent less power than DDR2 modules because it uses a lower voltage. The main benefit of DDR3, and the reason it doubles the data rate, isn't because of a raw increase in the pumping but because of the use of a deeper prefetch buffer. A prefetch buffer is an extra buffer on the RAM that allows quick access to data located on a common physical row in the memory. (A buffer is a simpler version of a cache.)

Generally speaking, most motherboards accept only one type of RAM: SDR, DDR, DDR2, or DDR3. Even if the motherboard is physically compatible with other types, it's programmed to work with RAM at a certain speed.

Physical Characteristics of RAM

There have been various sizes and shapes of RAM modules in PCs over the years. For the most part, PCs today use memory chips arranged on a small circuit board; an example is the *dual inline memory module (DIMM)*. The *dual* in DIMM refers to the fact that the module uses pins on both sides of the circuit board. DIMMs differ in the number of conductors, or pins, that each particular physical form factor uses. Some common examples include 168-, 184-, and 240-pin configurations, with 240 being the most common today. In addition, laptop memory comes in smaller form factors known as a *small outline DIMM (SODIMM)*. (Some laptops also use a smaller version known as a MicroDIMM.) Figure 1.19 shows the form factors for some popular memory modules. The top two are DDR3 and DDR2; notice how they basically look the same but the keying notches are different. The bottom one is a SODIMM for a laptop.

FIGURE 1.19   Memory module form factors

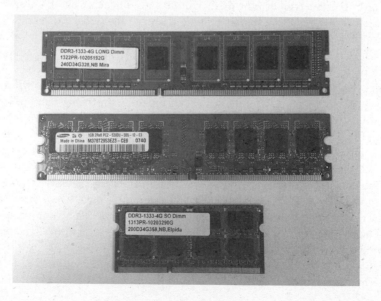

Different types of DIMMs and SODIMMs may be similar or even identical in overall size and shape and may even have the same number of pins. For example, DDR2 and DDR3 DIMMs both have 240 pins. The good news is each type of RAM has a uniquely placed notch in the edge that contains the pins. That notch makes the RAM fit only in a slot that has a correspondingly placed spacer and prevents people from installing the wrong type of memory. You could try, but the memory stick would likely break before you got it in there.

Exercise 1.3 helps you determine what type of RAM you have in your computer.

EXERCISE 1.3

Determining the Type of Installed RAM

1. Look in the documentation that came with your computer to see if there is anything about the RAM specifications. In the documentation, locate the information about installing a RAM upgrade. This will tell you where to find the RAM on your system.

2. Open the computer's case and locate the RAM. Identify whether it's DIMM or SODIMM. (Most notebook PCs use SODIMM, and most desktop PCs use DIMM.) To avoid damaging it with static electricity, avoid touching it. If you need to touch it, touch the metal frame of the PC's case first. You'll learn more about preventing static electricity damage in Chapter 12, "Environmental and Safety Concepts."

3. Examine the numbers or codes, if any, on the DIMM or SODIMM, looking for model numbers, speeds, or any other pertinent information.

4. Look at the data you gathered online to see if you can determine anything about the memory based on those numbers.

5. If you can't determine the RAM type by any of these methods, find the motherboard's brand and model number (look for this information printed on the motherboard itself). Then look up the motherboard online to see if information about its RAM requirements is available.

Exploring Storage and Expansion Devices

Beyond the "big three" of the motherboard, processor, and RAM, there are several other important devices located inside your computer. Broadly speaking, they fall into one of two camps. They either provide long-term storage, or they expand your system's functionality by giving you features such as video, audio, or network access.

Over the following sections, I will introduce you to six different types of devices. The first two, hard drives and optical drives, give you the ability to store data on a long-term basis. The last four, video cards, soundcards, network cards, and modems, provide features that take your computer from being a really good paperweight to being a helpful and fun device to use.

Hard Drives

Computers would be a lot less useful to us if they weren't able to store our data long-term. This is where hard drives come in. Hard disk drive (HDD) systems (called hard disks or *hard drives* for short) are used for permanent storage and quick access. They hold our data as well as files the system needs to operate smoothly. Drives differ in their capacity, speed (access time), and the type of materials they are made from (metal or glass platters coated with a magnetic coating).

Hard disks typically reside inside the computer, where they are semipermanently mounted with no external access (although there are external and removable hard drives), and can hold more information than other forms of storage. Hard drives use a magnetic storage medium and are known as conventional drives to differentiate them from newer solid-state storage media.

Inside the hard drive, you will find a sealed stack of metal platters, each with a read-write head on a retractable arm that reads data from and writes data to the platters by magnetizing bits of iron oxide particles on the platters in patterns of positive and negative polarity. As a hard disk operates, the platters rotate at a high speed, and the read/write heads hover just over the disk surfaces on a cushion of air generated by the spinning. Normally you won't see the inside of a hard drive, so you can see one in Figure 1.20. Once you open the metal box that it's encased in, you ruin the drive. The platters are typically 3½″ in diameter for full-size hard disk drives (for desktop PCs) and 2½″ for smaller hard disk drives used in notebook PCs.

FIGURE 1.20   Inside a hard drive

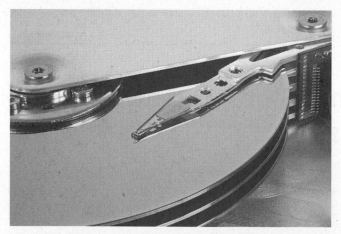

PHOTO CREDIT: ERIC GABA - WIKIMEDIA COMMONS USER: STING

You might hear old-timers talk about floppy disks and floppy disk drives (FDD). Floppy disks were square and held a thin, pliable disk of magnetic material, and they were written to and read from magnetically, just like hard drives. You would insert them into an FDD, which performed the reading and writing functions on the disk.

The two most common sizes were 3½" and 5¼", and they held 1.44 MB and 1.2 MB respectively. You won't need to know those numbers for the exam, but they give you good perspective on how little data they could hold. The one advantage they had was that they were portable. Now we have USB flash drives, with capacities in the gigabytes (and no special read/write device required), that make floppy disks obsolete.

Hard Drive Characteristics

When evaluating hard drives, there are really two factors that determine its performance: size and speed.

Size is fairly self-evident. Hard drives with larger capacity store more data. There isn't anything too tricky about it. You can easily find hard drives with capacities from several hundred gigabytes up to 4 terabytes. Table 1.2 has some conversions that will likely come in handy.

TABLE 1.2   Bit and byte conversions

How Many	Equals	Example
8 bits	1 byte	One text character.
1000 bytes	1 kilobyte (KB)	A 1000-character plain text file or a small icon.
1000 kilobytes	1 megabyte (MB)	A small photograph or one minute of music.
1000 megabytes	1 gigabyte (GB)	A full-length audio CD is about 800 MB; a two-hour DVD movie is about 4 GB.
1000 gigabytes	1 terabyte (TB)	A large business database.
1000 terabytes	1 petabyte (PB)	Data from a large government institution, such as the U.S. Internal Revenue Service.
1000 petabytes	1 exabyte (EB)	
1000 exabytes	1 zettabyte (ZB)	

The historical convention was always that the next level up equaled 1024 of the previous level, such that 1 MB = 1024 KB. Now, it's more or less accepted that we just round everything off to 1000 to make it easier to do the math.

Most people probably think that we don't need to think in terms of exabytes or zettabytes (not to mention yottabytes, which are 1000 zettabytes), but with 4 TB hard drives being relatively common today, these larger measures are probably right around the corner.

Speed is the other thing you will want to look at when considering a hard drive. Hard drive access is much slower than RAM access, so hard drives can often be the bottleneck in system performance. Over the years, though, technology has evolved to improve hard drive access time. To speed up data access, manufacturers increase the speed at which the platters spin from one generation of drives to the next, with multiple speeds coexisting in the marketplace for an unpredictable period until demand dies down for one or more speeds.

The following spin rates have been used in the industry for the platters in conventional magnetic hard disk drives:

- 5400 rpm
- 7200 rpm
- 10,000 rpm
- 12,000 rpm
- 15,000 rpm

A higher revolutions per minute (rpm) rating results in the ability to move data more quickly. The lower speeds can be better for laptops, where heat production and battery usage can be issues with the higher-speed drives.

Connecting a Hard Drive

There are two common hard drive standards in the marketplace today: Parallel ATA (PATA), also known as Integrated Drive Electronics (IDE), and Serial ATA (SATA). PATA/IDE has been around a lot longer (IDE came out in the late 1980s), and SATA is the newer and faster technology, launched in 2003.

Regardless of the standard, hard drives need two connections to function properly: power and the data cable. The power comes from the power supply, and the data cables connect to the motherboard. Figure 1.21 shows the back of two standard 3½″ desktop hard drives. The top one is PATA/IDE and the bottom one is SATA.

FIGURE 1.21   PATA/IDE and SATA hard drives

Figure 1.22 shows the ends of the data cables. Again, the top one is PATA and the bottom one is SATA. The connectors where the data cables plug into the motherboard were shown in Figure 1.9 and Figure 1.10.

FIGURE 1.22   PATA and SATA data cables

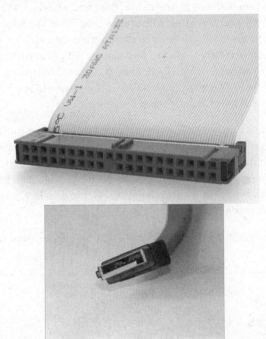

  There's a third connector type, called Small Computer System Interface (SCSI), that you might hear about. It uses a ribbon cable similar to IDE but wider. It was once popular for high-end systems, but the speed and lower cost of SATA has made SCSI fade in popularity. Few motherboards had SCSI controllers built onto them. If you wanted a SCSI hard drive, you needed to add an internal expansion board with a SCSI controller on it.

🌐 Real World Scenario

Connecting Multiple PATA Devices

Hard drives are important, and for many years the most common hard drive standard was PATA (at the time called IDE). Most motherboards came with two connectors; today, motherboards will have one, if they support PATA at all. When CD-ROM drives came out, they too used the same 40-pin connector as hard drives. If you had only two devices, this wasn't a problem. But what if you wanted two hard drives *and* a CD-ROM?

The 40-pin PATA ribbon cable has three connectors on it. One goes to the motherboard, and the other two—one in the middle of the cable and one at the other end—go to drives. If you have only one PATA drive, you use the connector at the far end of the cable, and the extra connector in the middle of the cable goes unused.

If you need to connect two devices to one cable, then you also need to tell the computer which device has priority over the other. Otherwise they fight like spoiled children and neither one will work. To do that, you need to configure each drive as either the master (MA) or the slave (SL) on that cable. Master and slave configuration is performed via jumpers on the back of the hard drive. If you look at Figure 1.18, the jumper block is the 10-pin block between the PATA data connector and the power block. The right two pins have a jumper placed over them, configuring the drive.

Some PATA cables will assign mastery or slavery to a drive based on the connector into which it's plugged. (That's called Cable Select (CS), with the master at the end and the slave in the middle.) To make this work, you must set the jumpers on each of the drives to the CS setting. Fortunately they are usually set to CS by default. The top of the hard drive might have a sticker showing you the jumper settings (the one in Figure 1.21 does), or you can check the manufacturer's documentation.

When a newly installed PATA drive doesn't work, it could be because the jumpers aren't set correctly.

Solid-State Drives

Unlike conventional hard drives, a *solid-state drive (SSD)* has no moving parts but uses the same solid-state memory technology found in the other forms of flash memory. You can think of them as bigger versions of the flash drives that are so common.

When used as a replacement for traditional HDDs, SSDs are expected to behave in a similar fashion, mainly by retaining contents even when the system is powered off. Connecting an SSD is just like connecting a regular HDD: they have the same PATA/SATA and power connectors. Most manufacturers also make them in the same physical dimensions as traditional hard drives.

As you might expect, SSDs have several advantages over their mechanical counterparts. These include the following:

- Faster start-up and read times
- Less power consumption and heat produced
- Silent operation
- Generally more reliable because of lack of moving parts
- Less susceptible to damage from physical shock and heat production
- Higher data density per square centimeter

Disadvantages of SSDs are as follows:

- All solid-state memory is limited to a finite number of write (including erase) operations. Lack of longevity could be an issue.

- The technology to build an SSD is more expensive per byte.

To summarize, SSDs are faster and produce less heat but are generally more expensive than conventional hard drives. In Exercise 1.4 you look at how to view information about your hard drive in Windows 7.

EXERCISE 1.4

Examining Hard Drives in Windows

1. In Windows 7, click Start ➤ Computer. A list of the drives on your PC appears.

2. Click the primary hard disk (C:) to select it, and look in the status bar at the bottom of the window. Figure 1.23 shows an example. The hard disk's total size, space used, space free, and file system information appear. Here is an example, but your hard drive will have different specifications.

FIGURE 1.23   Hard disk status

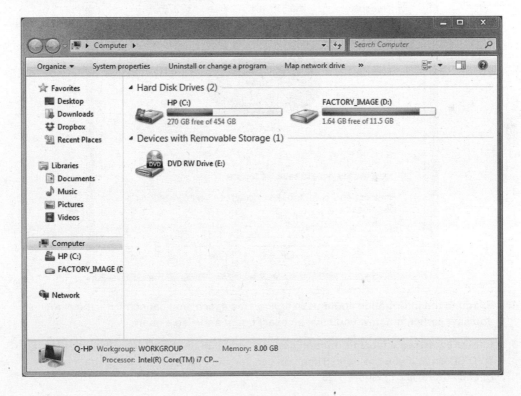

3. Right-click the hard disk, and click Properties. A Properties dialog box opens for that drive, as shown in Figure 1.24.

FIGURE 1.24 Hard disk properties

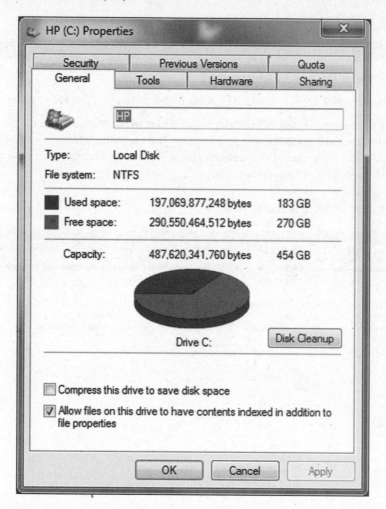

4. Examine the information about used space, free space, and capacity. It's the same as you saw earlier, but now you have an exact count and also a chart.

5. Click the Hardware tab. Information appears about all the disk drives, including your DVD/CD drive if you have one. Here you can see the brand name and model number of each drive, like in Figure 1.25.

FIGURE 1.25   Disk drives

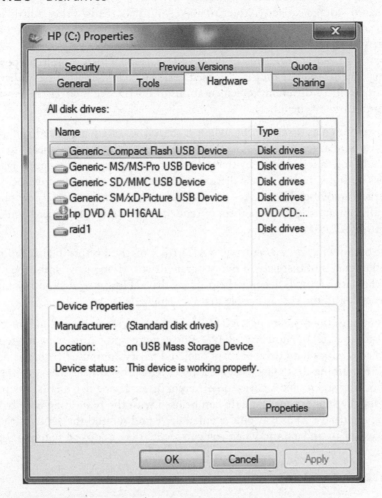

6.   Click Cancel to close the dialog box, and close the Computer window.

Combining Hard Drives

If having one hard drive is good, then having two hard drives is better. Perhaps you need additional storage space, so you add another drive. There's nothing wrong with doing that, but what happens if one (or both) of your hard drives fails? Having that extra drive didn't help. In fact, it added another potential point of failure for your computer. And adding that extra drive didn't speed up your system's performance. If anything, it might have slowed it down a bit if you added it to the same PATA cable as your existing hard drive.

There are ways you can add additional hard drives to a computer and get benefits beyond increased storage capacity. You can make your disk reads/writes a little faster, and you can also create *fault tolerance*, which means that you have extra protection against disk failures. You do this by implementing *RAID*.

RAID stands for *redundant array of independent disks*, which is multiple physical hard disks working together as a team for increased performance, increased reliability, or both. There are more than 10 different implementations of RAID. We'll cover the most popular (and important) three of them here.

RAID 0   Also known as *disk striping*, where a striped set of equal space from at least two drives creates a larger volume. *RAID 0* is not RAID in every sense because it doesn't provide the fault tolerance implied by the *redundant* component of the name. Data is written across multiple drives, so one drive can be reading or writing while the next drive's read-write head is moving. This makes for faster data access. However, if any one of the drives fails, all content is lost. Some form of redundancy or fault tolerance should be used in concert with RAID 0.

RAID 1   Also known as *disk mirroring*, *RAID 1* is a method of producing fault tolerance by writing all data simultaneously to two separate drives. If one drive fails, the other contains all the data and will become the primary drive. However, disk mirroring doesn't help access speed, and the cost is double that of a single drive.

RAID 5   Combines the benefits of RAID 0 and RAID 1, creating a redundant striped volume set. Unlike RAID 1, however, *RAID 5* does not employ mirroring for redundancy. Each stripe places data on all drives except one, and parity computed from the data is placed on the remaining disk. The parity is interleaved across all the drives in the array so that neighboring stripes have parity on different disks. If one drive fails, the parity information for the stripes that lost data can be used with the remaining data from the working drives to derive what was on the failed drive and rebuild the set once the drive is replaced. It's easier to understand when you can see it. Take a look at Figure 1.26.

FIGURE 1.26   RAID 1 and RAID 5

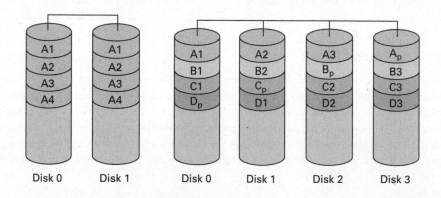

A minimum of three drives is required for RAID 5. If one drive fails, the system will continue to operate, but slowly. The loss of an additional drive, however, results in a catastrophic loss of all data in the array. RAID 5 does not eliminate the need to do data backups.

Optical Drives

Most computers today have an optical storage drive capable of reading the latest Blu-ray Disc (BD), a digital versatile disc—or digital video disc (DVD), or the legacy compact disc (CD) you have lying around. Each type of optical drive can be expected to also support the technology that came before it. Optical storage devices began replacing floppy drives in the late 1990s. Even though discs have greater data capacity and increased performance over floppies, they are not intended to replace hard drives.

The CDs, DVDs, and BDs used for data storage are virtually the same as those used for permanent recorded audio and video. The way data, audio, and video information is written to consumer-recordable versions makes them virtually indistinguishable from professionally manufactured discs.

Each of these media types requires an optical drive capable of reading them. Those devices are designated with a -ROM ending, for example, *CD-ROM*, *DVD-ROM*, or *BD-ROM*. If the drive is capable of writing to these discs (called a *burner*), it will have a different ending, such as -R (recordable) or -RW (rewritable). To make matters more confusing, there are two standards of DVD burners: DVD-RW and DVD+RW. Today's DVD readers can generally handle both formats, but older devices might not be able to. Burnable BD drives are designated BD-R or BD-RE (for re-recordable). Figure 1.27 shows a DVD-ROM. It's really hard to tell optical drives apart from each other, unless you see the logo that's on it.

FIGURE 1.27   A DVD-ROM

Each of the formats I have mentioned so far has different capacities. Table 1.3 lists the most common. Before getting to Table 1.3, though, I need to define a few more acronyms. Discs can be single sided (SS) or double-sided (DS), meaning information is written to one or both faces of the disc. In addition, DVDs and BDs can have multiple layers on the same side, otherwise known as dual-layer (DL). The ability to create dual layers nearly doubles the capacity of one side of the disc. Boldfaced capacities in the table are the commonly accepted values for their respective formats.

TABLE 1.3   Optical discs and their capacities

Disc Format	Capacity
CD SS (includes recordable versions)	650 MB, **700 MB**, 800 MB, 900 MB
DVD-R/RW SS, SL	4.71 GB (**4.7 GB**)
DVD+R/RW SS, SL	4.70 GB (**4.7 GB**)
DVD-R, DVD+R DS, SL	**9.4 GB**
DVD-R SS, DL	8.54 GB (**8.5 GB**)
DVD+R SS, DL	8.55 GB (**8.5 GB**)
DVD+R DS, DL	17.1 GB
BD-R/RE SS, SL	25 GB
BD-R/RE SS, DL	50 GB
BD-R/RE DS, DL	100 GB

SS: single-sided; DS: double-sided; SL: single-layer; DL: dual-layer

A double-sided, single-layer DVD will give you more storage space than a single-sided, dual-layer DVD. This is because there is a bit of inefficiency when writing a second layer on one side, so the second layer doesn't quite give you double the storage space versus just one layer.

So now you know why Blu-ray movies are so much better than those on DVD. Even the simplest BD can store nearly 50 percent more data than the most advanced DVD!

Video Cards

A video adapter (more commonly called a graphics adapter or even more commonly a *video card*) is the expansion card you put into a computer to allow the computer to display information on some kind of monitor. A video card is responsible for converting the data sent to it by the CPU into the pixels, addresses, and other items required for display.

Sometimes, video cards can include dedicated chips to perform some of these functions, thus accelerating the speed of display. This type of chip is called a *graphics processing unit (GPU)*. Some of the common GPUs are ATI Radeon and NVIDIA GeForce. Most video cards also have their own onboard RAM. This is a good thing, and just like the RAM on your motherboard, the more the better. Figure 1.28 shows a video card.

FIGURE 1.28   A video card

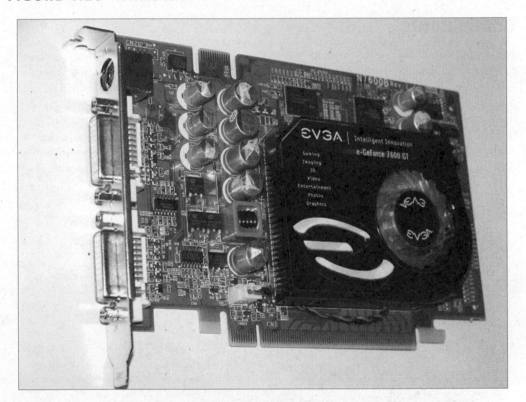

Most video cards sold today use the PCIe interface, but you might still see some older AGP cards out there. They both work the same way, except that AGP is very slow compared to PCIe.

Video cards can have one or more external plug-ins for monitors or other display devices. You will see that the card shown in Figure 1.28 has three—one S-video port and two DVI ports. Those will be covered in more detail in Chapter 2. Also notice that this card has a rather large fan attached to it. This is because the card has its own processor and memory and generates a lot of heat. Secondary cooling is necessary to keep this card from melting down.

NOTE To save space and money, some systems (primarily laptops) will have the GPU built into the CPU or otherwise on the motherboard. These systems will also split the system RAM between video and other system functions. (Usually in these cases, the amount of RAM dedicated to video can be configured in the BIOS or in Windows.) There's nothing wrong with this type of configuration, other than it's slower than having separate components. If you are a gamer, or otherwise have high video processing needs, you will want a separate video card with as much RAM on it as you can get.

Sound Cards

Just as there are devices to convert computer signals into printouts and video information, there are devices to convert those signals into sound. These devices are known as *sound cards* (or audio cards). Although sound cards started out as pluggable adapters, this functionality is one of the most common integrated technologies found on motherboards today. A sound card typically has small, round, ⅛-inch (3.5mm) jacks on the back of it for connecting microphones, headphones, and speakers as well as other sound equipment. Many sound cards used to have a DA15 game port, which can be used for either joysticks or MIDI controllers (used with external keyboards, etc.). Figure 1.29 shows an example of a legacy sound card with a DA15 game port.

FIGURE 1.29   A typical sound card

The most popular sound card standard in the market is the Sound Blaster, which is made by Creative Labs.

Network Cards

It seems like every computer participates on a network these days, whether it's at the office or at home. A *network interface card (NIC)* is an expansion card that connects a computer to a network so that it can communicate with other computers on that network. It translates the data from the parallel data stream used inside the computer into the serial data stream that makes up the frames used on the network. It has a connector for the type of expansion bus on the motherboard (PCIe, PCI, and so on) as well as a connector for the type of network (such as fiber connectors, RJ-45 for UTP, antenna for wireless, or BNC for legacy coax). Figure 1.30 shows a wireless network card designed for a desktop PC.

FIGURE 1.30   A wireless desktop NIC

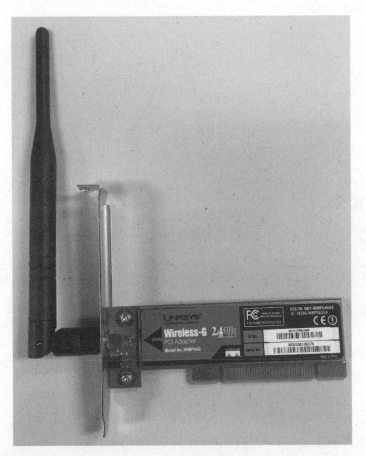

A large number of computers now have the NIC circuitry integrated into their motherboards. A computer with an integrated NIC wouldn't need to have a NIC expansion card installed unless it was faster or you were using the second NIC for load balancing, security, or fault-tolerance.

Modems

Any computer that connects to the Internet using an analog dial-up connection needs a modem, or *modulator/dem*odulator. A *modem* is a device that converts digital signals from a computer into analog signals that can be transmitted over phone lines and back again. These expansion card devices are easy to identify because they have phone connectors on the plate. Usually, as you can see in Figure 1.31, there are two RJ-11 ports: one for connection to the telephone line and the other for connection to a telephone. This is primarily so that a phone can gain access to the same wall jack that the computer connects to without swapping their cords. Keep in mind, though, that you won't be able to use the phone while the computer is connected to the Internet.

FIGURE 1.31   A modem

Before high-speed Internet became popular, a modem was the device people used to get on the Internet. Of course, this meant the phone line was in use and no one could call your home phone. This was back in the day when people still had land phone lines and mobile phones were a rare luxury. (I feel like my grandpa talking about the "olden days" when I say these things!) Modems are rarely used today.

Exploring Power and Cooling

Without electricity, there wouldn't be any computers. With too much electricity, you'll fry everything inside the box. The goal is to find a happy medium and provide consistent power to your computer.

Electronics components produce heat. The amount of heat depends on a variety of things, such as the number of transistors it has, the size of the piece, and the ventilation provided. Having components overheat is the most surefire way of having them fail, except perhaps for dousing them with water.

In these next two sections, you'll learn about providing your computer components with the right amount of power and then cooling them off so they last as long as possible.

Power Supplies

The device in the computer that provides power is appropriately named the *power supply* (Figure 1.32), sometimes called a power supply unit (PSU). That nondescript silver box with the tangle of cords coming from it converts 110V or 220VAC current into the DC voltages that a computer needs to operate. These are +3.3VDC, +5VDC, –5VDC (on older systems), +12VDC, and –12VDC. The jacket on the leads carrying each type of voltage has a different industry-standard color coding for faster recognition. Black ground leads offer the reference that gives the voltage leads their respective magnitudes. The +3.3VDC voltage was first offered on ATX motherboards.

FIGURE 1.32   A desktop power supply

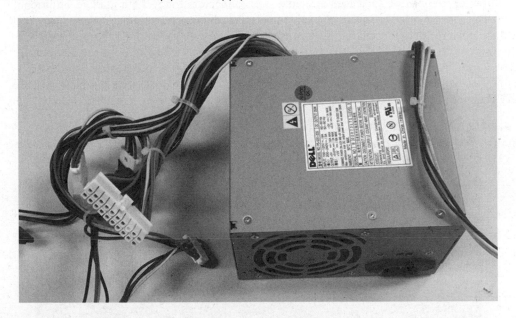

The abbreviation *VDC* stands for *volts DC. DC* is short for *direct current.* Unlike alternating current (AC), DC does not alter the direction in which the electrons flow. AC for standard power distribution does so 50 or 60 times per second (50 or 60 Hz, respectively).

WARNING   Power supplies contain transformers and capacitors that can discharge *lethal* amounts of current even when disconnected from the wall outlet for long periods. They are not meant to be serviced, especially by untrained personnel. Do not attempt to open them or do any work on them. Simply replace and recycle them when they go bad.

Power supplies are rated in watts. A watt is a unit of power. The higher the number, the more power your computer can draw from the power supply. Think of this rating as the capacity of the device to supply power. Most computers require power supplies in the 250- to 500-watt range. Higher-wattage power supplies might be required for more advanced systems that employ power-hungry graphics technologies or multiple disk drives, for instance. It is important to consider the draw that the various components and subcomponents of your computer place on the power supply before choosing one or its replacement.

Power supplies have an input plug for the power cord (shown on the left in Figure 1.33), a connector to power the motherboard, and then other connectors to power peripherals such as hard drives and optical drives. Each has a different appearance and way of connecting to the device. Newer systems have a variety of similar, replacement, and additional connectors, such as dedicated power connectors for SATA and PCIe, additional power connectors for the motherboard, and even modular connections for these leads back to the power supply instead of a permanent wiring harness. Figure 1.34 shows the ATX power connector that goes to the motherboard. Notice that it's keyed so it can't be put in the wrong way. Figure 1.35 shows three different types of peripheral power connectors: a four-pin Molex connector for PATA hard drives and optical drives, a six-pin PCIe (called a PEG connector), and a SATA connector.

FIGURE 1.33   Power supply in the case

FIGURE 1.34   A 20-pin ATX power connector

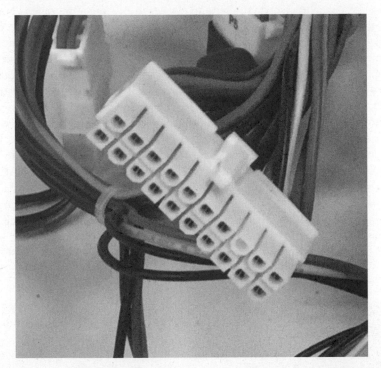

FIGURE 1.35   Peripheral power connectors

Most power supplies have a recessed, two-position slider switch, often a red one, on the rear that is exposed through the case. You can see it in Figure 1.33. Selections read 110 and 220, 115 and 230, or 120 and 240. This dual-voltage selector switch is used to adjust for the voltage level used in the country where the computer is in service. For example, in the United States, the power grid supplies anywhere from 110 to 120VAC. However, in Europe, for instance, the voltage supplied is double, ranging from 220 to 240VAC.

Although the voltage is the same as what is used in the United States to power high-voltage appliances, such as electric ranges and clothes driers, the amperage is much lower. The point is the switch is not there to match the type of outlet used in the same country. If the wrong voltage is chosen in the United States, the power supply expects more voltage than it receives and might not power up at all. If the wrong voltage is selected in Europe, however, the power supply receives more voltage than it is set for. The result could be disastrous for the entire computer. Sparks could also ignite a fire that could destroy nearby property and endanger lives. Always check the switch before powering up a new or recently relocated computer. In the United States and other countries that use the same voltage, check the setting of this switch if the computer fails to power up.

Laptop computers don't have big, bulky power supplies like the one shown in Figure 1.32 but instead use smaller AC adapters. They function the same way, converting AC current into DC power for the laptop's components. AC Adapters are also rated in watts and selected for use with a specific voltage just as power supplies are. One difference is that AC adapters are also rated in terms of DC volts out to the laptop or other device, such as certain brands and models of printers. One is shown in Figure 1.36. You can see the circular connector on the laptop for the adapter.

FIGURE 1.36   Laptop power supply

Because both power supplies and AC adapters go bad on occasion, you should replace them both and not attempt to repair them yourself. When replacing an AC adapter, be sure to match the size, shape, and polarity of the tip with the adapter you are replacing. However, because the output DC voltage is specified for the AC adapter, be sure to replace it with one of equal output voltage, an issue not seen when replacing desktop power supplies, which have standard outputs. Additionally, and as with power supplies, you can replace an AC adapter with a model that supplies more watts to the component because the component uses only what it needs.

Cooling Systems

The downside of providing power to electronic components is that they produce heat. The excess heat must be dissipated or it will shorten the life of the components. In some cases (like with the CPU), the component will produce so much heat that it can destroy itself in a matter of seconds if there is not some way to remove this extra heat. All computer systems today come with some cooling systems to reduce and remove heat. Here, we'll look at two broad categories of cooling systems: case cooling and CPU cooling.

Case Cooling

The most common method used to cool computers is air cooling. With air cooling, the movement of air removes the heat from the component. Sometimes, large blocks of metal called heat sinks are attached to a heat-producing component in order to dissipate the heat more rapidly.

When you turn on a computer, you will often hear lots of whirring. Contrary to popular opinion, the majority of the noise isn't coming from the hard disk (unless it's about to go bad). Most of this noise is coming from the various fans inside the computer. Fans provide airflow within the computer.

Most PCs have a combination of these fans:

Front Intake Fan   This fan is used to bring fresh, cool air into the computer for cooling purposes.

Rear Exhaust Fan   This fan is used to take hot air out of the case.

Power Supply Exhaust Fan   This fan is usually found at the back of the power supply and is used to cool the power supply. In addition, this fan draws air from inside the case into vents in the power supply. This pulls hot air through the power supply so that it can be blown out of the case. The front intake fan assists with this airflow. The rear exhaust fan supplements the power supply fan to achieve the same result outside the power supply.

In addition, you can buy supplemental cooling devices for almost any component inside your computer. For example, you can get cooling systems specifically for hard drives, RAM, chipsets, and video cards. Ideally, the airflow inside a computer should resemble what is shown in Figure 1.37.

FIGURE 1.37   System unit airflow

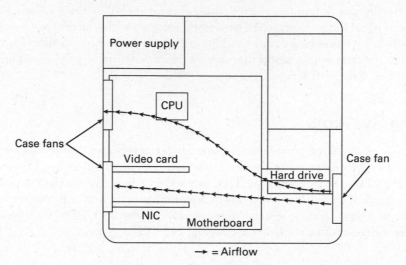

Note that you must pay attention to the orientation of the power supply's airflow. If the power supply fan is an exhaust fan, as assumed in this discussion, the front and rear fans will match their earlier descriptions: front, intake; rear, exhaust. If you run across a power supply that has an intake fan, the orientation of the supplemental chassis fans should be reversed as well. The rear chassis fan(s) should always be installed in the same orientation as the power supply fan runs to avoid creating a small airflow circuit that circumvents the cross flow of air through the case. The front chassis fan and the rear fans should always be installed in the reverse orientation to prevent them from fighting against each other and reducing the internal airflow.

CPU Cooling

Without a doubt, the greatest challenge in computer cooling is keeping the CPU's temperature in check. It is the component that generates the most heat in a computer; if left unchecked, it will fry itself in a matter of seconds. That's why most motherboards have an internal CPU heat sensor and a CPU fan sensor. If no cooling fan is active, these devices will shut down the computer before damage occurs.

There are a few different types of CPU cooling methods, but the two most common can be grouped into two categories: air cooling and liquid cooling.

Air Cooling

The parts inside most computers are cooled by air moving through the case. The CPU is no exception. However, because of the large amount of heat produced, the CPU must have (proportionately) the largest surface area exposed to the moving air in the case. Therefore, the heat sinks on the CPU are the largest of any inside the computer. A CPU heat sink is shown in Figure 1.38.

FIGURE 1.38   CPU heat sink

The metal fins on the heat sink in Figure 1.38 attach to the processor, and the fan on top helps dissipate the heat. You will find a variety of different types of processor heat sinks on the market, but most of them involve both the metal heat spreaders and a fan.

 Don't touch a CPU heat sink until your computer has been turned off for at least several minutes!

The CPU fan often blows air down through the body of the heat sink to force the heat into the ambient internal air, where it can join the airflow circuit for removal from the case. However, in some cases, you might find that the heat sink extends up farther, using radiator-type fins, and the fan is placed at a right angle and to the side of the heat sink. This design moves the heat away from the heat sink immediately instead of pushing the air down through the heat sink. CPU fans can be purchased that have an adjustable rheostat to allow you to dial in as little airflow as you need, aiding in noise reduction but potentially leading to accidental overheating.

Liquid Cooling

Liquid cooling is the second most popular way to cool processors, but it's not often found in the PC market. Liquid cooling uses a special water block to conduct heat away from the processor (as well as from the chipset). Water is circulated through this block to a radiator, where it is cooled.

The theory is that you could achieve better cooling performance through the use of liquid cooling. For the most part, this is true. However, with traditional cooling methods (which use air and water), the lowest temperature you can achieve is room temperature. Plus, with liquid cooling, the pump is submerged in the coolant (generally speaking), so as it works, it produces heat, which adds to the overall liquid temperature.

The main benefit to liquid cooling is that it's quiet. There is only one fan needed: the fan on the radiator to cool the water. So a liquid-cooled system can run extremely quietly.

Liquid cooling, while more efficient than air cooling and much quieter, has its drawbacks. Most liquid-cooling systems are more expensive than supplemental fan sets and require less-familiar components, such as a reservoir, pump, water block(s), hose, and radiator.

The relative complexity of installing liquid cooling systems, coupled with the perceived danger of liquids in close proximity to electronics, leads most computer owners to consider liquid cooling a novelty or a liability. The primary market for liquid cooling is high-performance systems and servers.

Summary

In this chapter, you started your survey of fundamental IT concepts with a tour inside the case of a computer. Considering that computers are collections of hardware, with software that lets you interact with that hardware, it makes sense to know what all of the components inside that metal and plastic box do.

First, you looked at motherboards, CPUs, and memory. The motherboard is the most important component in the system, because it connects everything together and provides pathways for communication. If the motherboard fails, your computer will not work. Processors are analogous to the brain of the computer, but what they really do is math. They do it very quickly, and they generate a ton of heat. Much like the motherboard, if the processor fails, you don't have a computer. Memory is critical too. It's a temporary storage area for data; that data is lost when your system is turned off. Generally speaking, the more memory your system has, the better.

Second, you looked at storage and expansion devices. Hard drives give you the permanent storage you need to make computers useful. They can be either conventional hard drives or newer solid-state drives. You can also store data on optical discs such as CD-, DVD-, or BD-ROMs. Expansion devices add functionality to your computers. Video cards let you see pictures on your screens, sound cards give you music, network cards are pretty much necessary to communicate with other computers, and modems, well, modems used to be important for getting on the Internet but are now nearly extinct.

Finally, I talked about power supplies and system cooling. Computers are electronics, so of course they need power. Power supplies take AC power from our wall outlets and convert it into DC power that the computer components need. The use of all this electricity generates heat, and too much heat can cause your components to fail. Most systems have built-in heat-mitigation systems such as fans and heat sinks. CPUs generate the most heat and therefore have the most pressing need to be adequately cooled.

Exam Essentials

Understand the purpose of motherboards, CPUs, and RAM.   Motherboards connect all of the components together and provide electrical pathways for data. CPUs perform mathematical operations on data, and RAM is used as a temporary storage area for data that the processor and applications need.

Know the difference between conventional hard drives and solid-state drives.   First, they both do the same thing, which is store data. Conventional hard disk drives have spinning platters and read/write heads, whereas SSDs use flash memory. SSDs are faster but generally more expensive than their conventional HDD counterparts.

Know the features of optical discs.   Optical discs store data but are not designed to replace hard drives. BD-ROMs store more data than DVD-ROMs, which store more than CD-ROMs.

Understand what different expansion devices do.   Video cards produce images for display devices such as monitors. Audio (sound) cards produce sound. Network cards and modems are for communication. Network cards communicate via network cable or wirelessly, whereas modems use conventional telephone lines.

Understand the importance of system cooling.   Computers generate heat. Processors in particular generate a lot of heat. They need to be cooled off in order to survive. Case fans are generally good enough for computers. CPUs require more active cooling methods, such as a combination of a heat sink and a fan or advanced systems like liquid cooling.

Written Labs

You can find the answers to the written labs in Appendix A.

In this lab, you are being given the task of buying a new computer for a relative. You've been given a strict budget. Based on that budget, you found three systems of the same price. Your relative will use the computer for browsing the Internet, paying bills, and occasionally playing some games. They also take a lot of family photos and videos and like to edit them on their computer. See Table 1.4 for the specifications of each of the three systems you found.

TABLE 1.4   Shopping comparison

Specification	System A	System L	System D
Processor speed	3.6 GHz	3.1 GHz	3.4 GHz
Cache memory	8 MB	6 MB	8 MB
System memory (RAM)	8 GB DDR3	12 GB DDR3	8 GB DDR3
RAM expandable to	Non-expandable	32 GB	32 GB
Hard drive type	SATA 7200 RPM	SATA 7200 RPM	SATA SSD
Hard drive size	2 TB	1 TB	240 GB
Optical drive	DVD±RW/CD-RW	DVD±RW/CD-RW	DVD±RW/DVD±R/CD-RW
Graphics	Intel integrated	NVIDIA GeForce	Intel integrated
Video memory	Shared	2 GB dedicated	Shared
Sound card	8-channel integrated	7.1 channel support	7.1 channel integrated
Network card	GBLAN	GBLAN	GBLAN
Expansion slots	1 PCIe x1, 1 PCIe x16	3 PCIe x1, 1 PCIe x16	1 PCI, 1 PCIe x1, 2 PCIe x16
USB ports	5 USB 2.0	8 USB 2.0	10 USB 2.0
Other ports	HDMI	HDMI	USB 3.0, DVI, display port
Media card reader	Yes	Yes	No
Operating system	Windows 8.1	Windows 8.1	Windows 7 Professional

1. Based on the system specifications, which one would you recommend and why?

2. What specifications made you not choose the others?

3. If you were looking for a computer for someone who played a lot of online action games, would you change your recommendation? Why?

4. Which computer has the best expansion capabilities?

Review Questions

You can find the answers to the review questions in Appendix B.

1. Which components in your computer store data? (Choose three.)
    A. RAM
    B. SSD
    C. PCI
    D. PSU
    E. BD-ROM

2. What type of expansion card allows your computer to talk to other computers, without network cables?
    A. Modem
    B. NIC
    C. PSU
    D. PCIe

3. Which type of expansion slot provides the fastest data transfer speeds?
    A. PCI
    B. PCIe x1
    C. PCIe x16
    D. PCIe x64

4. Which of the following optical discs will store the most data?
    A. CD-ROM
    B. DVD-ROM DL
    C. DVD-ROM DS
    D. BD-ROM

5. What is the name of the component that controls communication between the processor and memory?
    A. Motherboard
    B. Chipset
    C. CPU
    D. Expansion bus

6. Your friend Joe wants to add another hard drive to his computer. What should he check to make sure his system will support it?

    A. PSU

    B. Expansion slots

    C. CPU

    D. RAM

7. Which of the following devices is most likely to have a joystick port on it?

    A. Video card

    B. Sound card

    C. Network card

    D. Modem

8. You want to upgrade your computer to give it a faster boot time and more space for your files. What should you purchase?

    A. RAM

    B. HDD

    C. SSD

    D. CPU

9. If your computer runs low on RAM, what will it use instead?

    A. Cache

    B. SSD

    C. Optical drive

    D. Virtual memory

10. Which of the following are hard drive connector types? (Choose two.)

    A. PATA

    B. SATA

    C. PCIe

    D. AGP

11. When you turn on your computer, it tells you that it does not have the time and date set and asks you to enter setup. What likely needs to be replaced?

    A. CMOS battery

    B. BIOS chip

    C. CPU

    D. Time controller

12. A user named Monika wants to upgrade the memory in her laptop. What memory form factor will she need?

  A. DIMM

  B. SODIMM

  C. DDR3

  D. DDR2

13. Which device is connected to the motherboard with a 24-pin block connector?

  A. HDD

  B. SSD

  C. RAM

  D. PSU

14. Which of the following is faster than RAM?

  A. Cache

  B. HHD

  C. SSD

  D. BD-ROM

  E. None of the above

15. You are helping a neighbor buy a computer, and based on a recent experience he insists that his system needs to remain working even if a hard drive fails. What should you suggest he buy?

  A. SATA

  B. PATA

  C. RAID 0

  D. RAID 1

16. You just installed more memory in your computer, but it's not recognized. Your friend suggests you upgrade your BIOS. What's the best way to do this?

  A. Order a new BIOS chip from the motherboard manufacturer.

  B. Order a new BIOS chip from the memory manufacturer.

  C. Flash the BIOS.

  D. You can't upgrade a BIOS.

17. Which component inside a computer produces the most heat?

  A. PSU

  B. CPU

  C. GPU

  D. RAM

18. Which of the following uses a 240-pin connector?

    A. SODIMM

    B. DIMM

    C. SATA

    D. PATA

19. Your boss wants to you justify your suggestion to purchase solid-state hard drives. What are advantages of solid-state drives? (Choose three.)

    A. Faster than HDDs

    B. Generate less heat than HDDs

    C. Quieter than HDDs

    D. Cheaper than HDDs

20. Which of the following are communications devices for computers? (Choose two.)

    A. NIC

    B. Modem

    C. PCIe

    D. Sound card

Chapter

2

Peripherals and Connectors

THE FOLLOWING COMPTIA IT FUNDAMENTALS EXAM OBJECTIVES ARE COVERED IN THIS CHAPTER:

✓ **2.1 Identify basic wired and wireless peripherals and their purpose**

- Output devices
  - Printer
    - Laser
    - Inkjet
    - Thermal
  - Display devices
    - Flatscreen
    - CRT
    - Projector
  - Speakers
- Input devices
  - Keyboard
  - Pointing devices
    - Mouse
    - Touchpad
    - Joystick
    - Stylus pen
    - Trackball
  - Scanner
  - Microphone
  - Webcam

- Input & Output devices
  - Fax
  - External storage devices
    - Flash drive
    - External hard drive
    - CD/DVD/Blu-Ray
    - Network Attached Storage
    - Memory card
    - Mobile media players
    - Smartphone
  - Touchscreen display

✓ **2.2 Compare and contrast common computer connector types**

- Video
  - VGA
  - DVI
  - HDMI
  - Display port/Thunderbolt
  - USB
  - S-video
  - Component – RGB
- FireWire
- eSATA
- Thunderbolt
- USB
- PS/2
- Parallel
- Serial
- RJ–45
- RJ–11
- Audio

The hardware inside your computer's case is critical for operation, no doubt about it. By contrast, the peripheral hardware outside the case is optional. Your computer doesn't need a monitor or a keyboard to work properly. Granted, these devices add functionality that you really want. No one is going to bother using a computer without a monitor for very long.

In this chapter, you'll learn about three different categories of computer peripherals: those that provide output, those that give input, and those that do both. I will group the peripheral devices the best I can, but one challenge you will run into is that some devices, such as the multifunctional printer, fall into multiple camps.

Along with the devices themselves, there are lots of different connector types to talk about. Even though I have many to discuss (16 to be exact), the good news is it's hard to plug something into the wrong spot. I'm not saying you can't do it (I know some of you like a good challenge), but it's pretty tough to do. At the end, I'll summarize all of the connectors and important features you will probably need to know.

Audio, Video, and Printers

In this first section, you'll look at devices that are generally classified as output devices. Now, this designation doesn't completely hold true, as you will see. For example, sound cards have connections for microphones, which allow users to input, and many printers today are multifunctional devices that provide scanning or faxing services as well. Regardless, most of what I cover here will be specifically related to computer output, and I'll talk about the exceptions as I move through the chapter objectives.

Audio Connectors

Audio and audio connectors are a pretty easy topic in the grand scheme of computers, so let's tackle it first and get it out of the way. As you learned in Chapter 1, computers can have internal sound cards (or audio cards) that will let the computer produce music, sound for games, or even the voices of your friends and loved ones.

In order to hear the sound, though, you need speakers. Speakers come in a variety of shapes and sizes, from very simple and cheap headphones to complex speaker systems that rival those found in high-end home theaters. Depending on what you want to use your computer for, you can choose the right kind for your needs. Laptops almost always have speakers built into them.

Figure 2.1 shows you the back panel connectors of a desktop system. You can tell that these connectors are all built into the motherboard because of their location. If this system had a separate sound card, it would be in an expansion slot. On the right side you see three round audio connectors, designed for ⅛″ (3.5 mm) plugs. This system also gives you a handy icon next to each plug, letting you know which one is for audio input, which one is for speakers (it's usually green), and which one is for the microphone (usually pink).

FIGURE 2.1   Audio connectors

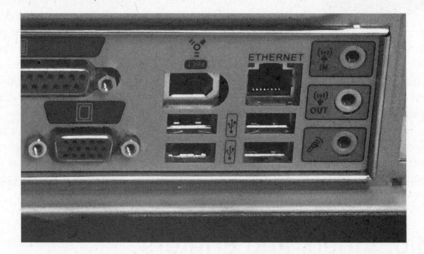

The example in Figure 2.1 is pretty basic. Some sound cards give you a few more plugs, such as the one in Figure 2.2. In this one, the black plug is for a subwoofer (if you have one), green is for speakers, and pink is still for the microphone. It's really hard to see, but on sound cards such as this, there are small icons scratched into the metal plate to let you know what should be plugged into each port. To me, decoding them is a little like trying to read hieroglyphics. This sound card also has a DA15 connector on the right, called a game port, which can be used to plug in older-style joysticks.

FIGURE 2.2   Sound card with game port

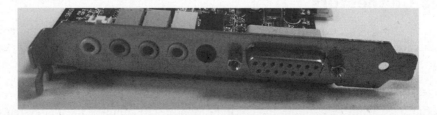

 Game ports have been made obsolete by USB ports, which I will talk about shortly. Joysticks you find today will most likely be USB.

So, this is the first example of a component (the sound card) handling both input and output duties. Speakers most definitely provide output, and microphones and joysticks are input devices. But they both plug into the same device—either the sound card or the audio ports built into the motherboard.

Display Devices and Connectors

Can you imagine not having monitors on computers? Well, the earliest computers didn't have video output, and academics and scientists still used them. Granted, they also took up the entire room and had a fraction of the computing power of your wristwatch, but they were still computers. It's a good thing that technology has come a long ways since then. It's doubtful that computers would enjoy the popularity they have today if they weren't visual.

In Chapter 1 you learned about video cards. Here, I'll talk about the other end of that system, which is the display device. After that, I'll spend some time talking about the types of connectors that you will use to join the display and computer together. Finally, you will look at how to configure some common video settings on your computer.

Display Devices

When it comes to display devices, you have quite a few choices in the marketplace. In many ways, choosing a display device for a computer is much like shopping for a television. They use similar technologies and give you similar features. Here, I'll group display devices into four broad categories:

- CRTs
- Projectors
- Flatscreens
- Touchscreens

In the next sections I'll discuss each one, in order from oldest to newest technology.

CRTs

Legacy monitors and a few specialty monitors contain a *cathode ray tube (CRT)*. In a CRT, a device called an electron gun shoots a beam of electrons toward the back side of the monitor screen (see Figure 2.3). Color CRTs often use three guns, one each for red, green, and blue image components. The back of the screen is coated with special chemical dots called phosphors (often zinc sulfide combined with other elements for color variation, but no phosphorus, ironically) that glow when electrons strike them. Each pixel on the monitor is formed by a triangle of a red, green, and blue phosphor called a triad. Each electron gun works only on dots of a certain color. So, for example, if a certain pixel is supposed to be purple, the red and blue guns will fire at it, but the green gun won't.

The beam of electrons scans across the monitor from left to right, as you face it, and top to bottom in a raster pattern to create the image on the screen. There are two ways to measure a CRT monitor's image quality: dot pitch and resolution. Dot pitch is a physical characteristic of the monitor hardware, but resolution is configurable through software.

Dot Pitch   *Dot pitch* is the measurement between triads on the display. Expressed in millimeters or dots per inch, the dot pitch tells how sharp the picture can be. The lower the measurement in millimeters or the higher the number of dots per inch, the closer together the phosphors are, and as a result, the sharper the image can be. An average dot pitch is 0.28 mm to 0.32 mm. Anything closer than 0.28 mm is considered exceptional.

FIGURE 2.3   Cutaway of a CRT monitor

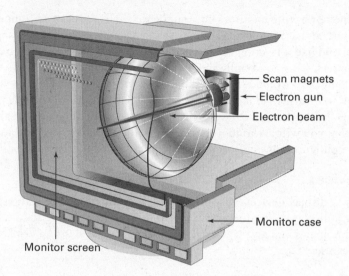

Resolution   *Resolution* is defined by how many software picture elements (pixels) are used to draw the screen. An advantage of higher resolutions is that more information can be displayed in the same screen area. A disadvantage is that the same objects and text displayed at a higher resolution appear smaller and might be harder to see. Resolution is described in terms of the visible image's dimensions, which indicate how many rows and columns of pixels are used to draw the screen. For example, a resolution of 1024×768 means 1024 pixels across (columns) and 768 pixels down (rows) were used to draw the pixel matrix. Resolution is a software setting that is common among CRTs, LCDs, and projection systems as well as other display devices.

Projectors

Another major category of display device is the video projection system, or projector. Portable *projectors* are incredibly useful if you travel a lot or if you can't afford projectors for every conference room in your office. Interactive whiteboards have become popular over the past decade to allow presenters to project an image onto the board as they use virtual markers to electronically draw on the displayed image. Remote participants can see the slide on their computer, as well as the markups made by the presenter. The presenter can see the same markups because the board transmits them to the computer to which the projector is attached, causing them to be displayed by the projector in real time.

Another popular implementation of projection systems has been the rear-projection television, in which a projector is built into a cabinet behind a screen onto which the image is projected in reverse so that an observer in front of the TV can view the image correctly. Early rear-projection TVs as well as ceiling-mounted home-theater units used CRT technology to drive three filtered light sources that worked together to create an RGB image. Today's projectors are more likely to use liquid crystal display (LCD) technology.

Projection systems are required to produce a lighted image and display it many feet away from the system. The inherent challenge to this is that ambient light tends to interfere with the image's projection. The best way to fight this problem is to ensure that your projector has a high brightness rating, which is measured in lumens. Projection systems are usually rated and chosen for purchase based on lumens of brightness, once a maximum supported resolution has been chosen. In a relatively darkened room a projector producing as little as 1300 lumens is adequate. However, in a very well-lit area, you may need 5000 to 6000 lumens for the image to be readily visible to viewers. By way of comparison, a 60W standard light bulb produces about 800 lumens.

 Bulb replacements tend to be relatively expensive, so treat your projector with care when moving it!

Flat Screens

Flat screen monitors are by far and away the most popular type of display device you will encounter today. *Flat screens* are much thinner and lighter than conventional CRTs, and they also consume significantly less power.

The rise of flat screen displays coincides with the rise in popularity of laptops. Said a better way, it's very likely that flat screen technology—which made laptops far smaller and more portable than they ever had been—helped laptops explode in popularity.

Flat screen devices can use one of several technologies to produce their image. The most common types of flat screens you will find are these:

Liquid Crystal Display Monitor   A *liquid crystal display (LCD) monitor* has two polarized filters, between which are liquid crystals. In order for light to appear on the display screen, it must pass through both filters and the crystals. The second filter, however, is at an angle to the first, so by default nothing passes through. By applying current to the crystal, you can cause it to twist, which also twists the light passing through it. If the light twists so that it matches the angle of the second filter, it can pass through the filter and light up an area of the display. On a color LCD, an additional filter splits the light into separate cells for red, green, and blue.

Light-Emitting Diode Monitor   If you can't tell the difference between an LCD display and a *light-emitting diode (LED) monitor*, you're not alone. LED displays are just LCD panels with light-emitting diodes (LEDs) as light sources instead of the fluorescent bulbs used by conventional LCD monitors. LED displays rival plasma displays in clarity and variations in luminance.

Plasma   From a functional standpoint, *plasma* monitors offer the greatest clarity and color variation. Their technology is a little more complicated, though. Plasma display panels (PDPs) create a cloud from an inert gas, such as neon, by placing electrodes in front of and behind sealed chambers full of the gas and vaporized mercury. This technology of running a current through an inert gas to ionize it is shared with neon signs and fluorescent bulbs. The downsides to plasma are that they can wear out quicker than LCDs or LEDs and they have a history of "burning" images into the screen. Technology advances have reduced this, but it can still be an issue.

Touchscreens

Touchscreens have exploded in popularity in recent years. They are pretty much standard fare for smartphones, and they are becoming more and more popular for tablet and laptop computers as well. The idea is pretty simple; it looks like any other display device, but you can touch the screen and the system senses it. It can be as simple as registering a click, like a mouse, or it can be more advanced such as capturing handwriting and saving it as a digital note. It's both an output device and an input device.

Although the technical details of how touchscreens work are beyond the scope of this book, there are a few things to know. One is that some touchscreens will work with any object touching them, whereas others require a conductive input, such as your finger. iPhones are a great example of this, as anyone who lives in cold climates and wears gloves can attest to. The second thing is that some touchscreens are coated with a film that is sensitive to touch. Cleaning these screens with regular glass cleaner can ruin the touchscreen nature of the device. It's best to clean those devices only with a damp cloth as needed.

What about Webcams?

Since I'm discussing video devices in this section, this is probably the best place to talk about webcams. A *webcam* is a small camera attached to your computer that allows you to capture video. It does not record it itself but transmits the video signals to the computer for displaying or processing. Those signals can be recorded or streamed live in a webcast or web chat. A lot of laptops now have webcams built in to their cases, while desktop webcams generally connect to the computer via USB or FireWire.

Video Connectors

Now that I have talked about the characteristics of different display devices, let's discuss how to plug them into a computer. The CompTIA IT Fundamentals exam lists seven different types of video connectors you need to know. I will start with the oldest technologies and work toward the present, and I'll show you what each connector looks like.

Component Video: RGB

Component video has been around as an analog video technology since the 1950s. (There's a digital version of it today as well.) The concept behind component video is that you get better-quality video by separating the video channels into three: red, green, and blue. Consequently, component video cables are easy to identify because they have three RCA-style plugs, often color-coded as red, green, and blue, as shown in Figure 2.4.

FIGURE 2.4   Component video cable

You're more likely to find component video on A/V (audio/video) equipment than you are on PCs, but there are video cards with RGB plugs on them. At best, they're rare in the PC world.

VGA

The *Video Graphics Array (VGA) connector* was the de facto video standard for computers for years and is still in use today. First introduced in 1987 by IBM, it was quickly adopted by other PC manufacturers. The term *VGA* is often used interchangeably to refer to generic analog video, the 15-pin video connector we're talking about here, or a 640×480 screen resolution. Figure 2.5 shows you a VGA connector, as well as the male connector that plugs into the monitor.

FIGURE 2.5   VGA connectors

VGA technology has been superseded by newer digital standards such as DVI and was supposed to be phased out starting in 2013. A technology this widely used will be around for quite a while, though, and you'll still see a lot of these in the wild.

S-video

S-video is a component video technology that was introduced around the same time VGA came out. It's analog component video, like composite video, but because it combines the three color channels into one, the video quality is not quite as high as that of composite. It was used a lot with older analog video cameras.

An S-video connector is shown on a video card in Figure 2.6. It's the round, seven-pin mini-DIN (small round) connector on the left. It also comes in other configurations, but seven-pin and four-pin are the only official standards.

FIGURE 2.6   Video card with three video connectors

   All of the video connector types introduced from here on are digital standards.

DVI

Digital Visual Interface (DVI) was introduced in 1999. It's the first widely used digital video standard for computers, but it also supports analog signals. It's shown in Figure 2.6—it's the white blocky connector in the middle. Figure 2.7 shows you what the connector looks like coming from the monitor.

FIGURE 2.7   DVI connector

The designers of DVI were smart to make it compatible with analog signals, as well as VGA technology. If you have a monitor with a DVI cable but a computer with only a VGA port (or vice versa), you can buy an adapter to connect the two together.

USB

Universal Serial Bus (USB) is the ubiquitous connector, so it should come as no surprise that there are USB display devices. The first widely used standard was USB 1.1, which was released in 1998, but it was pretty slow (only 12 Mbps) so it was really only used for keyboards, mice, and printers. When USB 2.0 came out in 2000 with a high-speed transfer rate of 480 Mbps, video devices were possible. I am guessing that everyone has seen USB, but if not, look back at Figure 2.1; the four identical connectors in the bottom center of the picture are USB.

 Throughout this chapter, I will refer to speeds in terms of bits per second (bps). In the case of USB, it's megabits per second (Mbps).

Perhaps the nicest feature of USB display devices is that they can draw their power from the USB cable, so you do not need to plug in a separate power cord for the display.

HDMI

One of the newest standards, and a very popular one in the home theater market today, is *High-Definition Multimedia Interface (HDMI)*. It was introduced in 2002, which makes it seem kind of old in technology years, but it's a great, fast, reliable connector that will probably be around for several more years to come. An HDMI cable and port on a motherboard are shown in Figure 2.8.

FIGURE 2.8   HDMI cable and connector

The HDMI standard is very fast; the most current version, HDMI 2.0 (released in 2013), has a data rate of 18 Gbps. Like USB, HDMI also has an advantage over DVI and other older standards in that it can carry audio signals as well as video.

DisplayPort/Thunderbolt

The way that DisplayPort and Thunderbolt are listed in the objectives makes them seem like they're one and the same, but they're actually not. *DisplayPort* was introduced in 2008 by the Video Electronics Standards Association (VESA); it was designed to be an industry standard and replace VGA and DVI. It's also backward compatible with VGA and DVI by using adapters. A display port on a laptop is shown in Figure 2.9. A display port is intended to be for video devices only, but like HDMI and USB, it can transmit audio and video simultaneously.

FIGURE 2.9   Display port

Thunderbolt was developed as an offshoot of the DisplayPort technology. The short history is that Apple announced a mini display port (MDP) standard in late 2008 and that the standard would have no licensing fee. In early 2009, VESA responded by saying that MDP would be included in the upcoming display port 1.2 specification. Apple was not pleased about this and teamed up with Intel to rework the specification. They added in support for PCIe, renamed it Thunderbolt, and launched it in 2011. Thunderbolt supports not only video devices but also several other types of peripherals. In terms of versatility, it's really only second to USB. We'll talk more about Thunderbolt in the "External Storage Connectors" section later in the chapter. All Apple laptops made right now contain a Thunderbolt port; other laptops can too if the manufacturer licenses the technology from Apple. It looks a lot like a DisplayPort, only smaller, and has the characteristic lightning bolt icon, as shown in Figure 2.10.

FIGURE 2.10   2 Thunderbolt ports

Adjusting and Configuring Displays

Now that we've talked about the different types of display devices and how you can hook them up to your computer, let's shift gears a bit and talk about how to keep monitors behaving properly once they're connected. First, we'll start with the adjustments on the monitor itself.

When you change the monitor resolution (via the display driver properties in the Control Panel in Windows, for example), the onscreen image may shift in one direction or become slightly larger or smaller than it was before. Most monitors have onscreen controls that can be used to adjust the image size, image position, contrast, brightness, and other factors. Inexpensive or old CRTs may have just a couple of thumbwheels or knobs for monitor adjustment; newer and more sophisticated monitors will have a complete digital menu system of controls that pop up when you press a certain button. You then move through the menu system by pressing buttons on the monitor or moving a wheel or stick on the front or back of the monitor. If you're unsure of what the buttons do, check the monitor's manual to figure out how the controls work; they're different for each model. Exercise 2.1 will give you practice in adjusting a monitor.

On a CRT, there may be a *Degauss* button. You press this button to discharge a built-up magnetic field within the monitor that may be causing the picture to be distorted. LCDs don't have this problem, so they don't have a Degauss feature. It's named after Carl Friedrich Gauss, a researcher who studied magnetism.

EXERCISE 2.1

Adjusting a Desktop Monitor

1. Locate the buttons on your monitor that control its image.

2. Experiment with the buttons to see if you can determine what they do. Or, look up the buttons in the monitor's documentation or on the manufacturer's website.

On a notebook PC's built-in monitor, adjustment controls are usually not on the monitor itself but built into the keyboard. Several of the keys on your keyboard, most often the F keys near the top of the keyboard, will have extra symbols, sometimes in a contrasting color. In Figure 2.11, you can see several of these on a laptop's F3–F8 keys.

FIGURE 2.11 Video adjustment keys including F4 (LCD toggle), F7 (dim), and F8 (brighten)

Pressing these keys in combination with the *Function (Fn) key,* as shown in Figure 2.12, activates that special function. For example, there may be a key with a picture of the sun with an up arrow that increases the display brightness like the F8 key in Figure 2.11.

FIGURE 2.12 Function (Fn) key

It's fairly common for laptop users to plug in an external display device such as a larger monitor or a projector. When you do this, you might need to toggle your video output to the correct device. In the example of Figure 2.11, you would press Fn and F4 at the same time. Options usually include displaying on the internal or external monitor only, displaying the same image on both, or extending the desktop to stretch across both devices. Figure 2.13 shows you what these options might look like on your laptop.

FIGURE 2.13   Laptop video toggle

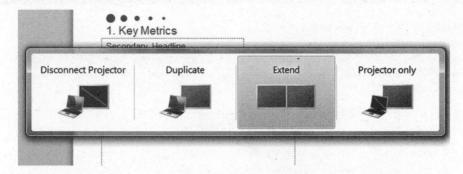

Some older laptops just cycle through the choices without giving you this visual, but many newer laptops show you what's happening. Once you have a second monitor attached, you can configure various aspects of it, such as if it's the primary or secondary display and if it appears to the left or the right of your laptop monitor (so if you move your mouse to the edge of one screen, it automatically flows to the other screen). Exercise 2.2 walks you through some multiple-monitor configuration options.

EXERCISE 2.2

Changing the Settings for Multiple Monitors

1. Right-click a blank portion of the Desktop.

2. Click Screen Resolution, as shown in Figure 2.14. You will see a screen similar to the one in Figure 2.15.

FIGURE 2.14   Screen Resolution

FIGURE 2.15 Multiple displays

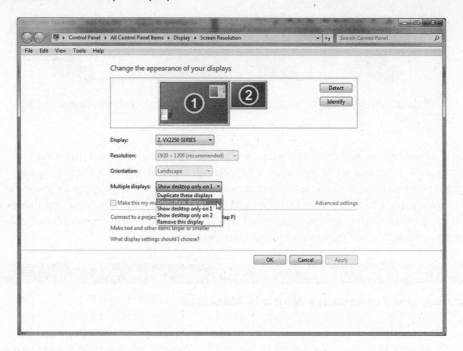

3. Click the picture of the monitor with the number 2 on it.

4. Pull down the menu labeled Multiple Displays, select Extend These Displays, and click Apply to produce an appropriate image of the second display's size and shape.

5. Click Keep Changes in the pop-up dialog that appears, like the one in Figure 2.16, before the 15-second timer expires.

FIGURE 2.16 Keep Changes button

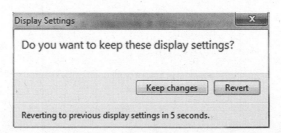

6. Click and drag the second monitor to the desired virtual position around the primary monitor. This affects the direction in which you drag objects from one display to the

other. You can see in Figure 2.17 that I placed one on top of the other. This affects how your mouse will move between the two screens.

FIGURE 2.17   Rearranging monitors

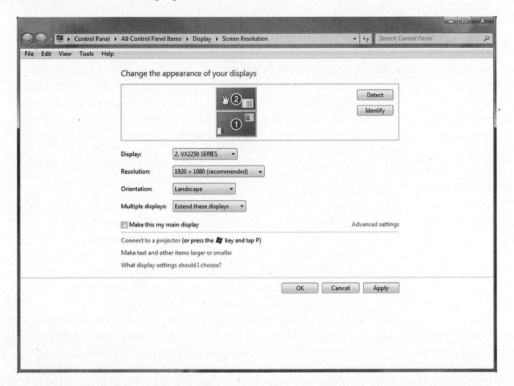

7.   Click OK to save your changes and exit.

Also notice that on the Screen Resolution screen you saw in Exercise 2.2 you can also configure the resolution of your monitor, as well as the refresh rate if you have a CRT display.

Printers

Printers are electromechanical output devices that are used to put information from the computer onto paper. They have been around since the introduction of the computer. Other than the monitor, the printer is the most popular peripheral purchased for a computer because many people want to have paper copies of the documents they create. Even though our society keeps inching farther toward electronic documents, there are times when a paper copy makes more sense or is required.

In this section, I will discuss the details of three major printer technologies, including inkjet printers, laser printers, and thermal printers. I will also talk about additional functionality that many printers now have built in, such as scanning and faxing. Once I cover printer technologies, I'll talk about how to connect your printer and some basics on installing and configuring it.

Printer Technologies

At the end of the day, all the printer needs to do is make an image appear on paper. Most of the time this is done with ink, but there are other ways too. You can use several different technologies to get an image on paper; the list of printer types includes impact, solid ink, dye-sublimation, inkjet, thermal, laser, and plotters. The IT Fundamentals exam wants you to focus on three of the most common ones used today, which are inkjet, laser, and thermal printers.

Inkjet Printers

One of the most popular types of printers in use today is *inkjet printers*. You might also hear these types of printers referred to as bubble-jet printers, but the term *Bubble Jet* is copyrighted by Canon. These printers spray ink on the page to form the image. Older inkjet printers used a reservoir of ink, a pump, and a nozzle to accomplish this. They were messy, noisy, and inefficient. Bubble Jet printers and newer inkjet printers work much more efficiently and are much cheaper. For all practical purposes, consider them one and the same because their components and printing processes are nearly identical.

Inkjet printers are simple devices. They contain very few parts and thus are inexpensive to manufacture. It's common today to have a $40 to $50 inkjet printer with print quality that rivals that of basic laser printers. These types of printers can use normal copy paper, and most of them can print fairly high-quality photos on glossy photo paper as well.

The primary consumable for inkjet printers is the *ink cartridge*. This is a small plastic container that holds the liquid ink the printer uses to create images. Printers that print only in black and white need only a black cartridge, whereas color printers need black in addition to cyan, magenta, and yellow. Color printers can have one of three cartridge configurations:

- All ink in one cartridge. These are often referred to as CMYK (cyan, magenta, yellow, black) cartridges.
- One black cartridge and a separate CMY color cartridge.
- Four cartridges total, one for each color.

From a print-quality standpoint, it doesn't matter that much which configuration you get. From a money standpoint, though, it can matter quite a bit. Most people use a lot more black ink than color ink. If you have a CMYK cartridge and run out of black, you'll need to replace the entire cartridge even if there are other colors remaining. In Figure 2.18, you can see that my printer has two cartridges: one color and one black.

FIGURE 2.18   Inkjet printer cartridges

Ink cartridges are held in place by plastic clips. They are folded back above the cartridges in Figure 2.18. To replace a cartridge, you release the clip, slide out the old cartridge, slide in the new one, and lock it into place. Make sure that the ink cartridges are the right size for your printer—in Figure 2.18 you can see that these are HP 61.

Laser Printers

A *laser printer* works much like a photocopier. The main difference is that a photocopier scans a document to produce an image, whereas the laser printer receives digitized data from a computer. Laser printers are generally bigger, faster, and more expensive than inkjet printers. Thus, you're more likely to find them in office settings than in homes. Laser printers also do not use ink. They use a dry powdery plastic resin called *toner*, which is stored in a replaceable toner cartridge. Toner cartridges are more expensive than ink cartridges, but they produce many more pages and are generally more cost-effective on a per-page basis.

A laser printer contains a large cylinder known as a *drum*, which carries a high negative electrical charge. During the print process, the printer directs a laser beam to partially neutralize the charge in certain areas of the drum. When the drum rotates past a toner reservoir, the toner clings to the areas of lesser charge, and the page image is formed on the drum. Then the drum rotates past positively charged paper, and the toner jumps off onto the paper. The paper then passes through a fuser that melts the plastic particles of the toner so that they stick to the paper.

Laser printers are available in color or monochrome models. To print in color, a laser printer must make four passes across the same page, laying down a different color each time. Such a printer has four separate toner cartridges: cyan, magenta, yellow, and black.

> Although you're unlikely to do so, if you spill any toner, let it settle before you clean it up. Toner is a fine powder and is carcinogenic. A *carcinogen* is a product that, with long-term continued exposure, may cause cancer. Also, don't use a normal vacuum cleaner to try to pick up toner. The powder is so fine that it will pass through the vacuum's filters and out the vent. Use a special computer vacuum that is designed with finer filters to catch the toner.

Thermal Printers

The two types of printers you have already learned about, inkjet and laser, comprise the vast majority of printers you will see in the market. *Thermal printers* are unique because they don't actually use ink. They use a special heat-sensitive paper.

Inside the printer is a print head the width of the paper. When it needs to print, a heating element heats certain spots on the print head. The paper below the heated print head turns black in those spots. As the paper moves through the printer, the pattern of blackened spots forms an image on the page of what is being printed. Another type of thermal printer uses a heat-sensitive ribbon instead of heat-sensitive paper. A thermal print head melts wax-based ink from the ribbon onto the paper. These are called thermal transfer or thermal wax-transfer printers.

Thermal printing technology is used in many point-of-sale terminals and older fax machines (newer fax machines usually use inkjet or laser technology). Thermal printers typically have long lives because they have few moving parts. The only unique part that you might not be as familiar with is the paper feed assembly, which oftentimes needs to accommodate a roll of paper instead of sheets. The paper is somewhat expensive, doesn't last long (especially if it is left in a very warm place, like a closed car in summer), and produces poorer-quality images than most of the other printing technologies.

Other Technologies Often Bundled with Printers

A lot of the printers you see on the market today combine printing with additional features, such as scanning and faxing. Such printers are called *multifunctional printers* or all-in-one printers. Adding in additional features changes the printer from being solely an output device to being an input device as well.

You will rarely see stand-alone scanners, which are input devices, or fax machines, which can be input and output devices.

Connecting Printers

For your printer to work properly, you must have a connection to it. The printer can be connected directly to your computer, or you can connect to one via the network. In this section, we'll look at various types of connectors that have been popular for printers over the years.

Serial Connections

When computers send data serially, they send it 1 bit at a time, one after another. The bits stand in line like people at a movie theater, waiting to get in. In Chapter 1 I talked about how old-time serial connections were painfully slow, but that new serial technology makes it a more viable option than parallel. In this particular instance, the serial I'm talking about is the old-school variety.

Specifically, older-style serial connectors were based on a standard called RS-232 and were called *serial ports*. They came in 9-pin (DE9) and 25-pin (DB25) varieties; the male DE9 is shown in Figure 2.19. It's conveniently labeled "Serial."

FIGURE 2.19   Back-panel connectors, including serial and parallel ports

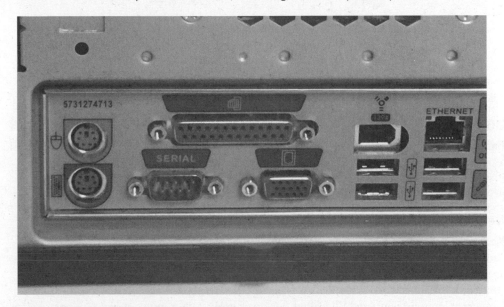

Serial connections like this really aren't used for printers any more. Modems used serial connectors too, but they have also gone the way of the dinosaur. About the only time you will see serial connections used today are for server, router, and switch consoles that can be used for management and diagnostics.

Parallel Connections

When a printer uses parallel communication, it is receiving data 8 bits at a time over eight separate wires (one for each bit). Parallel communication was the most popular way of communicating from computer to printer for many years, mainly because it's faster than serial. In fact, the *parallel port* became so synonymous with printing that a lot of companies simply started referring to parallel ports as printer ports. In Figure 2.19, the 25-pin parallel port has a printer icon above it.

A parallel cable consists of a male DB25 connector that connects to the computer and a male 36-pin Centronics connector that connects to the printer. Parallel cables work best when they are less than 10′ long, and they should be IEEE 1284 compliant. Figure 2.20 shows a typical printer cable, with the parallel connector on the left and the Centronics connector on the right.

FIGURE 2.20   Parallel cable

USB

Earlier in the chapter you learned that USB stands for Universal Serial Bus, but the *U* could as easily stand for "ubiquitous." USB is everywhere and seemingly connects everything. Printers are no exception. USB is the most common connector type you will see used with printers today.

Networked Printers

Rather than connect the printer to your computer, you can connect it to the network. This setup is very popular in businesses and is becoming more popular in home networks as well. When connecting a printer to the network, you have two choices. The first is to connect it via a network cable, which typically uses an RJ-45 connector. (It looks like a bigger telephone plug, and I'll talk about them in the "Communications Connectors" section later in this chapter.) The second is to connect it via wireless networking. You'll examine that topic in detail in Chapter 6, "Network Sharing and Storage."

 In addition to connecting the printer, you need to install a special piece of software called a printer driver so the operating system knows how to talk to the printer. I will talk about drivers and how to install them in Chapter 4, "Software Applications."

Input Devices

Even though artificial intelligence has made rapid strides in recent years, computers are still unable to truly "think" for themselves. This is probably a good thing, but my goal isn't to kick off a debate on cyber-ethics here. My point is that computers don't do anything until they are given input telling them what to do. The input can be as simple as a single keystroke or click or as complicated as millions of lines of computer code. Either way, input is critical.

The very earliest computers used punch cards as input; for example, ENIAC (which is recognized as the first electronic general-purpose computer) used punch cards for input and output in 1946. Keyboards were already widely available in the form of typewriters and were introduced as computer input devices by 1948. Pointing devices actually preceded them, with the trackball being invented in 1946. (Mice didn't really become popular until much later, in 1984.) Today, keyboards and pointing devices are still the two most common types of input devices, so we'll discuss both of them in the upcoming sections.

 Other input devices you need to be aware of for the IT Fundamentals exam are scanners, microphones, and webcams, but I already covered them when I talked about printers, audio connectors, and video.

Keyboards

The *keyboard* owes its history to that of the typewriter. The typewriter was first patented in 1868, and as of 1877 they were in mass production. In the 1930s the keyboard was combined with the telegraph and also with punch card systems to create keypunches. For entering data, the typewriter keyboard was the technology of choice. So it shouldn't come as a surprise that computer makers adopted the technology as well.

The most common keyboard configuration for Latin script languages is called QWERTY, named for the first six letters on the top row, from left to right. Keys were laid out as they were to minimize jamming of the metal arms within mechanical typewriters; the most commonly used letters were spaced farther apart to avoid issues. The Remington company, which was the leader in typewriter production in the 1870s, popularized the design, and the rest, as they say, is history.

Today, of course, we still use keyboards that have this configuration even though we don't need to worry about mechanical arms running into each other in the inner workings of our typewriters. Even when keyboards are built into devices such as the Blackberry or reproduced on our smartphone screens, the default layout has not changed. After video displays, keyboards are pretty much the most essential thing we plug into our computer.

Connecting Keyboards

The most common way to connect keyboards today is through your USB port. But wait, what about wireless keyboards, you ask? They're also usually connected via USB, just with a wireless USB receiver, as shown in Figure 2.21.

FIGURE 2.21 Wireless USB receiver

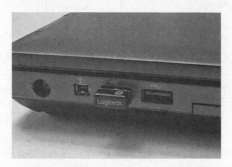

Prior to USB, the standard for several years was the *PS/2 port* (also known as a mini-DIN 6 connector), which was a keyboard and mouse interface port first found on the IBM PS/2 (hence the name). It is smaller than previous interfaces (the DIN 5 keyboard port and serial mouse connector), and thus its popularity increased quickly. It's shown in Figure 2.22. You'll notice that in addition to having an icon next to each port, the keyboard port is usually purple and the mouse port is usually green.

FIGURE 2.22 Keyboard and mouse PS/2 ports

Keyboard Configuration Options

There are two directions I am going to take this. First, let's take the physical configuration of your keyboard. Keyboards haven't changed a great deal over the last 140 or so years, but newer advances in ergonomics have led to some more comfortable (and interesting-looking) typing options. If your wrists or arms get sore or numb from typing too much, you might have bad form, and typing on a standard keyboard (or especially a small laptop keyboard) can actually be part of the problem. One design that's been out for several years is called the natural keyboard. It's shown in Figure 2.23 and is designed to promote more natural hand and arm positions.

FIGURE 2.23   A natural keyboard

A newer option is simply called an ergonomic keyboard, and it looks kind of futuristic, if you ask me. The example shown in Figure 2.24 is available from www.safetype.com. If the natural keyboard still does not help ease the pain in your wrists, this one might do the trick. If nothing else, it's a great conversation starter!

FIGURE 2.24   Ergonomic keyboard from safetype.com

FIGURE 2.24 IS OWNED BY SAFETYPE.COM AND IS REPRINTED WITH PERMISSION.

Second, you have some configuration options within your operating system. One of the more interesting ones is that you can change your keyboard layout. If you have programs in which you type using a different alphabet than Latin-based, you can change it to a different character type. In addition, there's another Latin-based layout called Dvorak, which is an alternative to QWERTY. It's designed to place more commonly used letters in better spots, increasing your typing speed. After all, we don't need to worry about mechanical keys sticking together on our typewriters any longer! Personally, I think it would take a lot of frustrating time to get used to it, but a former boss of mine used it and swore by its efficiency. It could also be fun to change it on an unsuspecting co-worker, not that I would recommend that. Exercise 2.3 shows you how to change your keyboard layout in Windows 7.

EXERCISE 2.3

Changing Your Keyboard Layout in Windows 7

1. Click Start ≻ Devices And Printers. (If your keyboard is not shown in the Devices and Printers window, open the Region and Language app in Control Panel, and then skip to step 3.) You will get a window similar to the one in Figure 2.25.

FIGURE 2.25 Devices And Printers window

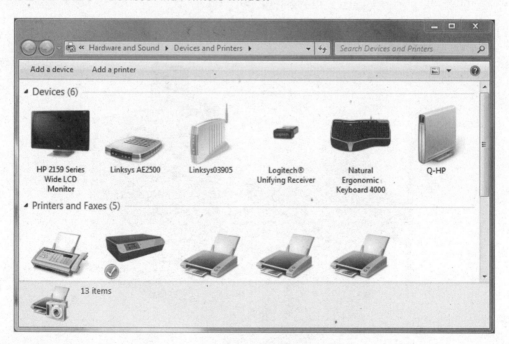

2. Right-click your keyboard, and choose Region And Language.

3. Select the Keyboards And Languages tab.

4. Click the Change Keyboards button, like the one shown in Figure 2.26.

FIGURE 2.26   Change Keyboards

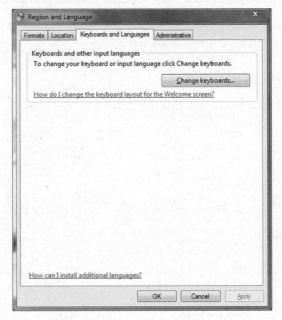

5.   In the Text Services And Input Languages dialog, like the one shown in Figure 2.27, click Add.

FIGURE 2.27   Text Services And Input Languages

6. The Add Input Language dialog will appear. Scroll down to English (United States) and choose United States-Dvorak, as shown in Figure 2.28.

FIGURE 2.28   Add Input Language

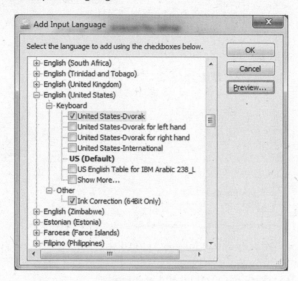

7. If you want to see what the layout looks like, click the Preview button, and you'll see the screen shown in Figure 2.29. Otherwise, click OK.

FIGURE 2.29   Dvorak layout

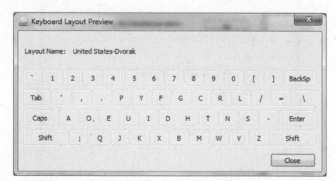

8. The Text Services And Input Languages dialog will now be back up. In the Default Input Language drop-down, choose Dvorak. Click OK.

9. Exit out of the dialogs, and Dvorak is your keyboard layout.

Pointing Devices

Pointing devices are so named because they allow you to move your cursor around the screen and point at what you want; they're a convenient handheld tool that lets you easily navigate onscreen. Pointing devices have been in use since the beginning of mankind, if you include the index finger. They've pretty much been available for computers as long as computers have existed. For example, the trackball was developed in 1946 to replace the joystick as an input device for an early electronic radar-plotting system. The mouse came along in the 1960s but didn't gain much popularity until Apple came out with the Macintosh 128K in 1984.

You might think that a mouse or another pointing device is basically required for today's PCs, but it's not. When I teach classes for computer technicians, one of the activities I like to have them do is disconnect their mouse and then navigate through Windows with just their keyboard. It can be difficult to get used to, but it's a very helpful skill if you find yourself stuck with a broken mouse at some point.

 You should open up Solitaire on your computer and play a game without the mouse. Hint: use your arrow keys and the Enter key.

Mice are the most popular pointing device you'll see today, although touchpads are a close second. I'll talk about both of those, as well as joysticks, stylus pens, and trackballs in the next section.

Types of Pointing Devices

There are five different types of pointing devices in the CompTIA IT Fundamentals exam objectives. I'll cover each of them here.

Mouse

The *mouse* is the most common pointing device in use today. It's named because the original mice that were created had the connector cord (a tail) leading from the rear of their body, pointing toward the user. Later designs put the cord at the head of the unit, but by then the name had stuck.

For most of its existence, the mouse had a ball inside it that touched two rollers, one positioned to detect vertical movement and one positioned to detect horizontal movement. By moving the mouse around on a solid surface, the ball would roll, causing movement in the rollers, which would get translated into electrical signals and move the cursor on your screen. Slippery surfaces would cause the ball to skid, making the mouse less useful, so people started using mouse pads to compensate.

The progression of technology allowed mice to lose their tails and their balls (replaced by a light that senses movement), and so most mice you see today are wireless or optical or both. Figure 2.30 shows a typical wireless optical mouse.

FIGURE 2.30 Wireless optical mouse

Mice come in a variety of shapes, sizes, and styles. Some are very small, designed to be more portable and used with laptops and tablets. As with keyboards, ergonomic designs exist as well. The ergonomic mouse in Figure 2.31 is one such option, courtesy of www.safetype.com. Most mice will have two or more buttons for left- and right-clicking, as well as a wheel to scroll up and down. You'll find some variance, such as mice for Macs, which have historically had only one button.

FIGURE 2.31 Ergonomic mouse

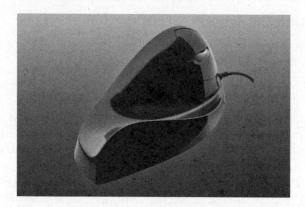

THIS IMAGE IS OWNED BY SAFETYPE.COM AND IS REPRINTED WITH PERMISSION.

Touchpad

Instead of using an external device such as a mouse, you can do as our ancient ancestors did and point at something using your finger. Granted, they didn't have a *touchpad* to use, because touchpads didn't rise to prominence until the laptop computer became commonplace. Functionally, a touchpad works just like a mouse, in that you can move your finger around to control your cursor, and you'll often have two buttons, one for left-clicking and one for right-clicking. Many touchpads also let you tap the pad itself to indicate a click. Figure 2.32 shows a typical touchpad.

FIGURE 2.32   Touchpad

You'll notice that the touchpad is conveniently placed right below the laptop keyboard, which happens to be where your palms rest when you type. Sometimes this will cause problems, because you can inadvertently cause your mouse cursor to do random things like jump across the screen. Most touchpads today have settings to allow you to control the sensitivity, and they will also differentiate between a palm touching them and a finger. In addition, if you have a sensitive touchpad that is giving you trouble, you can disable it altogether. Let's do that in Exercise 2.4.

EXERCISE 2.4

Disabling a Touchpad

1. Open the Hardware And Sound window within Control Panel. You can do so by clicking Start ➤ Control Panel, and then clicking Hardware And Sound, as shown in Figure 2.33.

2. Click Mouse near the top of the screen, and then go to the Device Settings tab, as shown in Figure 2.34.

3. Highlight your touchpad. In this example, it's named LuxPad. If you are curious to see what the configuration options are, click the Settings button to get a screen similar to the one shown in Figure 2.35.

EXERCISE 2.4 *(continued)*

FIGURE 2.33 Hardware and Sound

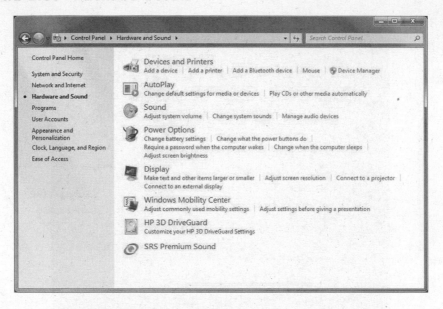

FIGURE 2.34 Device Settings tab of the Mouse Properties window

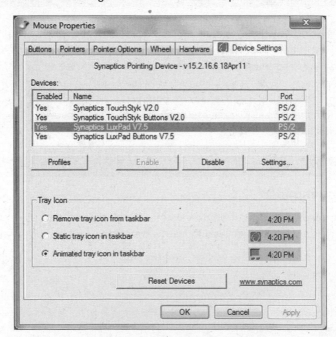

FIGURE 2.35   Touchpad configuration options

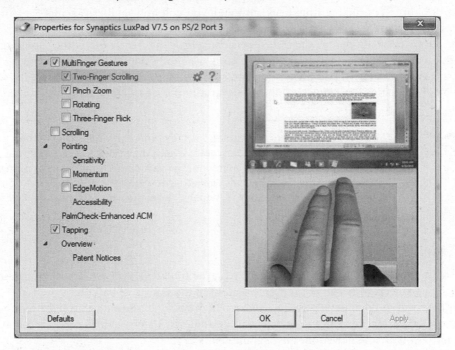

4. On the Device Settings tab, with your touchpad highlighted, click the Disable button.

5. Click OK to close this window.

Although touchpads are primarily used with laptop computers, you can also buy external touchpads that connect to a computer just as a mouse would.

Joystick

Joysticks were used in aviation before computers were invented; the first electrical *joystick* was patented in 1926. There were a few early, specialized computers that used joysticks in the 1940s. Back then those systems were mostly for military use, and the joysticks were pretty simple—a stick and a button or two to indicate action. Modern joysticks can get a lot more complicated in terms of the buttons and triggers on them, and today joysticks are mostly used for game playing (especially games like flight simulators). They're not normally an everyday pointing device like a mouse or a touchpad. Game controllers such as those used on the PlayStation or Xbox are offshoots of the joystick.

Stylus Pen

In terms of history, the *stylus pen* has been around a lot longer than other computer pointing devices—centuries in fact. The ancient Romans used small stylus-like devices to write on wax tablets.

A stylus can come in any number of shapes and sizes, just like a pen. Most of them are similar looking to normal writing pens, although you will find smaller variants for gaming devices and things like the PalmPilot.

For purposes of computing, the stylus is treated a little differently than other pointing devices for three reasons. One, it doesn't generally need to be connected to the computer in any way. Two, it's mostly used for writing and not moving a cursor around. Three, the screen that you are touching with it needs to be some variation of a touchscreen for it to work.

You may be wondering, what about the credit card machines in the supermarket or convenience stores, where the stylus used to sign the screen is connected to the machine? In most cases, that's purely a security measure to keep people from walking away with the stylus. Some do have a very slight electrical charge, which is how the screen senses where the pen is touching.

Trackball

As noted in the introduction to pointing devices, the *trackball* has been around for quite some time—since 1946. The original trackball used the same size ball that's used in Canadian five-pin bowling: it's about 5 inches (12.7 cm) in diameter and weighs around 3.5 pounds (1.6 kg). Hardly convenient by today's standards! Later versions used a standard-sized billiard ball, and newer ones use smaller balls yet.

You can think of a trackball as a sort of inverted mouse with a ball. It uses sensors like a mouse with a ball did; it's just that the ball is exposed and you roll it around with your thumb and/or fingers. Figure 2.36 shows a common trackball. From a usage standpoint, the trackball functions just as a mouse or a touchpad would. Many people who use them claim that they're more ergonomic than the traditional mouse.

FIGURE 2.36   A trackball

Connecting Pointing Devices

This section can almost be summed up with one acronym: USB. By far and away, USB is the most common connector you will see used with pointing devices.

Before USB was invented, mice would be connected via PS/2 ports, just as keyboards were. For a refresher on what that looks like, refer back to Figure 2.22. The mouse port is the green one at the top. Prior to PS/2, mice and other pointing devices were connected via RS-232 serial ports. A serial port is shown in Figure 2.19.

Remember that joysticks used to connect through the 15-pin (DA15) game port, which was often built into soundcards.

Pointing Device Configuration Options

For as simple as pointing devices such as mice are, there are actually quite a few configuration options you can set on them. For example, you can change the button configuration so that the mouse becomes more natural for left-handed people. You can also change how fast the cursor moves across the screen, what it looks like, and how quickly you need to click for the system to register it as a double-click. In Windows, all of these settings are configured through Mouse Properties in the Hardware And Sound app within Control Panel. Exercise 2.5 walks you through a few of the convenience-related options. Note that some of these are purely aesthetic, but others are very useful to some people with disabilities or who otherwise have difficulty using the pointing device.

EXERCISE 2.5

Configuring a Mouse

1. Open the Hardware And Sound window within Control Panel. You can do so by clicking Start ➤ Control Panel and then clicking Hardware And Sound.

2. Click Mouse, and the Mouse Properties window will appear, similar to the one shown in Figure 2.37.

3. Under Button Configuration, check the Switch Primary And Secondary Buttons check box.

4. Click the Pointer Options tab (you will need to use the other button now!), as shown in Figure 2.38.

5. In the Motion section, drag the pointer speed all the way to the Slow end. Notice how slowly the mouse moves. Slide the bar all the way to Fast to see what the difference is.

6. Click OK to save the changes if you want, or click Cancel.

FIGURE 2.37 Mouse Properties

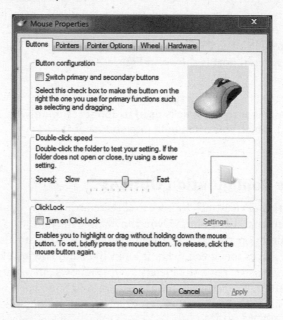

FIGURE 2.38 Pointer Options

External Storage and Other Connectors

In this section, you will look at two types of technologies: external storage and communications connectors. It might seem like an odd combination of technologies, and it's true that they don't always go together. External storage devices are pretty common to use today, and they require their own dedicated high-speed connections to work. I'll talk about the types of devices as well as those connections. Many external devices are network-compatible though, so that relates closely to communications (network) connections. I'll cover them both here to put the finishing touches on this chapter.

External Storage Devices

On first glance, it might seem like external storage devices are a relatively new technology in the computer world. The truth is, external storage was all computers had before internal hard drives were created. When PCs started becoming popular in the early 1980s, internal storage was more the exception than the rule. Practically every computer had two external floppy disk drives, usually of the 5¼″ variety. To boot your computer, you would put a boot disk in the primary floppy drive and turn the computer on. It would read the floppy drive and load the operating system into memory from there. Once the operating system was loaded, then you could take that disk out and put another one in with the program or data you needed. External storage was the norm, but it didn't resemble the external storage options we have today.

Now if you said that high-speed, ultra high-capacity external storage was relatively new to personal computing, you would be right. It's only really been since the early 2000s that external connection speeds were fast enough to support the data requirements of external hard drives. As speeds have increased, so have the options available for external storage. In this section, I will talk about several common types of external storage options, as well as the primary connectors you will see used with them.

 All of the external storage devices covered here should be considered both input and output devices.

Types of External Storage

As I have said before, we've come a long ways since the days of floppy disk drives. Even the smallest external storage devices used today hold one thousand or more times the data that the best floppy disks did. It's just another indication of how technology has progressed. We need the larger storage spaces because we have lots of pictures, videos, and presentations on our computers and we need to easily store and transfer them. These devices help us do just that.

Flash Drives

Flash drives have, for all practical purposes, replaced floppy disk drives in computers. You'll also hear them called thumb drives because they are roughly the size of someone's thumb. They're compact and cheap, store a lot (up to 256 GB at the time of writing), and are easy to use. As you can see in Figure 2.39, they have USB connectors. All you have to do is plug in the drive and wait for the system to detect it, and away you go. Most flash drives have a small light on them that illuminates when it's ready for use and blinks when data is being written to or read from it.

FIGURE 2.39   Two flash drives

Internally, flash drives use the same technology that solid-state drives (SSDs) use. There are no moving parts. Flash drives have about a 10-year shelf life, which I guess is a downside. In 10 years, the flash drive you have will be so hopelessly outdated you will want a new one anyway.

Memory Cards

From an internal comparison standpoint, *memory cards* works the same way that flash drives do. They look a little different, though (see Figure 2.40), and they require a special card reader. A lot of desktops, laptops, and printers have memory card readers built into them, like the desktop computer in Figure 2.41 does. If your system doesn't have a memory card reader, you can buy an external one that plugs into a USB port.

FIGURE 2.40   SD memory cards

FIGURE 2.41 Memory card slots

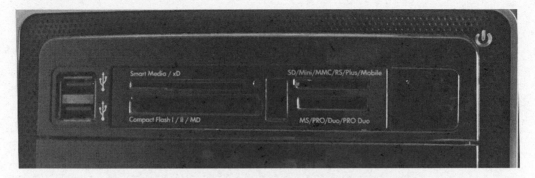

As you can see in Figure 2.41, there are several different standards of memory cards, and they're all slightly different sizes. The four standards shown here are:

- Smart Media
- Compact Flash
- Secure Digital (SD)
- Duo

Of the four, SD is the most popular and the one most likely to be built into your laptop or other device today. The standard SD cards are tiny—barely over an inch long (32 mm) and 0.08″ (2.1 mm) thick. You can easily find SD cards up to 256 GB in size, although the theoretical maximum for the current standard (called SD eXtended Capacity, or SDXC) is 2 TB. Memory cards are more expensive than flash drives of the same capacity.

SD cards also come in two smaller sizes, the mini SD and the micro SD. Smaller cards will fit into devices built for larger cards.

Memory cards are capable of storing any type of data, but their small size makes them popular for inserting into devices such as digital cameras and video cameras, as well as small portable gaming devices.

External Hard Drives

An *external hard drive* is basically the same thing as an internal hard drive, except that it's enclosed in a protective case and connects via an external connector. External drives can be conventional HDDs or SSDs. You can see that the one in Figure 2.42 has a USB connector on the back. This example is a little older; it's about six inches tall and can be set upright as pictured or laid flat. It has a light on the front to let you know it's working, and the light flashes when the drive is reading or writing.

FIGURE 2.42 External hard drive

External hard drives will connect via USB, FireWire, eSATA, or Thunderbolt connectors. I'll discuss the differences in the "External Storage Connectors" section later in this chapter.

 With current technology, regardless of the type of external hard drive connection you have, an external drive will be slower than using an internal SATA hard drive. USB 3.0, Thunderbolt, and eSATA are faster than internal PATA hard drives, however.

External Optical Drives

In the "External Hard Drives" section, I said that external drives are basically just like internal drives but with different connectors. The same holds true for external optical drives, whether they are CD, DVD, or Blu-ray devices. Like their external hard drive cousins, they will connect via USB, FireWire, eSATA, or Thunderbolt.

Network Attached Storage

A *network attached storage (NAS)* device takes hard drive storage to the next level. Based on its name, you can probably guess that it's attached to the network, which it is, but that's just the beginning. First, take a look at a simple NAS device in Figure 2.43.

FIGURE 2.43   NETGEAR NAS device

"NETGEAR READYNAS NV+" BY PJ - OWN WORK. LICENSED UNDER CC BY-SA 3.0 VIA WIKIMEDIA COMMONS

Looking at Figure 2.43, you can see that this is a self-enclosed unit that can hold up to four hard drives. Some hold more; some hold less. Nicer NAS systems will allow you to hot-swap hard drives, meaning that if one fails, you can remove it and replace it without shutting the NAS down. And remember RAID from Chapter 1? Most NAS systems will run that for you with very little intervention required. In addition to the hardware, the NAS device contains its own operating system, meaning it acts like its own file server. In most cases, you can plug it in, do some very minor configuration, and have instant storage space on your network.

As far as connectivity goes, NAS systems will connect to a PC through a USB, FireWire, or eSATA port, but that is primarily so you can use that PC to run the configuration software for the NAS. The NAS also connects to the network, and that is how all of the network users access the storage space.

If you are running a small office and need additional centralized storage, a NAS system is a good way to go.

Accessing a NAS server over the network will generally be slower than having an external hard drive on your computer. The advantage is that if you have multiple users on a network, everyone can easily get to it.

Mobile Media Players

There are a lot of different types of *mobile media players* on the market today. Some of them contain their own hard drives for storage, whereas others are simply wireless network-enabled devices that let you stream media online. Odds are you've heard of one or more of the examples here:

- Roku
- Apple TV
- Amazon Fire TV/TV Stick
- Google Chromecast
- PlayStation 4
- Slingbox

Most of those that I listed are streaming devices. That is, you hook them to your TV or computer, usually with an HDMI connection, and then you connect the device to your wireless network. Once on the network, you can stream (download in real time) the content.

There are other mobile media players that are basically high-capacity external hard drives, with software installed on them that allows you to play movies and see TV shows. Again, these typically attach to your TV or computer via HDMI cables.

Smartphones

Finally, we have *smartphones*. A smartphone is really a small computer masquerading as a telephone. Usually they have a touchscreen interface and built-in Internet connectivity to download files and apps. Oh—and you can use them to make telephone calls too. Popular examples include the iPhone, Samsung Galaxy, and Google Nexus series of phones.

While you can use your smartphone for external storage for your computer, that's not the most practical thing to do. For one, storage space on smartphones is far more limited than it is on computers. Second, viewing files on a smaller smartphone screen isn't as convenient as seeing them on a full-size laptop screen or desktop monitor. Granted, smartphones are getting bigger and bigger, and the line between smartphones and tablet computers is getting increasingly blurry.

Where external smartphone storage makes the most sense is for music and pictures. Those are items you typically want to take with you and have on the go, and they don't take up a ton of space.

Smartphones are connected to your computer (for downloads, uploads, and synchronization) via USB cable.

External Storage Connectors

In this section I want to focus on the four types of connectors you're most likely to see with external hard storage devices, specifically external hard drives. I've mentioned their names throughout this chapter, and we've already covered USB in a bit of depth. It's important, though, to cover all of them in the same place so you're able to compare and contrast the benefits of each, as well as differentiate what they look like.

USB

USB is the one I have talked about the most, but it's such a critical connector that it's good to review again. And here, I'll get into a bit more depth than I did before.

Like all other standards, USB has gone through several stages of evolution. The first published standard was USB 1.0, released in 1986. Because of some technical limitations, it didn't really catch on. Those limitations were fixed by 1998 when USB 1.1 was released. It caught fire in a hurry. It was slow by today's standards (only 12 Mbps), so it was primarily used for keyboards, mice, and printers. Since 1998, there have been three major upgrades to the USB standard; Table 2.1 shows the dates and important facts.

TABLE 2.1   USB specifications

Version	Year	Speed	Trade Name
USB 1.1	1998	12 Mbps	Full Speed
USB 2.0	2000	480 Mbps	High Speed
USB 3.0	2008	5 Gbps	SuperSpeed
USB 3.1	2013	10 Gbps	SuperSpeed+

USB 3.0 and USB 3.1 have people really excited. You can see the dramatic jump in speed between the USB 2.0 and USB 3.0 standards, and that jump put USB in the same ballpark as FireWire, eSATA, and Thunderbolt. USB 3.1 has a theoretical maximum of 10 Gbps, which would be faster than its competitors, but the overhead associated with it limits the actual throughput to about 7.2 Gbps. Still, that's fast.

The vast majority of USB ports you see in the market today are still USB 2.0. If you have a USB 3.x device, it will work while plugged into a USB 2.0 port, but it will just run at the slower speed. SuperSpeed cables and connectors are all supposed to be colored blue to easily differentiate them from older versions.

Regardless of the standard, low-power devices can get their power from the USB port itself. Devices with higher power requirements (such as the external hard drive shown back in Figure 2.42) can still use their own power sources. Up to 127 devices can be connected to one USB bus at once. As far as the types of devices that can be connected to USB, it's almost limitless. If you can think of a computer peripheral, odds are it comes in a USB version.

FireWire

Around 1986, engineers at Apple started playing with the idea of a high-speed serial digital connection. They named it *FireWire* after some of the thermal "noise" created in the connections when they ran it at high speeds. In 1995, Apple presented the standard to the Institute of Electrical and Electronics Engineers (IEEE), which is the group that ratifies electronics standards. The standard was confirmed as IEEE 1394. Right around that same time, Sony finalized its trademark iLink technology, which was also based on the same standard. Today, there are no practical differences between IEEE 1394, FireWire, and iLink. Figure 2.44 shows a FireWire connector on a laptop.

FIGURE 2.44   FireWire connector

As of 2000 Apple had incorporated it into its entire line of desktop and laptop computers. FireWire found a niche home with digital video cameras, but there were also plenty of FireWire hard drives out there as well. In addition, if you had workstations running the Macintosh OS X or Linux operating systems, you could create a small network using FireWire cables.

FireWire tops out at 3200 Mbps, and you can connect up to 63 devices on a single bus. As of 2011, Apple started replacing FireWire connections with Thunderbolt ones, and as of 2014 all new Macs have Thunderbolt instead of FireWire.

eSATA

In Chapter 1, I talked about the internal Serial ATA (SATA) hard drive connector. The external SATA (*eSATA*) connector is the same technology, only in an external connection. Figure 2.45 shows an eSATA connector. It came into the market in 2003, is mostly intended for hard drive use, and can support up to 15 devices on a single bus.

FIGURE 2.45   eSATA

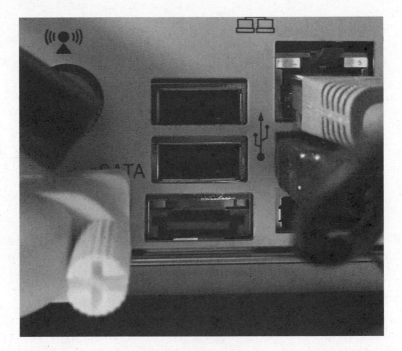

Table 2.2 shows some of the eSATA specifications.

TABLE 2.2   eSATA specifications

Version	Year	Speed	Names
Revision 1.0	2003	1.5 Gbps	SATA I, SATA 1.5Gb/s
Revision 2.0	2005	3.0 Gbps	SATA II, SATA 3Gb/s
Revision 3.0	2009	6.0 Gbps	SATA III, SATA 6Gb/s

You will commonly see the third generation of eSATA (and SATA) referred to as SATA 6 or SATA 6Gb/s. This is because if they called it SATA 3, there would be confusion with the second generation, which had transfer speeds of 3.0 Gbps.

An interesting fact about eSATA is that the interface does not provide power, which is a big negative compared to its contemporary high-speed serial counterparts. There is another eSATA port that you might see, which is called Power over eSATA, eSATA+, eSATAp, or eSATA/USB. It's essentially a combination eSATA and USB port. Since the port is combination of two others, neither sanctioning body officially recognizes it (which is probably why there are so many names—other companies call it what they want to). This port is shown in Figure 2.46.

FIGURE 2.46 USB over eSATA

You can see that this port is slightly different than the one in Figure 2.45, and it's also marked with a USB icon next to the eSATA one. On the market, you can purchase cables that go from this port to an eSATA device and provide it with power, via the eSATAp port.

Thunderbolt

I already talked about Thunderbolt a bit in the context of video connectors, because the technology was developed as an offshoot of display port technology. As a quick review, remember that Apple partnered with Intel and launched Thunderbolt in 2011. Figure 2.10 has a picture of the port, which has a lightning bolt next to it. And in terms of versatility, Thunderbolt is second to only USB in the types of devices made for it. You will find video devices, hard drives (both HDD and SSD), printers, laptop docking stations, audio devices, and PCIe expansion enclosures that use Thunderbolt.

Thunderbolt's speed will likely entice you to want to get it. The first generation of the technology boasted a 10 Gbps data rate. Thunderbolt 2, which was released in late 2013, joins two 10 Gbps channels together for 20 Gbps throughput. Apple has also announced plans for Thunderbolt 3, which will again double the throughput to 40 Gbps. Apple says it expects to start shipping products with Thunderbolt 3 connectors in late 2015 or early 2016.

 Real World Scenario

Choosing the Right Connection Technology

After reading about external storage connectors, you can see that you have several viable choices if you need to choose a technology. So which one do you choose?

A few factors to consider are compatibility, price, and future needs. First, think about compatibility. There are two vectors of this. The first one is compatibility with devices. What do you need to hook up? If it's basic devices such as a keyboard and a printer, then

USB is the right way to go. It's plenty fast and cheap. If you need a considerable amount of external storage at lightning-fast speeds, then Thunderbolt is probably a better choice, although USB 3.1 and eSATA can also meet your needs. (Then it might come down to cost.) The second compatibility vector is with your existing hardware. If you are looking to connect devices to your existing computer, what types of connectors do you have? That could make the decision for you, unless you're in the market for a new system as well.

Price can also be a consideration. USB is generally the cheapest, although since USB 3 is relatively new, those devices will be more expensive for a while.

Last, think about future expansion needs. Is this for your home office, and you aren't planning on adding extra devices for another five years or so? Then this isn't a big deal. But if you're working in a small business environment that is growing rapidly, you will want to think about future hardware needs and the speeds at which those devices need to run.

Many people are asking which one will win, Thunderbolt or USB? It's too early to tell, and really, maybe there shouldn't be one winner. Both technologies are great, and there's probably a place for both moving forward.

There's one last side note to this conversation. The blazing-fast speed of Thunderbolt and USB 3 is great, but if you use external HDDs, you're underutilizing the connection bandwidth. Mechanical HDDs simply can't spin fast enough to transfer data as fast as those connections will allow. The fastest conventional HDDs top out at just over 1500 Mbps—any of the technologies I talked about here (with the exception of USB 2.0) can easily handle that. If you want to truly take advantage of these fast speeds, you need to upgrade to SSDs, which will also cost you a lot more money per megabyte.

Communications Connectors

The last two connectors I have to talk about in this chapter are for communications. One will get you onto a network, and the other is designed to use telephone lines.

Network Connectors

To be fair, there are over a dozen different types of network connectors in existence. The connector used depends on the type of network cable you're using. For example, old-school coaxial cable (similar to cable TV cabling) uses different connectors than does twisted pair, and there are probably a dozen different fiber-optic cables alone. The good news for the CompTIA IT Fundamentals test is that there's only one they want you to know about, which is *RJ-45*.

The *RJ* in the connector name stands for *registered jack*. You'll find RJ-45 connectors on the ends of twisted-pair network cables, which you will hear people call Ethernet cables or sometimes Cat 5 or Cat 6 cables (*Cat* is short for *category*). It looks like a telephone plug, except that it's wider. A twisted-pair cable has four pairs of wires, so there are eight leads on the connector. You plug it in just as you would a telephone cord. The maximum speed depends on a lot of factors, such as the communication standard you are using and distance, but generally speaking the maximum you'll get from twisted pair is 1 Gbps. Figure 2.47 shows you two RJ connectors: RJ-11 on the left and RJ-45 on the right.

FIGURE 2.47   RJ-11 and RJ-45 connectors

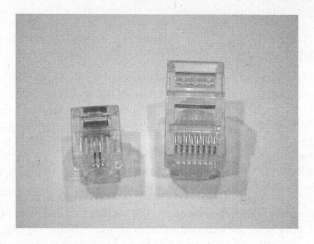

Telephone Connectors

The telephone connector you will see in use is called *RJ-11*. Telephone cables often have two pairs of wires, but only one is used. An RJ-11 is shown in Figure 2.47, and in Figure 2.48, you can see the two connectors on a laptop.

FIGURE 2.48   RJ ports

To use a telephone line, your computer must have a modem. As I talked about in Chapter 1, modems are all but extinct today. The biggest reason is lack of speed. The fastest modems ever produced had a transfer rate of 56 Kbps, but in practice the most you ever really got out of the connection was around 40 Kbps. That's barely fast enough to download text files without pulling out your hair, never mind music or videos!

Both RJ-45 and RJ-11 connectors have been in existence for over 50 years, but they were mandated as standards in 1976.

Reviewing Connector Types

We've covered a lot of different types of connectors in this chapter. Instead of having you bounce around between pages to compare and contrast them to each other, Table 2.3 lists them all. In it, I've included the approximate release date, the maximum speed of the newest standard in that family, and the types of devices that you will commonly see associated with the connector. For some of the maximum speeds I have listed n/a, because no one ever really talks about the speed of those connections. In cases like that, just assume that they're slow!

TABLE 2.3 Summary of connectors

Type	Released	Max Speed	Primary Uses
VGA	1987	n/a	Video (analog)
DVI	1999	3.96 Gbps	Video (digital and analog)
HDMI	2002	18 Gbps	Video (digital)
DisplayPort	2008	25.9 Gbps	Video (digital)
Thunderbolt	2011	20 Gbps	Video, hard drives, audio, docks, PCIe expansion
USB	1998	10 Gbps	Keyboards, mice, printers, and many others
S-video	1987	n/a	Video (analog)
Component - RGB	1950s	n/a	Video (analog and digital)
FireWire	1994	3.2 Gbps	Digital video cameras, hard drives, Mac OS X and Linux networks
eSATA	2003	6 Gbps	Hard drives and optical drives
PS/2	1987	n/a	Keyboards and mice
Parallel	1970	20 Mbps	Printers
Serial (RS-232)	1962	115 Kbps	Modem, printers, mice, control console for server and router management
RJ-45	1976	1 Gbps	Network cards
RJ-11	1976	56 Kbps	Modems

Summary

In this chapter, I talked about external peripheral devices and the connector types used to hook them to your computer. Broad categories of external peripherals are output devices, input devices, and input and output devices. Some devices, such as the printer, are output devices, but when you bundle in extra functionality such as scanning, you now have a device that does both input and output.

First, I covered output devices. To hear sound, you need a sound card in your system, as well as a set of speakers or headphones. To put ink on paper, you need a printer. Printers are one example of a device that can fall into multiple camps as far as input and output goes. A basic printer is just for output, but a multifunctional printer that also has scanning or faxing capabilities can be an input device as well. Video devices were our last group of output devices; I talked about different types of monitors and projectors, as well as the different video connectors that have been used or are used today.

Second, I shifted the focus to devices that are used primarily for input. These include keyboards and pointing devices like the mouse, touchpad, and trackball.

Finally, you learned about external storage and communications devices. There are many different types of external storage devices you'll use, from tiny memory cards and small thumb drives, to large-capacity network-attached storage, to mobile devices such as media players and smartphones.

Exam Essentials

Know which devices are considered output devices. The list includes printers, display devices, and speakers.

Know which devices are input devices. Keyboards, pointing devices, scanners, microphones, and webcams are input devices.

Know which devices can provide input and output. These devices are faxes, external storage devices, and touchscreen displays.

Understand the features of common video connectors. The video connectors you need to know are VGA, DVI, HDMI, DisplayPort, Thunderbolt, USB, S-video, and Component–RGB.

Understand the way in which each printer type creates images. Laser printers use a powdery toner, inkjet printers use liquid ink in small cartridges, and thermal printers use heat-sensitive paper.

Know which connection types are used for external storage. Connections that are used for external storage devices are USB, FireWire, eSATA, and Thunderbolt.

Know how to best connect keyboards and mice to computers. Keyboards and mice today all use USB. In the past, the PS/2 connector was used. Before PS/2, mice could use serial ports.

Written Labs

You can find the answers to the written labs in Appendix A.

Your friend Elise comes to you looking for help. You know that she is talented at producing videos and has recently started her own company to make videos for local restaurants and entertainment venues to put on their websites.

Elise tells you that business is growing quickly, and she's very excited. She's had so much business that she needed to bring in another friend, James, to do some work for her, and both of them have been very busy. Elise had purchased an external hard drive for additional storage, but now she is running out of room, and she needs a better solution, preferably one she and James can both use. Elise uses a MacBook Pro. James has some sort of Mac as well, but it's a few years old.

Elise's goals are, in order, to increase storage space, to make it easily available for her and James, and to have some protection against losing all of the data she has. She also doesn't want to spend a fortune, because she needs to keep costs down for her business to keep growing.

1. What types of hardware does Elise need to accomplish her goals?

2. Are there any peripherals that would let her accomplish all of her goals with one device?

3. How much will that option cost if she wants to get 1 TB of storage space?

4. Are there other options that Elise has that might save her money?

Feel free to use the Internet to research and come up with at least two options for Elise.

Review Questions

You can find the answers to the review questions in Appendix B.

1. Which of the following ports was developed by Apple and is found on MacBooks?
   A. eSATA
   B. S-video
   C. Thunderbolt
   D. Mac Video

2. If you want to plug in a keyboard, which types of connectors might you use? (Choose two.)
   A. Parallel
   B. Serial
   C. USB
   D. PS/2

3. What is the name of the connector that you are likely to find at the end of a twisted-pair network cable?
   A. RJ-11
   B. RJ-45
   C. HDMI
   D. FireWire

4. You want to use the video connector with the best resolution. Which one should you pick?
   A. HDMI
   B. HEMI
   C. DVI
   D. Component

5. What are the colors used by component video? (Choose three.)
   A. Red
   B. Blue
   C. Yellow
   D. Green
   E. White
   F. Black

6. Which type of printer uses a powdery substance to create images on paper?

   A. Powder

   B. Thermal

   C. Inkjet

   D. Laser

7. Rebecca points at a flat square below her keyboard on her laptop and asks what that is. What is it?

   A. Launchpad

   B. Touchpad

   C. Touchstick

   D. Webcam

8. Which of the following devices are both input and output devices? (Choose two.)

   A. NAS

   B. Flat screen

   C. Scanner

   D. Webcam

   E. Smartphone

9. What is the name of the round connector that is used for keyboards and mice?

   A. USB

   B. PS/2

   C. DIN

   D. Serial

10. You want to install a device in your office that allows for extra storage and has built-in fault tolerance. Which device do you need?

   A. NAS

   B. RAS

   C. SAS

   D. External hard drive

11. One of your friends asks you if you have any SuperSpeed devices. What type of device is she talking about?

   A. SSD

   B. CRT

   C. USB

   D. eSATA

12. You have a color inkjet printer. What type of ink cartridge does it most likely use?
    A. CMYB
    B. CMYK
    C. RGB
    D. ROYGBIV

13. In your office, you need to set up your computer for a video teleconference with another office. What peripheral do you need to make this work?
    A. Scanner
    B. CRT
    C. Projector
    D. Webcam

14. What type of connector do you plug into a modem?
    A. RJ-11
    B. RJ-15
    C. RJ-41
    D. RJ-45

15. Which type of printer uses a fuser that gets hot and melts the image into the paper?
    A. Thermal
    B. Inkjet
    C. Laser
    D. Fusing

16. Which of the following types of monitors is most likely to have a Degauss button on it?
    A. CRT
    B. Flat screen
    C. Touchscreen
    D. Projector

17. Your friend discovered a joystick in a box of his brother's items in the attic. What type of connector might this joystick have? (Choose two.)
    A. PS/2
    B. USB
    C. RS-232
    D. DA15

18. Which of the following statements is true about DVI connectors?

   A. They are digital only.

   B. They are analog only.

   C. They are digital and analog.

   D. They support hybrid video technology.

19. You have two Mac computers running OS X, and you want to connect them into a network. Which two types of connectors can help you accomplish this?

   A. RJ-11

   B. RJ-45

   C. FireWire

   D. eSATA

20. Robert complains that the cursor on his laptop screen often jumps around unexpectedly when he's typing. What can he do to solve the problem?

   A. Reinstall the mouse driver

   B. Reinstall the video driver

   C. Reboot the computer

   D. Disable the touchpad

   E. Stop typing

Chapter

3

Operating Systems

THE FOLLOWING COMPTIA IT FUNDAMENTALS EXAM OBJECTIVES ARE COVERED IN THIS CHAPTER:

✓ **1.1 Compare and contrast common Operating Systems and their functions and features**

- Types
  - Mobile
    - Apple iOS
    - Android
    - Windows Phone
    - Blackberry
  - Workstation
    - Windows
    - Mac
    - Linux
    - Chrome OS
  - Open source vs. commercial
- Software compatibility for different OS types and versions
- Awareness of hardware compatibility for OS support
  - 32bit vs. 64bit operating systems
- Basic functions of an operating system
  - Interface between user and machine
  - Coordination of hardware components
  - Provides environment for software to function
  - Monitors system health and functionality
  - Displays structure / directories for data management

✓ **5.2 Explain the basic methods of navigating an operating system**

- Executing programs
- Difference between shortcuts and files
- Manipulating files
  - Open
  - Edit
  - Save
  - Move
  - Copy
  - Cut
  - Paste
  - Delete
  - Rename
- Read-only vs. modifiable files
- Navigate a file structure
- Search, sort and display files
- Create screen captures
- Navigate with hot keys
- Folder and file size
- Accessibility options
- Folder and file permissions

Computers are pretty much useless without software. A piece of hardware might just as well be used as a paperweight or doorstop unless you have an easy way to interface with it. Software provides that way. While there are many types of software, or programs, the most important application you'll ever deal with is the operating system.

There are several types of operating systems on the market today, and each has its own unique functions and features. I'll cover eight different important ones in this chapter. Even though they are all somewhat different and all complex, at the end of the day they all need to accomplish the same basic functions. I'll talk about what those functions are, types of operating systems, and a bit of history in the "Operating System Fundamentals" section of this chapter.

Finally, you need to know how to navigate through an operating system to make it work effectively for you. The "Navigating an Operating System" section will give you an introduction to how folders and files are structured, as well as how to manage that structure and execute programs. That section closes with additional features of operating systems to make them easier for people to use. After reading this chapter, you should have a good fundamental understanding of what operating systems are and an appreciation for why they work the way they do.

Operating System Fundamentals

Before I begin discussing operating systems, it's important to take one step further back and talk about software in general. In computing, there are three major classifications of software that you will deal with: operating systems, applications, and drivers. Here's a description of each:

Operating System (OS) An *operating system* provides a consistent environment for other software to execute commands. The OS gives users an interface with the computer so they can send commands (input) and receive feedback or results (output). To do this, the OS must communicate with the computer hardware, as illustrated in Figure 3.1.

Once the OS has organized these basic resources, users can give the computer instructions through input devices (such as a keyboard or a mouse). Some of these commands are built into the OS, whereas others are issued through the use of applications. The OS becomes the center through which the system hardware, other software, and the user communicate; the rest of the components of the system work together through the OS, which coordinates their communication.

FIGURE 3.1   The operating system interacts with hardware.

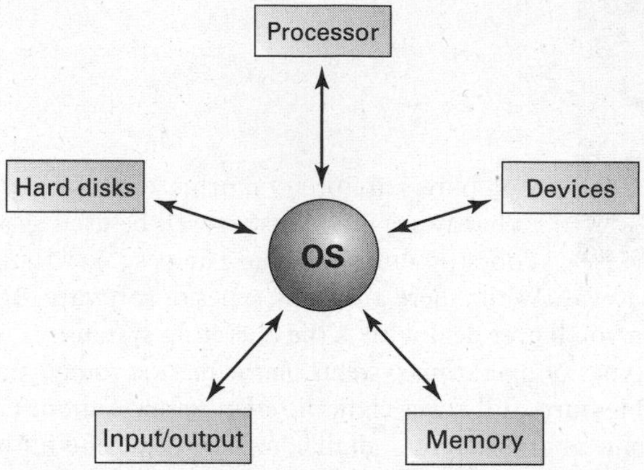

Application   An application is a piece of software used to accomplish a particular task; it is written to supplement the commands available to a particular OS. Each application is specifically compiled (configured) for the OS on which it will run. Examples of applications include complex programs such as Microsoft Word and Internet Explorer as well as simple programs such as a command-line file transfer program. I will cover applications in depth in Chapter 4, "Software Applications."

Driver   A driver is an extremely specific application written for the purpose of instructing a particular OS on how to access a piece of hardware. Each hardware device, like a printer or network card, has unique features and configuration settings, and the driver allows the OS to properly understand how the hardware works and what it is able to do. Drivers will also be discussed in depth in Chapter 4.

With those key software designations out of the way, let's take a trip back through time to understand where operating systems came from.

A Brief History of Operating Systems

First, I probably owe you a warning. You won't be quizzed on the history of operating systems on the CompTIA IT Fundamentals exam. What you *will* be tested on is the basic functions of an operating system and different varieties on the market. The reason I want to take you through some history is that I believe it will give you some good perspective on *why* OSs do what they do, why there are so many, and perhaps some appreciation for them as well. So even though it won't be on the test, don't skip this part!

Pre-OS

Let's go back to the dawning of the computer age, about 1946. A few electronic "computers" had been developed by that time, and the U.S. government, in partnership with the University of Pennsylvania, announced the development of a machine named the Electronic Numerical

Integrator And Computer (ENIAC). Like a lot of technology at the time, this one had the purpose of aiding the military. Among other projects, it helped calculate firing tables for artillery guns and also studied the feasibility of the nuclear bomb. It could do other things, though, and as such ENIAC is considered the first general-purpose electronic computer.

ENIAC was huge. Really huge. It was made up of nearly 18,000 vacuum tubes to go along with 70,000 resistors and 10,000 capacitors. It was 8 feet tall, 3 feet thick, and 100 feet long, weighing in at an impressive 27 tons. It consumed so much power that the joke was, when they turned it on, the power in the rest of Philadelphia dimmed. But it could run about 5,000 operations per second. Figure 3.2 shows a historical photo of this beast.

FIGURE 3.2   ENIAC

"ENIAC" BY UNKNOWN - U.S. ARMY PHOTO. LICENSED UNDER PUBLIC DOMAIN VIA WIKIMEDIA COMMONS - HTTP://COMMONS.WIKIMEDIA. ORG/WIKI/FILE:ENIAC.JPG#MEDIAVIEWER/FILE:ENIAC.JPG

In the introduction to this chapter I said that hardware is useless without software, and ENIAC was no exception. It was "programmed" by switching out thousands of connections in the patch panel. Instructions on what the computer was supposed to do had to be written by hand and then transcribed to punch cards, which were fed to the machine. Output was produced on punch cards as well, which were fed into a separate IBM punch card reader to produce printed output. It could take a team of five technicians a week to program ENIAC, troubleshoot, find errors, and fix the problem so the machine would produce the requested results. Clearly, improvements were needed.

By 1949, computers had memory. It wasn't much, and it was executed by using tubes filled with liquid mercury. Around the same time, other inventors were laying down the basic elements of programming languages. In 1952, the idea of reusable code (being able to run the same program multiple times with the same punch cards) surfaced. The assembler also appeared, which allowed programmers to write a command in a higher-level language, and it would be translated to assembly for the computer to take action.

> Assembly code is a low-level programming language that corresponds to direct action the computer needs to take.

These and other technological advancements started people on the path of developing the first operating system.

The Early Days

A group of IBM engineers put their heads together, and by 1954 they had developed the first computer programming language: Fortran. What Fortran allowed programmers to do was to create simple commands that told the computer (in assembly language) to execute several commands. It saved everyone a lot of time; simple programs could now be executed in just a few hours. Programmers started compiling multiple pieces of Fortran code together and sharing it with others, and the idea of a stable, consistent operating system started to gain traction.

> As old as it is, Fortran is still used today. Of course, revisions have been made over time to improve functionality. Fortran 2015 is scheduled to be released in 2015.

Throughout the 1950s and 1960s, various companies (including IBM and Bell Labs) and universities (Massachusetts Institute of Technology, Manchester University, University of Michigan, University of California–Berkeley, and others) started developing their own compilations of code and giving it names. These were the first operating systems, and they were each designed to work with a specific model of computer.

Standardization

Operating systems of the time were slow and were not compatible with each other. In 1969, a group of engineers from Bell Labs came out with UNIX. By 1973, they had released the fourth edition of it, which had some big benefits. First, it was written in a newer programming language (called C), which was easier to deal with than Fortran. Second, it could work on different hardware platforms. Third, it was a lot faster than anything else on the market. By 1975, many universities (and their students) were using UNIX, and its growth spread quickly.

An interesting and hugely impactful note to the history of UNIX is that at the time Bell Systems (which owned Bell Labs as well as the entire telephone infrastructure in the United States) was a regulated monopoly, so it couldn't get into the computer business. Therefore, since they couldn't make any money on UNIX, they distributed it for free. Users were also free to make any modifications they wanted to the OS, which means that UNIX was *open-source* code.

Open-source versus commercial (closed-source) code is still a matter of significant debate today—I'll get into that when we talk about different types of operating systems.

Through the late 1970s and early 1980s, operating systems were pretty basic. They had a command interpreter, the ability to load programs, and basic device drivers. That was about it. In 1981, IBM introduced the first personal computer, which was the first time this technology was brought to the masses. With the IBM PC came the need for an easy-to-use operating system. The one that frequently got bundled with it? It was called MS-DOS, short for Microsoft Disk Operating System.

Pretty Pictures and Modern Operating Systems

Also in 1981, Xerox introduced the Star workstation. It had the first window-based graphical user interface (GUI), mouse, and other conventions we take for granted today like Internet access and email. But it never really got very popular. Figure 3.3 shows how basic the interface is, yet it feels strikingly familiar today.

FIGURE 3.3 The first PC graphical user interface

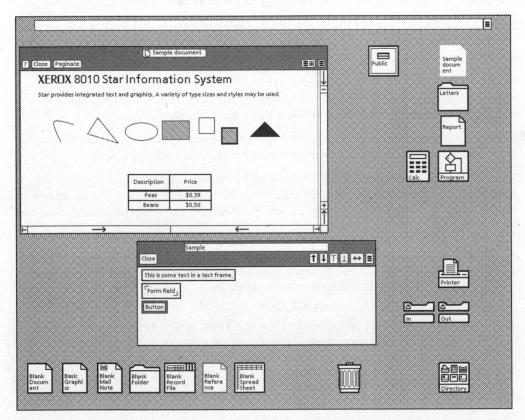

Apple licensed the operating system from Xerox, made some improvements, and introduced it on the Macintosh computer in 1984. It became immediately popular, and the world hasn't been the same since. (Apple was ahead of the curve even more than 30 years ago!) Up until this time, the only way you really interacted with your computer was with the keyboard, typing in commands, and all display was text-based. Not anymore. Graphical displays and windows were here to stay.

Microsoft tried (and failed) to popularize a graphical product until 1990, with their release of Windows 3.0. Even though it provided a graphical interface, it was still mostly based on its very popular MS-DOS operating system.

Linux came along in 1991, written by Linus Torvalds. It has its foundations in UNIX and is open source, but not exactly like UNIX. All of the modern operating systems we use today have their foundations in UNIX or Xerox Star.

Basic Functions of Operating Systems

Before we get too far into our discussion of what modern operating systems are expected to do, it will be useful to define a few key terms. The following are some terms you will come across as you study this chapter, and you should know them for computer literacy:

Kernel   The central part of the operating system. It controls all actions of the OS, including input and output, which processes get to use the CPU and memory, and translating between hardware and software components in the computer.

Version   A particular revision of a piece of software, normally described by a number that tells you how new the product is in relation to other versions of the product.

Source   The actual code that defines how a piece of software works. Computer operating systems can be open source, meaning the OS can be examined and modified by anyone, or they can be closed source, meaning that only an owner or developer can modify or examine the code.

Shell   A program that runs on top of the OS and allows the user to issue commands through a set of menus or other interface (which may or may not be graphical). Shells make an OS easier to use by changing the user interface.

Graphical User Interface (GUI)   A method by which a person communicates with a computer using graphical images, icons, and methods other than text. GUIs allow a user to use a mouse, touchpad, or another mechanism (in addition to the keyboard) to interact with the computer to issue commands.

Cooperative Multitasking   A multitasking method that depends on the application itself to be responsible for using the processor and then freeing it for access by other applications. This is the way very early versions of Windows managed multiple applications. If any application locked up while using the processor, the application was unable to properly free the processor to do other tasks and the entire system locked, usually forcing a reboot.

Preemptive Multitasking   A multitasking method in which the OS allots each application a certain amount of processor time and then forcibly takes back control and gives another application or task access to the processor. This means that if an application crashes, the OS takes control of the processor away from the locked application and passes it on to the next application, which should be unaffected. Although unstable programs still lock, only the locked application will stall—not the entire system. This is what is used today in modern operating systems.

Multithreading   The ability of a single application to have multiple requests in to the processor at one time. This results in faster application performance because it allows a program to do many things at once.

32-Bit   An operating system that is 32-bit is one that can not only run on 32-bit processors but can also fully utilize the capabilities of the processor. While this may sound simple, the truth of the matter is that it took many years after the 32-bit processor became available before operating systems (which were 16-bit at the time) were able to utilize their features. Just as you cannot mix racecars with a country road, you cannot mix 64-bit software with 32-bit hardware.

64-Bit   A 64-bit operating system is one that is written to utilize the instructions possible with 64-bit processors. Originally, these were more common with servers than desktops, but with prices dropping, 64-bit processors have become common on the desktop, as have operating systems that will run on them. As mentioned earlier, you cannot mix 64-bit software with 32-bit hardware (but you can run most 32-bit software on 64-bit hardware).

With those terms in mind, let's look at the key functions of an operating system. The functions that you will examine in more depth in the upcoming sections are as follows:

- Interface between the user and the hardware
- Coordinate hardware components
- Provide environment for software to function
- Display structure for data management
- Monitor system health and functionality

Coordinating Users and Hardware

Thank goodness we've moved beyond needing to spend an entire week manually moving connections around to just do a simple math problem. Even today, most people don't know how to tell the computer hardware (in assembly) to function, nor do they care to know how. We turn our computers on, and we expect that when we click something, it works, or when we press a key on the keyboard, that letter appears on our screen. The operating system coordinates all of that for us.

Most of us don't also really give much thought to the different types of hardware needed to execute what seem to be simple commands. If we open a document or a spreadsheet, it requires coordination of the mouse (or keyboard), the motherboard, processor, memory, and hard drive. If that file is on another computer on the network, it also requires our network card. Again, the operating system manages all of this for us so we don't have to think about it.

To talk to the hardware, operating systems use specialized programs called device drivers, or drivers for short. A driver tells the OS how to talk to the specific piece of hardware and how to use its features. I'll talk about drivers in Chapter 4.

If there is no driver for that OS, then the hardware will not be compatible with it. The biggest topic in compatibility today, though, is 32-bit versus 64-bit operating systems. What you can run is totally dependent on your processor. If you have a 32-bit processor, all you can run is a 32-bit OS. If you have a 64-bit processor, you can run either a 32- or 64-bit OS, although running a 32-bit OS on top of a 64-bit processor is a bit like replacing a sports car's engine with a hamster wheel and expecting it to perform.

Operating systems also keep us users in check. We're not allowed to perform any functions that would break the hardware, generally speaking. At a minimum, we're at least warned that what we are about to do will erase everything on our hard drive—are we sure that's what we want to do?

Another thing that OSs can do to help us silly people behave is to limit the resources we are allowed to access. If you work for a company, you probably don't need to see everyone's salary information unless you're the boss or in Human Resources. Many PC OSs allow for the creation of user accounts to manage who can get to what. This is done by assigning permissions—that is, specifying which users can access which files.

If you are the only person who uses your computer, user accounts and permissions aren't as big of a deal. But once you start getting into environments where more than one person is involved, they start to become important.

Working with User Accounts

A *user account* is an identity by which you're known when using the OS. Most OSs allow (or require) you to log in, identify yourself by your user account, and then adjust the system and user environment settings appropriately to match your user level and preferences. For example, your desktop background and available icons are linked to your user account.

Within most OSs are multiple levels of users, with each level having different security settings called *permissions*. This enables you to grant access to the system to someone whom you perhaps don't trust to have full access to it. For example, you might give a child permission to run applications on the system but not to make changes that affect other users, like changing system settings.

Three common levels of users are administrator, standard user (often just called user), and guest. In general, the administrator can do almost anything they want, the user can access files but not make system configuration changes, and the guest account has very limited permissions. In Figure 3.4, for example, there are four accounts: two with administrator privileges, one standard user, and a generic Guest account (which is built in with Windows). It's turned off, so it isn't visible at the login screen.

FIGURE 3.4 User accounts in Windows 7

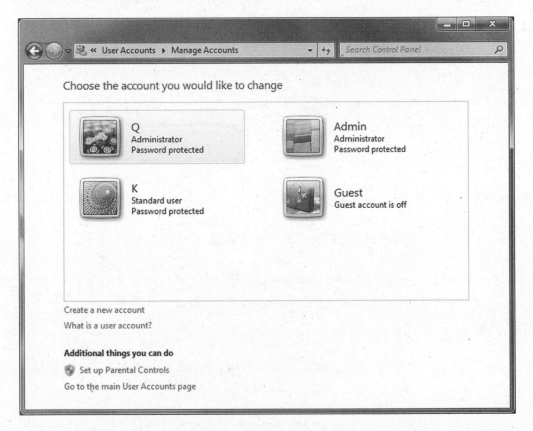

On a Mac, you have Standard and Administrator accounts available, plus a Managed with Parental Controls account and a Sharing Only account. As shown in Figure 3.5, you can make a user an administrator by selecting the Allow User To Administer This Computer check box, and you can impose parental controls with the Enable Parental Controls check box.

For Linux, the options available depend on the version you're using. For example, Ubuntu offers Administrator, Desktop User, and Unprivileged. Ubuntu also allows you to fine-tune the user's properties and privileges, as shown in Figure 3.6.

FIGURE 3.5   User settings in Mac OS X

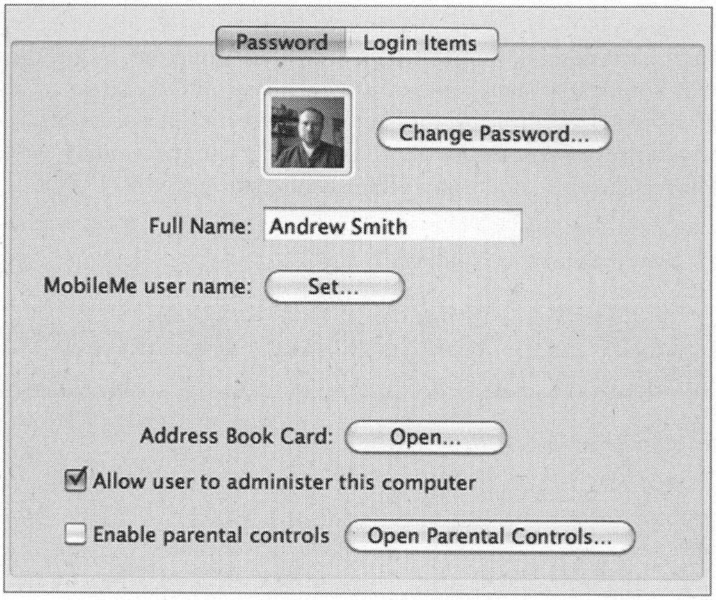

FIGURE 3.6   Ubuntu user properties

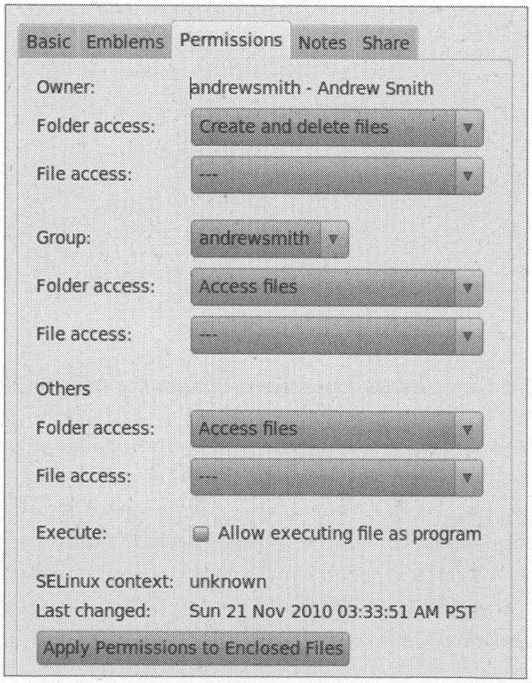

No matter which account type and OS you choose, it's a good idea to password-protect it. The only exception to that is the Guest account on a Windows system. It usually doesn't have a password because by its nature it's accessible to the public. It's also a good idea to keep that account disabled unless you have a specific reason for enabling it. Exercise 3.1 has you create a user account in Windows 7.

EXERCISE 3.1

Creating a User Account in Windows 7

1. In Windows 7, make sure you're logged in using an administrator account type.

2. Choose Start ➢ Control Panel.

3. Under the User Accounts And Family Safety heading, click Add Or Remove User Accounts. A list of the current accounts appears, like the one you saw earlier in Figure 3.4.

4. Click Create A New Account.

5. In the New Account Name box, type a name of your choice.

6. Leave the Standard User check box selected, as shown in Figure 3.7.

FIGURE 3.7   User account creation

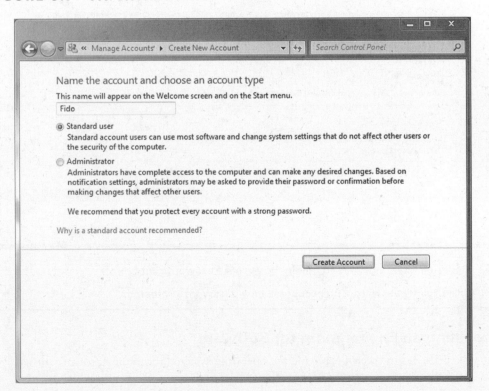

EXERCISE 3.1 *(continued)*

7. Click Create Account. The account appears on the list of accounts.

8. Click the new account's icon. A list of options appears that you can use to make changes.

9. Click Create A Password.

10. Type a password of your choice in the New Password and Confirm New Password boxes, as shown in Figure 3.8.

FIGURE 3.8 Creating a password

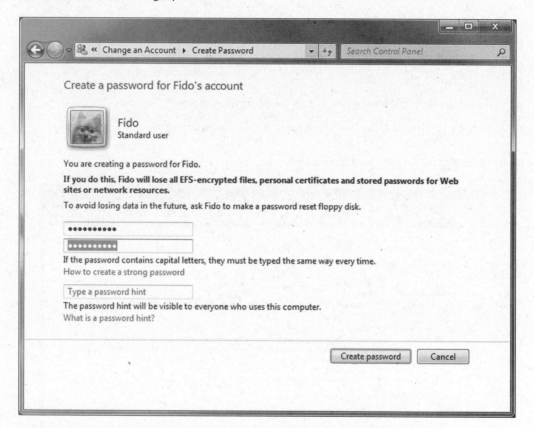

11. (Optional) Enter a password hint in the Type A Password Hint box.

12. Click Create Password. The account is now password-protected.

Providing an Environment for Software

We talked about how nice it is having the operating system talk to the hardware for us. Similarly, the OS gives software applications one standard interface with which to work.

Without an OS, each software application would need to know how to talk to each specific piece of hardware on the market—an impossible task for developers. So, the programmer creates a program that works with the OS, and then the OS figures out how to talk to the hardware.

Because each OS is created differently, though, applications are written for a specific OS and not compatible with different ones. For example, a game written for Mac OS X won't work on a machine running Windows or vice versa. Odds are the developer will have a different version that works just fine on Windows. Within versions of an OS family, compatibility isn't generally as big of a problem as it is across OS types. If an app works on Windows 8, it will probably run on Windows 7 or Vista as well. This isn't always true, and it starts becoming more problematic the farther apart generations of apps and operating systems become. For example, a game designed to run on Windows 95 (which is over 20 years old) might not work natively in Windows 8.

Providing Structure for Data Management

Hopefully by now, the idea that computers store data permanently shouldn't come as a shock to you. Data can be anything from files needed to run the OS to a spreadsheet with a work project to pictures and videos of a recent vacation. But how is it stored on the hard drive? Is it just a jumbled mess of bits? And if it were, then how do you easily find the data you need, when you need it?

In all actuality, the data stored on the hard drive does resemble a jumbled mess of bits. Fortunately, the OS comes to the rescue again by giving users a structured way to store and access those files and applications. OSs use a system of directories (often called folders) to store data in a hierarchical manner. It all starts with the root of the hard drive (typically C: on most PCs) and branches out from there; because of the branches you might hear it called a directory tree. So no matter where the data physically resides on the hard drive, the OS catalogs it in a logical manner so you can always get to what you need—if you remember where you put it.

The "Managing Folder and File Structures" section later in this chapter covers this topic in significantly more detail.

Monitoring System Health and Functionality

Finally, OSs will monitor the health of your system's hardware, giving you an idea of how well (or not) it's performing. You can see how busy your CPU is, or how quickly your hard drives retrieve data, or how much data your network card is sending, all to understand how efficient your computer is. Monitoring system performance can also alert you if a component is starting to fail, if its performance starts to deteriorate rapidly.

Different OSs use different tools to monitor system health. In most versions of Windows the utility is called Performance Monitor, and it's located in Administrative Tools in Control Panel. In Figure 3.9, you can see processor performance on my computer.

The longer spike in performance was when I opened a game, and the second, shorter spike was when I opened an Excel spreadsheet. But as you can see, my CPU isn't being taxed in any way.

FIGURE 3.9   Windows Performance Monitor

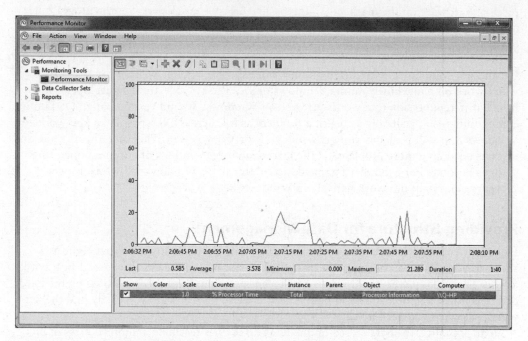

Most of the time, it's helpful to have context to decide if the data that these tools produce indicates a problem or not. For example, if 20 percent of my memory is being used, is that good or bad? It's probably not a problem, unless I haven't changed anything and it used to be consistently at 10 percent. What administrators often do is set up a *baseline* of performance for key hardware components (the CPU, memory, hard drive, and network) to know what normal performance looks like. Then, if the system is having issues, they can refer back to the baseline to see how bad the issue really is.

> Mac OS X's performance tool is called Activity Monitor. Ubuntu Linux has a similar graphical tool called System Monitor and a text-based one called saidar.

Configuring and using performance monitoring tools is beyond the scope of this book; just know that your operating system can perform these tasks for you.

Types of Operating Systems

You could literally spend a lifetime learning about all of the different types of operating systems in existence. There are OSs built specifically for servers, workstations, mobile devices, routers, home entertainment systems, and more. Within each of these designations you'll find dozens if not hundreds or thousands of variants, each with its own unique features. Understanding it all is an interesting hobby for some and an absolute nightmare for others.

Fortunately, the CompTIA IT Fundamentals exam doesn't ask you to memorize thousands of operating systems and their features. If they did, we would need several more books just to cover them. For this exam, you just need to know about a manageable list of eight OSs, which are grouped into two categories: workstation and mobile.

Workstation Operating Systems

Workstations are abundant in today's computer world. Everyone's computer at home is a workstation. On a network, the term *workstation* is synonymous with client computer. Workstations can be desktop computers or laptop computers. In this section, I'll take a look at four of the most important workstation OSs in the market.

Linux

Of the four OSs we're going to cover here, *Linux* is the least popular one for workstation installation. So why cover it first? Because it's easily the most influential. Linux was developed in 1991 by Linus Torvalds and is in many ways a derivative of UNIX.

First, I need to clarify one important thing: Linux isn't actually an operating system. Linux is a kernel, or the core of an operating system. To turn the kernel into a Linux-based OS, developers need to add other critical components such as daemons (services), a *shell*, shell utilities, a desktop environment (such as a *graphical user interface*), and desktop applications. The combination of all of these features is referred to as a *distribution*. Even though it's not technically an operating system, a lot of people still call it one. Here, I'll do the same, because it's a lot shorter than writing "the collection of Linux-based operating systems" every time I refer to it. Linux is also unique among our list of OSs because it's the only one that's open source.

 Most Linux distributions use what's called the Bash shell. Bash stands for Bourne-again shell, which was designed to replace an older commonly used shell called the Bourne shell. Bash is also the default shell of Mac OS X.

LINUX VERSIONS

If you'll recall, *open source* means that anyone who wants to can modify the code, and many developers have decided to take that challenge. They can't change the kernel, which is what defines Linux, but they can change anything else they want in the distribution. One developer might add lots of services, whereas another might keep it lean and quick. Some versions are 32-bit and others are 64-bit. Many distributions have a GUI, whereas others (mostly Slackware versions) have kept the default interface old-school command-prompt based. By my best count, I found over 350 current and well-known Linux distributions alive today. I am sure there are at least that many more that are retired or unpublished. Like any proper OS, Linux distributions have names. Examples include Ubuntu Linux, Linux Mint, Debian, KDE, and Red Hat. Figure 3.10 shows the desktop of Lubuntu, which is in the Ubuntu family. (It's basically Ubuntu with a "lighter" and quicker desktop, designed to speed up performance.)

You'll notice a similarity with other "Windows-like" desktops, complete with folders (such as the one that's open) and a menu to get to various applications and utilities.

FIGURE 3.10 Lubuntu desktop

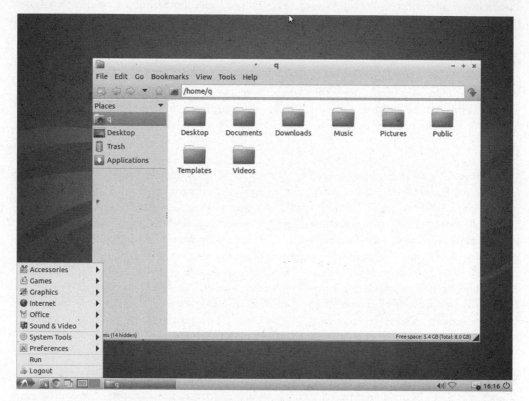

Most Linux distributions in the wild today come from one of three families: Debian, Slackware, or RPM, which were popular Linux versions around 1993–94. As is encouraged in the Linux community, developers took these versions, made changes, and redistributed them with different names. If you wanted to, you could take any existing version of Linux (except commercial ones), modify it, and call it whatever you wanted. Or, you could start from the ground up and develop your own, although that would take a considerable amount of work.

The website www.linuxfromscratch.org provides information on how to develop your own version of Linux, if the mood strikes you.

The vast majority of distributions are free of charge. The underpinning belief of the open-source community is that software, particularly software that aids in educational or scientific endeavors, should be free. Commercial (non-free) variants of Linux also exist, such as Red Hat Enterprise. In addition, several other OSs such as Android and Chrome are built upon a Linux foundation. You don't necessarily pay for those OSs, but they are bundled with devices that you do pay for, such as a smartphone or a Chromebook.

Distributions might or might not be backed by a corporation, which means technical support for issues can be hit or miss. In most cases, you will need to rely on online support forums, such as `wiki.ubuntu.com/lubuntu`. Members in the community are generally pretty responsive when others have questions or need help, but again, it depends on the version.

LINUX USAGE

Linux is immensely popular on servers and Internet devices. In fact, you can safely say that the Internet runs on Linux. (Do a Google search on the words "The Internet runs on" and see what the autofill is!) Some estimates have the Linux share of the server market at 50 percent. But, Linux is only installed on around 1–2 percent of all desktop and laptop computers. Why is that?

There are likely a few reasons. First, and most importantly, the vast majority of desktop and laptop PCs sold are bundled with a Windows-based OS. Related to that, considering the market share of Windows, most applications are written for that platform as well. There might or might not be a Linux version. Second, Linux has a bit of a reputation as being more technically challenging to run well—"geeky" if you will. This is based on its heritage as a UNIX derivative with a command-line interface, which probably turns off some users who might otherwise be interested in a free and efficient operating system.

For programmers or hardware developers, some version of Linux is generally the preferred choice. It has less overhead than other workstation OSs and is readily customizable for their needs. Even though it doesn't have a major install base in the workstation market, Linux is an incredibly powerful OS that we really don't want to live without.

Mac

Apple introduced the Macintosh computer in 1984, and behind a massive marketing campaign it became very popular. Its popularity can be attributed to the fact that it had a very easy-to-use interface—the first popular WIMP interface. The OS on the first Mac was simply called System, or sometimes *System Software*. Apple developed System in-house, as a combination of its own previous OS (called the Lisa OS) and features from the Xerox OS.

MAC OS VERSIONS

Early versions of System were relatively simple. They had an application called Finder, which allowed users to store and locate their files. One early challenge was that Finder created virtual folders for file storage, so those folders and files weren't visible in any program except for Finder. These early versions also could run only one application at a time.

Released in 1987, System 5 provided for cooperative multitasking with the MultiFinder application. This represented a big step forward for the OS. By then, files and folders were also integrated into the file system, so other applications could use them as well.

The next major version was System 7, which added some significant upgrades, including the following:

- Native support for virtual memory, so hard disk space could be used if the physical memory ran low

- Built-in cooperative multitasking (as opposed to multitasking being done through an app)
- The first 32-bit OS widely available for workstations
- A redesigned user interface
- The Trash can (for deleted file) no longer emptied by default automatically at shut down

System 7 was also the last version to use the "System" name. With update 7.6, Apple dropped the title and renamed it Mac OS.

Mac *OS X* was the tenth version of the Mac series of operating systems, and it marked a major departure from previous Mac OSs. Before we get into the details, let's pause and review some of the major versions of Mac OS to this point in Table 3.1.

TABLE 3.1 Selected Mac OS releases

Version	Year	Notes
System 1	1984	First widely popular GUI
System 2	1985	Introduces hierarchical file system
System 5	1987	Adds cooperative multitasking
System 7	1991	User interface redesign, virtual memory support, true 32-bit OS, and other enhancements
Mac OS 7.6	1997	Name change to make it easier for Apple to license OS to manufacturers of Mac clones
Mac OS X	1999	Major architecture change

The Mac clone market was short-lived—it lasted only about a year. Steve Jobs (one of the founders of Apple who was ousted by the board of directors in 1995) returned to Apple in August of 1997, and one of his major goals was to shut down Mac clones. He succeeded with the release of Mac OS 8 in late 1997.

Mac OS X for servers was released in 1999, and the desktop version followed in the spring of 2001. OS X was a major departure from Apple's previous OS, because it was UNIX-based. In fact, all of the most recent OS X versions are certified UNIX systems.

By the time OS X was released, Apple was in a challenging position. Windows was continuing to take market share, and Apple's OS interface was deemed a bit dated. OS X changed that with a new theme (layout) called Aqua. It's been updated several times, but the essence of Aqua still exists.

Since 2001, Mac OS X has gone through a number of revisions, each one adding new features. The name of the OS hasn't changed; instead, Apple has named each version after large cats and, since version 10.9, places in California. Table 3.2 shows you the versions of Mac OS X.

TABLE 3.2 Mac OS X versions

Version	Year	Name	Notes
10.0	2001	Cheetah	Panned by critics, loved by Mac enthusiasts. Aqua interface.
10.1	2001	Puma	Quick update released six months after Cheetah; improved system performance.
10.2	2002	Jaguar	The first version to use the code name for branding.
10.3	2003	Panther	Upgrade to UI and functionality. Improved interoperability with Microsoft Windows.
10.4	2005	Tiger	Added Spotlight search. First Apple OS installed on Macs with Intel processors.
10.5	2007	Leopard	First 64-bit support in Mac OS X family.
10.6	2009	Snow Leopard	Introduced support for Mac App Store. Only Intel-based Macs supported.
10.7	2011	Lion	Introduced the Launchpad, dropped support for 32-bit processors. iCloud debuted.
10.8	2012	Mountain Lion	Messages app replaced iChat. Apple commits to yearly OS release cycle.
10.9	2013	Mavericks	Improved battery life for laptops, integration of iOS features, announcement of free OS upgrades for life.
10.10	2014	Yosemite	Revamped interface, handoff between devices, and continued integration of iOS features.

At this point, Apple is committed to yearly updates of its OS X system, and it will give those upgrades out for free to qualified users. As I write this chapter, the name and the release date of OS X 10.11 are still mysteries. It's expected that it will be announced in the summer and released in the fall of 2015.

MAC OS USAGE

The Mac OS has been preinstalled on every Mac ever made. And as mentioned earlier, there was a very short period of time when Mac clones were made, and they had Mac OS as well. Today, you can buy any of several versions of Mac OS X on the Apple Store if you want and install it on a compatible system. Mac OS X has a relatively low share of the workstation market—only about 4–5 percent of the install base. Most of this is due to the fact that Apple has kept the OS mostly proprietary, whereas its main rival Windows has tried to be on every PC possible.

Macs tend to have very loyal users, and the general consensus is that if you're working on highly visual projects, Macs are the way to go. Macs also come with plenty of productivity software, but graphical applications are where Macs really shine.

As for using the interface, it's basically a lot like other WIMP interfaces out there. Figure 3.11 shows the Yosemite desktop. One difference versus some other interfaces is that OS X uses the dock, or the bar at the bottom of the desktop, for an easy way to activate icons of your favorite apps.

FIGURE 3.11   Mac OS X Yosemite

Windows

The Microsoft *Windows* family of operating systems has by far and away the largest installation base in the desktop and laptop PC market. This might not come as a surprise to you, but it might actually be a little surprising considering the inauspicious start the OS got off to. I'll get to that in a minute.

Windows has always been developed in-house by Microsoft and is seen as the flag bearer for closed-source software. Because of this, and because Microsoft has a history of strong-arming competitors, the company has faced a significant amount of scorn from the open-source community. The tide might be shifting a bit, though, based on some of Microsoft's actions. First, and most shocking, Microsoft's CEO Satya Nadella said, "Microsoft loves Linux." This might not seem like much, but those three words sent shockwaves throughout the computer industry. Second, Microsoft started partnering with various open-source companies to develop some of its platforms such as .NET. It's very possible that Microsoft got to the point where they decided there was too much development for them to take on and control themselves, so they needed to open up to compete in the new marketplace. Regardless of their motivations, it will be an interesting dynamic to watch over the next several years.

WINDOWS VERSIONS

Let's get back to the bad start that Windows had. The first version, Windows 1.0, was released in 1985 and was nothing more than a somewhat graphical front end to Microsoft's popular command-line MS-DOS operating system. Windows 2.0, released in 1987, didn't fare much better; Macintosh was clearly superior from a usability and aesthetics standpoint.

By the time Windows 3.0 rolled out in 1990, Microsoft and Apple were in a full-out battle with each other. Windows had copied, legally or not (depending on whom you talk to), a lot of the look and feel of Mac's System Software. In addition, Windows 3.0 supported cooperative multitasking and virtual memory. The Windows shell was called Program Manager, and it allowed users to graphically navigate the system to find files and start applications. Upgrades to Windows 3.0 included Windows 3.1 and Windows for Workgroups 3.11. Figure 3.12 shows the Windows 3.11 Program Manager.

FIGURE 3.12   Windows 3.11 Program Manager

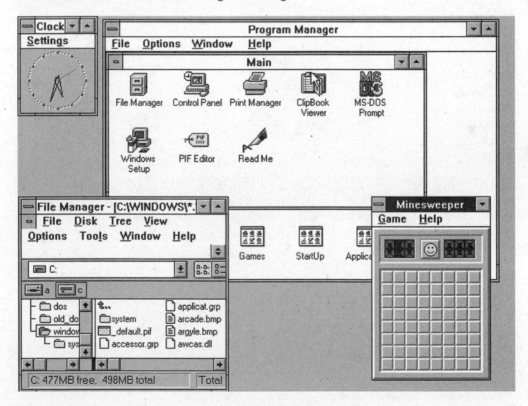

WINDOWS 3.11 PROGRAM MANAGER SCREENSHOT USED WITH PERMISSION FROM MICROSOFT.

The next major revision came in August of 1995: Windows 95. It replaced the Program Manager with a shell based on Windows Explorer and added a new feature called the Start button, as shown in Figure 3.13. It had some 32-bit features but employed 16-bit features as well, so it wasn't a true 32-bit OS. By most accounts, what had already been an easy operating system to use just got easier. Windows 95 exploded in popularity. Windows Explorer remained the default shell for Windows for 17 years, until Windows 8 was released in 2012.

FIGURE 3.13   Windows 95 desktop

WINDOWS 95 DESKTOP SCREENSHOT USED WITH PERMISSION FROM MICROSOFT.

Around the same time, Microsoft was working on a server-based operating system called Windows NT. (NT stood for New Technology, although critics claimed it stood for Nice Try.) Windows NT, using the 32-bit Windows NT kernel, was launched in 1993. At the time, of course, Microsoft was also busy working on Windows 95. Its goal was to unify the two operating systems into one platform, but that proved to be harder than they originally anticipated. Microsoft wouldn't be able to consolidate to one OS platform until Windows XP was released in 2001. XP was also the first version of Windows to come in a 64-bit version. From Windows XP on, all Microsoft OSs have used the Windows NT kernel.

Windows 8 was released in 2012 and marked the most significant appearance change for Windows since 1995. Figure 3.14 shows the Windows Start screen, which replaces the Start button. It provides tiles for the user, originally called the "Metro" design but since changed to "Windows Store app," intended to allow for faster navigation to the items the user wants. It's also intended to look very similar to Windows Phone and is optimized for devices with touchscreen displays.

FIGURE 3.14   Windows 8.1 Start screen

Unfortunately for Microsoft, Windows 8 has not achieved the commercial success they had anticipated. Critics complained about the lack of a Start button, noting that very few desktops or laptops have touchscreens. Due to some of the issues, Microsoft announced a free upgrade to Windows 8.1, which placed the Start button back on the desktop.

Windows 10 (Microsoft skipped Windows 9) is launching in late 2015. Among other features, it will keep the Start button, consolidate system settings into one place, add an area called Action Center to display notifications, and have a new web browser. The most anticipated feature of Windows 10 has to be Cortana, which is Microsoft's voice-activated personal assistant (think of Siri on the iPhone). That will run on your desktop or laptop, which sounds very cool. Finally, Microsoft is also further integrating its workstation and mobile OSs to make more seamless transitions between the desktop and mobile devices. One more thing that people will love too—Microsoft has announced that Windows 10 will be available as a free upgrade for Windows 7, Windows 8.1, and Windows Phone 8 users. Table 3.3 lists some key versions of Windows and associated features.

TABLE 3.3   Selected Windows versions

Version	Year	Notes
Windows 1.0	1985	A graphical interface for MS-DOS. Not widely received.
Windows 3.0	1990	The first serious competitor to Apple's graphical OS. Supported multitasking and virtual memory.
Windows 95	1995	Introduced the Start button.
Windows XP	2001	First Microsoft OS for home use with the Windows NT kernel. First 64-bit Microsoft OS version intended for home use.
Windows 7	2009	Available in 32- and 64-bit versions. Most popular desktop and laptop OS on the market today.
Windows 8	2012	Originally removed the Start button; optimized for touchscreen systems. Not as successful as Windows 7.
Windows 10	2015	Several major upgrades including Cortana and better integration with mobile devices.

WINDOWS USAGE

In your travels in the IT world, you will see a lot of Windows, because it is the most popular desktop and laptop OS in the world. That is mostly due to Microsoft's desire to get it onto as many systems as possible. Whereas Apple has traditionally combined the hardware and OS together as a package, Microsoft has not historically been in the hardware market. They produced an OS (and applications) and tried to make sure it was bundled with every PC that shipped. The strategy has had some clear success.

More specifically, Windows 7 is the most popular desktop and laptop OS in the world. As of early 2015, Windows 7 has an estimated 50 percent of the desktop and laptop market. The second most popular OS is Windows XP at around 24 percent. Windows 8 versions, despite all of the marketing money behind them, make up only about 13 percent of the market.

Chrome OS

Chrome OS was developed by Google and launched in 2011. In many important ways, it's unlike any of the other OSs we've discussed so far. The guiding principle behind the design of Chrome OS is that it's supposed to be lightweight and perform the most common tasks users need today. And what's the most common thing that all of us do? Get on the Internet.

Google had their Chrome browser, and their original intent was to make an OS based on the browser alone. That's it. Several rounds of testing showed that they were close but not quite on target with the ideal user experience. So they went back to the drawing board and incorporated the Gentoo Linux kernel and package management system with Chrome. Chrome OS was born. Looking at the Chrome desktop in Figure 3.15, you'll see that it looks like most other modern OS desktops, with a launcher in the lower-left corner, a taskbar, and status tray with a clock in the lower-right corner.

FIGURE 3.15   Google Chrome OS

What's particularly interesting about Chrome OS is that it stores little to nothing on the local computer. Everything is stored on the cloud.

CHROME OS VERSIONS

Chrome OS doesn't have major version names like Microsoft or Apple OSs do, at least not yet. As Google publishes updates, the new version is automatically downloaded to the system with no user intervention needed. There are no compatibility issues to worry about, because all of the apps themselves are stored on Google's cloud. For what it's worth, Chrome OS is 32-bit, and the version released in December 2014 was 39.0.2171.96. I doubt anyone will quiz you on that.

CHROME OS USAGE

Chrome OS was originally designed for small, portable computers called *netbooks*. Netbooks are like laptops, only smaller and very light. A netbook with Chrome is called a *Chromebook*. Netbooks have a processor, RAM, some ROM for storage, and a very, very small hard drive, typically SSD. Again, everything important is stored on the cloud. Recently, though, companies have started releasing desktop-type systems with Chrome OS as their operating system, called *Chromeboxes*. Regardless of your hardware platform, using Chrome OS requires an Internet connection because, again, everything is stored on the cloud.

 Chromeboxes often do have hard drives. Google insists that these be SSD drives because of their speed, and they are usually very small, such as 16 GB.

Google claims that they do not intend for Chrome OS to be a replacement for traditional desktop and laptop OSs. They say that Chrome OS is for secondary systems, with which people typically surf the Internet, send email, and use a few applications here and there.

The heavy lifting is still for other workstations. The launch of Chromeboxes makes some experts wonder if that's really the case.

Chrome OS has been one of the most popular OSs being sold in the last few years. As of the end of 2013, tablet sales eclipsed sales of PCs. During the 2014 November and December shopping season, Amazon listed Chromebooks as its three top-selling laptops. Its install base might not be huge today, but Chrome is easily the fastest growing OS and appears poised to continue on that trajectory for several more years.

Mobile Operating Systems

As the name of this section implies, here I will be talking about operating systems specifically designed for mobile devices. You'll see a lot of the same companies involved here, since Apple, Google, and Microsoft are all competitors in this arena as well.

Apple iOS

Apple is one of the dominant players in the mobile OS market with its iOS, running on the iPhone and iPad mobile platforms. Between those two devices, Apple has over 40 percent of the mobile and tablet market share. Figure 3.16 shows the home screen of iOS 8.

FIGURE 3.16   iOS 8 home screen

The *iOS* system is built on the same foundation as Apple's desktop OS X. In fact, early marketing literature for the iPhone simply referred to the OS as a version of OS X. Later on they renamed it to iPhone OS, but after the introduction of the iPad, they went to the shortened iOS. Throughout their history, though, the workstation and mobile versions have been fairly different and not directly compatible with each other. Apps built for one would not work on the other, but Apple is working to change that.

The first generation was released in 2007 concurrently with the first iPhone. With this launch, Apple thrust itself into a very competitive mobile market, with a product that in many ways was considered inferior to the established players. Apple got one thing very right, though, and that was the user experience. The iPhone was the first popular phone to have a touchscreen you could use with your fingers and not a stylus, and it used pinch-to-zoom and intuitive finger swipes to navigate the screen. It had only a few built-in apps (and no way to develop new ones) such as Google Maps and the Safari web browser, but it played music, videos, and movies, which you could get from the already-established iTunes store.

Apple released newer versions with better features, often synchronized with the release of new hardware. Table 3.4 highlights some of the major enhancements.

TABLE 3.4   iOS versions and features

Version	Year	Features
1.0	2007	First finger-based touchscreen, iTunes connectivity, Safari web browser, onscreen virtual keyboard
2.0	2008	App Store for third-party apps, full email support for Microsoft Exchange
3.0	2009	Voice control; the ability to cut, copy, and paste; Spotlight search; landscape keyboard
3.2	2010	Support for iPad, including iPad resolutions and Bluetooth keyboards
4.0	2010	Multitasking, FaceTime video chat, can create folders on home screen for apps
5.0	2011	Siri, iCloud, iMessage
6.0	2012	Siri enhancements, Passbook, Facebook integration
7.0	2013	New visual interface, Control Center, iTunes Radio, biometric thumbprint scanner
8.0	2014	Widgets (so third-party apps can update you in the Notification Center), several app upgrades, family sharing of photos, calendars, and purchases

With the release of OS X Yosemite, Apple is trying to make the experience between your workstation and your mobile device more seamless. Expect more of those types of efforts as Apple moves forward with new versions of iOS as well.

Android

Along with Apple, Google is the other dominant player in the mobile market with its *Android* OS. If you look at the smartphone market alone, Android has far more users thanks to a bigger presence in Asia than Apple. Many sources claim that there are more Android installations than all other OSs in the world combined, and Google itself in 2014 claimed to have over one billion active monthly users.

 Real World Scenario

Who's Really #1?

There's a lot of debate on the Internet about who is really the top player in the mobile space. Is it Android or iOS? Mark Twain is often quoted as saying, "There are three types of lies. Lies, damned lies, and statistics." In this case, the statistics can tell different stories, depending on how you slice them.

If you look at tablets, then iOS seems to have the edge. If you limit the discussion to phones, then the market leader is clearly Android. In the United States, it's relatively close, but globally, Android-based phones make up between 70 and 80 percent of shipments, depending on your data source.

Both platforms boast over one million apps in their respective application stores (App Store or Google Play). Internet usage (the number of searches, via NetMarketShare) favors iOS, as does business usage. Mobile usage alone (according to StatCounter) clearly favors Android. So it depends on who you ask and how you ask the question. Regardless, both platforms are very successful and likely will be for the next several years.

Android started off as its own company and was purchased by Google in 2005. Like Google's Chrome OS, Android is Linux-based. It's primarily installed on smartphones but also on specialized television, automobile, and wristwatch devices. It supports the use of similar touchscreen technology as Apple's iPhone. Figure 3.17 shows the Android 5.0 welcome screen.

Android was slightly later to the market than iOS, with Android 1.0 launching in 2008. Since its launch, though, it has quickly grown in popularity and is the top smartphone platform, thanks in large part to it being available on devices from several manufacturers such as Samsung, LG, HTC, Sony, and Motorola, along with Google's own hardware. (Apple, much like it does with its OS X platform, restricts iOS to Apple hardware, which limits its potential install base.) Highlights of Android versions and features are shown in Table 3.5.

FIGURE 3.17   Android 5.0 welcome screen

TABLE 3.5   Selected versions of Android OS

Version	Year	Name	Features
1.0	2008	(none)	Web browser, many Google apps, media player, Wi-Fi and Bluetooth support
1.5	2009	Cupcake	Widgets (mini apps that can be embedded in other apps and provide notifications), auto-rotation of screen

TABLE 3.5   Selected versions of Android OS *(continued)*

Version	Year	Name	Features
2.0	2009	Eclair	Microsoft Exchange email support, camera and keyboard improvements
2.2	2010	Froyo	Wi-Fi hotspot functionality, speed and memory optimizations
2.3	2010–11	Gingerbread	Support for multiple cameras, better power management, voice or video chat using Google Talk
3.0	2011	Honeycomb	First tablet-only version of Android
4.0	2011	Ice Cream Sandwich	Major improvements to "Holo" interface and system functionality
4.1	2012	Jelly Bean	Google Now personal assistant, swipe directly to camera, better clock, Bluetooth improvements
4.4	2013	KitKat	Wireless printing
5.0	2014	Lollipop	64-bit support, refreshed design

Moving forward, Android appears to be positioned to maintain its significant market presence due to the multi-vendor support it receives. The biggest question might be the futures of Chrome OS and Android as separate operating systems. Many experts believe that they compete with each other, whereas Google says that's not the case. Over the next few years, it's possible we could see a merging of the two into one platform.

Windows Phone

While Microsoft is the dominant player in the workstation PC market, it has a very small presence in the mobile world. The *Windows Phone* OS is manufactured by Microsoft and visually looks a lot like Windows 8, using the same NT kernel and Windows Store app start screen, as shown in Figure 3.18.

Microsoft started in the mobile space with Pocket PC back in 2000, mostly targeting corporate users and their mobile devices. In 2003 they changed the name to Windows Mobile, still targeting the same users. The software line was changed to Windows Phone in 2010, with more of an emphasis on telephones and home users. Table 3.6 gives you a quick tour of Windows Phone versions.

FIGURE 3.18 Windows Phone 8.1 start screen

WINDOWS PHONE START SCREEN SCREENSHOT USED WITH PERMISSION FROM MICROSOFT.

TABLE 3.6 Windows Phone versions and features

Version	Year	Features
Windows Phone 7	2010	Based on Windows CE.
Windows Phone 8	2012	Uses Windows NT kernel; apps can theoretically work on both platforms seamlessly.
Windows Phone 8.1	2014	Interface upgrades, Cortana voice assistant, dropped requirements for physical Start and Search buttons on device.

Windows 10, due out in late 2015, will provide additional support for mobile devices and further link Microsoft's workstation and mobile platforms together.

The biggest problem for Microsoft right now in the mobile space is their small share. They only have about 2 or 3 percent of users in the market. Microsoft is aggressively pursuing licensing options to help drive their share, but they have a long way to go in a very entrenched market.

BlackBerry

In 1999, a Canadian telecommunications company named Research In Motion (RIM) introduced what many consider to be the predecessor to the first modern smartphone. The first BlackBerry was basically a two-way pager with email support, but within a few years it would support mobile calls, email, text messaging, Internet faxing, and web browsing. With the focus on providing mobile email, BlackBerry quickly gained a significant presence in the mobile space.

One of the interesting features of the BlackBerry was that it had a full keyboard. It wasn't full-sized, but each letter had its own key, which made typing significantly easier than the cell phones in use at the time. Over the course of its history, the physical keyboard became both a symbol of BlackBerry as well as part of its downfall. Similarly to Apple, RIM produced both the hardware and the software together. The hardware devices ran the Java-based *BlackBerry OS*. The OS is shown on a BlackBerry 9620 in Figure 3.19.

FIGURE 3.19 BlackBerry OS

As far as the OS goes, it went through several revisions much like its competitors, adding new features. However, RIM was not as able to adapt quickly to changing market conditions as its competitors, and it went from being a strong player to being mostly irrelevant in the mobile space. As of 2009, BlackBerry commanded about a 20 percent share of the global mobile market and a 43 percent share in the United States. In 2011 the global figure had dropped to about 10 percent, and by 2014 it was down below 2 percent. The introduction of the iPhone severely hurt sales, and the Android launch a year later just made things worse. Critics complained that the BlackBerry had a dated look and feel, and it wasn't as good at browsing the Internet. The BlackBerry App World had apps but not enough. Moreover, RIM held a strong belief that consumers would not want to use a virtual keyboard, and it turned out they were wrong. The company did eventually introduce touchscreen smartphones, some with and some without physical keyboards, but by the time they did it, the damage had already been done.

In 2013, RIM changed its name to BlackBerry, released the BlackBerry 10 OS (based on the UNIX-like QNX platform), and announced that BlackBerry would stop producing operating systems. As of January 2015, rumors abound that BlackBerry will be purchased by another company.

Navigating an Operating System

Designers of operating systems go to great lengths to talk about how their OS is different and better than every other one on the market. Sure enough, if you look under the covers of each OS, you will see different methods of accomplishing similar tasks or different apps built in by default. The visual appearance is even more important, as programmers seem to try to out-design each other by creating things like the Aero interface starting with Windows Vista or blurred translucency effects in iOS7 and OS X Yosemite. A trip into the OS interface design world will introduce you to terms such as skeuomorph, dazzle you with color schemes, and amaze you with the moods that default system fonts generate.

As much as they try to differentiate themselves, it seems that most desktop operating systems since the launch of the Mac have looked, well, the same. Sure, there are differences, but the executional elements are all pretty similar. You have a desktop, a place to show you what's running, your system clock, and some sort of variation of a window. You'll run into some technical differences. For example, you can right-click a file to see its properties in Windows and most graphical versions of Linux, whereas to "right-click" with a Mac (which has only one mouse button) you hold down the Control key and click or turn on two-finger tapping in the trackpad preferences to right-click, as you would on a Chromebook with Chrome OS. But overall, using one desktop OS is very often like using any other OS. That's true even for Windows 8, which looks more different than any OS we've seen in some time.

Mobile operating systems have changed the game a bit due to their restricted real estate. But there again, the same concepts on how to open apps or swipe through screens remain relatively constant across systems.

The point is, learn how to use one OS and it will be relatively easy for you to figure out how to use another. In this section, you are going to learn some of the key features of using operating systems. First, I will cover the critical topic of managing file systems. Then, I'll look at additional important features of OSs such as accessibility options, hot keys, and taking screen captures.

Most of the examples I use in the following sections will be from Windows 7, because even though it's not the newest OS, it is still installed on about half of the workstations out there. The second most popular OS is Windows XP, and its functionality is nearly identical to that of Windows 7. Again, if you learn the concepts, you can almost always figure out how to make things happen, even on an unfamiliar operating system.

Managing Folder and File Structures

We all like the fact that computers store our files for us; the hard drive takes care of that. What we like even more is the ability to find our files when we need them; the operating system takes care of that. Stored on the hard drive, the data is nothing but a very long string of 0s and 1s. The operating system makes sense of all this, knowing where one file ends and the next one begins.

Of course, what we see is far less complicated than that mess. We're used to seeing a file with a name we recognize and opening it to get to the information we want. Perhaps that file is located in a folder (also called a directory), which might be in another folder. But how does the computer take that mess of those 0s and 1s and make sense of it?

Let's start from the hard drive and work our way to a more granular level. When a hard drive comes from the factory, there is basically nothing on it. That might not come as a surprise to you. Before anything can be stored on that drive, someone needs to properly prepare it for storage.

The first step is to create what is called a *partition*. A partition is a logical area created on the drive for storage. Every hard drive needs at least one partition, but there can be more than one on a single hard drive if there is enough space. If you think of a partition in a room, it divides the room. A hard drive partition divides the physical disk into logical sections. If you create one partition, it will typically get the drive letter C:. Additional partitions will get subsequent drive letters.

Once the partition is (or multiple partitions are) created, you need to format the partition before it can receive data. Formatting lays down the tracks for data storage, based on the type of *file system* you choose. The partition created the giant space for storage, and the formatting lays down tracks and sectors that are the right size to store data. (The exact size depends on the size of the partition and the file system you use.) Once the file system is in place, you can install files on that drive.

An analogy a lot of people use is that of a house. The partition is the foundation of the house, and the formatting is the framing. The file system is the type of walls you put in. Once the house is framed and the walls are in, then you can store stuff in it.

File systems are responsible for managing the following:

Disk Space and File Access   File systems organize the directories (folders) and files and keep track of their logical structure. When you save a new file to the disk, the file system determines where to physically put it on the disk. When you go to retrieve the data, the file system is responsible for finding it.

File Names and Directories   Some file systems have restrictions on how long a filename can be or what characters can be used; some file systems are case sensitive, whereas others are not.

Directories are treated just like files in many OSs; files that are in the directory will just point to that directory as a parent. Directory systems can be flat, meaning no other directories can be created in the parent directory, or hierarchical, meaning that several levels of directories can be placed inside each other.

File Metadata   Metadata is information such as the file's name, size, last time it was saved, and other attributes, such as read-only, hidden, or that the file has been changed since the last time it was backed up.

Security   Most file systems have built-in security. This allows an administrator or the creator of the file to allow some users to see the file, others to make changes to the file, and yet prohibit others from accessing it altogether.

Dozens of file systems have been created over the history of PCs, but only a handful are commonly used today. Most of the time, file systems are associated with a specific operating system. MS-DOS, for example, used File Allocation Table (FAT) as its default file system. Over the years, FAT was upgraded to FAT16 and FAT32, which provided additional functionality, such as larger maximum partition sizes. Since early versions of Windows sat on top of DOS, FAT also became associated with Windows. Table 3.7 gives you a list of common file systems you'll see.

TABLE 3.7   Common file systems

File System	Usual OS	Max Partition Size	Notes
File Allocation Table (FAT)	Windows	16 TB	Obsolete, no security
New Technology File System (NTFS)	Windows	256 TB	Default for Windows

TABLE 3.7   Common file systems *(continued)*

File System	Usual OS	Max Partition Size	Notes
Hierarchical File System (HFS)	Mac OS X	8 EB	Also used on read-only media such as CD-ROMs
third extended file system (ext3)	Linux	32 TB	Standard Linux file system; maximum of 32,000 subdirectories in a directory
fourth extended file system (ext4)	Linux	1 EB	Modern Linux file system, supports larger volumes; maximum of 64,000 subdirectories in a directory
Extended File System (XFS)	Linux	8 EB	High-performance file system, supports large partitions

 Chrome OS historically supported ext3 and ext4, but in 2014 Google dropped support for these file systems. Chrome OS now supports FAT and NTFS.

 The theoretical maximum partition size for NTFS is 16 EB, but in the newest versions of Windows OSs, the maximum size allowed is 256 TB.

In Exercise 3.2, you will look at metadata for your hard drive and begin a disk cleanup.

EXERCISE 3.2

Managing Your Storage Space

1. Open the Computer window by clicking the Start button and choosing Computer.

2. Find your C: drive, right-click it, and choose Properties. You will get a window similar to the one in Figure 3.20.

FIGURE 3.20   C: properties

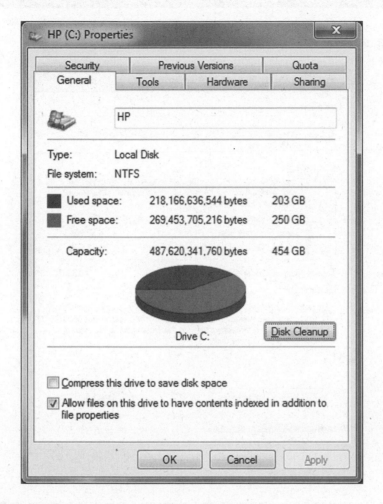

3. Identify the type of file system you have. If you run Windows, it's most likely NTFS.

4. Identify how much free hard disk space you have. Generally, you want to maintain at least 20 percent free space.

5. See how much space you can free up by cleaning up your hard drive; click Disk Cleanup. An example is shown in Figure 3.21.

6. If you want to clean up the files, click OK for it to begin.

FIGURE 3.21   Disk cleanup

Now that you understand how files are stored on the hard drive, let's get into specifics on managing a file structure within an operating system. First, we'll look at how to navigate through a file structure. Then, we will talk about viewing file properties. Finally, we'll examine how to "do something" to a file.

Navigating a File Structure

While trying to think of a good way to define what a file is, I decided to ask Google, because Google knows everything. *File* can be used as a noun—a folder or box for holding loose papers that are typically arranged in a particular order for easy reference. It can also be a verb—to place (a document) in a cabinet, box, or folder. So it seems that a "file" is where you put something, and "to file" is the act of putting that something somewhere. Thanks Google!

Relating this to computers, we typically think of a *file* as a collection of information or data that has a name. Based on this definition, nearly everything stored on a computer is a file. Applications, documents, spreadsheets, pictures, even directories (or folders; I will use the term interchangeably) are files. Folders are just specialized files that organize other files.

Files are stored in directories, which can be in turn stored in other directories. Because of this structure, you will sometimes hear the file system called a directory tree. At the base of this tree is the root, typically designated by your drive letter, such as C:. That drive letter represents the partition on the hard drive itself, but it will be represented on the computer like any other folder. Let's see what this really looks like in Figure 3.22. To get there, click the Start button and then choose Computer, which opens Windows Explorer.

FIGURE 3.22   Computer window

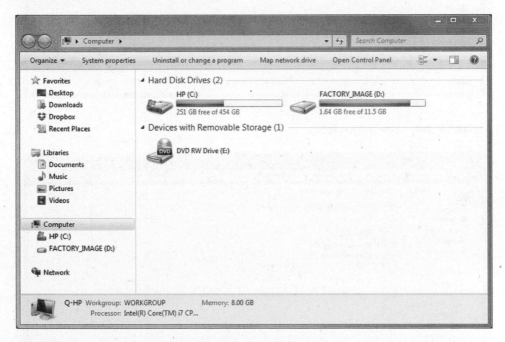

Among other things, you can see that my hard drive has two partitions. The C: drive is for data, and the D: drive is a factory image, which can be used to restore my OS to a factory state if needed. When you double-click the C: drive, you get the first level of directories, as shown in Figure 3.23.

All of the items you see on the left in these figures, such as Desktop, Downloads, Documents, and Pictures, are also folders on the C: drive. If you click Documents and then My Documents, you'll keep digging into further levels of folders. As you can see in Figure 3.24, I have highlighted a folder called IT Fundamentals Ch 3.

FIGURE 3.23   Directories in the C: drive

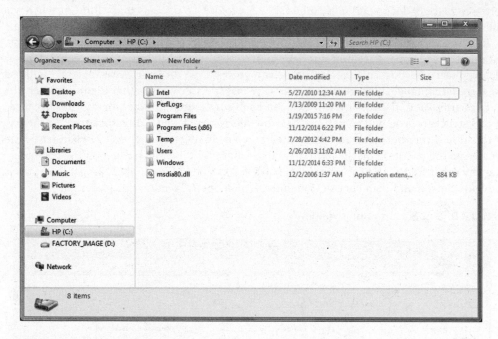

FIGURE 3.24   Several folders

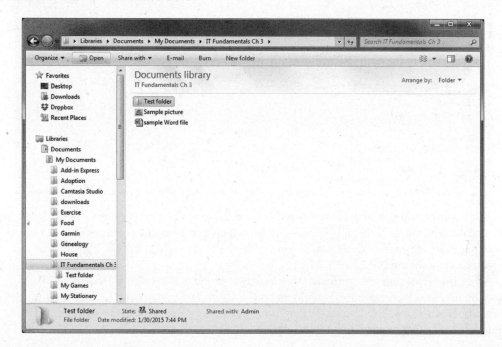

And, if you want to know where you are in the directory tree, all you have to do is click the address bar and it will tell you, as shown in Figure 3.25.

FIGURE 3.25   Address bar showing location

Using Windows Explorer, you can navigate to anywhere you want by double-clicking folders in the left pane. You can also click any of the directory names in the address bar (like the one at the top of Figure 3.24), and it will take you right to that directory. Clicking the little arrow to the right of the folder name in the address bar will let you go directly to any folder inside that folder.

You can also display the files in different ways, such as the filename only or more details. If you look back at Figure 3.24, you will see an icon directly to the right of the words New Folder (and bonus points if you can figure out how to create a new folder now!). Clicking that will let you change the way that files appear in the folder. I did that and chose Details, and I got the view shown in Figure 3.26.

FIGURE 3.26   Details view

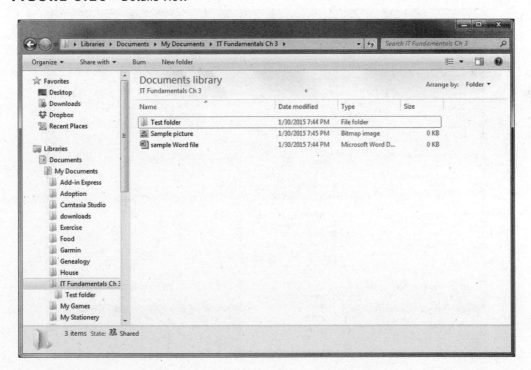

Looking at files this way can be convenient, because now you know when they were modified, the type of file, size, and the like. This view is also handy because you can sort the files how you want. There are two easy ways to do this. The first way is to click any of the information column headers. In Figure 3.26 you can see a small up arrow over the Name column. This shows how the files are sorted, with folders always first. Clicking Name again would sort the files in reverse alphabetical order. The second way is to use the Arrange By filter near the upper-right corner.

Also, you can search for files or text in a file by using the Search box, which is in the upper-right corner of Figure 3.26. Type in the word you want to search for and press Enter or click the magnifying glass icon. It will search that folder, any files in that folder, and any subdirectories and files in that folder. You can configure the search to just look for filenames, or to look in the files themselves, or to look for specific file types, date modified, size, or author. There are lots of choices for you here. The results will pop up in the same window where the files are currently displayed.

Viewing File Metadata

While in Windows Explorer, you can also easily view the metadata for your file. This includes the size, security, and all sorts of other useful information. To get there, right-click the file (or folder), as shown in Figure 3.27, and choose Properties.

FIGURE 3.27   Right-click a file

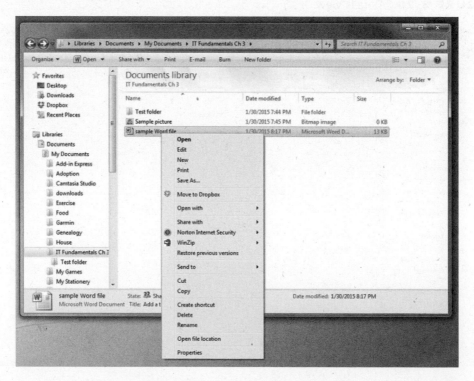

Remember the menu you see in Figure 3.27 because we will come back to it. For now, you should be looking at a window with your file properties, similar to the one shown in Figure 3.28.

FIGURE 3.28   File properties

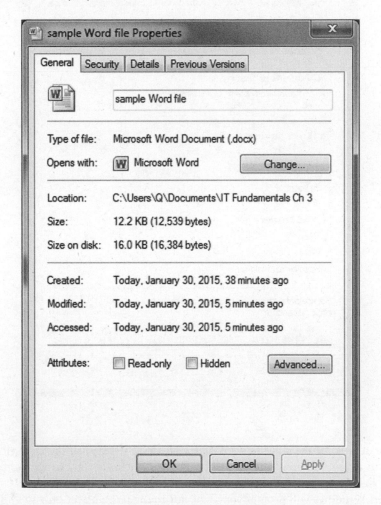

In this window, you can see the name, type of file, location, size, creation and most recent modification dates, and check boxes to make the file read-only or hidden. Those last two should be pretty self-explanatory. Check the Read-only box so no one can make modifications to the file, and check the second box to hide it from view. Click the Security tab to see the security details of the file, like those shown in Figure 3.29.

FIGURE 3.29   File security

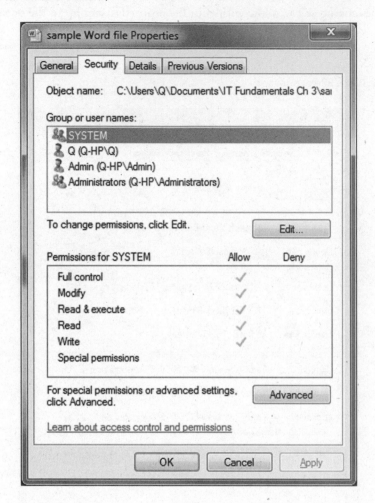

All of the details for the security settings are beyond the scope of the CompTIA IT Fundamentals exam, but now you know where to find them! If you change permissions (read-only), the hidden attribute, or security on a file, it affects only that file. If you change it on a folder, Windows will prompt you. You can change it to affect only the folder and its contents or all subdirectories and their files as well.

Manipulating Files and Executing Programs

When I discussed file metadata, I right-clicked the file to get the menu as shown in Figure 3.27. You probably noticed that there were quite a few different options on the menu. Your computer might have more or less than mine, depending on the software you have installed. For example, since I have Dropbox, Norton Internet Security, and WinZip, I have options to use those programs on my context menu. The rest of what you see on that menu is pretty standard for Windows. The CompTIA IT Fundamentals exam wants you to know about these nine options for manipulating files:

Open   Opens the file in the default program for that file. Sometimes you will also have the option Open With, which allows you to specify the program you want to open the file. You can also open a file by double-clicking it.

Edit   Opens the file in the default editor for that program. If it's a Word document, it will open Word just like the Open command will. For pictures, though, oftentimes you will have a different program to display the images versus edit the images.

Save   Saves the file with its current name and location. You might also have Save As, which will ask you where you want to save the file, and you can also choose to rename it.

Move   Takes the file from one folder and moves it to another. The original file content does not change, but the location in the directory tree does. On the hard drive, the file does not actually move. The metadata just gets modified, associating it with the folder where you moved the file to.

Copy   Copies the file to the clipboard (a temporary storage space in Windows). If you want to place the file somewhere else, you need to paste it there. The original file is not changed in any way. If you paste the file somewhere else, the OS will create a new version of the file, with the same name, in the new location. It also creates an additional version of it on the hard drive. You can also copy a file (or multiple files) by highlighting it and then pressing Ctrl+C (holding down the Ctrl key and then pressing C once) on your keyboard.

Cut   This is a lot like Copy, in the sense that it copies the file to the clipboard. Functionally it's more like Move, except that in order to complete the transaction you need to paste the file somewhere. You can also cut a file (or multiple files) by highlighting it and then pressing Ctrl+X on your keyboard.

Paste   If you have something on your clipboard, it will paste the contents into wherever you executed the Paste command. If you cut and paste a file, the file does not physically move on the hard drive. It gets executed like a Move command. The keyboard shortcut for Paste is Ctrl+V.

Delete   Removes the file from the directory it's in and moves it to the Recycle Bin (Windows) or Trash (Mac). It doesn't actually erase the file from the hard drive; it just changes the metadata to say it now belongs to the Recycle Bin or Trash directory. Emptying the Trash will erase it from the hard drive and free up disk space. You can also delete files by highlighting them and pressing the Del key on your keyboard.

Rename   Changes the metadata for the file, giving it a new name. Functionally it's very similar to Save As. You can't have more than one file with the same name in any directory.

In FAT or NTFS, you can't change file metadata, such as renaming or moving, when the file is open. Other file systems such as ext3 and ext4 do not have this restriction.

Exercise 3.3 has you manipulate files on your computer. Well, folders, really, but remember that folders are files too!

EXERCISE 3.3

Manipulating Files in Windows 7

1. Open the Documents folder by clicking Start ➢ Documents.

2. Create a new folder by clicking the New Folder menu option near the top or by right-clicking in the right pane and choosing New ➢ Folder.

3. Give the new folder a name, such as Ch3.

4. In your Documents folder, create another new folder named Happy.

5. Right-click Happy, and choose Cut. Notice how the folder icon now looks more transparent.

6. Right-click Ch3, and choose Paste. (You could also open up Ch3 first, and then right-click the right side and choose Paste, or just open Ch3 and press Ctrl+V.)

7. Double-click Ch3. The Happy folder should now be in there.

8. Right-click Happy, and choose Copy.

9. Navigate back to your Documents folder, and paste Happy there. Now, you should have a Happy folder in two locations.

10. Delete the folders Happy and Ch3 by highlighting both (click one and then Ctrl+click the other), right-clicking, and choosing Delete.

We already talked about two ways to open a file, which are to right-click it and choose Open or simply to double-click it. If what you are double-clicking is an application, it will execute that program. Additionally, you can open a file or execute a program using the Start menu. Click Start, find the file or program in the list, and click it. Or click Start, and in the Search Programs And Files box, type in the name of the program and hit Enter.

There's one last way, and that's to open a shortcut to the file or program. A *shortcut* is a file that points to the real file's location. Sometimes you will hear it referred to as a pointer file. Normally you will create these on your desktop to make it easier to access files or programs you run a lot. The shortcut itself doesn't contain the data, so you can delete a shortcut but not lose any data. You can identify a shortcut because it has a small arrow as part of the icon. Exercise 3.4 walks you through creating a shortcut.

EXERCISE 3.4

Creating a Shortcut for My Documents in Windows 7

1. Right-click an open area of your desktop and choose New ≻ Shortcut.

2. Click Browse, and a window will appear similar to the one in Figure 3.30.

FIGURE 3.30 Browse window

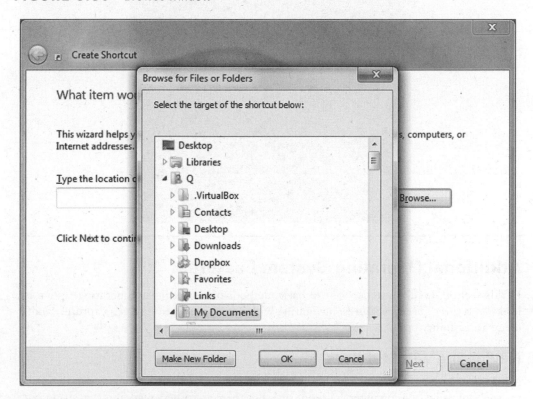

3. Find the My Documents folder in your directory tree, and click it.

4. Click OK and then Next.

5. Type in a name for your shortcut (if you want), and click Finish.

6. A new shortcut will appear on your desktop, like the one shown in Figure 3.31. Notice that it has a small arrow in the lower-left corner, signifying that it's a shortcut.

7. Double-click the shortcut, and notice that it opens your Documents folder.

8. (Optional) Delete the shortcut if you want. Remember that deleting the shortcut will not delete the files in the My Documents folder!

EXERCISE 3.4 *(continued)*

FIGURE 3.31   New shortcut

Additional Operating System Features

In this section, I will finish our tour of basic methods of navigating an operating system by looking at three specific features: navigating with hot keys, creating screen captures, and using accessibility options.

Navigating with Hot Keys

Many of us love to use our mouse. Some of us are even more than a little nervous at the prospect of using our computers without one. But there are others who find that using *hot keys* on their keyboard actually speeds them up when performing tasks.

The hot keys that you can use will depend somewhat on your keyboard. For example, the keyboard shown in Figure 3.32 has a lot of extra buttons at the top that can be used as hot keys, as well as more standard ones.

This particular keyboard has buttons for going to your Internet home page, search, and email, along with five customizable buttons, audio controls, and even a button to open the calculator all along the top. These can be pretty handy! You can also see a Start button between the left Ctrl and Alt keys and a right-click button between the right Ctrl and Alt keys. These two are a little more standard. Pressing the Start button will open your Start menu, and pressing the right-click button is just like right-clicking with your mouse. In addition, your F1 key is a hot key that opens up the Help file in Windows and many Windows-based programs. Table 3.8 lists some common Windows hot key combinations that you might find useful.

FIGURE 3.32   Keyboard with several hot keys at the top

TABLE 3.8   Windows hot key combinations

Combination	Function
Alt+F4	Closes the window or application you have open.
Alt+Tab	Switches between open applications.
Ctrl+F4	Closes the file you have open within a Microsoft Office application but leaves the program running.
Ctrl+Esc	Opens the Start menu.
Ctrl+S	Saves the file if you are in a program such as Word or Excel.
Ctrl+A	In Windows Explorer, selects all files and folders in your current location.
Ctrl+F	In Windows Explorer, opens the Search pane. Think of it as Ctrl+Find.
Ctrl+X	Cuts a highlighted file or highlighted text or information in a Microsoft Office application.
Ctrl+C	Copies a highlighted file or highlighted text or information a Microsoft Office application.
Ctrl+V	Pastes the cut or copied file or text.
Ctrl+Alt+Del	Lets you lock your computer or switch users (if your system is set up for multiple users) or open Task Manager. On older Windows and MS-DOS machines, it reboots the system. If you press Ctrl+Alt+Del twice in a row on a modern Windows system, it will reboot it as well.

For a list of useful Chrome OS hot keys, visit www.omgchrome.com/10-shortcuts-every-chromebook-owner-should-know. Mac OS X hot keys can be found at http://support.apple.com/en-us/HT201236.

For experience, you should go back through Exercise 3.3 and perform all of the tasks using hot keys instead of your mouse. The trickiest step might be to create the new folder. Here's a hint. When you open your Documents folder (step 2), hold down your Alt key for a second and then let go. Another menu will appear right under the address bar, like the one in Figure 3.33. Notice how the words have a letter underlined? You can now press that letter (such as F for File) and that menu will appear. Or, you can use your arrow keys to navigate. In the File menu, you have an option for New ➤ Folder.

FIGURE 3.33   Windows Alt key menu

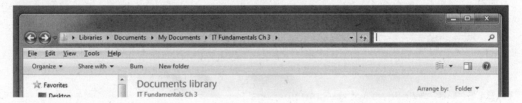

Other applications have their own hot keys, but there are too many to mention here. Suffice it to say, you can get around Windows just fine without a mouse if you put your mind to it.

Creating Screen Captures

I have to be honest here. I am not entirely sure why creating *screen captures* is part of the objectives for navigating an operating system. I'm not saying it's not important; it is. For example, I created most of the figures you see in this chapter using screen captures. And, if you are working with tech support (or you are tech support) on an issue, being able to capture the screen and error message exactly is incredibly useful.

There are third-party applications you can buy that perform screen captures for you, such as SnagIt (www.techsmith.com/snagit.html), TinyTake (www.tinytake.com), and many others. Most OSs also have built-in tools for screen captures, although without as many features as the purchased programs. Table 3.9 shows you some of the methods to take screen captures in various OSs.

TABLE 3.9   How to take screen captures

Operating System	Method	Captures
Windows Vista	Snipping Tool (In Start ➤ All Programs ➤ Accessories)	Full screen, windows, rectangles, or free-form
Windows	Shift+PrtScn	Entire screen

Operating System	Method	Captures
Mac OS X	Grab (In Utilities folder under Applications, or in Finder in Services and then Grab)	Entire screen, window, or selected area
Mac OS X	Command+Shift+3	Entire screen
Mac OS X	Command+Shift+4, then select an area or window	That area or window
Chrome OS	Press Ctrl and the Window Switcher key (the F5 key shown in Figure 3.34)	Full screen
Chrome OS	Ctrl+Shift+Window Switcher key	Selected area of the screen
Linux	PrtScn key	Entire screen
Linux	Kgrab or Ksnapshot	Entire screen or selected area
iOS	Press the power button and Home button at the same time	Entire screen
Android	Press the power button and the volume down button and hold for 1–2 seconds	Entire screen

FIGURE 3.34   Chrome Window Switcher (F5) key

If you use the Shift+PrtScn method in Windows, it will copy the screen capture to the clipboard. You will need to paste that image (Ctrl+V) into another application to use it. The PrtScn key in Linux will save the capture in your home folder.

Mac OS X screenshots are saved as files to the desktop. If you want to copy them to the clipboard, also hold down the Control key while you perform the other key sequence. Then you will need to paste the screen capture into the application you want it in.

Using Accessibility Options

Accessibility options are features built into most operating systems to make them easier to use for those who have physical disabilities that would otherwise make using a computer difficult. For example, some options will set the screen at very high contrast so it's easier for people who are visually impaired to see. Other options make it easier to use the keyboard or mouse, read text on the screen for those who are blind, or replace audio alerts with visual ones for those who have difficulty hearing. In Windows, accessibility options are located in Control Panel in the Ease of Access Center, as shown in Figure 3.35.

FIGURE 3.35   Windows Ease of Access Center

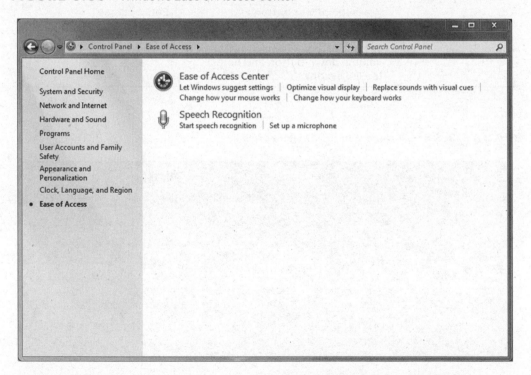

The accessibility options for Mac OS X are similar, with a screen reader called VoiceOver, available cursor and screen magnification, display inversion, dictation, and ways to configure the keyboard and mouse to be easier to use, such as sticky keys, slow keys, and mouse keys. To open the Accessibility Options window, press

Command+Option+F5 from an external keyboard or Function+Command+Option+F5 from a built-in laptop keyboard.

Chrome OS also has similar features. To configure them, click the status area where your account picture appears, choose Settings ➢ Show Advanced Settings (at the bottom), and scroll to the Accessibility section, as shown in Figure 3.36.

FIGURE 3.36   Chrome OS Accessibility settings

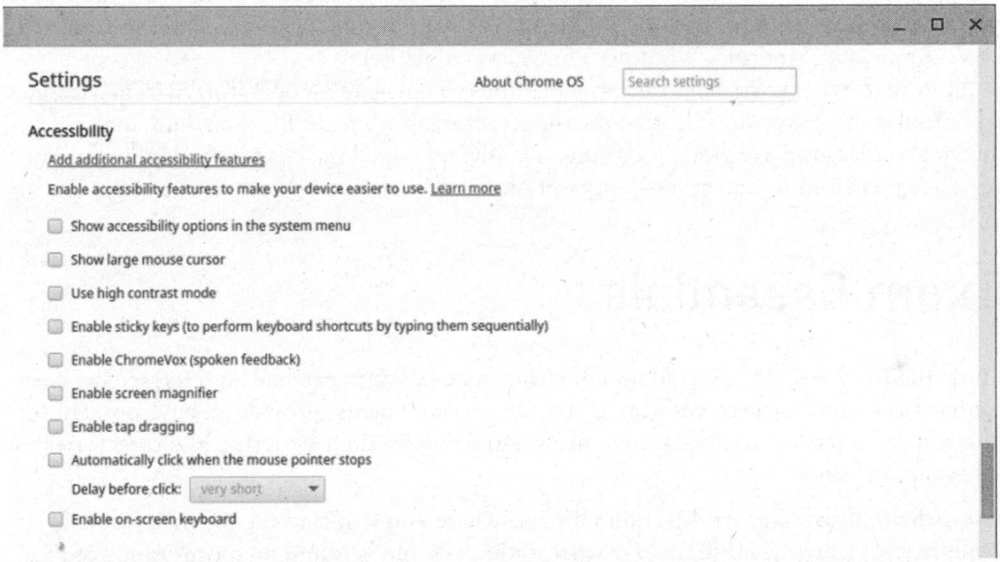

Exercise 3.5 shows you how to configure accessibility options within Windows 7.

EXERCISE 3.5

Configuring Accessibility Options in Windows 7

1. Click Start ➢ Control Panel ➢ Ease Of Access to open the Ease of Access Center, as shown previously in Figure 3.35.

2. Click Optimize Visual Display.

3. Check the box for Turn On Magnifier. This will help those who have poor vision see the screen better.

4. Click OK.

5. You should notice an immediate difference. Using the Magnifier settings, you can configure the zoom feature to be at the right level for the user.

6. Explore other options within the accessibility options. Close when finished.

Summary

In this chapter, we covered a wide variety of information about operating systems. First, I took you through a high-level history of operating systems, so you would have a better understanding of why they work the way they do. After that, we looked specifically at the basic functions that an OS performs.

Next, we moved into the types of operating systems. Specifically, we talked about four workstation OSs—Linux, Windows, Mac OS X, and Chrome OS—as well as four mobile OSs—Apple iOS, Android, Windows Phone, and BlackBerry.

After that, we talked about the basic methods to navigate an operating system. Among other topics, we covered navigating the file structure, looking at file metadata, making changes to files, and executing programs. Finally, we ended the chapter by looking at hot keys, screen captures, and accessibility options.

Exam Essentials

Know the five basic functions of an operating system.   OSs provide an interface between the hardware and the user, coordinate hardware components, provide an environment for software to function, monitor system health, and display data structure and directories for data management.

Know the four primary workstation OSs and where you will find them.   Microsoft Windows is by far the most popular workstation OS and is found on most brands of PCs. Mac OS X is a distant second in popularity and is found on Mac desktops and laptops. Linux is the only open-source OS on our list. (And it's not really an OS; it's just the kernel.) It can be installed on almost any PC. Chrome OS is made by Google and found on Chromebooks and Chromeboxes.

Know four mobile operating systems and where you will find them.   Apple's iOS is popular and found on iPhones and iPads. Android has the market leadership in cellphones and is found on devices made by several manufacturers. Windows Phone is not popular at all but will run on several devices as well. BlackBerry OS is found only on BlackBerry devices, which used to be fairly popular but have faded.

Understand how files are stored on computers.   Files are any items that have a filename. Files are stored in folders (or directories), which can in turn be stored in other folders on the hard drive.

Know how to view file properties.   Metadata is part of a file's properties. In Windows, you can right-click the file and select Properties to view the metadata.

Understand the difference between moving and copying files.   Moving a file within a file system removes it from the first folder and places it in another one. It does not physically move the file on the hard drive. Copying the file creates a replica in the new location and a new version on the hard drive.

Know how to use various hot keys and take screen captures.   Hot keys can enable you to navigate the computer and perform tasks more quickly than by using a mouse. There are several handy ones to remember, and they usually involve using the Ctrl or Alt key. Screen captures are images of what's on the screen, which can be useful for writing books or troubleshooting problems.

Understand how accessibility options can help users.   Accessibility options can help users with physical disabilities. For example, the screen can be magnified or read to visually impaired users, audio cues can be converted to visual cues for hearing-impaired users, and the keyboard and mouse can be made easier to use for those who have motor skills or coordination issues.

Chapter 3 Lab

Most people are familiar with Microsoft Windows, because it's so popular. Not everyone is as familiar with Linux, though. In this lab, you are going to install Lubuntu on your machine. The goal is to familiarize yourself with another OS and to understand that other operating systems aren't scary or mysterious. They all do similar things; it's just a matter of figuring out how.

Normally, installing a second OS involves a relatively complicated process where you need to dual-boot your computer. We're not going to do that here. You will use a technology called VirtualBox that allows you to create a new virtual system on your hard drive and not affect your existing Windows installation. I promise you that this lab will not mess up Windows on your computer! And when you're finished, you can just uninstall VirtualBox, if you want, and nothing will have changed on your system.

The first two steps are for preparation. You need to download the Oracle VirtualBox and a version of Lubuntu. Really, any version of Linux is fine, but I'll point you to a 32-bit version of Lubuntu, which should minimize any compatibility issues. Depending on your network speed, the download could take an hour or more.

1. Download Oracle VirtualBox from `https://www.virtualbox.org/wiki/Downloads`. Select VirtualBox For Windows Hosts, unless, of course, you have a Mac and then you need the one for OS X hosts. Save it to your desktop for ease of access.

2. Download Lubuntu from `http://lubuntu.net/tags/download`. There is a link on the left side for Lubuntu x86 CD. Choose that one. It will download a zipped file with an `.iso` extension. You will need that `.iso` file later; it will essentially act as a bootable CD for your OS installation.

    Now you begin the installation of VirtualBox.

3. Double-click the VirtualBox icon. If you get a security warning, click the Run button. Then click Next on the Setup Wizard screen.

4. On the Custom Setup screen, click Next and then Next again. It will give you a warning about your network interfaces. Click Yes. (Your network connections will come back automatically.)

5. Click Install. This may take several minutes. (You might also need to clear another security warning box.)

6. Once the install is complete, click Finish.

It's time to configure VirtualBox.

7. You might get a VirtualBox warning telling you that an image file is not currently accessible. That's fine. Click Ignore. You should see a screen similar to the one in Figure 3.37.

FIGURE 3.37   VirtualBox preconfiguration

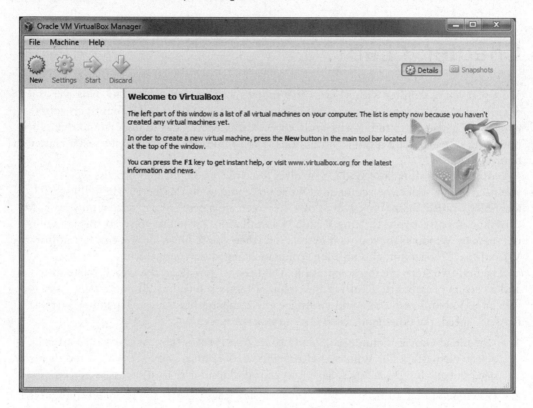

8. Click the blue New icon to create a new virtual machine. Give it a name. The Type and Version boxes aren't critical; they don't affect anything. If you type in Lubuntu for a name, it will automatically set the Type to Linux and the Version to Ubuntu. Click Next.

9. In the Memory Size window, click Next.

10. In the Hard Drive window, the default option is Create A Virtual Hard Drive. Leave that option selected and click Create.

11. It will ask you what hard drive file type you want to create. Leave it on VDI and click Next.

12. On the next screen, either Dynamically Allocated or Fixed Size is fine. If you are low on disk space, go with Fixed Size. Click Next.

13. In the File Location And Size window, it's probably best to leave it at the default size of 8 GB. Definitely don't make it smaller. Click Create. Now you will see a screen like the one shown in Figure 3.38.

    Great! You now have a virtual machine on your hard drive. Now you just need to put something, more specifically an OS, on it.

FIGURE 3.38   VirtualBox with a virtual drive

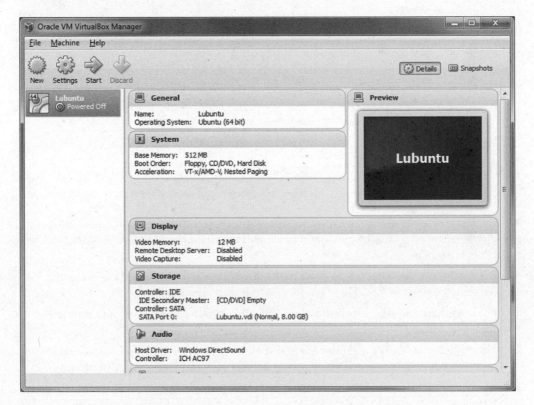

14. Click the Settings button.

15. In the Lubuntu - Settings window, click the Storage icon on the left.

16. Under one of your controllers, you should see something that looks like a disc icon that says Empty. It should look like Figure 3.39.

FIGURE 3.39   Lubuntu - Settings dialog

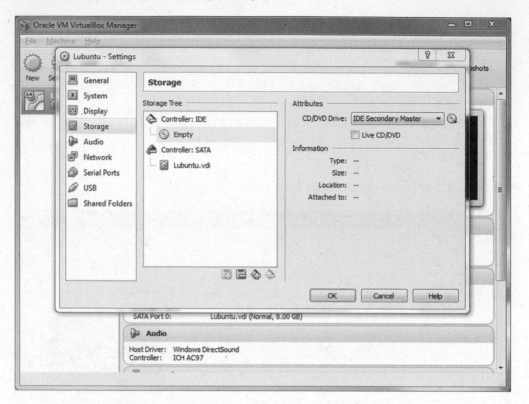

17. On the very right side of the window, you will have another disc icon with a little down arrow on it. Click that, and a menu will pop up. Select Choose A Virtual CD/DVD Disk File.

18. In the window that pops up, navigate to the directory where you stored the Lubuntu .iso file that you downloaded. Highlight the file, and then click Open.

19. Back on the Lubuntu - Settings dialog, your drive that was empty should now say Lubuntu. Click OK.

20. Now you are back to the Oracle VirtualBox Manager screen. With Lubuntu on the left highlighted, press the green Start arrow. This will begin installation of Lubuntu.

21. Choose a language, and then on the next screen choose Install Lubuntu and press Enter.

22. Follow the Lubuntu installation process.

23. You will get to a screen similar to the one in Figure 3.40, which asks you for an installation type. It looks scary, but choose the Erase Disk And Install Lubuntu option. This will install it on the virtual disk that you created earlier with VirtualBox, and it will *not* wipe out your entire hard drive.

FIGURE 3.40   Installing Lubuntu

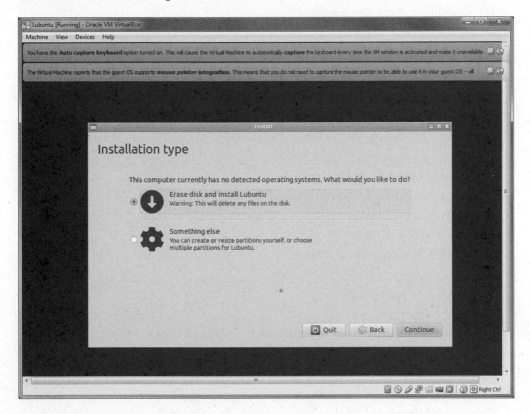

24. Continue with the installation process. When in doubt, choose the default and move to the next step.

25. When the installation is complete, click the Restart Now button.

Now that the installation is complete, play around in your new operating system! I strongly encourage you to go back through this chapter and do exercises 3.1–3.4 but this time in Lubuntu. The answers are provided in Appendix B, "Answers to Review Questions."

Review Questions

1. Which of the following is not a function of an operating system?

   A. Interface between the user and the machine

   B. Coordinate software applications

   C. Coordinate hardware components

   D. Monitor system health

2. Which of the following operating systems can you freely modify if you choose?

   A. OS X

   B. iOS

   C. BlackBerry

   D. Linux

3. Peter, a friend of yours, has a piece of software that was written for Mac OS X. Which of the following OSs will that software run on?

   A. Mac OS X only

   B. Mac OS X and Linux

   C. Mac OS X and Chrome OS

   D. Mac OS X, Linux, and Chrome OS

4. Your friend Michel just purchased a Chromebook and wants to know where his files are stored. What do you tell him?

   A. On the hard drive.

   B. In the system RAM.

   C. In the cloud.

   D. Chromebooks do not store files.

5. You just deleted a shortcut to an important work presentation. What happened to the data in the presentation?

   A. Nothing.

   B. It's in the Recycle Bin/Trash.

   C. It's deleted.

   D. It's in the recovery partition.

6. With which of the following file systems can you not rename a file when it's open?

   A. ext3

   B. ext4

   C. XFS

   D. NTFS

7. You are going to purchase a new iPhone. Which operating system will be installed on it?

A. iOS

B. OS X

C. iPhone OS

D. Android

E. iDontKnow

8. From the hard drive's perspective, moving a file is analogous to which of the following actions?

A. Copy and paste

B. Cut and paste

C. Delete and paste

D. Renaming

9. Fred, a co-worker, heard about new software called Lollipop. Which operating system is he referring to?

A. iOS

B. OS X

C. Android

D. Chrome OS

10. On which OS would you use the Ctrl+Window Switcher key to create a screen capture?

A. Windows

B. Linux

C. Mac OS X

D. Chrome OS

11. Linux is defined as a _____, which is also the core of an operating system.

A. Distribution

B. Version

C. Kernel

D. Shell

12. What are the utilities in an OS called that enable programs such as a screen reader?

A. Accessibility options

B. Reading options

C. User options

D. User account settings

13. You just copied a file from the Work directory to the Projects directory on your Windows PC. What happened to the file on the hard drive?

    A. Nothing.

    B. The file was removed from the Work directory and placed in the Projects directory.

    C. The file was not moved, but a new pointer record was created associating the file with the Projects directory.

    D. The file was copied to a new location on the hard drive and was associated with the Projects directory.

14. How many subdirectories are you allowed to create within a single directory in an OS?

    A. It depends on the OS

    B. 32,000

    C. 64,000

    D. Unlimited

15. The combination of Linux-based files that gets released as a product is called what?

    A. Distribution

    B. Version

    C. Kernel

    D. Source

16. Which of the following file systems does not have built-in security?

    A. ext3

    B. ext4

    C. FAT

    D. HFS

17. You need to prepare a brand-new replacement hard drive for storage. What is the first step needed to get it ready?

    A. Format the drive

    B. Install an OS

    C. Install a file system

    D. Create a partition

18. Which of the following is not a way to open the Start menu on a Windows-based computer?

    A. Ctrl+S

    B. Ctrl+Esc

    C. Click the Start button

    D. Press the Start key on the keyboard

19. Which of the following would not be considered metadata for a spreadsheet file?

    A. Read-only attribute

    B. Calculations inside the file

    C. Name of the file

    D. File size

20. Which of the following OSs uses the NT kernel?

    A. Windows 7

    B. Windows 3.11

    C. Mac OS X

    D. Chrome OS

Chapter 4

Software Applications

THE FOLLOWING COMPTIA IT FUNDAMENTALS EXAM OBJECTIVES ARE COVERED IN THIS CHAPTER:

✓ **1.2 Identify common programs, applications and their purpose**

- Types
  - Productivity Software
    - Word processing
    - Spreadsheet software
    - Email software
    - Basic database software
    - PDF viewers/creators
    - Presentation software
    - Desktop publishing software
    - Personal Information Manager
    - Remote desktop software
  - Collaboration Software
    - Online workspace
    - Document storage/sharing
    - Screen sharing software
    - Video conferencing software
    - Instant messaging software
    - Email software
  - Utility Software
    - Anti-malware

- Software firewalls
- Diagnostic/maintenance software
- Compression software
- Specialized Software
  - CAD
  - Graphic design
  - Medical
  - Scientific
  - Financial
  - Gaming
  - Entertainment
- Open source vs. commercial
- Platforms
  - Mobile
  - Desktop
  - Web-based
- Common file types
  - Documents
    - txt
    - rtf
    - doc/docx
    - xls/xlsx
    - ppt/pptx
    - pdf
  - Audio
    - mp3
    - wav
    - flac
    - aac
    - m4a

- Images
  - jpg
  - gif
  - tiff
  - png
  - bmp
- Video
  - mpg
  - mp4
  - flv
  - wmv
  - avi
- Executables
  - exe
  - msi
  - app
  - bat
  - scexe
- Compression formats
  - rar
  - tar
  - zip
  - dmg
  - iso
  - 7zip / 7z
  - gzip / gz
  - jar

✓ **1.3 Given a scenario, use software management best practices**

- Install / uninstall
- OS features

- Applications
- Drivers
- Patching / updates for OS, drivers, applications and security software
  - Scheduling
  - Frequency
  - Automatic updates
- Software version identification and compatibility
- Licensing
  - Product keys
  - Single / multi-license

✓ 1.4 Identify the following alternative technologies and their purpose

- VoIP
- Telepresence

All of the hardware and the operating system in computers just provide a base for what you really want to use computers for, and that's to run software applications. You want your computer to help you do something—often a lot of somethings—such as writing a letter, creating a presentation, managing your taxes, or playing a game. Thanks to the myriad of software titles out there, you can do all of these things and even more, quite often doing more than one of them at one time.

Applications are the second major classification of software (after operating systems), and that is the focus of this chapter. Topics will range from the types of applications you use to common file types to properly installing, uninstalling, and updating your programs. As part of this chapter, I will also group in the third classification of software, which is drivers. As you will learn later in this chapter, drivers are specialized software applications that let your operating system talk to your hardware.

By the end of this chapter, you will be familiar with several types of software available for use. You will also be able to recognize a large number of common file types and install, update, and uninstall applications, drivers, and your operating system. Software truly makes that box of parts sitting in front of you useful, so let's begin!

Common Software Applications and File Types

There are a lot of different software applications in the world—a lot. I wouldn't even know where to begin if asked to count them. The good news is if you want a piece of software that helps you accomplish a specific task, whether that task be productive or entertaining, you can probably find it. To make understanding software easier, in this section I'll lump applications into four different categories: productivity, collaboration, utility, and specialized.

Before getting into the types of applications and common file types, though, let's spend a little time talking about some key concepts related to how software works on computers.

Key Software Concepts

I'm going to go out on a not-so-shaky limb here and guess that you have used software before. If you have even touched a computer or a smartphone, you have. And the fact that you are reading this book means you're interested in computers, so it's an easy guess to get right. What you might not have done, though, is to take a step back and think about all of the things that need to happen for that application to run properly.

 Throughout this chapter, I will use the terms *software*, *application*, and *program* interchangeably.

You're probably used to double-clicking or tapping an icon and having that program open or the file opening in the right program. How does that happen? First, ask yourself the question, what does the application talk to? It talks to the operating system, which talks to the hardware. If you need to save a file, the application tells the OS that you need to save the file, and the OS talks to the hard drive to make it happen. Because of this process, the most critical thing for an app to run right is for it to be able to talk to the OS. This is why you will see software made for Windows, or for Mac OS X, or for another operating system. Software vendors might have different versions for different OSs, but software written for Windows will not work on a Mac, and vice versa.

Software Platforms

Let's broaden the Mac OS X versus Windows example a bit. We can say that Mac OS X and Windows are two different *software platforms*, because they require applications to be programmed differently. Taking that idea to the next level, there are generally three types of platforms that an application can belong to: desktop, mobile, and web-based. Applications written for the desktop and mobile platforms reside on that local computer's hard drive and are executed locally.

 For purposes of software platforms, the desktop group also includes laptops.

Web-based applications run on a server somewhere else, and your computer will connect to it and run it just like it's local. A great example of this is Google Docs, which comes with Chromebooks. The app itself is based on Google's cloud, and your Chromebook needs an Internet connection to be able to run the app. The good news is you don't need to worry about installing or updating the application, because Google does that for you. The bad news is you need to always have an Internet connection to use those apps or save files. In today's world this isn't usually a show-stopper, but there are places and times where you will be without the life-giving powers of the Internet.

Another difference between platforms is where you can find or buy new applications. For the desktop platforms, you can buy software at a brick-and-mortar store or download it from the Internet. Mobile devices have their own application store. For example, you can go to the App Store for iOS, Google Play for Android, or BlackBerry World for BlackBerry OS. Figure 4.1 shows an image of Apple's App Store.

FIGURE 4.1   App Store

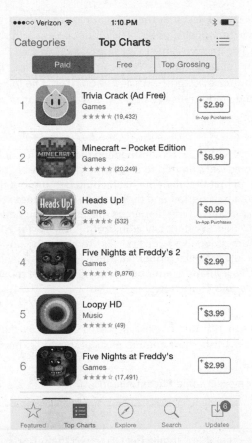

You can see in Figure 4.1 that there are apps you can purchase, as well as a category for free apps, the ability to search for apps, and an area to update the apps currently on your device. My phone has six apps with available updates that I should probably install. Buying an app from one of these stores will download that software to your device.

Chromebooks also allow you to add apps via the Chrome Web Store. Keep in mind, though, that these apps, just like other Chromebook apps, are run from the cloud and not your local computer.

In Figure 4.1 you might have noticed that there are categories for free apps as well as ones you pay for. The free ones are called *freeware*, whereas the ones you purchase are considered commercial. And just like OSs, you will run into some apps that are open source. Open source apps are generally distributed as freeware, but free apps might not necessarily be open source. Commercial apps are generally neither free nor open source.

File Extensions

Let's paraphrase the question I asked in the "Key Software Concepts" section: You double-click an icon and the program opens, or you click a document and the right app opens—how does this happen? The answer is file extensions.

All files on a computer have filenames. You've seen them before, items like `AcroRD32.exe`, `resume.doc`, `finances.xls`, or `summervaca.jpg`. The *file extension* is the "dot whatever" part at the end, and it tells the operating system what to do with the file.

The old FAT file system influenced filenames for quite some time. In FAT, filenames were limited to an 8.3 ("eight dot three") file-naming standard, meaning that the filename itself could be no more than eight characters followed by a period and then a three-character extension. It forced you to be very creative with filenames, because if you had something you wanted to call "Toys Western Division Profit Forecast for 2015" you might end up with something like `twdpf15.xls`. To someone not familiar with your work, that would look like gibberish. Today's predominant file systems do not have this limitation, although you will find that most file extensions are still three or four characters.

The file system knows that certain extensions are to directly execute a program—these are called *executables*. Table 4.1 lists some common executable file extensions you should know.

TABLE 4.1   Common executable file extensions

Extension	Use
.exe	Short for "executable," it tells the OS to run the program. Most Windows desktop programs use this extension.
.msi	For installation and removal of software within Windows. Opening an .msi file actually launches msiexec.exe, which reads the .msi file and does what it says. .msi files use Windows Installer, so think of it as standing for "Microsoft Installation."
.app	Executes a program within OS X (as .exe does in Windows).
.bat	Batch file. Used to execute multiple commands from the Windows command prompt (cmd.exe) within one file.
.scexe	Self-extracting firmware updates that Hewlett-Packard (HP) produces, commonly associated with Linux machines.

Never open an executable file you are sent via email or are otherwise unfamiliar with. Doing so is a good way to spread viruses.

Based on Table 4.1, you can see that if you're in Windows and you double-click an icon named `excel.exe`, it will open up Microsoft Excel, or `winword.exe` will open up Microsoft Word. What about files with different extensions? Why is it that if I double-click my `resume.doc` file, Word opens? (Not that we're complaining here, but how does the OS know to do that?) The OS keeps a list of known file extensions and associates them with specific applications. For example, if you open anything with a `.doc` extension, the OS knows that it needs to open Microsoft Word to read that file.

In Windows, you can go to Control Panel ≻ Programs to see and configure associations. Once in Programs, look for Default Programs and then a setting called "Make a file type always open in a specific program." That will open the Set Associations window, like the one shown in Figure 4.2.

FIGURE 4.2   Set Associations window

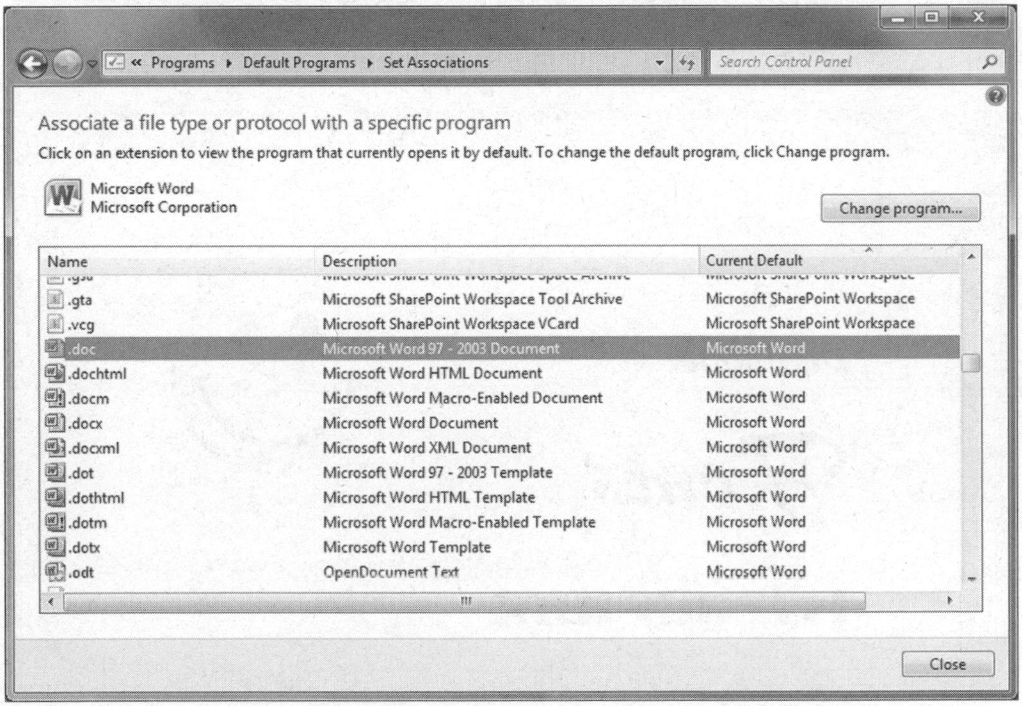

In Figure 4.2, you can see that there are actually quite a few different file extensions associated with Microsoft Word. If you wanted to change the association, you would highlight the extension and click the Change Program button. We will talk more about specific file extensions and the applications they are associated with throughout this chapter.

Productivity Software

The first group of software types that we will talk about is *productivity software*. The group gets its name because, well, it's designed to make you more productive. The software in this section will help you get more work done and hopefully make that work easier as well.

Word Processing Software

Word processing software is one of the most common types of applications used by business and home users alike. With this software, you can create everything from simple letters or resumes to detailed reports and flyers.

The most popular word processing program on the market today is Microsoft Word, which is part of the Microsoft Office suite. Figure 4.3 shows a simple Word document.

FIGURE 4.3   Word document

Within a word processor, you will have the ability to change fonts and styles; insert pictures, shapes, and tables; and manage many different facets of the document's appearance.

Of course, there are several other word processing programs out there, some of which are free and others that are not. Among the commercial offerings are Word Perfect and Corel Write. Free options include Google Docs, AbiWord, Jarte, and Writer from www.OpenOffice .org. Each one has slightly different menus and features, but in general they all do the same thing. With features, sometimes you get what you pay for. In addition, the biggest issue you might run into is compatibility between formats. It's not guaranteed that a Microsoft Word document will be readable in WordPerfect or Jarte, or anything else for that matter. For the most part, you won't run into any problems with simpler documents, but more complicated files with unique features can pose problems. Compatibility can also be influenced by the format you save it in. Simple text (.txt) files are more compatible across platforms than .docx files are. Table 4.2 lists some common file extensions for word processing software.

TABLE 4.2   Word processing file extensions

Extension	Use
.txt	Basic text file. Almost all word processors will open this, from the basic Notepad in Windows to Microsoft Word, and most other commercial and free apps as well. Generally, very few configuration options (such as fonts or inserting images) are available.
.rtf	Rich text format. A fairly basic document format developed by Microsoft and generally more compatible than .doc files.
.doc/.docx	Microsoft Word files. .docx files are newer and support more features than older .doc files.

The file extensions in Table 4.2 are the only ones on the CompTIA IT Fundamentals exam objectives, but know that other extensions exist too. For example, WordPerfect typically uses the .wpd extension, AbiWord uses .abw, and OpenOffice can use several, such as .odt, .ott, and .sxw.

I have talked about Google Docs before and how it's run from Google's cloud. Microsoft has introduced a cloud-based version of its popular Office software as well, called Office 365. It gives you fully functional versions of Office software and works on workstations, tablets, and Android-based phones. You buy a subscription to use it (either monthly or yearly) and store files online just as you would with Google Docs.

Spreadsheet Software

Spreadsheets serve an important niche, which is for managing numbers and small quantities of data, and are almost as popular as word processing programs. In fact, most office "suites" of software bundle word processing and spreadsheet applications together, along with basic database and presentation software. Microsoft Office includes Word (for documents) and Excel (for worksheets), and OpenOffice has Writer and Calc. Other versions include Quattro Pro, Google Sheets, and Gnumeric (for Windows and Linux). The .xls and .xlsx extensions are associated with Microsoft Excel; Figure 4.4 shows a basic Excel worksheet.

FIGURE 4.4   Microsoft Excel

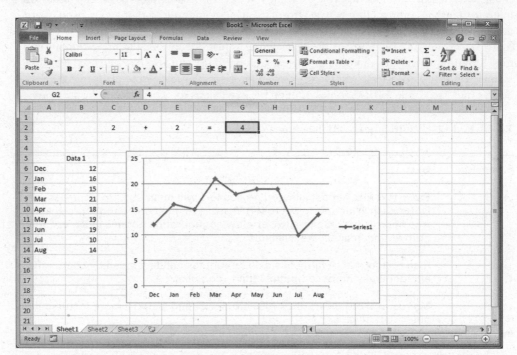

Spreadsheet software is mostly used for the management of numbers or lists of data. You can have it do math for you using formulas, sort data, create charts and graphs, and perform relatively complex data manipulation tasks using macros. If you have more sizeable data management needs, then it's more efficient to use database software.

Email Software

Email is by far and away the most commonly used productivity application today. The vast majority of people with computers or mobile devices use it daily. It's so prevalent that it can be a distraction for people; we could argue that it actually hurts productivity for some users. Regardless of if you think you can't live without email, or if you find the number of messages you get to be overwhelming, email is an entrenched part of our society.

 Because email software lets us collaborate with other users, it's also listed in the CompTIA IT Fundamentals exam objectives under Collaboration Software.

In order to use email, you need an email client. Email clients let you send and receive messages, manage your contacts and calendar, and assign yourself tasks with deadlines, and it will give you reminders when you need to follow up on something.

Most businesses will use one of two commercial email clients: Microsoft Outlook or IBM Notes (formerly Lotus Notes). There are literally dozens of other email clients that you can install on your computer, such as Eudora, GNUMail, and Mozilla Thunderbird. If you have an email account through your company, university, or other organization, you will likely use one of these clients and connect to an email server managed by that organization.

If you use Outlook and Microsoft Office, they synchronize pretty well together. Formatting Outlook emails is very similar to using Microsoft Word, and Outlook also links seamlessly with Microsoft's instant messaging software, which we'll talk about later in this chapter.

There are lots of free Internet email services that you can use as well. Examples include Gmail, Yahoo! Mail, AOL Mail, Outlook.com, and Mail.com. Each has different features and peculiarities. Most have the ability to use an instant messenger, link to your social media accounts, and work on your mobile device. Oftentimes, you also get presented with copious amounts of advertising. But they're free.

Basic Database Software

Databases come in all shapes and sizes, from small systems that hold a few hundred records to massive behemoths that hold hundreds of millions of records. Here, we'll focus on the smaller, more user-friendly variety.

 Database management is a lucrative career for many IT professionals.

In its simplest form, a database doesn't look like much more than a spreadsheet. It contains data in a logical structure, which should make it easy to access. Databases can be a lot more complex, though, with multiple tables interacting with each other to produce the data you need to use. Here are some basic database terms to be familiar with:

Tables   These are what look like worksheets, which contain your data. One database can (and often does) have multiple tables. Each row in a table is called a record. If you want to link multiple tables together, you need to structure the data in such a way that it makes it easy to identify which records belong with each other, such as with a customer identifier.

Forms   Forms are how data is entered into and often viewed from your database. You don't need forms to have a database, but they make database management a lot easier. For example, you can have one form that lets customer service agents enter in new client information, whereas another form lets a manager review all new clients entered in the last week.

Reports   Reports are generated to answer specific questions. For example, a manager could have an automatic report that generates the list of new clients in the last week, as opposed to viewing the list in a form.

Queries   Queries are the real power of databases. They let you mine through your data to find the specific information you need. If you have a database with millions of records, queries are the only realistic way you will find anything useful.

Macros and Modules   Macros and modules let you add functionality to your database. For example, if you want to do a monthly cleanup of all records older than a certain date, you can automate that by creating a module. For anything that you would have to run manually, you can probably create a macro to make the process faster.

You would want to go with a database instead of a spreadsheet if any of the following are true:

- You have too much data to manage in a spreadsheet.
- You have multiple users who need to access and regularly update the data.
- You allow customers to access any of the data, such as checking inventory levels through a website.
- Your data needs security measures.

As with other applications, there are plenty of basic database choices on the market, some free and some commercial. Microsoft Access comes with the Office Suite, and OpenOffice contains a database solution called Base. The key when looking for database software is to ensure that it's relatively easy to use, can expand to meet your storage needs, and has the security you require.

 The most popular large-scale database provider is Oracle. Microsoft also has a popular large database platform called SQL Server.

PDF Viewers and Creators

The .pdf file format, short for Portable Document Format, was created in the early 1990s by software maker Adobe Systems. Adobe's goal was to create a document format that would work regardless of the computer platform the user had, such as Windows, Mac OS, UNIX, or Linux. Instead of needing software such as Microsoft Word, which might or might not run on your computer, you needed a .pdf reader, such as Adobe Reader (called Acrobat Reader back then), which could be installed on any OS. Usually, .pdf files are documents, but they can be flyers, worksheets, presentations, or really anything you want them to be. Some organizations use .pdf files as a very basic way to do desktop publishing.

For most of its history, the .pdf format was proprietary and owned by Adobe. In 2008, they decided to relinquish control and make it an open standard, managed by the International Organization for Standardization (ISO), which is a volunteer organization that establishes international standards.

Background on ISO

ISO might seem like it should be abbreviated IOS, but it's an international organization with three official languages: English, French, and Russian. The organization's name would require different acronyms when translated into each of the languages, so they settled on ISO. Some of the more common standards they are known for are ISO 9000, quality management; ISO 27001, information security management; ISO 14000, environmental management; and ISO 22000, food safety management. ISO isn't a policing organization, so they can't enforce standards. Compliance is accomplished more through peer pressure; showing that you are ISO-compliant indicates to potential business partners that you take quality (or information security, or whatever) seriously, so you are a legitimate business partner.

The method to read a `.pdf` file hasn't changed much since the early 1990s—you still need a `.pdf` reader. Adobe Reader is distributed free, and there are other free readers on the market as well. Most web browsers (both workstation and mobile) either have the ability to read `.pdf` files natively or have a module you can download to make it happen.

One of the nice features of `.pdf` files is that normally when you distribute them, they are read-only. Other people can't modify the files unless they have `.pdf` editing software, and even then you can set passwords to protect the file's contents. Another cool feature is that you can enable the `.pdf` file for people to edit certain parts of it. For example, say that you are distributing a form to clients, and you want them to enter in their name and address, as well as choose from several options that they might be interested in (by checking boxes). You could create a `.pdf` file that lets users edit those fields but not the rest of the document.

To create or edit a `.pdf` file you need special software called a PDF creator. The most popular creator is Adobe Acrobat, and there are several versions available. You will also find numerous free PDF converters online that will take existing documents and convert them for you. Others will convert `.pdf` back to a format such as `.doc`, but usually you need to pay for software that does this. Finally, Microsoft Office 2010 and newer have a feature that lets you generate a `.pdf` file directly from the application. As shown in Figure 4.5, if you go to the File menu and navigate to Save & Send, you have two options for creating PDFs—one to create a PDF/XPS document and the other to attach a PDF copy of the document in an email. Or, you can choose Save As and then select PDF. Figure 4.6 shows what a PDF file looks like inside the viewer.

FIGURE 4.5 Creating a PDF file from Word 2010

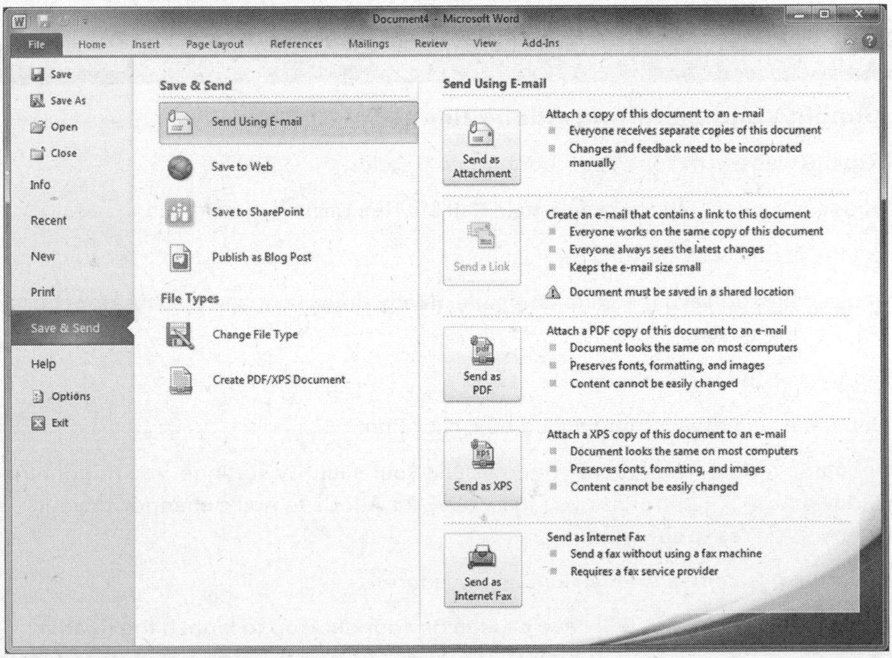

FIGURE 4.6   Viewing a PDF file

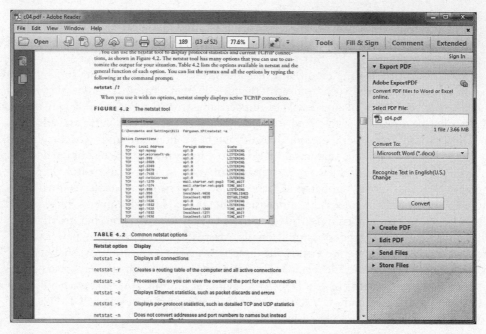

PDF viewers are commonly used, and there's no reason to not have one installed on your computer. Exercise 4.1 has you download Adobe Reader and install it on your computer.

EXERCISE 4.1

Downloading and Installing Adobe Reader

1. Go to the website `https://get.adobe.com/reader`.

2. Optional: Deselect the check box to install McAfee Security Scan Plus.

3. Click the Install Now button.

4. Choose where to save the installation file. (Many times I choose the Desktop, because then it's very easy to find.)

5. Double-click the installation file.

6. If you get a security warning dialog box, click Run.

7. Depending on your version of Windows and your security settings, you might have Windows Access Control ask you if it's okay for Adobe to make changes to your system. Click Yes to continue.

8. Follow the Adobe Reader installation procedure.

9. When it's complete, you will have an icon on your desktop to launch the Reader.

Presentation Software

You might find yourself in a situation where a meeting is coming up, and you need to convey a message to a group of people. Presentation software is designed to help you do that by letting you put your ideas down in slides and then share a full-screen slide show from your computer.

Within your presentation, you can add text, graphs, charts, pictures, and shapes; embed videos for playback; and even create special effects such as having text fade in or out and adding sound. You can also set it up such that the slides transition after a set amount of time. Some people do this and set up a recording of the presentation, to create what amounts to a presentation video to send to others.

As with other software types, you have plenty of presentation packages available, free and commercial, locally installed or web-based. Microsoft PowerPoint comes as part of the Microsoft Office suite and is a commonly used piece of presentation software. OpenOffice's equivalent is called Impress, and a popular Mac version is Keynote. Figure 4.7 shows you what editing a basic presentation in PowerPoint could look like. The .ppt and .pptx file extensions are associated with PowerPoint.

FIGURE 4.7   Microsoft PowerPoint

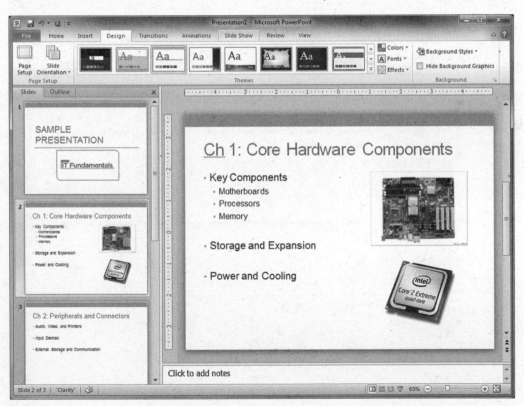

Desktop Publishing Software

If you wanted to create your own book or magazine, you would need software to help you do that, and desktop publishing is that software. Desktop publishers aren't limited to complicated offerings, though; they are perfectly capable of creating smaller projects such as pamphlets or flyers for distribution.

With today's software, there has been a blurring of the lines between what desktop publishing software can offer versus word processing applications. The long story short is word processors have gotten to the point where they offer so many features that they are almost as full-featured as desktop publishing packages out there (and in some cases more).

Stop me if you've heard this before, but there are several desktop publishing software packages available, both for free and commercial. Microsoft Office comes with Publisher, and Figure 4.8 shows what it looks like when it opens. Adobe PageMaker, QuarkXPress, and Apple Pages are other popular versions.

FIGURE 4.8 Microsoft Publisher

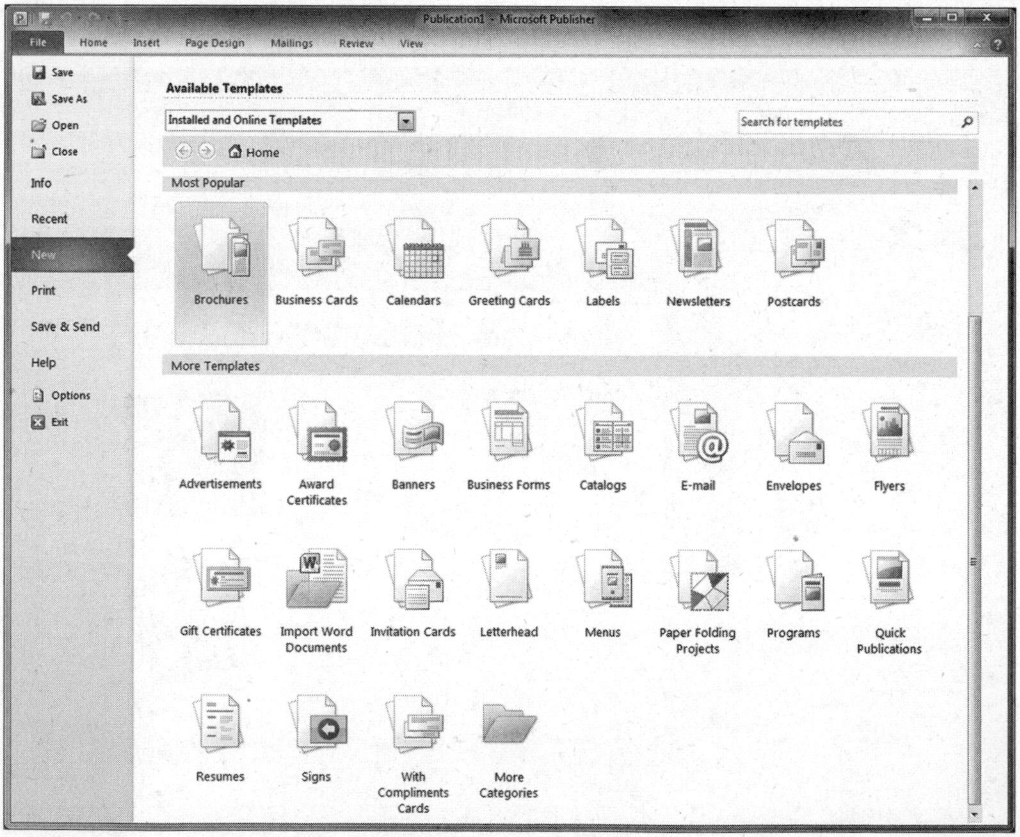

Perhaps the most obvious difference between Publisher and Word is that Publisher has several more built-in templates that you can choose from. Once you decide which type of document you want to create, editing that file is practically identical to using Word.

One thing that you might use more of with a desktop publisher than a word processor is image files. If you're going to create an eye-catching poster or flyer, you need to include pictures. Pictures are stored with specific file extensions, and some of the most common ones are included in Table 4.3.

TABLE 4.3   Image file extensions

Extension	Use
.jpg	Called a j-peg, and sometimes you will see files with a .jpeg extension. The JPEG standard defines how images are compressed and stored. Very commonly used by digital cameras.
.gif	Pronounced with a hard g like the word go, it stands for Graphics Interchange Format. Uses a different compression standard than JPEG. Commonly used on websites.
.tiff	Pronounced like a word and sometimes found as just .tif. Stands for Tagged Image File Format. Uses lossless compression, which preserves better image quality than JPEG or GIF.
.png	Portable Network Graphics. Designed as a lossless compression format to replace GIF. Very common on websites.
.bmp	Short for bitmap. One of the oldest and simplest image formats, usually for lower-quality pictures.

Any desktop publishing software will recognize all of the image file formats shown here. Most photo editing software will too. Occasionally you will run into photo software that only lets you edit a few of the formats, but again, most will work with any of the extensions in Table 4.3.

Personal Information Manager

If you're someone who finds yourself in a consistent state of disorganization, personal information manager (PIM) software could be just what you need. Here are some of the things that PIM software can help you organize:

- Address books
- Lists (including tasks)
- Important calendar dates
- Reminders
- Email and instant message archives
- Files, documents, photos, and videos
- Notes from meetings

If the previous list sounds like a lot of the things that you can manage in Microsoft Outlook or IBM Notes, you are right; those programs can be considered personal managers. You might also look at the list and think that your smartphone pretty much does all of that for you, and you'd also be correct. Part of the heritage of smartphones includes the personal digital assistant (PDA) such·as the Palm Pilot, and so smartphones can do these things too.

In addition to your email software or your smartphone, you can find specialized software packages branded as personal information managers. Most will manage everything included in the bulleted list and will also serve as a personal diary and note-taker. A few examples are EssentialPIM, Pimero, WinPIM, MyInfo, and Chandler Project, which is shown in Figure 4.9.

FIGURE 4.9 Chandler PIM

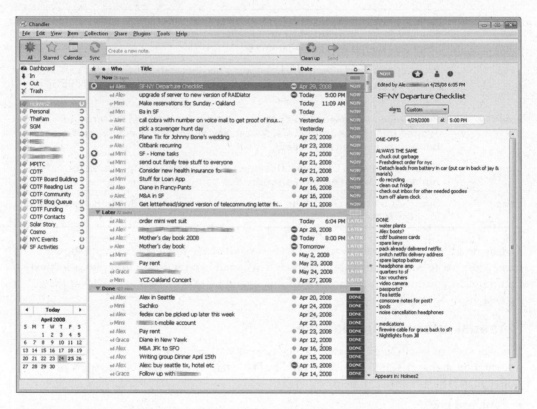

CHANDLER PIM SCREENSHOT COURTESY OF CHANDLERPROJECT.ORG, SHARED VIA CREATIVE COMMONS LICENSE, ATTRIBUTION ONLY 3.0.

Remote Desktop Software

Remote desktop software serves two purposes. One, it allows you to work on·a remote computer just as if you were sitting at it. For instance, let's say you are at home and your work computer is in the next area code (and powered on), but you need to email a co-worker a file in the next five minutes or both of you get fired. Remote desktop software can let you connect to the remote machine and work as if you were sitting at it. Two, it can give someone else the ability to control your computer. Why on Earth would you let anyone do that? Perhaps you need to call technical support to fix an issue. Using remote desktop, the tech support agent can take control of your system and perform the necessary steps to troubleshoot the problem rather than having to explain the steps to you. Regardless of how computer savvy you are, this is probably much more efficient.

In order to run a remote desktop, you obviously need two computers. One system will be the master or the host and the other the slave or the client. The host system will control the client. Getting access to the client computer depends on how you have the remote desktop software configured on it. In the first example we used, you would configure the client to allow access based on a login, typically your work login and password, over a secure Internet connection. In the tech support example, the agent would send a signal to your computer asking for permission to control the system. You would get a pop-up window on your screen asking if you want to grant the remote user control. You give the permission, and control is granted.

Microsoft developed the Remote Desktop Protocol (RDP) for remote management. The client computer must have RDP client software, which is installed by default on all Windows-based computers and is available for most other OSs including OS X, Linux, iOS, and Android. The master computer needs to be running a server version of the software, which Microsoft calls Remote Desktop Connection.

Other popular versions of remote desktop software include LogMeIn, TeamViewer, Chrome Remote Desktop, and RealVNC.

 Real World Scenario

Which Software Should You Choose?

You are consulting for a friend who owns a small business with about 20 employees. She is in the process of standardizing all of the software her employees use. They use a lot of productivity software, specifically presentation software, spreadsheets, and word processing applications. In addition, they quite often share the files with external agencies that collaborate on work with them. Your friend wants to keep costs down, but she also wants seamless integration with her external agencies. What should you advise her to choose?

You have probably two main choices: Microsoft Office or a free version such as OpenOffice. Both of them will provide the functionality that your friend's employees need, and odds are the employees are already familiar with Microsoft Office. The biggest concern might be sharing the files with external agencies. If the external agencies use Microsoft Office, then it will be much better for your friend's company to use it as well. If your friend is less concerned with occasional interoperability issues and more concerned about the bottom line, then the free option might be the better alternative.

Present both options along with pros and cons to your friend so she can make the most informed decision possible.

Collaboration Software

The world is more interconnected today than it has ever been. If you work in an office environment, it's entirely possible that some or all members of your work team will be located in different cities or on different continents. No matter the situation, you still need to get work done effectively as a team, just as if you were sitting in the cubicles next to each other. That's where *collaboration software* comes into play.

The goal of collaboration software is to blur the lines between those who work right next to you and those who do not. It's sort of fitting then that most collaboration software applications blur the lines between the categories of collaboration software listed in the CompTIA IT Fundamentals exam objectives. Said another way, one software package might be able to provide everything you need for collaboration, including working online, sharing and storing files, sharing screens, having videoconferences, and instant messaging each other. That said, we'll still look at each of the categories of collaboration software individually, mostly to address the specific goals of each type of software.

Document Storage and Sharing

If you are working with colleagues in a different location, being able to quickly and easily access the files your team needs to work on is a big deal. Today, there are multiple cloud-based services that let you store and share documents online. Examples include Google Drive, Microsoft Office Online, Box, Dropbox, Carbonite, IDrive, and OpenDrive. Some are more geared toward online backups, whereas others are focused more on making sharing easier.

Here are some key features to look for when considering online document storage and sharing:

Storage and Upload Maximums   How much data will the solution allow you to store, and what is the size limit on the files you upload? This might not be as big of a deal with a small team, but if you are considering a solution for an entire organization, size limits matter.

Backups   Is the data backed up? And if so, how often? There would be nothing worse than to trust someone else to manage your data and then to lose it because it hasn't been backed up.

File Synchronization   This can be a big deal if multiple people are working on a file at the same time and don't realize it. How does the system know, and what version does it keep? Also, some solutions allow you to keep a virtual copy of those files on your local system. Make sure those are synchronized with the online versions.

File Encryption   Are the online files encrypted when they are stored? They had better be. Storing plain-text data on a cloud-based resource is basically asking to have your data stolen.

Maintained Servers   Who owns and maintains the company's servers? Do they do it themselves or license it out to a third party such as Google? Companies that own their hardware have more control over that hardware and of course have a vested interest to make sure it runs properly. There's nothing inherently wrong with a company that uses a third party such as Google to manage their cloud, but it does introduce one more player into the mix, which introduces more potential issues.

Security Mechanisms   Can you set folder permissions and set different permissions for each folder? You should be able to. In addition, managing the security should be easy for anyone in your organization.

Mobile Platforms   It should work with mobile devices, and most online storage and sharing systems do. Almost all online systems will synchronize with mobile devices as well.

Help and Support   How accessible is their help and support system? Do they just have email support or can you get live chat if you need it?

There isn't really a one-size-fits-all solution for all business situations. The best idea is to research the different options, weigh the pros and cons, and then choose the best one for your needs.

Videoconferencing Software

The next three types of programs—videoconferencing, screen sharing, and online workspace—are very closely related to each other. In fact, most software that does any of these functions will do all of the functions. It just depends on how you want to use the service.

Videoconferencing is making a call, like a telephone call, to a remote location using your computer. As the name implies, you and the other people on the call can use webcams to see each other, as opposed to just hearing their voices. This type of solution has obvious advantages, but it also means you probably can't take calls lying around home in your pajamas anymore. Well, maybe you can—it depends on your co-workers!

The technology in this area has improved dramatically in recent years, with the goal of some of the higher-end videoconferencing suites to make you feel like you and the people on the other end of the line are actually in the same room. This has been termed *telepresence*. To make this seem like an authentic experience where everyone is in the same room, special videoconferencing rooms are set up. The rooms at both locations often have the same style of table and chairs and the same décor, including similar artwork and fake plants!

With most videoconferencing software packages, you have the ability to share what's on your screen. You can choose to share all applications or just one specific file. In addition, you will have options such as recording the session and allowing others to annotate on your screen. Recordings can be played back later for people who couldn't make the conference or if you want to review comments made by someone on the call.

There are dozens of software solutions available for those who want videoconferencing. Cisco WebEx, GoToMeeting, Fuze, join.me, and Adobe Connect are some popular commercial options. Free options include Skype, Google Hangouts, FaceTime, and Camfrog. The paid options usually have a Quality of Service (QoS) guarantee, whereas the free ones don't. The free ones might work fine one time and then be plagued by connection issues the next. In addition, the free ones are not as likely to have all of the same features of their commercial counterparts.

One technology that is often seen along with videoconferencing is *Voice over Internet Protocol (VoIP)*. It isn't a specific software package but rather a group of technologies that work to deliver voice communications over the Internet or other data networks. VoIP can give you voice-only transmissions over network cables or video along with voice, all over the same network connection.

 To see if you are using VoIP, look at where the phone plugs in to the wall. Does it plug into a standard phone jack or a network jack? If it's the latter, you are probably using VoIP.

The biggest advantage of VoIP and teleconferencing is that they help reduce travel costs. Instead of paying to fly people to a remote location for a meeting, you can simply connect with your business partners in another location. Good teleconferencing systems are pretty expensive, but with the travel savings, the systems pay for themselves very quickly.

Screen-Sharing Software

As the name implies, screen-sharing software focuses on sharing the contents of your screen with others. Most of the time this can be accomplished using videoconferencing software; you can share content as well as talk and see the person at the same time. Some instant messaging software programs will also let you share your screen. The same players that provide videoconferencing will give you screen sharing as well.

There are some specific screen-sharing programs that don't have videoconferencing but allow for audioconferencing and also have features like the ability for multiple people to control a mouse cursor on the screen. Screenhero is an example of this, as are Quick Screen Share and Mikogo.

Online Workspace

Online workspace specifically means that multiple people can collaborate on (and make changes to) the same file at the same time. This, of course, involves sharing the screen of the file you are working on with others. Screenhero and Mikogo are two examples of online workspaces. Features include a multiuser whiteboard, session recording, and instant messenger chat.

Instant Messaging Software

Instant messaging is sending a text note to another user in real-time. If you do it on your phone, it's typically referred to as texting. Instant message (IM) software will keep a list of contacts that you have added. Some, such as Microsoft Lync, will synchronize with your Microsoft Outlook address book to make finding connections easier. Many IM programs will also let you share your screen with those who you are chatting with.

There are dozens of IM applications, and most of them are free. In addition to Microsoft Lync, there are Yahoo! Messenger, Google Talk/Google Chat, ICQ, Messages (formerly iChat), Adium, FaceTime, AOL Instant Messenger (AIM), Pidgin, Telegram, Digsby, Trillian, Miranda IM, and many others. The key is the person you want to talk to needs to be on the same system; otherwise, you won't be able to connect. Some, such as Pidgin and Digsby, allow you to connect simultaneously across several messaging networks at the same time.

Utility Software

Many extra services that you can use on a computer are handy to have but are not necessarily ones that help you get your project done or communicate with others. These functions are managed by *utility software*. None of the programs in this section are mandatory, but all of them are pretty useful.

Anti-Malware

Malware is software that does harm to your computer. Why would software harm your computer? Well, because the unfortunate reality is that there are bad people in this world. It's sad in a way, because many people that are otherwise talented programmers choose to use their skills to harm others. It's reality, though, so you need to do what you can to protect your computer against malware.

The term *malware* is really a grouping of different types of bad programs. I am sure that many of their names will be familiar to you, such as viruses, worms, spyware, and rootkits. We'll talk about each of these in more detail in Chapter 8, "Security Threats," but for now we'll just look at how to keep them off your computer.

As the name of this section suggests, you use anti-malware software to keep the malware off of your machine. Some of the more popular programs in the anti-malware arena are Symantec's Norton Security (formerly Norton Antivirus), McAfee, AVG, Avast, Bitdefender, Kaspersky, and Malwarebytes. When choosing a software package, it's important to understand what it specifically protects against. Some apps protect against several types of threats, but others are specifically antivirus or anti-spyware packages. There's nothing wrong with those specialized products, as long as you're aware of the level of protection your computer has.

 WARNING Just because you have anti-malware installed does not mean you are guaranteed to be virus or spyware free! Still, going without the software is very dangerous for computers with an Internet connection.

How Anti-Malware Works

Generally speaking, anti-malware works by monitoring activity on your computer for any activity that appears suspicious. For example, an antivirus program is generally run in the background on a computer, and it examines all the file activity on that computer. When it detects suspicious activity, it notifies the user of a potential problem and asks the user what to do about it. Some antivirus programs can also make intelligent decisions about what to do. The process of running an antivirus program on a computer is known as *inoculating* the computer against a virus.

 For a listing of most of the viruses that are currently out there, refer to Symantec's AntiVirus Research Center (SARC) at www.symantec.com/ security_response/.

These programs have a database of known viruses and the symptoms each one causes. They look for those, as well as signatures, or specific patterns of computer code, that could be suspicious.

 Antivirus databases should be updated frequently. About once a week is good, although more often is better. Most antivirus programs will automatically update themselves if configured properly.

While a true antivirus program will scan for viruses, anti-malware programs are a superset of virus scanners and will look for more than just traditional viruses, such as spyware. The operating systems from Microsoft are the ones most affected by spyware, and Microsoft has released Microsoft Security Essentials and Windows Defender to combat the problem. (Microsoft Security Essentials is also available for Windows XP/Vista/7/8).

As with similar programs, for Windows Defender to function properly, you need to keep the definitions current and scan on a regular basis. In Exercise 4.2, you'll run Windows Defender.

EXERCISE 4.2

Run Windows Defender in Windows 7

1. Choose Start ➢ Control Panel and in the Search Control Panel window, type **Windows Defender**. Click the link to open it.

2. If you are prompted that Defender is not configured, choose to turn it on (this will bring up a User Account Control prompt to continue if UAC is toggled on).

3. From the drop-down list next to Help (a question mark in a blue circle), choose Check For Updates (again, if UAC is toggled on, you will be prompted to continue).

4. Click Scan.

5. Upon completion, the message Your computer is running normally should appear within the frame labeled No Unwanted Or Harmful Software Detected (see Figure 4.10). If anything else appears, resolve those issues.

6. Exit Windows Defender.

FIGURE 4.10   Windows Defender report

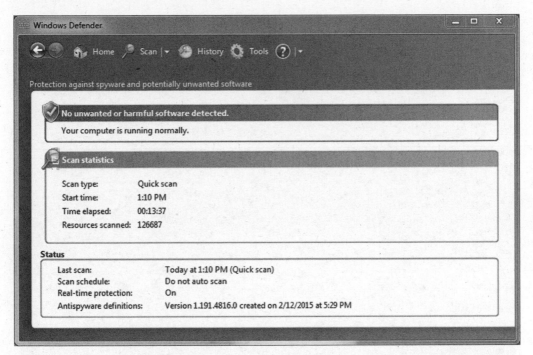

Configuring Anti-Malware

After you install your software, you need to configure it. For the most part, the default settings for the anti-malware program are going to be sufficient. The biggest thing will be to ensure that the software is set to update automatically. Figure 4.11 shows the main screen of Norton Internet Security.

In Figure 4.11, you can see the security settings to turn on or off, as well as the ability to scan your system immediately and other features. To get to the configuration of updates in this software, I clicked the Settings link next to Computer. It gave me the screen in Figure 4.12, and you can see that automatic updates are on.

Removing Malware

If you think you have an infected computer, you will want to remove the malware. The following discussion presents the information you need to know for removing the bad software:

1.   **Identify malware symptoms.** Before doing anything major, it is imperative to first be sure that you are dealing with the right issue. If you suspect malware, then try to identify the type (spyware, virus, and so on) and look for the proof needed to substantiate that it is indeed the culprit.

FIGURE 4.11   Norton Internet Security

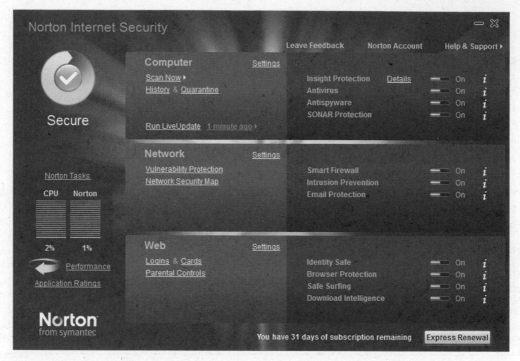

2. **Quarantine the infected system.** Once you have confirmed that malware is at hand, then quarantine the infected system to prevent it from spreading the malware to other systems. Bear in mind that malware can spread any number of ways, including through a network connection, email, and so on. The quarantine needs to be complete to prevent any spread.

3. **Remediate infected systems.** The steps taken here depend on the type of malware you're dealing with but should include updating antivirus software with the latest definitions and using the appropriate scan and removal techniques.

4. **Schedule scans and updates.** The odds of the system never being confronted by malware again are slim. To reduce the chances of it being infected again, schedule scans and updates to run regularly.

5. **Educate the end user.** Education should always be viewed as the final step. The end user needs to understand what led to the malware infestation and what to avoid, or look for, in the future to keep it from happening again.

Software Firewalls

A *firewall* is a hardware or software solution that serves as your network's security guard. They're probably the most important devices on networks that are connected to the

FIGURE 4.12   Automatic updates are on

Internet. Firewalls can protect you in two ways. They protect your network resources from hackers lurking in the dark corners of the Internet, and they can simultaneously prevent computers on your network from accessing undesirable content on the Internet. At a basic level, firewalls filter network traffic based on rules defined by the network administrator.

 Anti-malware software examines individual files for threats. Firewalls protect you from streams of network traffic that could be harmful to your computer.

Firewalls can be stand-alone "black boxes," software installed on a server or router, or some combination of hardware and software. In addition to the categorizations of hardware and software, there are two types of firewalls: network based and host based. A network-based firewall is designed to protect a whole network of computers and almost always is a hardware solution with software on it. Host-based firewalls protect only one computer and are almost always software solutions.

How Firewalls Work

To give you fair warning, note that you won't be tested on this section on the CompTIA IT Fundamentals exam. However, it's good basic knowledge to have anyway. And if this is an area that's interesting to you, then you can literally make a career out of network security.

Most network-based firewalls have at least two network connections: one to the Internet, or *public side*, and one to the internal network, or *private side*. Some firewalls have a third network port for a second semi-internal network. This port is used to connect servers that can be considered both public and private, such as web and email servers. This intermediary network is known as a *demilitarized zone (DMZ)*.

A firewall is configured to allow only packets (network data) that pass specific security restrictions to get through. By default, most firewalls are configured as *default deny*, which means that all traffic is blocked unless specifically authorized by the administrator. The basic method of configuring firewalls is to use an *access control list (ACL)*. The ACL is the set of rules that determines which traffic gets through the firewall and which traffic is blocked. ACLs are typically configured to block traffic by IP address, port number, domain name, or some combination of all three. Packets that meet the criteria in the ACL are passed through the firewall to their destination.

Enabling a Software Firewall

Windows comes with its own software firewall called Windows Firewall. There are also numerous software firewalls on the market. I'm not going to get too deep into how to configure Windows Firewall here; we'll play with it more in the "Software Management Best Practices" section later in this chapter. For now, know that turning it on is a good thing to help protect your computer from hackers, and it should be turned on by default.

Windows Firewall is found in Control Panel under System and Security. Figure 4.13 shows what Windows Firewall looks like.

Some third-party security software, such as Norton Internet Security, comes with its own software firewall. In cases where you have those types of programs installed, they will turn off Windows Firewall automatically.

Diagnostic and Maintenance Software

You usually take it for granted that when you push the power button on your computer, it will start up and work without any issues. Even though your system might seem to be working fine, small problems could be lurking under the surface, which could turn into bigger problems down the road.

Most operating systems come with light-duty diagnostic and maintenance software built in. For example, in Chapter 2, "Peripherals and Connectors," we looked at performance

FIGURE 4.13   Windows Firewall

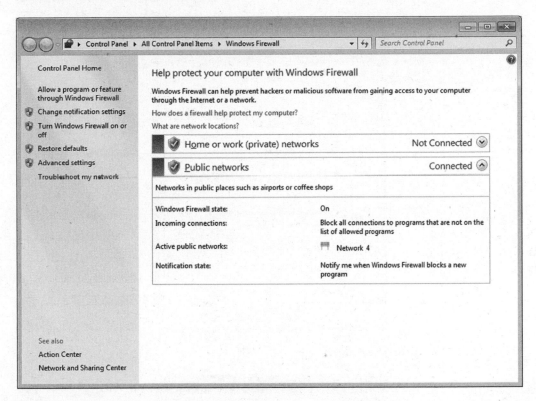

monitoring utilities. These can help you establish a baseline of system performance, and if the performance degrades, it could be a sign of trouble. Other tools can help with routine maintenance too, such as Disk Cleanup (which we talked about in Chapter 2), error checking on hard drives, and disk defragmentation. The latter two are shown in Figure 4.14, which I got to by opening Computer, right-clicking my C: drive, and selecting Properties, then selecting the Tools tab.

Clicking Check Now under Error-Checking will open up a dialog similar to the one in Figure 4.15. You can click Start to have the system scan your hard drive for errors and fix them. You would likely do this only if you're having disk read or write issues.

When Windows writes files to the hard drive, it looks for blocks of space large enough to accommodate the file being written. But because of file edits, moving files, and other OS shenanigans, this sometimes results in files becoming fragmented, or written in different parts of the drive. Excessive fragmentation can slow down hard drive reads and writes. Using Disk Defragmenter, as shown in Figure 4.16, you can rearrange the files on your hard drive to speed performance. In the case of Figure 4.16, you can see that it's automatically scheduled to run on this system, so no defragmentation is needed.

FIGURE 4.14 Hard drive properties

FIGURE 4.15 Error checking

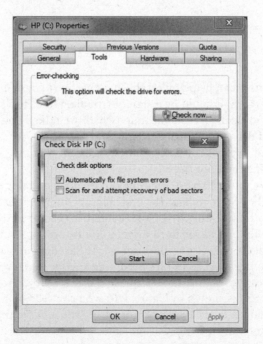

FIGURE 4.16   Disk defragmentation

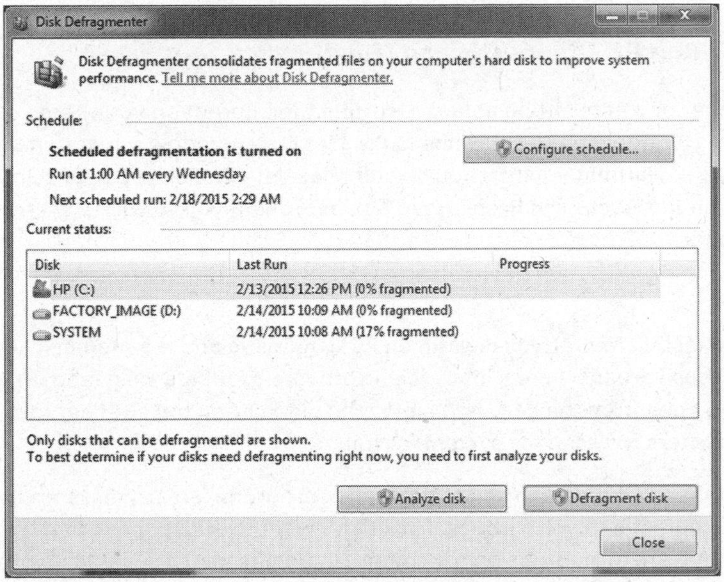

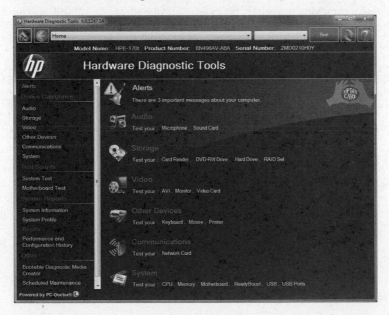

Other third-party utilities can do a much more thorough assessment of your computer hardware and determine if there are any issues. Figure 4.17 shows the HP Hardware Diagnostic Tools screen, which comes with most HP computers. It's based on a program called PC-Doctor.

FIGURE 4.17   HP hardware diagnostics

Real World Scenario

Do I Need to Run PC Diagnostic and Maintenance Software?

Here's the scenario: you're sitting at home, surfing the Internet on your home computer. All of a sudden a window pops up, which looks a lot like a window generated by your operating system, warning you that your system has detected slow performance and you should diagnose the issue. The flashing red box beckoning you to click it seems pretty legit. What do you do?

Don't click it.

I have to be honest; I am pretty lukewarm on PC diagnostic and maintenance software. This is one of those areas where a lot of scam software products exist, and it's really hard to tell the good ones from the bad. And I might be old-school, but I get nervous any time an application offers to "scan my system for free."

I'm not saying that all diagnostic and maintenance programs are scams; some legitimately do detect hardware issues. I just don't want to take the risk that it's not going to download spyware or pop-ups on my computer. Besides, let's say that your hard drive is indeed starting to fail. It's not like you can repair it. You can replace it, but you'll do that when it totally fails anyway. (And if you're backing up your data like you should, then you won't lose anything either.) Or if your RAM is failing, you are going to be getting occasional system errors letting you know there's a problem.

Running utilities that come with your OS to handle occasional maintenance such as defragmentation or removing temporary files that are taking up space is fine. But other than that, you can probably skip diagnostic and maintenance software and not be any worse for the wear.

What happens if you get an error message on your computer and you need to diagnose it? The best answer is Google it. Write down the error message and start typing it into Google. You'll find out what the error means, and likely get several ideas on how to fix the problem. Once again, Google comes to the rescue!

Compression Software

You probably share files with other people quite a lot, and sometimes those files get really big—so big that they can clog up your email pipes and not make it through the server. Other times, you have 20 files you want to share, but you really don't want to have to sit there and attach 20 separate files to an email. Compression software is the solution to both of these dilemmas.

 Compressing a file is often called zipping a file, named after one of the compression file extensions, which is `.zip`.

Compression software removes redundant information within files and by doing so makes them smaller than their original size. You will see different levels of compression based on the type of file you are trying to zip. Text files and worksheets often compress quite a bit, whereas pictures don't usually see much of a size reduction. As noted earlier, compression software can also take multiple files and compress them into the same archive, which can be uncompressed later and the original files retrieved.

The gold standard in compression software for many years has been WinZip. It's a great program, but it's not free. Other popular options include WinRAR, PKZIP, 7-Zip, gzip, and Express Zip. Table 4.4 lists common compression file formats and their use.

TABLE 4.4   File compression formats

Extension	Use
.rar	Compression format introduced by WinRAR program.
.tar	Short for tape archive, it's a format used in the UNIX and Linux environments. It's not compressed; a compressed .tar file would have the extension .tar.gz.
.zip	The most common compression format, supported by most compression software. Originally created by PKWARE, which makes the PKZIP program.
.dmg	Mac OS X disk image files.
.iso	Disk image archive files for optical media, such as CD-ROMs.
.7z	Compression files generated by the 7-Zip program.
.gz	Compression files generated by the gzip program, which is mostly found on UNIX and Linux systems. gzip is the replacement for the compress utility.
.jar	Short for Java archive; similar in format to .zip files. Usually used to distribute software programmed in the Java language.

In Exercise 4.3, you will download and install 7-Zip and create an archive.

EXERCISE 4.3

Installing and Using 7-Zip

1. Go to www.7-zip.org/download.html.

2. Click the Download link next to the file you want. For this exercise, I will download the .msi for 64-bit Windows.

3. Save the file to your desktop (or other location).

4. Double-click the `.msi` file to begin installation.

5. Click the box to accept the License Agreement and click Next.

6. Choose where to install the application (the defaults are fine) and then click Next.

7. Click Install to begin installation.

8. After installation is complete, click Finish to exit the installer.

9. Click Start, and you will have the 7-Zip file manager in your applications menu. Click it to open it. You will see a screen similar to the one in Figure 4.18. You can click any folder to navigate to it, or use the up folder arrow to the left of the location bar to move up one level.

FIGURE 4.18 7-Zip file manager

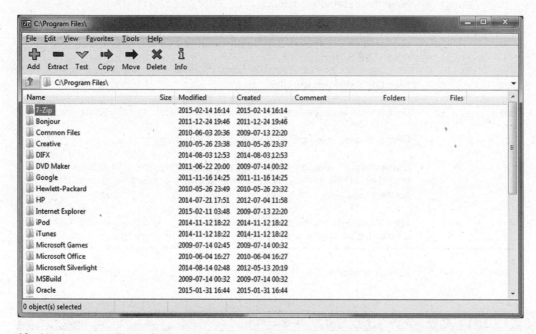

10. Navigate to a file or folder you want to add to the zipped archive, and click the green plus (Add) button. It will give you a screen similar to the one in Figure 4.19.

11. The defaults are fine to accept, but notice that you have options. The ones you are most likely to use pertain to renaming the file, the level of compression, and password protecting the file.

FIGURE 4.19   7-Zip archive options

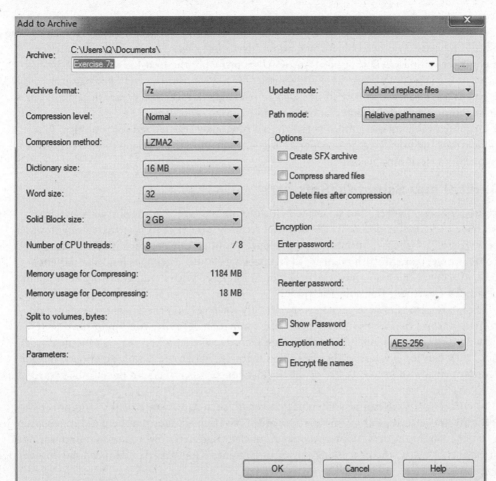

12. Click OK, and 7-Zip will create the file for you.

13. Compare the .7z file to the original. How much smaller is it?

Specialized Software

The final group of software we'll look at is specialized software. This could have also been called the "We couldn't think of a better name" group, but the truth is that each of these could rightfully be its own category. Most of them are designed to give added functionality for specific types of professions, such as graphical designers or medical doctors, but some are purely for fun.

Computer-Aided Design and Graphic Design

Computer-Aided Design (CAD) systems are used by designers of buildings and other structures as well as artists to create two- and three-dimensional drawings. If you're going to build a house, you need blueprints, and odds are they were created by an architect or engineer with a CAD program. AutoCAD is probably the best-known and most full-featured CAD package, but there are versions for novice users as well. For example, HGTV produces the HGTV Ultimate Home Design package that lets you create floorplans for a house, complete with full interior design, landscaping, and decks.

Graphic designers use similar software but obviously specialized for graphics. Practical applications include designing corporate logos, professionally altering photos (Photoshop, anyone?), or designing websites.

Medical and Scientific Software

Professionals in medical and scientific fields often have very specific software needs. If you have visited your doctor or the hospital recently, you've seen that there are computers everywhere. It's likely that those computers are running an electronic medical records (EMR) or electronic health records (EHR) package. These packages hold the patient's medical records but also allow the provider to interface with medical testing equipment such as an electrocardiogram (EKG) kit.

There are also software packages specifically for medical practice management and billing software that helps link to insurance companies. Finally, you might have seen software that lets patients link to their own records, so that when they get medical tests back, they can log in and see their results. Of course, when we're talking about medical records, privacy and security are of the utmost concern, so that's an issue to be aware of as well.

Scientific software can be somewhat universal, such as for statistical testing, or it can be highly specialized. For example, there are software packages that help aid in research in topics from bioinformatics to genetics to nuclear magnetic resonance to computational astronomy. Clearly, the processing power of computers has greatly advanced our knowledge of science.

Financial Software

Financial software has two major divisions: professional use and small business/home use. Professional investors or traders have specialized software packages that allow them to analyze the market and make trading decisions.

For small business owners or home users, there are a number of applications that help manage personal finance, such as Quicken, Microsoft Money, and iCash. Web-based apps are gaining traction in the market, led by Mint and doxo. Most of these programs allow you to set and track budgets, manage your banking, plan investment choices and retirement savings, generate reports, and pay bills automatically.

Tax preparation is another big area for small business and home users who might not want to pay for professional services. TurboTax and H&R Block's tax preparation software are the leaders in this field.

Gaming and Entertainment

For years, there has been a big debate among gamers as to which is better, PCs or consoles such as the PlayStation and Xbox. Now you can introduce mobile gaming into the equation as well, although most serious gamers would scoff and turn up their noses, noting that mobile gaming still has a long way to go.

If money is any indication, then PCs clearly dominate the gaming market. The PC gaming segment is twice the size of the console market, and it's growing, even in the midst of declining overall PC sales. Estimates have the PC gaming market at about a \$23–\$25 billion industry. So far in this chapter we've talked about all of these great software packages that can help productivity or ward off viruses, but gaming is a huge part of the computer industry.

It doesn't make sense to get too much into the types of games in the market today since they change over time. If you're curious, go to a retailer like Amazon.com and look under their video games section. There are numerous games available in almost every conceivable genre.

In addition to games, we love our computers because they play movies and music. Sure, we can get other devices to do those things too, but computers were made for this kind of stuff. While we're on the subject, we should talk about common video file extensions. For one, they are a test objective, and for two, you might find yourself needing to find the right movie player for the video file type you want to watch. Let's take a look at them in Table 4.5.

TABLE 4.5   Video file extensions

Extension	Use
.mpg	Called an m-peg file, it's short for Moving Picture Experts Group. These are compressed files commonly found on the Internet. Most video players can handle .mpg files.
.mp4	This an MPEG-4 file, or just a newer and better version of .mpg. Again, most video players can handle these files. It has the advantage over .flv of being supported natively on most mobile devices.
.flv	This is short for Flash Video, which is a format created by Adobe Systems. It's a competing technology to .mp4 and requires a Flash plug-in to play. It's still a common format on YouTube and Google Video.
.wmv	Short for Windows Media Video, it was created by Microsoft. It tends to work better on Windows-based computers than other OSs.
.avi	Audio Video Interleave was also developed by Microsoft. Typically it uses less compression than other formats. These files are usually more universally supported than .wmv files.

Music is a very popular form of electronic entertainment as well. The rise of mobile devices and the relatively small size of audio files have made this combination very lucrative. Table 4.6 lists the information you need to know about audio file extensions.

TABLE 4.6   Audio file extensions

Extension	Use
.mp3	This is short for MPEG-1 Audio Layer-3, and it's an audio-only compression format created by the Moving Picture Experts Group. It compresses files into about one-twelfth their original size yet maintains near-CD quality sound.
.wav	Waveform Audio File Format, or just called "wave," these are uncompressed files, and as such they have the best sound quality. They are also the largest.
.flac	Pronounced "flack," this is an open-source compression format. It's not widely supported, though, so it's possible that your mobile music player won't read these files.
.aac	Advanced Audio Coding was designed as a replacement for .mp3. It produces better sound quality at about the same file size. This is the file format used by iTunes.
.m4a	This stands for MPEG-4 Audio, and it uses the same compression as .aac. It's also a replacement for .mp3. Some media players won't play these files unless they are renamed to .mp4.

The easiest way to see if your file type is supported by your application is simply to try to open the file. If it doesn't work, and you desperately need to open the file, you can find file converters online that will convert it from one format to another.

Software Management Best Practices

Software management isn't too hard, as long as you follow a couple of basic rules—install and uninstall properly and update as needed. If you do those things, you will have relatively few problems with the software on your computer. And if or when you have a scenario where you are having problems with an application, rebooting your computer often takes care of the issue. If the issue keeps coming back, uninstall and reinstall, and you should be back up and running with no problems.

In this section, we will cover best practices for software management. First, we will talk about the stuff you need to think about before installing an application, such as whether it will work with your OS or not. Then, we'll move on to the proper way to install and uninstall features of your operating system, applications, and drivers. Finally, we'll talk about updating or patching software on your system.

Considerations for Installing Software

Before you buy any software, you need to make sure of a few critical things. The first is if the application works with your operating system, and the second is if your hardware is robust enough to support it. In addition, you should also consider the licensing requirements for that software and if your intended use falls within those requirements.

Software Compatibility

Sometimes you will find yourself standing in a store, looking at the box for a new application, and wondering, "Will this work on my computer?"

On the box for each retail application you buy, and in the documentation for each application available for download, you'll find a Minimum System Requirements section. This usually includes a list of compatible OS versions, a minimum processor speed, a minimum amount of RAM, and a minimum amount of hard disk space available. There may also be additional requirements, such as a particular display adapter, the amount of display adapter RAM, or a permanent Internet connection to use the software.

Besides the generic minimum requirements, you would also be wise to research compatibility issues before spending a lot of money on an application. For example, some applications (particularly games) have known problems with certain display adapters.

When judging whether you have enough hard disk space, keep in mind that at least 15 to 20 percent of the hard disk space should be left empty to ensure best performance. Don't assume that if your hard disk has 1 GB of space left on it, you can install an application that requires 1 GB of space.

If your system barely meets the requirements in one or more aspects, the application may install but performance may suffer. For example, the application may crash frequently, run slowly, or have poor graphic or sound performance.

If you want to run an older application that is designed for a previous version of Windows, you may find the Compatibility Mode feature in Windows to be useful. This feature enables a newer version of Windows to mimic an older version selectively when it deals with an individual application. For example, an application may require a lower display resolution than Windows 7 or Windows Vista provides; the Compatibility Mode feature can temporarily permit that lower resolution.

Some applications require an Internet connection in order to install them. Depending on the settings of your firewall software (such as Windows Firewall), a warning may appear when the Setup program tries to access the Internet. In most cases, you can click a button to let the firewall know that it's okay to proceed.

You may sometimes have to unblock certain port numbers manually in your firewall software in order to permit an application to access the Internet. (Ports are numbered pathways that help the OS keep Internet traffic routed to the right applications.) The exact steps for blocking and unblocking ports and allowing applications vary depending on the OS and the firewall software. Exercise 4.4 shows you how to do it in Windows 7. (Note that you would go through this process after installing the new software; otherwise the new software would not appear on the list.)

EXERCISE 4.4

Configuring Windows Firewall

1. Open Windows Firewall in Control Panel. To find it, you might need to choose Start ➢ Control Panel ➢ System And Security and, under the Windows Firewall heading, click Allow A Program Through Windows Firewall.

2. Change settings, scroll down to the bottom of the list, and click Windows Remote Management. Select the check box to its left, as shown in Figure 4.20. The Home/Work (Private) check box is automatically selected for that entry. This is the basic way to enable a program.

FIGURE 4.20 Windows Firewall allowed programs

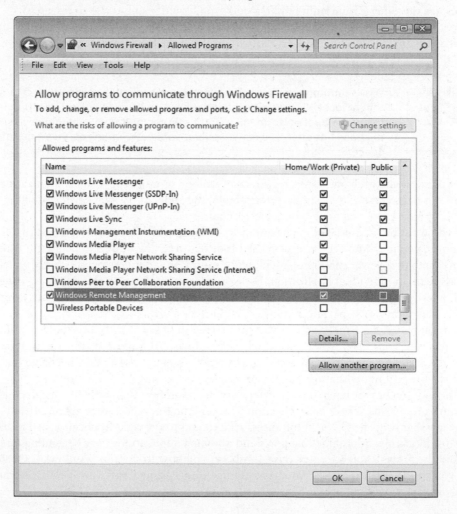

3. Clear the check box for Windows Remote Management, and click OK. Next, you'll learn how to open a particular port number by creating a new rule.

4. Back in the Control Panel's System And Security page, click the Windows Firewall heading.

5. In the pane at the left, click Advanced Settings. Advanced information for the firewall appears in the Windows Firewall With Advanced Security window.

6. Scroll down to the View And Create Firewall Rules section, and click Outbound Rules.

7. Choose Action ➢ New Rule. The New Outbound Rule Wizard dialog box opens.

8. Select the Port radio button, as shown in Figure 4.21, and click Next.

FIGURE 4.21   New Outbound Rule Wizard

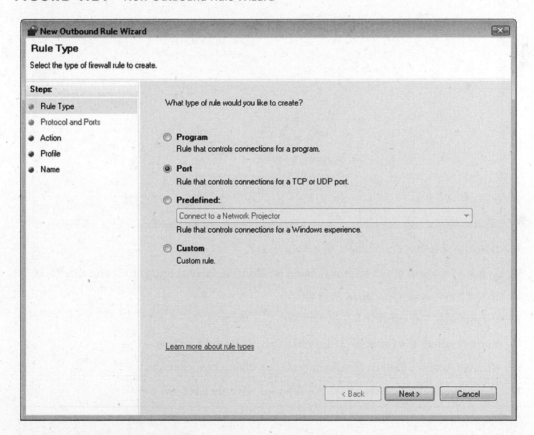

9. Select the TCP radio button.

10. Select Specific Remote Ports, and type 80 in the text box, as shown in Figure 4.22. Click Next.

FIGURE 4.22   Configuring an outbound port

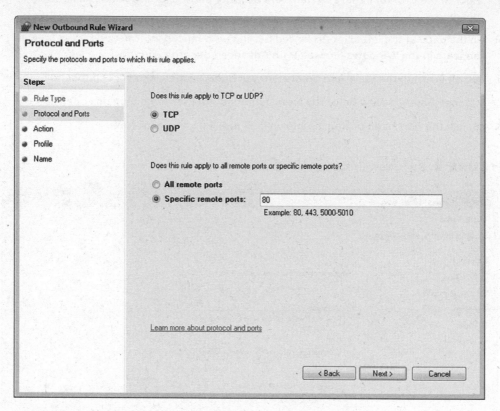

11. Select Allow The Connection, and click Next.

12. Leave all three of the check boxes selected (Domain, Private, and Public) and click Next.

13. In the Name box, type **Open Port 80**.

14. Click Finish. The rule is created.

15. Scroll through the Outbound Rules list, and select the new rule.

16. Choose Action ➢ Delete. In the confirmation dialog box, click Yes.

17. Close the Windows Firewall With Advanced Security window.

Software Licensing

When you buy an application, you aren't actually buying the application. Instead, you're buying the right to use the application in a limited way as prescribed by the licensing agreement that comes with it. Most people don't read these licensing agreements closely, but suffice it to say that they're pretty slanted in favor of the software manufacturer.

Don't like the terms? Too bad. No negotiation is allowed. If you don't accept the *license agreement*, your only recourse is to return the software for a refund. (And good luck finding a vendor that will take back an opened box. Still, the software manufacturer is required to take it back and refund your money if you reject the licensing.)

Although the majority of the applications you acquire will probably be commercial products, there are a number of alternatives to commercial software sales. Here are some of the license types you may encounter:

Freeware   Freeware is software that is completely free. On the small scale, you can get such software from download sites such as www.download.com or from the creator's personal website. Large companies like Google and Microsoft also sometimes offer products for free, because it serves the company's interests to have lots of people using that software. Examples include Google Chrome and Microsoft Internet Explorer. Freeware doesn't include source code, and users aren't allowed to modify the application.

Open Source   This software is freer than free: not only is the application free, but the source code (code used by programmers) is also shared to encourage others to contribute to the future development and improvement of the application. OSs such as Linux and applications like OpenOffice fit this category. Open source software can't be sold, although it can be bundled with commercial products that are sold.

Shareware   This is software that provides a free trial, with the expectation that you'll pay for it if you like it and decide to keep it. In some cases, a shareware version isn't the full product; in other cases, it expires after a certain amount of time. Some shareware provides a full and unlimited version, with payment requested on the honor system.

Multiuser   This is commercial software that you're allowed to install on more than one computer. For example, some versions of Microsoft Office allow you to install the same copy on two or three PCs.

Single User   This is commercial software for which the license restricts installation to a single PC. A common misconception is that a single-user license allows you to install the software on more than one computer as long as you use only one instance at a time, but that's not accurate. Commercial products sometimes have activation systems that lock the software to a specific PC once it's installed, so you can't install it elsewhere.

Concurrent   This license allows the software to be installed on many PCs but used concurrently by a smaller number. For example, you may have 1,000 computers with the application installed, but only 100 users can use it simultaneously. This is useful in situations where everyone needs to have an application available, but the application gets very little actual use.

Corporate, Campus, or Site   This license permits an organization to install the application on an agreed-upon number of PCs. For example, a school may buy a site license of an antivirus program and allow all students to download and install it freely to ensure that the school's network remains virus free.

If you buy any sort of commercial software, you will receive a *product key*, which you will need to enter during installation or the first time the application is opened. The product key might be emailed to you, or it could be located on the physical media if you got an installation CD-ROM. Figure 4.23 shows an example of a product key.

FIGURE 4.23   Microsoft product key

How Do I Buy the Right Licenses?

Consider this situation: After talking to your boss about software licenses, you decide to investigate the office productivity software on your department's computers. You are unable to find proper documentation that the correct software licenses were purchased, leading you to wonder whether the company has the right licenses. Your boss wants to avoid any potential legal issues and asks you to go buy enough copies of the latest version of Microsoft Office for the 20 users in your department. What do you do?

The first question to ask yourself is do all 20 people use their computers at the same time? If not, then you might be able to purchase a concurrent license for fewer than 20 users. If there's the possibility of all 20 users needing Office at once, then you definitely need licenses for everyone. You might purchase a corporate license as well. Now that you have figured out what to buy, how do you do it?

One option is to go to the local computer store, load up 20 boxes of Office (if they have that many in stock), and trudge up to the cashier. A second option is to go to Microsoft's volume licensing site at http://www.microsoft.com/licensing/about-licensing/office.aspx to learn about purchasing multiple licenses. Microsoft will direct you to an authorized reseller so you can purchase them; they will email you the list of license numbers to use when installing the software. Now you need just one physical (or down-loaded) copy to perform the installation.

Installing and Uninstalling Software

Software manufacturers have smartly made installing their products very easy. They understand that if the average user can't get the software onto their machine, then it won't get used and the company won't make money. The CompTIA IT Fundamentals exam lists three different objectives for installing and uninstalling software. Each requires a slightly different process, and we will cover them all here.

Operating System Features

Most operating system features are installed during the initial installation of the OS. There are some optional features that perhaps not all users need, but you do. For example, if Solitaire is not installed but you are bored at work and need to keep your sanity, you could install the games. (Not that I recommend installing or playing games at work.) Or conversely, if you're the boss and want to keep the slackers in your group from playing Solitaire, then you can remove it.

If you need to manage software that is already installed (and in this case, the OS is), you will do so through Control Panel. Exercise 4.5 walks you through how to do this in Windows 7.

EXERCISE 4.5

Installing and Uninstalling Operating System Features

1. Choose Start ➢ Control Panel ➢ Programs.

2. Under Programs And Features, choose Turn Windows Features On Or Off. (Note that you will need administrator-level privileges to do this.) You will get a screen like the one in Figure 4.24.

3. In this case, the Games box is checked, indicating that this component is installed. To uninstall it, uncheck the box and click OK. You will get a message asking you to wait while Windows makes changes to features. Once the process is complete, the message box will disappear.

4. Close Control Panel.

FIGURE 4.24   Turn Windows Features On Or Off

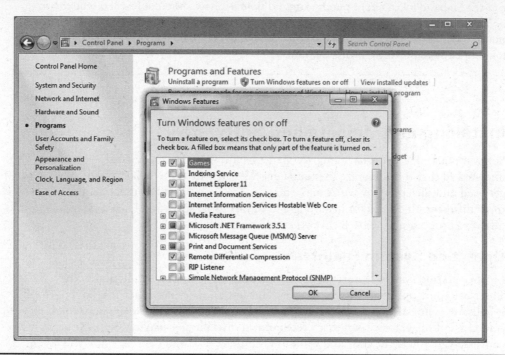

WARNING   Do not enable OS features unless you are sure that you need them! Enabling unused and unnecessary features can potentially open security holes in your system, making it easier for a hacker to exploit your computer.

Applications

You will get applications either on an optical disc or by downloading them from the Internet. Installing an application from a disc is simple. Just pop the disc into the drive, and the Setup program will generally start automatically. If it doesn't, double-click the drive icon for the drive. If that doesn't start the Setup program, it will open a list of files on that disc; locate and double-click the one named Setup (or something similar).

You can also download and install applications. If you download an executable Setup file (usually it will have an .exe or .msi extension), you can double-click that file to start the setup routine.

Occasionally, an application you download may come in a compressed archive, such as a Zip file. In such a case, you must extract the contents of the archive to a new folder on your hard disk and then run the setup from that new folder.

Applications are installed in similar ways regardless of your operating system. For example, most Mac applications come with an installer, similar to Windows. In other cases, you drag the program into the `Applications` folder. In either case, applications are often delivered in either a `.zip` file or a disk image, designated with a `.dmg` file extension. Double-click either of these file types to access the program or installer. Earlier in this chapter, we installed the 7-Zip program. Exercise 4.6 gives you more practice installing applications if you would like it.

EXERCISE 4.6

Installing Free Applications

1. Go to www.download.com, and locate a freeware or shareware program that interests you.

2. Download the Setup file for the program.

3. Run the Setup file to install the application. If any problems come up, such as system permission or firewall issues, troubleshoot and solve them.

Registering and Activation

Registering software—that is, providing your contact information to the software maker—isn't usually required, but software makers try to make you believe it's in your best interest to do so. In actuality, it's a trade-off. Yes, companies want to collect your personal information for marketing purposes, and yes, they may sell it to a third party. However, if you register, you may be eligible for discounts on new versions, free updates, and other goodies.

Activating software is a different story. Some products, especially expensive ones that are frequently pirated, include *activation* features that lock the installed copy (by installation key code) to a particular PC, so you can't use it on multiple PCs.

In a nutshell, here's how it works. The software company maintains an online database of all the installation key codes. When you install the software, you're prompted to activate it. (Usually you have 30 days to do so, or a certain number of uses, before it stops working.) The activation program examines the hardware on your system (processor, motherboard model, and so on) and generates a code that describes the general state of the hardware. It then sends that code to the activation server online. If you try to activate the software on a different PC, the activation server compares the hardware code it has on file to the new one coming in, and if they're too different, it assumes you're installing on a different PC and refuses to let you activate the software.

How is this code generated? Manufacturers are very cagey about that, because releasing too much information may give hackers what they need to thwart the system. Generally, a small hardware change on a PC, such as a different network card or display adapter, won't be a problem. However, if you replace the motherboard, the software probably won't reactivate through the automated system.

Most of the manufacturers that use activation allow you to phone in to request an activation reset, and they will give you no grief over it the first few times. But if you repeatedly call to request additional activation chances, they'll probably think you're trying to get around the license agreement and won't let you reset the activation anymore.

Uninstalling Applications

Removing an application that you no longer want can free up disk space. In addition, if that application has a component that runs constantly in the background, removing the application can free up the memory that was previously occupied by that function.

For Mac users, unless the application specifically has a Remove folder/application, you can delete the application by dragging it to the trash. Also delete any ancillary folders or files associated with that application that may be stored in other locations, such as in the `Library/Application Support` folder. Doing so removes all application files and associated system resources.

With Windows systems, uninstallation is best handled through the Programs section of Control Panel. (If there's an Uninstall command or icon in the folder where the application is stored, that will lead you to the same place.) Open Control Panel and look for the Uninstall A Program option under Programs (you can see it in Figure 4.24). After you click Uninstall A Program, Windows will compile a list of programs for you. Find the application you want to remove and highlight it. Above the applications list, you should have an Uninstall option. Figure 4.25 shows an example. Click Uninstall, and follow the prompts. Using this method is known as a *clean uninstallation*.

FIGURE 4.25 Uninstalling an application

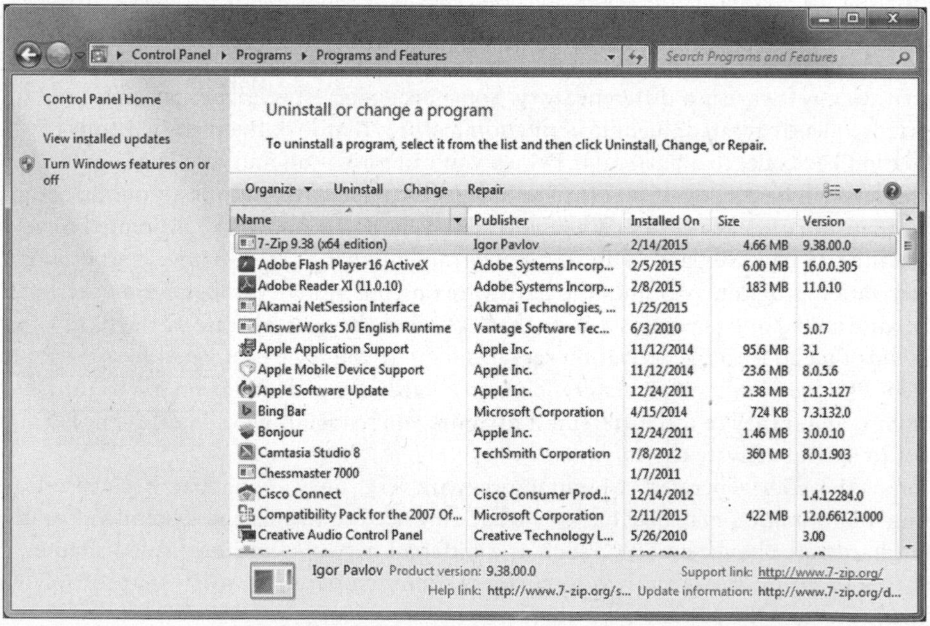

In Figure 4.25, you can see a Repair option next to Uninstall. If you have an application that is not working properly, you may be able to come here and repair it. If that doesn't work, you will probably need to uninstall and reinstall the program to get it to work properly.

In Uninstall Or Change A Program, you can also identify the software version of the installed applications on your computer.

During the uninstall process, you may be asked whether you want to keep certain data or configuration files. That's up to you. If you plan to reinstall the same application later (for example, if you're uninstalling to try to correct a problem rather than to get rid of the program entirely), you may want to save the configuration files. That's a double-edged sword, though, because if you're uninstalling to try to correct a problem, that problem could possibly be caused by one of those configuration files.

If you're using Linux, then depending on the version you may find different resources. Common versions such as Lubuntu have a Software Center window, as shown in Figure 4.26, where you can view and remove installed applications.

FIGURE 4.26 Lubuntu Software Center

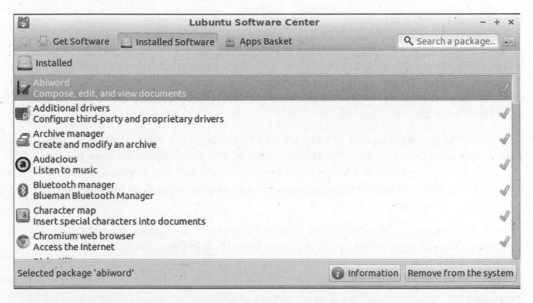

If for some reason you can't uninstall an application using the preferred clean method, you can remove it using a brute-force method that involves manually deleting the program's files and folders and perhaps manually editing Windows Registry to remove the references to it. This is known as an unclean uninstallation.

An unclean uninstall isn't a good idea, because the potential is great for accidentally deleting a file that is essential to some other application or making a change to the Registry that results in other problems. However, sometimes unclean uninstallations happen by accident. For example, you may accidentally delete the folder containing an application, or you may abort the standard Uninstall utility accidentally, resulting in a half-removed, unusable application that won't allow itself to be removed using the utility.

If you need to perform an unclean uninstallation for some reason, here are the basic steps for doing it:

1. Make sure the application isn't running. If it has a background component, turn that off.

2. Delete the folder containing the program files. It's probably in the `C:\Program Files` folder. If it's a 32-bit application on a 64-bit version of Windows, it may be in the `C:\ Program Files (x86)` folder.

3. Delete the program's icons or folders from the Start menu. To do so, open the Start menu, right-click the icon or folder, and choose Delete.

4. If you have enough information to know what to delete in the Registry, start the Registry Editor (click Start, type **regedit**, and press Enter) and make the needed changes. Be sure to always back up the Registry before you edit it!

 Real World Scenario

Removing Pop-Up Windows

Several months ago, a friend brought me her computer. She was complaining that Internet browsing was nearly impossible with all of the pop-up windows she was getting. In addition, sometimes when she tried to go to specific websites to shop, she would instead be redirected to other websites. She mentioned that it had only been happening for a few weeks, after she downloaded and installed a new application.

I went into the Software section of Control Panel to see what she had installed. In there, I sorted the apps by install date. It was pretty easy to find the app she had installed. On the same date, three additional applications were also installed that she was not aware of. I used the Uninstall feature to remove the three extra apps, and all of her pop-up and redirection problems disappeared.

There are two morals of the story. First, be careful what you download and install. Second, many software issues in Windows can be easily fixed through Control Panel.

Drivers

A *driver*, also known as a *device driver*, is a piece of software written to tell the operating system how to communicate with a specific piece of hardware. Without a driver, the piece of hardware will not function. Usually, the only time you think about drivers is when you install new hardware, such as a printer.

Most of the time when you plug in your new hardware device, your OS will recognize it and begin the driver installation process for you. Sometimes your OS will have a built-in driver that it can use. If not, it will ask you to provide one.

If you have to do it manually, installing a driver is often just like installing an application. Either it will come on a CD-ROM or, more likely, you will download it from the manufacturer's website. It will probably be an `.exe` file; double-click it and the installation process will begin.

Here are the basic steps to installing a printer driver:

1. Once you have connected and powered up the device, boot up the computer and wait for Windows to recognize the device.

2. Windows will pop up a screen indicating that it has detected new hardware and is installing it. If it does not have a driver, it will ask you for one. Provide the location of the CD-ROM drive or downloaded driver file.

3. Installation will finish.

If the new printer (or other device) isn't automatically detected, you can start the process manually by going to Start ➤ Devices And Printers, which will open a screen similar to the one in Figure 4.27. Click Add A Device or Add A Printer, depending on what you are trying to add.

FIGURE 4.27   Devices And Printers window

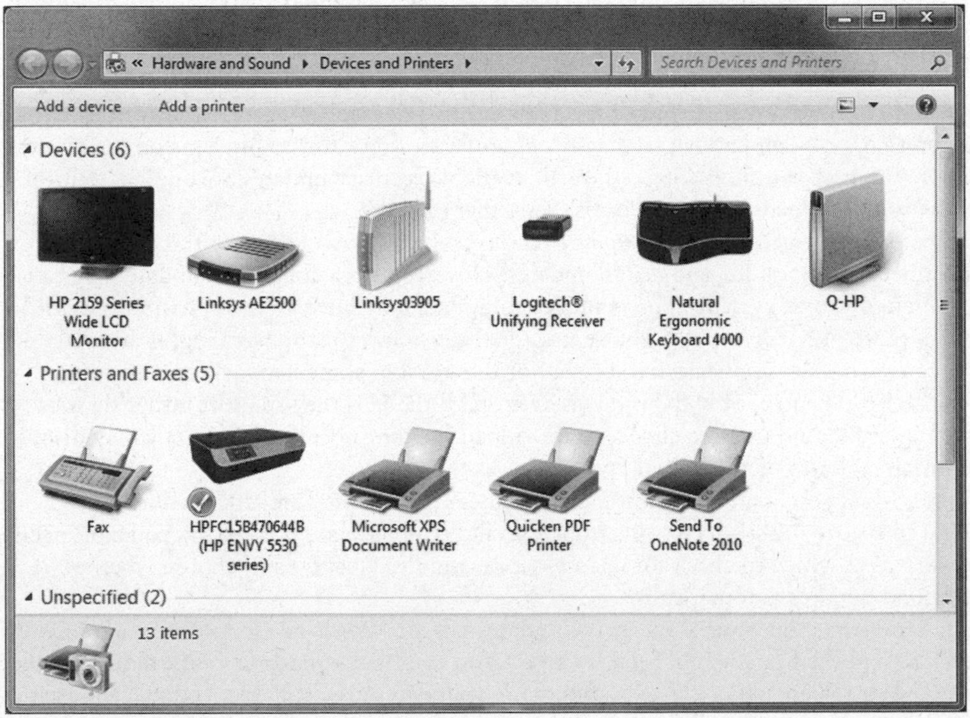

You will specify the type of device, and then Windows will ask you for the driver.

Updating and Patching Software

Newer versions of existing software products are frequently released. These newer versions might fix known bugs with the application, while others will add functionality that didn't exist before. The frequency of version releases depends on the software manufacturer and the severity of the issue. If it's an update or a patch to solve an issue within the program, the manufacturer will provide that update for free.

In this section, we will look at updating and patching OSs, applications (including security software), and drivers. Here we will focus on how often you should update, scheduling updates, and automatic updates.

Updating and Patching Operating Systems

The OS is the platform on which everything else sits, so it's important that it be a stable and reliable platform.

> Don't confuse updating with upgrading. Upgrading refers to replacing your current OS with a newer or more feature-rich release. For example, if you have Windows 7 and you install Windows 10 to replace it, that's an upgrade. It's also an upgrade if you go from a more basic to a more advanced version of the same OS, such as from Windows 7 Home Basic to Windows 7 Ultimate Edition. On the other hand, if you apply a free patch from Microsoft that's designed to correct a problem or provide a minor enhancement, that's an update.

You don't always have to have the most recently released OS version, but you do need a version that's current enough so that all the software you want to use runs on it. Whatever version you use, you should make sure all available security updates are applied to it to avoid problems due to viruses, worms, and other exploits.

Most OSs have an *automatic update* feature, which relieves users of the burden of remembering to look for and install updates. However, occasionally an update may cause a problem on some systems. For example, an update may have an incompatibility with a certain piece of hardware that you've installed, causing it to stop working, or an update may cause an older application to crash. For this reason, some network administrators prefer to keep control of updates themselves on all the PCs they support rather than enabling individual users to choose to download them or not; therefore, they may disable automatic updates on individual PCs.

On a Mac, you control the automatic updates via the Software Update dialog box, shown in Figure 4.28. (Access this from System Preferences on the Dock.) You can specify an interval at which to check for updates (for example, Weekly) and choose whether to download updates automatically.

In Windows, you control automatic updates via the *Windows Update* section of Control Panel. (It's in the System And Security area.) You can turn updating on/off, manually check for updates, review update history, and more. If updates are available, you can choose to install them or hide the notification of them without installing them (see Figure 4.29).

FIGURE 4.28　Automatic updates on a Mac

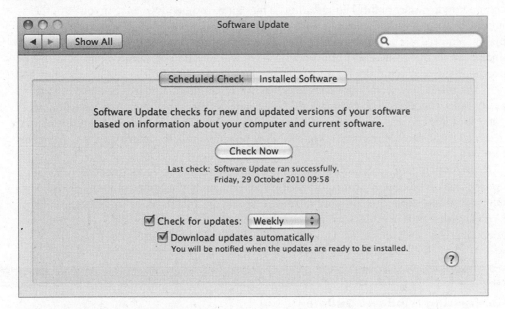

FIGURE 4.29　Windows Update

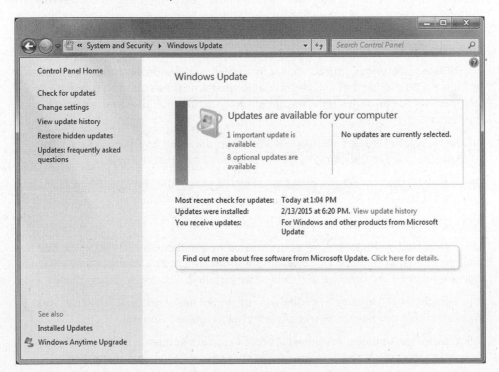

When you're installing updates, be aware that some updates require you to reboot the computer when they're finished installing. This can be an inconvenience if you're in the middle of an important project or have many open windows and applications. When an update requires a reboot, you can decline to restart until a more convenient time. If it's an update where a reboot is very important, the OS will remind you until you do it, letting you postpone the next reminder for a certain amount of time, from a few minutes to a few hours.

Although it may seem more convenient to avoid automatic updates because of that pesky restarting directive, there are risks associated with ignoring an available update. Some updates address critical security flaws. If you don't install updates promptly that are designed to protect your system, your PC may be vulnerable to security attacks from the Internet.

Windows Update (or Software Update on the Mac) can also recommend and install updates for certain applications, especially those made by the same company as the OS itself. Also, depending on your hardware, it may be able to make updates for your hardware drivers available, such as a new version of a display-adapter driver or network-adapter driver. In Exercise 4.7 you will configure Windows Update.

EXERCISE 4.7

Configuring Windows Update

1. Open Windows Update in Control Panel. To find it, you might need to choose Start ➤ Control Panel ➤ System And Security ➤ Windows Update. Review whether there are any updates to be installed. (In Figure 4.29, for example, there is one important update shown.)

2. Click Change Settings. Options appear for configuring Windows Update, as shown in Figure 4.30. Notice that you can schedule what time these updates occur. If your computer is not on at this time, the update will not run until after you power your system on.

3. In the Important Updates section, open the drop-down list and choose Check For Updates But Let Me Choose Whether To Download And Install Them.

4. Make sure all the other check boxes are selected except the last one (Show Me Detailed Notifications When New Microsoft Software Is Available).

5. Click OK to return to the main Windows Update window.

6. Click View Update History. A list of the previously installed updates appears, like the one shown in Figure 4.31. Review this information, noting whether they were successful, their importance, and their dates installed.

7. Click the Installed Updates hyperlink near the top of the window. A list of updates appears. From this screen, you could remove an installed update.

8. Click one of the updates. An Uninstall button appears at the top of the list. If you wanted to remove this update, you would click Uninstall to begin that process.

FIGURE 4.30   Windows Update settings

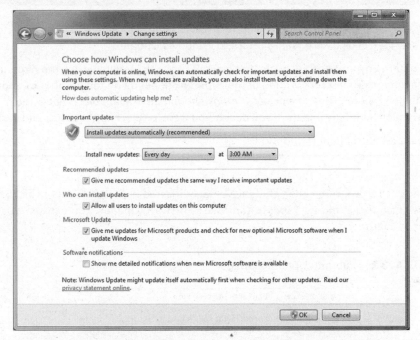

FIGURE 4.31   Windows Update history

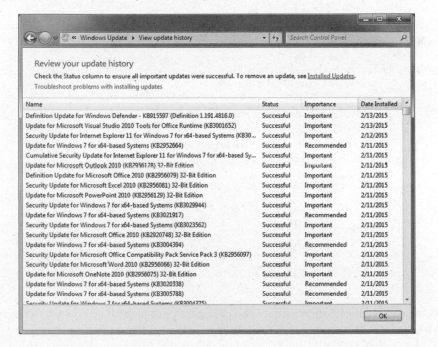

9. Click the back button (blue left-pointing arrow) to return to the View Update History list, and then click back again to return to Windows Update.

10. If there are any updates available that haven't yet been installed, click the hyperlink to view them. The exact wording of the hyperlink depends on the number of updates available; if there is one, it will say *1 important update is available*. Review the information about the update. If you decide you want it, select its check box and click OK.

11. Close the Control Panel window.

Lubuntu has a program called Update Manager located in System Tools, which functions much like Windows Update and Mac's Software Update. You can see what it looks like in Figure 4.32.

FIGURE 4.32 Lubuntu Update Manager

Clicking the Settings button will let you configure options such as how often the system checks for updates as well as if they are automatically installed or not.

Major updates to the OS are typically rolled out to consumers as a service pack. A service pack is like any other update except for its scope; it typically alters the inner workings of the OS in a deeper way than a regular update.

Updating and Patching Applications

Updating or patching an application generally isn't as critical as the operating system, with the exception of your security software. As I mentioned in the last section, Windows Update and other OS updating software can sometimes find updates for your applications as well. If not, the application manufacturer will release updates and patches as downloadable files on their website. These updates are installed just like the application, with an .exe, .msi, .zip, or other file you open to begin the installation.

Security software is the one major exception. You always want to make sure that your security software is up to date, which includes its definitions library. Earlier in this chapter we looked at Norton Internet Security and its setting for automatic updates. Regardless of the antivirus or other security program you have installed, automatic updates are a good idea. They keep you from forgetting and then ending up having not updated in several months. If you do want to manually control your security updates, it's recommended that you run them at least once per week.

Updating Drivers

Drivers also require infrequent updates. Usually the only time you will want to update a driver is if you are having problems with your hardware. For example, I was having issues with my video card. Occasionally when I would resize windows in Windows, the display would freeze, go black, and then return to normal. I would see an error message stating that my display device driver had stopped responding. I updated the driver and the problem went away.

 The best place to get drivers is always the manufacturer's website.

You can get to your device drivers to check for updates in a few different ways. One of the easiest ways in Windows is to open Device Manager by clicking Start and then right-clicking Computer and choosing Manage. Device Manager is in the Computer Management app shown in Figure 4.33.

In Figure 4.33, you can see the hardware devices in the center pane. If you right-click any of the devices, you will get an option that says Update Driver Software. Click that and you will get a screen similar to the one shown in Figure 4.34.

You can let Windows search the Internet for an updated driver, or you can point Windows to the location of a driver if you have downloaded one. If Windows searches and does not find an updated driver, it will let you know. Otherwise you can install it.

FIGURE 4.33 Device Manager

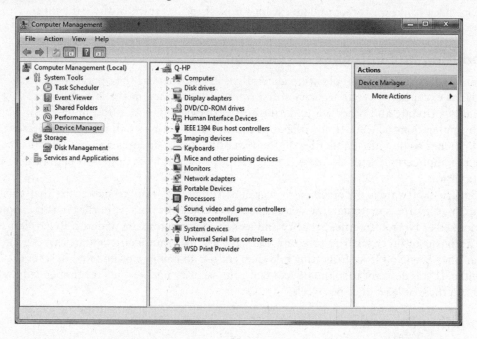

FIGURE 4.34 Update Driver Software screen

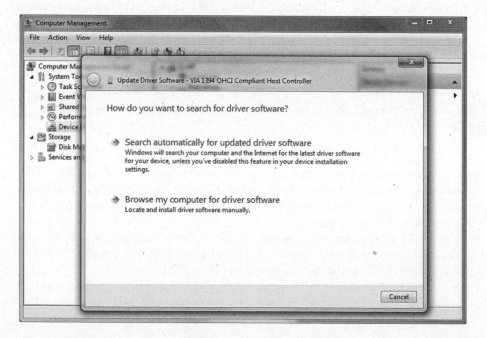

Another way to manage drivers is to right-click the device and choose Properties. Then go to the Drivers tab, as shown in Figure 4.35. From there you can look at driver details, update the driver, roll back the driver, disable the device, or uninstall the driver.

FIGURE 4.35   Driver management

Occasionally you will run into issues where you install a driver update and it causes more problems than you originally had. In situations like that you can roll back the driver. This basically uninstalls the current version of the driver and reinstalls the previous version. From there, you can continue to troubleshoot the situation as needed.

Summary

In this chapter, I covered a wide range of information on software applications. I started with software concepts, such as the platform the software can run on (which OS as well as desktop, mobile, and web based), compatibility, and file extensions.

Next, you learned about different classifications of software. The first was productivity software, which helps you get your job done. Examples include word processing, spreadsheets, email, presentation software, and desktop publishing. Collaboration software was next, and that includes videoconferencing, online workspaces and storage, and instant messaging. The third category was utility software, which includes the important anti-malware and firewall software apps, as well as diagnostic software and compression programs. The last category we looked at was specialized software, really seven categories in one. Examples included CAD and graphic design; medical, scientific, and financial software; and games and entertainment.

The next major section was on best practices for software management. There, you learned about more details on software compatibility as well as licensing types and requirements. Then, we talked about installing and uninstalling software. Finally, I ended the chapter with patching and updating software on computer systems.

Exam Essentials

Know executable file extensions.   Executable file extensions include .exe, .msi, .app, .bat, and .scexe.

Understand examples of productivity software.   Productivity software includes word processing, spreadsheets, email, basic databases, PDF viewers and creators, presentation software, desktop publishing, personal information manager, and remote desktop software.

Know document file extensions.   Document file extensions include .txt, .rtf, .doc/.docx, .xls/.xlsx, .ppt/.pptx, and .pdf.

Know image file extensions.   Image file extensions include .jpg, .gif, .tiff, .png, and .bmp.

Be able to give examples of collaboration software.   Collaboration software includes online workspace, document storage and sharing, screen sharing, videoconferencing, instant messaging, and email.

Know some examples of utility software.   Utility software includes anti-malware, software firewalls, diagnostic and maintenance software, and compression utilities.

Know file compression formats.   File compression formats include .rar, .tar, .zip, .dmg, .iso, .7z, .gz, and .jar.

Understand video file extensions.   Video file extensions include .mpg, .mp4, .flv, .wmv, and .avi.

Know the common audio file extensions.   Audio file extensions include `.mp3`, `.wav`, `.flac`, `.aac`, and `.m4a`.

Understand licensing and activation processes.   Software that you purchase comes with a license to use it, which defines how you can use the software and how many people can use it. Some software packages require you to activate them before they will work, linking that software to your computer.

Know how to install and uninstall applications.   Installing applications is typically done by double-clicking the `.exe` or other installation file or by inserting the CD and letting it auto-run. Software manager tools within your OS are generally used to uninstall applications.

Know where to configure OS auto-updates.   Windows automatic updates are configured through Windows Update. Macs use Software Update, and while Linux systems can differ, many will have a feature similar to Lubuntu's Update Manager.

Chapter 4 Lab

Chapter 4 introduced a lot of software concepts that are good to know and some that are absolutely critical to the safety of your computer. For this lab, you are going to actually do two separate activities.

First, you should familiarize yourself with software that you have not used before. Most people are familiar with Microsoft Office, but not everyone has seen a competing office suite. So for the first part of the lab, go to `www.openoffice.org` and download Apache OpenOffice. Install it and open it. In particular, play with Writer and Calc, or whichever Microsoft Office equivalent you are most familiar with. Can you find what you need in the menus? Also, if you have a `.doc` or an `.xls` file, see if you can open it in OpenOffice. Does it work like it's supposed to?

For the second part of your lab, you need to make sure that your computer is secure and up to date on its important patches. Here are some steps you can take:

1. If you don't have antivirus or anti-malware software, install some! Options are suggested in the chapter, and you can also Google search for recommended options from reputable sources.

2. If you do have antivirus software, open it up and see when the last time it updated its definitions was. It should be within the last week. If not, update them.

3. Make sure that your OS is scheduled to receive automatic updates. Perhaps you have a good reason why you might not want them installed automatically, but for the most part, installing automatically is the best bet.

Review Questions

1. Which of the following file formats were designed to replace .mp3? (Choose two.)

   A. .mp4

   B. .flac

   C. .aac

   D. .m4a

2. Rose opens her software application and gets a message stating that she has only 16 more uses of the product available. Given this scenario, what is her best course of action in order to use it more than 16 additional times?

   A. Activate the software.

   B. Register the software.

   C. Uninstall and reinstall the software.

   D. Not close the application any more.

3. Which of the following file formats indicates a program that can be run on a Macintosh computer?

   A. .msi

   B. .bat

   C. .app

   D. .prog

4. You have just purchased licensed software and want to install it. Which of the following are you required to enter to install this software?

   A. Your name and contact information

   B. The product key

   C. The serial number of your processor

   D. None of the above

5. Which file format is used on optical media, such as CD-ROMs?

   A. .iso

   B. .dmg

   C. .rar

   D. .zip

6. John purchases a single-user software license for an application and installs it on his desktop. Then he installs it on his laptop computer. In this scenario, which of the following statements is true?

    A. John can use the application on both computers at the same time.

    B. John can use the application on both computers but only one at a time.

    C. John can use the application on only one of the computers.

    D. John can share the application with his friends to install on their computers.

7. Which of the following image formats produces the best quality images?

    A. .tiff

    B. .bmp

    C. .jpg

    D. .gif

8. Word processing, spreadsheets, and presentation software are examples of what?

    A. Productivity software

    B. Collaboration software

    C. Utility software

    D. Operating system add-ins

9. Mac OS X disk image files have what extension?

    A. .osx

    B. .img

    C. .dmg

    D. .iso

10. What software is designed to let the OS talk to hardware?

    A. Driver

    B. Application

    C. Patch

    D. Virtual

11. Which one of the following compression file extensions doesn't actually use compression?

    A. .rar

    B. .tar

    C. .7z

    D. .gz

12. When thinking of software compatibility, which two factors matter most? (Choose two.)

    A. If the software will work with other software on the computer

    B. If the software will work with the operating system

    C. If the minimum hardware requirements are met

    D. If the software comes with automatic updates

13. You have just plugged in a new HP printer to your Mac. You can't find a printer driver. What should you do given the circumstances?

    A. Use the default HP printer driver for Mac OS X.

    B. Visit Apple's website to download the printer driver.

    C. Visit HP's website to download the printer driver.

    D. Run Software Update to automatically install the printer driver.

14. Susan wants to play the games that come with Windows on her computer, but they are not on the Start menu. What should she do in this scenario?

    A. Install the games from Control Panel.

    B. Install the games from Windows Update.

    C. Install the games from System Update.

    D. Delete and reinstall Windows.

15. Which of the following file extensions is a worksheet created in a Microsoft spreadsheet application likely to have?

    A. .spd

    B. .ppt

    C. .mss

    D. .xls

16. You just installed an antivirus program on your laptop computer. Given a scenario in which you want to maintain proper levels of security, how often should you update the software?

    A. At least once a week

    B. At least once a month

    C. At least once a year

    D. Only when a new virus is discovered

17. Which file extension is used for files that execute multiple commands from within a Windows command prompt?

    A. .cmd

    B. .bat

    C. .exe

    D. .scexe

18. Your boss calls you on the phone while he is trying to install software. It is telling him that he needs a product key. Where should you tell him to look for it? (Choose two.)

    A. On the package the installation CD came in

    B. In an email from the manufacturer

    C. On the screen in the Options menu

    D. In Windows Update

19. A .ppt file is what type of file?

    A. Spreadsheet

    B. Database

    C. Compression

    D. Presentation

20. Michael receives an email from an unknown user with a file attachment in it that has an .exe extension. What should Michael do in this situation?

    A. Delete the email.

    B. Double-click the file to open it.

    C. Save the file to his desktop and then open it.

    D. Right-click the file to identify its product key, and then install it.

Networking Technologies and Wireless Routers

THE FOLLOWING COMPTIA IT FUNDAMENTALS EXAM OBJECTIVES ARE COVERED IN THIS CHAPTER:

✓ **3.2 Given a scenario, use security best practices**

- Open WiFi vs. secure WiFi

✓ **4.1 Given a scenario, set up and configure a basic SOHO router (wired / wireless)**

- Verify wired connection, if applicable
- Set WEP vs. WPA vs. WPA2
- Change SSID from default
- Apply a new wireless password
- Change admin password for router
- Connect to the new network
- Verify internet connectivity
- Update firmware if necessary

✓ **4.2 Compare and contrast cellular, wireless and wired data connections**

- High vs. low mobility
- High vs. low availability
- High vs. low throughput/bandwidth
- High vs. low reliability
- Connection delay
- Number of concurrent connections
- Levels of security

It seems like nearly everyone is on the Internet these days. Media that used to be restricted to desktop and laptop computers is now accessible by small handheld devices like smartphones and even smart wristwatches. This chapter is called "Networking Technologies and Wireless Routers," but it could just as easily be called "Getting on the Internet."

Now to be fair, this chapter is about setting up a small network for your small office/home office (SOHO) environment, which means it's about connecting computers to each other and not just the Internet. It just happens that many of us get twitchy when we have to go more than a few hours without getting our update on what's going on in the world.

To start off this chapter, I'll cover network connection types and features. If you're new to networking, this will be a good primer for you to understand the different types of connections you can make both within a network and when connecting your network to the outside world. As part of that discussion, I'll compare and contrast the different types of connections so you can make the best decision possible for your needs.

The second major section of this chapter will focus on setting up a SOHO router. First, I'll talk about network connectivity essentials—details you need to know about how computers communicate with each other over a network. I will then take that base of information and dive into the specifics of setting up a small router to give you what you really want: that reliable connection to other computers (and the Internet!).

Connection Types and Features

There are a lot of analogies we can make between humans and computers. You've already heard analogies for hardware, such as the motherboard being the nervous system of a computer and the processor being the brain. These comparisons can continue when it comes to connecting computers together.

For people to communicate with one another, they need to be connected somehow. It used to be that people needed to be in the same physical location to speak to each other. Then, technology improved, and by 1876 people could say things like, "Mr. Watson, come here. I want to see you," into a little box with wires sticking out of it, and other people could hear them in the next room. That technology worked well enough, but then humans figured out how to communicate via radio waves. Today, humans are so advanced as a species that when some apparently crazy person walks down the street seemingly talking loudly to himself, he might actually be talking to a good friend by using a small wireless device hooked to his ear. The line between insanity and technology-enabled has possibly blurred a bit, but that's not the point of this section.

The point is computers need to be connected to each other to communicate as well. And the same holds true for our other mobile electronic devices. The first computer networks relied on wired physical connections, and technology has evolved to provide relatively high-speed wireless communications as well.

There are several available options when it comes to connecting devices together. In this first section, I will talk about how these types of connections work. After that, I will compare and contrast their features so you can make an informed decision on which type of connection is best for your situation.

Choosing a Connection Type

The CompTIA IT Fundamentals exam objectives list three different types of connections you need to be familiar with:

- Wired
- Wireless
- Cellular

Cellular connections (think of your smartphone) are certainly wireless, but wireless networking and cellular communications technologies work in different ways.

These three designations are important to know, and I will use them throughout this chapter. This section will be organized a bit differently, though, into connections you will make within your network and those you will make to connect your network to other networks.

There are two reasons for organizing this way. First, later in this chapter you will learn to set up and configure a basic SOHO router. That process alone is fine, but the assumption is that you will have computers (or mobile devices) connected to this router, and you will also have this router connected to the rest of the world. It's hard to know how to make these connections without the right background. Second, the three technologies you need to understand have different pros and cons, which make some better suited for external connections than for internal connections and vice versa.

Finally, you also need to think about the future. When choosing a connection type, think about not only what the needs are today but also what the needs could be in two or three years. There is no sense in going overboard and buying a top-of-the-line solution if it's not needed, but you do want to plan for expansion if that's a possibility.

Choosing External Network Connections

By "external" connection, I really mean "Internet" connection, because that's the most common connection type, by a significant margin. Internet connections can be broadly broken into two categories: dial-up and broadband. It used to be that you had to weigh the pros and cons and figure out which one was best for your situation. Today, the choice is easy. Go broadband. The only time you would want to use dial-up is if broadband isn't available, and if that's the case, I'm sorry!

Your Internet connection will give you online service through an *Internet service provider (ISP)*. The type of service you want will often determine what your ISP choices are. For example, if you want cable Internet, your choices are limited to your local cable companies and a few national providers. I'll outline some of the features of each type of service and discuss why you might or might not want a specific connection type based on the situation.

Dial-up/POTS

One of the oldest ways of communicating with ISPs and remote networks is through dial-up connections. Although this is still possible, dial-up is rarely used anymore because of limitations on modem speed, which tops out at 56 Kbps. Dial-up uses modems that operate over regular phone lines—that is, the *plain old telephone service (POTS)*—and cannot compare to speeds possible with broadband. In 2000, about 74 percent of American households used dial-up Internet connections. By 2013 that number had dropped to 3 percent, according to the Pew Research Center. Most of the people who still use dial-up do it because it's cheaper than broadband or because high-speed access isn't available where they live.

The biggest advantage to dial-up is that it's cheap and relatively easy to configure. The only hardware you need is a modem and a phone cable. You dial into a server (such as an ISP's server), provide a username and a password, and you're on the Internet.

Companies also have the option to grant users dial-up access to their networks. As with Internet connections, this option used to be a lot more popular than it is today. Microsoft offered a server-side product to facilitate this called Remote Access Service (RAS), as did many other companies. Today you might still hear people talking about connecting remotely to your company's network as "remote access."

It seems that dial-up is considered to be a relic from the Stone Age of Internet access. But there are some reasons why it might be the right solution:

- The only hardware it requires is a modem and a phone cord.
- It's relatively easy to set up and configure.
- It's the cheapest online solution (usually $10 to $20 per month).
- You can use it wherever there is phone service, which is just about everywhere.

Of course, there are reasons why a dial-up connection might not be appropriate. The big one is speed. If you need to download files or have substantial data requirements, dial-up is probably too slow. In addition, with limited bandwidth, it's really good only for one computer. It *is* possible to share a dial-up Internet connection by using software tools, but it's also possible to push a stalled car up a muddy hill. Neither option sounds like much fun.

DSL

One of the two most popular broadband choices for home use is *digital subscriber line (DSL)*. It utilizes existing phone lines and provides fairly reliable high-speed access. To use DSL, you need a DSL modem (shown in Figure 5.1) and a network card in your computer. The ISP usually provides the DSL modem, but you can also purchase them in a variety of electronics stores. You use a network cable with an RJ-45 connector to plug your network card into the DSL modem (Figure 5.2) and the phone cord to plug the DSL modem into the phone outlet.

FIGURE 5.1   A DSL modem

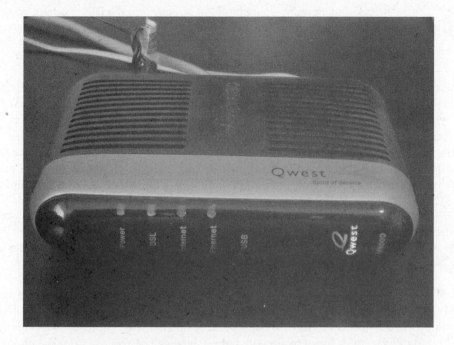

FIGURE 5.2   The back of the DSL modem

Instead of plugging your computer directly into the DSL modem, you can plug your computer into a router (such as a wireless router) and then plug the router into the DSL modem. This allows multiple devices to use the DSL connection.

There are actually several different forms of DSL, including *high bit-rate DSL (HDSL)*, *very high bit-rate DSL (VDSL)*, *rate-adaptive DSL (RADSL)*, *symmetric DSL (SDSL)*, and *asymmetric DSL (ADSL)*. The most popular in-home form of DSL is ADSL. It's asymmetrical because it supports download speeds that are faster than upload speeds. Dividing up the total available bandwidth this way makes sense because most Internet traffic is downloaded, not uploaded. Imagine a 10-lane highway. If you knew that 8 out of 10 cars that drove the highway went south, wouldn't you make 8 lanes southbound and only 2 lanes northbound? That is essentially what ADSL does.

ADSL and voice communications can work at the same time over the phone line because they use different frequencies on the same wire.

The first ADSL standard was approved in 1998 and offered maximum download speeds of 8 Mbps and upload speeds of 1 Mbps. Today, you will see telephone companies offer maximum DSL download speeds of around 30 Mbps with 5 Mbps uploads. The speed you actually get will vary on a lot of factors, including the distance you are from the phone company's equipment.

Some phone companies might offer speeds up to 1 Gbps. These are fiber-optic connections, which are not technically DSL, and are covered later.

One major advantage that DSL providers tout is that with DSL you do not share bandwidth with other customers, whereas that may not be true with cable modems.

To summarize, here are some advantages to using DSL:

- It's *much* faster than dial-up.
- Your bandwidth is not shared with other users.
- It's generally very reliable (depending on your ISP).

There are some potential disadvantages as well:

- DSL may not be available in your area. There are distance limitations as to how far away from the phone company's central office you can be to get DSL. Usually this isn't a problem in metro areas, but it could be a problem in rural areas.
- DSL requires more hardware than dial-up: a network card, a network cable, a DSL modem, and a phone cord. And you usually pay a monthly rental fee for the DSL modem.

- The cost is higher. Lower-speed packages often start off at around $30 to $40 per month, but the ones they advertise with the great data rates can easily run you $100 a month or more.
- If you are in a house or building with older wiring, the older phone lines may not be able to support the full speed you pay for.

That said, DSL is a popular choice for both small businesses and home users. If it's available, it's easy to get the phone company to bundle your service with your landline and bill you at the same time. Often you'll also get a package discount for having multiple services. Most important, you can hook up the DSL modem to your router or wireless router and share the Internet connection among several computers. The phone companies don't like the fact that you can do this (they want you to pay for more access), but as of now there's not a lot they can do about it.

 To see if DSL is available in your area, go to www.dslreports.com. You can also talk to your local telephone service provider.

With many people using their cell phones as their home phones and landlines slowly fading into history, you may wonder if this causes a problem if you want DSL. Not really. Many phone providers will provide you DSL without a landline (called *naked DSL*). Of course, you are going to have to pay a surcharge for the use of the phone line if you don't already use one.

Cable

The other half of the popular home-broadband duet is the *cable modem*. These provide high-speed Internet access through your cable service, much like DSL does over phone lines. You plug your computer into the cable modem using a standard Ethernet cable, just as you would plug into a DSL modem. The only difference is that the other connection goes into a cable TV jack instead of the phone jack. Cable Internet provides broadband Internet access via a specification known as Data Over Cable Service Internet Specification (DOCSIS). Anyone who can get a cable TV connection should be able to get the service.

As advertised, cable Internet connections are generally faster than DSL connections. While cable is generally regarded as faster than DSL, a big caveat to these speeds is that they are not guaranteed and they can vary.

One of the reasons that speeds may vary is that you are sharing available bandwidth within your distribution network. The size of the network varies but is usually between 100 and 2,000 customers. Some of them may have cable modems too, and access can be slower during peak usage times. Another reason is that cable companies make liberal use of bandwidth throttling. If you read the fine print on some of their packages that promise the fast speeds, one of the technical details is that they boost your download speed for the first 10 MB or 20 MB of a file transfer, and then they throttle your speed back down to your normal rate.

It may seem as though I am a bit negative about cable modems, but you need to understand exactly what you are getting. In practice, the speeds of cable modems are pretty comparable to those of DSL. Both have pros and cons when it comes to reliability and speed of service, but most of that varies by service provider and isn't necessarily reflective of the technology. When it comes right down to it, the choice you make between DSL and cable (if both are available in your area) may depend on which company you get the best package deal from: phone and DSL through your telephone company or cable TV and cable modem from your cable provider.

To summarize, here are the advantages to using cable:

- It's *much* faster than dial-up, and it can be faster than DSL (particularly for uploads).
- You're not required to have or use a telephone landline.
- It's generally very reliable (depending on your ISP).

As with anything else, there are possible disadvantages:

- Cable may not be available in your area. In metro areas this normally isn't a problem, but it could be in rural areas.
- Cable requires more hardware than dial-up: a network card, a network cable, and a cable modem. Most ISPs will charge you a one-time fee or a monthly lease fee for the cable modem.
- Your bandwidth is shared with everyone on your network segment, usually a neighborhood-sized group of homes. Everyone shares the available bandwidth. During peak times, your access speed may slow down.
- The cost is higher. Lower-speed packages often start off at around $20 to $30 per month, but the ones they advertise with the great data rates can easily run you $100 a month or more.

Cable modems can be connected directly to a computer but can also be connected to a router or wireless router just like a DSL modem. Therefore, you can share an Internet connection over a cable modem.

For detailed information about broadband Internet availability and performance, check out www.highspeedinternet.com.

Fiber-Optic Internet

Fiber-optic cable is pretty impressive with the speed and bandwidth it delivers. For nearly all of fiber-optic cable's existence, it's been used mostly for high-speed telecommunications and network backbones. This is because it is much more expensive than copper to install and operate. The cables themselves are pricier, and so is the hardware at the end of the cables.

Technology follows this inevitable path of getting cheaper the longer it exists, and fiber is really starting to embrace its destiny. Some telephone and media companies are now offering fiber-optic Internet connections for home subscribers.

An example of one such option is FiOS, offered by Verizon. It offers *Fiber-to-the-Home (FTTH)* service, which means that the cables are 100 percent fiber from their data centers to your home. At the time we were writing this book, the fastest speeds offered were 500 Mbps download and 35 Mbps upload. That means you could download a two-hour HD movie in about two minutes. That's ridiculous.

Are there any downsides to a fiber Internet connection? Really only two come to mind. The first is availability. It's still pretty spotty as to where you can get it. The second is price. That great fast connection can cost you about $200 a month.

Satellite

One type of broadband Internet connection that does not get much fanfare is satellite Internet. *Satellite Internet* is not much like any other type of broadband connection. Instead of a cabled connection, it uses a satellite dish to receive data from an orbiting satellite and relay station that is connected to the Internet. Satellite connections are typically a lot slower than wired broadband connections, often maxing out at around 4 Mbps.

The need for a satellite dish and the reliance on its technology are one of the major drawbacks to satellite Internet. People who own satellite dishes will tell you that there are occasional problems due to weather and satellite alignment. You must keep the satellite dish aimed precisely at the satellite or your signal strength (and thus your connection reliability and speed) will suffer. Plus, cloudy or stormy days can cause interference with the signal, especially if there are high winds that could blow the satellite dish out of alignment. Receivers are typically small satellite dishes (like the ones used for DIRECTV or Dish Network) but can also be portable satellite modems (modems the size of a briefcase) or portable satellite phones.

Satellite Internet is often referred to as "line of sight" wireless because it does require a clear line of sight between the user and the transmitter.

Another drawback to satellite technology is the delay (also called *connection delay*), or *latency*. The delay occurs because of the length of time required to transmit the data and receive a response via the satellite. This delay (between 250 and 350 milliseconds) comes from the time it takes the data to travel the approximately 35,000 kilometers into space and return. To compare it with other types of broadband signals, cable and DSL have a delay between customer and ISP of 10 to 30 milliseconds. With standard web and email traffic, this delay, while slightly annoying, is acceptable. However, with technologies like VoIP and live Internet gaming, the delay is intolerable.

Online gamers are especially sensitive to latency. They often refer to it as *ping time*. The higher the ping time (in milliseconds), the worse the response time in the game. It sometimes means the difference between winning and losing an online game.

Of course, satellite also has advantages or no one would use it. First, satellite connections are incredibly useful when you are in an area where it's difficult or impossible to run a cable or if your Internet access needs are mobile and cellular data rates just don't cut it.

The second advantage is due to the nature of the connection. This type of connection is called *point-to-multipoint* because one satellite can provide a signal to a number of receivers simultaneously. It's used in a variety of applications from telecommunications and handheld GPSs to television and radio broadcasts and a host of others.

Here are a few considerations to keep in mind regarding satellite:

Installation can be tricky.   When installing a satellite system, you need to ensure that the satellite dish on the ground is pointed at precisely the right spot in the sky. This can be tricky to do if you're not trained, but some have a utility that helps you see how close you are to being right on (you're getting warmer… warmer…).

Line of sight is required.   Satellite communications also require line of sight. A tree between you and your orbiting partner will cause problems. Rain and other atmospheric conditions can cause problems as well.

Latency can be a problem.   Because of the long distance the message must travel, satellites can be subject to long latency times. While it happens with wired connections, it disproportionately affects satellite transmissions. Have you ever watched a national news channel when a reporter is reporting from some location halfway across the world? The anchor behind the desk will ask a question, and the reporter will nod, and nod, and finally about five excruciating seconds after the anchor has finished speaking, the reporter will start to answer. That's latency.

Most satellite connections are also pretty slow compared to the other broadband methods. Average speed for downloads is often 256 Kbps to 1.5 Mbps, and uploads are in the 128 Kbps to 256 Kbps range. In addition, many providers set thresholds on the amount of data you can download per month. Going over that amount can result in extra charges.

 Real World Scenario

All in the Name of Entertainment

As a teenager, I worked for a local television station during the summer. Each summer, the television station would broadcast a Senior PGA golf tournament that was held on a nearby mountain course.

Before the tournament, the crew would spend three days setting up the control truck, cameras, and link back to the station. (It was a network with TV cameras instead of workstations!) Because of the remote location, the crew had to set up a satellite uplink to get the signals back to civilization. From the control truck, a transmitter was pointed at a relay station on the side of the mountain, which in turn was pointed at a satellite orbiting the earth. It took a team of four engineers to get it set up. Two engineers would stay at the truck, and two others would board ATVs and journey up the remote mountainside. Once in position, they would set up the relay station, which looked a lot like a keg of beer with a few antennas. The engineers at the truck would adjust their directional microwave transmitter until the relay station received a strong signal. Then the engineers on the mountainside would perform the arduous task of pointing their transmitter at the satellite.

It was a long and tedious process, and that's really the point of the story. Satellite was the *only* option available to complete the network, but satellite networks can be a challenge to set up and configure.

Cellular (Cellular Networking)

The cell phone, once a clunky brick-like status symbol of the well-to-do, is now pervasive in our society. It seems that everyone—from kindergarteners to 80-year-old grandmothers—has a cell. The industry has revolutionized the way people communicate and, some say, contributed to furthering an attention-deficit-disorder-like, instant-gratification-hungry society. In fact, the line between cell phones and computers has blurred significantly with all of the new smartphones on the market. It used to be that the Internet was reserved for "real" computers, but now anyone can be online at almost any time.

Regardless of your feelings about cell phones, whether you are fanatical about checking in every time you visit a local eatery to ensure you're the "mayor" or you long for the good-old days when you could escape your phone because it had a functional radius as long as your cord, you need to understand the basics of cell technology.

Cellular Technical Specifications

For years, there have been two major cell standards used around the world. The Global System for Mobile Communications (GSM) is the most popular, boasting over 1.5 billion users in 210 countries. The other standard is code division multiple access (CDMA), which was developed by Qualcomm and is available only in the United States.

Both are considered 3G (or third-generation) mobile technologies, and each has its advantages. GSM was introduced first, and when CDMA was launched, it was much faster than GSM. GSM eventually caught up, though, and the two now have relatively similar data rates. The biggest issue is that GSM and CDMA are not compatible with each other. Whatever technology you get is based on the provider you sign up with. Sprint and Verizon use CDMA, and AT&T and T-Mobile use GSM. That means that if you have a CMDA phone through Verizon, you can't switch (with that phone) to AT&T. And, your CDMA phone won't work outside the United States.

Now we have 4G technology available, which is the new global standard designed to make 3G obsolete. If you turn on the TV, you can't help but be bombarded with commercials (if you don't fast-forward through them) from cell providers pitching the fastest or widest or whatever-est *4G LTE (Long-Term Evolution)* network.

The biggest enhancement in 4G LTE over 3G is speed. Whereas with 3G technology you were limited to about 500 Kbps downloads, some 4G LTE networks will give you download speeds of 10–20 Mbps and upload speeds of 3–10 Mbps. (The theoretical maximum for LTE is 300 Mbps download and 75 Mbps upload.) The range of 4G LTE depends on the tower and obstructions in the way. The optimal cell size is about 3.1 miles (5 km) in rural areas, and you can get reasonable performance for about 19 miles (30 km).

Mobile Hotspots

Many cell phone providers offer network cards (or they incorrectly call them modems) that allow your laptop computer or other non-cellular device to connect to the cellular network (and the Internet) from anywhere you can get a cell signal. This is called a *mobile hotspot*. Some providers will bundle that service with your normal monthly cell service at no additional charge, while others will charge you an incremental fee. The term you'll hear a lot in connection with this is *MiFi*. Figure 5.3 shows a Verizon MiFi hotspot.

FIGURE 5.3 MiFi hotspot

A MiFi card such as this allows you to connect up to five Wi-Fi–enabled devices as a MiFi cloud to get Internet access. After you purchase a MiFi device, you first connect it to your laptop via USB cable for activation and setup. Once that step is complete, you can go entirely wireless. MiFi supports Wi-Fi security such as WEP, WPA, and WPA2, which we will talk about later in this chapter.

Table 5.1 summarizes the connection types you have just learned about. In Exercise 5.1, you will scout out the Internet connection options in your area.

TABLE 5.1 Common Internet connection types and speeds

Designation	Maximum Download Speed	Description
Dial-up	Up to 56 Kbps	Plain old telephone service. A regular analog phone line.
DSL	Up to 30 Mbps	Digital subscriber line. Shares existing phone wires with voice service.
Cable	Up to 50 Mbps	Inexpensive broadband Internet access method with wide availability.
Fiber-optic	Up to 500 Mbps	Incredibly fast and just as expensive.
Cellular	Up to 20 Mbps (realistically)	Great range; supported by cell phone providers. Best for a very limited number of devices.
Satellite	Up to 4 Mbps	Great for rural areas without cabled broadband methods.

Sometimes, the Choices Are Limited

Before you decide which broadband connection sounds the most appealing to you, you should also factor in something very important: what is available in your area. DSL is available at different rates of connectivity based on distance from a central station. If you live far enough from a central station, or near a central station that has not been updated lately (such as in the middle of rural America), DSL may not be an option. Similarly, not all cable providers are willing to take the steps necessary to run a connection in all situations.

Make certain you know the available options—not just the technological options—before you spend too much time determining what is best for you.

EXERCISE 5.1

Pricing Internet Connectivity

1. Visit the website for a telephone provider in your area, and see what offers are available for DSL. What is the most basic package that you can get, and what does it cost? What is the fastest package you can get, and what does it cost?

2. Visit the website for a cable television provider in your area, and see what offers are available for cable Internet. What is the most basic package that you can get, and what does it cost? What is the fastest package you can get, and what does it cost?

3. Visit the website for a satellite Internet provider. If you're not familiar with one, www.hughesnet.com is a popular provider. What's the fastest package you can get, and what does it cost?

4. (Optional) Can you find a dial-up ISP in your area? How much does it cost?

Choosing Internal Network Connections

Along with deciding how your computers will get to the outside world, you need to think about how your computers will communicate with each other on your internal network. The choices you make will depend on the speed you need, distance and security requirements, and cost involved with installation and maintenance. It may also depend some on the abilities of the installer. You may feel comfortable replacing Category 6 cables but not so much when it comes to fiber-optic. Your choices for internal connections can be lumped into two groups: wired and wireless.

Many networks today are a hybrid of wired and wireless connections. Understand the fundamentals of how each works separately; then you can understand how they work together. Every wireless connection eventually connects back to a wired network point somehow.

Wired Network Connections

Wired connections form the backbone of nearly every network in existence. Even as wireless becomes more popular, the importance of wired connections remains strong. In general, wired networks are faster and more secure than their wireless counterparts.

When it comes to choosing a wired network connection type, you need to think about speed, distance, and cost. Your two choices are *unshielded twisted pair (UTP)*, which is copper, and *fiber-optic*. You'll run one of the two (or maybe a combination of the two), with UTP being by far the most common choice. The most common configuration when you use either of these is to connect all computers to a central connectivity device, such as a hub or a switch. If you're using a wireless router with some wired ports, that works too.

The first question you need to ask yourself is, "How fast does this network need to be?" For most networks, the 100 Mbps provided by UTP running Fast Ethernet is probably sufficient. If you have higher throughput requirements, then you can start looking into Gigabit Ethernet (1 Gbps) or faster (10 Gbps).

What Is Ethernet?

Ethernet is a standard for wired computer network communications, as defined by the IEEE 802.3 specification. It specifies that only one computer can talk on the network at one time; a computer will listen on the network, and if it doesn't hear any traffic it will transmit. If two or more computers attempt to talk at once, the network packets will collide, and no communication will get to its destination. The sending computers will detect this, wait a short random amount of time, and then resend their data. This whole process is called Carrier Sense Multiple Access with Collision Detection (CSMA/CD).

In 1990, the Ethernet specification called for transmissions of 10 Mbps over twisted-pair copper cable. At the time, the cable standard was Category 3 (Cat-3) UTP. By 1991, a standard was developed for Cat-5 cable, and it could handle speeds of 100 Mbps. (They increased the number of twists per foot in the cable.) The Ethernet standard was updated to account for this faster speed and was called Fast Ethernet.

The Cat-5e (enhanced) cable standard was introduced in 2001 and could handle speeds of 1 Gbps, so running Ethernet over Cat-5e became known as Gigabit Ethernet. Category 6a came along in 2008, supporting speeds of 10 Gbps (10-Gigabit Ethernet).

In the real world, you'll hear people ask if you have an "Ethernet cable," which is typically synonymous with the words "network cable" and twisted-pair cable. Most of the time, people don't differentiate between the standards, assuming that you just have Cat-5e or better. It's usually a good assumption, considering it's hard to find anything older. If you know that you're running 10-Gig E, then you might want to specify a Cat-6a cable.

The second question is then, "What is the maximum distance I'll need to run any one cable?" In most office environments, you can configure your network in such a way that

100 meters will get you from any connectivity device to the end user. If you need to go longer than that, you'll definitely need fiber for that connection unless you want to mess with signal repeaters.

As you're thinking about what type of cable you will go with, also consider the hardware you'll need. If you are going to run fiber to the desktop, you'll need fiber network cards, routers, and switches. If you are running UTP, you'll need network cards, routers, and switches with RJ-45 connectors. If you're going to run Gigabit, all of your devices will need to support it.

The third question to ask yourself is, "How big of a deal is security?" Most of the time, the answer lies somewhere between "very" and "extremely"! Copper cable is pretty secure, but it does emit a signal that can be intercepted, meaning people can tap into your transmissions (hence the term *wiretap*). Fiber-optic cables are immune to wiretapping. Normally this isn't a big deal because copper cables don't exactly broadcast your data all over as a wireless connection does. But if security is of the utmost concern, then fiber is the way to go.

Fourth, "Is there a lot of electrical interference in the area?" Transmissions across a copper cable can be ravaged by the effects of electromagnetic interference (EMI), which is interference from objects like motors, power cables, and fluorescent lights. Fiber is immune to those effects.

Finally, ask yourself about cost. Fiber cables and hardware are more expensive than their copper counterparts. Table 5.2 summarizes your cable choices and provides characteristics of each.

TABLE 5.2 Cable types and characteristics

Characteristics	Twisted-Pair	Fiber-Optic
Transmission rate	CAT-5: 100 Mbps CAT-5e: 1 Gbps CAT-6a: 10 Gbps	100 Mbps to 10 Gbps
Maximum length	100 meters (328 feet)	~25 miles
Flexibility	Very flexible	Fair
Ease of installation	Very easy	Difficult
Connector	RJ-45	Special (SC, ST, and others)
Interference (security)	Susceptible	Not susceptible
Overall cost	Inexpensive	Expensive
NIC cost	100 Mbps: $15–$40 1Gbps: $30 and up	$100–$150; easily $600–$800 for server NICs
10m cable cost	CAT-5/5e: $8–$12 CAT-6/6a: $12–$15	Depends on mode and connector type, but generally $20–$40
8-port switch cost	100 Mbps: $30–$100 1 Gbps: $70–$400	$350 and up

Understand that the costs shown in Table 5.2 are approximate and are for illustrative purposes only. The cost for this equipment in your area may differ. Fiber has gotten considerably cheaper in the last 5 to 10 years, but it's still far more expensive than copper.

Fiber-optic cabling has some obvious advantages over copper, but as you can see it may be prohibitively expensive to run fiber to the desktop. What a lot of organizations will do is use fiber sparingly, where it is needed the most, and then run copper to the desktop. Fiber will be used in the server room and perhaps between floors of a building as well as any place where a very long cable run is needed.

Wireless Network Connections

People love wireless networks for one major reason: convenience. Wireless connections enable a sense of freedom in users. They're not stuck to their desk; they can work from anywhere! (I'm not sure if this is actually a good thing.) Wireless isn't as fast and it tends to be a bit more expensive than wired copper networks, but the convenience factor far outweighs the others.

Wireless LAN (WLAN)

When thinking about using wireless for network communications, the only real technology option available today is IEEE 802.11. Bluetooth and infrared (which I'll cover in just a bit) can help mobile devices communicate, but they aren't designed for full wireless LAN (WLAN) use. Your choice becomes which 802.11 standard you want to use. Table 5.3 summarizes your options.

TABLE 5.3   802.11 standards

Type	Frequency	Maximum Data Rate	Indoor Range	Outdoor Range
a	5 GHz	54 Mbps	35m	120m
b	2.4 GHz	11 Mbps	40m	140m
g	2.4 GHz	54 Mbps	40m	140m
n	2.4/5 GHz	600 Mbps	70m	250m
ac	5 GHz	1300 Mbps	35m	120m

Not So Fast...

The maximum data rates shown in Table 5.3 are theoretical maximums and should be taken with a large grain of salt. First, the distance from the wireless access point to your device makes a huge difference. Second, interference from other electronics and obstructions will lower the data rate. Third, wireless bandwidth is shared among all devices connecting on that wireless network. Real-world testing shows that 802.11n devices typically max out at 50–150 Mbps, and 802.11ac tops out around 300–350 Mbps.

Also keep in mind that the maximum ranges are ideal estimates too. The farther away you get from the wireless access point, the slower the connection will be.

So how do you choose which one is right for your situation? You can apply the same thinking you would for a wired network in that you need to consider speed, distance, security, and cost. Generally speaking, though, with wireless it's best to start with the most robust technology and work your way backward.

Security concerns on wireless networks are similar regardless of your choice. You're broadcasting network signals through air; there will be some security concerns. It really comes down to speed and cost.

In today's environment it's almost silly to consider 802.11a or 802.11b. Deciding that you are going to install an 802.11b network from the ground up at this point is a bit like saying you are going to build a mud house. You could, but why?

That brings you to your most likely choices: 802.11n and 802.11ac. Devices are plentiful and are backward compatible with the previous versions. (You will see some products branded as 802.11g/n, which means they support both standards.) It will come down to cost. In Exercise 5.2, you will go shopping for Wi-Fi gear to understand the cost differences.

EXERCISE 5.2

The Cost of Networking

1. Visit the website for an electronics store. If you're unfamiliar with any, try www.bestbuy.com or www.frys.com.

2. Find an 802.11ac wireless router. How much is it?

3. Find an older standard. See if you can find an 802.11b one. If not, go for 802.11g. How much is it?

4. Now price out wired network cards. Find a fiber-optic card, and price that versus an Ethernet card that offers similar speeds. Also look at the price of a 25m Cat-6 (or Cat-5) cable versus a 5m fiber-optic cable. How much difference is there?

Bluetooth

Bluetooth is not designed to be a WLAN but rather a wireless personal area network (WPAN). In other words, it's not the right technology to use if you want to set up a wireless network for your office. It is, however, a great technology to use if you have wireless devices that you want your computer to be able to communicate with. Examples include smartphones, mice, keyboards, headsets, and printers.

Nearly every laptop comes with built-in Wi-Fi capabilities, but they don't necessarily come Bluetooth enabled. To use Bluetooth devices, you will need to add an adapter, such as the one shown in Figure 5.4.

FIGURE 5.4   Bluetooth USB adapter

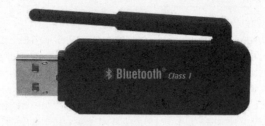

    Almost all smartphones and other mobile devices today support Bluetooth.

Bluetooth devices can belong to one of three classes. Most mobile Bluetooth devices are Class 2 devices, which have a maximum range of 10 meters.

    Like 802.11b/g, Bluetooth uses the unlicensed 2.4 GHz range for communication. To avoid interference, Bluetooth can "signal hop" at different frequencies to avoid conflicts with devices using other technologies in the area. Thanks to technology improvements, interference with Wi-Fi is unlikely, but it can still occur.

One of the unusual features of Bluetooth networks is their temporary nature. With Wi-Fi, you need a central communication point, such as a wireless access point or router. Bluetooth networks are formed on an ad hoc basis, meaning that whenever two Bluetooth devices get close enough to each other, they can communicate directly with each other. This dynamically created network is called a *piconet*. A Bluetooth-enabled device can communicate with up to seven other devices in one piconet.

Infrared

Infrared waves have been around since the beginning of time. They are longer than light waves but shorter than microwaves. The most common use of infrared technology is the television remote control, although infrared is also used in night-vision goggles and medical and scientific imaging.

In 1993 the *Infrared Data Association (IrDA)* was formed as a technical consortium to support "interoperable, low-cost infrared data interconnection standards that support a walk-up, point-to-point user model." The key terms here are *walk-up* and *point-to-point*, meaning you need to be at very close range to use infrared, and it's designed for one-to-one communication. Infrared requires line of sight, and generally speaking, the two devices need to be pointed at each other to work. If you point your remote away from the television, how well does it work?

 More information on the IrDA standard can be found at the organization's website: http://www.irda.org.

Some laptops and mobile devices have a built-in infrared port, which is a small, dark square of plastic, usually black or dark maroon. For easy access, infrared ports are located on the front or side of devices that have them. Figure 5.5 shows an example of an infrared port.

FIGURE 5.5 Infrared port

Current IrDA specifications allow transmission of data up to 1 Gbps, and IrDA claims that 5 Gbps and 10 Gbps standards are being worked on. Because infrared does not use radio waves, there are no concerns of interference or signal conflicts. Atmospheric conditions can play a role in disrupting infrared waves, but considering that the maximum functional range of an IrDA device is about 1 meter, weather is not likely to cause you any problems.

Security is not much of an issue with infrared. The maximum range is about 1 meter with an angle of about 30 degrees, and the signal does not go through walls, so hacking prospects are limited. If someone is making an attempt to intercept an infrared signal, it's going to be pretty obvious. The data is directional, and you choose when and where to send it.

Different Infrared Technologies

You might have read the 1 meter distance limitation in the Infrared section and thought, "But my television remote works at longer distances than that"—and you are right. Television and other consumer electronics remote controls are not governed by IrDA. They use a different infrared technology, based on the RC-5 protocol developed by Philips in the late 1980s. The maximum functional distance of these remote controls is about 15-20 feet, depending on the device.

Computer communications standards using infrared are managed by IrDA, and the maximum distance is about 1 meter. There are methods that IR manufacturers can use to modify this, but the general specification guarantees data rates at only 1 meter.

Comparing and Contrasting Data Connections

After all of that material on which network connections to choose, I hope you feel much more knowledgeable about the options available to you. The most popular way to set up a home or small office network today is to pick DSL or cable as your broadband connection and then run wireless inside your home or office. Mobile devices can easily participate on wireless networks, and then they can use cellular service when you're not in range of your wireless router.

The CompTIA IT Fundamentals exam objectives ask you to compare and contrast cellular, wireless, and wired data connections on seven different attributes. The fact that there are several different types of wired and wireless connections could complicate things, but in general, it's safe to assume that you'll need to compare 4G LTE cellular, Wi-Fi (802.11), and twisted-pair connections. I talked about several of their attributes in the previous sections, but it will be good to summarize them here all in one place:

Mobility   Cellular clearly wins here, since you can take your phone almost anywhere you want. Once you're out of the range of one cell tower, you will be handed off to the next one automatically. Wi-Fi has good mobility; at least it lets you untether from your desk. With a wired connection, you're pretty much limited to the length of your leash.

Availability and Reliability   These are two different objectives, but the answers are really the same for all three types of networks. Wired networks will be the best in these two areas, simply because you're directly connected and not usually worried about interference. Cellular and wireless networks will have lower availability and reliability than wired networks. For the most part, cellular networks perform well on both attributes. If they didn't, they would lose customers. It depends on the carrier, though. Everyone knows of a dead spot where their mobile phone just refuses to work. Wireless networks are probably the lowest on these two attributes, because it's you and me managing them as opposed to an organization that's worried about losing money.

Throughput/Bandwidth   This one is easy. Wired networks are the best, followed by wireless, and then cellular.

Connection Delay   Here too, wired networks are the king. Electricity on the wire travels a lot faster than radio waves. Wireless networks are second, because you're sending the signal no more than a few hundred feet, at most. Cellular signals have to go to a tower that could be several miles away, so they have the most delay.

Number of Concurrent Connections   On this one, both wired networks and cellular networks score high. Wired networks, if configured properly, can easily support thousands of users, and in most cases thousands of users are in range of a single cell tower. Wireless networking falls behind here. For an 802.11n network, you should really limit it to no more than 30–40 users per access point, and 802.11ac networks should be limited to 90–100 users per access point.

Levels of Security   For security, I need to make the assumption that everything is configured properly. That might be a big assumption, but it's all I can go on. Wired networks will be the best, simply because you're not throwing your signals into the air. Wi-Fi will be second best, because if nothing else the range is far more limited than cellular. Cell networks do use encryption, but the fact remains that you could be sending a signal several miles through the air, which means it has a higher likelihood of being intercepted.

Network Connectivity Essentials

The ultimate goal of this chapter is to teach you how to successfully set up your own SOHO network. Sure, the objectives say you need to set up a router, but that more than implies that you're setting up a network. In order to do it right and really understand what you're doing, it's important to know some critical details. After all, there's a difference between plugging in a box and having it work and being able to make it work if things don't quite go smoothly.

In the first section of this chapter, you learned how to physically connect your computers to the Internet, as well as to each other via cables or wireless connections. That's the first part. But now that they're connected to each other, *how* do they communicate? That's just as important, and that's what I'll cover here in the second part.

The "how" is by using a protocol. Specifically, this section will teach you the basics of TCP/IP, which is the language that most computers speak when they talk to each other on a network.

Networking Protocol Basics

Networking protocols are a lot like human languages in that they are the language that computers speak when talking to each other. Technically speaking, a *protocol* is a set of rules that govern communications. If computers don't speak the same language, they won't be able to talk to each other. To complicate matters, there are dozens of different languages that computers can use. Just like humans, computers can understand and use multiple languages. Imagine you are on the street and someone comes up to you and speaks in Spanish. If you know Spanish, you will likely reply in kind. It doesn't matter if both of you know English as well because you've already established that you can communicate. On the other hand, it's going to be a pretty quick conversation if you don't know Spanish. This same concept applies to computers that are trying to communicate. They must have a network protocol in common in order for the conversation to be successful.

Throughout the years, hundreds of network protocols have been developed. As the advent of networking exploded, various companies developed their own networking hardware, software, and proprietary protocols. Although a few achieved long-term success, most have faded into oblivion. The one protocol suite that has sustained is TCP/IP. While it has some structural plusses such as its modularity, it didn't necessarily succeed because it was inherently superior to other protocols. It succeeded because it is the protocol of the Internet.

This is why I focus on TCP/IP. It is the protocol used on the Internet, but it's also the protocol used by the vast majority of home and business networks today. I'll start by taking a quick look at the history of TCP/IP, the model on which it's based, and a few of the common protocols you'll hear about. Then, I'll spend some time on IP addressing, which is essential for proper communication. Entire books have been written on TCP/IP—there's no way I could cover it entirely in one chapter. Instead, I'll give you the foundation you need to understand it well and set up your own network.

 For a more detailed discussion of networking protocols and TCP/IP, read the *CompTIA A+ Complete Study Guide* by Quentin Docter, Emmett Dulaney, and Toby Skandier. The A+ certification is a great one to get after you pass your CompTIA IT Fundamentals exam!

TCP/IP Essentials

Every computer protocol that's created needs to accomplish a specific set of tasks for communication to be successful. To give some structure to these tasks, theoretical networking models were developed in the 1970s. TCP/IP's structure is based on a model created by the United States Department of Defense: the *Department of Defense (DoD) model*. The DoD model has four layers that specify the tasks that need to happen: Process/Application, Host-to-Host, Internet, and Network Access.

The *Transmission Control Protocol/Internet Protocol (TCP/IP) suite* is based on the DoD's theoretical model. While the protocol suite is named after two of its hardest working protocols, Transmission Control Protocol (TCP) and Internet Protocol (IP), TCP/IP actually contains dozens of protocols working together to help computers communicate with one another. Figure 5.6 shows the DoD model's four layers and the TCP/IP protocols that correspond to those layers.

FIGURE 5.6   TCP/IP protocol suite

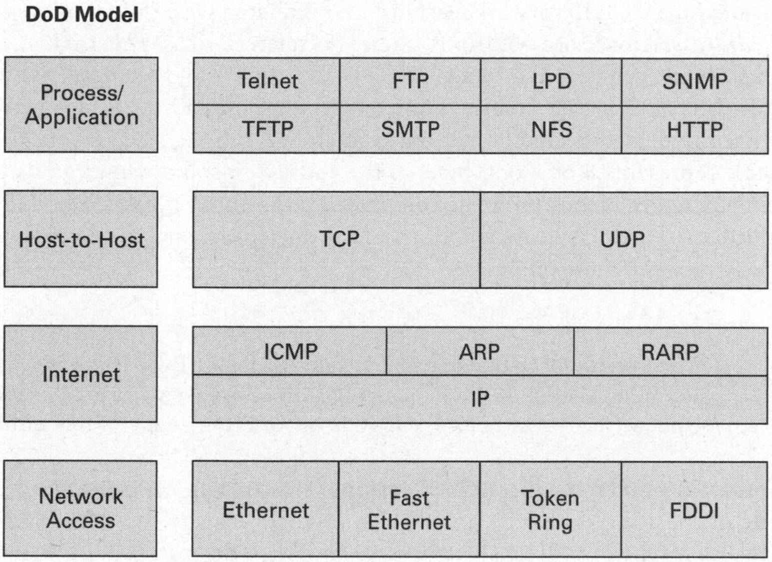

DoD Model

Process/ Application	Telnet	FTP	LPD	SNMP
	TFTP	SMTP	NFS	HTTP

Host-to-Host	TCP		UDP	

Internet	ICMP	ARP		RARP
	IP			

Network Access	Ethernet	Fast Ethernet	Token Ring	FDDI

Don't feel the need to memorize the components of the TCP/IP suite—yet. When you move on to more advanced exams, more detailed knowledge will be required.

Think of TCP/IP as a puzzle. You need one item from each layer to make the puzzle fit together. The majority of TCP/IP protocols are located at the Process/Application layer. You might already be familiar with a few of these, such as *Hypertext Transfer Protocol (HTTP)* and *File Transfer Protocol (FTP)*.

If you've used the Internet, you've used HTTP. When you're in your web browser, nearly all of the websites you visit will have an http:// in front of them. This specifies the use of HTTP. FTP is used for file downloads.

At the Host-to-Host layer, there are only two protocols: TCP and User Datagram Protocol (UDP). Most applications will use one or the other to transmit data, although some can use both but will do so for different tasks.

The most important protocol at the Internet layer is IP. This is the backbone of TCP/IP. Other protocols at this layer work in conjunction with IP, such as Internet Control Message Protocol (ICMP) and Address Resolution Protocol (ARP).

You'll notice that the Network Access layer doesn't have any protocols per se. This layer describes the type of network access method you are using, such as Ethernet, Token Ring, Wi-Fi, or others.

Understanding IP Addressing

To communicate on a TCP/IP network, each device needs to have a unique address, which is called an *IP address*. Any device with an IP address is referred to as a *host*. This can include servers, workstations, printers, and routers. If you can assign it an IP address, it's a host.

An IP address is a 32-bit hierarchical address that identifies a host on the network. It's typically written in dotted-decimal notation, such as 192.168.10.55. Each of the numbers in this example represents 8 bits (or 1 byte) of the address, also known as an *octet*. The same address written in binary (how the computer thinks about it) would be 11000000 10101000 00001010 00110111. As you can see, the dotted-decimal version is a much more convenient way to write these numbers!

> The version of IP that uses 32-bit addresses is IPv4. There is a newer version called IPv6, which uses 128-bit addresses and is slowly being phased in. The structure of IPv6 is beyond the scope of this book.

The addresses are said to be hierarchical, as opposed to "flat," because the numbers at the beginning of the address identify groups of computers that belong to the same network. Because of the hierarchical address structure, we're able to do really cool things like route packets between local networks and on the Internet.

A great example of hierarchical addressing is your street address. Let's say that you live in apartment 4B on 123 Main Street, Anytown, Kansas, USA. If someone sent you a letter via snail mail, the hierarchy of your address would help the postal service and carrier deliver it to the right place. First and broadest is USA. Kansas helps narrow it down a bit, and Anytown narrows it down more. Eventually they get to your street, the right number on your street, and then the right apartment. If the address space were flat (for example, Kansas didn't mean anything more specific than Main Street), or you could name your state anything you wanted to, it would be really hard to get the letter to the right spot.

Take this analogy back to IP addresses. They're set up to logically organize networks to make delivery between them possible and then to identify an individual node within a network. If this structure weren't in place, a huge, multinetwork space like the Internet wouldn't be possible. It would simply be too unwieldy to manage.

Each IP address is made up of two components: the *network ID* and the *host ID*. The network portion of the address always comes before the host portion. Because of the way IP addresses are structured, the network portion does not have to be a specific fixed length. In other words, some computers will use 8 of the 32 bits for the network portion and the other 24 for the host portion, while other computers might use 24 bits for the network portion and the remaining 8 bits for the host portion. Here are a few rules you should know about when working with IP addresses:

- All host addresses on a network must be unique.

- On a routed network (such as the Internet), all network addresses must be unique as well.

- Neither the network ID nor the host ID can be set to all 0s. A host ID portion of all 0s means "this network."

- Neither the network ID nor the host ID can be set to all 1s. A host ID portion of all 1s means "all hosts on this network," commonly known as a broadcast address.

Computers are able to differentiate where the network ID ends and the host address begins through the use of a *subnet mask*. This is a value written just like an IP address and may look something like 255.255.255.0. Any bit that is set to a 1 in the subnet mask makes the corresponding bit in the IP address part of the network ID. The rest will be the host ID. The number 255 is the highest number you will ever see in IP addressing, and it means that all bits in the octet are set to 1.

Here's an example based on two numbers I have used in this chapter. Look at the IP address of 192.168.10.55. Assume that the subnet mask in use with this address is 255.255.255.0. This indicates that the first three octets are the network portion of the address and the last octet is the host portion. Said another way, the network ID is 192.168.10, and the unique host ID is 55.

All of this is important to know because it governs how computers communicate. If a computer wants to send a message to another computer on the same network, it just spits the message out on the wire (or wireless) and the other computer receives it. If the destination is on a different network (as determined by the network address), then the router comes into play. The sender will forward the message to the router to send to the destination. In this case, your router is called a *default gateway*. It's basically the door from your network to the outside world.

 All of this TCP/IP stuff can get a little heady. The keys to remember are that in order to communicate using TCP/IP, each computer is *required* to have an IP address and a correct subnet mask. And, if you want to connect your network to other networks (such as the Internet), a default gateway is also required.

DHCP and DNS

Two critical TCP/IP services you need to be aware of are Dynamic Host Configuration Protocol (DHCP) and Domain Name System (DNS). Both are services that are typically installed on a server (or in the case of DHCP, a router) and both provide key functionality to network clients. I'll talk about them now because they're important components of TCP/IP, and you will see them come up when you configure your router.

DHCP servers can be configured to automatically provide IP configuration information to clients. The following configuration information is typically provided:

- IP address
- Subnet mask
- Default gateway
- DNS server address

DHCP servers can provide a lot more than the items on this list, but those are the most common.

The alternative to DHCP is for an administrator to enter in the IP configuration information manually on each host. This is called *static IP addressing* and is administratively intensive as compared to DHCP's dynamic addressing.

DNS has one function on the network, and that is to resolve hostnames to IP addresses. This sounds simple enough, but it has profound implications.

Think about using the Internet. You open your browser, and in the address bar you type the name of your favorite website, something like www.google.com, and press Enter. The first question your computer asks is, "Who is that?" (Remember, computers understand only 0s and 1s.) Your machine requires an IP address to connect to the website. The DNS server provides the answer, "That is 72.14.205.104." Now that your computer knows the address of the website you want, it's able to traverse the Internet to find it.

Each DNS server has a database where it stores hostname-to-IP-address pairs. If the DNS server does not know the address of the host you are looking for, it has the ability to query other DNS servers to help answer the request.

Think about the implications of that for just a minute. We all probably use Google several times a day, but in all honesty how many of us know its IP address? It's certainly not something we are likely to have memorized. Much less, how could you possibly memorize the IP addresses of all of the websites you visit? Because of DNS, it's easy to find resources. Whether you want to find Coca-Cola, Toyota, Amazon.com, or thousands of other companies, it's usually pretty easy to figure out how. Type in the name with a .com on the end of it and you're usually right. The only reason this is successful is that DNS is there to perform resolution of that name to the corresponding IP address.

DNS works the same way on an intranet (a local network not attached to the Internet) as it does on the Internet. The only difference is that instead of helping you find www.google.com, it may help you find Jenny's print server or Joe's file server. From a client-side perspective, all you need to do is configure the host with the address of a legitimate DNS server and you should be good to go.

Automatic Private IP Addressing

Automatic Private IP Addressing (APIPA) is a TCP/IP standard used to automatically configure IP-based hosts that are unable to reach a DHCP server. APIPA addresses are in the 169.254.0.0 range with a subnet mask of 255.255.0.0. If you see a computer that has an IP address beginning with 169.254, you know that it has configured itself. If this is the case, that computer will not be able to get on the Internet.

Typically the only time you will see this is when a computer is supposed to receive configuration information from a DHCP server but for some reason that server is unavailable. Even while configured with this address, the client will continue to search for a DHCP server so it can be given a real address once the server becomes available. In Exercise 5.3, you will find your computer's IP configuration information.

EXERCISE 5.3

Finding Your IP Configuration Information in Windows

1. Click Start, and in the box type **cmd** and press Enter. This will open a command prompt.

2. At the prompt, type **ipconfig** and press Enter. This will display IP configuration information for your computer. Can you find your IP address, subnet mask, and (optional) default gateway? A sample output is shown in Figure 5.7.

FIGURE 5.7   Ipconfig output

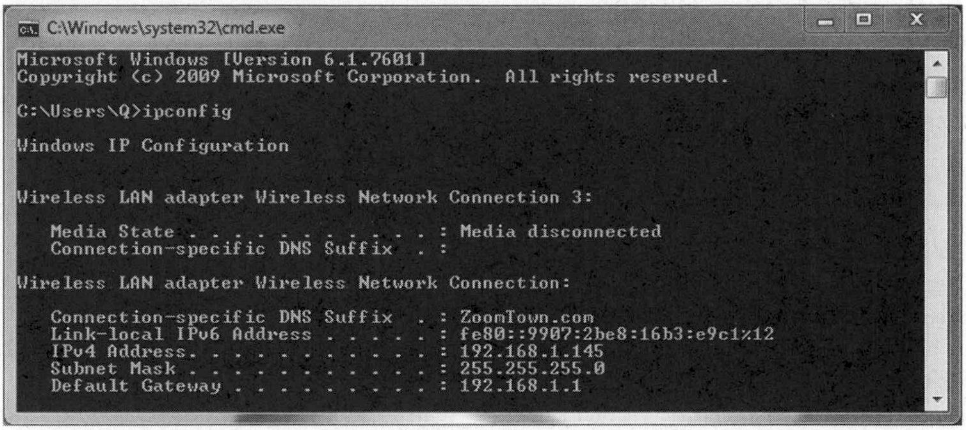

```
C:\Windows\system32\cmd.exe                                    _  □  X

Microsoft Windows [Version 6.1.7601]
Copyright (c) 2009 Microsoft Corporation.  All rights reserved.

C:\Users\Q>ipconfig

Windows IP Configuration


Wireless LAN adapter Wireless Network Connection 3:

   Media State . . . . . . . . . . . : Media disconnected
   Connection-specific DNS Suffix  . :

Wireless LAN adapter Wireless Network Connection:

   Connection-specific DNS Suffix  . : ZoomTown.com
   Link-local IPv6 Address . . . . . : fe80::9907:2be8:16b3:e9c1%12
   IPv4 Address. . . . . . . . . . . : 192.168.1.145
   Subnet Mask . . . . . . . . . . . : 255.255.255.0
   Default Gateway . . . . . . . . . : 192.168.1.1
```

The link-local address shown is an IPv6 address, which is written in hexadecimal.

3. At the prompt, type **ipconfig /all** and press Enter. This will show you much more information, including the address of your DHCP and DNS servers, if you have them.

4. Type **exit** and press Enter to close the command prompt.

 To get IP configuration on a Mac, open the terminal by pressing Cmd+spacebar and typing **terminal**. At the prompt, type **ifconfig**. The ifconfig command also works in Linux.

Public vs. Private IP Addresses

All of the addresses that are used on the Internet are called public IP addresses. They must be purchased, and only one computer can use any given public address at one time. A problem quickly arose—the world was running out of public IP addresses while the use of TCP/IP was growing. Additionally, the structure of IP addressing made it impossible to "create" or add any new addresses to the system.

To address this, a solution was devised to allow for the use of TCP/IP without requiring the assignment of a public address—private IP addresses. Private addresses are not routable on the Internet (meaning, they won't work on the Internet). They were intended to be used on private networks only. Because they weren't intended to be used on the Internet, it freed us from the requirement that all addresses be globally unique. This essentially created an infinite number of IP addresses that companies could use within their own network walls. Table 5.4 shows what the private IP address ranges are.

TABLE 5.4 Private IP address ranges

IP Address Range	Subnet Mask	Number of Hosts
10.0.0.0–10.255.255.255	255.0.0.0	16.7 million
172.16.0.0–172.31.255.255	255.255.0.0	1 million
192.168.0.0–192.168.255.255	255.255.255.0	65,536

When you did Exercise 5.3, if you were on a corporate network or even on your home network, I'd give it about a 90 percent probability that your IP address was in one of those ranges. And, you can likely get on the Internet right now. So what's going on here?

The fact is that private addresses cannot be used on the Internet and cannot be routed externally. However, your router (that gateway to the Internet) has a capability called *Network Address Translation (NAT)* that was created to address this problem. NAT runs on your router and handles the translation of private, nonroutable IP addresses into public IP addresses.

This is how it works: You or your network administrator sets up a NAT-enabled router, such as a wireless router, which functions as the default gateway to the Internet. The external interface of the router has a public IP address assigned to it that has been provided by the ISP, such as 155.120.100.1. The internal interface of the router will have an administrator-assigned private IP address within one of these ranges, such as 192.168.1.1. All computers on the internal network will then also need to be on the 192.168.1.0 network. To the outside world, any request coming from the internal network will appear to come from 155.120.100.1. The NAT router translates all incoming packets and sends them to the appropriate client. This type of setup is very common today.

By definition, NAT is actually a one-to-one private-to-public IP address translation protocol. There is a type of NAT called *Port Address Translation (PAT)*, which allows for many private IP addresses to use one public IP address on the Internet.

So that's why when you look at your own computer, which probably has an address in a private range, you can still get on the Internet. The NAT router technically makes the Internet request on your computer's behalf, and the NAT router is using a public IP address.

Setting Up a SOHO Router

Finally, the part you have been waiting for! This is the section where I will show you how to configure a router for your SOHO network. The exam objectives mention wired/wireless routers, because most of the routers you buy today for SOHO use are wireless but have around four wired ports as well. Plugging your computer into one of those ports makes you wired, but you still use the router to get to the Internet as a wireless client would.

Each wireless router manufacturer uses different software, but you can usually configure their parameters with the built-in, web-based configuration utility that's included with the product. While the software is convenient, you still need to know which options to configure and how those configurations will affect users on your networks. The items that require configuration depend on the choices you make about your wireless network. I will divide this part into three sections: basic configuration, security options, and additional services.

Basic Configuration

The Wi-Fi Alliance (www.wi-fi.org) is the authoritative expert in the field of wireless LANs. It lists five critical steps to setting up a secured wireless router:

1. Change the router's SSID.
2. Change the administrator username and password. Make sure it's a strong password.
3. Enable WPA2 Personal with AES encryption.
4. Choose a high-quality security passphrase.
5. From the clients, select WPA2 and enter the security passphrase to connect.

This list has a few new acronyms in it, and I'll get to what each of those means in just a minute. The CompTIA IT Fundamentals exam objectives cover those five crucial steps (in slightly different words) and also list a few additional items you need to do for basic router setup and configuration:

- Verify wired connection, if applicable
- Connect to the new network
- Verify Internet connectivity
- Update firmware if necessary

I will cover each of those steps here. To do that, I am going to walk you through the setup of a Linksys EA3500 wireless router, because that's what I have. Its setup will be pretty similar to other routers on the market. A prerequisite step I have already taken is to get DSL set up through my phone provider, so I have my DSL modem ready to go. (Of course, you could use a cable modem or other broadband connection as well.)

The Linksys router comes with a setup CD. I put it in my CD-ROM drive and let it automatically run the setup program. Now, you get a guided tour of setup.

Step 1: Accept the License Agreement

As you will recall from reading in Chapter 4, "Software Applications," this is a non-negotiable step. If you want to use their product, check the box and click Next. The screen is shown in Figure 5.8. There's no sense in fighting the system here, so I checked the box and clicked Next.

FIGURE 5.8   Router setup initial screen

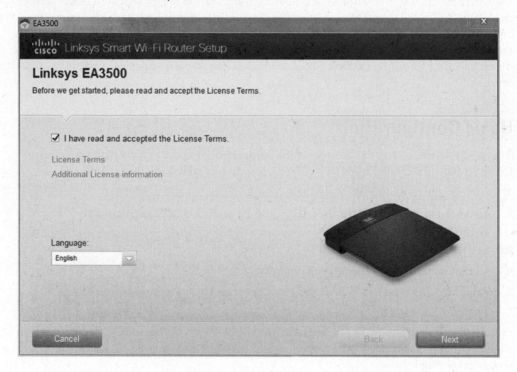

Step 2: Connect the Router

This step corresponds to the "verify wired connection, if applicable" test objective. I am trying to set up a connection to the Internet, so this step is applicable. The screen showing you what to do is shown in Figure 5.9, and it gives you a pretty good explanation of what to do: plug the router into an outlet, and connect a network cable between the router and the modem. After verifying my connection, I dutifully clicked Next.

From here, your computer will look for the router to begin setting it up, as shown in Figure 5.10.

FIGURE 5.9   Verify wired connection.

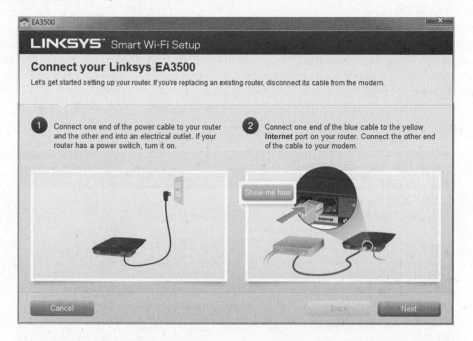

FIGURE 5.10   Connecting to the router

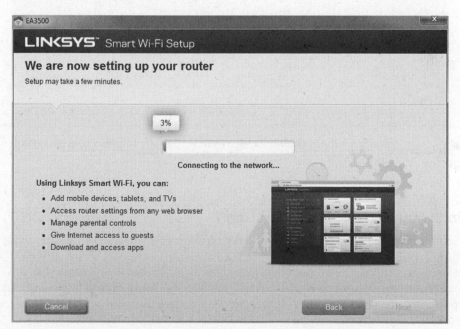

Sometimes after running for a few minutes, your computer will return an error message that it couldn't find the router, as you can see in Figure 5.11. If this happens to you, you can try a few troubleshooting steps. Of course, the first step is to check the easy stuff: make sure that your computer is near the router, your wireless is enabled, and the router is powered on. Then click Next and try it again. If it still doesn't detect your router, the best course of action is to plug in a network cable from your computer to your router and try again. Sometimes these things can be a little finicky.

FIGURE 5.11   Error message: Can't find router

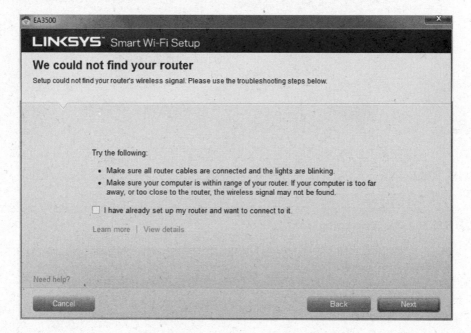

 Have a network cable handy when setting up wireless routers, just in case you need it.

Step 3: Finish Basic Configuration

The setup process will continue and eventually finish, giving you a screen similar to the one in Figure 5.12.

It's important to notice a few things here. First, your router is operational at this point. Second, the important settings are all defaults, meaning that your network name and password are so easy to guess that most seven-year-olds could probably hack your network.

FIGURE 5.12   Router is configured.

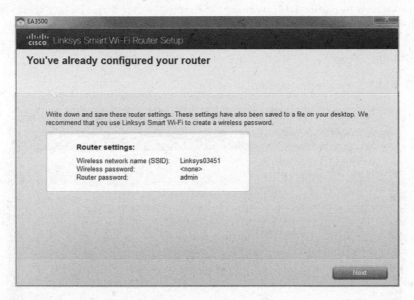

If you click Next, this particular router asks if you want to create a Linksys Smart Wi-Fi account, as shown in Figure 5.13. It's a good idea to do this, just so you have another way to manage your router. Keep in mind that the account and password you create are *not* the same as your local router password. You can make them be the same, but that increases your security risk a bit.

FIGURE 5.13   Create a Linksys account.

I chose not to do this, because I already have an account, and clicked Continue. Then, I received the screen in Figure 5.14, warning me that my router is not in fact set up properly because it is unsecured. Check the box and click Continue. You will be asked to sign in to the router, as shown in Figure 5.15. Remember that the password is still the default. In this case, it's admin.

FIGURE 5.14   Your network is not secure.

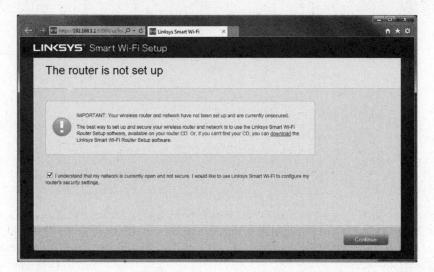

FIGURE 5.15   Sign in to the router.

Once you're signed in to the router, you will get the main configuration screen like the one in Figure 5.16. Here is where you'll be able to set up the other parameters you need to in order to make your network secure. It doesn't matter in which order you take the next two steps, but both need to be performed for your network to have any security.

FIGURE 5.16   Linksys Smart Wi-Fi configuration screen

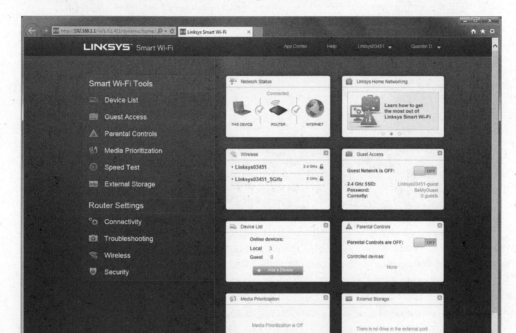

Step 4: Secure the Network

The next three parameters you need to configure all happen to be on the same screen in this configuration utility. To get to it, I clicked the Wireless option in the left navigation area (Figure 5.17).

The three parameters you're looking for here (which correspond to test objectives and are smart to configure in real life) are these:

- Change SSID from default
- Set security (WEP versus WPA versus WPA2)
- Apply a new wireless password

FIGURE 5.17   Wireless configuration

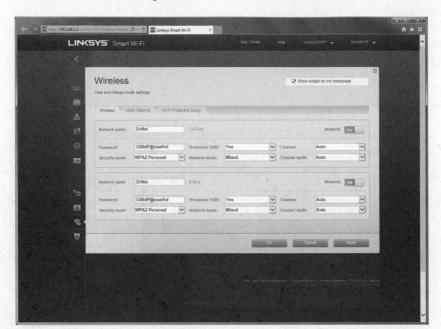

The parameter that you will configure first is the *Service Set Identifier (SSID)*, which is your wireless network name. An SSID is a unique name given to the wireless network. All hardware that is to participate on the network must be configured to use the same SSID. When you are connecting clients to a wireless network, all available wireless networks will be listed by their SSIDs. As you saw in Figure 5.16, the default network name was Linksys03451. You need to change the default to something more memorable.

 For better security, you should set your network name to something that doesn't identify to whom it belongs. This keeps potential hackers from coming after you personally or possibly being able to guess your password based on information about you. I am probably setting a bad example in Figure 5.17 by naming my network something close to my last name.

The second option you need to configure is the security mode. You can see in Figure 5.17 that I chose WPA2 Personal. WPA2 is the best of the options and I'll tell you why in the "Wireless Router Security" section. The third critical option on this page is the wireless password (it just says Password in Figure 5.17.) This is the password that clients will need to enter to join your network. It should be something that's not too easy to guess; otherwise you defeat the purpose of setting up security in the first place. Whether you as the admin type it into the client computers or you tell your users what to type in is up to you. Obviously, the former is more secure and makes it harder for people to set up devices on your wireless network that are unknown to you.

Once you've finished configuring these options, you can click Apply to save the changes and leave the screen open, or click OK to save the changes and close the screen.

Step 5: Change the Administrator Password and Update Firmware

The password I configured in step 4 was for the clients to join. My router still has the default password of admin, and this is a huge security issue. By clicking the Connectivity option on the left, I got the screen shown in Figure 5.18.

FIGURE 5.18   Connectivity options

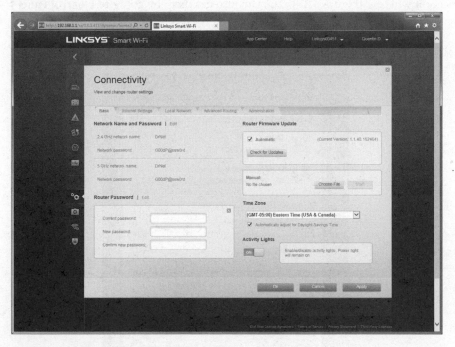

You'll notice that I can also configure my wireless network name and password here, and they are displayed for me. The administrator password is under the section Router Password. Give your router a very strong password. For the love of all that's secure in this world, please make it different than the network password!

If you forget your wireless router's administrator password, you won't be able to make any configuration changes. Wireless routers have a recessed reset button on them, usually on the bottom. You will need a pen or a paperclip to be able to push it. Push that button in and hold it for about 20 to 30 seconds. The router's lights will flash several times, and it will reset to factory settings. Then, launch your configuration utility to set up the router again.

This screen also lets me configure my time zone and update the router's firmware. I checked the box for it to update automatically, which is a good option. I could also click Check For Updates if I wanted to manually update the firmware.

Step 6: Connect to the Network and Verify Internet Connectivity

Having a wireless router with no clients is like having a port with no ships. The reason the first exists is to support the second! To connect your wireless clients to the router, you need the network password. Here are two examples of how to connect a wireless client to the router.

Windows clients will likely have an icon in their System tray (next to the clock) that looks like cell phone signal strength bars. Clicking that will open the Wireless Network Connection window (Figure 5.19). You can also get there by going to Control Panel ➢ Network And Internet and selecting Connect To A Network.

FIGURE 5.19   Wireless Network Connection window

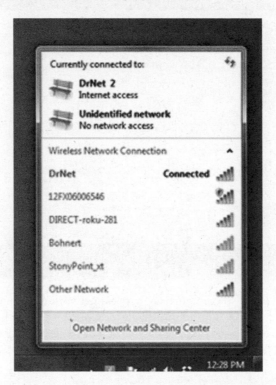

To connect to a network, click it in the list. A Connect button will appear under it. Click that button, and you will be asked for the network password. Enter the correct password and you will connect.

Mobile clients will follow a similar procedure. On an iPhone, go to Settings ➢ Wi-Fi and you will have a list of available networks like the one in Figure 5.20. You can see which ones are secured because they have a padlock icon next to their signal strength indicator. Tap the network you want to join, enter the password, and you should connect.

FIGURE 5.20   Wireless networks on an iPhone

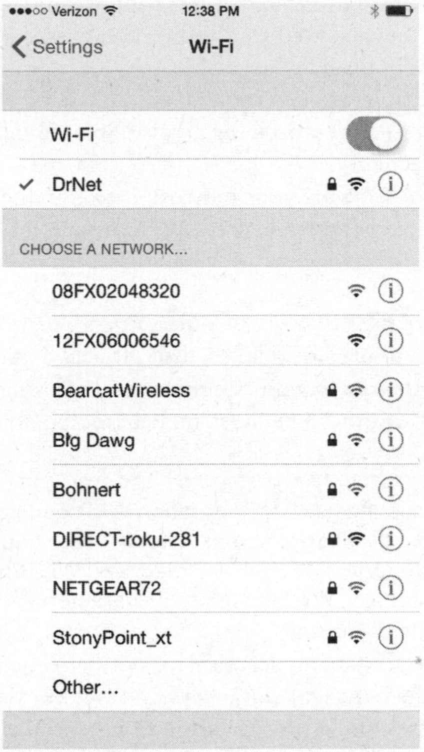

If you are unable to connect with the right password, it could be a security mismatch. Most clients today will autodetect the security type (such as WPA or WPA2) needed by the router. If not, and the client and router are set up to use different security methods, the connection will fail.

Once you are connected to the network, verify Internet connectivity. Do this by opening the browser of your choice and seeing if you can get to a website such as www.google.com.

Wireless Router Security

By their very nature, wireless routers are less secure than their wired counterparts. The fact that their signals travel through air makes them a little harder to contain. Here I'll review a few things you can do to increase the security of your wireless installation. Specifically, you can implement the following:

- Wireless encryption
- Disabling SSID broadcasts
- MAC filtering

Wireless Encryption Methods

The growth of wireless systems has created several opportunities for attackers. These systems are relatively new, they use well-established communications mechanisms, and they're easily intercepted. Wi-Fi routers use SSIDs to allow communications with a specific access point. Because by default wireless routers will broadcast their SSID, all someone with a wireless client needs to do is search for an available signal. If it's not secured, they can connect within a few seconds.

The most effective way of securing your network is to use one of the several encryption methods available. Examples of these are WEP, WPA, and WPA2.

WEP

Wired Equivalency Protocol (WEP) was one of the first security standards for wireless devices. WEP encrypts data to provide data security. It uses a static key (password); the client needs to know the right key to gain communication through a WEP-enabled device. The keys are commonly 10, 26, or 58 hexadecimal characters long.

> You may see the use of the notation WEP.*x*, which refers to the key size; 64-bit and 128-bit are the most widely used, and 256-bit keys are supported by some vendors (WEP.64, WEP.128, and WEP.256). WEP.64 uses a 10-character key. WEP.128 uses 26 characters, and WEP.256 uses 58.

The protocol has always been under scrutiny for not being as secure as initially intended. WEP is vulnerable due to the nature of static keys and weaknesses in the encryption algorithms. These weaknesses allow the algorithm to potentially be cracked in a very short amount of time—no more than two or three minutes. This makes WEP one of the more vulnerable protocols available for security.

Because of security weaknesses and the availability of newer protocols, WEP is not used widely. It's still better than nothing, though, and it does an adequate job of keeping casual snoops at bay. But if you have any other options, it's best to avoid WEP.

WPA

Wi-Fi Protected Access (WPA) is an improvement on WEP that was first available in 1999 but did not see widespread acceptance until around 2003. Once it became widely available, the Wi-Fi Alliance recommended that networks no longer use WEP in favor of WPA.

This standard was the first to implement some of the features defined in the IEEE 802.11i security specification. Most notable among them was the use of the *Temporal Key Integrity Protocol (TKIP)*. Whereas WEP used a static 40- or 128-bit key, TKIP uses a 128-bit dynamic per-packet key. It generates a new key for each packet sent. WPA also introduced message integrity checking.

When WPA was introduced to the market, it was intended to be a temporary solution to wireless security. The provisions of 802.11i had already been drafted, and a standard that employed all of the security recommendations was in development. The upgraded standard would eventually be known as WPA2.

WPA2

Even though their names might make you assume that WPA and WPA2 are very similar, they are quite different in structure. *Wi-Fi Protected Access 2 (WPA2)* is a huge improvement over WEP and WPA. As mentioned earlier, it implements all of the required elements of the 802.11i security standard. Most notably, it uses Counter Mode CBC-MAC Protocol (CCMP), which is a protocol based on the *Advanced Encryption Standard (AES)* security algorithm. CCMP was created to address the shortcomings of TKIP, so consequently it's much stronger than TKIP.

> The terms CCMP and AES tend to be interchangeable in common parlance. You might also see it written as AES-CCMP.

Since 2006, wireless devices have been required to support WPA2 to be certified as Wi-Fi compliant. Of the wireless security options available today, it provides the strongest encryption and data protection.

Other Security Options

Setting up Wi-Fi encryption is the best thing you can do. There are two other options as well, but neither is truly secure. They will do a decent job of thwarting casual amateur hackers, but real hackers will defeat these next two measures very quickly.

Disabling SSID Broadcasts

Disabling the SSID broadcast makes it a little harder to find your network—not impossible, just harder. (Figure 5.17 shows you where to disable this on the example router.) Casual hackers won't be able to "see" your network, but someone with a wireless packet sniffer could still detect your network transmissions and attempt to hack in. The only downside to disabling your SSID broadcast is that the SSID won't appear on the network list for your legitimate clients. You will have to configure client computers manually with the network name.

MAC Address Filtering

The last one to look at is MAC filtering. The *Media Access Control (MAC)* address is the unique hardware address associated with every network adapter. All NICs, wired or wireless, have a unique MAC address. By enabling MAC filtering, you can limit the computers that have access to your network.

> You can find the MAC address of your network card by using the `ipconfig/all` command. Look for the Physical Address parameter. The address will have six hexadecimal parts and look something like 08-00-24-03-A0-4C.

On my sample router, the MAC filter is in the Wireless configuration under the MAC Filtering tab (Figure 5.21). You check the Enabled box, choose to deny or allow those on the list, and then click Add MAC Address to enter your MAC addresses.

FIGURE 5.21 MAC filtering

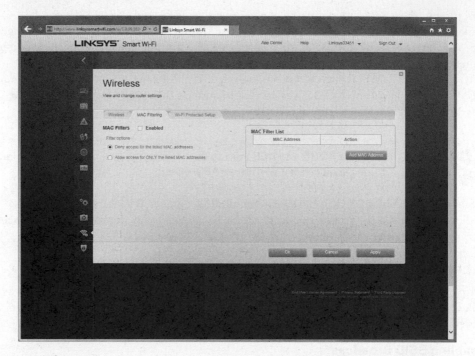

As with most other security options, MAC filtering isn't totally foolproof either. If a hacker wanted to badly enough, they could spoof a MAC address of one of your wireless clients and get access.

Always be sure that your router has the most current firmware. Older firmware versions may have security holes, and newer versions will patch those as well as possibly offer you new features.

Additional Wireless Router Services

Wireless routers offer many more services than I've been able to cover to this point, and most of them are out of the scope of IT Fundamentals exam training. Still, there are a few items covered earlier in this book that I want to cover while on the subject.

Guest Access

Clients who access your wireless network can see other clients on the network and access their resources that are shared. (Chapter 6, "Network Sharing and Storage," covers this in depth.) If you have clients who need Internet access but you don't want them to see the rest of the network, you can let them on as guests.

As a security precaution, leave your guest network disabled unless you have a specific reason to enable it.

Guest clients will need to know the SSID of your guest network as well as the password. Of course, make sure this password is different than the other ones you have configured so far. Figure 5.22 shows the guest network configuration on my router.

FIGURE 5.22   Guest network configuration

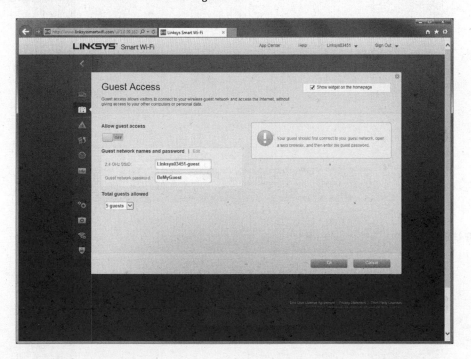

DHCP

Earlier in this chapter I talked about DHCP and how it automatically configures your clients with IP addresses. This router has it enabled (Figure 5.23), and you can see some of the configuration options. For the most part, you won't need to change any of these, unless perhaps you want to allow more than the default of 50 clients onto your network. Odds are if you have that many clients, you will need a second wireless access point to handle the traffic.

NAT

If you'll recall, Network Address Translation allows you to use a private IP address internally but still get to the Internet. Figure 5.23 showed you the DHCP range for this router, which is a private range. You might assume that means NAT is enabled on this router, and sure enough it is. Figure 5.24 shows that the NAT box is checked.

FIGURE 5.23   DHCP configuration

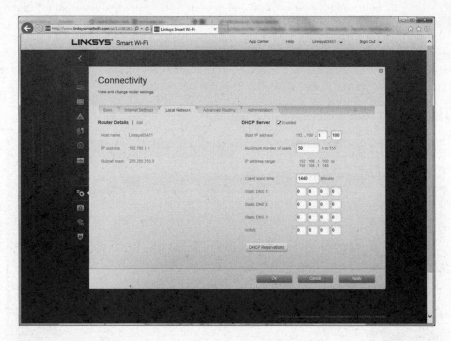

FIGURE 5.24   NAT enabled

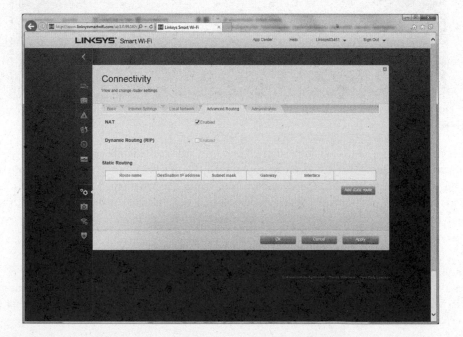

Firewall

I talked about software firewalls in Chapter 4, "Software Applications." A router is often used as a hardware firewall to protect several computers. Figure 5.25 shows you the Security section of the router's configuration, which allows you to set up your firewall rules.

FIGURE 5.25   Firewall settings

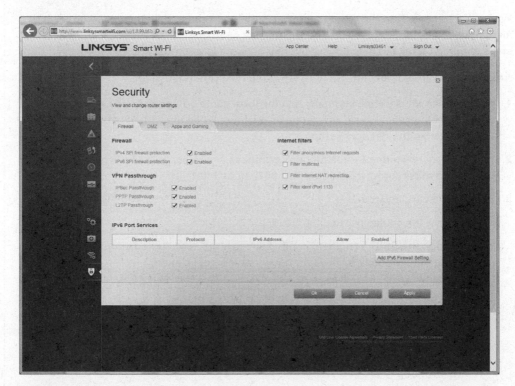

On these three security tabs, you can set an Internet access policy and block protocols such as HTTP, FTP, and others. You can also block websites by URL and limit Internet access times by using the Parental Controls feature.

Real World Scenario

Configuring a Small Office Network

You are helping a friend who is opening a small tax preparation firm. She needs to set up an office network for five users. Her office will need Internet access, and because she is dealing with confidential financial information, security is a big concern.

When clients come into the office, some bring their laptops to help the tax preparer find all of the documentation needed. The clients may need Internet access for this. What steps should you take to help her configure a network in the most appropriate way?

Answers can vary somewhat, but here are some recommended steps:

1. Contact the local phone company and the local cable company to see what the best deal is for Internet access, and set up an account. Once the DSL or cable modem arrives, begin the network setup.

2. While you are waiting for the modem, purchase a wireless router. It's generally best to get the most current technology, so 802.11n or 802.11ac is the best choice.

3. Set up the wireless router:

    a. Plug in the cables per the instructions.

    b. Change the SSID from the default. If she is highly concerned about security, using her company name is probably not the best option.

    c. Set the network to use WPA2 security. Do not leave the network open to Wi-Fi access!

    d. Change the network password to something difficult to guess. Random characters are good, but she might want something she can remember if for some reason she needs to add a client to the network. Maybe Tx$pr4y2 (Tax dollars prep for you too).

    e. Change the admin password to something equally difficult to guess, if not more so. Go with something like 7ygH$2p*.

    f. Enable the guest network. The SSID can be easier to use than the regular network SSID, such as TaxPrepGuest. The password should be challenging but not overly so. Something like tpg$2015.

    g. Update the firmware on the router, or set it to update automatically.

4. Add the client computers to the network. Verify Internet connectivity.

5. Using your laptop, verify that the Guest network works and that you are able to get on the Internet using it.

Summary

This chapter was the first in-depth discussion of networking concepts in this book. You started off by learning about connection types and features of each. For example, external connections to the Internet are generally broadband today, and the most popular choices are DSL and cable Internet. For internal networking, you have two primary choices: wired and wireless. Wireless networking really means Wi-Fi, which is based on the IEEE 802.11 standard. Other wireless connection types include Bluetooth and infrared, but those are specialized connection types not intended for full-scale networking.

Next, you compared and contrasted wired, wireless, and cellular connections on several vectors: mobility, availability, reliability, throughput/bandwidth, delay, number of concurrent connections, and security. Generally speaking, wired connections are the most secure and reliable and give you the most bandwidth with the least delay but are also the most constraining from a mobility standpoint.

The next topic was network communication basics. You learned about protocols and in particular the most important protocol used today, TCP/IP. You learned about IP addresses, subnet masks, and default gateways. In addition, you learned what DHCP and DNS do for you, as well as about private addresses, NAT, and APIPA.

This chapter finished with a detailed look at how to set up a wireless/wired router. Important facets included changing the SSID, setting up the best security possible, and making sure clients can access the Internet.

Exam Essentials

Understand what the common options are for Internet access.   Options include dial-up, DSL, cable modems, fiber-optic Internet, satellite, and cellular.

Know the two types of internal network connections and pros and cons of each.   The two choices are wired and wireless. Wired is more secure and faster, but wireless is popular because of its vastly superior mobility.

Understand how to compare wired, wireless, and cellular connections in regard to mobility, availability, reliability, throughput, delay, concurrent users, and security.   In general, wired connections are less mobile but more available and reliable, and they have greater throughput, lower delay, a larger number of users, and better security. Cellular has the best mobility but the lowest throughput, the worst security, and the highest delay.

Know which IP configuration options are required.   To communicate on a network, every host needs an IP address and a subnet mask. If you want to get on the Internet, you also need a default gateway (such as a wireless router).

Understand what DHCP and DNS do for you.   DHCP automatically assigns TCP/IP configuration information to clients. DNS resolves user-friendly hostnames such as www.google.com to an IP address.

Know the best wireless security options.   WPA2 is the best, followed by WPA, and as a minimum, WEP.

Understand other available security options.   You should not rely on these methods to protect you from hackers, but you can also disable SSID broadcasts and enable MAC filtering.

Chapter 5 Lab

The Chapter 5 lab has two parts to it. In part 1, you will set up your own secure network. In part 2, you will see how well others around you have done.

Part 1: Setting Up Your Wireless Router

1. Plug in your router per the manufacturer's instructions, and configure the connection to your Internet device (if applicable).
2. Run the setup routine.
3. Set your SSID.
4. Set security to WPA2.
5. Change the wireless password to something that is challenging to guess.
6. Change the administrator password to something that's even harder to guess.
7. Connect your client computer to the network.
8. Verify Internet access.
9. Update the firmware; set the firmware to automatically update if you would like.

Part 2: Testing Your Neighbors

In this part, you will check to see how well your neighbors have set up their wireless networks.

1. Open the list of available networks on your client computer (or mobile device). How many do you see available?

    If you live in a densely populated area, especially an apartment or condominium, you will probably have a really long list of available networks.

2. How many of those networks are unsecured?

    Don't try to connect to neighbors' unsecured networks. One big reason is it's illegal. Another reason is that it could expose your computer to potential threats on that unsecured network.

Review Questions

1. You are configuring a computer to participate on a network. Which of the following are mandatory? (Choose two.)

   A. IP address

   B. Default gateway

   C. DHCP server

   D. Subnet mask

2. Which one of the following types of network connections can give you the highest data transfer rates?

   A. Wired

   B. Cellular

   C. Broadband

   D. Wireless

3. You are configuring a wireless router to let clients get on the Internet while using private IP addresses. In this scenario, which of the following services do you need to make sure is enabled on the router?

   A. DHCP

   B. DNS

   C. NAT

   D. APIPA

4. You have a scenario where you need to disable the guest network on your wireless router. You try to log in, but your password does not work. After several attempts you realize you forgot your password. What can you do?

   A. Use the password reset option in your router configuration utility.

   B. Unplug the router and plug it back in.

   C. Use the default password of admin.

   D. Hold the reset button down for 30 seconds to reset the router.

5. On Monday, you log into your computer at work, but you are not able to access any network resources. You run `ipconfig` and see that your IP address is 169.254.18.53. What is the most likely cause of the problem?

   A. The DNS server is down.

   B. The DHCP server is down.

   C. The NAT server is down.

   D. Your default gateway is set incorrectly.

6. This question refers to the scenario at the end of the chapter, in "Configuring a Small Office Network." When connecting client computers to the network, what password do they need to enter?

   A. tpg$2015

   B. 7ygH$2p*

   C. Tx$pr4y2

   D. No password is required.

7. Your friend Maria asks you which of the following are the most secure. What do you tell her?

   A. 802.11n

   B. Infrared

   C. Cellular

   D. UTP

8. Which one of the following addresses is considered a private IP address?

   A. 192.168.100.101

   B. 168.192.100.101

   C. 19.21.68.100

   D. 172.15.100.101

9. Your friend Michael is setting up a wireless network and asks you which security option he should choose to make the network the most secure. What do you suggest?

   A. WEP

   B. WPA

   C. WPA2

   D. NAT

10. Which of the following connectivity options gives you the best mobility?

    A. Cellular

    B. Wireless

    C. Wired

    D. Broadband

11. You need to set up a wireless network. Which standard will give you the highest speed?

    A. 802.11a

    B. 802.11ac

    C. 802.11g

    D. 802.11n

12. Your friend Barbara needs to set up an Internet connection. In this scenario, which of the following options will give her the best speed? (Choose two.)

   A. Cable Internet

   B. DSL

   C. Satellite

   D. Cellular

13. Which one of these connection types has the longest delay?

   A. Wireless

   B. Infrared

   C. Wired

   D. Cellular

14. Of your internal network connection options, which one can provide the fastest speeds?

   A. UTP

   B. Fiber

   C. Infrared

   D. 802.11n

15. You have decided to retire to a remote mountain cabin and write books. You need an Internet connection to send material to your publisher. What is the option most likely to work for you?

   A. DSL

   B. Cable Internet

   C. Dial-up

   D. Satellite

16. You configured a wireless network for your neighbor, and he wants to implement additional security measures beyond the standard wireless encryption. What options does he have? (Choose two.)

   A. Use NAT.

   B. Disable SSID broadcasts.

   C. Enable DHCP.

   D. Use MAC filtering.

17. What command would you use on a Mac to determine your TCP/IP configuration information?

   A. ifconfig

   B. ipconfig

   C. ipinfo

   D. tcpipconfig

18. By definition, what is an SSID?

    A.   A wireless network name

    B.   A wireless network security protocol

    C.   A wireless network security password

    D.   A wireless network authentication method

19. When configuring a wireless router, which of the following should you always do? (Choose two.)

    A.   Enable DHCP.

    B.   Change the SSID.

    C.   Change the admin password.

    D.   Configure the firewall.

20. This question refers to the scenario at the end of the chapter. Your friend wants the tax prep agents to be able to let their clients connect their wireless devices to the network. Which password should she tell the agents to give to clients?

    A.   7ygH$2p*

    B.   tpg$2015

    C.   Tx$pr4y2

    D.   No password is required.

Chapter

6

Network Sharing and Storage

THE FOLLOWING COMPTIA IT FUNDAMENTALS EXAM OBJECTIVES ARE COVERED IN THIS CHAPTER:

✓ **1.4 Identify the following alternative technologies and their purpose**

- Virtualization
  - Physical machine vs. virtual machine
- Cloud computing
  - Streaming media (audio/video)
- Web applications

✓ **4.3 Compare and contrast different methods of sharing and storage**

- HTTP vs. HTTPS
  - Browser-based file downloads
- FTP vs. FTPS vs. SFTP (Secure File Transfer Protocol)
- Local vs. hosted storage
  - Cloud-based services
    - Cloud-based collaborative applications
    - Cloud-based storage
  - File and print sharing
    - Workgroup
    - Homegroup
- Network drives
- Network attached storage
- Direct attached storage
- External hard drives

- Peer-to-peer
    - Local adhoc network
        - Bluetooth sharing
    - Direct link (PC-to-PC)
    - Online peer-to-peer network
- Network vs. local printing
    - USB
    - Wireless / wired network

In Chapter 5, "Networking Technologies and Wireless Routers," you learned the basics of computer connectivity and setting up your own network. As part of setting up your own network, knowledge of TCP/IP is important to understand how computers talk to each other in a networked environment. In this chapter, you'll take the next step forward and learn *how* you actually share resources such as files, printers, and applications over the network.

This chapter starts off with a section on local network sharing. First, I will cover some core network concepts that will help your general understanding of networking. After that, I will spend time on storage options, and then I'll finish up with a discussion on how to share files and printers with other users.

Then this chapter takes a wider view of network sharing, by looking at web-based sharing and access. Many of the concepts are similar to those in local network sharing, but there are some exceptions. Most notable for the discussion here are cloud computing and accessing resources via the Internet. After this chapter, not only will you know how to connect computers together on a network, but you will be able to share resources between them as well.

Local Network Sharing

People use networks to get access to resources they normally wouldn't have. One big example is that we use networks to get on the Internet, which gives us access to an endless stream of information on news events, shopping, sports, hobbies, or whatever else we could be interested in. Closer to your home or office, perhaps you want to purchase only one printer and share it among your co-workers or family. That definitely saves money, and the only way everyone can use it is with a network.

In this section you are going to learn details of local network sharing, which is also the foundation for more distributed-resource sharing that is covered later in this chapter. First, you will learn about different types of networks. This will give you the background and vocabulary needed to understand the concepts throughout the chapter. After that, you will learn about local storage options. After all, the files everyone needs have to be stored somewhere, right? This section will end with a discussion on sharing files and printers on your network, so everyone has access to the resources they need.

Network Types

You might have read the title to this section and thought, "Wait a minute, I learned about wired and wireless networks in the last chapter. Aren't those network types?" The answer is yes, they are definitions of physical network types, but there are other ways you can categorize networks too, such as by the proximity of computers to each other or based on the roles computers on them play.

LANs, WANs, PANs, and MANs

Local area networks (LANs) were introduced to connect computers in a single office or building. *Wide area networks (WANs)* expanded the LANs to include networks outside the local environment and also to distribute resources across long distances. Generally, it's safe to think of a WAN as multiple, disbursed LANs connected together. Today, LANs exist in many homes (wireless networks) and nearly all businesses. WANs are becoming more common as businesses become more mobile and as more of them span greater distances. WANs were historically used only by larger corporations, but many smaller companies with remote locations now use them as well.

Having two types of network categories just didn't feel like enough, so the industry introduced two more terms. The *personal area network (PAN)* is a very small-scale network designed around one person. The term generally refers to networks using Bluetooth technology. On a larger scale is the *metropolitan area network (MAN)*, which is bigger than a LAN but not quite as big as a WAN.

LANs

By the 1980s, offices were beginning to buy PCs in large numbers. Portables were also introduced, allowing computing to become mobile. Neither PCs nor portables, however, were efficient in sharing information. As timeliness and security became more important, floppy disks were just not cutting it. Offices needed to find a way to implement a better means to share and access resources. This led to the introduction of the first type of PC local area network: ShareNet by Novell, which had both hardware and software components. LANs are simply the linking of computers to share resources within a closed environment. The first simple LANs were constructed a lot like the LAN in Figure 6.1.

FIGURE 6.1   A simple LAN

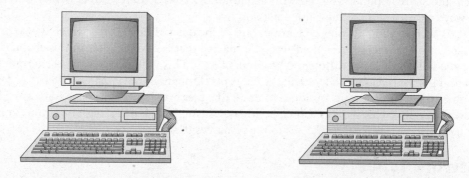

After the introduction of ShareNet, more LANs sprouted. The earliest LANs could not cover large distances. Most of them could only stretch across a single floor of the office and could support no more than 30 users. Further, they were still very rudimentary and only a few software programs supported them. The first software programs that ran on a LAN were not capable of being used by more than one user at a time (this constraint was known as *file locking*). Nowadays, multiple users can access a program or file at one time. Most of the time, the only limitations will be restrictions at the record level if two users are trying to modify a database record at the same time.

WANs

By the late 1980s, networks were expanding to cover large geographical areas and were supporting thousands of users. Wide area networks (WANs), first implemented with mainframes at massive government expense, started attracting PC users as networks went to this new level. Employees of businesses with offices across the country communicated as if they were only desks apart. Soon the whole world saw a change in the way of doing business, across not only a few miles but across countries. Whereas LANs are limited to single buildings, WANs can span buildings, states, countries, and even continental boundaries. Figure 6.2 gives an example of a simple WAN.

FIGURE 6.2   A simple WAN

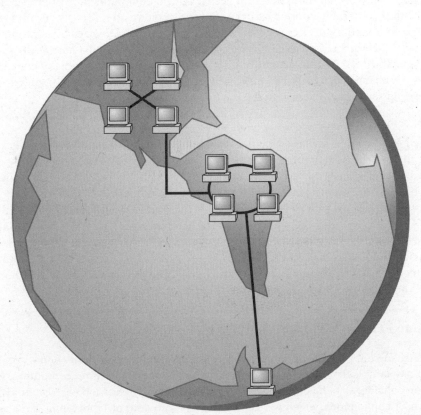

Networks of today and tomorrow are no longer limited by the inability of LANs to cover distance and handle mobility. WANs play an important role in the future development of corporate networks worldwide.

PANs

In 1998, a consortium of companies formed the Bluetooth Special Interest Group (SIG) and formally adopted the name *Bluetooth* for its technology. The technical specification IEEE 802.15.1 describes a *wireless personal area network (WPAN)* based on Bluetooth version 1.1.

The first Bluetooth device on the market was an Ericsson headset and cell phone adapter, which arrived on the scene in 2000. While mobile phones and accessories are still the most common type of Bluetooth device, you will find many more including wireless keyboards, mice, and printers.

 If you want to learn more about Bluetooth, you can visit www.bluetooth.com.

One of the unusual features of a Bluetooth WPAN is its temporary nature. With other popular networking standards, you need a central communication point, such as a hub, switch, or router. Bluetooth networks are formed on an ad hoc basis, meaning that whenever two Bluetooth devices get close enough to each other, they can communicate directly with each other. This dynamically created network is called a *piconet*. A Bluetooth-enabled device can communicate with up to seven other devices in one piconet. Two or more piconets can be linked together in a *scatternet*. In a scatternet, one or more devices would serve as a bridge between the piconets.

MANs

For those networks that are larger than a LAN but confined to a relatively small geographical area, there is the term *metropolitan area network (MAN)*. A MAN is generally defined as a network that spans a city or a large campus. For example, if a city decides to install wireless hotspots in various places, that network could be considered a MAN.

One of the questions a lot of people ask is, "Is there really a difference between a MAN and a WAN?" There is definitely some gray area here; in many cases they are virtually identical. Perhaps the biggest difference is who has responsibility for managing the connectivity. In a MAN, a central IT organization such as the campus or city IT staff is responsible. In a WAN, it's implied that you will be using publicly available communication lines and there will be a phone company or other service provider involved.

Blurring the Lines

In the 1980s and '90s, LANs and WANs were often differentiated by their connection speeds. For example, if you had a 10 Mbps or faster connection to other computers, you were often considered to be on a LAN. WANs were often connected to each other by very expensive T1 connections, which have a maximum bandwidth of 1.544 Mbps.

As with all other technologies, networking capacity has exploded. In today's office network, anything slower than 100 Mbps is considered archaic. Connections of 1 Gbps are fairly common. WAN connectivity, although still slower than LAN connectivity, can easily be several times faster than the T1. Because of the speed increases in WAN connectivity, the old practice of categorizing your network based on connection speed is outdated.

Today, the most common way to classify a network is based on geographical distance. If your network is in one central location, whether that is one office, one floor of an office building, or maybe even one entire building, it's usually considered a LAN. If your network is spread out among multiple distant locations, it's a WAN.

Peer-to-Peer and Client-Server Networks

In a peer-to-peer network, computers act as both service providers (servers) and service requestors (clients). An example of a peer-to-peer resource model is shown in Figure 6.3.

FIGURE 6.3   The peer-to-peer resource model

Peer-to-peer networks are great for small, simple, inexpensive networks. This model can be set up almost immediately, with little extra hardware required. Many versions of Windows (Windows 7, Vista, XP, 2000), Linux, and Mac OS are popular operating system environments that support a peer-to-peer resource model. Peer-to-peer networks are also referred to as *workgroups*.

Generally speaking, there is no centralized administration or control in the peer-to-peer resource model. Every station has unique control over the resources the computer owns, and each station must be administered separately. However, this very lack of centralized control can make it difficult to administer the network; for the same reason, the network isn't very secure. Moreover, because each computer is acting as both a workstation and server, it may not be easy to locate resources. The person who is in charge of a file may have moved it without anyone's knowledge. Also, the users who work under this arrangement need more training because they are not only users but also administrators.

Peer-to-peer resource models are generally considered the right choice for small companies that don't expect future growth. Small companies that expect growth, on the other hand, should not choose this type of model.

A rule of thumb is that if you have no more than 10 computers and centralized security is not a key priority, a workgroup may be a good choice for you.

The other option is to have machines that are dedicated servers on your network. The client-server (also known as server-based) model is better than the peer-to-peer model for large networks (say, more than 10 computers) that need a more secure environment and centralized control. Server-based networks use one or more dedicated, centralized servers. All administrative functions and resource sharing are performed from this point. This makes it easier to share resources, perform backups, and support an almost unlimited number of users. This model also offers better security. However, the server needs more hardware than a typical workstation/server computer in a peer-to-peer resource model needs. In addition, it requires specialized software (a network operating system) to manage the server's role in the environment. Server-based networks can easily cost more than peer-to-peer resource models. However, for large networks, it's the only choice. An example of a client-server resource model is shown in Figure 6.4.

FIGURE 6.4 The client-server resource model

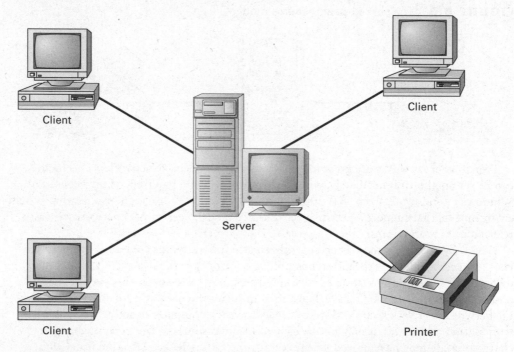

Server-based networks are also known as *domains*. The key characteristic of a domain is that security is centrally administered. When you log into the network, the login request is passed to the server responsible for security, sometimes known as a *domain controller*. (Microsoft uses the term *domain controller*, whereas other vendors of server products do not.) This is different from the peer-to-peer model, where each individual workstation validates users. In a peer-to-peer model, if the user jsmith wants to be able to log into different workstations, she needs to have a user account set up on each machine. This can quickly become an administrative nightmare! In a domain, all user accounts are stored on the server. User jsmith needs only one account and can log onto any of the workstations in the domain.

Client-server resource models are the desired models for companies that are continually growing, need to support a large environment, or need centralized security. Server-based networks offer the flexibility to add more resources and clients almost indefinitely into the future. Hardware costs may be higher, but with the centralized administration, managing resources becomes less time consuming. Also, only a few administrators need to be trained, and users are responsible for only their own work environment.

If you are looking for an inexpensive, simple network with little setup required, and there is no need for the company to grow in the future, then the peer-to-peer network is the way to go. If you are looking for a network to support many users (more than 10 computers), strong security, and centralized administration, then consider the server-based network your only choice.

Storage Options

From Chapter 1, "Core Hardware Components," you know that files are stored on hard drives. Regardless of whether the files you are accessing are on a local computer or across a network, they are stored on a hard drive *somewhere*. The question is just *where* and *how* you get to them.

Direct Attached Storage

The first option is *direct attached storage (DAS)*, which is a fancy term for a very simple idea. It simply refers to any hard drive attached to a local computer. The hard drive that comes in your computer is a prime example of DAS, as is any external hard drive you might add.

DAS has an advantage in that it's the easiest of the storage systems to install and manage. If you can plug in a hard drive, either internally or externally, you can install and manage it. You can also make these hard drives accessible to others on the network via file sharing, which I will cover in a few sections. One downside to DAS is that if for any reason your computer is not accessible, such as if it's powered down or you are traveling for work, then other people can't access the files on the drive. A second is that different operating systems don't always play nicely with each other. If you are sharing your external hard drive on a Windows computer, someone with a Mac or Linux client might not be able to access it. This isn't always the case, but it can be an issue.

Network Attached Storage

Chapter 2, "Peripherals and Connectors," introduced network attached storage (NAS) devices. If you'll recall, they are self-contained, external storage devices that typically contain two or more hard drives. In addition, NAS devices also have their own operating system and file-sharing mechanisms.

NAS solutions tend to be more expensive than DAS ones, and they can be a little harder to set up and manage. For example, they are connected to the network instead of your computer, and they come with their own software package for management. But the upside far outweighs the downside. First, since it's connected to the network, the NAS is available regardless of whether an individual computer is online or not. Second, you don't run into any file system compatibility issues between clients with different operating systems. Third, most NAS devices also come with extra utilities, such as built-in RAID or backup programs. If you're looking for something quick and cheap, DAS might do the trick. If you want something a little more permanent, stable, and flexible, then NAS is a better option.

Network Drives

A network drive is simply a hard drive on another computer that you are accessing. In most cases it's located on a server. From your computer's perspective, it doesn't matter if that drive is internal or external to the server, a NAS device, or anything else. Your computer just needs to know the location of that drive.

The way to connect to a network drive is pretty simple. You need to know the server name (or whatever computer is serving it up) as well as the name of the shared folder. Then, you can click Start and in the search box type *server**sharename*, where *server* is the name of the computer and *sharename* is the name of the shared folder. If the remote computer is online, and you have appropriate permissions, access will be granted to the resource.

It might be a pain to have to do this every time you want to access a network drive, so Windows and other operating systems give you the ability to *map* to a network drive and reconnect every time your computer boots up. In Windows, you click Start and right-click Computer. There you will have the option Map Network Drive. Click that, and it will open a screen similar to the one in Figure 6.5.

FIGURE 6.5   Mapping a network drive

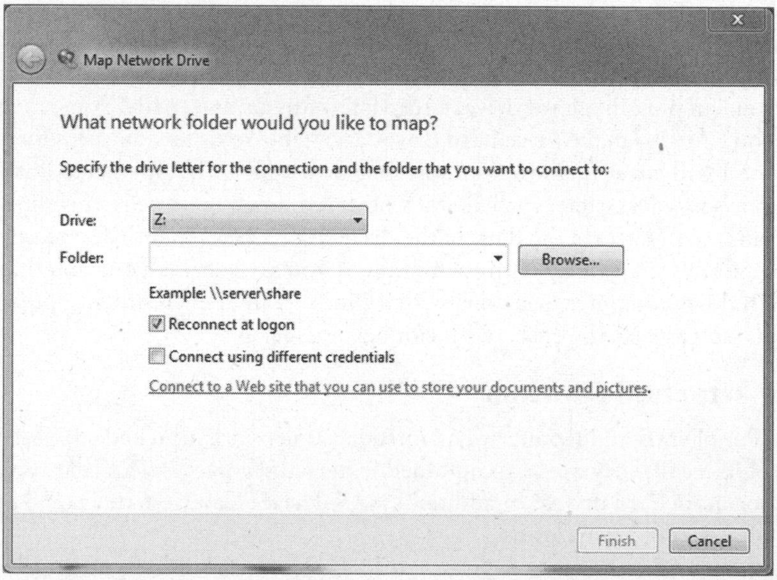

When mapping a network drive, you first assign it a drive letter. It can be any letter you want that's not already in use on your computer. Then you type in the path to the folder or browse for it on the network. Finally, you can choose to reconnect at logon, and you can also use different credentials (username and password) to log on versus the ones you used to log onto your system. After you set your parameters, click Finish, and if you did everything right, you will now be able to access that shared resource. In fact, if you click Start ➢ Computer, that drive letter should now appear in your list of available drives. Exercise 6.1 has you practice doing this, but you will need access to a server or a second computer with a shared folder for this exercise to work.

EXERCISE 6.1

Connecting to a Shared Folder

1. Find the name of the server and the shared folder. (You can get this from your administrator or instructor if you're in a classroom setting. If you are doing this at home with a second computer, you can browse for the shared folder on the network. Alternatively, you can go to the server computer, right-click the folder you shared, and choose Properties. On the Sharing tab, it will tell you the share name.

2. On the client computer, click Start, right-click Computer, and choose Map Network Drive.

3. Choose a drive letter.

4. Enter the shared path, or use the Browse button to locate it on the network.

5. Check the boxes for either of the options you want, and click Finish.

 Real World Scenario

What "R" Drive?

This is a situation you might run into with co-workers; I know I have had this happen several times.

You ask a co-worker where a file you need is, and the response is, "Oh, it's on the R drive." (Or pick a letter, any letter.) Now, perhaps the R drive is a corporate standard that everyone knows about, and you can just open it on your computer. But perhaps not. If not, then knowing that it's the R drive is like asking someone where some sand is and they tell you, "In the desert." Thanks, but not helpful.

Most people don't realize that the R drive on their computer might not be the same as any drive on your computer, and most of them probably also don't realize that the R drive is actually located on another computer and not theirs. In situations like this, calmly thank them, and then ask them if you can see the path to the R drive so you can connect to it yourself.

Types of Local Sharing

Resources located on your computer or on a server somewhere aren't automatically available to other users on the network. This is a very good thing, because you probably have files that are private and no other users need to get to. Even on a server, there are files that no one has business getting to across the network. In order to make these resources available to users on different systems, you have to *share* them. After the resources are shared, the computer uses security permissions to determine who can get to the resources and what they can do once they get there, such as only read the file or make changes to the file.

Here, you will learn about two different types of sharing: peer-to-peer, which is designed more for ad hoc and temporary connections, and file and print sharing, which is usually more permanent in nature.

Peer-to-Peer Sharing

Based on its name, you can guess that *peer-to-peer (P2P) sharing* does not involve the use of servers. Both computers or mobile devices used in this arrangement are peers. One will serve the material to the other but does not have any other predetermined higher level of importance.

Ad Hoc Bluetooth Sharing

For mobile devices, Bluetooth sharing can be a quick and easy way to transfer files—most often pictures, videos, or contacts—from one device to another. As you learned earlier in this chapter, when two Bluetooth-enabled devices are close enough to each other, they can automatically create a network called a piconet.

Be sure that Bluetooth is enabled on your phone before attempting a file transfer.

To transfer files between devices, though, you need an app. Each mobile's app store will have plenty of options to choose from, so go with the one you like. Figure 6.6 shows a few popular options from the iTunes store.

After downloading the app, transferring files is pretty simple. Although the specific steps might differ based on your platform, this is generally how you do it:

1. Get in range of the other person with the Bluetooth-enabled device.
2. Open the app and locate their device.
3. Find the picture or file you want to share, tap it, and tap Share.
4. Choose Bluetooth as your sharing medium.
5. The person on the receiving end accepts the file.

Unless you are actively sharing a Bluetooth file or using a Bluetooth device such as a hands-free headset, disable Bluetooth on your device. It will save battery life and also make you less vulnerable to potential Bluetooth-based hacking attempts.

FIGURE 6.6   Bluetooth sharing apps on iTunes

Once you've finished, you can close the app, turn off Bluetooth, and go about your day.

PC-to-PC Direct Link

This is the simplest of PC-based networks, because it involves only two computers directly connected to each other. A direct link network is typically used only for temporary situations. If you want a more permanent network, it's best to use a connectivity device like a hub or wireless router.

You have a few options to directly connect the PCs together. The first is to use a network cable with RJ-45 connectors. An ordinary network cable (called a patch cable) will not work, though; you need a *crossover cable*. Here's why. On a normal Cat 5 patch cable, four wires are used: 1, 2, 3, and 6. The wires, of course, connect to the pins on the connector in the network card. Pins 1 and 2 send data, and pins 3 and 6 receive data. If you were to try using a regular patch cable, the first computer would send data out pins 1 and 2 and straight to pins 1 and 2 (the send pins) of the second computer. That won't work. Instead, the crossover cable flips pins 1 and 3 and pins 2 and 6 on one end of the cable. That way the signals sent from one end get to the receiving pins on the other end. The second option is to use a direct-link USB cable.

After you connect the two computers, you need to share the directory or drive on the host computer that you want to access from the client computer. I will show you how to do that later in the "File and Print Sharing" section.

Online Peer-to-Peer Network

The PC-to-PC direct link solution works only if both computers are in the same location. If not, it can be hard to make the cable reach from one to the other. Fortunately there are online solutions that allow you to create an online P2P network to share movies, music, games, and other files.

P2P networks have existed since the late 1990s and have at times attained controversial status. One of the earlier examples of an online P2P network was Napster, which was set up to share music files. It worked by having users indicate which music files they wanted to share, and other users could search for music they wanted. The Napster servers indexed the content to make searching easier. After a match was made, the two computers were connected directly to each other for the file transfer.

The upside for users was that Napster allowed them to get music for free from other users. The downside, according to the music industry, was that it was illegal. After a series of lawsuits, Napster was shut down as a free service. Other services followed, which allowed for transfer of files other than music as well.

For business purposes, you can find several online tools that let you make a connection to another computer on the Internet to exchange files. Examples include JustBeamIt and FilesOverMiles. Others also exist that require you to download their client software onto your computer, such as BitTorrent.

Here are a few things to watch out for with online P2P networks:

- Make sure your security software is current. P2P apps can easily download malware to your computer.

- Related to that, always scan your downloads for viruses.

- Observe the laws. Don't download anything illegal or upload anything that you don't own the legally transferrable copyright to.

- Be careful which folders and files you share. You don't want your private information on display on the Internet. That's almost like asking to have your identity stolen.

- Close down the P2P session after you have finished to reduce your security risks.

If you are transferring work-related files between two computers, also be aware of potential security risks. The files and the transfers might or might not be encrypted, so it isn't the best idea to transfer secret information this way. Online P2P networks can be fast, but if you have any concerns about security or malware, just don't use them.

File and Print Sharing

Unlike P2P connections, setting up file and print sharing implies a longer-term connection. It also lets you make connections between more than two devices at a time. With file and print sharing, you can make folders or printers available to everyone in your office or all members of your family. There are two different ways I will talk about sharing resources here: using workgroups and using homegroups.

 The common way for sharing files and printers on a large network is to use a domain. It's much easier to configure and centrally control security in a domain than it is in a workgroup. You won't be tested on setting up domains on the IT Fundamentals exam.

Configuring Workgroups for Sharing

Before I get too far into configuring a workgroup, I should stop for a minute and define what one is. A *workgroup* is a collection of peer-to-peer computers without centralized security. The limit you will see in Microsoft literature is that they are limited to 20 computers, but realistically anything more than 10 is too cumbersome to manage. Other features of workgroups include the following:

- To join the workgroup, only the workgroup name is required. No password is needed.

- Clients with various operating systems can join, such as any version of Windows and Mac OS X.

- Every computer on the workgroup needs to manage its own set of user accounts. This is one reason why administration becomes challenging.

- Every computer shares the resources it needs to share. This is another reason why administration becomes challenging.

- All computers must be on the same local network.

By default, your Windows computer will join the default workgroup, conveniently named WORKGROUP. You can see your system's workgroup configuration by going to Control Panel ➢ System And Security ➢ System (Figure 6.7). To change the workgroup name, you click Change Settings, which brings up the System Properties window, and then click the Change button to rename the computer or the workgroup (Figure 6.8).

Because there is no password required, it's quite easy to join a workgroup. That can also be a bad thing, because you can't stop a local computer on your network from joining the workgroup if you don't want it to. Macs can join workgroups as well; Exercise 6.2 shows you how.

FIGURE 6.7 Workgroup name

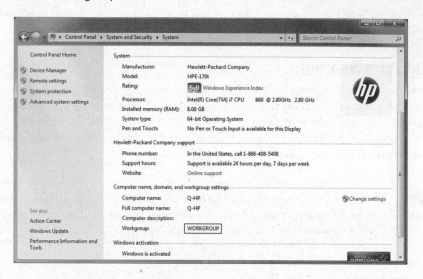

FIGURE 6.8 Changing the computer and workgroup name

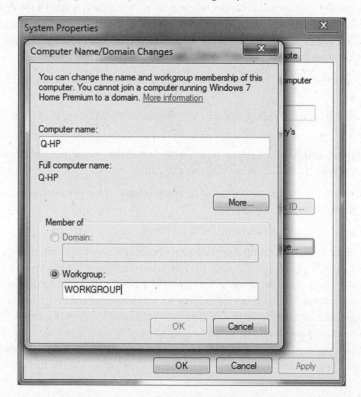

EXERCISE 6.2

Connecting a Mac to a Workgroup

1. Open System Preferences ➤ Internet & Network ➤ Network.

2. Click the network connection you use to connect to Windows computers (such as Ethernet). Click the Advanced button.

3. Click the WINS button at the top of the window.

4. Click the NetBIOS field, and enter the name you want your Mac to be known as in the workgroup.

5. Click the Workgroup field and enter the name of the workgroup.

6. Click OK and then Apply. Close Network Preferences and reboot.

7. After rebooting, click the File menu at the top of the screen and choose New Finder Window. You should see the available shared folders under the Shared heading on the left side.

GRANTING ACCESS TO SHARED RESOURCES

Granting access to a resource involves two steps: sharing the resource and assigning permissions. To share a folder, right-click the folder in Windows Explorer, choose Properties, and click the Security tab, as shown in Figure 6.9.

Clicking Advanced Sharing will bring up the Advanced Sharing window (Figure 6.10), and here is where you check the box to share the folder, give it a share name (it doesn't need to be the same as the folder name), and limit the number of concurrent users if you choose to. Also, you can click the Permissions button to set access restrictions on the folder (Figure 6.11). You'll see in Figure 6.11 that by default, the Everyone group has Read access to this folder. This raises two questions. One, who is Everyone, and two, what do the three permissions mean?

Everyone means every person who has an account on this local computer. Keep in mind that we are still talking about accessing a shared resource across the network. This means that in your workgroup of 12 people, if you have a folder that everyone needs, you need to have user accounts for all 12 of those people on your computer. If the user accounts don't exist, you need to create them. If a user changes his password on one computer, it won't change on yours. Can that get confusing? You bet it can. Playing this out even further, you can imagine how fun this scenario gets when everyone has resources to share. Twelve workstations with 12 accounts each means 144 user accounts in total.

There is a way around that, but it's not recommended because it weakens your security. If you look back at the Sharing tab shown in Figure 6.9, you will see a link at the bottom of the window for the Network and Sharing Center. Click that, and then click the down arrow across from Home Or Work. It will open up a screen like the one shown in Figure 6.12. Here you have an option called Password Protected Sharing. If you turn this off, then people don't need a user account on your system to access files. It will make your life easier, but it's not recommended. Remember, people don't need passwords to join your workgroup. They only need to be on the local network, which could mean they are sitting in the parking lot (in a black car with dark tinted windows), using their laptop, and connecting via your wireless network.

FIGURE 6.9   Sharing tab

As for the second question, there are three share permissions: Full Control, Modify, and Read. Here's what they allow:

- Full Control allows the user to do anything to the folder, its files, and subfolders, including deleting them all, changing permissions, and giving themselves ownership.

- Modify lets the user do almost everything Full Control does, except users can't change permissions, delete subfolders or files, or give themselves ownership.

- Read lets the user read the contents of the file or folder or execute an application.

FIGURE 6.10   Advanced Sharing window

FIGURE 6.11   Sharing permissions

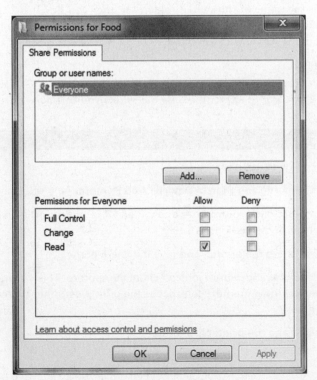

FIGURE 6.12   Network and Sharing Center

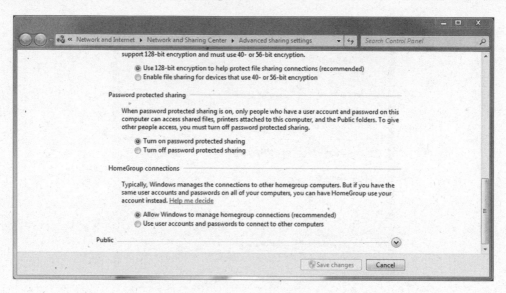

Once the resource is shared, users on the network can access it by clicking Start and in the search box typing ***server**sharename***, where *server* is the name of the computer and *sharename* is the name of the shared folder. Or, they can find it by clicking Start ➢ Computer (or opening any Windows Explorer window) and then looking under the Network heading in the left navigation pane.

SHARING PRINTERS

Sharing a printer in a workgroup is similar to sharing a folder; you just need to locate the printer instead of the folder to share. Exercise 6.3 walks you through sharing a printer.

EXERCISE 6.3

Sharing a Printer in Windows

1. Find your printer by clicking Start ➢ Devices And Printers.

2. In that window, right-click your printer and choose Printer Properties, and then click the Sharing tab, as shown in Figure 6.13.

3. Check the box to share the printer, and give it a share name.

4. Also check the box to render print jobs on client computers. This will make client computers use their own memory to process the print jobs rather than using your computer's memory.

5. Click Apply or OK, and the printer is shared.

FIGURE 6.13   Sharing a printer

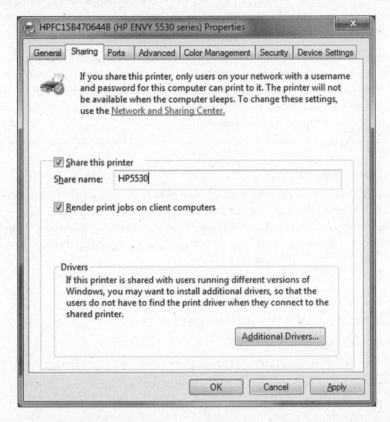

There are two different ways printers can be attached to the network: they can connect to your local computer using a USB cable, or they can connect to the network directly with a network cable or wireless.

If the printer is connected to your machine, users need an account on your computer to use it, just as they would for shared files. In addition, if your computer is off for any reason, the printer is not available. Finally, clients using tablets or smartphones will not be able to print to the printer. Connecting directly to the network is much easier. Your computer can be off yet others can still print, and mobile users will be able to print as well. Networked printers are typically shared through their own interface (most will have their own touchscreen display) as opposed to through a workstation.

Sharing and Accessing Shared Resources in Mac OS X

Sharing folders on Mac OS X is easy. Open System Preferences ➢ Sharing and choose the items you want to share. You can also share folders from Finder by selecting the folder, going to the File menu and choosing Get Info, and enabling Shared Folder.

To access shares on a remote computer, in Finder choose Go ➢ Connect To Server. From there you can type the name of the server in the Server Address field or choose Browse to look for it on the network. When you locate the server, click it and then click Connect As. Unless the server allows you to connect as Guest, you will need a valid user account and password on the machine you are connecting to.

Sharing in Homegroups

A *homegroup* is a group of computers on a home network that can share files and printers. It sounds a lot like a workgroup, doesn't it? In some ways they are analogous, but there are some major differences. Microsoft introduced homegroups in Windows 7, and only Microsoft Windows 7 and newer operating systems can participate in them. In addition, homegroups have the following features:

- An unlimited number of computers can join.
- A password is required to join the homegroup.
- Members do not need to be on the local network.
- IP version 6 is required.
- Sharing files and printers is easier than sharing them in a workgroup.

How do you know if you are in a homegroup? First, if you are not running Windows 7 or newer, then the answer is easy: no, you're not. If you are running Windows 7 (or newer), you can open Control Panel ➢ Network And Internet ➢ Network And Sharing Center (Figure 6.14) and look at the screen. Next to the network connection, it will say HomeGroup: Joined. If it says anything else, you are not in a homegroup.

Changing homegroup settings or sharing resources is easily accomplished by going to the HomeGroup page shown in Figure 6.15. You can get there by clicking the Joined link in Figure 6.14, clicking HomeGroup in the Network and Sharing Center, or by choosing HomeGroup from Control Panel ➢ Network And Internet.

In Figure 6.15, you can see that you just check boxes to share or stream data, and you have links to view and change the homegroup password, leave the homegroup, change advanced settings, or troubleshoot problems. The best part is that unlike a workgroup, the users in your homegroup don't need accounts on your computer to access files, so network administration is a lot easier.

FIGURE 6.14   Member of a homegroup

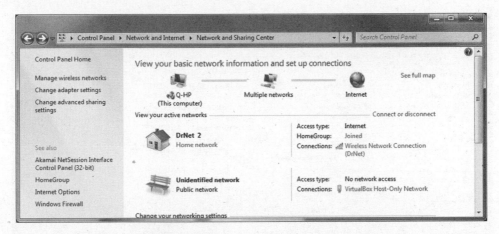

FIGURE 6.15   HomeGroup settings

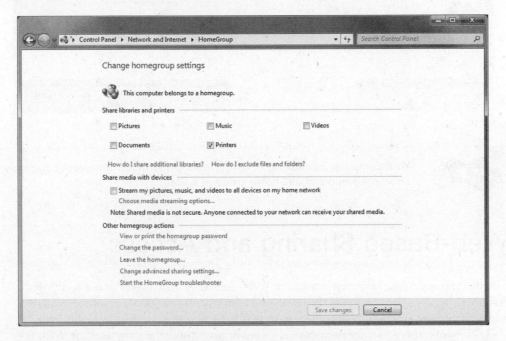

If you don't want to share all of the files on your computer with members of your homegroup, you can stop sharing of specific folders. Stopping the sharing affects files in that folder as well as any subfolders. To do that, find the folder you want to stop sharing, right-click, and choose Share With ➤ Nobody, as shown in Figure 6.16. Or, you can choose to share only with Specific People, and then you are essentially back to managing user accounts just as you would with workgroup sharing.

FIGURE 6.16   Share with Nobody

 Your computer can belong to both a workgroup and a homegroup but only one workgroup and one homegroup at a time.

Web-Based Sharing and Access

Sharing and accessing resources across the Web bears very little resemblance to sharing resources locally. The concept is the same—an administrator makes a resource available and a client user accesses it—but the way in which it's accomplished is quite different.

At the same time, you are probably very used to accessing resources over the Web. It's likely that you are on the Internet every day, or at least a few times a week, and when you are, you're accessing resources across the Web. It might be as simple as reading about news or celebrities or sports, or it might be downloading a new application for your computer.

This section is broken into two parts. In the first, I will talk about concepts related to cloud computing and demystify what it really means. In the second, I will cover specific methods and protocols used to access resources across the Internet.

Cloud Concepts

You hear the term a lot today—*the cloud*. What exactly is the cloud? The way it's named, and it's probably due to the word *the* at the beginning, it sounds like it's one giant, fluffy, magical entity that does everything you could ever want a computer to do. Only it's not quite that big, fluffy, magical, or even one thing.

Cloud computing is a method by which you access remote servers to store files or run applications for you. There isn't one cloud but hundreds of commercial clouds in existence today. Many of them are owned by big companies such as Microsoft, Google, HP, Apple, Netflix, Amazon, and others. Basically, they set up the hardware and/or software for you on their network, and then you use it.

Using the cloud sounds pretty simple, and in most cases it is. From the administrator's side, things can be a little trickier. Cloud computing uses a concept called *virtualization*, which means there isn't necessarily a one-to-one relationship between a physical server and a logical (or virtual) server. In other words, you might have one physical server that virtually hosts cloud servers for a dozen companies, or you might have several physical servers working together as one logical server. From the end user's side, the idea of a physical machine versus a virtual machine doesn't even come into play, because it's all handled behind the scenes.

Cloud providers generally offer one of three types of services:

Software as a Service (SaaS)   SaaS handles the task of managing software and its deployment. This is the one you are probably most familiar with, because it's the model used by Google Docs, Microsoft Office 365, and even storage solutions such as Dropbox. The advantage of this model is to cut costs for software ownership and management; usually you sign up for subscriptions to use the software.

Platform as a Service (PaaS)   PaaS can be very helpful to software developers, because the vendor manages the various hardware platforms. This frees up the software developer to focus on building their application and scaling it.

Infrastructure as a Service (IaaS)   Let's say you need extra network capacity, including processing power, storage, and networking services (such as firewalls), but you don't have the money to buy more network hardware. Instead, you can purchase IaaS, which is a lot like paying for utilities—you pay for what you use. Of the three, IaaS requires the most network management expertise from the client.

Running a cloud is not restricted to big companies over the Internet either. You can purchase virtualization software to set up your own cloud within your own network. That type of setup is referred to as a *private cloud*, as opposed to the *public clouds* I mentioned earlier.

The upside of using a cloud is that it's generally cheaper than needing to buy your own hardware or software and install and manage it all. Plus, if there is a hardware failure within the cloud, the provider handles it for you. If the cloud is set up right, you won't even know a failure occurred. The biggest downside has been security. You're storing your data on someone else's server and sending it back and forth via the Internet. Cloud providers have dramatically increased their security over the last few years, but this can still be an issue, especially if you are dealing with highly sensitive material or personally identifiable information (PII).

Cloud-Based Storage

Storage is the area in which cloud computing got its start. The idea is simple—you store files just like you would on a hard drive but with two major advantages. One, you don't need to buy the hardware. Two, users can access the files regardless of where they are physically located. You can have users in the United States, China, and Germany, and all of them have access via their web browser.

There is no shortage of cloud-based storage providers on the market today. Each one offers slightly different features. Most of them will offer limited storage for free and premium services for more data-heavy users. Table 6.1 shows you a comparison of some of the more well-known providers. Please note that the data limits and cost can change; this is for illustrative purposes only. Most of these providers offer business plans with unlimited storage as well, for an additional cost.

TABLE 6.1   Cloud providers and features

Service	Free	Premium	Cost per year
Dropbox	2 GB	1 TB	$100
Apple iCloud	5 GB	200 GB	$48
Box	10 GB	100 GB	$60
Microsoft OneDrive	15 GB	200 GB	$48
Google Drive	15 GB	1 TB	$120

Which one should you choose? If you want extra features such as web-based applications, then Google or Microsoft is probably the best choice. If you just need data storage, then Box or Dropbox might be a better option.

> **NOTE**   Nearly all client OSs will work with any of the providers, with the exception of Linux, which natively works only with Dropbox.

Most cloud storage providers offer synchronization to the desktop, which makes it so you have a folder on your computer, just as if it were on your hard drive. And importantly, that folder will always have the most current edition of the files stored in the cloud.

Accessing the sites is done through your web browser. Once you are in the site, managing your files is much like managing them on your local computer. In Figure 6.17 you can see the Google Drive interface, with three folders and two files in it.

You have a few options to share a folder with another user. One way is to right-click the folder and choose Share ➢ Share (Figure 6.18). You'll be asked to enter their name or email address and indicate whether they can view or edit the file. To share multiple items, you can check the boxes in front of folder names (as the box is checked in Figure 6.18) and then click the icon that shows a person and a plus sign right above the check box. That will take you to the same sharing menu, which asks for the name and email address.

FIGURE 6.17   Google Drive

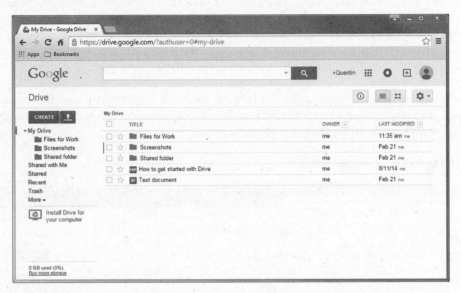

FIGURE 6.18   Sharing a folder on Google Drive

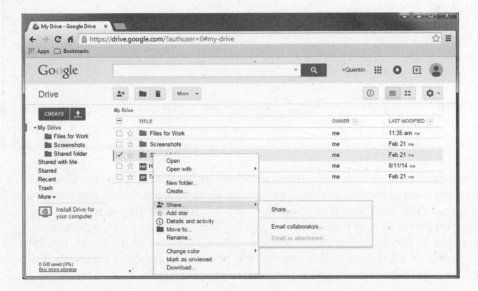

Cloud-Based Applications

Google really popularized the use of web-based applications. After all, the whole Chromebook platform, which has been very successful, is based on this premise! Other companies have gotten into the cloud-based application space as well, such as Microsoft with Office 365. The menus and layout are slightly different than PC-based versions of Office, but if you're familiar with Office, you can easily use Office 365. And, all of the files are stored on the cloud.

Cloud-based apps run through your web browser. This is great for end users for a few reasons. One, your system does not have to use its own hardware to run the application. Two, different client OSs can run the application (usually) without worrying about compatibility issues.

To create a new document using Google Docs, you click the Create button shown on the left side of Figure 6.18 and then choose Document from the menu. It opens a new browser window with Google Docs, shown in Figure 6.19.

FIGURE 6.19   Google Docs

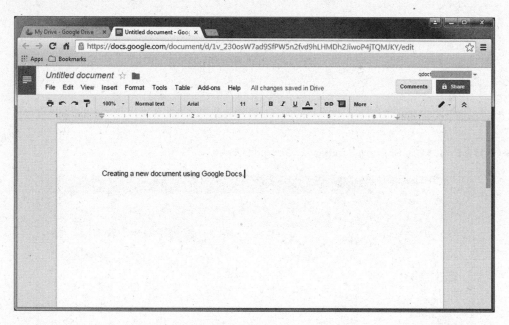

The newest trend in web applications and cloud storage is the streaming of media. Companies such as Netflix, Amazon, Pandora, and others store movies and music on their clouds. You download their client software, and for a monthly subscription fee you can stream media to your device. It can be your phone, your computer, or your home entertainment system. Before the advent of broadband network technologies, this type of setup would have been impossible, but now it is poised to become the mainstream way that people receive audio and video entertainment.

Accessing Web-Based Resources

Browsing the Internet is something you probably do most days of the week, so spending time here telling you how to do that isn't the most productive thing to do. Instead, I will talk about some of the things that are going on behind the scenes, so you understand what's really happening.

First, remember that everything on the Internet revolves around TCP/IP, which you learned about in Chapter 5. If you'll recall, accessing another computer on the Internet requires knowing the remote computer's IP address. Think of it in terms of delivering a package. If you tell the driver to deliver the package to James White, and that's all you tell him, you will probably get a blank stare. But if you tell the driver that James White lives at 123 Main Street in Buffalo, New York, then the driver knows where to go. DNS servers help out a lot, because they resolve host names to IP addresses. Summarizing the process of accessing an Internet site looks something like this:

1. You open your web browser, type in www.google.com, and press Enter.

2. Your computer looks to find the IP address of a DNS server. If there is no DNS server configured, you will get a message that the server cannot be found. If you do have a DNS server configured, your system will ask the DNS server for the address to www.google.com.

3. The DNS server replies that www.google.com is 173.194.219.99.

4. Your computer sends a message to 173.194.219.99 (via your router) asking to make a connection.

5. The server at 173.194.219.99 responds with its content, which is the file set up as its default home page.

The actual process is a bit more complicated, but this covers the most important parts. One thing I need to add to it, though, is the use of ports. Think of a port as a communications channel. It's like cable television. You get 500 channels delivered to your address, but when you want to watch a show you need to turn to a specific channel. The same sort of thing happens on the Internet. When you make the connection to 173.194.219.99, you do it using the appropriate port (channel) for the request. For example, normal web browsing uses HTTP on port 80. So technically you are communicating to 173.194.219.99:80. The combination of the IP address and port number is called a *socket*. Ports let servers differentiate and keep track of incoming and outgoing traffic for better data management.

Web Browsing

The TCP/IP protocol used the most often, by far, is the *Hypertext Transfer Protocol (HTTP)*. It's used to manage communications between web browsers and web servers, and it opens the right resource when you click a link. HTTP is optimized to deliver text, graphics, and hyperlinks to other resources. As I mentioned in the previous paragraph, HTTP uses port 80.

While HTTP is a great, versatile protocol, it has one glaring weakness—it's unsecure. Fortunately, there is a solution for that, and it's *Hypertext Transfer Protocol Secure (HTTPS)*. HTTPS connections are secured using either *Secure Sockets Layer (SSL)* or *Transport Layer Security (TLS)*, and HTTPS uses port 443. If you want to access secure information online, such as personal banking or anything that has you type in a password, make sure the site is using HTTPS and not HTTP.

> I can't emphasize this enough: websites using only HTTP send all of the information back and forth across the Internet in plain text. Before typing in *anything* that you wouldn't want others to see, make sure the site uses HTTPS.

From the client side, the most common issue you will encounter when HTTPS is in use on a website is that users may not know what the proper context is. To access most websites, you use http:// in the address bar. To get to a site using HTTPS, you need to use https:// instead.

 Real World Scenario

How Secure Is It?

You have probably heard before that you should not enter personal information (such as a credit card number) into an unsecure website. But what does that really mean?

First, know what to look for. If you are entering information into a website form and the address of the site begins with just http://, you're just asking for someone to steal the information! HTTP transmits data in plain text, meaning that there is no encryption at all between your computer and the server. On the other hand, HTTPS encrypts the data transmissions as they cross the wire.

To use HTTPS, the website needs to obtain an SSL certificate from a reputable web host, which verifies the identity of the website. So the good news is that if you are accessing a site with https:// in the header, you know that the site is what it says it is (and not a Trojan horse) and that transmissions between your computer and that site are encrypted. Once the data is on the website's server, though, HTTPS is no longer relevant and other protection methods are needed to keep your data secure.

Exercise 6.4 shows you what to look for to verify that it's a secure site using HTTPS.

EXERCISE 6.4

Verifying HTTPS

1.   Open your web browser.

2.   In the address box, type www.bankofamerica.com and press Enter.

3.   Look at the title bar. Figure 6.20 shows you what a secure site looks like in Internet Explorer, and Figure 6.21 shows you the same site in Google Chrome.

FIGURE 6.20   Secure site in IE

FIGURE 6.21   Secure site in Chrome

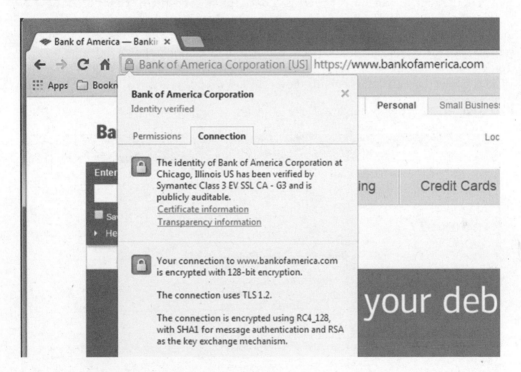

4.   Notice that the address bars have HTTPS in them and are colored green (not all secured sites will be green).

5.   If you want to verify the connection, click the padlock icon, as is shown in Figure 6.21. This will provide additional security details.

6.   Close your web browser.

If you use your web browser to initiate a file download, it will process those requests (either in the background or overtly) using FTP, which I am going to cover next.

File Downloads

Just as HTTP is optimized for web traffic, the *File Transfer Protocol (FTP)* is optimized to do what it says it does—transfer files. This includes both uploading and downloading files from one host to another. FTP is both a protocol and an application. Specifically, FTP lets you copy files, list and manipulate directories, and view file contents. You can't use it to remotely execute applications. FTP uses ports 20 and 21.

Whenever a user attempts to access an FTP site, they will be asked for a login. If it's a public site, you can often just use the login name *anonymous* and then provide your email address as the password. Of course, there's no rule saying you have to give your real email address if you don't want to. If the FTP site is secured, you will need a legitimate login name and password to access it. If you are using a browser such as Internet Explorer to connect via FTP, the correct syntax in the address window is `ftp://username:password@ftp.ftpsite.com`.

If you're used to the pictures and hyperlinks on web pages, you will probably be a bit disappointed by the Spartan look of FTP sites. Remember that FTP is designed for file transfers, so there really are no bells and whistles in the example shown in Figure 6.22. You will see directories and files. The directories contain sample images of files from the various books that Sybex has published over the last several years.

FIGURE 6.22 Sybex public FTP site

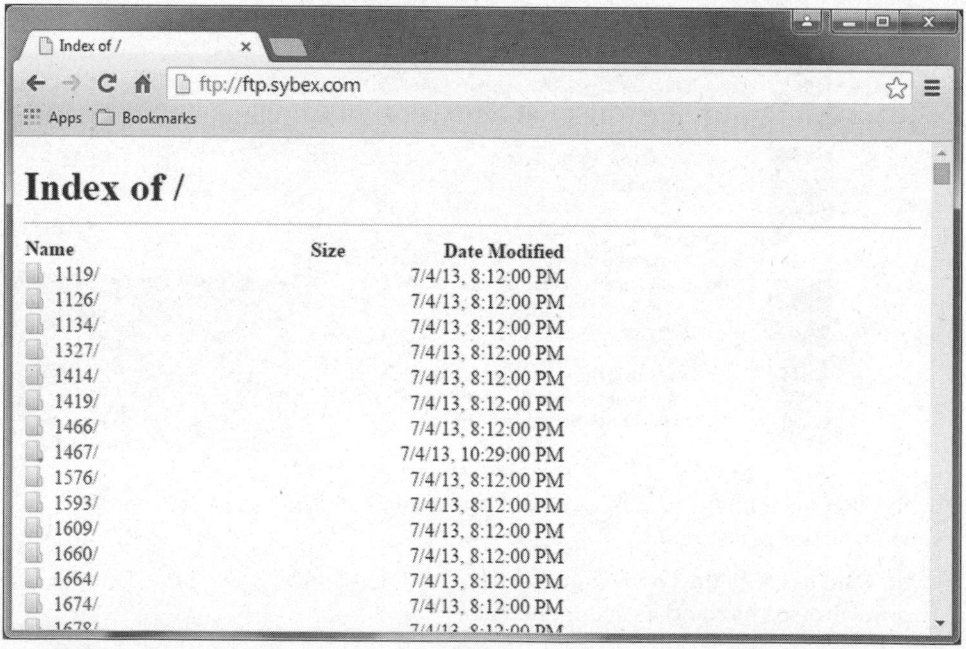

The only problem with FTP is that all data is sent in clear text, just like HTTP. If you need to make your FTP transfer secure, then you'll use SFTP. *Secure File Transfer Protocol (SFTP)*, also called SSH File Transfer Protocol, is used when you need to transfer files over an encrypted connection. It uses a Secure Shell (SSH) session, which encrypts the connection on port 22. Apart from the secure part, it's used just as FTP is—for transferring files between computers on an IP network, such as the Internet.

The final option you should know about is *File Transfer Protocol Secure (FTPS)*. It's like HTTPS in that it uses SSL or TLS to secure the connection. Because of this, it requires a third-party-issued security certificate, which is an extra step that most administrators don't want to deal with. In addition, it doesn't have as many features as SFTP. Honestly, I am kind of surprised that it's an exam objective because since the introduction of SFTP in 1997, it's hardly ever used in the real world. FTPS can run on port 990 or port 21.

 To use HTTP or FTP on your own network, you need to set up a computer as an HTTP or FTP server. Doing so is beyond the scope of the IT Fundamentals exam, but know that you can do it. For example, FTP works well if you need to transfer large files between remote segments of a network.

Summary

In this chapter, you learned about sharing and accessing local and web-based resources. First, you learned about network types, such as LANs, WANs, PANs, and MANs, as well as the differences between client-server and peer-to-peer networking models. Then, you read about storage options such as direct attached storage and network attached storage and how to connect to network drives.

Next, you learned about different peer-to-peer sharing models. Examples included ad hoc Bluetooth networks, direct link peer-to-peer, and online peer-to-peer connections. Then the P2P model was expanded a bit to cover workgroups and homegroups and the differences between them. This included sharing printers.

Finally, you learned about web-based sharing and resource access. One of the hot buzzwords in computing today is *the cloud*. You learned that the cloud isn't a single thing but a collection of hardware and software that you can use for your storage and application needs. The chapter finished with a discussion on accessing web resources using HTTP and HTTPS, as well as transferring files with FTP, SFTP, and FTPS.

Exam Essentials

Know the difference between DAS and NAS. Direct attached storage means a hard drive attached to your computer, whether it's an internal or external drive. Network attached storage is a hard drive unit with file management software that's directly attached to the network with a network cable.

Understand the difference between a peer-to-peer network and a client-server network. In a peer-to-peer network, there is no centralized security, and all systems on the network are considered equals. Resources may be shared from any system. In a client-server network, you have centralized security and resource management.

Know the different types of peer-to-peer sharing methods.   Options include ad hoc Bluetooth networks, direct link PC-to-PC, and online peer-to-peer networks.

Understand the difference between local and network printing.   If the printer is connected directly to your computer, it's local. You can share your local printer for others on the network to use, but if your computer is off, no one can use it. A network printer is attached to the network and is easier to share among several users.

Know how cloud-based storage and applications work.   Third-party companies supply the hardware and software. Storage solutions such as Google Drive and Dropbox let you store files for access by anyone in the world through their web browser. Cloud-based apps like Google Docs and Microsoft Office 365 let you run an application through your web browser without needing the software installed on your computer.

Know the protocols used to access web-based resources.   The protocols for websites are HTTP and HTTPS. For file downloads, you would use FTP, FTPS, or SFTP.

Chapter 6 Lab

This lab gives you experience with using cloud-based storage and applications. You can use any cloud provider you like, and in fact, it's better if you experience the differences in how providers store files and let you manage and manipulate them. For this example, you will use Google Drive and its associated apps.

This lab will work best if you have someone to work with. For example, in a classroom setting you can partner with someone. If you are studying at home, you can create multiple accounts and get the same experience. You will just need to log off and on with your other account to see the shared files.

1.   Open Google at www.google.com.

2.   If you do not already have a Google account, you will need to create one. This will let you use their online apps and storage, as well as give you a Gmail account.

3.   Once you're logged in, click the Apps icon in the upper-right corner. It's the one that has nine small squares (Figure 6.23).

4.   In Apps, click Drive. This will open Google Drive, as shown in Figure 6.24.

5.   Create a folder and share it with another account. Also create a document or spreadsheet using Google's online software. How easy or difficult was it?

6.   Now access the resources that were shared for you. How easy or difficult was it?

Here are some questions based on Google Drive.

1.   How do you create new files or folders?

2.   How do you upload files or folders from your computer?

FIGURE 6.23   Google icons

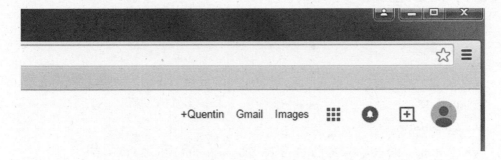

FIGURE 6.24   Google Drive

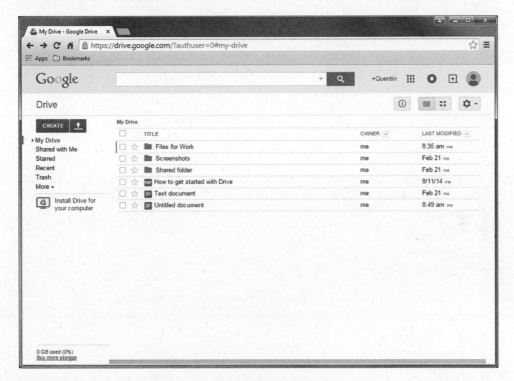

3.   How do you see your most recent activities performed?

4.   How do you synchronize files with your hard drive?

5.   If you need another app, how do you get one?

6.   How do you see how much storage space you have used?

7.   Where do you change your display language or time zone or update your Google profile?

Review Questions

1. Which of the following types of networks offers centralized security and resource administration?

   A. LAN

   B. WAN

   C. Peer-to-peer

   D. Client-server

2. Which of the following are required to join a homegroup? (Choose two.)

   A. All computers on the same local network

   B. A password

   C. File and print sharing enabled

   D. Windows 7 or newer

3. If you were setting up a network on one floor of an office building, what type of network would that most likely be?

   A. LAN

   B. WAN

   C. Peer-to-peer

   D. Client-server

4. You want to share files among six computers, all running Windows 8. You do not want to have to create user accounts for each user on all six computers. What should you use?

   A. Workgroup

   B. Homegroup

   C. Client-server

   D. Ad hoc network

5. What kind of network is specifically associated with Bluetooth devices?

   A. LAN

   B. WAN

   C. PAN

   D. MAN

6. You have shared a folder with Mary, another user on your network. What share permissions should you give her if you want her to be able to edit a file but not give access to others?

   A. Full control

   B. Modify

   C. Edit

   D. Read

7. Susan has configured a peer-to-peer network at her company with her four co-workers. Each co-worker will share vital files from their computer with everyone else in the workgroup. How many total user accounts are needed on this network?

   A. 5

   B. 10

   C. 20

   D. 25

8. Martha has a printer attached to her workstation with a USB cable. Monday morning she calls in sick and her computer is off. Which of the following is true?

   A. Other users will be able to print to the printer with no problems.

   B. Other users need to turn the printer on, and then they can print with no problems.

   C. Other users should map it as a network printer, and then they can print with no problems.

   D. Other users will not be able to print.

9. What type of network model is also called a domain?

   A. LAN

   B. WAN

   C. Peer-to-peer

   D. Client-server

10. Google Docs is an example of which type of cloud computing?

    A. SaaS

    B. IaaS

    C. PaaS

    D. GaaS

11. Your computer is quickly running out of hard drive space, and you need to transfer several large files from another computer to yours. You need a fast and cheap solution. What type of storage should you get?

    A. NAS

    B. DAS

    C. Network drive

    D. P2P

12. What is the secure file transfer protocol that uses SSH for security?

    A. FTPS

    B. SFTP

    C. HTTPS

    D. SHTTP

13. You need to map your R drive to a local server. What is the proper context to map a shared drive?

    A. *servername**sharename*

    B. *servername**sharename*

    C. ::*servername**sharename*

    D. >*servername*>*sharename*

14. You want to reconnect to a shared folder on a server every time your laptop restarts. What do you need to configure?

    A. DAS

    B. NAS

    C. Network drive

    D. Cloud storage

15. Which of the following storage devices is an external hard drive with its own file management software?

    A. NAS

    B. DAS

    C. Network drive

    D. Cloud

16. Which technology refers to online storage, and means that there is not a one-to-one relationship between the hardware and the server?

    A. Cloud computing

    B. Virtualization

    C. Server farm

    D. Spanning

17. Michael needs to connect two PCs directly to each other for large file transfers. What options does he have? (Choose two.)

    A. Cat 5 crossover cable

    B. Cat 5 patch cable

    C. Cat 5 duplex cable

    D. USB direct link cable

18. Users on a network are complaining that they can't access web servers. External email is coming through fine, and someone was able to access a secure web server. Which port was most likely accidentally blocked on the firewall?

    A. 20

    B. 21

    C. 80

    D. 443

19. You have eight computers located in one office building and want to share resources among them. All computers are running Windows 7. What is the easiest option to configure to share files and folders?

A. Workgroup

B. Homegroup

C. PAN

D. LAN

20. HTTPS uses which of the following to secure its connection? (Select two.)

A. SSSH

B. TLS

C. SSL

D. HASH

Chapter

7

Mobile Devices

THE FOLLOWING COMPTIA IT FUNDAMENTALS EXAM OBJECTIVES ARE COVERED IN THIS CHAPTER:

✓ **1.4 Identify the following alternative technologies and their purpose**

- Gesture-based interaction
  - Swiping
  - Pinch-to-zoom
  - Kinetics

✓ **1.5 Explain the basic software features and functions of wireless devices**

- Unlocking/security
- Bluetooth pairing
  - Hands free
  - Data transfer
- Wireless connection setup
  - Verify wireless capabilities
  - Turn on WiFi
  - Locate SSID
  - Enter wireless password (if applicable)
  - Verlfy Internet connection
- Email configuration
  - POP3
  - IMAP
  - SMTP
- Screen orientation
- Synchronization configuration
- Airplane mode
- Stores for mobile applications

As technology evolves, the natural progression is for it to get smaller, faster, and cheaper. As those three happen, manufacturers start bundling technologies together that previously resided on separate devices, such as a telephone and GPS. For evidence of all of those factors coming together, you need to look no further than mobile computing.

You can be pretty certain that the inventors of ENIAC or any other early computer would be absolutely astonished by the capability of the smartphones in the market today, ones that are easily several thousands of times more powerful than the room-sized behemoths of their day. And in another 40 or 50 years, who knows what types of devices will exist? The youth of that generation may look back on our smartphones as quaint curiosities, much like the youth of today look at black-and-white televisions or cassette tapes.

The popularity of mobile devices today is unquestioned, as mobile operating systems greatly outpace workstation operating system sales. And why wouldn't they? Today you can get a hand-held device that lets you surf the Internet, take pictures, play music and movies, and stay in touch with your friends. With that kind of functionality there is almost no need to be tied down to a desk, except for perhaps when you want a bigger screen or a real keyboard to do some work.

Earlier I mentioned that technology gets smaller as it progresses, which is true. For example, in the last 20 years or so, cell phone and laptop manufacturers have been in an arms race to miniaturize, in part to show how advanced their technology was. In the last few years though, there has been an interesting trend in actually making some devices *bigger*. For example, smartphone commercials tout having bigger screens as a reason to buy a particular model. Because of this, you are seeing an increased blurring of the lines between devices. Some phones are big enough now that you might wonder if they're tablets. And many tablets can make phone calls, so what's the difference between them and a phone anyway? This chapter covers the mobile devices that have shot to the top of sales charts and the front of our consciousness, specifically smartphones and tablet computers.

Using Wireless Devices

Even if you are a holdout who doesn't own a smartphone or a tablet, odds are that you know someone who has one. Or maybe you know several people who own them, and they give you grief for not being part of the twenty-first century. Regardless of whether you own one or not, you need to understand how they work and how to set one up to get proper functionality.

The CompTIA IT Fundamentals exam objectives say *wireless devices*; I will use the term *mobile devices* interchangeably with *wireless* throughout this chapter.

To understand how mobile devices work, you need to know a bit about hardware, operating systems, and networking, because they all come together in a small package. Those topics have already been covered in earlier chapters. Here, the focus is on two areas: specific usability features of mobile devices and setting up a wireless device for network and email.

Wireless Usability Options

With this new generation of devices came new ways of interacting with personal electronics. Their small size necessitated new ways, because traditional input devices such as the keyboard and mouse were far too large. The touchscreen and onscreen keyboard became the new tools for working with your device.

For the examples in this chapter, I am going to use iOS 8 on an iPhone as well as Android as you would see it on a tablet computer. Before getting into the specifics of wireless usability options, familiarize yourself with the home screen for the operating system. Figure 7.1 shows you a home screen in iOS 8 and Figure 7.2 shows you an Android home screen.

FIGURE 7.1   iOS 8 home screen

FIGURE 7.2 Android home screen

 The Android screen shots you will see in this chapter are coming from Andy the Android emulator. This free emulator works on PCs and Macs, and you can find it at www.andyroid.net.

With iOS, the home screen contains several apps, and the one you will use to set most configuration options will be Settings. In Android, you can get to settings by tapping the Settings icon—it's the fifth one from the left on the bottom, the one that looks like it has slider bars on it. (From left to right, the icons are Chrome browser, Email, ES file explorer, Apps, Settings, Camera, and Play Store.)

Interacting with Mobile Devices

When most users first experience a mobile device, there is a lot of uncertainty. There are no keyboard and no mouse. How do you possibly interact with this thing? If you have an iPhone, there's only one button on the front (called the Home button). Android devices have three or four buttons. New users need to get used to the functionality of a touch screen in a hurry.

Mobile devices are built around a concept called *gesture-based interaction*, whereby users use their fingers and various movements to interact with their touch screen. The good news is the device doesn't require complicated interpretive dance patterns to work, although it has sensors built in that could detect your dance movements if you wanted it to. The three gestures you need to know are tap, swipe, and pinch, and there is a fourth closely related concept called kinetics.

Tap A tap of the finger is all it takes to get a lot done on a mobile device. It's a bit like clicking on a Mac or double-clicking on a PC. Tapping an icon will open that app. In this manner, your finger acts a lot like the mouse pointer does on a PC.

Swipe To swipe, you press your finger to the screen and then brush it in a direction. It's almost like the gesture of turning a page in a book. You will use this to move pages or scroll up or down. Swiping your finger up will scroll the page down, for example.

Pinch   By placing two fingers apart and then pinching them together (while touching the screen, of course), you can zoom out. Placing two fingers together and then slowly spreading them apart will zoom in. (It's kind of a reverse pinch.) This feature doesn't work in all apps, but is particularly helpful when looking at maps.

Kinetics   Kinetics refers to the sense of motion. iPhones and other devices have an amazing array of kinetic sensors built in. For example, the iPhone 6 has a gyroscope, accelerometer, linear acceleration sensor, magnetometer, altitude sensor, and gravity sensor. These sensors let your device act like a GPS and compass, and they also detect movements such as tilting or shaking the device that many apps take advantage of.

Screen Orientation

One of the nice features of the gyroscope is that it can change the screen orientation from portrait to landscape depending on how you hold your device. This can be particularly helpful when using the onscreen keyboard to type. If you look at Figure 7.3, you'll see that it shows a new email in the Mail app in portrait mode.

FIGURE 7.3   Portrait mode

By keeping the screen facing you and rotating the device 90 degrees to the left or right, the phone automatically detects the rotation and switches to landscape mode, as shown in Figure 7.4.

FIGURE 7.4   Landscape mode

The keys on the virtual keyboard are now a little larger, potentially making it easier to type. Some games also work better in landscape mode. Not all apps are built to use the gyroscope, so you won't get the rotation with everything.

Mobile Locking and Security

One final feature of interacting with mobile devices that new users need to get used to is security. Mobile devices are much easier to steal than desktop computers, so it's important to secure the device. When you try to access the device, you will get a screen similar to the one in Figure 7.5.

FIGURE 7.5   iOS security lock

In order to use the device, you need to enter the correct password, which is generally a minimum of four digits. Newer phones such as the iPhone 5S and Samsung Galaxy S5 series (and newer) have thumbprint biometric scanners built into the Home button. Instead of using a passcode, you can be authenticated with your fingerprint or thumbprint. Exercise 7.1 shows you how to change the security settings on iOS 8.

EXERCISE 7.1

Changing Security Settings on iOS 8

1. Tap the Settings app to open it.

2. Scroll down to Touch ID & Passcode (Figure 7.6) and tap it.

FIGURE 7.6   iPhone Settings

3. Enter your current passcode and tap Done.

4. On the Touch ID & Passcode screen (Figure 7.7) you can see the security settings. Tap Change Passcode to change your passcode.

FIGURE 7.7 Touch ID & Passcode

5. Enter your old passcode and tap Next.

6. Enter your new passcode and tap Next.

7. Re-enter your new passcode and tap Done.

Even if you have enabled a biometric sensor on an iPhone, when you power the device on, you must always type in the passcode to access the device the first time.

Configuring External Connections

The overall process to set up a mobile device is pretty straightforward. You buy it from a mobile provider, charge it with its USB cable, turn it on, and follow the prompts to configure it and get connected to your cellular provider. The manufacturers and wireless providers have spent a lot of time to make the setup process accessible and easy to navigate. When it comes to setting up wireless devices, the main areas to focus on are the external connections that fall outside the scope of cellular connections. I will cover each of these in the following sections:

- Wireless
- Email
- Bluetooth
- Synchronization
- Airplane mode

Setting Up a Wireless Connection

When you get a mobile device, you generally have a cellular connection to a provider such as AT&T, Verizon, T-Mobile, or others. You pay for a certain amount of data each month, and if you go over that amount you will be charged extra—often, a lot extra. The other primary data connection you can make is to a Wi-Fi network. When you are using Wi-Fi, you are not using your wireless data plan, so essentially your data is unlimited. If you're doing a lot of downloading, using a Wi-Fi connection can save you money, plus it's generally a lot faster than cellular.

The first thing to do when setting up a wireless connection is to verify that your device has wireless capabilities. If not, then this whole process won't work. The vast majority of mobile devices support Wi-Fi, but you will want to confirm that yours does too.

After verifying that your device supports wireless, you want to turn on Wi-Fi. On the iPhone, tap Settings to open the Settings app (Figure 7.8). The second option down is

FIGURE 7.8   iOS Settings

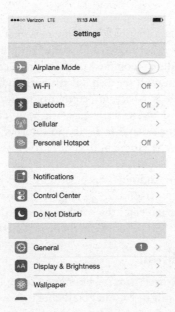

Wi-Fi, and you can see that in this case it's turned off. Tap anywhere on the Wi-Fi line to open the Wi-Fi screen (Figure 7.9). There you see a slider bar to the right of Wi-Fi. Use your finger to slide that to the right into the On position (Figure 7.10). Once you do that, you will see the SSIDs of networks in range under the heading Choose A Network.

FIGURE 7.9   Wi-Fi is off.

My phone is configured to automatically join my network (you can see that it's done so in Figure 7.10), but to join any other network, I would simply tap the SSID I want in the list of SSIDs. Networks with a padlock icon next to them are secured and require a password to join. Next to the padlock you will see a signal strength indicator and an information button. The information button is where you configure options like DHCP.

Once you enter the password and join the network, it will appear underneath Wi-Fi with a check mark next to it. The final step is to verify an Internet connection. To do this, go back to the home screen (push the Home button once to close Settings) and open up Safari. Visit a website, and you are finished!

The process is very similar on Android—open Settings, and you will see Wi-Fi in the left menu under Wireless & Networks (Figure 7.11). The list of networks appears on the right; you select the SSID you want to join and enter the wireless password as needed. Once it's connected (it will say Connected under the SSID), verify Internet connectivity by opening Chrome.

Setting Up Wireless Email

The BlackBerry was one of the first "smart" phones to come out, and one of the most revolutionary features it had built in was an email client. Now, practically all smartphones and tablets have built-in clients for several email providers.

FIGURE 7.10   Wi-Fi is on, with available networks.

FIGURE 7.11   Android settings

If you set up email to a standard service such as Yahoo! Mail or Gmail, you won't be asked to input parameters for the mail server name. When connecting to a corporate or other email account you will. You need to be familiar with three protocols that are part of the TCP/IP suite when setting up these types of email accounts:

Post Office Protocol 3   *Post Office Protocol 3 (POP3)* is an incoming email protocol, which uses port 110 or 945 when configured to use Secure Sockets Layer (SSL) security. POP3 allows for the downloading of email from the server to a client.

Internet Message Access Protocol   A newer incoming email protocol is *Internet Message Access Protocol (IMAP)*. The most current version is IMAP4, which allows you to download only selected messages (as opposed to all of them) and also lets you preview a message as opposed to needing to download all of it. IMAP also supports search functions with email and lets you store messages and interact with them on the server instead of just downloading to the client. IMAP uses port 143 or 993 with SSL.

Simple Mail Transfer Protocol   The protocol used to send email is *Simple Mail Transfer Protocol (SMTP)*. It doesn't have a lot of features like IMAP does, because it doesn't really need them. You press Send, and SMTP handles the transfer to the server. SMTP uses port 25, or 465 with SSL.

Most of the time, the same email server manages incoming and outgoing email and can handle all three protocols. You just need to tell your client which one to use to receive mail. Exercise 7.2 walks you through setting up an email account in iOS.

EXERCISE 7.2

Configuring Email on an iPhone

1.   From the home screen, tap Settings and scroll down until you see Mail, Contacts, Calendars (Figure 7.12).

FIGURE 7.12   Mail, Contacts, Calendars

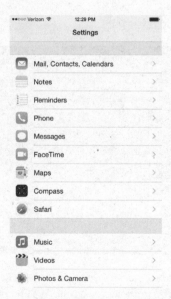

2.   Tap Mail, Contacts, Calendars. It will show you accounts as well as the configuration settings for email, contacts, and calendars.

3.   Tap Add Account (near the top) and it will give you a screen similar to the one shown in Figure 7.13.

FIGURE 7.13   Add Account

4. If you have email with any of the listed services, tap it to configure your client. For this example tap Other ➤ Add Mail Account. Either way, you will get a screen similar to the one shown in Figure 7.14. Here you can add your name, email address, password, and an optional description. Tap Next.

FIGURE 7.14   Adding a new account

5. In the New Account screen (Figure 7.15), choose IMAP or POP. If your server supports it, IMAP is preferable. Here you also configure the names of the incoming and outgoing mail servers. Most organizations will have one server handle both functions. Once you have entered the correct information, click Next.

FIGURE 7.15   Configuring email servers

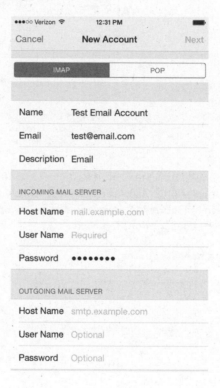

6. The iPhone will make connections to the server(s) to verify the username and password. If successful, you will get a screen asking which content you want to receive, similar to the one shown in Figure 7.16. Make your selections and tap Save. It will add your account.

7. Now you can use the Mail icon on the home page to retrieve email. Note that you can have several email accounts configured to receive email in this app.

8. (Optional) To delete an account, repeat steps 1 and 2 in this exercise. On the Mail, Contacts, Calendars screen (Figure 7.17) tap the account you want to delete.

FIGURE 7.16   Email account content options

FIGURE 7.17   Accounts list

9.   (Optional) Tap Delete Account (Figure 7.18) to remove it from this client.

FIGURE 7.18   Deleting an account

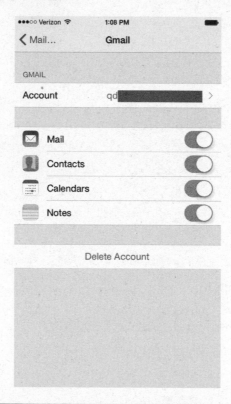

The same principles that you used to add email in iOS also apply in Android. Of course, the process is just a little different. Exercise 7.3 walks you through how to do it.

Configuring Email in Android

1.   Tap Settings, and scroll down to the Accounts section on the left side. Tap Add Account (Figure 7.19).

2.   Tap the type of account you want to add. In this example I chose Personal (IMAP).

3.   Enter your email account name and tap Next.

FIGURE 7.19   Add An Account

4.   Enter your password and tap Next. You will get a screen similar to the one shown in Figure 7.20.

FIGURE 7.20   Incoming Server Settings

5.   Note that the port is 143 because I chose IMAP. If you tap anywhere on the setting next to Security Type, you can change the security to SSL/TLS. That will automatically change the port number to 993. Tap Next. Android will contact the server and verify the server settings.

6. After verifying a connection to the server, you can choose account options like the ones shown in Figure 7.21. Choose the ones you want and tap Next.

FIGURE 7.21 Email account options

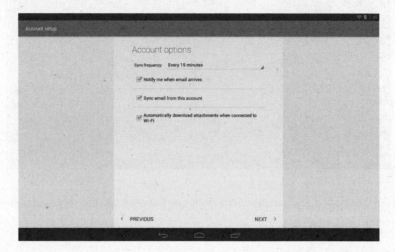

7. You will get an account confirmation page, where you can edit the account name that gets displayed as well as your name that gets displayed on outgoing messages (Figure 7.22). Tap Next.

FIGURE 7.22 Account setup options

8. The new account will appear in your accounts list in Settings. You can access your email through the Gmail app on the home page.

Configuring Bluetooth

Bluetooth isn't a technology you use for full-scale networking, but it works great for short-range connectivity with peripheral devices such as mice, keyboards, and hands-free communication devices.

To enable two Bluetooth devices to communicate with each other, you need to work through a process called *Bluetooth pairing*. Essentially, it's a setup process that tells both devices that it's okay to communicate with one another. This process is required as an extra security step—you wouldn't want someone you don't know connecting to your Bluetooth-enabled phone in an airport and downloading your email or pictures!

The exact process for Bluetooth pairing will differ by your mobile OS and the device you are connecting to. In general, though, these are the steps:

1. Turn on the Bluetooth hands-free device. Some devices will be "discoverable" when they first turn on, and others you will have to make discoverable. Check your documentation to be sure.

2. Use your mobile device to locate and select the Bluetooth device.

3. Enter the Bluetooth device's passcode.

4. Confirm pairing on the Bluetooth device by pressing a button or a combination of buttons.

Here's a specific example from when I paired my iPhone to the hands-free audio system in my car.

1. First, I enabled the Bluetooth pairing in my car. It will often involve using menu or voice commands to begin the pairing process.

2. When the car was ready, I went into Settings ➤ Bluetooth and slid the switch to enable Bluetooth, as shown in Figure 7.23. It found the car's multi-media system.

3. I tapped the Car Multi-Media device, and it took me to the PIN screen where I entered the four-digit PIN, as shown in Figure 7.24. (The car's setup program told me what the PIN was; your device documentation will tell you the default PIN, or you can try 0000.) I then tapped Pair.

4. My iPhone showed me that the device was connected and ready for use (Figure 7.25).

5. If I want to un-pair the devices, I can tap the information icon next to the word Connected and then tap Forget Device.

For specific instructions on how to pair your devices together, check the instructions for the Bluetooth device you are pairing with.

WARNING   Disable Bluetooth on your mobile devices unless you know you are going to use it. There are two reasons. The first is that enabling Bluetooth will run down your battery faster than if it's disabled. The second is as a security precaution. When Bluetooth is enabled, you may be vulnerable to *Bluejacking* or *Bluesnarfing*. Bluejacking is the sending of (usually) harmless messages to your device via Bluetooth—think of it as Bluetooth spam. Bluesnarfing occurs when someone connects to your device without your knowledge and has access to all of the data (pictures, contacts, emails, etc.) on your device. They can then hack your data or copy it to their device for later use.

FIGURE 7.23 Bluetooth device found

FIGURE 7.24 Entering the PIN

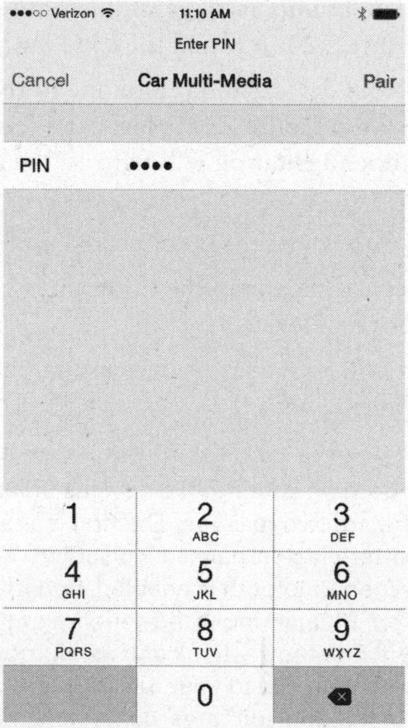

FIGURE 7.25   Paired Bluetooth

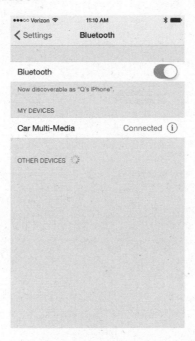

You can also perform data transfers between devices using Bluetooth by setting up an ad hoc network. Most often this will be used to transfer pictures, videos, or contacts from one device to another. To do this, you need to download a Bluetooth sharing app from your device's app store and then pair the devices. More details on this process are covered in Chapter 6, "Network Sharing and Storage."

Configuring Synchronization Options

Synchronizing your device has two benefits. The first is that you can access your files online or from your device. The second is that it provides a backup of your files in case you need to restore your device. Hopefully you'll never need to use the second option, but having backups of your important data is always important.

iPhones and iPads can sync to iTunes on a desktop or laptop computer or to the iCloud. On the device itself, you can configure various options through Settings ➢ iCloud or Settings ➢ iTunes & App Store. Figure 7.26 shows the sync summary of the iTunes app on a desktop computer. To get to this screen, you need to have the device plugged in. Then, click the icon that looks like a phone near the upper-left corner. You can see in Figure 7.26 that the phone icon is highlighted in blue.

Within this app you can see the summary or configure synchronization options for individual types of media or apps. You can also set the backup options to back up to the iCloud or the local computer. The choice comes down to whatever is more convenient for you. There are additional options on this page such as to sync automatically when the phone is connected and to sync over Wi-Fi.

FIGURE 7.26 iTunes sync

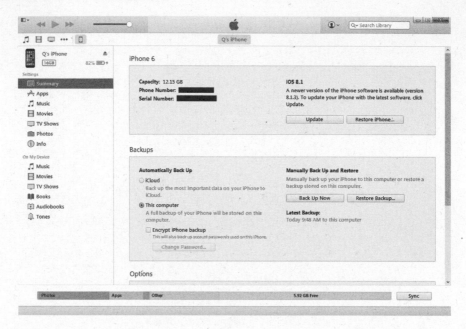

Setting up sync is easy within Android as well. You will find it in one of two places. Either open the Backup & Reset app and look in Settings, or tap the Apps icon and then go to Settings, as shown in Figure 7.27. From there, tap 1ClickSync and you can configure your sync options for the Google Play store, Google+, or Google App (Figure 7.28). All of your data will be synched to Google Drive.

FIGURE 7.27 Settings apps on Android

FIGURE 7.28   1ClickSync options

Using Airplane Mode

Airplane mode isn't as much about setting up connections as it is disconnecting from everything. Enabling Airplane mode shuts off all of your wireless connections, including cellular, Wi-Fi, and Bluetooth. You can get to Airplane mode on an iPhone in a couple different ways. One is to open Settings, and it's the first option you'll see (Figure 7.29). When you slide it on, notice how all of the other connections are turned off.

FIGURE 7.29   Airplane mode on iOS 8

The other way is to access it from the Control Center. You can do this from both the lock screen and the home screen. Simply swipe your finger up from the very bottom of the iPhone's touchscreen, and you will get the Control Center, similar to what's shown in Figure 7.30.

FIGURE 7.30   iPhone Control Center

Tap the airplane icon in the upper-left corner to enable Airplane mode. Notice that you also have a few other handy features in the Control Center, such as the ability to control music, turn on your flashlight, and use your calculator or camera.

To enable Airplane mode in Android, open Settings and then tap More under Wireless & Networks (Figure 7.31). Tap the check box next to Airplane Mode and you're all set.

Getting Additional Apps

The first BlackBerry smartphones didn't have additional apps to download—you simply got what the manufacturer gave you. Newer devices came along that gave you the option to customize, and part of the reason BlackBerry declined so quickly was its slowness to adapt to that change. Now, downloading apps to mobile devices is a pretty common thing for mobile users to do, whether it's to increase your productivity or maintain your sanity with a new distraction.

FIGURE 7.31   Airplane mode in Android

Each mobile platform has its own specific application store. Much like workstation apps are built for a specific OS, so are mobile apps. If you are using iOS, you get to the *iTunes* app store by tapping the App Store icon on the home screen. The app will look similar to the one shown in Figure 7.32. There are categories for the top free and paid apps and the ability to search for specific apps and update the ones currently on your device.

FIGURE 7.32   iTunes app store

The *Google Play* app store is where to go for Android-based devices. You get to it by tapping the Play Store app from the home page. You will get a screen similar to the one in Figure 7.33. Here, you have six categories to browse for apps as well as some popular apps to choose from. You can also search by using the magnifying glass icon in the upper-right corner.

FIGURE 7.33   Google Play Store

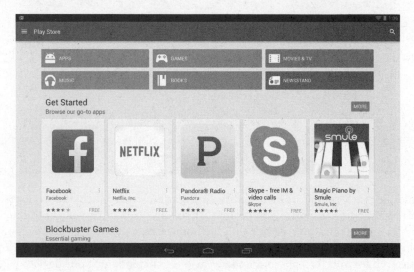

To install the app you want, tap it. You will be able to see more information on it including what it does and reviews from other users. Then tap Install or Get. If apps have additional in-app purchases they will tell you, like the example in Figure 7.34 does. If it's not a free app, it will tell you (instead of the Install or Get button, it will have a button with the cost), and then you can make the decision to purchase it or not.

FIGURE 7.34   Install an app

🌐 Real World Scenario

Avoiding Unpleasant and Expensive Surprises

The explosion of mobile devices has given billions of people instant access to data at their fingertips. What used to be friendly arguments with no provable answer now quickly turn into a chorus of "Just Google it!" Constant access has also led to some unpleasant side effects, though.

Either you have seen stories like this on the news, or maybe it's happened to you or someone you know. The exact details change but the general premise is like this: Joe or Jane user gets a bill from their cellphone or credit card company with several hundreds or thousands of unexpected charges on it. Ultimately it gets traced back to their smartphone or tablet and the fact that the user unwittingly did something to rack up those huge costs. What happened?

It's usually one of a few things:

- Using too much data
- Roaming charges (especially internationally)
- In-app purchases

When you register a mobile device with provider, you will buy a data plan. Maybe you'll get only 2 GB of data per month or maybe you'll get 20 GB. But if you go over the allotted amount, the charge for extra data can be pretty expensive. Perhaps under normal circumstances you don't go over your data plan, but let's say you go on vacation. While in the car or at your destination you choose to download some music, check email, and surf the Web like you normally do. Only now you're using your minutes and data plan as opposed to using your Wi-Fi at home. You might not realize it at the time, but your idle surfing is costing you a lot of money.

If you're travelling internationally, the problem can get even worse. Check your plan to see what the provision is for travelling out of your home country. Some providers will automatically charge those minutes and that data as roaming, which will make it very expensive in a hurry.

The last one is in-app purchases. It might have been free to download the game and even to play it, but perhaps you can buy some gems or coins or something to level up even faster. Why wait around when you can become level 50 with just a few dollars? Maybe you have restraint when it comes to this, but maybe you don't. And maybe it's not you. Last year, one of my friends let her three-year-old son play Candy Crush Saga on her tablet while in the car. The next month a bill came for nearly $500 for in-app purchases. It wasn't what she considered money well spent.

So how do you protect yourself against unexpected bills? First, be sure to understand your wireless plan, including minutes, data maximums, and roaming charges. If you are going to travel, it might be worth it to increase your plan for a month or two as opposed to paying overuse fees.

Second, you can change settings on your phone to potentially minimize the damage. In iOS 8, you can go to Settings ➢ Cellular ➢ Roaming to tell your phone how to behave, as shown in Figure 7.35. Turning off roaming is a good way to avoid unexpected surprises.

FIGURE 7.35   iOS 8 cellular settings

Finally, configure your app store account and apps so that new apps and in-app purchases require a password—and make sure your child or friends don't know it! (My friend: "Well, I guess he saw me type it in enough that he figured it out.") A few simple steps can potentially save you a lot of money—it's always a good idea to know how your device is being used and what you are and are not required to pay for.

Summary

This chapter gave you the essential background of how to use mobile devices and some of the unique features that users of these devices need to be familiar with. First, you learned how to interact with a device that doesn't have the traditional computer input methods. Examples include tapping, swiping, and pinching; as well as the kinetic sensors built into the devices. You also learned about screen orientation and locking and security.

Next, you learned how to configure external connections. Mobile devices come readily equipped to handle cellular connections. Beyond that, you can configure Wi-Fi connections, email, Bluetooth pairing, and synchronization. Airplane mode is used to turn all external connections off.

Finally, you learned about the two most popular app stores to enhance the functionality of mobile devices, including where to find apps and how to install them.

Exam Essentials

Understand the unique methods you can use to interact with mobile devices.   Examples include tapping, swiping, and pinching, as well as interacting through the use of built-in kinetic sensors.

Know how to configure external connections.   Most connections are configured through the Settings app. Examples include Wi-Fi, email, Bluetooth, synchronization, and Airplane mode.

Understand incoming and outgoing email protocols.   The protocols used to receive mail are POP3 (port 110) and IMAP (port 143). The protocol used to send email is SMTP (port 25).

Know how to quickly turn off Wi-Fi and cellular connections on your mobile device.   This is accomplished by enabling Airplane mode.

Know where to get new apps for mobile devices.   For iOS devices, use iTunes, which is accessed through the App Store icon on the home screen. Android devices use the Google Play Store icon on the home screen.

Chapter 7 Lab

IT professionals need to know how to use a variety of operating systems in order to configure items properly and help clients fix issues. Even if you're not pursuing an IT career, knowing different operating systems can help you easily navigate through problems when you encounter something unfamiliar to you. After all, users do the same types of tasks on nearly all computers, regardless of the OS. The trick is to figure out how to do it on a system you are not as familiar with. This lab will have you install the Andy emulator on your computer and familiarize yourself with the Android operating system.

To install Andy, visit www.andyroid.net and click the Download button. Follow the prompts to install it on your computer. It will not damage your computer's operating system or other software. Once installed, you should have a Start Andy icon on your desktop. Use that shortcut to launch Andy. Here are some questions for you to answer:

1. There are three buttons at the bottom in the black area of the window. What are they called and what do they do?

2. What's the easiest way to do a Google search?

3. How do you see the apps installed on this virtual device?

4. What is the functionality of each of the seven icons on the bottom of the home page?

5. How do you see what apps have recently been opened, and how do you close them?

6. Where do you configure accessibility options for disabled users?

7. How do you change security settings for this device?

8. Install a new app of your choice. Was it easy or difficult? How do you launch the app? How do you delete the app icon from your home page? Does it delete the app?

9. Create a new group for your app, and then move the app there. How did you do it?

Review Questions

1. Using an Android phone, you want to scroll down. What do you do to accomplish this?

   A. Swipe up

   B. Swipe down

   C. Pinch fingers together

   D. Start with pinched fingers and separate them

2. Ronnie is configuring a new iPad to receive email from the corporate email server, which supports POP3. What port number does POP3 use?

   A. 25

   B. 110

   C. 143

   D. 443

3. While using an iPhone which of the following motions enables you to zoom in on a map?

   A. Tap

   B. Double tap

   C. Pinch

   D. Reverse pinch

4. When configuring your manager's new iPad, she asks you what protocol is used by the email client to send email. What do you tell her?

   A. IMAP

   B. POP3

   C. SMTP

   D. SNMP

5. Rachel is using her iPad to view pictures. She turns the iPad 90 degrees and the image turns as well. Which sensor allowed this to happen?

   A. Accelerometer

   B. Magnetometer

   C. Turnometer

   D. Gyroscope

6. Which port does IMAP use by itself, and which port does it use when combined with SSL security?

   A. 143 and 993

   B. 143 and 945

   C. 110 and 993

   D. 110 and 945

7. Francis is trying to change the settings on his iPhone. He opens the Settings app. In order to see them better, he turns his phone 90 degrees but nothing happens. What is the most likely cause?

    A. The gyroscope is broken.

    B. The Settings app does not support rotation.

    C. He needs to enable app rotation in Settings first.

    D. He needs to turn off the device and turn it back on to reset the rotation feature.

8. What is the term used that refers to connecting two Bluetooth devices together for communications?

    A. Synching

    B. Netting

    C. Pairing

    D. Partnering

9. Agi has an iPhone with a biometric scanner enabled. What methods can she use to unlock her phone?

    A. Fingerprint only

    B. Passcode only

    C. Fingerprint or passcode

    D. Fingerprint, passcode, or iris scan

10. What term refers to having data stolen from your device via Bluetooth connection?

    A. Pairing

    B. Bluesurfing

    C. Bluejacking

    D. Bluesnarfing

11. Your friend recently got a new Android phone and comes over to your house. What app does your friend use to set up a Wi-Fi connection with your wireless router?

    A. Wi-Fi

    B. Settings

    C. Networking

    D. Connections

12. Which of the following are the right protocol and port number for sending email from a wireless device?

    A. SMTP and 25

    B. SMTP and 110

    C. IMAP and 25

    D. IMAP and 110

13. You are setting up a new Wi-Fi connection on your Android phone. What step do you take after turning on Wi-Fi?

A. Verify wireless capabilities.

B. Enter the wireless password.

C. Verify the Internet connection.

D. Locate SSID.

14. You want to enable backups of your new iPhone. Which two options do you have? (Choose two.)

A. iDrive

B. iCloud

C. iTunes

D. iBackup

15. Sally is configuring an email account on an Android phone. Which two protocols are used to retrieve mail? (Choose two.)

A. IMAP

B. POP3

C. SMTP

D. SNMP

16. Which of the following accurately describes what Airplane mode does on an iPhone?

A. Turns off the Wi-Fi connection

B. Turns off the Bluetooth connection

C. Turns off the cellular connection

D. Turns off all wireless connections

17. Your co-worker Ryan is setting up email on his director's new iPad. Ryan does not know the name of the SMTP server, but the iPad needs to be set up in the next 10 minutes. What advice should you give him?

A. Leave it blank.

B. Enter the same server name as the IMAP server.

C. Enter smtp.*company.com*.

D. Configure the iPad to send email using IMAP instead.

18. You need to find a new productivity app for your Android-based tablet. Where should you look?

A. iTunes

B. Google Drive

C. Google Apps

D. Google Play

19. You are configuring an email account on an Android tablet and choose the IMAP protocol. What port number does IMAP use?

   A. 25

   B. 110

   C. 143

   D. 443

20. Rebecca wants to get a copy of the newest game she heard about for her iPad. Where should she go to find and download it?

   A. iTunes

   B. iApps

   C. iPlay

   D. Google Play

Chapter

8

Security Threats

THE FOLLOWING COMPTIA IT FUNDAMENTALS EXAM OBJECTIVES ARE COVERED IN THIS CHAPTER:

✓ **3.1 Define basic security threats**

- Malware
    - Virus
    - Trojan
    - Spyware
    - Ransomware
- Phishing
- Social engineering
- Spam
- Password cracking
- Physical security
    - Hardware theft
    - Software/license theft
    - Shoulder surfing
    - Dumpster diving

In an ideal world, computer security systems let in the right people and applications without any hassle and keep out the wrong people and applications. The world isn't ideal, though, and computer security certainly isn't either. There are two extremes to access. The first is you can open everything up and let anyone access anything. While this is simple, it's not secure. The other extreme is to lock everything down tight. It's secure, but it kind of defeats the purpose of having a network—you want to share resources with others. It follows then that effective computer security is a constant balance between safety and convenience.

The fact that you have to open up your systems to allow others to access resources has an inherent flaw, which is that opening can allow people who shouldn't have access to try to get in anyway. Those people might be simply curious, or they could be serious criminals who want to steal data or damage businesses. Either way, they're out there and they're writing malware and trying to get unauthorized access to computer networks right now. In the world of computer security, paranoia is a good thing. You don't need to be part of the tinfoil hat–wearing brigade, but a healthy dose of wariness can save you a lot of grief.

In this chapter, you'll learn about the many types of threats to safety, security, and privacy, because what you don't know *can* hurt you. I am going to break the discussion of threats into three groups—physical threats, people-based threats, and software threats collectively known as malware. I will also talk about some mitigation techniques, although most of those will be covered in Chapter 9, "Security Best Practices."

Before looking at specific types of threats, though, take a step back for just a moment and think about the people making those threats. What are they trying to do and why? After that, you will learn about some of the specific techniques they may use.

Understanding Hacking

Hacking refers to a variety of computer crimes that involve gaining unauthorized access to a computer system or its data, usually with the intent of stealing private information from, or causing harm or embarrassment to, the rightful owner.

The word *hacker* also has a benign meaning, referring to a computer expert who is thoroughly familiar with, and enthusiastic about, the inner workings of a computer system. This meaning is older, but the newer meaning, which associates the term *hacker* with criminal activities, is now more prevalent.

Some examples of hacking are as follows:

- Stealing passwords or personal information
- Gaining remote access to a server or an operating system
- Logging in locally and stealing data
- Changing a website's content
- Gaining access to the contents of a database (perhaps one that contains passwords or credit card information)
- Surreptitiously analyzing network traffic
- Installing software designed to cause harm or steal data
- Creating a condition in which a computer or network no longer works well
- Modifying existing software so that it no longer performs as it should or so that it secretly does harmful things in addition to its usual activity

Much of this chapter is devoted to helping you understand how hackers target computer systems to gain access or cause damage. If hackers can gain access to certain system files, for example, they may be able to retrieve the Administrator password for the system. To prevent this type of attack, you might use BIOS-level security to prevent a PC from booting from a disk other than the hard disk.

Wireless networks are great for users, but they also can open up huge security holes on our networks. Hackers may try to connect to your wireless network looking for computers or data that isn't protected. To prevent this type of attack, you can employ wireless networking security techniques, which I introduced in Chapter 5, "Networking Technologies and Wireless Routers," such as WPA2.

Or perhaps a hacker might take advantage of open network ports to access a computer remotely. Firewalls can help guard against this type of attack. Finally, hackers might install software on your computer that causes damage or causes additional security breaches. The trick is to get you to install it for them without knowing! Anti-malware software can help out in some of these cases, and safe web-browsing and emailing practices can thwart others.

The point is that criminal hackers generally want to make money from their exploits or cause damage to businesses or individuals. The bigger impact they can have, the better. And they have plenty of tools at their disposal. It's time to learn more about specific security threats.

 Real World Scenario

Different Motivations

There are various factions within the hacking community, and they are motivated by different goals. As I mentioned earlier, some are motivated by money or the thrill of causing damage. Within the last few years, you have seen major business hacks make news headlines, such as the Target breach during the 2013 holiday shopping season. In fact, the prevalence of such activities has caused some major news publications to ask, tongue in cheek, who hasn't reported a breach? (Although to be fair, most major retailers have not been hacked—yet.)

Others are motivated by the challenge of getting into a system that is hard to penetrate—literally just so they can say they did it and gain admiration from fellow hackers. These hackers may leave clues to their attack for the hacked network administrators to find, along with helpful suggestions on how to breach the hole they exploited. Still others are interested in doing damage to organizations whose views differ from their own—in a sense they want to make their own political statement.

In fact, within many of the professional hacking circles, the idea of hacking for monetary gain is frowned upon. You won't find these groups trying to steal credit card data—that type of petty criminality is beneath them. They are oftentimes more motivated by moral or political beliefs and trying to expose organizations they consider dishonest or unethical. The WikiLeaks group qualifies here. Their self-reported profile is that they are an "international, non-profit journalistic organization which publishes secret information, news leaks, and classified media from anonymous sources." Organizations that have had their information published by WikiLeaks definitely call them hackers, but clearly WikiLeaks sees itself in a much more altruistic light.

Understanding Security Threats

If you are walking around in a bad neighborhood at two in the morning, you know to keep your eyes open for anything that might be suspicious or could cause you harm. If you see a creepy-looking person hanging out at the park, you will probably pay extra attention to their actions. And it seems like today when you board an airplane, everyone is eyeing everyone else to see if they're a potential threat. Sometimes it's feels easy to identify threats, but of course that's not always the case. It's even harder in the computer world, because the threat could be on the other side of the world and you don't even know it exists.

In this chapter I am going to focus on three different groupings of security threats:

- Physical security threats
- People-based security threats
- Software-based security threats

Each one poses different problems and therefore requires its own mitigation techniques. I will talk some about mitigation here, but the more in-depth conversation on preventing and dealing with threats will be in Chapter 9. The primary goal in this chapter is to raise awareness, so you have an idea of what to look out for.

Physical Security Threats

Organizations lose millions of dollars of equipment every year through thefts and hundreds of millions through the data that goes along with them. Therefore, it's important to secure your computer hardware physically in whatever environment you place it. You also need to take preventive measures to protect your data from physical theft.

Hardware Damage

Within your own company's offices, solutions for securing computers and peripherals focus mainly on securing the environment overall, rather than securing an individual piece of hardware. For example, some possible measures include the following:

- Requiring a security keycard for access to the office area
- Having a professional security presence in large organizations
- Keeping doors and windows locked
- Being prepared to challenge anyone who isn't normally a part of your work environment

Physically securing your area prevents two types of problems: hardware damage and hardware theft (covered in the next section). If an attacker can get to your computer with a hammer, it doesn't matter how good your firewall is or if you are using the latest and most secure encryption technology. That person can do some damage.

Hardware damage can also be inadvertent. For example, one company I used to work for was having roof repairs done. The workers left it unfinished over the weekend, when there happened to be an unusually heavy rain storm. The roof leaked and water flooded into the server room causing tens of thousands of dollars in damage.

Hardware Theft

The risk of hardware theft varies with the environment, of course. Leaving a laptop unattended at an airport is a very different matter from leaving it unattended in your own office when you go to lunch.

When travelling with a notebook PC or other portable technology device, the emphasis should be placed on the physical security of the individual device. Here are some pointers:

- Know where the device is at all times—preferably within your sight.
- Don't leave the device unattended, even for a minute.
- Carry the device in an unconventional bag, rather than an expensive-looking laptop bag.
- Install an alarm that beeps if your device gets more than a certain distance away from a transponder that you keep close to you (such as on your keychain or belt).

Mobile devices such as cellphones are even easier for a thief to walk away with. The principles for these devices are the same as other mobile devices, but you need to be even more astute in your defense. It's best to never set your phone down at all.

If you aren't in a secured area (and even if you are), it may be appropriate to use locks and other devices that physically attach the hardware to a desk or other fixed object in order to prevent it from "walking away." There are various types of locks, cages, and racks designed to make it difficult for someone to remove a computer from its location.

Many notebook computers have a K-slot, which is short for Kensington security slot. Kensington is a company that makes a type of lock that fits into that slot. The lock is then attached to a security cable, and the other end of is bolted to the wall or furniture. The locks are secured with either a key or a combination. Figure 8.1 shows an example of a security cable attached to a K-slot on a notebook PC.

FIGURE 8.1   A laptop security cable

 Services are available, such as LoJack, that can track stolen hardware via a small radio installed inside the device and disable a stolen computer remotely so the data that resides on it won't be compromised. LoJack functionality comes preinstalled in the BIOS of many major brand-name notebook computers, including Dell, Lenovo, HP, Toshiba, and Fujitsu. The radio-tracking unit comes free with the computer, but you must pay to install and use the software that enables it. You can learn more about this software at http://lojack.absolute.com. In addition, many mobile phones and tablets have built-in "kill switches" that permanently disable the device in the event that it is stolen. The state of California will require that all mobile phones sold in the state as of July 2015 come with the kill switch enabled by default.

Data, Software, and License Theft

You might not think of data theft as a physical issue, but it is. It's true that data can be stolen over networks, but physical security lapses in securing access to computers or storing computer backups is an issue as well. Data theft can cost a company even more than hardware theft in the long run. For any organization, the loss of data can equate to the following:

▪ Loss of trust from your customers/clients when they discover that someone else has their personal information

- Serious embarrassment if there are public media reports that your company has lost control of its data
- Legal liabilities from either regulatory authorities or angry customers whose data you've compromised
- Loss of competitive advantage when commercially sensitive data falls into the hands of rivals

A thief doesn't need to steal a computer to steal data; someone can sit down at your computer, plug in a USB memory stick, and be gone with important data files in a couple of minutes. For this reason, some organizations have OS security policies that disable the USB ports on PCs that contain sensitive data.

One way to prevent others from booting from a device other than the hard disk is to modify the BIOS Setup settings so that a password is required to save changes to BIOS Setup. That way, nobody can change the system's boot order to prefer a USB port over the main hard disk.

Locking your computer as you leave your desk (via the OS's lock command), as well as having your screen saver set to resume on password after a short period of time, will help reduce the risk of someone using your computer while you're away. In Exercise 8.1, you will practice setting up a secure screen saver.

EXERCISE 8.1

Securing a Windows 7 PC from Unauthorized Local Use

1. In Windows 7, right-click the desktop and choose Personalize.

2. Click Screen Saver. The Screen Saver Settings dialog box opens, like the one in Figure 8.2.

3. Open the Screen Saver drop-down list, and pick any of the screen savers (for example, Bubbles).

4. Select the On Resume, Display Logon Screen check box.

5. In the Wait box, change the value to 1 minute.

6. Click OK.

7. Wait 1 minute for the screen saver to start.

8. Move the mouse to awaken the computer. The logon screen appears.

9. Click your user account, and retype your password to resume.

10. Repeat steps 1–7, returning to your previous screen saver settings.

11. Choose Start ➢ Lock (it's an option that appears when you click the right arrow next to Shut Down). The logon screen appears.

12. Click your user account, and retype your password to resume.

FIGURE 8.2   Screen Saver Settings

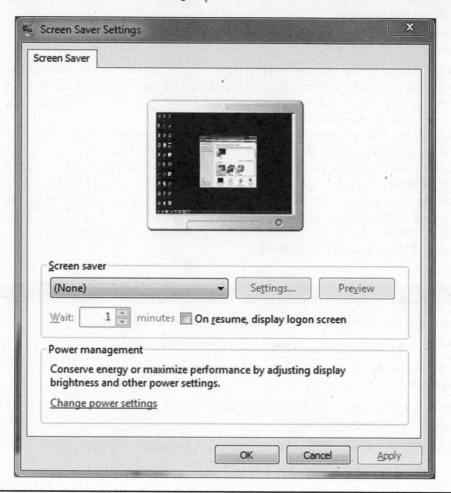

Securing Backup Media

Large companies typically back up their data using their network, with the backups stored on the same type of secure servers on which the data itself resides. However, smaller companies sometimes rely on data backups to external hard disks, optical media, and even memory sticks and tape drives. The data is no safer than the physical safety of these backup devices.

Keep in mind that data can be stolen from backup devices just as easily as from the original storage locations. Physically secure all backup devices and media, both from theft and from accidents and disasters, such as fires and flooding. Data should be stored offsite, in a fireproof safe.

Preventing Software and License Theft

If someone can get to your physical installation media, such as a CD-ROM, they can steal that for their own use. A lot of CD-ROM cases or sleeves will have a sticker with the product's license code on them, meaning that once the physical media is stolen, so is the license. The way to prevent this from happening, of course, is to physically secure the media as well.

If you purchased licenses in bulk, you will get an email with your software license numbers. Protect that file! Don't print off that list and post it anywhere or leave it lying around. Software licenses are expensive and should be guarded.

Dumpster Diving

Although it might sound like a made-up term from Wall Street takeover movies, *dumpster diving* is a real thing. It is pretty much what it sounds like—people can go through the dumpster, or your garbage, and steal information. In many places there are laws that prohibit such behavior, but we're talking about people who generally ignore such inconveniences anyway.

The best way to avoid being a victim of dumpster diving is to not throw away anything that can cause you problems later. Be sure to shred all papers in a good shredder. When disposing of media such as hard drives or flash drives, reformatting isn't enough to ensure that the data can't be read again. Damaging the drive physically and then taking it to a recycling center is a better way to go. I've seen some professionals recommend opening the case of your hard drives and using a drill to drill through the platters to make them completely useless. Whether or not you choose to go that far is up to you. Regardless, ruining the device beyond repair isn't a terrible idea, and you should always recycle old computer parts to dispose of them properly.

Social Engineering

Hackers are more sophisticated today than they were 10 years ago, but then again, so are network administrators. Because most of today's sys admins have secured their networks well enough to make it pretty tough for an outsider to gain access, hackers have decided to try an easier route to gain information: they just ask the network's users for it.

These are relatively low-tech attacks and are more akin to con jobs, so it's relatively astounding how often they're successful. If someone random called you up and said, "Give me your bank account number," there's no way you would provide it. At least I hope not! But if that same someone calls you up and pretends to be a co-worker in a remote office with your company, who really needs help and has a plausible story, then things might be different. These types of attacks are called social engineering.

Social engineering is a process in which an attacker attempts to acquire information about you or your network and system by social means, such as talking to people in the organization. This isn't a new concept—people have been trying to defraud others for centuries. A social engineering attack may occur over the phone, by email, or even in person. The intent is to acquire sensitive information, such as this:

- User IDs and passwords
- Preferred email address
- Telephone numbers and physical addresses
- Personal information such as date and location of birth, maiden name, or mother's maiden name
- Other information that can help them guess passwords, such as the school(s) you went to, your favorite sports team, or the type of music you listen to

Social engineering works because the personal touch is often the hardest for people to resist, and because the individuals concerned are normally very good at encouraging you to reveal personal information. It's more difficult when you're unsure if they're genuine—it's unpleasant to mistrust everyone.

Here's how it might work over the phone. Let's say you get a call to your desk at work from "Joe" in IT. He says he's noticed some unusual activity on your network account and wants to check it out, but for security purposes, he needs your permission first. So he proceeds to confirm your login, and then he tells you he needs to enter your password into the network tracker. He asks, "What's your password?" What do you do? To protect yourself from this one, all you need to do is confirm *his* information and verify it with your IT department *before* you give him any of your data. Just because "Joe" knows your login doesn't mean he's on the up-and-up.

In fact, if you ever get a call from someone whom you're unsure of, start asking questions: "Who did you say you are? What department? Oh—who is your manager? You know I am kind of busy right now, what number can I call you back at?" Many times once you start asking questions, the person at the other end will figure you're not worth the trouble and will hang up. But even if "Joe" hangs up on you, you should still report the call to IT or security.

How did Joe get your login and telephone number? Maybe he did some network reconnaissance and found a company phone directory on the Web. Even if it isn't published, maybe Joe did some earlier homework by calling one of your coworkers and, pretending to be a colleague at another site, asked for your phone number. But what about the username? On most networks, your username is the same as your email address because that makes things easier for your sys admin. This means that knowing that information is probably just a good guess on the attacker's part. Maybe Joe the Hacker has gotten an email from someone at your company and knows what your email format is, and he may have some other information to help him figure out your network login. And even if the number on your caller ID when Joe called was an internal phone number, it doesn't mean a thing—hackers have software that can allow them to spoof phone numbers.

Exercise 8.2 gives you some good ways to test others on how likely they are to be susceptible to a social engineering attack. The steps are suggestions for tests; you may need to modify them slightly to be appropriate at your workplace. Before proceeding, make certain your manager knows that you're conducting such a test and approves of it.

EXERCISE 8.2

Testing Social Engineering

1. Call the receptionist from an outside line when the sales manager is at lunch. Tell her that you're a new salesperson, that you didn't write down the username and password the sales manager gave you last week, and that you need to get a file from the email system for a presentation tomorrow. Does she direct you to the appropriate person or attempt to help you receive the file?

2. Call the human resources department from an outside line. Don't give your real name, but instead say that you're a vendor who has been working with this company for years. You'd like a copy of the employee phone list to be emailed to you, if possible. Do they agree to send you the list, which would contain information that could be used to try to guess usernames and passwords?

3. Pick a user at random. Call them and identify yourself as someone who does work with the company. Tell them that you're supposed to have some new software ready for them by next week and that you need to know their password to finish configuring it. Do they do the right thing?

The best defense against any social engineering attack is education. Make certain the employees of your company would know how to react to the requests presented here.

The golden rule is don't ever give any of your information or anyone else's to anyone you're not absolutely sure should have it. And if they are someone who should have it, they probably already do, and they shouldn't be contacting you for it!

The social engineering examples so far have been phone-based, but they are more commonly done over email or instant messaging.

Phishing

Phishing is a form of social engineering in which someone uses email to ask you for a piece of information that they are missing by making it look as if it is a legitimate request. The email will often look like it comes from an official source, such as a bank, and will contain some basic information like your name.

These types of messages often state that there is a problem with your account or access privileges. You will be told to click a link to correct the problem. After you click the link— which goes to a site other than the bank's—you are asked for your username, password, account information, and so on. The person instigating the phishing can then use this information to access the legitimate account.

One of the best countermeasures to phishing is to simply mouse over the Click Here link and read the URL. Almost every time the URL is an adaptation of the legitimate URL as opposed to a link to the real thing.

The only preventive measure in dealing with social engineering attacks is to educate your users and staff to never give out passwords and user IDs over the phone or via email or to anyone who isn't positively verified as being who they say they are.

When you combine phishing with Voice over IP (VoIP), it becomes known as *vishing* and is just an elevated form of social engineering. While crank calls have been in existence since the invention of the telephone, the rise in VoIP now makes it possible for someone to call you from almost anywhere in the world, without the worry of tracing/caller ID/and other features of the land line, and pretend to be someone they are not in order to get data from you.

Two other forms of phishing to be aware of are *spear phishing* and *whaling*, and they are very similar in nature. With spear phishing, the attacker uses information that the target would be less likely to question because it appears to be coming from a trusted source. Suppose, for example, you receive a message that appears to be from your spouse and it says to click here to see that video of your children from last Christmas. Because it appears far more likely to be a legitimate message, it cuts through your standard defenses like a spear, and the likelihood that you would click the link is higher. Generating the attack requires much more work on the part of the attacker and often involves using information from contact lists, friend lists from social media sites, and so on.

Whaling is nothing more than phishing, or spear phishing, for so-called "big" users, thus the reference to the ocean's largest creatures. Instead of sending out a To Whom It May Concern message to thousands of users, the whaler identifies one person from whom they can gain all the data they want—usually a manager or business owner—and targets the phishing campaign at them.

Shoulder Surfing

One form of social engineering is known as *shoulder surfing* and involves nothing more than watching someone when they enter their sensitive data. They can see you entering a password, typing in a credit card number, or entering any other pertinent information.

Shoulder surfing is listed under physical security in the exam objectives. It can be considered a physical security risk as well as a form of social engineering.

The best defense against this type of attack is simply to survey your environment before entering personal data. It might also help to orient your screen such that people walking by can't easily see it. If it's impossible to adequately hide the monitor from unauthorized lookers, and if the data on the screen is highly confidential, you may find a screen filter useful. A screen filter (also called a *privacy screen*) directs the light from the display at a restricted angle so that anyone who isn't viewing it straight on won't be able to read it clearly.

It's common courtesy when someone else is typing in a password to make an obvious effort to look away.

> ## 🌐 Real World Scenario
>
> ### Don't Make It Too Easy
>
> As a teenager, before I got into IT, I was a clerk in a retail store. The company had just opened up a new store, and the store manager, Robert, asked me to come with him to look at an area of the store. During this time, he needed to check something on our computer system (which was new to all of us), so he went to one of the terminals and logged in.
>
> When he typed in his password, I did not make an obvious effort to look away (I didn't know the common courtesy tip yet), but I wasn't exactly trying to look at what he typed, either. I basically just saw his arm movements, and I knew from previous experience that he was a "pecker" (meaning he typed with the index finger on each hand only). What I semi-observed was three slowly typed letters, left-right-left, followed by a pause, and three rapid left keystrokes.
>
> After we took care of our task, I got to thinking about the situation, and quickly realized that he had given me his password—it was his first name! I never did anything with that information, but imagine the access I might have had to the system. I am quite certain that I would have been able to view information that I had no business seeing, had I tried.
>
> There are two big problems in this scenario. First, he clearly was not practicing good password selection (which I'll talk about in detail in Chapter 9), especially considering his level of importance in our company. Second, I should have made the attempt to avoid shoulder surfing. The moral of the story is don't make it too easy for others to hack in on your behalf. Make sure you choose tough passwords, and also make sure that you are aware of your surroundings when entering sensitive information.

Software-Based Security Threats

Software-based threats are by far the widest ranging group of security threats you need to be worried about. It seems that the creators of malicious software applications have no shortage of imagination. The broad term for software designed to do harm to your computer is *malware*, and it covers anything that has been installed on anyone's computer without their intent and intended to cause mischief. In the realm of malware, here are most of the categories you need to be aware of:

Exploits   These take advantage of flaws in the OS or an application.

Viruses   These are used to cause damage and/or disruption.

Worms   These are used to transmit malware.

Trojan Horses   These are applications that mask their true intent.

Adware   These are used to display unwanted advertisements.

Spyware   These are used to report on your computer and possibly steal data.

Ransomware   These are used to extract payments from the infected user.

Rootkits   These conceal themselves on the host OS, allowing for full-control access of the computer at a later date.

Backdoors   These open ports or other routes into your system.

Keyloggers   These record every keystroke and then use that data for identity theft.

In the following sections, you'll learn more about each of these types of malware. In addition, you will learn about spam and password cracking. The last two don't technically qualify as malware because most of the time they're not software installed on an unsuspecting user's computer. They are horribly annoying, though, so they deserve to be covered here as well.

OS and Application Exploits

All OSs and applications have potential vulnerabilities that criminals can exploit. A *vulnerability* exists when flaws in the programming create the potential for misuse, an attacker is aware of the flaw, and a tool or technique that the attacker can use to exploit that vulnerability for malicious purposes is readily available. When criminals use a vulnerability to attack a system, it's called an *exploit*.

Although some OSs are considered to be more secure than others, the reality is that all OSs have weaknesses that, when discovered, are exploited. To guard against exploits, operating systems have mechanisms to update and patch themselves automatically as programmers become aware of vulnerabilities. That's why it's important to download and install all available updates and service packs for your OS promptly. Refer back to Chapter 4, "Software Applications," for details on Windows Update.

 Real World Scenario

My Mac Is Safe from Viruses, Right?

A common misperception among computer users is that Windows is the only operating system that is vulnerable to viruses or other malware attacks. It's not true.

Mac and Linux systems aren't immune to malware attacks, but Windows systems do run a greater risk of infection. There are two reasons for this. The first is that some hackers have an axe to grind against Microsoft, so that's who they target. The second and biggest reason, though, is because of the popularity of Windows. It's by far the most widely used OS, so any financial gain a criminal might get from malware would be maximized by targeting Windows systems.

Applications can also be exploited, although it happens less frequently because an application is a smaller and less-appealing target to a criminal. Widely used applications such as Microsoft Office are most often the targets of application exploit attempts.

As an application or OS ages, more and more security patches become available for it, to the point that rolling them all out individually to users becomes unwieldy. At that point, the OS or application manufacturer typically releases a service pack. A *service pack* is a collection of critical updates (and sometimes minor enhancements) that are released as a group. A service pack is much like a regular update except that it takes longer to download and install, and you can't usually remove it after installing it.

Viruses

A *virus* is computer code that inserts itself into an executable file. When that file is run, the virus's code executes along with the application's code. The virus hides itself inside its host file, so it's not obvious that it's there. A virus's code can cause all manner of mischief, from annoying but harmless things like displaying a message, to really destructive things like deleting all files of a certain type or causing your OS to stop working. Most viruses also have a self-replicating component that causes them to spread from one executable file to another. This usually happens via RAM. When the infected file executes, the virus code is copied into RAM, and from there it can attach itself to other executable files.

Many other types of malware are often called viruses as well, even though they are not because they don't hide themselves in executable code. Instead they may be worms or Trojan horses, which will be explained in later sections.

Viruses can be classified as polymorphic, stealth, retrovirus, multipartite, armored, companion, phage, and macro viruses. Each type of virus has a different attack strategy and different consequences.

Estimates for losses due to viruses are in the billions of dollars. These losses include financial loss as well as lost productivity.

The following sections introduce the symptoms of a virus infection, explain how a virus works, and describe the types of viruses you can expect to encounter and how they generally behave. You'll also see how a virus is transmitted through a network and look at a few hoaxes.

Symptoms of a Virus/Malware Infection

Many viruses will announce that you're infected as soon as they gain access to your system. They may take control of your system and flash annoying messages on your screen or destroy your hard disk. When this occurs, you'll know that you're a victim. Other viruses will cause your system to slow down, cause files to disappear from your computer, or take over your disk space.

You should look for some of the following symptoms when determining if a malware or virus infection has occurred:

- The programs on your system start to load more slowly. This happens because the virus is spreading to other files in your system or is taking over system resources.

- Unusual files appear on your hard drive, or files start to disappear from your system. Many viruses delete key files in your system to render it inoperable.

- Program sizes change from the installed versions. This occurs because the virus is attaching itself to these programs on your disk.

- Your browser, word-processing application, or other software begins to exhibit unusual operating characteristics. Screens or menus may change.

- The system mysteriously shuts itself down or starts itself up and does a great deal of unanticipated disk activity.

- You mysteriously lose access to a disk drive or other system resources. The virus has changed the settings on a device to make it unusable.

- Your system suddenly doesn't reboot or gives unexpected error messages during startup.

This list is by no means comprehensive. What is an absolute, however, is the fact that you should immediately quarantine the infected system. It is imperative that you do all you can to contain the virus and keep it from spreading to other users, or other computers if you are on a network.

How Viruses Work

A virus, in most cases, tries to accomplish one of two things: render your system inoperable or spread to other systems. Many viruses will spread to other systems given the chance and then render your system unusable. This is common with many of the newer viruses.

If your system is infected, the virus may try to attach itself to every file in your system and spread each time you send a file or document to other users. Figure 8.3 shows a virus spreading from an infected system either through a network or by removable media. When you give removable media to another user or put it into another system, you then infect that system with the virus.

FIGURE 8.3   Virus spreading from an infected system

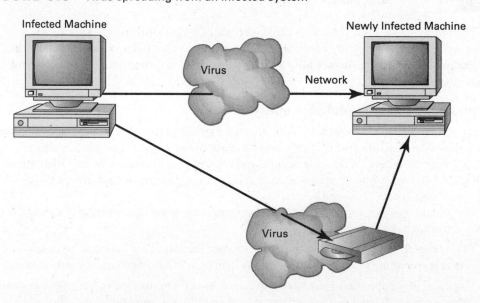

Many viruses today are spread using email. The infected system attaches a file to any email that you send to another user. The recipient opens this file, thinking it's something you legitimately sent them. When they open the file, the virus infects the target system. The virus might then attach itself to all the emails the newly infected system sends, which in turn infects computers of the recipients of the emails. Figure 8.4 shows how a virus can spread from a single user to literally thousands of users in a very short time using email.

FIGURE 8.4   Email viruses can spread quickly.

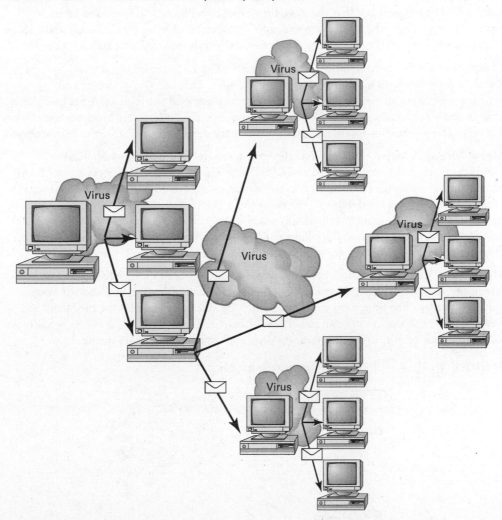

Types of Viruses

Viruses take many different forms. The following list briefly introduces these forms and explains how they work.

These are the most common types of viruses, but this isn't a comprehensive list:

Armored Virus   An *armored virus* is designed to make itself difficult to detect or analyze. Armored viruses cover themselves with protective code that stops debuggers or disassemblers from examining critical elements of the virus. The virus may be written in such a way that some aspects of the programming act as a decoy to distract analysis while the actual code hides in other areas in the program.

From the perspective of the creator, the more time it takes to deconstruct the virus, the longer it can live. The longer it can live, the more time it has to replicate and spread to as many machines as possible. The key to stopping most viruses is to identify them quickly and educate administrators about them—the very things that the armor makes difficult to accomplish.

Companion Virus   A *companion virus* attaches itself to legitimate programs and then creates a program with a different filename extension. This file may reside in your system's temporary directory. When a user types the name of the legitimate program, the companion virus executes instead of the real program. This effectively hides the virus from the user. The infected program may perform its dirty deed and then start the real program.

Macro Virus   A *macro virus* exploits the enhancements made to many application programs, such as Microsoft Word and Excel. Word, for example, supports a mini-BASIC programming language that allows files to be manipulated automatically. These programs in the document are called *macros*. For example, a macro can tell your word processor to spell-check your document automatically when it opens. Macro viruses can infect all the documents on your system and spread to other systems via email or other methods. Macro viruses are one of the fastest growing forms of exploitation today.

Multipartite Virus   A *multipartite virus* attacks your system in multiple ways. It may attempt to infect your boot sector, infect all of your executable files, and destroy your application files. The hope here is that you won't be able to correct all the problems and will allow the infestation to continue. The multipartite virus depicted in Figure 8.5 attacks a system's boot sector, infects application files, and attacks Word documents.

FIGURE 8.5   A multipartite virus attacking a system

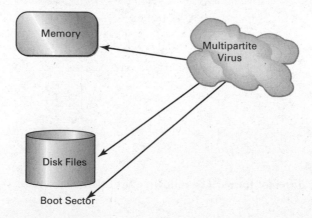

Phage Virus   A *phage virus* alters other programs and databases. The virus infects all of these files. The only way to remove this virus is to reinstall the programs that are infected. If you miss even a single incident of this virus on the victim system, the process will start again and infect the system once more.

Polymorphic Virus   *Polymorphic viruses* change form to avoid detection. These types of viruses attack your system, and may display a message on your computer and also delete files. The virus will attempt to hide from your antivirus software. Frequently, the virus will encrypt parts of itself to avoid detection. When the virus does this, it's referred to as *mutation*. The mutation process makes it hard for antivirus software to detect common characteristics of the virus. Figure 8.6 shows a polymorphic virus changing its characteristics to avoid detection. In this example, the virus changes a signature to fool antivirus software.

FIGURE 8.6   The polymorphic virus changing its characteristics

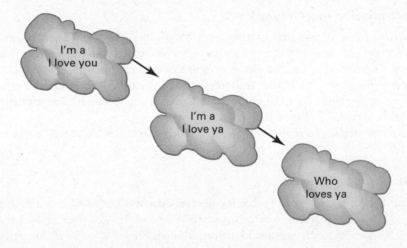

 A *signature* is an algorithm or other element of a virus that uniquely identifies it. Because some viruses have the ability to alter their signature, it is crucial that you keep signature files current, whether you choose to manually download them or configure the antivirus engine to do so automatically.

Retrovirus   A *retrovirus* attacks or bypasses the antivirus software installed on a computer. You can consider a retrovirus to be an anti-antivirus. Retroviruses can directly attack your antivirus software and potentially destroy the virus definition database file. Destroying this information without your knowledge would leave you with a false sense of security. The virus may also directly attack an antivirus program to create bypasses for itself.

Stealth Virus   A *stealth virus* attempts to avoid detection by masking itself from applications. It may attach itself to the boot sector of the hard drive. When a system utility or program runs, the stealth virus redirects commands around itself to avoid detection. An infected file may report a file size different from what is actually present. Figure 8.7 shows a stealth virus attaching itself to the boot sector to avoid detection. Stealth viruses may also move themselves from file A to file B during a virus scan for the same reason.

FIGURE 8.7   A stealth virus hiding in a disk boot sector

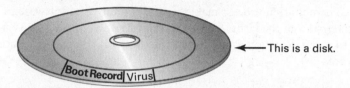

←——This is a disk.

Boot Record | Virus

Virus Transmission in a Network

Upon infection, some viruses destroy the target system immediately. The saving grace is that the infection can be detected and corrected. Some viruses won't destroy or otherwise tamper with a system; they use the victim system as a carrier. The victim system then infects servers, file shares, and other resources with the virus. The carrier then infects the target system again. Until the carrier is identified and cleaned, the virus continues to harass systems in this network and spread.

Viruses are detected and removed using antivirus software, which I will cover in depth in Chapter 9.

Worms

A *worm* is different from a virus in that it can reproduce itself, it's self-contained, and it doesn't need a host application to be transported. Many of the so-called viruses that have made the news were actually worms. However, it's possible for a worm to contain or deliver a virus to a target system. If a worm carries additional malware, that malware is called a *payload*.

Worms can be active or passive: active worms self-transport without human intervention, whereas passive worms rely on the user's innocence to transport themselves from one location to another, normally through email or social engineering. Active worms use email, vulnerabilities in your OS, TCP/IP, and Internet services to move their payload around a network infrastructure. Most antivirus programs can detect and remove worms.

Trojan Horses

A *Trojan horse* (often known as a Trojan) is a rogue application that enters the system or network disguised as another program. Some will pretend to offer services that you want. For example, one insidious type of Trojan horse is a program that claims to scan your system for malware but instead causes system problems (which it tries to get you to pay to get rid of) or installs its own malware, such as a keylogger. A *keylogger* records all keystrokes and sends the information to a file or to a remote location. The hacker can get your usernames and passwords that way and use them to impersonate you.

Trojan horse programs don't replicate themselves, so they aren't viruses, technically speaking. The most common way that Trojan horse programs spread is via worms. Most antivirus programs can detect and remove Trojan horses.

Adware

Adware is a category of application that displays unasked-for ads on your computer. The most common type of adware comes in the form of an add-on toolbar for your web browser that supposedly provides "advanced" or "helpful" search services, but that also has the side effect of causing pop-up ads to appear whenever you use your web browser. Adware makers make money when people click the ads they display.

Strictly speaking, not all adware is illegal, and not all adware makers are involved in criminal activity. If you're seduced into downloading a particular web toolbar or application, and then you aren't happy with what it does, or there are too many ads to make it worth the value you're getting from it, you're free to remove it. Removal may not be easy, though; the uninstall option for the toolbar may or may not appear in the Control Panel in Windows, and you may need to connect to a website or go through some extra steps to complete the removal.

Some adware is an out-and-out annoyance, with no pretense of being anything else. Such programs are typically very difficult to remove, much like a virus infection. Your antivirus software may be of some help; you also may need to do a web search on the removal process to find Registry-editing instructions to help you stamp out the adware.

Spyware

Spyware is software that (usually secretly) records your computer usage. Keyloggers are a form of spyware; so are programs that track the websites you visit and what ads you click and send that information back to their owners. Spyware makers get revenue from collecting consumer marketing data, either specifically about you or about all users in general. Most spyware is illegal, works surreptitiously, and can be difficult to remove.

Spyware isn't self-replicating, and it relies on low-level social engineering to spread. The most common way to get infected with spyware is to install a free application from a website. Be very careful what sites you use to download executable files! Another way to get spyware is to run an ActiveX or Java component on a website you visit. A website may seem like a good deal because it's free, but there are many unscrupulous site owners, particularly in the adult entertainment industry, who exploit site visitors by infecting their computers with spyware or adware.

Some antivirus software detects and removes spyware. There are also applications designed specifically to remove spyware and adware from your system, such as Windows Defender (which was discussed in Chapter 4).

Ransomware

Ransomware is a particularly insidious type of malware that extorts the infected users for money. Even though it's been around since 1989, it's only gained significant popularity since about 2012. Generally contracted through a Trojan or exploits in software such as a Flash player, the ransomware will pop up a message telling the user to pay up or else.

Some ransomware tries to look official. For example, one version attempted to look like an official notice from a police group, stating that the user had been in violation of several laws and needed to pay a fine to have the issue resolved. Others are far more direct—they will encrypt files on your hard drive and tell you that if you want them back, you'll pay the money. This type of threat is called *cryptoviral extortion.* The ransomware will give you a handy link to pay the fine, which redirects you to another site to enter your payment information.

Of course, this starts to introduce other problems. Clicking the link to visit the website means that other malware can be loaded onto your system, such as a rootkit, spyware, or keylogger. And, the hackers will give you the convenient option of entering your credit card information to pay them off. What could go wrong there?

Fortunately, most antivirus software will block ransomware as well. If you are infected and your files are locked or encrypted, your only recourse may be to wipe your system and restore from backup, provided of course that your backup files aren't infected as well.

Rootkits

Rootkits are software programs that have the ability to hide certain things from the operating system; they do so by obtaining (and retaining) administrative-level access. With a rootkit, there may be a number of processes running on a system that don't show up in Task Manager or network connections that don't appear in networking tools—the rootkit masks the presence of these items. It does this by manipulating the operating system to filter out information that would normally appear.

Unfortunately, many rootkits are written to get around antivirus and antispyware programs that aren't kept up to date. The best defense you have is to monitor what your system is doing and catch the rootkit in the process of installation.

In UNIX systems, *root* is the name of the all-powerful administrator account. The term *rootkit* was coined because it's a tool that gives you root-level access to a system.

Backdoors

A *backdoor* is a method of circumventing the normal security system on a computer. Instead of needing a password, a hacker with a backdoor could log in by providing no credentials. Backdoors can be stand-alone programs or can be incorporated into other malware such as rootkits or worms.

Another source of backdoor issues is user error. Not changing a default password can allow for unauthorized access. In addition, debugging routines built into software, and not removed before release into production, can sometimes function as backdoors as well.

Spam

Spam is different than the software-based threats I've covered so far, because it's not software that gets installed on your computer. Rather, *spam* is the deluge of unsolicited messages that you receive electronically. Most spam comes via email, but it can be generated in instant messaging, blogs, online classifieds, mobile phones, Internet forums, and message groups.

Most spam is advertisements, and there is little or no cost for the spammers to send these types of messages. All the spammer needs is a program to generate the spam (called a *spambot*) and email lists. There is cost for Internet service providers, businesses, and users, though, because ISPs and businesses need to install and maintain hardware or software solutions to deal with the volume. It's estimated that over nine trillion spam messages get sent per year. Clearly, legislation that has made spam illegal in many areas has not had much effect.

In addition, while a large percentage of spam is advertising, a lot of it is purely an attempt to defraud people who click links inside the note. While it's becoming more common for users to realize that clicking a link in an email from someone you don't know is a no-no, it still happens. In addition, spammers can often make the emails look like they come from a legitimate source, such as a real business, your ISP, or even a contact in your mailing list, making it more likely that someone will click a link and download a virus or other malware.

In addition to email spam, someone who posts the same message repeatedly in an online forum is considered a spammer. Their goal is usually to be obnoxious and hijack the thread or conversation for some reason.

The best way to deal with spam that gets into your inbox is to delete it. Most email clients will have a junk mail or spam filter, and you can flag the note as spam. This will redirect future emails from that sender straight into your junk email or spam folder.

Password Cracking

Most of us are used to typing in passwords, probably several times a day. It's kind of a fact of life that you need a username and password to get to most of your resources. Of course, there are people out there who would love to gain unauthorized access to your data as well, and one way they can do that is by attempting to crack your password.

Password cracking can take many forms. Perhaps the easiest is for the attacker to try the default password for a device or service. If the attacker knows your password for a different resource or website, they can try that one too, because a lot of us reuse our passwords across different sites. A third way is to guess passwords based on things they know about you, such as children's or pet's names, favorite teams or music, important dates, and things like that. Finally, there's the brute force method. An automated computer program can start trying random strings of characters in an attempt to guess your password. Given enough time, password cracking software will eventually guess your password—and it doesn't take as much time as you think. A regular desktop or laptop computer outfitted with password-cracking software can try about three billion password keys per second, meaning that a random 8-character password with numbers, mixed case, and symbols can be cracked in about 15 minutes. A computer designed specifically for password cracking can crank out about 90 billion password keys per second.

 Password-cracking software is not illegal, and in fact there are many legal uses of it. If you have lost or need to reset a password, this type of software can be very helpful. Trying to get into a system you don't own is illegal, though.

Fortunately, most websites and computer systems have limits to the number of login attempts that can be tried before the account is locked, usually around five attempts. Regardless, don't make it easy on someone to guess your password. You will learn more about specific steps to take for good password management in Chapter 9.

Summary

This chapter attempted to make you paranoid by introducing you to security threats that you can face every day. It started off with a discussion on hackers and the type of information they try to steal or the damage they try to cause.

The first group of threats you learned about were physical threats. For example, if an attacker can physically get to your hardware, they could damage the device to make it unusable or steal the device to either sell it to someone else or attempt to steal data from the device. Data, software, and software licenses are also targets of thieves looking to make money. Some attackers will go as far as to sift through garbage, called dumpster diving, in an attempt to gain unauthorized access to information.

The second type of threats you learned about are ones that use people as targets. The broad classification of these threats is social engineering. It preys upon people's desires to be helpful to others, which unfortunately makes them easy targets for attackers pretending to be someone they're really not. One common way social engineering is done is over the phone. If the attempt is made over email it's referred to as phishing. A third social engineering method is to simply look over someone's shoulder, which is appropriately called shoulder surfing.

Software-based threats are the third group you learned about. This is the largest group, and the list of possible maladies is long: exploits, viruses, worms, Trojans, adware, spyware, ransomware, rootkits, backdoors, and keyloggers are all types of malware that affect your computer. In addition to that, spam and password cracking can also threaten your computer's security.

Exam Essentials

Understand what physical security threats to be aware of.   Physical threats include hardware damage and theft, software and license theft, and dumpster diving. The exam objectives also list shoulder surfing as a physical threat, but that can also be considered social engineering.

Know what social engineering is.   Social engineering is preying upon people to provide information that will allow an attacker to gain access. This is often done over the phone. Email social engineering is called phishing.

Understand the different types of malware that can affect your computer.   Malware includes operating system and application exploits, viruses, worms, Trojan horses, adware, spyware, ransomware, rootkits, backdoors, and keyloggers.

Understand why spam and password cracking are security threats.   Spam can be simply annoying, or it can contain viruses or other malware that get downloaded to your computer when you click a link. Password cracking is an attempt to gain unauthorized access to a system.

Chapter 8 Lab

Chapter 8 introduced a large number of threats to your computer's security. Most threats are in the malware group, and new viruses and threats are released on a regular basis to join the cadre of those already in existence. It's a good idea to be aware of the threats that are out there and keep up to date on new ones being introduced into the wild.

One great source to find this information is the CERT/CC Current Activity web page at www.us-cert.gov/current/current_activity.html. Here you'll find a detailed description of the most current viruses as well as links to pages on older threats. You can also find updates on most anti-malware companies' websites, such as www.symantec.com (for Norton Security) and www.mcafee.com. Google searches can also make you aware of threats or provide news on recent attacks.

Here are a few specific questions for you to answer:

1. Pick a recent date. How many viruses and malware were "discovered" on that date? (Alternate question: how many were added to your antivirus program on a given date?)

2. Are there any serious security threats currently?

3. Which virus or worm caused the most damage in history? How many computers did it infect and how fast did it spread?

4. Can you find example names of some different types of viruses? Choose a few, such as a polymorphic virus, a boot virus, and a multipartite virus.

5. What is the most popular ransomware in history?

6. What is the name of the most common backdoor you can find?

7. What are examples of password-cracking software?

Review Questions

1. Which of the following are activities that a hacker might attempt?

   A. Stealing usernames and passwords

   B. Modifying website content

   C. Disrupting network communications

   D. Analyzing network traffic

   E. All of the above

2. You receive a security warning from your antivirus software provider stating that a new virus is directly attacking the antivirus software. What type of virus is this?

   A. Macro

   B. Phage

   C. Retrovirus

   D. Armored

3. Which of the following are considered physical security risks? (Choose two.)

   A. Hardware theft

   B. Password cracking

   C. Phishing

   D. Software theft

4. What is the name of an application that appears to look like a helpful application but instead does harm to your computer?

   A. Virus

   B. Worm

   C. Malware

   D. Trojan horse

5. Someone was recently caught sifting through your company's trash looking for confidential information. What is this an example of?

   A. Trash snooping

   B. Dumpster diving

   C. Phishing

   D. Social engineering

6. IT security recently found a program on your co-worker's computer that apparently tracked all of the words that they typed into the computer. What kind of malware is this?

    A. Keylogger

    B. Keyblogger

    C. Trojan horse

    D. Keystroke virus

7. You have been asked to lead a class on preventing social engineering. What two topics should you be sure to cover? (Choose two.)

    A. Viruses and worms

    B. Shoulder surfing

    C. Hardware theft

    D. Phishing

8. What type of malware is best known for carrying other malware as a payload?

    A. Virus

    B. Worm

    C. Trojan horse

    D. Rootkit

9. You receive an email from your bank, telling you that your account has been compromised and you need to validate your account details or else your account will be closed. You are supposed to click a link to validate your information. What is this an example of?

    A. A security breach at your bank that needs to be resolved

    B. Spam

    C. Ransomware

    D. Phishing

10. Rose just installed a new search engine on her laptop. Now whenever she searches the Internet, she gets several pop-up windows directing her to websites to buy products. What does Rose have?

    A. Ransomware

    B. Spyware

    C. Adware

    D. Trojan horse

11. What is it called when a co-worker sitting next to you always seems to look your way when you try to enter your user ID and password to log onto the network?

    A. Phishing

    B. Social engineering

    C. Shoulder surfing

    D. Coincidence

12. The system administrator in your office quits unexpectedly in the middle of the day. It's quickly apparent that he changed the server password and no one knows what it is. What might you do in this type of situation?

    A. Use a Trojan horse to find the password

    B. Use a password cracker to find the password

    C. Use social engineering to find the password

    D. Delete and reinstall the server

13. Which of the following operating systems are susceptible to viruses?

    A. Windows

    B. Windows and Mac OS X

    C. Windows, Mac OS X, and Linux

    D. Windows, Mac OS X, Linux, and Android

14. What type of software is used to circumvent normal security processes on a computer?

    A. Backdoor

    B. Trojan horse

    C. Spyware

    D. Phage virus

15. A virus that covers itself in protective code, making it harder to find and eradicate, is called what?

    A. Stealth virus

    B. Polymorphic virus

    C. Armored virus

    D. Trojan horse

16. You were browsing the Web on a questionable website, and now you get a pop-up window stating that if you do not pay $100 within one hour, all files on your computer will be destroyed. What is this an example of?

    A. Heistware

    B. Theftware

    C. Extortionware

    D. Ransomware

17. You believe that your computer has contracted a virus that has affected your Excel files only. What type of virus is most likely to do this?

A. Macro

B. Retrovirus

C. Phage

D. Excel virus

18. What does the term *spam* refer to in computing?

A. Excessive pop-up windows

B. Unsolicited emails

C. Social engineering attempts

D. Installing malware on a computer

19. If a virus attacks the boot sector of your hard drive as well as files in the file system, what type of virus is it?

A. Polymorphic

B. Multipartite

C. Companion

D. Macro

20. David just heard of a program that if installed on your computer gives the attacker administrator-like access to your machine. What type of software is he talking about?

A. Trojan horse

B. Spyware

C. Ransomware

D. Rootkit

Chapter

9

Security Best Practices

THE FOLLOWING COMPTIA IT FUNDAMENTALS EXAM OBJECTIVES ARE COVERED IN THIS CHAPTER:

✓ **3.2 Given a scenario, use security best practices**

- Password management
  - Password complexity
  - Change default passwords
  - Password confidentiality
  - Password expiration
  - Password reuse
  - Awareness of Single Sign On
- Device hardening
  - Disable unused features
    - Disable Bluetooth
    - Disable NFC
  - Timeout / lock options
  - Enable security software/features
    - Software firewall
    - Anti-malware
  - Encryption options
- Open WiFi vs. secure WiFi
- Multifactor authentication
- Suspicious emails
  - Attachments
  - Hyperlinks

- Act on security software alerts
- Admin vs. user vs. guest account

✓ **3.3 Given a scenario, use web-browsing best practices**

- Recognize a secure connection/website
  - https
  - lock symbol
- Recognize invalid certificate warnings
- Recognize suspicious links
- Recognize suspicious banner ads
- Recognize adware symptoms
  - Constant popups
  - Home page redirection
  - Search engine redirection
- Limit the use of personal information (PII)
- Update browsers and plugins
  - Avoid use of legacy browsers
- Disable unneeded/suspicious browser plugins, toolbars and extensions
- Disable autofill forms/passwords
- Clear browser cache/history/cookies
- Recognize untrusted source warnings
- Risks of using public workstations

Chapter 8, "Security Threats," introduced you to a wide range of attacks and threats to your computer. While it's true that you need to be vigilant when protecting your computer, the good news is that there are many steps you can take to help secure your system. Even if you follow all of the best steps to protect your computer, you can still find yourself the victim of an attack—there is no guarantee that you're safe. Your goal though is to make a would-be attacker's life as miserable as possible. The harder your computer is to get into, the more likely it is that the attacker will look for easier victims. Following the proper steps dramatically decreases the odds of an attack being successful versus having an unprotected system.

This chapter builds upon Chapter 8 by showing you steps you can take to protect your computer and your data. As part of that, you will learn how to harden your computer, manage user accounts properly, and protect yourself on a network, with particular emphasis on Internet and email safety. This chapter contains practical advice, as well as scenarios to help you understand preventive measures, what to look for in regard to suspicious activity, and what to do in case your system becomes compromised.

Computer and Network Security Best Practices

The best computer security plans are always multifaceted; there are parts of the plan to implement on the local computer as well as the network, and there are activities you should avoid doing to be safe. Odds are you wouldn't walk down a dark alley at night—this section will show you what the computerized version of that dark alley is so you can avoid it.

In this section, you will learn details on three different classifications of computer and network security. It starts off with device hardening, moves to user account management, and finishes with network security.

Device Hardening

The term *device hardening* has to be one of the best terms in all of computing. It sounds strong and powerful and like it will make your computer invincible. While the invincibility part is a bit of a stretch, device hardening helps protect your computer by reducing its vulnerabilities.

If you think about it, the very act of networking computers is what makes them vulnerable to attacks. An old adage in the IT industry is that "a server is totally secure until you install the network card." The pragmatic paradox is, of course, without that network card the server can't really serve anyone. The adage holds true for all computers, and so does the paradox. Device hardening is one proactive step you can take at the local machine to reduce the likelihood of a successful attack. Here, you will learn about the following device-hardening techniques:

- Disabling unused or potentially dangerous features
- Locking the system
- Enabling encryption
- Utilizing security software and features

Disabling Unused or Dangerous Features

You've probably heard the phrase, "out of sight, out of mind." This is the first thing I think of when it comes to unused features. Because they're not used, they are forgotten about, so you don't bother to ever monitor them to see if they were used and you didn't realize it. Unused features with potential security holes are things that hackers love. Think of a scenario where an attacker exploits a bug in an unused feature and remains undetected; this allows them to continue their tasks without deterrents. It's like being able to eat all of the cookies in the cookie jar knowing that no one will look for crumbs—almost too good to be true!

Disabling Unused Communication Methods

With the prevalence of smartphones today, hacking via wireless network or other communication methods has become quite popular. The best way to protect yourself is to disable those services.

Imagine a situation where you are in a crowded public place, and you receive an unsolicited popup message on your smartphone inviting you to buy a new product. You have just been bluejacked! The message you received is probably harmless advertising, but it's not something you asked for and it could be more serious. Solve this by disabling Bluetooth. On your iPhone or Android phone, this is done in Settings. Figure 9.1 shows you the setting in iOS, and Figure 9.2 shows it to you in Android.

FIGURE 9.1 Disabled Bluetooth in iOS

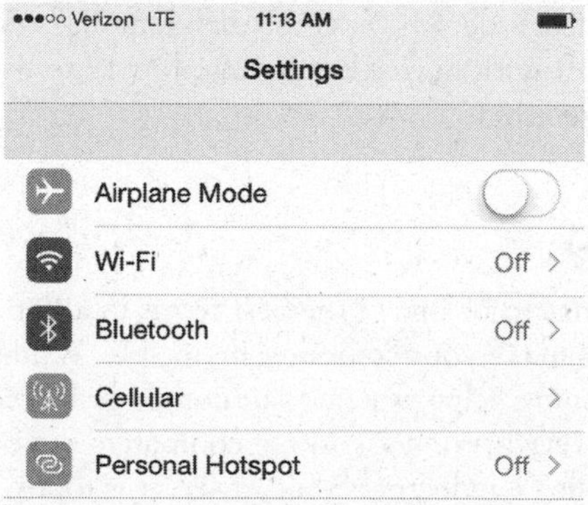

FIGURE 9.2 Disabled Bluetooth in Android

Another potentially dangerous short-range communication method is *near field communication (NFC)*. It's a convenient technology that lets you do things like hold your phone next to someone else's and transfer data, or bump your phone to a receiver at a store to pay for your purchase. That convenience can also be a door into your system, though, so if you're not actively using it, disable it!

Disabling Unused Services

Within Windows and other operating systems, various system functions are implemented as services. For example, the process of managing a print job falls to the print spooler service, and logging into a domain controller is managed by a service called Netlogon. To run these services, your operating system logs itself on temporarily as a quasi-user with elevated privileges to perform the task and then logs itself back off.

An attacker could use an exploit of a service to attempt to gain unauthorized access to your machine. Most of the time, unused services are disabled by default, so the point is to not enable services unless you know you need them. Services are found in Windows in Computer Management. Exercise 9.1 shows you how to start and stop services in Windows 7.

EXERCISE 9.1

Starting and Stopping Services in Windows 7

1. Open Computer Management by clicking Start and then right-clicking Computer and choosing Manage.

2. On the left side of the Computer Management window, click Services under Services And Applications, as shown in Figure 9.3.

3. You will see the Bluetooth Support Service, as highlighted in Figure 9.3. Notice that it is not started and starts up manually. The other choices for startup are Automatic and Disabled.

FIGURE 9.3 Windows Services

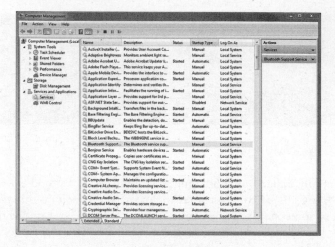

4. To start the service, either click the green Start arrow above the Name column or right-click the service and choose Start. The status will change.

5. To stop the service, click the Stop button above the Name column or right-click the service and choose Stop.

6. To change the startup type for a service, right-click and choose Properties. Use the drop-down menu next to Startup Type to make your selection, as shown in Figure 9.4, and then click OK.

FIGURE 9.4 Bluetooth Support Service properties

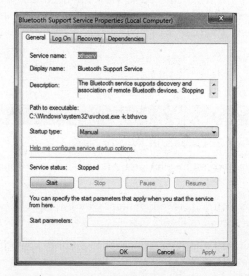

Although disabling unused services can help harden your system, don't disable services in your operating system unless you know what they do and you know you don't need them. Disabling necessary services can cause your system to not function properly.

Disabling AutoPlay

AutoPlay is branded as a convenient feature that lets you insert media into your system and have it run automatically. Unfortunately this can also introduce a security risk.

It is never a good idea to put any media in a workstation if you do not know where it came from or what it is. The reason is that the media (CD, DVD, USB) could contain malware. Compounding matters, that malware could be referenced in the AUTORUN.INF file on the media, causing it to be summoned simply by inserting the media in the machine and requiring no other action. AUTORUN.INF can be used to start an executable, access a website, or do any of a large number of different tasks. The best way to prevent your system from falling victim to such a ploy is to disable the AutoPlay feature on the workstation.

AutoPlay may also be called Autorun on your computer.

The AutoPlay settings are located in Control Panel under Hardware And Sound. If you open Control Panel don't see it, type AutoPlay in the Search box and it will appear. Open AutoPlay, and you will see a screen similar to the one shown in Figure 9.5.

FIGURE 9.5   AutoPlay options

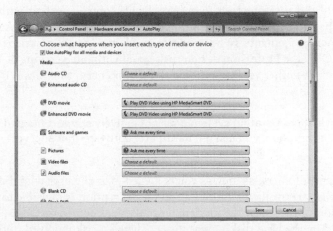

The easiest way to disable AutoPlay is to uncheck the box at the top of the page. You can also control the settings for individual media types. For example, in Figure 9.5 you can see that for software and games the system will prompt the user as to which action to take. This is far better than just running the media automatically.

Locking the System

Locking the system can mean two things. The first is physically locking the system to a desk or in a drawer so it can't be stolen. The second is to software lock the system when you leave your desk. You learned about both of these security options in Chapter 8.

As a quick reminder, a screensaver should automatically start after a short period of idle time, and a password should be required before the user can begin the session again. This method of locking the workstation adds one more level of security. Better yet, users should automatically lock their computer as soon as they leave their desk. This is done by pressing Ctrl+Alt+Del and choosing Lock Workstation. The user's password will be required to unlock the machine.

A popular phrase associated with this security step is "Control Alt Delete when you leave your seat!"

Setting NTFS Permissions and Enabling Encryption

In Chapter 6, "Network Sharing and Storage," you learned about sharing resources over the network and the permissions used to control access to shared files. Those permissions apply only when people are connecting to the computer via the network. When different users log into the same computer locally, though, you need to employ other methods to keep their private data separate.

One way is to set certain folders to be inaccessible to other local users. To do this in Windows, use the Security tab in the folder's Properties dialog box. It contains file-sharing permission settings that apply to local access. You can also *encrypt* certain folders so their content is scrambled if someone tries to browse the file content, such as with a disk-editor utility. To encrypt a folder, in the folder's Properties dialog box, click the Advanced button and select the Encrypt Contents To Secure Data check box. You'll practice these skills in Exercise 9.2. Only the Professional, Enterprise, and Ultimate versions of Windows 7 support encryption; in other versions, the check box for encrypting files is unavailable.

If your operating system does not natively support file and folder encryption, you can get third-party software that encrypts data.

When you encrypt folders, as long as you're logged in as the user who did the encrypting, the files are available normally and the encryption is invisible to you. However, if you log in as some other user, the files are inaccessible. Encryption is based on security certificates stored on the hard disk for each user. There's a risk involved, though, because if the security certificate becomes corrupted or deleted, you won't be able to access files that are legitimately yours. It's therefore important to back up your certificate before you start relying on encryption to protect your files locally. A lost or damaged certificate can be recovered but not easily. Exercise 9.2 has you practice encrypting files and setting security permissions, and Exercise 9.3 provides practice in backing up a security certificate. For the exercises to work, you will need Windows 7 Professional, Ultimate, or Enterprise editions.

EXERCISE 9.2

Securing and Encrypting Local Folders in Windows 7

1. If you don't already have at least two user accounts on your PC, create one. To do so, follow these steps:

    a. Choose Start ➢ Control Panel ➢ User Accounts (or User Accounts And Family Safety, depending on your Windows version) ➢ Add Or Remove User Accounts.

    b. Click Create New Account.

    c. Type the new account name.

    d. Click Create Account.

2. Open the Documents folder. Click New Folder, type **Private** as its name, and press Enter to accept the new name.

3. Right-click the Private folder, and choose Properties.

4. On the Security tab, click Edit. The Permissions For Private dialog box opens.

5. Click Add. The Select Users Or Groups dialog box opens.

6. In the Enter The Object Names To Select box, type the username for the other user on this PC that you want to use for the exercise.

7. Click Check Names. The username appears, preceded by the computer name, as shown in Figure 9.6.

FIGURE 9.6   Giving a user permissions

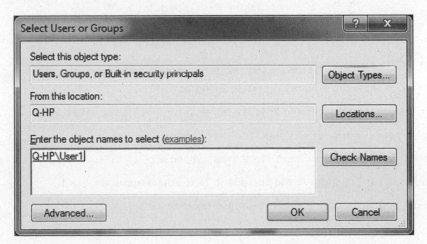

8. Click OK. Now that user appears on the Group Or User Names list in the Private Properties dialog box.

9. With the user's name selected, notice the permissions in the lower pane. As Figure 9.7 shows, the Full Control and Modify check boxes aren't selected.

FIGURE 9.7   User permissions

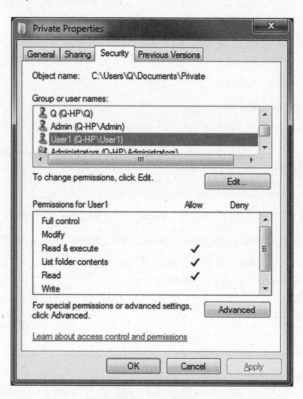

10. Click OK.

11. Click OK to close the Private Properties dialog box.

12. Copy a document file into the `Private` folder.

13. Log off your current user account, and log in as the other user.

14. Attempt to open the document. Note what happens.

15. Attempt to save changes to the document. Note what happens.

16. Log off, and log in again using the original username.

17. Open the Documents folder. Right-click the Private folder, and choose Properties.

18. On the General tab, click Advanced.

19. In the Advanced Attributes dialog box, select the Encrypt Contents To Secure Data check box if it's available.

Note: You must have the Professional, Ultimate, or Enterprise edition of Windows 7 to encrypt a folder's contents as detailed in step 19. On any other Windows 7 version, the check box will be grayed out.

20. Click OK.

21. Click OK to close the Private Properties dialog box.

22. Log off your current user account, and log in as the other user.

23. Attempt to access the Private folder, and note what happens. If you chose to encrypt the contents in step 19, it isn't accessible.

24. Log off, and log in again using the original username. Delete the Private folder.

EXERCISE 9.3

Backing Up a Windows Security Certificate

1. In Windows, click Start, type **certmgr.msc**, and press Enter. The Certificate Manager utility opens.

2. Click the Personal folder to expand it.

3. Click Certificates.

4. Click the certificate that shows Encrypting File System in the Intended Purposes column.

5. Choose Action ➢ All Tasks ➢ Export. The Certificate Export Wizard runs.

6. Click Next.

7. Click Yes, export the private key, and then click Next.

8. Make sure Personal Information Exchange is selected, and click Next.

9. In the Password box, type a password of your choice. Type it again in the Type And Confirm Password box. Then click Next.

10. In the File Name box, type the name you want to use to save the backup file. For example, if your username is jsmith, you might use jsmith-certbackup.

11. The default storage location for the backup is your Documents folder. If you want to place it somewhere else, click Browse, change locations, and then click Save.

12. Click Next. The Completing The Certificate Export Wizard screen appears.

13. Click Finish.

14. In the confirmation dialog box, click OK.

15. Close the Certificate Manager window.

On a Mac, local encryption can't be applied to individual folders and files; you must encrypt the entire disk. You can do this via the Disk Utility, as shown in Figure 9.8, or encrypt the home folder using FileVault as shown in Figure 9.9.

FIGURE 9.8   Encrypting a disk in Mac OS X

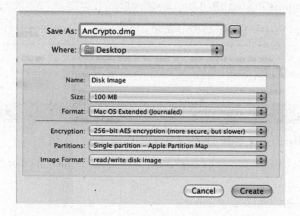

FIGURE 9.9   The Mac FileVault

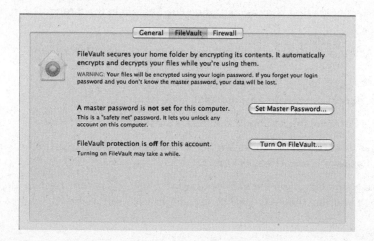

The easiest way to encrypt files and folders on a Linux system is via the command-line interface using the `openssl` libraries. `openssl` allows encryption and decryption by selecting which cipher to use. For example, you can use `des3` (Triple Data Encryption Standard) as the encryption algorithm. In Linux, you specify the cipher, followed by defining the key derivation routine, such as `salt`, when encrypting. Then you specify the original input file followed by the encrypted output file. An example looks like this:

```
openssl des3 -salt -in originalfile.txt -out encryptedfile.txt
```

To decrypt, the only differences are that you use the `-d` option (which means decrypt) and you put the encrypted filename before the unencrypted output file. An example looks like this:

```
openssl des3 -d -salt -in encryptedfile.txt -out unencryptedfile.txt
```

Using Security Software and Features

Having a system infected with malware is one of the most likely security risk scenarios you will encounter. There are four main classes of applications to help protect your system against malware and hackers:

- Antivirus software defends against viruses, worms, and Trojan horses.
- Antispyware software defends against adware and spyware.
- Antispam software reduces the amount of junk email you receive.
- Software firewalls block potentially dangerous network traffic.

There are also suites available that combine multiple security functions; for example, the Norton Security suite includes antivirus, antimalware, and antispam features, along with identity-protection tools, a software firewall, a backup tool, and a PC tune-up tool. McAfee's LiveSafe is similar. In addition, there is some overlap between the types of threats each application guards against; for example, an antivirus program may also target some types of non-virus malware.

Antivirus Software

Antivirus software attempts to identify virus infections by scanning all the files on your hard disk (or a subset of files that are most likely to contain viruses). Popular antivirus programs include Norton Security (formerly Norton Antivirus) and McAfee AntiVirus.

The website www.av-comparatives.org provides a comprehensive comparison and review of current antivirus applications. Take the time to look through this site and draw your own conclusions about what may be the best antivirus application for you.

Viruses are often concealed by a simple deception. They embed themselves inside an application, redirecting the application's commands and code around themselves while running as a separate task. One way antivirus programs detect a virus is by opening the file and scanning the code, looking for this type of redirection. Some programming languages, such as C++ and Java, generate code in a style that is sometimes wrongly accused by an antivirus program of being infected.

Another way antivirus programs work is to scan the code of each executable file looking for virus signatures. A virus's signature is an identifying snippet of its code, sometimes called a virus definition. The antivirus program maintains a database of known virus definitions; when it finds a match between its database and some code it finds in a file it scans, it signals a warning that there may be an infection. As new viruses and other threats are discovered, the company updates the virus-definition file for its antivirus program and downloads it to users as an update. Having the most up-to-date definitions is critical for effective virus protection, so you must regularly update your antivirus software (or better yet, set it to update itself automatically).

In addition, many antivirus programs create an MD5 for each application. MD5 stands for Message Digest Version 5, a math calculation that results in a unique value used to reflect the data being checked. If the MD5 changes, this may be treated as a virus attack.

Antivirus applications are normally resident, meaning they're continuously running in the background, analyzing your system and any programs when they're opened or closed as well as any files that are opened or closed. Some antivirus programs check incoming and outgoing email too, as well as web pages you visit. You can also tell your antivirus program to do a complete scan of all your files any time you like. (It will probably offer to do one right after you install the antivirus software.)

When your antivirus program finds something suspicious, a message appears, giving you the choice of deleting or quarantining the infected file(s). Deleting a file removes it from your system. Quarantining it places it in an off-limits area so it can't be run but keeps it on your system. You might quarantine a file that you wanted to share with an IT professional who was tracking virus infections on your network, for example. Exercise 9.4 gives you the steps needed to install and use an antivirus program.

If your security software pops up an alert, it's best to act upon it immediately. The alert will tell you what the suspected problem is and recommend a course of action. Unless you have a specific reason not to, follow your security software's recommended actions!

EXERCISE 9.4

Installing and Using an Antivirus Application

1. If you don't already have an antivirus application, download and install one. For Windows systems, Microsoft's Home Security Essentials program is free, and it will work well for this exercise. You can download it at windows.microsoft.com/en-us/windows/security-essentials-download. Or, if you already have an antivirus application, open it.

2. Using whatever antivirus software you have installed, do the following:

    a. Update the virus definitions.

    b. Run a complete system scan.

3. If any viruses are found, quarantine or delete the files that contain them.

Antispyware Software

Antispyware applications look for known spyware and adware programs and offer to disable them or remove them from your system. Like antivirus applications, antispyware programs look for definitions—that is, code snippets that identify a spyware or adware component.

Most antispyware applications also can remove lesser security and privacy threats, such as tracking cookies. Many antivirus applications include antispyware protection too, so you may not have to bother with a separate antispyware application.

Some antispyware applications run all the time in the background, like an antivirus application. Others run only when you specifically open them and initiate a scan.

Windows Defender is a free antispyware tool that comes with Windows. There are also many other free and commercial antispyware programs available, such as Spybot Search & Destroy (www.safer-networking.org).

As with antivirus applications, antispyware applications are most effective when their definitions are up to date.

Antispam Software

Spam refers to unwanted junk email. People send spam to try to sell products because doing so is economical—it costs almost nothing to send millions of emails, so even if only a very small percentage of people respond, it's still a money-making proposition. People also send spam to perpetrate fraud, either by trying to sell useless or nonexistent products or by trying to trick people into visiting phishing websites or sites where a virus or other malware will be downloaded.

Many email applications include filters and other tools to manage spam. Microsoft Outlook has its own junk-mail filter, for example. However, these built-in filters often fail to catch a lot of the spam because their algorithms for differentiating between spam and legitimate mail aren't sophisticated.

Some antivirus applications include an antispam component, and you can also buy add-on antispam programs or get them for free. For example, SpamBayes, available for free at spambayes.sourceforge.net, is an extremely sophisticated email differentiator that uses a ranking system that evaluates each message on multiple criteria to determine its spam probability. It's available for Windows, UNIX, Linux, and Mac OS X.

Diagnosing and Fixing Malware Infections

Even if you have an antimalware application installed, it's not perfect. Occasionally a virus or other malware may get around it, especially a new threat (and especially if you haven't updated your definitions lately). When a system is infected with a virus, a worm, a Trojan horse, or other malware, you may experience some of these symptoms, either immediately or on a particular day or time when the malware triggers itself:

- Your antivirus software may be disabled, and you can't re-enable it. Or, if you didn't already have antivirus software and you're just now installing it, it may not install. This is a very common side effect of virus infection, because it makes it difficult for you to remove the virus.

- Your system may run sluggishly, taking much longer than normal to open windows or applications. Many malware infections bog down a system or cripple it.

- CPU and memory usage may be high even though you aren't doing anything that would cause them to act in this manner. This can happen if the malware is hijacking your system for its own computing purposes.

- A warning or message box may appear onscreen and refuse to go away. For example, there may be a message that your system is infected with a virus and demanding that you enter a credit card to "buy" software that will fix the problem.

- Your friends may let you know that they have been receiving strange emails from you that you didn't send.

- When you use your web browser, you may be bombarded with pop-up ads.

If you start experiencing these symptoms, your own antivirus program may not be much help because a virus may have gotten around it and disabled it. If it's running—great. Do a full virus scan immediately.

If you can't use your local antivirus program, your best bet is an online virus checker. Trend Micro offers a good free one at housecall.trendmicro.com, for example. Scan your system with that, and then follow the advice the scanner recommends. If the system is infected to the point that it won't operate even to open a web browser, try booting into Safe Mode with Networking. Doing so may disable some of the virus's components temporarily. If you still can't rid of the virus, you may need to consult an IT professional at your local computer shop.

After you've removed the infection, you may need to repair or reinstall your antivirus software and download updates to it.

Software Firewalls

You learned about software firewalls in Chapter 4, "Software Applications." If you will recall, firewalls can protect you in two ways. They protect your network resources from bad traffic generated by hackers, and they can simultaneously prevent computers on your network from accessing undesirable content on the Internet. Firewalls perform these tasks by monitoring and filtering network traffic. Windows comes with its own software, appropriately named Windows Firewall. If you want to obtain a different firewall, you can find them as stand-alone products or part of a security suite such as Norton Security. If you are unsure of what security measures are in place on your system, the Windows Action Center, shown in Figure 9.10, can show you what security measures are set on your system.

FIGURE 9.10   Windows Action Center

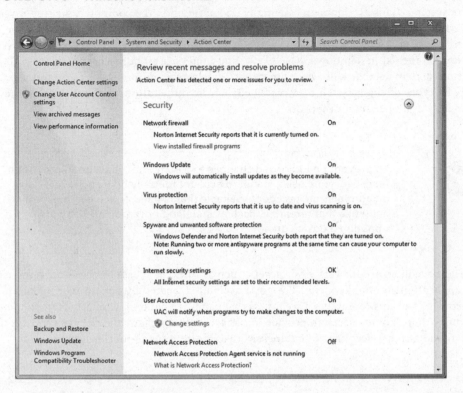

User Account Management

Users represent the weakest link in the security chain, whether harm comes to them in the form of malware, social engineering, or simply avoidable mistakes. Aside from some of the obvious things, like training users (or yourself) to be on the alert for social engineering, there are several tasks you can perform to decrease the security risks related to user accounts. These include proper management of user account types, password management, and authentication systems.

Managing User Account Types

All computer operating systems come with multiple levels of user accounts, each with predefined sets of permissions. While the specific names of the accounts might differ between OSs, the types of accounts generally fall into these three categories, from most to least powerful:

- Administrators
- Users
- Guests

The administrator is sometimes shortened to admin and is called root on UNIX and Linux systems. This account can essentially do anything on the computer, making it very powerful. Because of this, you want to be very careful deciding who has administrator rights.

Next on the list in Windows, Mac OS X, and Linux are standard user accounts. They can't make changes that will affect other users, whereas an administrator account can make all types of changes. This prevents people from uninstalling applications that they personally don't need but others do.

> To prevent unauthorized changes to a computer, it's a good practice to have everyone use a standard account for daily operations and have an administrator account available that is used only when performing activities that require it, such as installing or removing software or updating a device driver.

Guest accounts are for very basic access, such as Internet access only or access to just one application at a public kiosk. The guest account is created by default when Windows is installed, and this represents a weakness that can be exploited by an attacker. While the account cannot do much, it can provide initial access to a system and the attacker can use that to find another account or acquire sensitive information about the system.

> Some operating systems have additional classifications of user accounts, such as Power Users, which have some basic administrative rights but not total control.

To secure the system, disable all accounts that are not needed, especially the Guest account. Next, rename the accounts if you can (Microsoft won't allow you to rename some). For example, change Administrator to something more difficult to guess. If an attacker knows the username, all they have to do is crack the password. If they don't know either, their job just became that much more difficult.

Managing Passwords

Imagine this scenario: you just installed four computers on a wireless network, enabled the best Wi-Fi security (WPA2), installed antimalware and a software firewall on all computers, and then you find out that one of the users has the word password for their login password. How secure is that?

Password management is a critical security feature that tends to get overlooked. It involves proper user training and is aided by restrictions a network administrator can set on users if their computers are part of a domain.

One of the first things that users should know is to change their default passwords and make the passwords they choose complex. Also teach your users to not share their password with anyone—passwords are to remain confidential in order to protect the network.

Creating Effective Passwords

A *strong password* is one that is difficult for someone to guess. Strong passwords have these characteristics:

Long   The longer, the better. At least eight characters are optimal.

Varied   The password contains at least one capital letter and at least one number and/or symbol.

Unusual   The password doesn't appear in a dictionary and isn't a proper noun.

Passwords that are easy to guess are considered *weak passwords*. Some of the worst passwords of all are things like `qwerty`, `12345`, the user ID, and the word `password`. Only slightly better are the names of people, pets, and places. Even though a password should be difficult for others to guess, it's okay to make it easy for you to remember. To do this, try combining numbers and letters that make sense to you but won't make sense to other people. For example, suppose you have a cousin Sam who grew up in Wichita, and you used to call him a lot, so you remember that his phone number was 555-1192. An effective password might be `Sam-Wich#1192`. Notice that this password is long (13 characters), varied (uppercase, lowercase, numeric, and symbol characters), and unusual, yet it's fairly easy for you to remember just by thinking about your cousin.

Here are some other techniques for creating passwords that are easy to remember but difficult to guess:

Substitute Zero for the Letter O in Words   For example, `St0rageR00m`.

Substitute Numbers for Letters   To make it easier to remember, use the numeral that represents the letter of the alphabet (for example, b=2) or use the numeral that represents the position in the word (for example, take the word *teacher* and substitute numerals for the second and fourth digits, like this: `t2a4her`.

Combine Two or More Unrelated but Memorable Words   For example, `GroceryCandleFlowerpot`.

Substitute a Symbol for a Letter That It Resembles   For example, $ looks like an *S*, as in `$ubstitution$alary`; and ! looks like a capital *I*, as in `!temized`.

As tempting as it may be to reuse the same password for multiple systems or sites, you're safer using a different password for every site you access. That way, if one site is hacked, it won't affect your security on another site.

If you can't remember all the passwords in your head, one possible solution is to store them in a password-protected file on your hard drive. Yes, someone could steal that file from your hard disk and possibly even unencrypt it, but the chances of that happening are slim compared to the chances of a server being hacked where your password for a certain site is stored.

Another possible solution is to reuse the same password for sites that don't store any financial information. For example, you might use the same password for logging into message boards and chat rooms at various sites, because if your password is discovered at those sites the consequences are generally mild. Someone might log in and impersonate you, causing you some temporary embarrassment, but you haven't lost any money. On the other hand, you should use a different password for each of your important banking or other financial accounts, because a thief could cause you significant financial problems on these sites.

Password Changes

Some companies' IT policies require that you change your password at regular intervals, such as every 90 days. The rationale is that the longer you keep a password, the more likely that someone has surreptitiously seen you type it, or you've written it down somewhere, or some other security breach has occurred.

Even if a system doesn't require you to change your password on a certain timetable, you may want to take the initiative to change it yourself, especially on sites where you manage your financial affairs.

To help you remember your password in a frequently changing environment, you may want to develop a structured system of changes. For example, suppose your password is `video$Furrier`. When you change it, you might add the two-digit number of the month in which you changed it. For example, if you change it in February, you can make it `video$02Furrier`. Then, when you change it again in May, you can change it to `video$05Furrier`.

In addition to not reusing your password on different sites, you also shouldn't reuse passwords after being required to change it. Recycling old passwords can make it easier for hackers to guess your password and gain unauthorized access.

User Authentication

User *authentication* happens when the system you are logging into validates that you have proper credentials. Oftentimes, this is as simple as entering a username and password, but it could be more complex.

Multifactor Authentication

To increase security, your computer or network might require *multifactor authentication*, which as the name implies requires multiple pieces of information for you to log in. Generally speaking, in addition to a username, multifactor authentication requires you to provide two or more pieces of information out of these three categories: something you know, something you have, or something you are.

Something you know is generally a password. Something you have can be one of a few different things, such as a smart card or a security token.

A smart card is a plastic card, similar in dimensions to a credit card, that contains a microchip that a card reader can scan, such as on a security system. Smart cards often double as employee badges, enabling employees to access employee-only areas of a building or to use elevators that go to restricted areas, or as credit cards.

Smart cards can also be used to allow or prevent computer access. For example, a PC may have a card reader on it through which the employee has to swipe the card, or that reads the card's chip automatically when the card comes into its vicinity. Or, they're combined with PIN numbers or used as an add-on to a standard login system, to give an additional layer of security verification. For someone to gain unauthorized access, they have to not only know a user's ID and password (or PIN) but also steal their smart card. That makes it much more difficult to be a thief!

A security token, like the one shown in Figure 9.11, displays an access code that changes about every 30 seconds. When received, it's synchronized with your user account, and the algorithm that controls the code change is known by the token as well as your authentication system. When you log in, you need your username and password, along with the code on the token.

FIGURE 9.11 RSA SecurID

Finally, the system could require something totally unique to you to enable authentication. These characteristics are usually assessed via *biometric devices*, which authenticate users by scanning for one or more physical traits. Some common types include fingerprint recognition, facial recognition, and retina scanning.

Law enforcement agencies have been using fingerprint recognition for over 100 years, and no two prints have yet been found to be identical, even in genetically identical twins. That's because fingerprints develop in the womb, and they aren't preprogrammed at conception. More recently, computerized fingerprint scanners have taken the place of manual ink prints, and the technology for reading fingerprints has become so affordable that it's built into many computer systems, including consumer-level notebook PCs and smart phones. Some fingerprint scanners use a rapid laser to detect the ridges in a person's fingers; others have an electrostatically sensitive pad that detects the current formed by the small quantities of water in a fingerprint.

Facial recognition software works in conjunction with a camera (like the webcams built into some notebook computers) to scan the face of the person who is logging in. The facial scan is matched with existing previous scans of that same person stored on the computer. Some consumer-level notebook PCs now come with an option of logging into the OS via facial recognition as an alternative to typing a login password.

Retina scanning is very similar to facial recognition, but it looks specifically at your eye and the pattern of blood vessels on your retina. Apparently, your retinal blood vessel pattern is as unique as your fingerprint is.

Single Sign-On

One of the big problems that larger systems must deal with is the need for users to access multiple systems or applications. This may require a user to remember multiple accounts and passwords. The purpose of a *single sign-on (SSO)* is to give users access to all the applications and systems they need when they log on. This is becoming a reality in many network environments.

Single sign-on is both a blessing and a curse. It's a blessing in that once the user is authenticated, they can access all the resources on the network with less inconvenience. It's a curse in that it removes potential security doors that otherwise exist between the user and various resources.

> While single sign-on is not the opposite of multifactor authentication, they are often mistakenly thought of that way. One-, two-, and three-factor authentication merely refers to the number of items a user must supply to authenticate. After factor authentication is done, then single sign-on can still apply throughout remainder of the user's session.

Network Security

As you learned in Chapter 5, "Networking Technologies and Wireless Routers," wireless (Wi-Fi) networks can be either open (no encryption) or secured (using encryption). Encryption is set at the router, so whether or not a network has encryption on it is determined by the router settings. The router, in turn, connects its users to the Internet.

If a network is secured, you must type its encryption key (password) when connecting to it. If it's not, anyone may connect to it. However, connecting to a network may not be sufficient to gain access to all its services (such as Internet access). Additional login information may be required. When you open a web browser window, a redirect operation displays a login page in which you may need to accept a user agreement, enter a username and password (or create one), and/or provide credit-card information to buy Internet access.

> If it's your network, you should always secure it by using WPA2 to protect your resources. Also be sure to guard your encryption key carefully so that it does not fall into the wrong hands.

There are security risks associated with connecting to any network but especially a free public network. Although most of your fellow users who share that network just want to use the Internet, as you do, hackers occasionally lurk about who may try to browse or even steal files from your computer via your shared network connection.

To minimize the risk associated with connecting to a specific network, you can change your file-sharing settings to more restrictive ones while you're connected to that network.

In Windows, when you connect to a new network, you're prompted to select whether it's a Home, Work, or Public network. If you choose Public, file- and printer-sharing features are disabled on that network connection. This makes it more difficult for someone to snoop or harm your computer.

Internet Security Best Practices

When surfing the Web was relatively new, most of the people who did it (or emailed regularly) were relatively computer-savvy early adopters. Over time, as the Web and email became more mainstream, less-savvy people joined in the fun, which opened up many more opportunities for hackers to prey on them. A shadow industry of charlatans and other questionable business providers grew to take advantage.

At this point, it's probably safe to say that this whole "Internet" thing isn't just a passing fad. The Internet is cemented as an integral part of most of our daily routines, and now it seems our goal is to get it on every electronic device imaginable. It's also safe to say that Internet users as a whole are savvier than ever before, either because they were a victim of a cybercrime themselves or they know someone who was. Even though the collective user awareness of potential issues has increased, there are still plenty of targets out there. And as you learned in Chapter 8, it's pretty easy for attackers to automate their bad intent.

This section covers many of the warning signs you should recognize as potential Internet or email issues, so you can both browse safely yourself and educate family, friends, and co-workers on dangerous habits they might have. It's broken into three parts: preparation and maintenance, Internet browsing, and safe emailing. Armed with this knowledge, you should be able to face potentially dangerous Internet scenarios and navigate safely.

Web Browsing Preparation and Maintenance

There's a certain amount of preparation you can take before browsing the Internet that will make your experience safer. Even if you have never done it before, it's a good idea to go and review these items on your system to see what your settings are. In addition, you should periodically perform maintenance to ensure that these settings are still correct and everything is properly updated. All of the settings you are going to learn about are managed in your Internet browser. The two most common PC-based browsers are Internet Explorer (IE) and Google Chrome.

Managing Internet Browser Versions

The first thing for you to do is to make sure that the Internet browser you are using is the most current version available. Older versions, called *legacy browsers*, may have security holes or fewer features that can protect you as you browse the Web. IE will update automatically if you tell it to, and Chrome automatically updates—this is a good thing. Before looking at where that setting is, though, familiarize yourself with each browser's options or settings menu. In both IE and Chrome, you click an icon in the upper-right corner. IE's looks like a gear (as shown in Figure 9.12), whereas Chrome's looks like a list (Figure 9.13).

FIGURE 9.12 Internet Explorer 11 options

FIGURE 9.13 Chrome version 41 options

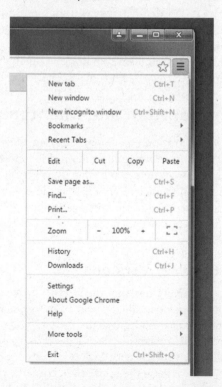

Both browsers have relatively similar menus, which makes it convenient to find the option you're looking for. And if worse comes to worst, you can always click around in the browser until you find the option you need. To see what version your browser is, click the settings icon and choose About Internet Explorer or About Google Chrome. You will see IE's window in Figure 9.14 and Chrome's in Figure 9.15.

FIGURE 9.14   About Internet Explorer

FIGURE 9.15   About Chrome

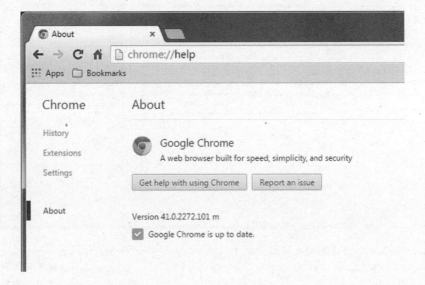

In addition to making sure your browser is up to date, you should also be sure to update needed plugins. A *plugin* is just a piece of software that gives your browser additional functionality—think of it as a bit like a driver, except it's for software. For example, if you need to run a video that requires Flash, you need a Flash plugin. If you try to run media that requires a plugin that your browser doesn't have, your browser will give you a message and the opportunity to download the needed software. If there is a newer version available, you will get a pop-up message telling you that when you start the plugin. Again, make sure plugins are up to date as well.

Managing Plugins, Toolbars, and Extensions

Plugins, toolbars, and extensions are all software components added to your browser to give it additional functionality. When managed right, these features are convenient and enhance your Internet browsing experience. On the flip side, installing too many toolbars and extensions can slow your browser down. Even worse, some toolbars and extensions can make your system do things that you don't want it to do, such as always redirecting you to a specific site regardless of where you really want to go.

In Internet Explorer, you manage your plugins, toolbars, and extensions by clicking Settings and then Manage Add-ons; the Manage Add-ons window is shown in Figure 9.16. You can also get to the same window by clicking Settings ➢ Internet Options ➢ Programs ➢ Manage Add-ons.

FIGURE 9.16 Manage Add-ons in IE 11

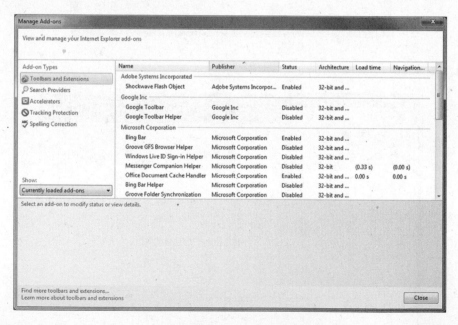

Within the Manage Add-ons window, IE doesn't really differentiate between plugins, toolbars, and extensions. For example, Shockwave Flash is a plugin, Google Toolbar is clearly a toolbar, and Windows Live ID Sign-in Helper is an extension. This non-differentiation is fine because they all pretty much just add functionality. What you see is a list of what's installed, the publisher, whether it's enabled, and some other information. To disable one of these enabled items, highlight it in the list (as shown in Figure 9.17), and click Disable. If the feature is currently disabled, the button will say Enable instead.

FIGURE 9.17 Disabling an add-on in IE 11

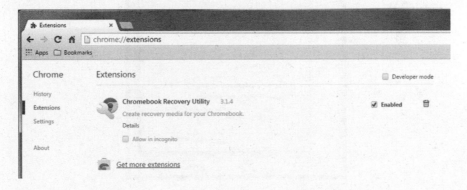

To get to extensions in Chrome, open Settings and click Extensions on the left side, as shown in Figure 9.18. To disable the extension (or plugin or toolbar), uncheck the Enabled box.

FIGURE 9.18 Extensions in Chrome

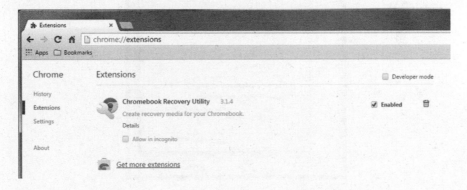

All plugins or extensions that affect Internet browsing should appear in the windows shown in Figure 9.17 or 9.18, so you can disable them if you want to. Some suspicious add-ons won't show up there, which makes them a little more inconvenient to remove. These items should show up in your installed programs in Control Panel. To disable (or better yet uninstall) these, to go Uninstall A Program in Control Panel.

Managing Autofill

Autofill is a feature that automatically populates fields in a form on a web page for you. For example, say you visit a website that wants your name and address. Instead of needing to type it all in, once you start typing your first name in the First Name field, the rest of the fields will automatically fill in for you. Autofill can also save and enter in credit card payment information too. While this can be incredibly convenient, it can also pose a security risk.

If you are the only one using a home computer, or maybe it's just you and trusted members of your family, enabling Autofill isn't a terrible thing to do. One could argue that you shouldn't enable it on laptops because they are easier to steal. If it's a public workstation though, definitely disable Autofill. If you are using a public workstation and it asks you anything about saving your information for Autofill, politely decline.

Internet Explorer calls this option AutoComplete. To get to it in IE, choose Settings ➤ Internet Options ➤ Content and click the Settings button in the AutoComplete section. The settings are shown in Figure 9.19. Letting the address bar of IE autocomplete when you are typing in website names is the least threatening of these options. For safety, disable AutoComplete in forms and for usernames and passwords.

FIGURE 9.19 AutoComplete settings

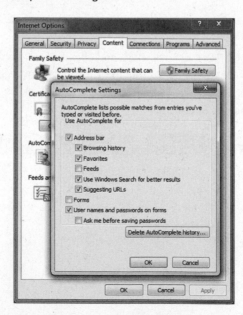

The Autofill settings in Chrome are under Settings ➤ Show Advanced Settings, as shown in Figure 9.20. By clicking Manage Autofill Settings, you can specify information you want in your Autofill (if you're using it) such as your address and credit card information.

FIGURE 9.20 Autofill in Chrome

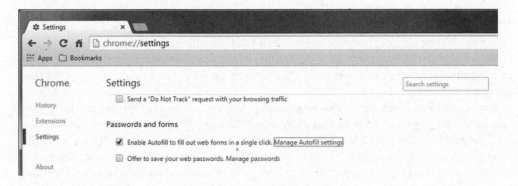

 Real World Scenario

The Risks of Using Public Workstations

Every so often, you might find yourself in a situation where you want or need to use a public workstation. Perhaps you are stuck at the auto repair shop and they have convenient computers for their guests to use. Maybe you are staying at a hotel and they have computers available in their business center. No matter the reason, you should be aware of the risks of using public workstations.

Public systems can be fine to use, but they are also highly susceptible to attacks or acts of fraud because so many people use them. Some of the more severe risks include identity theft, because a hacker or an unscrupulous owner could have installed a keylogger on the computer. Also, public computers often use unsecured Wi-Fi networks, which present a major issue because they transmit all communications without encryption. You don't want your credit card information announced to a crowd with a bullhorn. So what can you do to protect yourself? Here are a few suggestions:

- If it's on an unsecured wireless network, don't use it except for basic web news surfing or entertainment. Don't enter in any personally identifiable information (PII) or usernames or passwords.

- Don't enter in any confidential information, such as bank or credit card information.

- Make sure Autofill isn't being used and passwords are not being remembered.

- Don't save any files to the local computer.

- Delete your browsing history, cache, and cookies after you have finished.

- Always pay attention to your surroundings. Obviously, some locations are safer than others. Public places are great for shoulder surfing—don't be on the wrong side of that.

Configuring Security Settings

Using the wrong security settings in your web browser can result in a variety of security risks, such as running content on your computer that you don't want executed. Fortunately, in most browsers, you can easily set the most common security settings by accepting the defaults.

Internet Explorer lets you set security under Settings ➢ Internet Options on the Security tab, as shown in Figure 9.21. IE uses the concept of security zones, where websites can be classified into different groups that have different security settings. In Figure 9.21, the Internet zone is chosen, which by default has a Medium-High security setting. Trusted sites are Medium, and Local intranet sites Medium-Low. You can drag a slider to choose your security settings. Medium-High is the best balance between functionality and security in most cases.

FIGURE 9.21 Internet security options

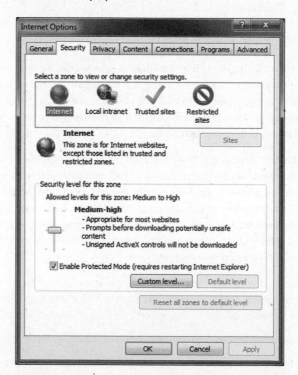

Another prudent security measure is to make sure Protected Mode is enabled for the Internet and Restricted security zones. (It's that way by default.) Protected Mode prevents many different security exploits by displaying content in a low-privileges mode.

> If you attempt to download a file from a website that is not in your Trusted zone, you will get a pop-up on your screen warning you that you are about to download a file from an untrusted source. You can click OK to continue or cancel. If you initiated the download, you generally click OK. But some malicious websites will try to download materials without your knowledge, and this warning can help protect you from that content.

You may also want to enable ActiveX Filtering. Some websites use ActiveX controls to display content, but ActiveX can also be a security threat. In IE, open the Tools menu (if it's not displayed, press your Alt key and the menus will appear) and choose ActiveX Filtering. When it's checked, ActiveX controls are suppressed.

Chrome also allows you to configure security, but it does not use the zones concept like IE does—all websites are treated the same. You can configure security options under Settings ➤ Show Advanced Settings ➤ Privacy and clicking the Content Settings button. Some of the content settings are shown in Figure 9.22.

FIGURE 9.22   Chrome content settings

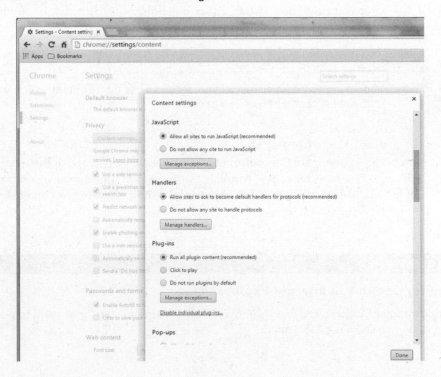

Managing Cookies

A *cookie* is a plain-text file that a web page (or an ad on a web page) stores on your hard disk for tracking purposes. A cookie can tell an advertiser that you've previously viewed a certain ad, for example, or can keep track of the items in your shopping cart on an e-commerce site.

Cookies are harmless 99.99 percent of the time, and they can actually perform useful functions that you want, such as remembering your preferences when you return to an oft-visited website. However, there are two risks involved with cookies. One is a privacy threat: a cookie can deliver personally identifiable information to a website. The other is a security threat: a virus or Trojan horse may copy a stored password from a cookie and deliver it to someone who can then steal your login information for a site to commit identity theft or some other type of fraud.

There are four different types of cookies. A *first-party cookie* is placed on your computer by a website you visit. For example, when you go to www.amazon.com, a cookie provides your name so that the site can welcome you by name. A *third-party cookie* is placed on your computer by an ad on a website, where the ad's parent company isn't related to the owner of the website. For example, as you browse on Facebook, a third-party cookie may record the ads you've clicked, indicating your potential interest in certain products.

A *session cookie* lasts only as long as your web browser is open. When you finish your web-browsing session, session cookies are deleted. A *persistent cookie* stays on your hard disk after you close the browser, either indefinitely or for a certain number of days.

Some legitimate websites will not let you view their content unless your browser is configured to accept cookies.

All browsers can be configured to control how your system stores each of the types of cookies. You can create rules for cookie handling, set certain sites from which you'll allow or deny cookies, and delete existing cookies. Exercise 9.5 shows how to view and delete cookies in Internet Explorer 11.

EXERCISE 9.5

Managing Cookies in Internet Explorer 11

1.   Open Internet Explorer, and choose Tools ➢ Internet Options. (You may need to press the Alt key to show the Tools menu.)

2. On the Privacy tab, as shown in Figure 9.23, drag the slider to Medium if it isn't already set there. Examine the information that appears describing the Medium setting.

FIGURE 9.23   Privacy tab in IE 11

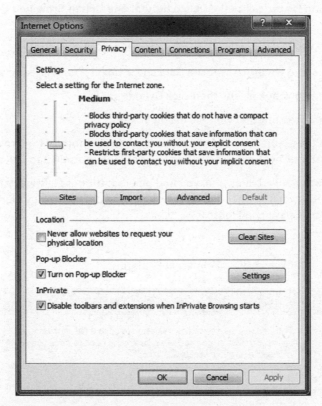

3. Click the Sites button. The Per Site Privacy Actions dialog box opens.

4. In the Address Of Website box, type **www.emcp.com**, and then click Allow.

5. Click OK.

6. Click the Advanced button. The Advanced Privacy Settings dialog box opens.

7. Select the Override Automatic Cookie Handling check box.

8. Under Third-Party Cookies, click Prompt.

9. Select the Always Allow Session Cookies check box.

10. Click OK.

11. Select the Never Allow Websites To Request Your Physical Location check box.

12. Click Clear Sites.

13. Click the General tab.

14. Under Browsing History, click the Delete button. The Delete Browsing History dialog box opens.

15. Select the Cookies And Website Data check box if it isn't already selected.

16. Select the Preserve Favorites Website Data check box if it isn't already selected.

17. Clear all other check boxes, and then click Delete.

18. Click OK to close the Internet Options dialog box.

19. Click the X on the status message that appears at the bottom of the browser window, telling you that Internet Explorer has finished deleting the selected history.

20. Visit several popular websites until you find one that triggers a Privacy Alert dialog box that prompts you whether to save a certain cookie. The privacy alert will be similar to the one shown in Figure 9.24.

FIGURE 9.24 Cookie warning in Internet Explorer

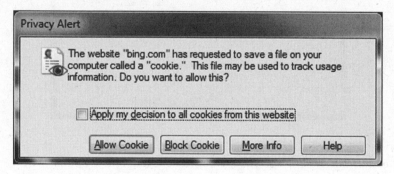

21. Click Block Cookie.

22. Change the setting back to Allow for third-party cookies as you did in steps 6–10.

In Exercise 9.5 you deleted your browser cache and history as well. The cache is a temporary copy of settings you had configured on websites, similar to preferences on the site. The history shows the historical record of sites you have visited in that browser.

If you use Chrome and want to delete your cookies, cache, and history, open Settings ➤ Show Advanced Settings, and then under Privacy click the Clear Browsing Data box. You will get a screen similar to the one in Figure 9.25.

FIGURE 9.25   Clearing browsing data in Chrome

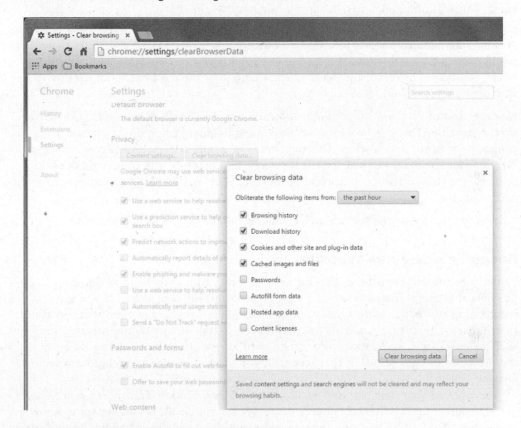

Safe Internet Browsing

Web browsers work by downloading and displaying web pages, which are essentially programming scripts. The script is rendered as a formatted web page by your web browser on your local PC.

The trouble is, at the moment when that page is downloaded, there are numerous opportunities for a hacker to take advantage of the connection in various ways. For example, your requests for pages can be intercepted on their way to the server. This can compromise your privacy, because someone can see what pages you're requesting. More important, however, it can compromise any login information you may be sending to a financial or business site. Scripts can also contain malicious code that infects your system, making it perform unwanted activities like sending your private information to a third party or displaying countless ads. Web pages can also have embedded Flash or Java applications that can do harm in some cases.

Before getting into specific things you should recognize, here are two basic safe web-browsing tips:

Do Not Visit Questionable Sites   This one might seem self-evident, right? Part of the problem might be identifying a questionable site, much like you can't always identify a "bad person" simply based on their looks. Some sites are pretty obvious, though. Sites that claim to offer free software downloads for programs you know aren't normally free, sites that offer hate-themed material, and adult websites tend to be the most notorious for providing your computer with unwanted content.

Limit the Use of Personally Identifiable Information   *Personally identifiable information (PII)* is anything that can be used to identify an individual person on its own or in context with other information. This includes your name, address, other contact information, the names of your family members, and other details you would consider private. You should also be judicious in providing your email address to websites to avoid getting spam.

Now, on to specific tips for safe web browsing and things you should recognize.

Recognizing Secure Websites

Sometimes you might surf the Web for fun, but other times you need to do business that might include checking your email or personal banking. If you are rummaging through celebrity news gossip sites, you're probably not too worried about Internet security at that moment. But if you need to type in any secure information, such as a username and password or credit card information, security should be at the forefront of your mind. In that scenario, you need to be able to recognize a secure website.

A *secure website* is one that uses Secure Sockets Layer (SSL) or Transport Layer Security (TLS) to encrypt transmissions between the server and the client. It's important to know that although SSL or TLS secures the transmission, that's where its job ends. Once the data such as your credit card information is stored on the server, it needs to be secured using other means, which could be something like local encryption.

WARNING

Information transmitted to an unsecure website not using SSL or TLS is transmitted in *plain text*, meaning that anyone snooping on the wire could easily read that information. Simply put, *do not ever* enter confidential information such as your username, password, or financial data unless the site is secured.

It's pretty easy to identify a secure website. First, the URL will begin with `https://` rather than `http://`. Second, your browser will provide a few indicators, such as a lock icon in the address bar, and many browsers will turn the address bar or some text in the address bar green. Figure 9.26 shows both of these indicators.

FIGURE 9.26   A secure website will have a lock and in most cases green in the address bar.

In order for a website to use HTTPS, the owners of the site must have been granted a security certificate from a *certificate authority (CA)*. Think of issuing authorities as the notary publics of the Internet. A security certificate contains information including a serial number, the person or organization that issued the certificate, and a range of dates it's valid to and from. If a site has a certificate, you can be reasonably assured that it's legitimate and not a fake out to steal your information. There have been a few reported cases of certificate theft, but they are rare.

    Remember that HTTPS uses port 443, and HTTP uses port 80.

By clicking the lock icon in the address bar, you will get a screen similar to the one shown in Figure 9.27, which lists general information about the company that owns the certificate and the issuing authority. In the case of Apple iTunes, the CA is Symantec. By clicking the Certificate Information link, you can see additional details such as the date through which the certificate is valid and the serial number.

FIGURE 9.27   Apple iTunes security certificate information

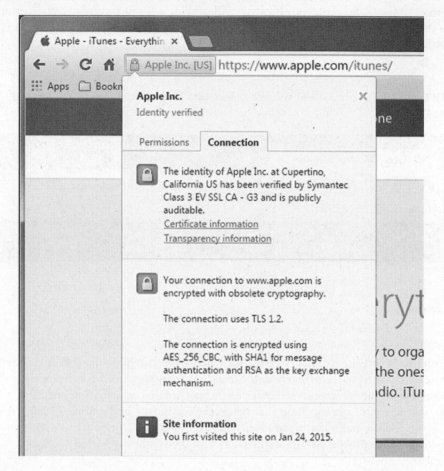

With almost any web browser, it's easy to review and monitor what certificates have been installed, who the issuing authorities are, and what details are held within each certificate. Exercise 9.6 shows where to find security certificate information in Internet Explorer 11.

EXERCISE 9.6

Viewing Security Certificates in Internet Explorer

1. Open Internet Explorer, and choose Tools ➢ Internet Options. (You may need to press the Alt key to show the Tools menu.)

2. On the Content tab, click the Certificates button. A list of security certificates appears. There are multiple tabs in the dialog box for different certificate publishers and authorities.

3. Click the Trusted Root Certification Authorities tab, as shown in Figure 9.28, and browse the list. These are all companies that issue and verify certificates.

FIGURE 9.28 Root certification authorities

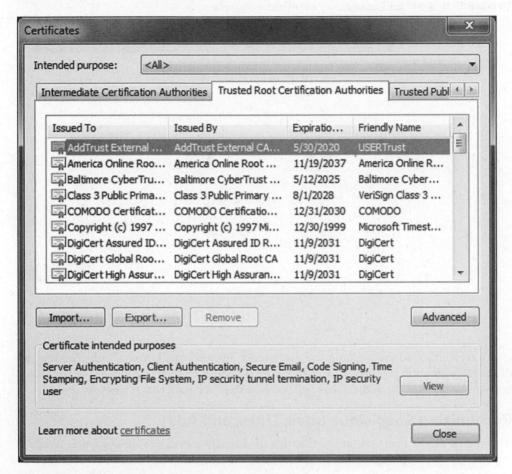

4. Double-click one of the certificates to see its information. Then click OK to close its box.

5. Click Close to close the Certificates dialog box, and then click OK to close the Internet Options dialog box.

In Chrome, you can open the same security certificates window by going to Settings ➤ Show Advanced Settings, and clicking Manage Certificates in the HTTPS/SSL section.

If there is a problem with a certificate or the web server's use of a certificate (for example, it has expired or has been stolen), you will get a warning when you visit that site.

While the format of the warning may differ, it should be very clear that the website is not secure. Figure 9.29 shows an example.

FIGURE 9.29 Invalid security certificate example

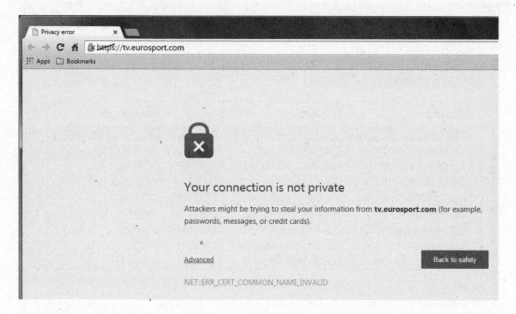

It's recommended that you not use that site for any purpose. If you are absolutely sure of the site's identity, you may be able to ignore the warning and continue to the site. Most browsers will color the address bar red as a persistent warning that it's not secure.

Recognizing Suspicious Sites, Links, and Ads

It would be nice if sites that intended to download malware on to your computer would just let you know. Perhaps they could have a big flashing warning informing you that they intend to steal your identity and cause you hundreds of hours of misery. Obviously, that's not the case. Creators of sites who have bad intentions do everything they can to make sure their site resembles a legitimate site as much as possible. This can include copying web page layouts and company logos to convince people to visit the site and click the links.

Creating a site that masquerades as a legitimate secure site but actually steals your information is called *phishing* (or *spoofing*). Phishing employs many tactics, which are continually evolving. One common scheme to watch out for is getting an email that claims to be from your bank, ISP, or other institution, asking you to follow a link to its site to update your details. The email looks authentic, and when you follow the link, the site looks very much like the site of the bank or ISP—except the page probably isn't secure, and some links on the page may not be operational.

When people talk about phishing, it's generally in context of suspicious email, because that's how the term originated. Hackers sent out messages hoping to get someone to take the bait. The term has evolved a bit to encompass any electronic activity designed to defraud someone, which can and often does include the use of fake websites.

So what does a suspicious site, link, or ad look like? Unfortunately that's a bit like asking what a criminal looks like. There's no one specific answer. Here are some things you can look out for though:

If Visiting a Website, Look for Signs of Security   These were covered in the last section, but look for `https://`, the lock symbol, and green in the address bar.

Websites That Have Incorrect Spelling   If someone is spoofing a website, they may try to get spelling very close to the real site, hoping that people won't look closely and click. A made-up example is something like `www.micro.soft.com` or `www.micros0ft.com`. Neither of those are the Microsoft company, but the URLs could be chosen to attempt to impersonate Microsoft.

Incorrect Spelling or Bad Grammar   Big companies do not send out mass emails to their clients unless they have been professionally edited and spell checked.

Threats   If you're being threatened that your account will close or your card won't work or whatever unless you enter in security information, it's probably not legitimate.

Deals That Are Too Good to Be True   If it sounds too good to be true, it probably is. That's a good adage to follow in life, and it's especially true in cyberspace. The flashier or more attention-grabbing the banner ad, the more suspicious you should be of its legitimacy.

If you find yourself wondering if a link or banner ad is legitimate, just don't click it!

Your web browser can likely help defend you against some phishing attacks, because most browsers have some phishing protection built-in. That's part of the role of the different-colored background of the address bar in Internet Explorer. For example, if it's green, that indicates the phishing filter has determined the site is legitimate. A yellow background indicates caution because there is a problem with the verification, and a red background indicates that this site probably isn't what it seems to be and should be avoided.

In Internet Explorer, the phishing filter is called the *SmartScreen filter*, and it can be enabled or disabled. Normally you should leave it enabled, because it provides information and doesn't prevent you from doing anything. Its assessment is fairly accurate, as well. The only drawback (and it's very minor) is that if you leave automatic checking turned on, the browser checks every page you visit, resulting in slightly slower browser performance. If you seldom visit secure sites and you want to check only the specific sites about which you have a question, you can turn off this feature. Exercise 9.7 shows you how to configure the SmartScreen filter in Internet Explorer.

EXERCISE 9.7

Configuring SmartScreen in Internet Explorer 11

1. Choose Tools ➤ SmartScreen Filter ➤ Turn Off SmartScreen Filter. (To display the Tools menu, you might have to press the Alt key on your keyboard first.) A dialog box will open similar to the one in Figure 9.30, with Turn Off SmartScreen Filter already selected.

FIGURE 9.30   Turning off SmartScreen Filter

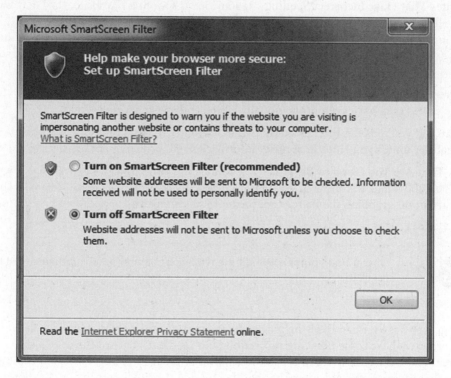

2. Click OK.

3. Type in the address www.paypal.com and press Enter.

4. Choose Tools ➤ SmartScreen Filter ➤ Check This Website. The first time you do this, you will see a message stating that the address will be sent to Microsoft. Click OK.

5. A box appears telling you that SmartScreen Filter checked this website and didn't report any threats, like the one in Figure 9.31.

FIGURE 9.31   No threats detected in this website

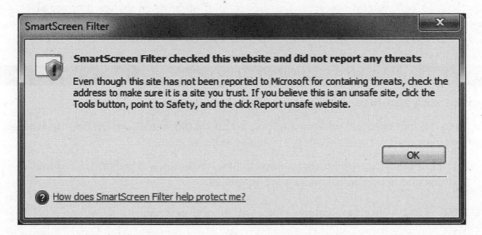

6.   Click OK.

7.   Choose Tools ➢ SmartScreen Filter ➢ Turn On SmartScreen Filter. A dialog box opens
     with Turn On SmartScreen Filter already selected. Click OK.

8.   Notice that in Tools ➢ SmartScreen Filter, you also have the option to report sites for
     suspicious behavior.

Google Chrome also has built-in phishing protection. It's enabled by going to Settings ➢
Show Advanced Settings ➢ Privacy and checking the Enable Phishing And Malware
Protection box.

Recognizing Adware Symptoms

Adware is an obnoxious form of malware, but it's not generally destructive. Instead, what
adware attempts to get you to do is see advertisements only from companies it wants you
to see or direct your Internet activity to where it wants you to go. Of course, the companies
that get traffic directed to them have paid the adware producers to generate traffic. You've
already learned about malware symptoms, but this section looks at three symptoms related
specifically to adware.

Controlling Pop-Ups

A *pop-up* is an extra, usually small browser window that appears automatically when you
display a certain web page or click a certain button on a page. Pop-ups can serve useful functions,
such as displaying the amount of time you've been logged in at a public Wi-Fi location that
charges you by the minute or displaying details for you to download a file you want. However,
pop-ups are more often used to display advertisements or fake dialog boxes that trick you into
doing something you really don't want to do, like branching to another company's website.

Your web browser most likely has a pop-up blocker built into it. You can enable it
or disable it, and in some cases you can configure it to be more or less aggressive about

blocking pop-ups. Not all browsers' pop-up blockers are very effective, though; sometimes they can miss certain pop-up types. Third-party pop-up blocker applications are also available and are often more effective than the web browser blockers. Exercise 9.8 shows you how to configure Internet Explorer's pop-up blocker.

EXERCISE 9.8

Configuring the Internet Explorer Pop-Up Blocker

1. Open Internet Explorer, and choose Tools ➢ Pop-Up Blocker ➢ Turn Off Pop-Up Blocker. (You may need to press the Alt key to show the Tools menu.)

2. Choose Tools ➢ Pop-Up Blocker ➢ Pop-Up Blocker Settings. The Pop-Up Blocker Settings dialog box opens, shown in Figure 9.32.

   FIGURE 9.32 Internet Explorer 11 Pop-Up Blocker settings

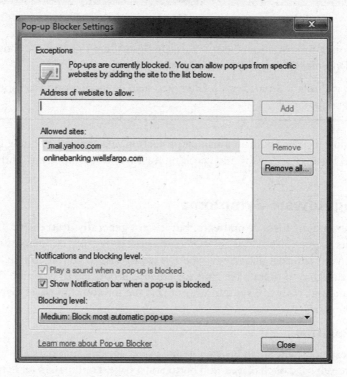

3. Open the Blocking Level drop-down list, and click High: Block All Pop-Ups.

4. In the Address Of Website To Allow box, type ***.emcp.com** and click Add. The asterisk is a wildcard that allows any text in that position. For example, this entry covers `www.emcp.com`, `support.emcp.com`, and so on.

5. Click Close.

Chrome's pop-up blocker is easy to configure as well. It's found in Settings ➤ Show Advanced Settings ➤ Privacy ➤ Content Settings. Figure 9.33 shows you what the option looks like. You can click the Manage Exceptions button to add exceptions like you did for Internet Explorer in Exercise 9.8.

FIGURE 9.33 Chrome's pop-up blocker

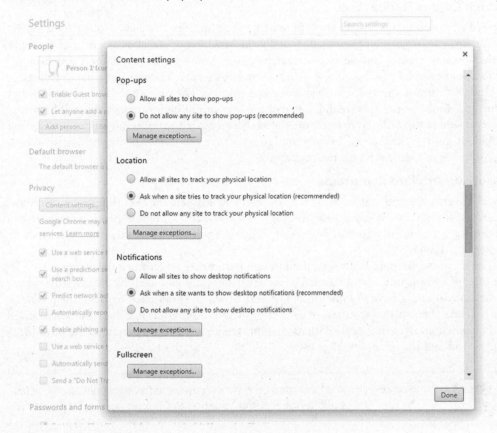

Browser Redirection

A second tactic that adware might use is redirecting your browser. This could be as simple as changing your home page to the home page of its client. You can change the home page back to what you want it to be, but the next time you open your browser, the adware will take over again and change it back to the unwanted page.

A more dangerous form of browser redirection is called *pharming*. Pharming is a form of redirection in which traffic intended for one host is sent to another. For example, you might experience a situation where you attempt to go to a site only to be redirected to another. For example, suppose Illegitimate Company ABC creates a site to look exactly like the one for Giant Bank XYZ. The pharming tricks users trying to reach Giant Bank XYZ into going to Illegitimate Company ABC's site, which looks enough like what they are used to seeing that they give username and password data.

As soon as Giant Bank XYZ realizes that the traffic is being redirected, it will immediately move to stop it. But although Illegitimate Company ABC will be shut down, it was able to collect data for the length of time the redirection occurred, which could vary from minutes to days.

Search Engine Redirection

A third common tactic for adware is to redirect your Internet searches. No matter what you search for, you are always presented virtually the same list of websites as hits. For example, perhaps you are using Google as your search engine. You want to search for a new bowtie (who doesn't need a new bowtie), so you type in your terms. You will get a list of results, in Google's format and fonts, with sites for you to click. The only problem is Google didn't return those sites—the adware did. Some of the sites might be businesses that sell bowties, whereas others might be completely unrelated. If you search for organic produce next, you will likely get the exact same (or very similar) sites that you got with your bowtie search. Again, some might be relevant but probably not.

Resolving Adware Symptoms

If you are experiencing any of the three symptoms of adware, the best thing to do is remove the adware. One option might be to disable it if it's loaded as a plugin or an extension. You learned where to do that in the "Managing Plugins, Toolbars, and Extensions" section earlier in this chapter.

The other—and more likely—method to remove adware is to uninstall it from your list of applications in Control Panel. The adware might not call itself by an easy-to-find name, so you might have to look for it. The best way is to think back to when the problem started, and then sort your software by date of installation. Odds are that you downloaded and installed an item that came with an unexpected and unwelcome present. Remove the application and the issue should go away.

> For additional information on how to remove software applications, refer to the "Uninstalling Applications" section in Chapter 4.

Browsing Undercover

If you want to protect your privacy while surfing the Internet (or perhaps feel like a super-secret spy), you can use undercover features of your browser. Internet Explorer calls it InPrivate browsing, and Chrome calls it Incognito.

Internet Explorer versions 8 and higher include InPrivate browsing mode. When you start an InPrivate session, none of the history is stored, regardless of your browser's normal history settings. No passwords and login information are stored, and no cookies or temporary Internet files are kept. This mode is very useful when you're visiting a site where safety may be questionable, because in this mode Internet Explorer won't permit the website to affect your computer in any way.

To turn on InPrivate Browsing in Internet Explorer, choose Tools ➤ InPrivate Browsing. A new Internet Explorer window opens (Figure 9.34), along with a message letting you know that InPrivate Browsing is enabled, and an indicator appears on the address bar. Close the browser window when you're finished.

FIGURE 9.34   InPrivate browsing

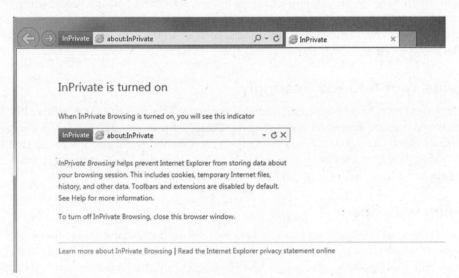

Chrome's Incognito feature functions in much the same way as InPrivate does. To open an Incognito window, open Chrome and then click Settings ➤ New Incognito Window, or press Ctrl+Shift+N. A new window will appear similar to the one in Figure 9.35. Chrome puts an icon that looks like a spy in the upper-left corner of the browser window.

FIGURE 9.35   Incognito browsing

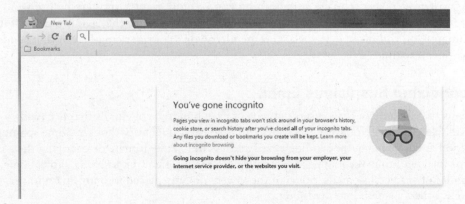

Using Email Safely

Most people rely on email today as a way of communication. For businesses, it may be the only way that things get done. It's so much faster and cheaper than traditional (snail) mail, there's no wondering why it's so popular.

Anything that's popular on the Internet today invites the attention of attackers, who are looking to have the biggest impact for the lowest effort and cost possible. Sending thousands or even millions of emails automatically and searching for potential victims is an efficient way. This section gives you an idea of what to look for in suspicious emails and how to use your email safely.

Provide Your Address Sparingly

The first tip is to provide your email address sparingly. This is in the same vein as PII. If you enter your email address at every website that asks for it, you will get email spam—lots and lots of email spam. Several people I know have a second email address set up that is their "public" address they enter into websites, where they don't care if they get spam, and their private address they give to only friends and family.

Dealing with Spam

While *spam* is not a virus or malware, it is one of the most annoying things users and network administrators contend with. Spam is defined as any unwanted, unsolicited email, and not only can the sheer volume of it be irritating, it can often open the door to larger problems. For instance, some of the sites advertised in spam may be infected with viruses, worms, and other unwanted programs. If users begin to respond to spam by visiting those sites, then viruses and other problems will surely follow.

Just as you should install good antivirus software programs, you should also consider similar measures for spam. The good news is most Internet service providers and companies take care of this for you. One of the issues to watch out for with antispam programs is false positives. Occasionally, a legitimate email will get tagged as spam and make its way into your Spam or Junk Email folders. It's a good idea to scan those folders just to make sure nothing you actually want is in there before you delete everything. In most email programs, if an email is sent to the Spam folder but it's legitimate, you can mark it as such, and the filter won't consider email from that sender malicious next time.

Recognizing Suspicious Email

It seems that on a daily basis, users get tens or even hundreds of emails that are easily identifiable as spam. Not every piece of spam is so easy to identify though. Some spammers are good at customizing the sending email address to look legitimate or changing the title of the email to make it appear customized to the recipient. Figure 9.36 shows some examples of suspicious emails. Some of these were directly placed into my Spam folder, whereas others made it into my Inbox.

FIGURE 9.36   Suspicious emails

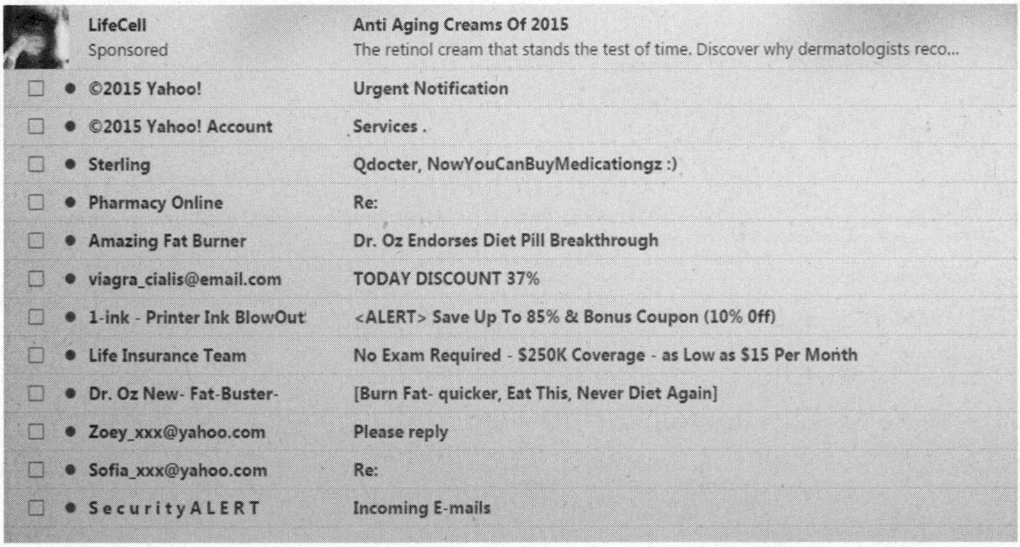

LifeCell Sponsored	**Anti Aging Creams Of 2015** The retinol cream that stands the test of time. Discover why dermatologists reco...	
©2015 Yahoo!	Urgent Notification	
©2015 Yahoo! Account	Services .	
Sterling	Qdocter, NowYouCanBuyMedicationgz :)	
Pharmacy Online	Re:	
Amazing Fat Burner	Dr. Oz Endorses Diet Pill Breakthrough	
viagra_cialis@email.com	TODAY DISCOUNT 37%	
1-ink - Printer Ink BlowOut	<ALERT> Save Up To 85% & Bonus Coupon (10% Off)	
Life Insurance Team	No Exam Required - $250K Coverage - as Low as $15 Per Month	
Dr. Oz New- Fat-Buster-	[Burn Fat- quicker, Eat This, Never Diet Again]	
Zoey_xxx@yahoo.com	Please reply	
Sofia_xxx@yahoo.com	Re:	
S e c u r i t y A L E R T	Incoming E-mails	

There are several classic examples of things to watch out for in Figure 9.36. Here are some to recognize:

- The top two appear to come from my email provider. These spammers were at least smart enough to know that Yahoo! uses an exclamation point at the end of its name—many times it's not included.

- The one from Sterling (whoever he is) uses my username in the subject line—very clever! (Or not.)

- The email from Sterling also spells *medications* wrong. Sometimes you will see words with characters such as @ replacing the letter *a* and ! for the letter *i*, in an effort to get through spam filters.

- Unsolicited pharmacy emails. Just delete them, even if they do promise amazing deals.

- Threats are common. The ones supposedly from Yahoo! or the security alert team warn me that if I don't act, I will lose my email. Figure 9.37 shows the content of one of these warning emails.

The email in Figure 9.37 is pretty standard hacker fare. They did include the Yahoo! logo and even put the copyright symbol in the message title. Those are nice touches. The grammar in the email is bad, and if my limit really was 1 GB, then how did the service really let me get to 99.8 GB of usage? Fortunately, they provide me a handy link I can click to restore my email account. Even better, they are concerned with my privacy so they provide a helpful suggestion at the bottom. Admittedly, I am curious to see exactly what would happen if I clicked the link. I'm not curious enough to want to spend the next week cleaning up whatever mess that creates, though.

FIGURE 9.37   The contents of a fraudulent email

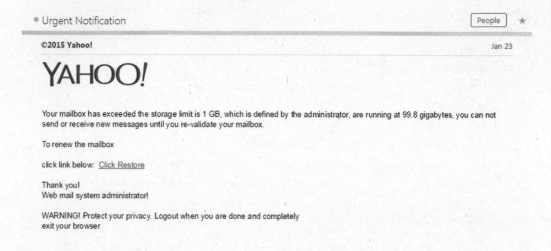

This brings me to the two cardinal rules of suspicious email:

- Never open any attachments.
- Never click any hyperlinks.

Either of those two actions will give you a direct link to acquiring malware for your computer. Even if you have the best antimalware software on the market, don't click attachments or links—don't subject your antimalware software to an obvious test.

Finally, consider the case of getting an email from what appears to be your bank or other financial institution, and you really are concerned that there could be a problem. In those situations, call them. Don't click anything in the email or use phone numbers provided in the email or suspicious site. Close your browser or email, and look up the contact information separately. If it's a legitimate problem, you can discuss it with a real representative over the phone.

Understanding Hijacked Email

One of the easiest ways to spread malware is to capture the email contacts of a user and send it as an attachment to all of those in their circle. The recipient is more likely to open the attachment because it seemingly comes from a trusted source. So instead of getting an email from a random person, you get an email from someone you know, with an attachment or link and instructions to click it because it's "amazing" or "the best thing ever."

If you get an email like this, call or text your acquaintance and ask them if they sent it. If they really did send it and the link is amazing, then you can click it and enjoy. Otherwise, practice safe emailing and ignore the message.

Summary

In this chapter, you learned about security best practices for your computer and network as well as safely browsing the Internet and using email.

The first section was on securing your computer and network, which started with device hardening. This includes disabling features such as Bluetooth, unused services, and AutoPlay. You should also lock your system, both physically to the desk in the case of laptops (and some desktops) and by using a software lock when you are away from your computer. To protect the data on your system from theft or access by other users, you can encrypt the data on your hard drive. And one of the most important device-hardening measures is to ensure you're using antimalware programs such as antivirus and antispam software.

User accounts should be carefully managed to ensure the best security. Grant Administrator account access only to those who really need it, and even administrators should use a regular user account unless they need to perform an administrative task. Disabling the Guest account also helps protect against attacks. Passwords need to be carefully managed as well. They should be sufficiently complex, changed regularly, and not reused. You also learned about authentication and the concepts of multifactor authentication and single sign-on.

The last section in computer and network best practices was on network security. Specifically, you should never use an open or unsecured network, and always be sure to enable the strongest encryption on your own networks. And be careful of public workstations!

Next, you learned about Internet usage best practices. Before you use the Internet, you can perform some preparatory tasks to ensure a safer browsing experience. These include updating your web browsers to the latest editions; managing plugins, toolbars, and extensions; disabling Autofill; configuring browser security; and managing cookies.

While browsing the Web, you should enter confidential information only into secure websites. In addition, avoid any suspicious-looking sites, links, or advertisements. If you do have odd activity happening on your computer such as excessive pop-ups, browser redirection, or search engine redirection, it's possible you have adware and need to remove it. You also learned about browsing InPrivate or Incognito.

Finally, you learned about email safety. Specifically, you should avoid giving out your email address too often. In addition, you should be on the lookout for suspicious email, and never click a hyperlink or attachment in an email from an unknown source.

Exam Essentials

Understand the actions you can take to accomplish device hardening. Device hardening makes it more difficult for attackers to exploit. Some actions you can take include disabling unused services and communication channels such as Bluetooth or NFC and disabling AutoPlay.

Know how to lock your system. If you have a laptop or other mobile device, it should be secured to the desk with a security cable. If you leave your workstation, use Ctrl+Alt+Delete to secure your seat!

Know what encryption does.   Encryption scrambles your files so no other local users can read them. Only the user who encrypted the files can decrypt them.

Know how to protect your computer against malware.   The best way is to avoid malware in the first place, but this isn't always possible. To protect yourself, use antimalware software, such as antivirus, antispam, and antispyware applications.

Understand three classifications of user accounts and what they are for.   The Administrator account is for system administration and should be carefully guarded. Regular user accounts are for everyday usage. Guest accounts are for temporary access and should be disabled if not in use.

Know good practices for password management.   Always change default passwords. Passwords should be sufficiently complex to avoid being guessed or hacked, kept confidential, changed regularly, and not reused on other sites or in the future after they have been changed.

Understand what multifactor authentication is.   Multifactor authentication requires at least two pieces of information from these three groups: what you know (such as a password), what you have (like a smart card), and what you are (such as a fingerprint).

Know the basics of how to secure your wireless network.   Enable the strongest encryption (WPA2), and avoid using unsecure networks and public workstations.

Know how to configure your browser for safe Internet browsing.   Update it to the latest version, including any necessary plugins, toolbars, and extensions. Disable Autofill, enable security, and manage cookies properly.

Understand how to browse the Internet safely.   Avoid unscrupulous sites. If you are going to enter confidential information such as passwords or financial information, make sure the site is secure. Avoid suspicious links and ads.

Know how to tell if a website is secure.   Secure websites will start with `https://` instead of `http://` and have a lock icon in the address bar. In addition, many browsers will color at least a portion of the address bar green.

Know what the symptoms of adware are.   Symptoms include excessive pop-ups, browser redirection, and search engine redirection.

Know how to safely use email.   Avoid giving out your email address unless you need to. Don't click hyperlinks or attachments in emails from people you don't know. If you get an email from a contact with an attachment or link urging you to click it, verify that the contact actually sent the email before clicking it.

Chapter 9 Lab

Chapter 9 covered a wide range of security measures you can implement on your computer, your network, and when you browse the Internet. This lab provides you with a checklist of things you can do to improve your security. It's recommended that you go through each of the tasks and understand how to perform them on your system.

Tasks you should be able to do:

1. Disable Bluetooth or NFC.
2. Disable unused services.
3. Disable AutoPlay.
4. Set up a screensaver password and engage it.
5. Enable file encryption.
6. Install and configure antimalware.
7. Disable or enable the Guest user account.
8. Create complex passwords that are easy for you to remember.
9. Update your web browser to the latest version.
10. Configure Autofill.
11. Configure browser security.
12. Manage and delete browser history and cookies.
13. Recognize secure websites.
14. Recognize symptoms of adware.
15. Know how to browse InPrivate or Incognito.
16. Recognize suspicious emails.

Review Questions

1. Due to a recent string of thefts in your office, you need to harden your local system. What two actions are most appropriate for your situation? (Choose two.)

   A. Install a hardware lock

   B. Disable unused services

   C. Install antimalware

   D. Enable encryption

2. What option can you configure on your workstation to increase security when you leave your desk?

   A. File encryption

   B. Multifactor authentication

   C. Single sign-on

   D. Screensaver password

3. You have just landed at the airport and have an unexpected six-hour layover. You want to use your smartphone to get some work done. What should you disable as a precautionary device hardening measure to help prevent potential attacks? (Choose two.)

   A. Autofill

   B. Bluetooth

   C. NFC

   D. FFC

4. Claire, a co-worker, is browsing the Internet and wants to know if it's safe to enter her credit card information into a website. What do you tell her to look for?

   A. HTTPS://

   B. HTTP://

   C. SSL://

   D. TLS://

5. You enabled file encryption on your local computer. While you were on vacation, one of your co-workers managed to get on your computer and share your important files with other users. How did they do this?

   A. They logged on and disabled encryption.

   B. They used the Disk Recovery tool to access the encrypted files.

   C. All users logging into the system have access to encrypted files.

   D. They logged on with your username and password.

6. Ray, a co-worker, is concerned that his computer is infected with adware. What symptoms should you tell Ray to look for to confirm his suspicions? (Choose three.)

    A. Excessive pop-ups

    B. Browser redirection

    C. Search engine redirection

    D. Multifactor login redirection

7. Which type of software will help protect your computer from malicious network traffic?

    A. Software firewall

    B. Password complexity tool

    C. Antispyware

    D. Antivirus

8. You are using Google Chrome and you want to browse a website but not have the website stored in your browsing history. What should you do?

    A. Log in as someone else to browse the site

    B. Configure independent browsing

    C. Use InPrivate

    D. Use Incognito

9. Your manager just got a new workstation and is not part of a domain. He wants to know which user accounts he should disable to increase security. What should you tell him to disable?

    A. Guest

    B. Users

    C. Power Users

    D. Administrator

10. Which of the following actions is not considered a web-browsing best practice?

    A. Limiting the use of PII

    B. Disabling Autofill

    C. Closing untrusted source warnings

    D. Updating plugins and toolbars

11. The managers at your company have decided to implement stricter security policies. Which of the following login schemes will help them achieve this goal?

    A. Single sign-on

    B. Multifactor authentication

    C. Password confidentiality

    D. HTTPS

12. Your coworker Rachel has recently discovered that when she starts typing her name into a field in a web browser, her whole name appears as well as her address in the appropriate boxes. What is this due to?

   A. Adware infection

   B. Single sign-on

   C. Suspicious hyperlinks

   D. Autofill

13. You have been asked to give training on network security. For your section on password management, which options should you recommend to users? (Choose two.)

   A. Do not use complex passwords because they are easy to forget.

   B. Change default passwords on systems.

   C. Use the same password on multiple systems so they are easy to remember.

   D. Do not reuse the same password after you are required to change it.

14. You are in a library that has free computers to use for Internet browsing. Which of the following should you possibly be concerned about?

   A. Shoulder surfing

   B. Keyloggers

   C. Unsecured wireless network

   D. A and B

   E. A, B, and C

15. Which two of the following statements are true regarding single sign-on?

   A. It is convenient for users.

   B. It can potentially cause security issues.

   C. It requires the use of multifactor authentication.

   D. It does not work across different operating systems.

16. Which of the following are considered characteristics of a strong password? (Choose two.)

   A. Long

   B. Uses patterns

   C. Uses symbols, numbers, and letters

   D. Contains PII

17. You just read an article about an Internet worm recently causing problems. What type of software should you install to protect yourself from this worm?

   A. Software firewall

   B. Antispyware

   C. Antivirus

   D. Antispam

18. You receive an email in your Inbox from your friend Sara. The title of the email is "This is so cool!" and inside the email is an attachment with an `.exe` extension. What should you do?

 A. Delete the email.

 B. Click the attachment.

 C. Run virus scan, then click the attachment.

 D. Call Sara to see if she sent you the email.

19. You recently received a new workstation and need to properly secure it before browsing the Internet. Which actions should you take? (Choose two.)

 A. Enable Autofill.

 B. Enable acceptance of cookies.

 C. Upgrade your browser to the newest version.

 D. Configure browser security zones.

20. Which of the following statements is true regarding web browser plugins, toolbars, and extensions?

 A. They should be updated to the newest versions.

 B. They are dangerous and should be deleted.

 C. They will be detected and removed by antivirus software.

 D. They only function in Internet Explorer.

Chapter

10

Buying and Configuring a Workstation

THE FOLLOWING COMPTIA IT FUNDAMENTALS EXAM OBJECTIVES ARE COVERED IN THIS CHAPTER:

✓ **5.1 Perform appropriate steps to set up a basic workstation**

- Plug in cables
- Power on computer
- Follow initial operating system setup wizard
  - Localization settings
  - Screen resolution
  - Audio settings
- Install security software
- Configure peripherals (if applicable)
- Uninstall unneeded software (if applicable)
- Configure and verify internet connection
- Install additional software (if applicable)
- Run software and security updates
- Other user accounts (if applicable)
- Basic cable management

As an IT professional, you are expected to know a great amount about computers. You must know hardware, software, networking, and security. Each of those areas covers a broad range, considering the number of different client operating systems in use or the plethora of hardware you might have to deal with. Even if it's not your area of expertise, you must have a pretty good understanding of all components of a computer. Your knowledge also needs to extend to all aspects of a computer's life cycle, starting with pre-purchase decisions and ranging to setup, operation, and finally proper disposal.

This chapter focuses on the early stages of computer life. It starts with a discussion on what questions to ask and what to look for when buying a computer. Then it covers the appropriate steps to set up a basic workstation.

Buying and Configuring a Workstation

When you think about working on computers, most of the time you imagine people sitting at desks, frantically punching away at a keyboard trying to get work done, or a high-tech server room with the constant whirring of cooling fans. The technicians tinker with broken systems until someone calls with a problem and desperation in their voice—the tech will save the day. (Whether the tech wears a cape or not is up to their individual discretion.)

In many cases, that scenario holds fairly true (including optional capes), but techs are also involved in the purchase and setup of computers. Junior technicians are often the ones handed the assignment of setting up new systems, while the senior technicians tackle tougher operability challenges.

Adding to that, once people realize that you know about computers (because you are CompTIA IT Fundamentals certified), you will get questions. Friends, loved ones, and total strangers will ask you, "What computer should I get?" It's not a one-size-fits-all answer. In the next section, you will learn the right questions to ask and what to look for in order to match the right computer to the user. After that, you will learn the proper steps to set up a workstation.

Selecting the Right Computer

Selecting the right computer can be a lot like selecting the right person to date. There are many options, and each one has different qualities. You know that if you pick the right one, things can be wonderful. If you pick the wrong one, though, you might have a miserable experience that includes needing to replace parts. Okay, so perhaps choosing the right block of metal and plastic isn't quite as important as choosing someone for a relationship, but you do want to make sure you get a system that meets your needs.

Before digging into the details of computer selection, take a step back for a moment and think about the big picture of what computers are—a collection of hardware and software. So really you just need to pick the right pieces from each of those groups. In the hardware group, processors, memory, video cards, and displays are your main options, and in software you have the operating system and applications. Now it's just a matter of putting them all together. With all of that in mind, the next sections will address the questions you should ask to determine the right kind of computer for the situation.

Determining the Use

What will this computer be used for? Is it for a home user or an office user? If the sole purpose of the computer is to browse the Internet and check email, the requirements are very different than those for someone who will be doing video editing or massive amounts of calculations in workbooks. This should be the first question to ask because it will help you narrow the choices the fastest.

Deciding on a Platform

The next thing to think about is whether the user needs mobility. If not, then a desktop might be a viable solution. The main advantage of desktop computers is that they offer much better performance at lower prices than laptops. If the user needs a computer with the fastest of everything and maximum memory for online gaming, then a desktop is the best choice. You also can get a bigger screen. Desktop displays of 21 inches and greater are pretty common. You *can* get a laptop with a 21-inch display, but would the user really want to lug that thing around everywhere? Probably not.

Many users today need mobility. It could be that they work in an office and need to take their system from meeting to meeting. It could also be that they like to surf the Web while watching television on the couch, and desktops don't lend themselves well to sitting on laps. With the advances in wireless networking technology, laptop computers often have connectivity that's just as good (if not better) than their desktop counterparts with the added advantage of mobility.

If you've decided that a mobile solution is needed, then you also need to decide on a traditional laptop versus a tablet or a netbook. Netbooks are great for surfing the Web and sending email but not much else. The user can create occasional documents or worksheets, but netbooks are not designed to be fully operational workstations. Tablets range in sizes from those that are about the size of netbooks but offer a little more in the area of office functionality to those that are barely bigger than smartphones.

Choosing to Build or Buy

If a desktop is the right solution, then the next question is whether you want to build your own system or buy a prebuilt one. Building your own system, often lovingly called a Frankenstein, ensures that you get exactly the components you want. You choose everything—the case, power supply, motherboard, processor, memory, hard drive, video card, network card, and whatever else you want to put into it. You can make it the biggest and fastest system possible, and in a year when the new technology has made your system obsolete, you can upgrade any components you want. It can be cheaper than similarly configured prebuilt systems as well. This route does require some technical expertise and is daunting to some people.

There are a few potential downsides to building your own computer. First, you need to purchase your own software, including the operating system. Alternatively, you could use Linux and other open-source software to save money. Second, there is no tech support—you are the tech support. This might not bother you, but if you're building 20 systems for a business, you might not want to always be on the hook to troubleshoot and replace a component if it fails.

If you decide to build your own system, find a good local computer store you can trust or a reputable online retailer to get parts from. That way, you can make sure you are getting good prices as well as staying on top of the new technology that becomes available. A friendly return policy is incredibly helpful as well, because electronic components do sometimes fail.

There is no shame in buying a machine built by a major manufacturer such as HP, Apple, Dell, Lenovo, Asus, or Acer. There are smaller companies that produce their own systems as well—you might find a local computer company that makes great computers.

Some desktop computers come prepackaged with a monitor (and sometimes a printer), while with others the monitor is a separate purchase.

When choosing a prebuilt system, the most important factor is to comparison shop. You will find a wide range of prices on computers that have similar configurations. You might be able to save money by choosing one manufacturer over another or perhaps get more memory and processing speed for the same price. Reading reviews is a good practice too. Finally, visit the manufacturer's website. Several of them let you build your own custom system online and will ship it to you, meaning you get what you want and customer service too.

Also check for refurbished systems on manufacturer websites. They will be less expensive and often have the same warranty as new systems. A friend once said to me, "As long as it has the same warranty, I don't care if they dragged it out of a dumpster."

Finding the Right Laptop

With laptops, you don't have to make the build-or-buy decision—you buy. Most parts used in laptops are custom built for the manufacturer and even for that specific laptop case design. Hard drives and memory are really the only choices when it comes to internal components.

Laptops are designed to be mobile but still provide good computing power. Because of the design and purpose of laptop computers, there are specific features you will want to pay attention to:

Display Size   This is the biggest determinant of weight. The bigger the screen, the heavier it will be and the faster it will drain the battery. Common sizes are around 15″ and 17″, although you can find both bigger and smaller. Displays smaller than 15″ tend to be impractical for all-day use, and those bigger than 17″ practically require you to lift weights regularly to be able to carry them around.

Battery Life   Sometimes the user is near a power outlet, and but there are times when they can't find one when they desperately need it. Longer battery life is better, and it can be affected by the display size as well as processor speed and how many peripherals are connected. If the user travels a lot, a second backup battery is a worthwhile investment.

Wireless Networking   All laptops have built-in Wi-Fi today, but some perform better than others. Make sure that the mobile device supports at least 802.11n but preferably 802.11ac. Some laptops, particularly cheaper ones, suffer from intermittent wireless access due to poor design. In situations like that, consider getting an extra USB or other expansion slot network card.

Processors and Memory   Faster processors and more memory are good things, but they also cost money. Generally speaking, though, it's best to get the fastest CPU and most memory you can realistically afford; not only does it help performance, but it keeps the computer relevant longer.

Hard Drives   Laptops often have limited storage space. Many laptops are moving toward using SSD hard drives, which is great for speed and quieter use but also means less storage space.

There is a huge range in laptop prices and features. If you buy cheap laptops, expect to replace them every few years. More robust systems should last four to five years before needing to be replaced.

Comparing laptops from different manufacturers for features and prices is smart. Also consider reading reviews to see if the manufacturer has a good reputation.

Choosing a Tablet

The primary reason for choosing a tablet is the small size and portability. In choosing one, you recognize that you are giving up power for size. There are three primary factors to consider when deciding among tablets:

Operating System   The choices here are iOS, Android, and Windows Mobile. Kindle Fire technically counts too, but that is uncommonly used in business settings. Android and iOS dominate the market, with Windows having a tiny share. If the use is familiar with the iPhone or has a Mac, iOS could be the best choice. Android has the benefit of being designed around Google, which provides great apps (including productivity ones such as Google Docs) and search capability.

Size and Weight   You can find tablets that are essentially overgrown smartphones or that are the size of small laptops. The bigger ones, of course, will be heavier but will have larger screens, which make them easier to use over the course of a day. Screens commonly range from about 7″ to 12.5″ in size.

Storage Space   Tablets are very limited in storage due to their small size. Typically you can get between 8 and 64 GB of built-in storage space, although some higher end models will come with 128 or 256 GB of SSD hard disk space.

Selecting an Operating System

When purchasing a prebuilt computer, you don't have a wide range of choices for an operating system. It will be either some version of Windows or Mac OS X. If you really want the Mac OS, that dramatically limits your choices of hardware, because the OS is installed only on Mac systems. If you are building your own computer, you can add Linux into the mix as well.

Which operating system you choose depends on a few big factors:

- What the user will use the computer for. If they work with creative content such as videos or music, Mac OS X is generally regarded as the better choice.

- The other computers the user has or what their co-workers use. If everyone in the office uses a PC with Windows, it might be easier for interoperability to get Windows too.

- Personal preference. Perhaps they really like one specific operating system or dislike another.

Other factors are involved too, such as the availability of software applications for your chosen OS. Nearly every type of program you can think of is available for almost all operating systems today, but it's still a good thing to check if you require a certain program.

Determining a Budget

Ah yes—money. The user might want a high-end gaming machine but might not be able to afford it. It's hard to purchase a five-star dinner on a ramen noodle budget.

The features of a computer determine the cost. It's really quite simple—the more performance they want, the more they will pay for it. This is why it's important to understand what the computer will be used for, so you're not tempted to spend more than necessary to accomplish the tasks it will perform. At the same time, don't go too cheap. Cutting the cost might seem like a good way to stay on budget, but if the system doesn't perform how it should, they will become frustrated and need to replace the system sooner. It's usually better to slightly over-purchase than under-purchase when it comes to computers, provided that their budget can afford it.

Apple computers tend to be more expensive than similarly powered PC equivalents, and laptops are also more expensive than similar desktops. In Exercise 10.1, you will compare and contrast prices for different laptops.

EXERCISE 10.1

Comparing Windows and Mac Laptop Prices

1. Create an easy and quick computer comparison grid. You can do it on a computer screen or a piece of paper. Down the side, list components such as screen size, processor type and speed, memory, hard drive, network, weight, battery life, and price. Add other components if you would like. Across the top, you can list the models you research.

2. Go to the website of a major electronics retailer. Examples could be www.bestbuy.com or www.frys.com.

3. Search for a MacBook. For example, find a MacBook Pro with a 13.3″ display, Intel i5 CPU, 8 GB RAM, and 128 or 256 GB SSD hard drive. Enter the specifications on your comparison grid.

4. Search for a second MacBook. Pick one with a 15.4″ display and more power than the first model. List the specifications on your comparison grid. What are the big differences between these two MacBooks?

5. Search for a PC laptop with similar specifications to your first MacBook, and list them. What are the differences?

6. Search for a PC laptop with similar specifications to your second MacBook, and list them. What are the differences?

The goal of Exercise 10.1 isn't to simply show that Macs are generally more expensive. You can perform the same exercise with three similarly configured PC laptops from different manufacturers and find different prices. The goal is to show that you should always research the best options for your needs and the current prices on the market.

Categories of Home and SOHO Computers

Based on the questions discussed in the previous section, you can imagine that there are dozens or even hundreds of possible solutions to meet the end user's needs. It's hard to wrap your mind around so many different solutions, but it's easier if you can categorize the general type of system that users will need.

In this section, you will learn about several categories of home or small office/home office (SOHO) computers. That way, when you are asking your questions, you can categorize the user's needs (to make your task easier), and then tweak the system as needed based on their specific intended use. The list of computer types discussed here is by no means exhaustive, but it will give you a good foundation. The following types of systems are covered:

- Standard workstations
- Gaming PCs
- Graphic design workstations
- Audio/video editing workstations
- Home theater PCs
- Home/SOHO server PCs

For each of these types of computers, you will need to think about the components that are most important. You know the standard list of components such as processor, memory, video card, and network card. Some of these systems might also require more specialized equipment such as advanced cooling, a television tuner, a custom case, or other items.

Standard Workstations

A standard workstation computer isn't anything special but rather the baseline from which all other configurations are measured. Standard workstation computers can be desktops, laptops, or tablets, based on the user's needs.

There are no specific hardware or software requirements for standard workstation computers, other than what is needed to run the operating system. Not even a network connection is required, although it would be incredibly rare to see a computer without network capabilities in today's environment.

If your client is looking for a basic workstation that allows them to do office work or just browse the Web and read email, this is the configuration to start with. You can decide to buy more or less powerful components based on the user's needs and budget.

Gaming PCs

Gaming PCs aren't built for Solitaire but for the advanced, action-packed and graphically intensive games on the market today. Some of the games have become incredibly realistic, while other animated games have quality that rivals cinematic productions. If you or someone you know is into PC gaming, then you realize that gaming PCs need to be fast and powerful systems on the forefront of technology. The specific components that need to be optimized are the processor, memory, and video. Upgrading the sound card and adding an enhanced cooling system to the computer should be considered as well.

Modern action games require the processor to perform millions of calculations per second over extended periods of time. For that reason, a gaming PC should have the fastest processor possible with the most cores possible. A quad-core or six-core processor is standard fare. Memory is also critical because it speeds up system performance, so the more memory the better. Video cards should have their own memory (as much as possible) and not share regular system memory. The monitor also needs to be high end to handle the quick and detailed output the video card provides. Finally, all of the heat generated from the fast processor and powerful video card might require a specialized cooling system, such as extra fans or liquid cooling.

As you might expect based on this description, gaming systems are generally quite a bit more expensive than standard workstations. For those who are seriously into gaming, though, the performance is worth every penny.

Some manufacturers sell "gaming laptops," which are fairly powerful and expensive laptop computers. Serious gamers will tell you that there is no such thing (at least not today) as a gaming laptop—no matter how powerful, they're just not good enough. For that reason, most gaming systems are desktop computers.

Graphic Design Workstations

Graphic designers, publishers, and architects are great examples of the types of users who will require a graphic design workstation. These systems run specialized software to render art, create designs, lay out publications, and design blueprints for construction projects. The most important components to aid in the design process are the CPU, RAM, and video system.

While graphic design isn't a matter of virtual life-or-death like gaming can be, graphics programs render very complex 3D designs quickly and need to be able to rotate, spin, and zoom without causing delays. All of this work is very processor and memory intensive. Generally speaking, it's important to maximize the CPU and RAM in these types of systems. In addition, since designers are focused on visual outcomes, the video system, including video card and monitor, should be of high quality as well.

Audio/Video Editing Workstations

Users who edit multimedia files have their own unique set of needs. Specifically, they need high-end video enhancements, exceptional audio performance, and lots of storage space.

A video card with its own dedicated memory and GPU is required. It's also often necessary to have video cards with multiple video inputs and outputs, either for different components or for multiple monitors. Many times, video editors need to use multiple screens simultaneously.

The audio system is critical as well. Most sound cards today support basic 5.1 or 7.1 analog surround sound. While this might be sufficient for video editing, it's more likely that digital audio will be needed.

Finally, video files take up huge amounts of space. Storage space will be critical for audio/video workstations—several terabytes may be required. Depending on the situation, if multiple people are editing, it might make more sense to buy a standalone network attached storage (NAS) device as opposed to storage on individual machines. Many editors greatly prefer the speed of SSD over standard spinning hard drives.

Home Theater PCs

The home theater industry and computers are a beautiful marriage of technologies. Many users seek theater-quality entertainment in their own homes, and computer systems designed to augment that experience are becoming more and more common. In fact, there is a form factor called home theater PC (HTPC) that is specifically designed for home theaters. HTPC systems often look like other audio/video equipment, so they fit right in with the rest of the user's components. Many of these systems will have large touch-screen displays, large volume knobs, and silent cooling systems.

In addition to the case, home theater PCs should have upgraded video enhancements, high-quality audio, and Blu-ray and may include a television tuner.

High-quality video almost goes without saying, but home theater PCs should have good video cards with multiple HDMI plugs built in. Ideally these video cards will have both HDMI input and HDMI output capabilities. HDMI supports 7.1 surround sound audio, so if the system has HDMI, you might not even have to worry about good audio—it's already built in. Many HTPCs also include built-in Blu-ray players, so you don't need an external device. Finally, many systems will have embedded television tuner cards, allowing the user to watch or record live television from one or more inputs simultaneously.

Home/SOHO Servers

This last type isn't really a workstation, but it often has similar hardware and operating systems to a workstation—a home or small office/home office (SOHO) server. The following enhanced features might be required in a home or SOHO server:

- File and print sharing services
- Fault tolerance
- Faster networking
- Media streaming capabilities

The main idea behind using a server is to share commonly used information among several users, and a SOHO server is no different. Thus, having built-in file and print services is generally a requirement. With Windows 7 and newer, you can use homegroups to easily share files and printers with clients. (Keep in mind that only Windows 7 and newer clients can use homegroups.) If you have a mixed OS environment or older clients, you can use workgroups and standard file and print sharing. To help protect files you should also implement fault tolerance, such as RAID 1 or RAID 5.

If you have several users who need access to a large number of common files, it might make sense to install a NAS device along with the SOHO server. NAS devices typically have built-in RAID as well, freeing up processor capacity from the server, which no longer needs to manage fault tolerance.

Home servers might also need a faster network connection if they are serving multiple clients. For example, they could have Gigabit Ethernet. They should be physically attached to a gigabit-capable port on the network switch or wireless router.

Even if the client computers support Gigabit Ethernet, run them at Fast Ethernet (100 Mbps) instead. This frees up server bandwidth to serve multiple clients simultaneously, without one client being able to monopolize the server's gigabit bandwidth.

Finally, SOHO servers may need to provide media streaming for clients. Exercise 10.2 shows you how to configure Windows 7 for media streaming.

EXERCISE 10.2

Configuring Windows 7 for Media Streaming

1. In Control Panel, open Network And Sharing Center. (It may be under Network And Internet, depending on how you have Control Panel configured.)

2. Click the Change Advanced Sharing Settings link (shown in Figure 10.1) in the left frame.

FIGURE 10.1   Network and Sharing Center

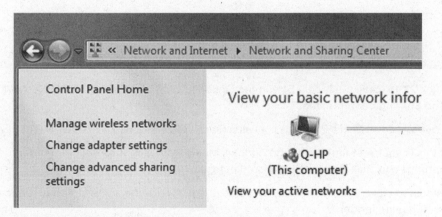

3. Click the down arrow to the right of Home Or Work to expand that configuration section.

4. In the Media Streaming section, click the Choose Media Streaming Options link.

5. In the Media Streaming Options dialog, like the one shown in Figure 10.2, pull down the buttons labeled Blocked and change them to Allowed for each computer on the network that you want to be able to stream from the local PC.

FIGURE 10.2 Media Streaming Options

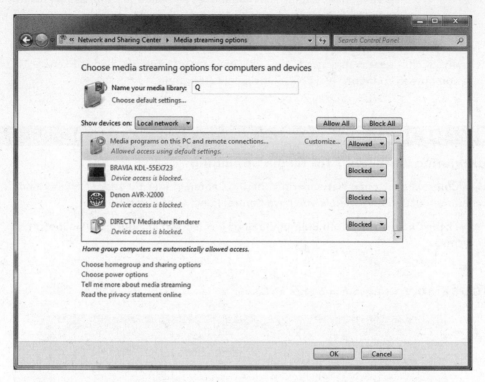

6. Click OK to leave the Media Streaming Options dialog and then close the Network And Sharing Center dialog.

7. Open Windows Media Player by choosing Start ➤ All Programs ➤ Windows Media Player.

8. If this is your first time opening Windows Media Player, choose Recommended Settings and click Finish. Otherwise skip to step 9.

9. Switch to Library mode, if necessary (the grid icon with the arrow pointing left in Now Playing mode).

10. Ensure that streaming is enabled by clicking Stream ➤ Turn On Media Streaming (or Turn On Media Streaming With Homegroup). This option is hidden if streaming is already on.

11. On one of the remote systems, start Windows Media Player.

12. In the left frame, click Other Libraries.

13. Expand the remote library you just shared and see if you can play music, watch videos or recorded TV, or view pictures.

That "New Car Smell"

You might be familiar with the adage that once you drive a new car off the dealer's lot, it loses half its value. It's not technically true, but there are shreds of truth in it, and it sticks in people's minds. The computer version of that phrase should be "as soon as you buy a computer, it's obsolete." Again, it's not technically true but there are shreds of truth buried in the idea.

If you just bought a computer, the best advice is to not look at computer prices for several months. Prices will inevitably drop and possibly quickly. If you bought a great computer and got a great deal, its price could drop enough that it all of a sudden looks like a bad deal, even if that wasn't the case at the time. Or maybe you will discover that a month later you could have gotten a faster processor or more RAM for the same money. It will only cause buyer's remorse! Take time to enjoy your new computer—comparison shopping right after you bought it won't help you do that.

Setting Up a Workstation

You just purchased a new workstation and brought it home. Or maybe you purchased a dozen workstations and are now staring at a small mountain of cardboard boxes. Now what do you do? If it's your own new system, you are probably excited to try it out. If you need to set up a dozen systems, you might be feeling a bit of anxiety and are hoping that everything works properly. Regardless of the situation, it's time to start setting up the computer(s). This section focuses on the appropriate steps to set up a basic workstation.

Plugging in Cables

After removing the computer from the box, always be sure to immediately check for visible signs of damage. Manufacturers do a very good job of securely packaging their products, but sometimes accidents happen during shipping. Small dings or scratches in the case aren't likely to affect the computer's performance, but large dents or cracks or broken components are a bad sign.

If your visual inspection uncovers no problems, the next step is to plug in all of the cables. Manufacturers have made this very easy based on two things they have done. First, they have color coded and keyed most of the connectors. The color coding is fairly self-evident—the blue plug goes with the blue connector. The connectors are also keyed, meaning that they will connect only one way, the right way. If the plug is upside down or reversed, it won't connect. You could try to force it, but if you feel like you need to do that, something is wrong.

The second thing manufacturers have done to help people set up computers is provide setup guides or quick start guides in the box. Figure 10.3 shows a sample quick start guide. These guides are usually posters with very few words, and they show how to connect the components of the computer by using pictures.

FIGURE 10.3 HP quick start guide

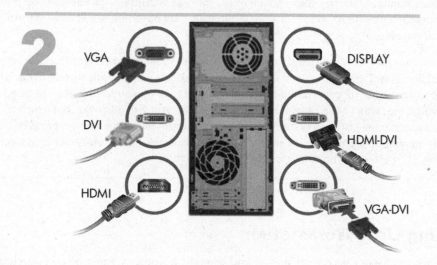

Figure 10.3 shows step two of the guide, which demonstrates how to plug in the monitor based on the connector you have. If you have set up several systems in your life, you probably don't need this poster. For novice users, though, it's quite helpful. If the computer you purchased doesn't have a poster or quick start guide and you need one, you should be able to find one on the Internet. (You will need to use a different computer to search for it!)

At a minimum, for a desktop you need to plug in the power cord, the monitor (unless it's an all-in-one model), and the keyboard. Usually you plug in a mouse, network connection, and speakers as well. If you have other peripherals such as a printer, USB hub, webcam, or external storage, don't plug them in just yet. Connect the basics and verify that the system works, and configure the extra peripherals later.

The setup process for laptops and tablets has fewer steps. You might need to plug in the power cord or charging cord, but that's about it. Open the system (if applicable), and move on to the next step.

Powering on the Computer

Computers need power. Hopefully this does not come as a surprise to you. Power the computer on. If you're not sure where the power button is, the quick start guide will show you. Figure 10.4 shows where the power button is on a few different cases that this poster might have shipped with. Don't forget to power the monitor on if it's separate from the computer!

FIGURE 10.4 Quick start guide showing power buttons

 Occasionally, you will have a laptop that will not power on when you press the power button, even if it's plugged into a wall outlet and the battery is charged. If this happens, turn the laptop over and detach the battery. There will be a small release lever or two on the bottom of the laptop for this purpose. Reattach the battery, and then try the power button again. It should power up.

Setting Up the Operating System

A prebuilt computer will have an operating system installed at the factory. After you power it on, you will need to configure it to your liking. All current workstation OSs will have some sort of menu system or setup wizard to help guide you through the choices. For the most part the choices are relatively simple, such as selecting the region you're in, setting the time and date, configuring the screen resolution, and choosing audio settings. If you don't configure the system exactly the right way during the initial setup wizard, you can always go back later and change the settings in Control Panel.

Localization Settings

A *localization setting* simply specifies where in the world the computer operates. An example of a localization setting screen is shown in Figure 10.5. Based on the choice of country, the computer will set other parameters such as the language; the format of date, time, and numbers; and the keyboard layout. In addition to specifying a location, you will likely be asked to select a time zone and confirm the date and time.

FIGURE 10.5   Choosing a localization setting

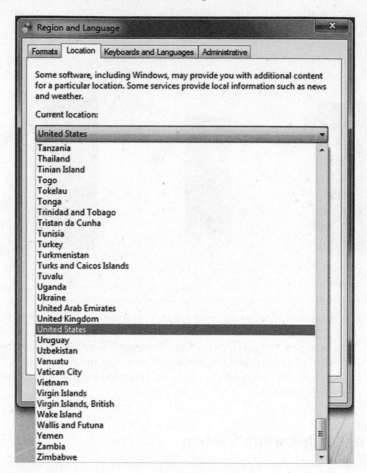

Screen Resolution

The *screen resolution*, also known as resolution, determines how many horizontal dots and vertical dots make up the rows and columns of your display. Higher resolutions make items appear crisper on the screen but require more video memory because there are more dots on the screen to manage. Higher resolutions also make items such as icons and words in documents appear smaller, which could be a problem for users without great vision.

Here's an example of how it works. Say that you have set the monitor resolution to 500 × 400 (it's not a real resolution, but that's okay for this example), which means that the monitor will display 500 pixels in each horizontal line and 400 pixels in each vertical column. And suppose that an icon on your desktop is programmed to be 100 pixels wide.

It will take up approximately one-fifth of the width of your screen. Now if you change the resolution to 1000 × 800, the same icon, still programmed to be 100 pixels wide, now takes up only one-tenth of the screen width. It will look much smaller because of the resolution change.

The monitor must also support the resolution you choose; otherwise the image won't display properly or at all. Your system shouldn't let you select a resolution that's not supported by the hardware. When you choose a resolution, the system will switch to it temporarily to ensure it displays properly and give you a choice of keeping the resolution or reverting to the previous one. If you don't choose to keep it (for example, if it doesn't display properly or you can't see anything), the resolution will revert to the previous setting in about 15 seconds. Figure 10.6 shows you the resolution settings in Control Panel. There are options to change the monitor type, resolution, and orientation (landscape or portrait). You rarely need to change the monitor type, but sometimes the monitor isn't properly detected, and a generic monitor driver is installed. If this happens, you might not be able to choose resolutions that are as high as what your monitor can support. In these situations, finish the setup, and download and install the monitor driver manually.

Choosing the wrong resolution can prevent all items from fitting on the screen, or your images will appear distorted, because resolutions are designed for displays with specific ratios of dimensions. Older monitors that were squarer in shape fit

FIGURE 10.6   Resolution settings in Control Panel

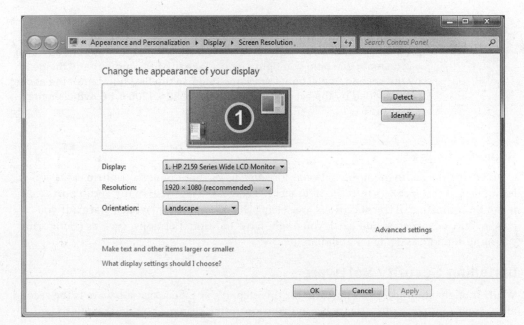

the 4:3 aspect ratio, meaning that the display area was 4 units wide by 3 units high. All resolutions were in multiples of this. For example, the VGA standard resolution is 640 × 480. Widescreen computer monitors typically have an aspect ratio of 16:10. High-definition televisions, which follow the ATSC 1080i/1080p standard, have an aspect ratio of 16:9. Table 10.1 shows you a few video standards and their corresponding resolutions and ratios.

TABLE 10.1   Video standards and resolutions

Standard	Resolution	Aspect Ratio
VGA	640 × 480	4:3
Super VGA	800 × 600	4:3
ATSC 720p	1280 × 720	16:9
ATSC 1080i/1080p	1920 × 1080	16:9
Widescreen XGA (WXGA)	1280 × 800	16:10
WUXGA	1920 × 1200	16:10

 If you're presented with a video resolution that you don't know the aspect ratio to (and therefore are unsure if it will work with the monitor you have), a little math will help you figure it out. Take the first number and divide it by the second. It will equal the same thing as the first number of the aspect ratio divided by the second. For example, 1920 ÷ 1200 = 1.6, which is the same as 16 ÷ 10.

Audio Settings

Configuring the audio might be optional for some users, but doing so confirms that you at least plugged the speakers into the right jack. (There are usually so many audio ports that it can be confusing!) Typical options are setting the volume and playback status. If you have a more advanced sound card, you might have additional options, such as configuring surround sound or setting up audio inputs.

Installing Security Software

While it might seem like it's a bit early for this step, it's not. Security software is the second most important piece of software behind your operating system. You don't want to be connected to the Internet for long without security software enabled, or you will likely contract something nasty.

Many prebuilt systems will have installed security software from companies such as Norton or McAfee, with a free trial period. Enabling the trial product is certainly better than nothing, but you will want to have a permanent plan in place. Either extend the trial to a full subscription (usually around $50 per year), or install the security software of your choice. A good practice is to make sure that you have antimalware software as well as a software firewall (or Windows Firewall) in place.

> Running security updates is an optional step later in the setup process, but if your Internet connection is already working, it's perfectly fine (and recommended) to update the security software right after you enable it, just to ensure that your protection is up to date.

Configuring Peripherals

Configuring peripherals is an optional step, because you might not have any additional peripherals to configure. If you are installing a printer, external hard drive, specialized keyboard or pointing device, webcam, or other device, you can now plug it in and configure it. Configuring peripherals involves three steps:

1. Plug in the device.
2. Install the driver.
3. Verify functionality.

If the peripheral you are installing is an internal device, you will want to ensure the computer is off before installing it. If the device is external, the computer will most likely detect it automatically after you plug it in and will begin the driver installation process. Your OS will try to locate a driver for the device or ask you for the location of the driver. A driver should have come with the device; if not, check the device manufacturer's website.

Uninstalling Unneeded Software

Uninstalling unneeded software is an optional step. Many prebuilt machines will have software packages on them, bundled on the computer by the manufacturer. Some of the applications will be useful, whereas others will be trial versions that pester you with pop-ups to buy them or programs you would never use. One advantage of building your own system is that you don't have to deal with unwanted junk software!

Removing programs in Windows is done through the Uninstall A Program app in Control Panel, as shown in Figure 10.7. Highlight the program and click Uninstall. On a Mac, some apps will have a Remove folder/application that deletes the app and all related files. If not, find the icon and drag it to the trash. Many Linux versions will have a Software Center app that lets you delete software in a similar fashion to Windows Control Panel.

FIGURE 10.7 Uninstall A Program in Windows

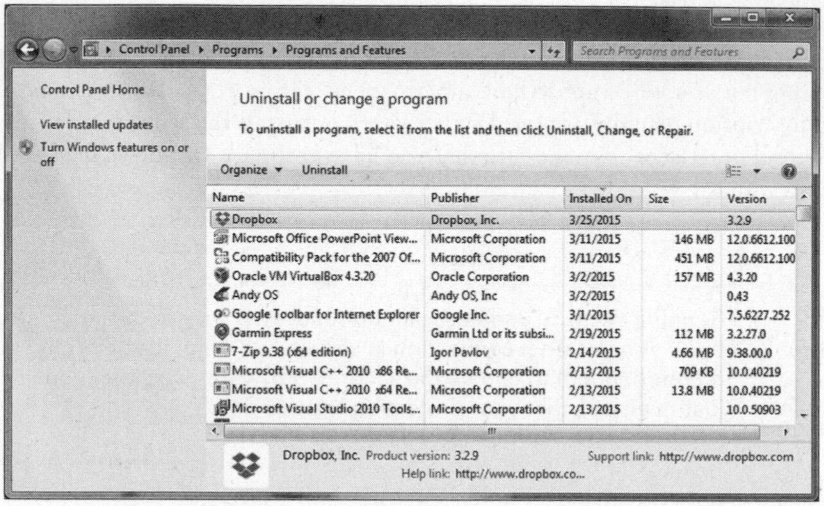

Configuring the Internet Connection

You probably don't need a reminder of how important Internet connections are to most users today. So instead, here's a reminder that configuring an Internet connection in Windows is done in the Network And Sharing Center within Control Panel, as shown in Figure 10.8. Mac network connections are configured by going to the Apple menu and choosing System Preferences ➢ Network.

FIGURE 10.8 Network And Sharing Center

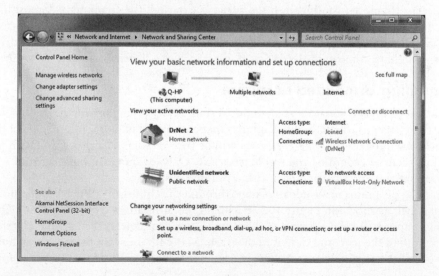

After configuring the Internet connection, be sure to verify that it works. Open a web browser and connect to a site such as www.google.com and perform a quick search to ensure that everything is working properly.

Installing Additional Software

The user might not need additional software, so this is an optional step. If needed, install any additional programs by inserting the installation media and running the installation program or by downloading the program and running the installer. After installing the software, verify that it works.

Running Software and Security Updates

By now, the security software and other optional applications are installed, and the Internet connection is working. The next step should be to run security updates to ensure that your antimalware definition files are up to date, if you haven't done so already. Also use this time to update software programs on the computer. Many programs, such as Microsoft Word shown in Figure 10.9, will have a Check For Updates or similar feature in the Help section.

FIGURE 10.9   Check For Updates

Creating User Accounts

If more than one person will use this computer, and it's not a member of a security domain, you will need to create additional user accounts. Creating accounts is something that only a user with administrative privileges can do. For a refresher course on creating user accounts, visit the "Working with User Accounts" section of Chapter 3, "Operating Systems."

Managing Cables

The last step in setting up a computer is to tidy up the area where the computer is located. This includes mundane tasks such as removing the garbage and setting the monitor in the right place. One task that often gets overlooked is managing cables. Loose cables can be a workplace hazard, so at a minimum you should tuck the cables away and get them as out of the way as you possibly can. You want to avoid situations where users could kick the cables and disconnect them, which might result in a call to the IT help desk. Worse yet, loose cables could present trip hazards, which could cause injury or other damages. If there are a few cables that run through the same area, you can use cable ties (Figure 10.10) to hold them together and in place. If cables will be running across a walkway, use a floor cable guard (Figure 10.11). These serve two functions—they keep users from tripping, and they also protect the cables from damage.

FIGURE 10.10   Cable ties

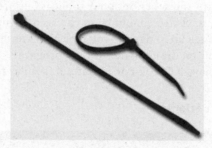

FIGURE 10.11   A floor cable guard

Summary

In this chapter, you learned how to pick out the right workstation and then set it up and configure it. First, you learned the right questions to ask to determine what type of system is right for the user. Find out what the computer will be used for. Determine the right platform, such as a desktop or laptop. Then, select an operating system, and also consider budget limitations.

Next, we discussed different categories of home and small office computers. Options included a standard workstation, gaming computers, graphic design systems, audio/video editing workstations, home theater systems, and small office/home office servers.

Finally, the chapter covered the appropriate steps needed to set up a basic workstation. The steps are to plug in cables, power on the computer, follow the initial operating system setup wizard, install security software, configure peripherals, uninstall unneeded software, configure and verify Internet connectivity, install additional software, update security and other software, create additional user accounts, and perform basic cable management functions.

Exam Essentials

Know the steps to set up a basic workstation.   The steps are to plug in cables, power on the computer, follow the initial operating system setup wizard, install security software, configure peripherals, uninstall unneeded software, configure and verify Internet connectivity, install additional software, update security and other software, create additional user accounts, and perform basic cable management functions.

Know what is configured in localization settings.   Localization settings always configure the country the computer will operate in. They often also include the time zone, date and time, and language.

Understand the importance of configuring screen resolution.   If the screen resolution is not configured properly, the display might not work or it may appear distorted.

Chapter 10 Lab

The primary focus of Chapter 10 was acquiring and setting up a new workstation. The best way to reinforce the concepts in this chapter is to perform them. Therefore, that's what the Chapter 10 lab will have you do. On a new workstation, perform the following steps:

1. Plug in the cables.
2. Power on the computer.
3. Follow the initial operating system setup wizard.
4. Install security software.
5. Configure peripherals.
6. Uninstall unneeded software.
7. Configure and verify Internet connectivity.
8. Install additional software.
9. Update security and other software.
10. Create additional user accounts.
11. Perform basic cable management functions.

Review Questions

1. You have been asked to purchase a computer for a client. What is the first question you should ask to determine the right computer to buy?

   A. What it will be used for

   B. What operating system they want

   C. What platform they want

   D. What their budget is

2. You are setting up a workstation and have configured the screen resolution. After choosing a resolution, the image on the screen appears distorted. What is the most likely cause of the problem?

   A. The monitor is failing.

   B. The resolution is set too high for the monitor.

   C. The resolution is set too low for the monitor.

   D. The resolution is at the wrong aspect ratio.

3. Which of the following operating systems tends to be associated with workstations that are more expensive than their counterparts?

   A. Android

   B. Windows

   C. Linux

   D. OS X

4. You have been asked to set up a workstation for a client. You have performed all of the steps up to and including configuring and verifying the Internet connection. What should you do next?

   A. Install security software.

   B. Create additional user accounts.

   C. Run software and security updates.

   D. Install additional software.

5. When choosing a laptop for a client's use, which of the following items should be primary criteria? (Choose two.)

   A. Weight

   B. CPU speed

   C. Battery life

   D. If it has a car adapter

6. You are configuring a workstation and are setting the video resolution. After selecting the resolution, the screen goes black. What should you do?

   A. Wait 15 seconds for the image to reappear.

   B. Turn off the monitor and turn it back on.

   C. Reboot the workstation.

   D. Restart the operating system setup wizard.

7. When choosing a tablet computer, which of the following operating systems are most likely to come preinstalled? (Choose two.)

   A. OS X

   B. iOS

   C. Linux

   D. Android

8. What aspect ratio do widescreen computer monitors typically use by default?

   A. 16:9

   B. 16:10

   C. 4:3

   D. 3:2

9. Your friend Joe has decided that he needs a powerful gaming computer with the best technology. Which of the following is the best reason that Joe might consider building his own?

   A. He can choose his own operating system.

   B. There's no additional software to uninstall.

   C. He gets free technical support.

   D. He can choose his hardware components.

10. When configuring a new workstation with Windows 8, you choose the wrong localization setting for this particular user. What is the easiest way to fix this setting?

   A. Delete and reinstall Windows 8.

   B. Reboot the computer and rerun the OS setup wizard.

   C. Change the option in Control Panel.

   D. Use the localization rollback option in the setup wizard configuration utility.

11. Your friend Gloria is a graphic designer and wants your help in selecting a new workstation. Which of the following are likely going to be advanced hardware needs for her line of work? (Choose two.)

   A. Memory

   B. Hard drive

   C. Monitor

   D. Sound card

12. You are installing a new computer and have just created additional user accounts. What is the next step you should perform?

   A. Update security and software.

   B. Configure peripherals.

   C. Configure and verify Internet connection.

   D. Perform cable management tasks.

13. You are building a home theater system. Which components will likely need to be upgraded over a standard workstation?

   A. GPU

   B. CPU

   C. RAM

   D. Network card

14. You are configuring a new workstation for an engineer who has a special printer he needs attached to his system. When should you perform this task?

   A. When plugging in all of the cables

   B. Before installing security software

   C. After installing security software

   D. After configuring and verifying the Internet connection

15. Your friend Daphne is purchasing a new workstation to support her small but growing video production business. What components should she upgrade over a standard workstation? (Choose two.)

   A. CPU

   B. RAM

   C. GPU

   D. HDD

16. You are configuring a new workstation for a user. After configuring the computer to have an Internet connection, what should you do next?

   A. Install additional software (if applicable).

   B. Run software and security updates.

   C. Create other user accounts (if applicable).

   D. Verify the Internet connection.

17. You recently purchased a workstation and brought it home. After unpacking it, what is the first step you should perform to set it up?

   A. Power on the computer.

   B. Perform computer registration.

   C. Plug in the cables.

   D. Configure the Internet connection.

18. A friend of yours bought a computer from a major manufacturer. On it is bundled software that she does not want. When is the appropriate time during the setup process to uninstall this software?

   A. After installing security software

   B. After configuring peripherals

   C. During the initial operating system setup wizard

   D. After configuring and verifying the Internet connection

19. You are setting up five workstations for a small office. After completing the OS configuration process, what is the next step to take?

   A. Install security software.

   B. Configure peripherals.

   C. Create user accounts.

   D. Perform cable management.

20. After purchasing a new Windows laptop, you are beginning to configure it. You don't want to receive reminders to purchase bundled software. What is the recommended way to remove software that you don't want?

   A. Remove it during the initial OS setup wizard.

   B. Delete the icons on the desktop.

   C. Use Control Panel.

   D. Delete and reinstall Windows from the factory backup image.

Chapter
11

Computer Support and Backups

THE FOLLOWING COMPTIA IT FUNDAMENTALS EXAM OBJECTIVES ARE COVERED IN THIS CHAPTER:

✓ **5.3 Given a scenario, implement basic support concepts**

- Check for external issues
  - Loose cables/connections
  - Power
  - Physical damage
- Manufacturer documentation
- Manufacturer websites
- Technical community groups
- Internet search engine
- Contact technical support

✓ **5.4 Explain basic backup concepts**

- Importance of backups
- Scheduling
- Frequency
- Storage mediums
  - Locally attached storage
  - Offsite/cloud-based
  - Network attached storage
- Backup verification and testing

Computer systems, whether they are powerful servers or portable handheld devices, have become an omnipresent part of society today. People use them for business, recreation, entertainment, to stay in touch with friends and family, and multiple other reasons. Ten to fifteen years ago, it was becoming more common for households to have PCs. Now, if you include mobile devices (which you should), most households have several. Computers are so common that we tend to take them for granted—until they don't work like they're supposed to.

This chapter covers two key topics related to dealing with computer problems—troubleshooting and support, and backups. When that inevitable problem happens, you need to be familiar with the best methods to isolate and fix the problem to get the computer up and running as quickly as possible. If the problem is with the hard drive, then what do you do? Hopefully the user backed up their data. Many of us consider data, whether it is financial data or family pictures or something else, to be our most important and irreplaceable assets. Without that backup, a hard drive failure can cause catastrophic loss. In this chapter, you'll learn proper methods for troubleshooting and how to manage computer backups.

Basic Computer Support Concepts

Computer support isn't typically thought of as one of the sexy jobs in IT, but it's definitely one of the most critical and visible jobs. Users don't care how elegant your network design is, how bulletproof your security model is, or how user-friendly your website is if their computer won't boot up. And when it won't boot up, their best friend is the computer support person.

Sometimes you will fix computers in person, while other times you'll deal with challenging situations over the phone. In either case, you need to be prepared to quickly diagnose the problem and implement a solution. The user will be counting on you—and you get to be the hero! Okay, so maybe the user won't treat you like a hero, and there probably won't be a parade in your honor, but you will definitely know that they appreciate your help.

Computer support is synonymous with troubleshooting. To troubleshoot well, you need to understand the theory and process of troubleshooting. This includes the basic concepts and resources that apply in most situations. In addition, there are common scenarios you will encounter—knowing how to solve the common issues will help you think about how to solve the difficult ones as well.

Understanding Troubleshooting Theory

When troubleshooting, you should assess every problem systematically and try to isolate the root cause. Yes, there is a lot of art to troubleshooting, and experience plays a part too. But regardless of how "artful" or experienced you are, haphazard troubleshooting is doomed to fail. Conversely, even technicians with limited experience can be effective troubleshooters if they stick to the principles. The major key is to start with the issue and whittle away at it until you can get down to the point where you can pinpoint the problem—this often means eliminating, or verifying, the obvious.

Although everyone approaches troubleshooting from a different perspective, a few things should remain constant. First, always back up your data before making any changes to a system. Hardware components can be replaced but data often can't be. For that reason, always be vigilant about making data backups.

Second, establish priorities—one user being unable to print to the printer of their choice isn't as important as a floor full of accountants unable to run payroll. Prioritize every job and escalate it (or de-escalate it) as you need to.

Third, but perhaps most important, document everything—not just that there was a problem but also the solution you found, the actions you tried, and the outcomes of each.

Troubleshooting theory can be broken down into the following steps to follow:

- Identify the problem.
- Establish a theory of what's wrong.
- Test the solutions.
- Establish a plan of action to fix the problem.
- Verify functionality.
- Document the findings.

In the next few sections I will take you through each step of the troubleshooting process.

Identifying the Problem

While this may seem obvious, it can't be overlooked: If you can't define the problem, you can't begin to solve it. Sometimes problems are relatively straightforward, but other times they're just a symptom of a bigger issue. For example, if a user isn't able to connect to the Internet from their computer, it could indeed be an issue with their system. But if other users are having similar problems, then the first user's difficulties might just be one example of the real problem.

Ask yourself, "Is there a problem?" Perhaps "the problem" is as simple as a customer expecting too much from the computer.

Problems in computer systems generally occur in one (or more) of four areas, each of which is in turn made up of many pieces:

- A *collection of hardware pieces* integrated into a working system. As you know, the hardware can be quite complex, what with motherboards, hard drives, video cards, and so on. Software can be equally perplexing.

- An *operating system*, which in turn is dependent on the hardware.

- An *application* or software program that is supposed to do something. Programs such as Microsoft Word and Excel are bundled with a great many features.

- A *computer user*, ready to take the computer system to its limits (and beyond). Sometimes it's easy to forget that the user is a very complex and important part of the puzzle.

Talking to the Customer

Many times you can define the problem by asking questions of the user. One of the keys to working with your users or customers is to ensure, much like a medical professional, that you have good bedside manner. Most people are not as technically hip as you, and when something goes wrong they become confused or even fearful that they'll take the blame. Assure them that you're just trying to fix the problem but that they can probably help because they know what went on before you got there. It's important to instill trust with your customer. Believe what they are saying, but also believe that they might not tell you everything right away. It's not that they're necessarily lying; they just might not know what's important to tell.

 Real World Scenario

Is the Power On?

It's a classic IT story that almost sounds like a joke, but it happens. A customer calls technical support because their computer won't turn on. After 20 minutes of troubleshooting, the technician is becoming frustrated...maybe it's a bad power supply? The technician asks the user to read some numbers off of the back of his computer, and the user says, "Hold on, I need to get a flashlight. It's dark in here with the power out."

Help clarify things by having the customer show you what the problem is. The best method I've seen of doing this is to say, "Show me what 'not working' looks like." That way, you see the conditions and methods under which the problem occurs. The problem may be a simple matter of an improper method. The user may be performing an operation incorrectly or performing the operation in the wrong order. During this step, you have the opportunity to observe how the problem occurs, so pay attention.

Here are a few questions to ask the user to aid in determining what the problem is:

Can you show me the problem?   This question is one of the best. It allows the user to show you exactly where and when they experience the problem.

How often does this happen?   This question establishes whether this problem is a one-time occurrence that can be solved with a reboot or whether a specific sequence of events causes the problem to happen. The latter usually indicates a more serious problem that may require software installation or hardware replacement.

Has any new hardware or software been installed recently?   New hardware or software can mean compatibility problems with existing devices or applications. For example, a newly installed device may want to use the same resource settings as an existing device. This can cause both devices to become disabled. When you install a new application, that application is likely to install several support files. If those support files are also used by an existing application, then there could be a conflict.

Has the computer recently been moved?   Moving a computer can cause things to become loose and then fail to work. Perhaps all of the peripherals of the computer didn't complete—or weren't included on—the move, meaning there's less functionality than the user expects.

Has someone who normally doesn't use the computer recently used it?   That person could have mistakenly (or intentionally) done something to make the computer begin exhibiting the irregular behavior.

Have any other changes been made to the computer recently?   If the answer is yes, ask if the user can remember approximately when the change was made. Then ask them approximately when the problem started. If the two dates seem related, there's a good chance the problem is related to the change. If it's a new hardware component, check to see that it was installed correctly.

Be careful of how you ask questions so you don't appear accusatory. You can't assume that the user did something to mess up the computer. Then again, you also can't assume that they don't know anything about why it's not working.

 Real World Scenario

The Social Side of Troubleshooting

When you're looking for clues as to the nature of a problem, no one can give you more information than the person who was there when it happened. They can tell you what led up to the problem, what software was running, and the exact nature of the problem ("It happened when I tried to print"), and they can help you re-create the problem, if possible.

Use questioning techniques that are neutral in nature. Instead of saying, "What were you doing when it broke?" be more compassionate and say, "What was going on when the computer decided not to work?" Frame the question in a way that makes it sound like the computer did something wrong and not the person. It might sound silly, but these things can make your job a lot easier!

While it's sometimes frustrating dealing with end users and computer problems, such as the user who calls you up and gives you the "My computer's not working" line (okay, and what *exactly* is that supposed to mean?), even more frustrating is when no one was around to see what happened. In cases like this, do your best to find out where the problem is by establishing what works and what doesn't work.

Gathering Information

Let's say that you get to a computer and the power light is on and you can hear the hard drive spinning, but there is no video and the system seems to be unresponsive. At least you know that the system has power and you can start investigating where things start to break down. (It sound like there is a reboot in your future!)

The whole key to this step is to identify, as specifically as possible, what the problem is. The more specific you can be in identifying what's not working, the easier it will be for you to understand why it's not working and fix it. If you have users available who were there when the thing stopped working, you can try to gather information from them. If not, you're on your own to gather clues. It's like *CSI* but not as gory.

So now instead of having users to ask questions of, you need to use your own investigative services to determine what's wrong. The questions you would have otherwise asked the user are still a good starting point. Does anything appear amiss or seem to have been changed recently? What is working and what's not? Was there a storm recently? Can I reboot? If I reboot, does the problem seem to go away?

> If a computer seems to have multiple problems that appear to be unrelated, identify what they are one at a time and fix them one at a time. For example, if the sound is not working and you can't get on the Internet, deal with those separately. If they seem related, such as not being able to get on the Internet and you can't access a network file server, then one solution might solve both problems.

The key is to find out everything you can that might be related to the problem. Document exactly what works and what doesn't and, if you can, why. If the power is out in the house, as in the story related earlier, then there's no sense in trying the power plug in another outlet.

DETERMINING IF THE PROBLEM IS HARDWARE OR SOFTWARE RELATED

This step is important because it determines the part of the computer on which you should focus your troubleshooting skills. Each part requires different skills and different tools.

To determine whether a problem is hardware or software related, you can do a few things to narrow down the issue. For instance, does the problem manifest itself when the user uses a particular piece of hardware (a DVD-ROM or USB hard drive, for example)? If it does, the problem is more than likely hardware related, which can also mean a problem with the device driver.

This step relies on personal experience more than any of the other steps do. You'll without a doubt run into strange software problems. Each one has a particular solution.

Some may even require reinstallation of an application or the operating system. If that doesn't work, you may need to resort to restoring the entire system (operating system, applications, and data) from a data backup done when the computer was working properly.

DETERMINING WHICH COMPONENT IS FAILING (FOR HARDWARE PROBLEMS)

Hardware problems are usually pretty easy to figure out. Let's say the sound card doesn't work, you've tried new speakers that you know do work, and you've reinstalled the driver. All of the settings look right but it just won't respond. The sound card is probably the piece of hardware that needs to be replaced.

With many newer computers, several components such as sound, video, and networking cards are integrated into the motherboard. If you troubleshoot the computer and find a hardware component to be bad, there's a good chance that the bad component is integrated into the motherboard and the whole motherboard must be replaced—an expensive proposition, to be sure.

 Laptops and a lot of desktops have components (network card, sound card, video adapter) integrated into the motherboard. If an integrated component fails, you may be able to use an expansion device (such as a USB or PC Card network adapter) to give the system full functionality without a costly repair.

Establishing a Theory

Way back when, probably in your middle school or junior high school years, you learned about the scientific method. In a nutshell, scientists develop a hypothesis, test it, and then figure out if their hypothesis is still valid. Troubleshooting involves much the same process.

Once you have determined what the problem is, you need to develop a theory as to why it is happening. No video? It could be something to do with the monitor or the video card. Can't get to your favorite website? Is it that site? Is it your network card, the cable, your IP address, DNS server settings, or something else? Once you have defined the problem, establishing a theory about the cause of the problem—what is wrong—helps you develop possible solutions to the problem.

Eliminating Possibilities

Theories can either state what can be true or what can't be true. However you choose to approach your theory generation, it's usually helpful to take a mental inventory to see what is possible and what's not. Start eliminating possibilities and eventually the only thing that can be wrong is what's left. This type of approach works well when it's an ambiguous problem; start broad and narrow your scope. For example, if the hard drive won't read, there is likely one of three culprits: the drive itself, the cable it's on, or the connector on the motherboard. Try plugging the drive into the other connector or using a different cable. Narrow down the options.

A common troubleshooting technique is to strip the system down to the bare bones. In a hardware situation, this could mean removing all interface cards except those absolutely required for the system to operate. In a software situation, this usually means booting up in Safe Mode so most of the drivers do not load.

Once you have isolated the problem, slowly rebuild the system to see if the problem comes back (or goes away). This helps you identify what is really causing the problem and determine if there are other factors affecting the situation. For example, I have seen memory problems that are fixed by switching the slot that the memory chips are in.

Using External Resources

Sometimes you can figure out what's not working, but you have no idea why or what you can do to fix it. That's okay. In situations like those, it may be best to fall back on an old trick called reading the manual. As they say, "When all else fails, read the instructions." The service manuals are your instructions for troubleshooting and service information. Virtually every computer and peripheral made today has service documentation on the company's website, or on a DVD, or although unlikely, even in a paper manual. Don't be afraid to use them!

The Internet can be your troubleshooting friend as well. I've joked before that Google knows everything, but if you have a problem or a specific error message, a Google search may give you a solution or point you in the right direction. Besides the manufacturer's documentation and website (which should generally be your first resources), there may be technical community groups that can help. If a similar question to yours has been posted, there could be an answer. If you don't see your problem, post the question on the board. Always remember to be as clear as possible about the problem, and be polite and friendly. No one is going to answer a question if they think you are a troll. If none of that works out, you can always call the manufacturer's technical support line to seek help.

Finally, if you're lucky enough to have experienced, knowledgeable, and friendly co-workers, be open to asking for help if you get stuck on a problem.

Before starting to eliminate possibilities, check the vendor's website for any information that might help you. For example, if you are getting an error message saying, "PC Load Letter" and you don't know what it means, typing it into the vendor's website might take you directly to specific steps to fix the problem.

Testing Solutions

You've eliminated possibilities and developed a theory as to what the problem is. Your theory may be pretty specific, such as "the power cable is fried," or it may be a bit more general, like "the hard drive isn't working" or "there's a connectivity problem." No matter your theory, now is the time to start testing solutions. Again, if you're not sure where to begin to find a solution, the manufacturer's website is a good place to start!

Check the Simple Stuff First

This step is the one that even experienced technicians overlook. Often, computer problems are the result of something simple. Technicians overlook these problems because they're so simple that the technicians assume they *couldn't* be the problem. Here are some examples of simple problems:

Is it plugged in?   And plugged in at both ends? Cables must be plugged in at *both ends* to function correctly. Cables can easily be tripped over and inadvertently pulled from their sockets. Rule number one is to always check the cables first.

 Real World Scenario

"Is It Plugged In?" and Other Insulting Questions

Think about how you feel if someone asks you this question. Your likely response is, "Of course it is!" After all, you're not an idiot, right? You'll often get the same reaction to similar questions about the device being turned on. The reality is, making sure it's plugged in and turned on are the first things you should always do when investigating a problem.

When asking these types of questions, it's not what you say but how you say it. For example, instead of asking if it's plugged in, you could say something like, "Can you do me a favor and check to see what color the end of the keyboard plug is? Is that the same color of the port where it's plugged into on the computer?" That generally gets the user to at least look at it without making them feel dumb. For power, something like, "What color are the lights on the front of the router? Are any of them blinking?" can work well.

Ask neutral and nonthreatening questions. Make it sound like the computer is at fault, not the user. These types of things will help you build rapport and be able to get more information so you can solve problems faster.

Is it turned on?   This one seems the most obvious, but we've all fallen victim to it at one point or another. Computers and their peripherals must be turned on to function. Most have power switches with LEDs that glow when the power is turned on.

Is there physical damage?   Sometimes physical damage is obvious, such as if someone hit a computer with a hammer. Other times it will be more subtle. For example, you might see a brown patch on a motherboard where it got burnt due to a power issue.

Is the system ready?   Computers must be ready before they can be used. *Ready* means the system is ready to accept commands from the user. An indication that a computer is ready is when the operating system screens come up and the computer presents you with a menu or a command prompt. If that computer uses a graphical interface, the computer is ready when the mouse pointer appears. Printers are ready when the Online or Ready light on the front panel is lit.

Do the chips and cables need to be reseated? You can solve some of the strangest problems (random hang-ups or errors) by opening the case and pressing down on each socketed chip, memory module, and expansion card (known as *reseating*). This remedies the chip-creep problem, which happens when computers heat up and cool down repeatedly as a result of being turned on and off, causing some components to begin to move out of their sockets. In addition, you should reseat any cables to make sure they're making good contact.

> Always be sure you're grounded before operating inside the case! If you're not, you could create a static charge (ESD) that could damage components. You will learn more about ESD in Chapter 12, "Environmental and Safety Concepts."

Check to See If It's User Error

User error is common but preventable. If a user can't perform some very common computer task, such as printing or saving a file, the problem is likely due to user error. As soon as you hear of a problem like this, you should begin asking questions to determine if the solution is as simple as teaching the user the correct procedure. A good question to ask is, "Were you *ever* able to perform that task?" If the answer is no, it could mean they are doing the procedure wrong. If they answer yes, you must ask additional questions to get at the root of the problem.

If you suspect user error, tread carefully in regard to your line of questioning to avoid making the user feel defensive. User errors provide an opportunity to teach the users the right way to do things. Again, what you say matters. Offer a "different" or "another" way of doing things instead of the "right" way.

 Real World Scenario

Problems Faxing

Several years ago when I was doing computer support over the phone, I had a user call with a problem with their fax modem. (I told you it was a long time ago!) He said he tried faxing several times, but nothing would ever go through.

I started with the basics, like determining if the computer was on (it was) and the phone line was connected (it was). We even checked the modem to be sure it picked up the line properly and dialed numbers. The hardware seemed fine. My thoughts turned to an issue in the fax software. I had him open the application, verify that he typed in the right phone number, and confirm several other options. Just like with the hardware, everything seemed fine. I was getting really confused as to why it wasn't working.

Finally I started asking the right questions. When I asked what he was trying to fax, he said it was a piece of paper he needed to send to his insurance company. Okay, that's a good start... a piece of paper? I followed up by asking him to walk me through the steps of how he was trying to fax it. He responded by telling me that he opened the fax program and typed in the number. He then held the piece of paper up to the monitor and clicked the Send button on the fax program. And—he thought it was difficult to click the Send button when he couldn't see it because the paper was in the way. But it didn't work.

Clearly, the process he was following wasn't going to work, so it was an opportunity for user education. And while it's always good to start with the basics, such as checking the connections, the moral of the story is to always understand what the user is actually doing when they try to accomplish a task.

Restart the Computer

It's amazing how often a simple computer restart can solve a problem. Restarting the computer clears the memory and starts the computer with a clean slate. If restarting doesn't work, try powering down the system completely and then powering it up again (*rebooting*). More often than not, that will solve the problem.

> If you (or the user) experience a problem on a computer for the first time, reboot the computer and see if the problem goes away. If it does, then you've finished fixing it. If the problem is a persistent one, though, it indicates a larger issue that needs further investigation. There could be failing hardware or an application that needs to be reinstalled.

Establishing a Plan of Action

If your fix worked, then you're brilliant! If not, then you need to reevaluate and look for the next option. After testing possible solutions, your plan of action may take one of three paths:

- If the first fix didn't work, try something else.
- If needed, implement the fix on other computers.
- If everything is working, document the solution.

Try, Try Again

So you tried the hard drive with a new (verified) cable and it still doesn't work. Now what? Your sound card won't play and you've just deleted and reinstalled the driver. Next steps? Move on and try the next logical thing in line.

> When trying solutions to fix a problem, make only one change to the computer at a time. If the change doesn't fix the problem, revert the system to the way it was and then make your next change. Making more than one change at a time is not recommended for two reasons: One, you are never sure which change actually worked. Two, by making multiple changes at once, you might actually cause additional problems.

When evaluating your results and looking for that golden "next step," don't forget other resources you might have available. Use the Internet to look at the manufacturer's website. Read the manual. Talk to your friend who knows everything about obscure hardware (or arcane versions of Windows). When fixing problems, two heads can be better than one.

Spread the Solution

If the problem was isolated to one computer, this step doesn't apply. But some problems you deal with may affect an entire group of computers. For example, perhaps some configuration information was entered incorrectly into the router, giving everyone the wrong configuration. The router is now fixed, but all of the clients need to renew their IP configuration information.

Document the Solution

Once everything is working, you'll need to document what happened and how you fixed it. If the problem looks to be long and complex, I suggest taking notes as you're trying to fix it. It will help you remember what you've already tried and what didn't work. I'll discuss documenting in more depth in the section "Documenting the Work" later in this chapter.

Verifying Functionality

After fixing the system, or all of the systems, affected by the problem, go back and verify full functionality. For example, if the users couldn't get to any network resources, check to make sure they can get to the Internet as well as internal resources.

Some solutions may actually cause another problem on the system. For example, if you update software or drivers, you may inadvertently cause another application to have problems. There's obviously no way you can or should test all applications on a computer after applying a fix, but know that these types of problems can occur. Just make sure that what you've fixed works and that there aren't any obvious signs of something else not working all of a sudden.

Another important thing to do at this time is to implement preventive measures, if possible. If it was a user error, ensure that the user understands ways to accomplish the task that don't cause the error. If a cable melted because it was too close to someone's space heater under their desk, resolve the issue. If the computer overheated because there was an inch of dust clogging the fan...you get the idea.

Documenting the Work

Lots of people can fix problems. But can you remember what you did when you fixed a problem a month ago? Maybe. Can one of your co-workers remember something you did to fix the same problem on that machine a month ago? Unlikely. Always document your work so that you or someone else can learn from the experience. Good documentation of past troubleshooting can save hours of stress in the future.

Documentation can take a few different forms, but the two most common are personal and system based.

Probably the best thing you can do is to always carry a personal notebook and take notes. The type of notebook doesn't matter—use whatever works best for you. The notebook can be a lifesaver, especially when you're new to a job. Write down the problem, what you tried, and the solution. The next time you run across the same or a similar problem, you'll have a better idea of what to try. Eventually you'll find yourself less and less reliant on it, but it's incredibly handy to have!

System-based documentation is useful to both you and your co-workers. Many facilities have server logs of one type or another, conveniently located close to the machine. If someone makes a fix or a change, it gets noted in the log. If there's a problem, it's noted in the log. It's critical to have a log for a few reasons. One, if you weren't there the first time it was fixed, you might not have an idea of what to try and it could take you a long time using trial and error. Two, if you begin to see a repeated pattern of problems, you can make a permanent intervention before the system completely dies.

There are several different forms of system-based documentation. Again, the type of log doesn't matter as long as you use it! Often it's a notebook or a binder next to the system or on a nearby shelf. If you have a rack, you can mount something on the side to hold a binder or notebook. For client computers, one way is to tape an index card to the top or side of the power supply (don't cover any vents!) so if a tech has to go inside the case, they can see if anyone else has been in there to fix something too. In larger environments, there is often an electronic knowledge base or incident repository available for use; it is just as important to contribute to these systems as it is to use them to help diagnose problems.

Troubleshooting Examples

There isn't one single book you can read to learn everything you need to know to troubleshoot every situation. There are just too many pieces of hardware, software applications, operating systems, and security configurations in the market for there to be one comprehensive guide. A lot of what you will know comes from experience. Remember though, even if you're relatively inexperienced, you can still do a good job of troubleshooting by following a disciplined and methodological approach. It isn't always the fastest way but it's the best, and you will get faster as you gain experience.

Knowing that there isn't one book that can cover all troubleshooting scenarios, I am still going to provide some basic examples of issues you might run into and possible solutions. This will give you a good foundation for working on problems. Here, I've created four groups of common types of problems:

- Computer won't boot up
- Operating system errors
- Application failures
- Hardware failures

Computer Won't Boot

Telling someone that a computer won't boot is a pretty general statement. It can mean anything from a hardware failure to an operating system problem. In these scenarios, the key is that the OS won't load. And because the operating system provides the platform from which you launch all the activities you do with a computer, nothing productive can happen until you fix it. Depending on the OS and version, the steps involved for troubleshooting will vary. The following sections present some general guidance and introduce some troubleshooting tools that may be useful.

Nothing on the Monitor

If you turn on the computer and nothing happens—no fan spinning, no nothing—you probably have some type of power problem. Check that the computer is plugged in. A bad motherboard or CPU can also cause the computer to appear dead. Those failures, however, are less likely if the computer has been working in the past than if you're assembling a new one from scratch.

If you hear fans spinning but nothing shows up onscreen, there's probably an issue with the monitor, display adapter, memory, or motherboard. It can be difficult to figure out which of these may be faulty without an error message to guide you. If you have a spare display adapter or memory module, you can try swapping it out, but it may be easier to take the computer to a repair shop at this point.

If you're determined to troubleshoot on your own, a device called a *POST card* may be useful. POST stands for "power-on self-test." Most desktop computers will beep once after a successful POST, where all critical components are checked. If you hear no beeps, or a series of beeps, you might have a hardware problem. A POST card is a circuit board you insert into an open slot in the motherboard, which can help you diagnose the issue. The card displays a two-digit numeric code on its LED to tell you where the system is in the booting process. A book that accompanies the POST card tells what each number represents. When the boot process stalls, read the code on the POST card and look it up to figure out where the boot process has broken down, and that may tell you which component has failed.

Black-Screen or Blue-Screen Error Message

A plain-text error message (gray text on a black screen) is usually a message from the BIOS prior to the OS load. A failed or soon-to-be-failed hard disk most often triggers such a message. The exact wording of the BIOS-thrown error messages varies depending on the BIOS company and version; you may see a message like "Disk Drive Failure" or "No Boot Disk Found."

Although hard-disk errors are the most common errors that appear before the OS load, they aren't the only possible errors at this point. You may see a message that the keyboard has a key stuck, for example, or that there is an error involving RAM.

If the error message appears as gray or white text on a bright blue background, that's a *STOP error.* It's called a STOP because the first word on the screen is usually STOP, and the PC freezes up when it appears, requiring you to power the PC off and back on again to continue. Some techie types call this error a *Blue Screen of Death (BSOD).* This type of error often means that a piece of hardware (usually something like a network adapter, sound card, or modem) is defective or incompatible with your Windows version, but there are also other reasons for STOP errors, specific to the error code that displays.

To diagnose a STOP error, look up the error code on a website that provides a directory of such errors. Here are a few good sources to get you started:

http://www.aumha.org/a/stop.php

http://pcsupport.about.com/od/findbyerrormessage/tp/stop_error_list.htm

Based on what you discover, you may need to remove or replace a hardware component or reinstall or repair the OS.

Windows Won't Load

Windows requires certain files to be present, usable, and in the expected location in order to start up. These files are mostly stored in the C:\Windows\System32 or C:\Windows\SysWOW64 folder, and they include WinLoad.exe, Ntoskrnl.exe, Hal.dll, WinLogon.exe, and others. If any of these files are unavailable, Windows won't load, and an error message will tell you what's missing. You may need to reinstall or repair Windows in order to fix the problem. If you have the setup DVD available for your version of Windows, you may be able to boot into the Recovery Environment (Windows Vista or newer) or the Recovery Console (Windows XP) to repair Windows. (See the section "Using the Recovery Environment" later in this chapter for details.)

Assuming Windows has all the critical files it needs to load, it reads information from the Registry as it boots up. The Registry informs it of the settings to use, what device drivers to load, and what programs should start up automatically in the background. If any of the files called for during this process are unavailable, an error message appears or the boot process simply hangs, usually after the Windows logo has briefly appeared onscreen.

You may be able to boot the PC using Safe Mode, which bypasses all noncritical startup options; if the problem is with one of the noncritical files, that problem will be temporarily disabled enough to start the system. After starting up Windows (in Safe Mode if necessary), if the problem was caused by a recently installed item of hardware or software, you may be able to use System Restore to return the system configuration to its earlier state, undoing whatever action caused the problem to occur.

USING SAFE MODE

When Windows won't start normally, you can often boot into Safe Mode for access to your Windows Desktop. *Safe Mode* is a low-functionality mode that bypasses all optional components, both hardware and software, loading only the minimum required to display the Desktop. You shouldn't use the computer for normal tasks in Safe Mode because of its limited functionality; stay in Safe Mode only long enough to implement whatever fixes are needed to allow Windows to boot normally again.

To enter Safe Mode, restart the computer and, as soon as you see any text on the screen, begin pressing the F8 key. Doing so displays the Advanced Options menu, a text-based menu system. Using the arrow keys, select Safe Mode (or Safe Mode With Networking) from the menu, and press Enter to start the computer in Safe Mode. Or, you can use MSCONFIG (discussed later in this chapter) to boot into Safe Mode as well.

In Safe Mode, the display adapter uses a generic driver, so the screen resolution is very low and uses only a limited color set. Nonessential hardware doesn't work, such as sound cards and modems; and unless you chose Safe Mode With Networking at the Advanced Options menu, the network doesn't work either (and that includes the Internet).

If the computer starts fine in Safe Mode but doesn't start normally, you can assume that the startup problem lies in one of the nonessential hardware drivers or software applications that Safe Mode blocks from starting. From here it's just a matter of elimination.

Here are some things to try once you're in Safe Mode:

- Disconnect all nonessential external hardware devices, such as modems, external hard disks, webcams, and so on. Try to boot normally. If you can, then plug the devices back in one at a time, rebooting after each one, until you find the one with the problem.

- If you've recently installed new internal hardware, remove it and see if the problem goes away.

- If you've recently installed a new application, remove it using the Control Panel (see Chapter 4, "Software Applications") and reboot to see if the problem goes away.

- Use System Restore, as described in the next section, to return your computer to an earlier configuration point before the problem started.

- Run the System Configuration utility (MSCONFIG), as described later in this chapter, to prevent all noncritical applications from loading at startup. Then re-enable them one by one, rebooting each time, until you find the problem.

Exercise 11.1 shows you how to boot into Safe Mode.

EXERCISE 11.1

Booting into Safe Mode in Windows 7

1. Restart your PC, and as soon as you hear the single beep and see text on the screen, start pressing the F8 key. The Advanced Options menu opens.

2. Press the down-arrow key to highlight Safe Mode With Networking, and press Enter. The system starts up in Safe Mode.

3. Explore Safe Mode, looking for differences from normal operation.

4. Restart the computer normally.

USING SYSTEM RESTORE

The *System Restore* feature in Windows makes a backup copy of the important system configuration files once a day (by default), called a *restore point*. You can also make additional copies at any time, such as immediately before you install new and untried hardware or software. Then, if the system doesn't work anymore after you install the new item, you can revert the system files to the earlier versions, removing all traces of anything the new item may have brought with it.

 System Restore backs up Windows configuration files only, not personal data files!

If Windows won't start normally, or if it runs poorly all of a sudden after previously running fairly well, it's often easier to revert to a System Restore point than to spend a lot of time trying to pinpoint what happened. Start System Restore from the Start menu (Start ➤ All Programs ➤ Accessories ➤ System Tools ➤ System Restore). Then follow the prompts to select a previously saved restore point and restore that copy. Exercise 11.2 provides an opportunity to try this.

EXERCISE 11.2

Using System Restore in Windows 7

1. Open the System app in Control Panel (it may be in System And Security ➤ System).

2. In the navigation pane at the left, click System Protection. The System Properties dialog box opens with the System Protection tab displayed, as shown in Figure 11.1.

FIGURE 11.1 System Protection

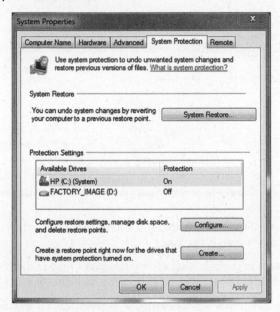

3. Click the Create button. A System Protection dialog box opens.

4. Type **Test 1** in the text box.

5. Click Create to create the restore point, and wait for the restore point to be created. It should take a minute or two.

6. Click Close to close the message box that tells you the restore point was created.

7. Close all open windows and dialog boxes.

8. Right-click the Desktop, and click Personalize.

9. Choose a different Desktop background, and then close Control Panel.

10. Choose Start ➤ All Programs ➤ Accessories ➤ System Tools ➤ System Restore. The System Restore application opens.

11. Click Next to continue.

12. In the list of restore points, click Test 1, as shown in Figure 11.2.

FIGURE 11.2   Choosing a restore point

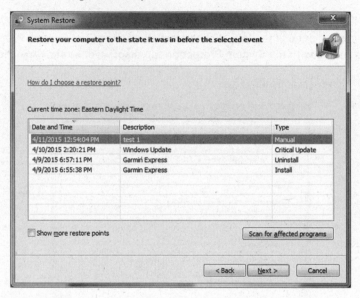

13. Click Next, and then click Finish. A warning appears that once started, System Restore can't be interrupted. Click Yes.

14. Wait for your system to restart. After it restarts, click Close to dismiss the dialog box that tells you the System Restore operation completed successfully.

15. Choose Start ➤ All Programs ➤ Accessories ➤ System Tools ➤ System Restore. The System Restore application opens.

16. Click Next to continue.

17. In the list of restore points, click Restore Operation. Notice that its type is Manual; you're going to undo the System Restore you just did.

18. Click Next, and then click Finish. A warning appears that, once started, System Restore can't be interrupted. Click Yes.

19. Wait for your system to restart. After it restarts, click Close to dismiss the confirmation dialog box.

USING THE SYSTEM CONFIGURATION UTILITY

The *System Configuration utility*, also known by its executable filename of *MSCONFIG*, allows Windows users to selectively disable certain applications and services that automatically load at startup. This can be a great benefit when you're trying to troubleshoot a startup problem that you're fairly sure involves one of your startup applications, but you have no idea which one.

This utility isn't found in the Windows menu system, so you have to run it using its name. Click the Start button, type **MSCONFIG**, and press Enter to open the System Configuration window shown in Figure 11.3. It's available in Safe Mode too.

FIGURE 11.3   System Configuration utility

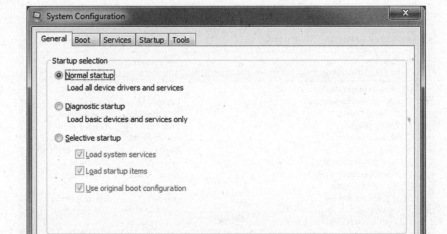

Notice that by default, Normal Startup is selected. That means everything that the Registry specifies should be loaded is loaded. The alternatives are Diagnostic Startup (which turns off everything nonessential and is useful in determining, in general, whether something loading at startup is causing the problem) and Selective Startup (which starts up using only the specific items you haven't excluded).

The Startup tab is the main feature of this utility. Click Startup to see a list of all the programs that load at startup. The length of the list may surprise you. You can drag the column widths to widen them so that you can see the text in them more clearly. The names, manufacturers, and commands can give you clues as to each program's origin and purpose. You can also use an online resource, such as the Task List reference found at www.answersthatwork.com. Exercise 11.3 walks you through how to use System Configuration.

EXERCISE 11.3

Using the System Configuration Utility in Windows 7

1. In Windows 7, click Start, type **MSCONFIG**, and press Enter. The System Configuration window opens.

2. Click the Startup tab.

3. Widen the Startup Item column by dragging the divider between the column headings until you can see all the names in that column, as shown in Figure 11.4.

FIGURE 11.4 MSCONFIG Startup tab

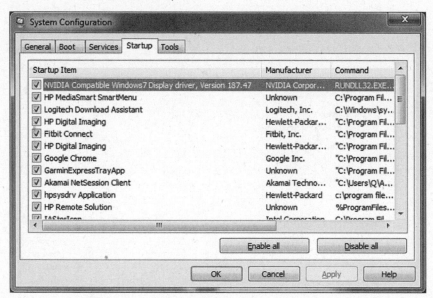

4. Clear the check mark next to one of the items. Pick any one you like, because you aren't actually going to apply your changes.

5. Click the General tab. Notice that Selective Startup has been marked. It became marked when you cleared the check box in step 4. Notice that Load System Services is still checked, and the Load Startup Items check box is solid blue, indicating that some but not all startup items are marked.

6. Click the Services tab, and clear one of the check boxes there.

7. Click back to the General tab. Notice that now the Load System Services check box is solid blue too, indicating that some but not all services are marked.

8. Click the Normal Startup option button to clear the changes you made.

9. Click the Tools tab, as shown in Figure 11.5. Notice that many of the troubleshooting tools available in Windows 7 are also available here from the central point, including Action Center, Windows Troubleshooting, and Event Viewer.

FIGURE 11.5 MSCONFIG Tools tab

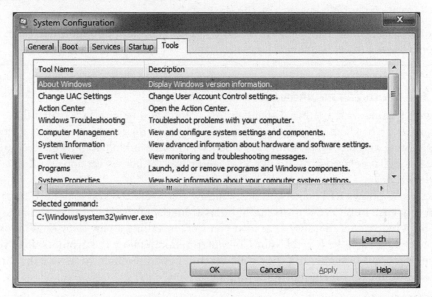

10. Click Cancel to close the System Configuration utility without making any changes.

 You might want to go through the list of items on your Startup tab to see what's loading when you boot. There might be applications starting that you are unaware of and might not want on your computer. In addition, the more items you load on startup, the slower your operating system will boot. Some items are critical, but if they're not, you can speed up the boot process by disabling them from starting up automatically.

This utility not only provides easy access to your startup options but also offers links to many of the most commonly used troubleshooting utilities in Windows. Therefore you may want to create a shortcut for it on your Desktop. Exercise 11.4 shows you how.

EXERCISE 11.4

Creating a Desktop Shortcut for MSCONFIG

1. Right-click the Desktop, and choose New ≻ Shortcut. The Create Shortcut dialog box opens.

2. In the Type The Location Of The Item text box, type **MSCONFIG**. Click Next.

EXERCISE 11.4 *(continued)*

3. In the Type A Name For This Shortcut text box, type **System Configuration Utility**, replacing the default name that's there.

4. Click Finish. A shortcut appears on the Desktop.

5. Double-click the shortcut to confirm that it opens the System Configuration utility. Then close the utility window.

USING THE RECOVERY ENVIRONMENT

Windows XP came with a rather difficult-to-use command-line interface called the *Recovery Console*, which you could use to access the hard disk and run a limited set of troubleshooting and recovery commands when Windows wouldn't start. The Recovery Console has been replaced in Windows Vista and newer Windows versions with the *Windows Recovery Environment (Windows RE)*.

To access Windows RE, boot from the Windows setup DVD. (You may need to change the boot sequence in BIOS Setup so that it boots from the DVD drive rather than the hard disk.) The Windows Setup utility runs as if you were installing a new copy of Windows. When prompted, click the Repair Your Computer option. Follow the prompts until you get to System Recovery Options, and then click Startup Repair. Follow the advice that Startup Repair gives to repair your Windows installation.

Mac OS X Won't Load

Macs go through the same basic process for startup as PCs. If there's a disk error, such as the ones on the black screen that a PC's BIOS may display, you'll see a flashing question-mark icon.

The flashing question-mark icon means the startup process can't find a hard disk or can't find a system folder on the hard disk. The hard disk may be disconnected, its driver may be bad, or its cable may be loose; or if it's an old enough system to still have a floppy disk drive, there may be a disk in that drive that the OS is trying to boot from instead of the hard disk.

On a Mac, the hard drive must have a System folder that contains such items as accessories, fonts, and system utilities, plus the System file and Finder. Without these, the computer won't boot. The question-mark icon appears if this folder is missing or corrupted or doesn't contain the needed files.

Any other OS problem on a Mac results in a red circle with a diagonal line through it, called a *prohibition icon*. (Earlier versions of the Mac OS used a "sad Mac" icon in these cases.) Along with this icon, you'll see an error code that you can look up online. Try a Google search or the Apple support website.

Operating System Error Messages

Each OS has its own error messages that it displays in various circumstances. In most cases, you can look up these error messages online at the OS maker's website or third-party sites to determine what they mean.

For example, to troubleshoot issues with Mac OS X, see the article "Isolating Issues in Mac OS X" on Apple's support knowledge base: `https://support.apple.com/en-us/HT203161`.

Other OS manufacturers will have their own support sites as well, listing common error messages and fixes. Here are a few Windows error messages you may encounter and what they mean:

Windows Has Recovered From A Serious Error   This message means something major has crashed, and Windows has restarted itself as a result. If you see this error once, it's probably a fluke; but if you see it frequently, you may need to repair Windows or take a critical look at what programs are loading at startup that may be causing the error.

The System Is Low On Virtual Memory. Windows Is Increasing The Size Of Your Virtual Memory Paging File.   This message describes what is happening when your system has run out of memory. Do you have too many applications running for the amount of memory installed? As a result, Windows increases the paging file size so that it won't happen again (presumably). If the PC is running slowly, try rebooting.

Data Error Reading/Writing Drive   This message means Windows is having trouble reading from or writing to whatever drive letter it lists in the error message. Run CHKDSK (it's called Error Checking on the drive's Properties dialog box on the Tools tab), and select the Scan For And Attempt Recovery Of Bad Sectors check box to assess the drive.

A Runtime Error Has Occurred. Do You Wish To Debug?   This is an Internet Explorer error message, normally caused by badly written code being delivered from the website. It isn't your PC's fault. If you find this message annoying, you can change a setting in Internet Explorer to prevent it from appearing. From Control Panel, choose Network And Internet, and then Internet Options. On the Advanced tab, in the Browsing section, select the Disable Script Debugging (Internet Explorer) check box.

The Event Viewer utility in Windows can sometimes provide information about an error event that has occurred, helping you to narrow down what may have caused it. You can access the Event Viewer from the Control Panel in the Administrative Tools section.

OS Slowdown or Lockup

Sometimes you may be working along in your OS when, all of a sudden, everything slows to a crawl. Simple things like opening an application and closing a window take much longer than usual. There are two basic reasons why slowdowns happen. One is that the physical memory is mostly used up, so the system is relying more on its paging file than usual. Because the paging file is on the hard disk, and the hard disk is slower than real RAM, operations involving heavy use of the paging file take longer. The other reason is that the CPU is being heavily used, so each operation that needs the CPU's attention has to wait its turn.

That begs the question: what causes the RAM and/or the CPU to be used heavily? They can be legitimately used by applications if you run a lot of applications at once, especially those that require a lot of processing power. Big graphics-editing programs like

Photoshop qualify, for example. The RAM and CPU can also be improperly hijacked by a malfunctioning program or by a virus or other malware application.

When you first start up the OS, it's normal for application-related activities to take longer than normal, because the OS continues to finish loading behind the scenes for up to several minutes after the OS interface becomes usable. If you try to start up several applications immediately after starting the PC, and they don't start up quickly enough to suit you, be patient. Within a few minutes, your computer should be running normally.

To check the memory and CPU usage in Windows, use the Task Manager. Right-click the taskbar, and choose Start Task Manager. Then, on the Processes tab, sort by the Memory column and look for a process that is using an inordinate amount of memory. Terminate it if necessary to get back normal control of your computer. You can also look on the Performance tab to see the RAM and CPU usage statistics.

If the OS locks up completely, usually including the mouse pointer, the most common cause is overheating. If the CPU or another chip on the motherboard overheats, the system locks up. The OS can lock up like that for other reasons than overheating, such as a corrupted system file (repair the OS to fix that), but that's less likely. By halting rather than continuing to operate in an overheated state, the motherboard preserves the valuable CPU chip, which may be damaged if it continued to run. The monitor may go blank, or it may keep displaying the last information it was sent, so the image on the screen appears frozen in time.

If your OS has locked up, shut off the PC if it didn't shut itself down. Open the case, and let the PC sit for 10 to 15 minutes so everything cools off. Then, with the case open, turn on the computer again and see whether any fans aren't spinning. The problem may be as simple as a faulty fan. There should be a fan inside the power supply, a fan on (or very near) the CPU, and possibly other fans that circulate air through the case. No faulty fans? Let the PC boot up the OS again, and let it sit. Don't run any applications. If it boots up just fine but then locks up after a few minutes without you doing anything to it, something is definitely overheating.

Application Failures

Applications are more likely to cause problems than OSs, because there are so many different applications, all made by different manufacturers, and all expected to play nicely with each other, with your hardware, and with different versions of the OS.

Application Fails to Install or Fails to Run

Usually, when an application fails to install or fails to run, it's because it's somehow incompatible with your system. It could be that your OS version isn't supported or the application doesn't like a piece of hardware you've installed (most likely the sound or display adapter). The hardware may be inadequate (check the minimum requirements for the application) or simply incompatible.

Check the application's specs to make sure your system meets the minimum requirements in every way. If your system meets the requirements but the application still won't install, check out the Support section of the application manufacturer's website. There may be a patch you can download that will fix the problem, or there may be suggestions regarding workarounds. For example, in some cases, installing an updated driver for your display adapter or sound card can make an application work that previously didn't.

If the program meets all the hardware requirements but not the OS requirements, you can try running the Setup program in *compatibility mode* (in Windows). Compatibility mode tricks the application into thinking you have a different version of the OS than you actually have, bypassing any version requirements that may be built into the software. It doesn't always work, because different applications implement version requirements in various ways, and some of those ways have nothing to do with the version-specific bits and pieces that compatibility mode offers the application.

Another possible source of trouble when installing applications is overzealous security. The OS itself may prevent you from installing an application, for example. If you're logged in as a standard user, you may need to log out and then log in again as an administrator. If the application being installed requires Internet access to complete the installation, you may need to tell your firewall that it's OK to let that application through. And finally, the application may make a system change that your antivirus program or security suite detects as a threat (falsely), causing the security program to prevent the change from being made. Exercise 11.5 shows you how to run an application in compatibility mode in Windows 7.

EXERCISE 11.5

Running an Application in Compatibility Mode

1. In Windows, choose Start ➤ All Programs, and then right-click an application and choose Properties. The Properties dialog box opens for that shortcut. You should not choose an application that is preinstalled with the OS (such as Paint or Calculator) because for these you may not be able to set Compatibility.

2. Click the Compatibility tab.

3. Select the Run This Program In Compatibility Mode For check box.

4. Open the drop-down list below the check box, and examine the available OSs. Click Windows 98 / Windows Me.

5. In the Settings area, select the Run In 256 Colors check box, as shown in Figure 11.6.

FIGURE 11.6   Configuring an application for compatibility mode

6. Click OK.

7. Select Start ➢ All Programs again, and click the program to run it. It may run, or it may not. It doesn't matter; you're just testing.

8. Close the application (if it ran).

9. Choose Start ➢ All Programs, and then right-click the same application and choose Properties again.

10. Click the Compatibility tab, and clear the Run This Program In Compatibility Mode For check box.

11. Clear the Run In 256 Colors check box.

12. Click OK to close the Properties box.

A Previously Working Application Won't Work Anymore

If an application stops working that previously worked, something has changed on your system—obviously. But what was it? If any of the files belonging to the application have been deleted, you may need to reinstall the application. To save yourself some time, though, look in the Recycle Bin first and see if you may be able to restore the deleted files from there. If you put all the files back where they belong, the application may start working again.

A virus infection can cause programs to run slowly, poorly, or not at all. Many viruses affect the entire system, though, not just one program. Thus, if you're having troubles with only one application, a virus isn't likely to be the cause. There's one exception to that: viruses sometimes target antivirus software specifically, so if everything's working other than your antivirus software, you're probably infected.

Some programs have limited-time licenses, so it's possible that an application that previously worked may stop working due to a license expiration. In such cases, though, a helpful dialog box will usually appear to let you know how to pay the software maker, so there's not much doubt what's happening.

If you've recently installed an OS or application update, and then suddenly an old familiar application won't work anymore, it's probably the update's fault. You can try removing the update (if possible), or contact the application manufacturer's support department for help.

Application Crashes

Crash is the term used to describe a situation when an application stops working. It may stop working due to a programming error in its own code or due to a conflict or compatibility issue with a device driver, with the OS, or with another application.

When an application stops working, it may terminate all by itself, or you may have to terminate it manually. To do so in Windows, right-click the taskbar and choose Start Task Manager. Then, in the Task Manager window, on the Applications tab, click the application. The task may have Not Responding in the Status column. Click End Task.

On a Mac, to force-quit an application, choose Force Quit from the Apple menu (or press Command+Option+Esc) and then select the unresponsive application in the Force Quit window and click Force Quit.

If an application crashes only once, it may be a fluke. However, if the same application keeps crashing repeatedly, it's time to do a little detective work to try to figure out what may be the problem. If an error message appears, make a note of it. Try closing all other applications, including any background applications you don't need, and running the application again to see if that helps. If it does, the problem stems from a conflict with some other program. You may need to uninstall and reinstall the crashing application or check the manufacturer's website for troubleshooting tips.

Device Failures

Any hardware component can fail, and the longer you keep your computer, the more likely it is that you'll experience at least one hardware failure. Usually you'll know a device has failed simply because functionality you were expecting to work doesn't work.

Hardware/Driver Compatibility

A *driver* is a file (or set of files) that contains information needed for the OS to communicate with a hardware device. One way to think of a driver is as a language translator between the OS, which speaks one language, and the hardware, which speaks an entirely different one.

The skill of the interpreter makes all the difference in any communication, and a driver that can accurately translate between the OS and the hardware is essential for satisfactory hardware functionality. Therefore, it's important to pick the best driver available. If an unsatisfactory driver is installed (perhaps one that's not designed specifically for the OS or device being used or one that has been corrupted), the device may behave strangely or not work at all.

The best driver is one that is (1) specifically for that device (most important), (2) specifically for that OS (moderately important), and (3) the most recent version available (least important).

When you install a hardware device, you have a choice of drivers, and your challenge is to figure out which of them fits the criteria the best. Your choices may include the following:

- The OS may supply a driver for the device and install it automatically.

- The device may come with a setup CD or DVD that contains an appropriate driver.

- A driver may be available on the device manufacturer's website that is even more current than the one that came with the device.

If the device has never worked, the driver is a good place to start. If it was working but just stopped, it's more than likely not a driver issue, unless the driver was somehow uninstalled.

Malfunctioning Input Devices

An input device, such as a keyboard or mouse, may malfunction for a variety of reasons. For example, the wrong driver may be installed for it (see the previous section), or it may be incompatible with your OS. For example, some mice and trackballs are specifically designed for Macintosh computers, and they won't work if you plug them into a Windows-based PC.

After you've eliminated incompatibility and bad drivers as the cause of an input device malfunction, next look at the device itself. Is there anything physically wrong with it? If it's an optical mouse, does the light turn on? (It could be a dead battery.) If it's a keyboard, will all the keys press? Is the cord or connector damaged? Has something spilled on the device? Has it been dropped or hit?

If there's nothing physically wrong with the device, try plugging it into a different computer if possible. If it works there, then the problem is the relationship between the device and the original computer and not the device itself. Investigate things like driver issues, incompatibility, and the connector on the PC into which the device connects. If it doesn't work on the other computer, the device is probably defective.

An input device that gradually stops working well over time or that malfunctions only in a specific way (such as a certain key not working on a keyboard or a mouse that moves in only one direction) may be dirty. Try cleaning the device.

Troubleshooting Network Connectivity

Hardware is often, but not always, to blame when a user can't log onto the local network or can't connect to the Internet. Here are some general troubleshooting tips:

1. If you can't browse network resources:

   a. Confirm that the computer's network adapter is installed and working. In Windows, look in Device Manager to make sure it's there and doesn't report any errors.

   b. Confirm that a cable or wireless connection is established between the network adapter and the router, switch, or wireless access point. If it's a wired connection, trace the cable from the PC to the router or switch. If wireless, check to make sure the OS recognizes the wireless connection.

   c. Make sure the right networking protocols are in place (TCP/IP being the most common). Exercise 11.6 shows you how to do this in Windows and how to use TCP/IP to troubleshoot an Internet connection problem.

2. If your network login keeps getting rejected on a corporate network:

   a. Check that Caps Lock isn't on and that you're typing your username and password accurately.

   b. Check with your network administrator to make sure there are no known problems with the network that may be preventing everyone from logging on (not just you).

   c. Check with the network administrator to ensure that the account has not been locked out, for example, due to a number of incorrect login attempts.

3. If the problem is lack of Internet connectivity:

   a. You may need to reset or power-cycle your cable or DSL modem.

   b. Your Internet service provider (ISP) may be temporarily unavailable. Sometimes there are brief outages with even the most reliable services. Wait it out for a few hours before contacting your ISP.

   c. The Internet itself may be experiencing temporary delays or outages. This is likely the case if you can get to some but not all websites, or you can get email but not web access, or vice versa.

EXERCISE 11.6

Checking TCP/IP Connectivity

1. In Windows, open a command prompt window. To do so, click Start, type **cmd**, and press Enter. You can also do this exercise on Linux or Mac systems by opening a command prompt.

2. At the command prompt, type **ping 127.0.0.1** and press Enter, as shown in Figure 11.7. 127.0.0.1 is the loopback address, that is, the IP address that refers to the machine that is issuing the command. If you get a reply from this command, you know your network adapter is working. This eliminates all problems within the PC from the troubleshooting process. You can also type **ping localhost** to get the same results.

EXERCISE 11.6 *(continued)*

FIGURE 11.7 Pinging the loopback address

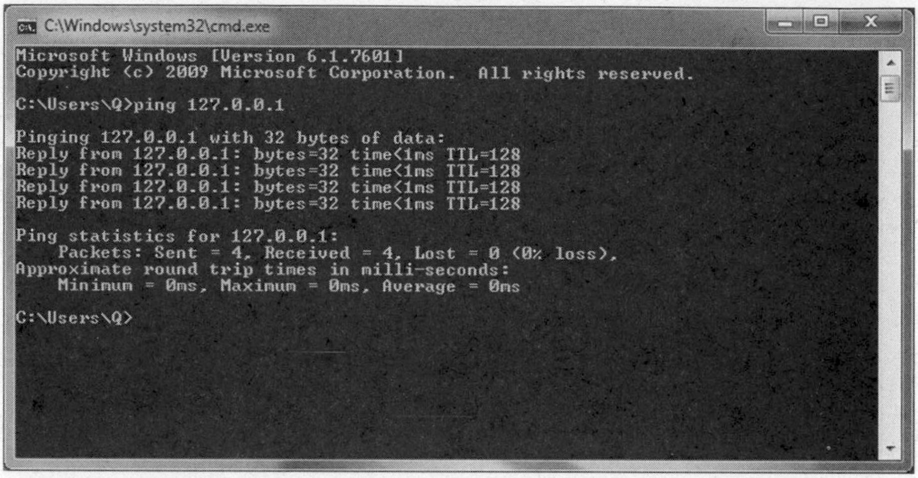

3. At the command prompt, type **ipconfig** and press Enter. The IP addresses for all the network adapters in your system appear. Some of them may show Media Disconnected, meaning that adapter isn't in use. (Mac and Linux computers will use **ifconfig** instead.)

4. Find the network adapter you use to connect to the network, and look at the IPv4 address for it. For example, in Figure 11.8, it's 192.168.1.144. IP addresses that begin with 192.168 are common on small home networks.

FIGURE 11.8 Ipconfig output

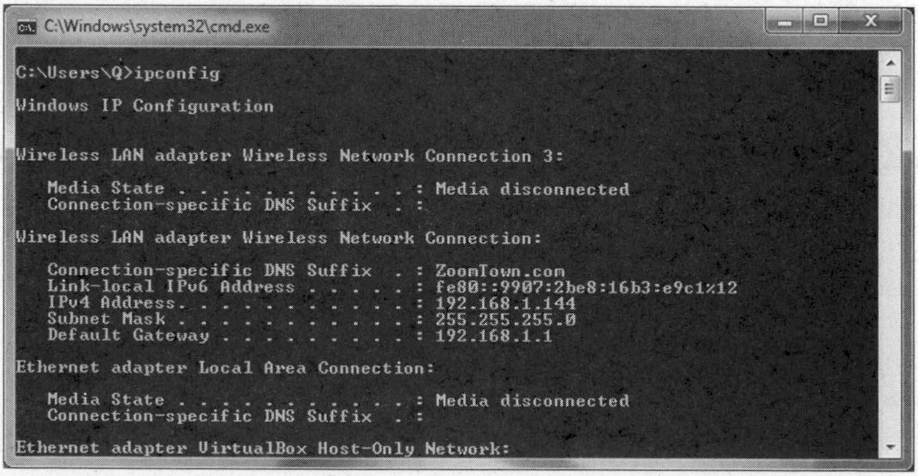

5. For that same network adapter, make a note of the default gateway. That's the address of the router that provides the exit point from the local network and connects you to the larger network (for example, the Internet). In the previous figure, it's 192.168.1.1.

6. Ping the default gateway to make sure it's reachable. To do this, type **ping**, a space, and then the address of the default gateway that you noted in step 5—for example, **ping 192.168.1.1**. If the default gateway is reachable, you should get back multiple Reply lines. If not, you'll get back multiple Timed Out lines.

7. Ping a website to see if you have web connectivity. To do so, type **ping**, a space, and then either an IP address or a URL of a website. For example, type **ping www.google.com** and press Enter, as shown in Figure 11.9.

FIGURE 11.9   Successful ping results

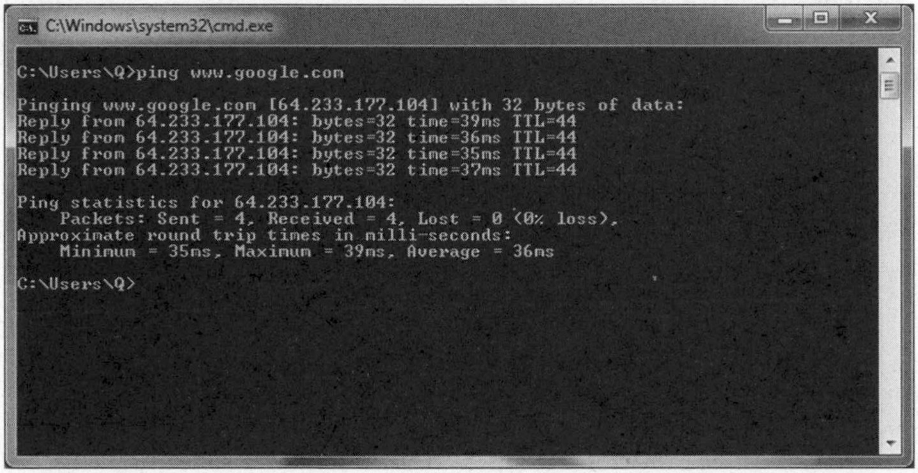

```
C:\Windows\system32\cmd.exe

C:\Users\Q>ping www.google.com

Pinging www.google.com [64.233.177.104] with 32 bytes of data:
Reply from 64.233.177.104: bytes=32 time=39ms TTL=44
Reply from 64.233.177.104: bytes=32 time=36ms TTL=44
Reply from 64.233.177.104: bytes=32 time=35ms TTL=44
Reply from 64.233.177.104: bytes=32 time=37ms TTL=44

Ping statistics for 64.233.177.104:
    Packets: Sent = 4, Received = 4, Lost = 0 (0% loss),
Approximate round trip times in milli-seconds:
    Minimum = 35ms, Maximum = 39ms, Average = 36ms

C:\Users\Q>
```

If you don't get a reply from the first site you try, try some other addresses. Some websites block ping inquiries as a matter of company policy.

8. If you can't get through to a particular website, you can use another command, **tracert** (short for "trace route"), to see the hops the message takes from router to router across the Internet. This can help you see where the transmission is breaking down. Type **tracert google.com**, and press Enter. Information comes back about each of the routers the message passes through on the way, up to a maximum of 30 hops. Your results will look different than the one shown in Figure 11.10, because your computer will take a different path to Google's servers than mine did.

FIGURE 11.10 Successful tracert results

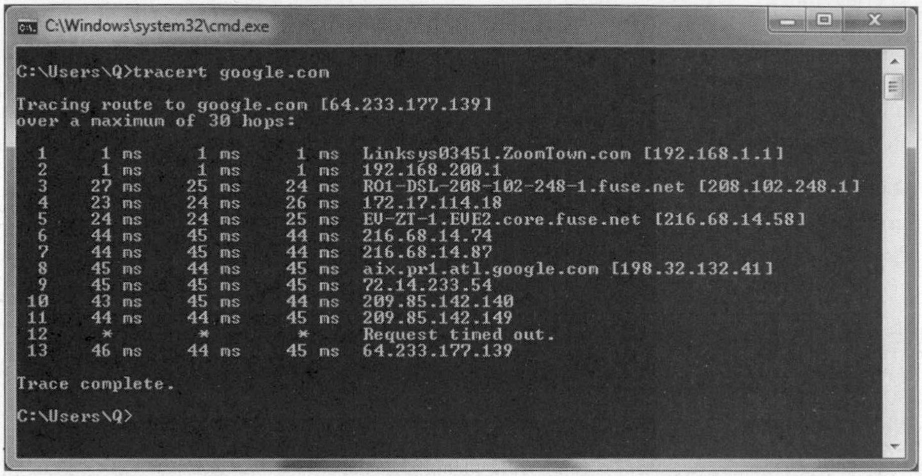

```
C:\Windows\system32\cmd.exe

C:\Users\Q>tracert google.com

Tracing route to google.com [64.233.177.139]
over a maximum of 30 hops:

  1     1 ms     1 ms     1 ms  Linksys03451.ZoomTown.com [192.168.1.1]
  2     1 ms     1 ms     1 ms  192.168.200.1
  3    27 ms    25 ms    24 ms  RO1-DSL-208-102-248-1.fuse.net [208.102.248.1]
  4    23 ms    24 ms    26 ms  172.17.114.18
  5    24 ms    24 ms    25 ms  EU-ZT-1.EUE2.core.fuse.net [216.68.14.58]
  6    44 ms    45 ms    44 ms  216.68.14.74
  7    44 ms    45 ms    44 ms  216.68.14.87
  8    45 ms    44 ms    45 ms  aix.pr1.atl.google.com [198.32.132.41]
  9    45 ms    45 ms    45 ms  72.14.233.54
 10    43 ms    45 ms    44 ms  209.85.142.140
 11    44 ms    44 ms    45 ms  209.85.142.149
 12     *         *         *   Request timed out.
 13    46 ms    44 ms    45 ms  64.233.177.139

Trace complete.

C:\Users\Q>
```

9. Close the command prompt window.

Computer Backups

Simply put, your data is probably the most important thing you have. Hardware can be replaced, but if you lose your data, you could be in serious trouble. From a personal standpoint, you could lose important pictures or other information you can never replace. For businesses, large-scale data losses often lead to catastrophic results.

The way to prevent total data loss is to ensure that you are backing up your data. A *backup* is a restorable copy of any set of data that is needed on the system. Sometimes you will hear people call it an archive, but technically an *archive* is any collection of data that is removed from the system because it's no longer needed on a regular basis.

If you work for a company, that organization's *backup policy* dictates what information should be backed up and how it should be backed up. If you are only concerned with your own system, you should still create a plan for backups, including what type you will make and how often you'll make them. Along with making the backup, you also need to consider who can get to the backup. If data is valuable enough to spend the resources required to back it up, it is clearly important enough to protect carefully.

When considering a backup solution, the following questions are pertinent:

▪ How often do you plan to back up? For business-critical data, every day is appropriate. For casual home users and their personal files, once a week or even once a month may be enough.

- How large are the files? Backing up a large amount of data takes more time and takes up more disk space. You may choose to back up large files like videos and music less often than other files for this reason.

- What backup software is available? Many different applications will do local and online backups and system images. Some have more features and higher price tags than others.

- Should each backup recopy all files, or should there be smaller backups done that copy only files that have changed?

Understanding the Importance of Backups

Computer users often take their data for granted, forgetting the large quantity of important and irreplaceable documents, images, and music files they collect over the years. A hard disk failure or virus can wipe out years of stored memories, not to mention files of significant value to a business.

There are many ways to ensure that a system failure doesn't result in data loss. For example, you can use a multi-disk RAID system to protect against data loss caused by a physical hard disk failure by mirroring a drive (RAID 1) or striping data across multiple drives (RAID 5). RAID isn't enough, though, because multiple hard disk failures will still doom you. Even if you use RAID, you should perform backups of your data.

 Real World Scenario

The Importance of Data

Several years ago when I did technical support, I received a call from a user with hard drive problems. After some quick troubleshooting, I determined that his hard drive had failed and would need to be replaced. After telling him the news, he asked, "So how do I get my data back?" I asked if he had backed up his data, and he had not.

He was a doctoral student in his final year, and his dissertation was stored on that hard drive. (Key word: *was.*) He had no backups. I could hear the desperation and agony in his voice as he frantically sought options to get his data back. He had spent years of his life hard at work on something that was now gone—simply gone. Had he taken a few moments to back up the data, there would have been no problems. At the time, data recovery cost several hundred dollars per megabyte.

Now, data recovery companies that will take damaged hard drives and attempt to recover data from them are not as expensive as they used to be, but their services are not cheap. Some of the least expensive online services cost $200–300, and others can cost several thousand dollars. Back up your data, and you won't have to feel the sting of paying that cost.

While the general theme of this section is "Back up your data," it might not be necessary based on the situation. If what's on the hard drive is unimportant and it's not a big deal to lose it, then don't bother backing up. This could be the case for a public workstation. Otherwise, it's a critical step that most people forget to do.

Understanding How Backups Work

Backup programs generally work by looking at an attribute of the file known as an *archive bit*. When a file is created or modified, the archive bit is set to 1, indicating that the file has not been backed up in its current state. When a backup is made, that archive bit may be cleared—that is, set back to 0—to indicate that the file has been backed up. Some backup types do not clear the archive bit.

There are a couple of quick and easy ways you can see if the archive bit for a file is or is not set. The first is in Windows Explorer. Navigate to a file, such as a Word document, right-click it, and choose Properties. At the bottom of the General tab, you will see an Advanced button. Click the Advanced button to display a window like the one in Figure 11.11.

FIGURE 11.11   Advanced file attributes

If the File Is Ready For Archiving box is checked, that means that the archive bit is set. If you uncheck the box, then the archive bit is set back to 0.

The second way is from a command prompt. In a directory, type **attrib** and press Enter. You will see a directory listing. If off to the left of the filename you see the letter *A*, that means that the archive bit is set. The attrib command can be used to clear and set this bit. For help with this, type **attrib /?** at the command prompt.

Understanding Backup Options

When performing a data backup, you will have several decisions to make on various options. The first is which backup program you want to use. Windows comes with a backup utility, named Windows Backup, which will meet the needs of most users. There are also network-based backup programs that can back up multiple systems across a network. Finally, online and cloud-based backup utilities have gained significant popularity over the last few years.

Other options you will need to think about are the type of backup you want to perform, the location in which you will store the backup files, and frequency and scheduling of backups.

Backup Types

Some backup programs are rather simplistic in the types of backups they offer—you choose the files to back up, and they get backed up. Others give you far more options as to how you want to back things up. Windows Backup, for example, gives you two options (Figure 11.12): Let Windows Choose or Let Me Choose. The intent for most backup programs is to back up user files and not standard files that the operating system requires to run.

FIGURE 11.12 Windows Backup options

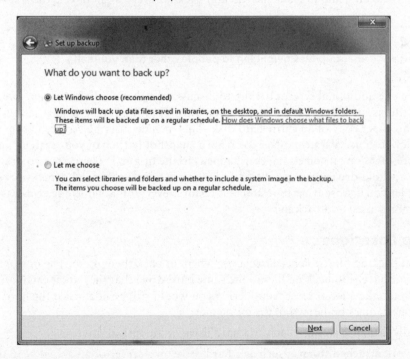

Other programs give you far greater options on the type of backup you want to do. In general, there are five different types of backups you can perform:

Normal Backs up selected files and clears the archive bit. Takes the longest to back up but is the fastest to restore.

Copy Backs up selected files but does not clear the archive bit.

Incremental   Backs up selected files only if they were created or modified since the previous backup, and clears the archive bit. Tends to be the fastest in terms of backup speed but slower to restore.

Differential   Backs up selected files only if they were created or modified since the previous backup, but does not clear the archive bit. In between Normal and Incremental on backup and restore speeds.

Daily   Backs up files that were created or modified today. It doesn't look at the archive bit but only the date when the file was modified.

The most thorough backup is Normal, because it will back up everything you've selected. When you choose to back up files using Windows Backup, this is the type of backup performed. But since this backs up everything, it can take the longest amount of time. At one company where I used to consult, it took over 16 hours to make a full backup of one of their file servers! This is obviously something they couldn't do every night, nor did they need to since not all files changed every day. Their solution was to start a full (Normal) backup on Saturday evening and to make incremental backups every night during the week.

 For security purposes, you must have administrative rights to be able to back up files belonging to people other than yourself.

There's one additional type of backup to discuss, and that's called a *system image*. Some backup utilities, including the one that comes with Windows 7, can make a system image, which is an exact copy of an entire hard disk. This includes user files as well as operating system files. You use a system image to create a snapshot in time of your system, and then you restore that copy if something ever happens to the original. There are two drawbacks. First, it's a whole-drive image, so it takes a long time to make. Second, when you restore, it doesn't let you choose what to restore—it restores everything. For these two reasons, it's not commonly used as a backup type.

Backup Locations

When you back up files, you need to choose where to back them up to. The one option you will *not* have is to back up files to the same hard drive that they are located on. Doing so wouldn't make a lot of sense, considering you would still be at a loss if the hard drive failed. Your choices boil down to the following:

- Locally attached storage, such as a hard drive or an optical drive
- Network attached storage, such as a hard drive on a server or an actual NAS device
- Internet or cloud-based

Local backups will always be the fastest. To back up your computer locally, you can use a second internal hard drive, an external hard drive, or an optical drive. Tape backup drives used to be fairly common but are rarely used anymore. If you are using an external hard drive or an optical drive, be sure to secure the drive or disc after the backup has been made. It could be very easy for someone to casually walk away with a DVD that contains all of your personal data.

Network backup solutions can be handy for corporate networks. These types of backups are generally configured by an administrator, and the user doesn't need to do anything. Security is also controlled centrally. As the end user, you probably don't know if it's being backed up on a server or a NAS device or somewhere else, but it really doesn't matter as long as you can get your files back when you need them. For a lot of companies, backing up everyone's local workstation is far too cumbersome, and they rely on the individual users to make backups of their own systems.

Internet and cloud-based backups have gained a lot of popularity over the last few years. You pay for a certain amount of storage space, and your cloud provider takes care of the backups and security. Before using one of these services, be sure you understand how often they perform backups and what security measures they have in place.

Frequency and Scheduling

This is one of the areas where most users, and even most companies, fail to manage properly. At the same time, it's one of the most important. Backups serve several key purposes, such as protecting against hard drive failure, protecting against accidental deletion, protecting against malicious deletion or attacks, and making an archive of important files for later use. Any time you make major changes to your system, including installing new software, you should perform a backup of important files before making those changes.

All Windows versions since Windows 2000 allow you to schedule backups, which is a great feature that not all versions of Windows have had.

Now that you know you can schedule backups to make your life easier, and of course you want to make backups because it's the right thing to do, the question becomes: How often do you need to back up your files?

The answer depends on what the computer does and what you do on the computer. How often does your data change? Every day? Every week or every month? How important are your files? Can you afford to lose them? How much time or money will it cost to replace lost files? Can they be replaced? By answering these questions, you can get an idea of how often you want to run scheduled backups. As a rule of thumb, the more important the data is and the more often it changes, the more often you want to back up. If you don't care about losing the data, then there's no need for backups—but most of us do care about losing our stuff. Exercise 11.7 walks you through setting up a backup in Windows 7, including scheduling.

EXERCISE 11.7

Setting Up a Backup in Windows 7

1. Open Windows Backup. In Control Panel, it's called Backup and Restore and is located in the System and Security section. Figure 11.13 shows what Backup and Restore looks like.

FIGURE 11.13   Windows Backup

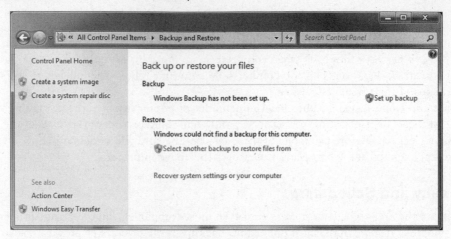

Notice in Figure 11.13 that the option to create a system image is on the left side.

2. Click Set Up Backup. Windows will ask you to choose the location to save your backup, as shown in Figure 11.14.

FIGURE 11.14   Choosing a backup location

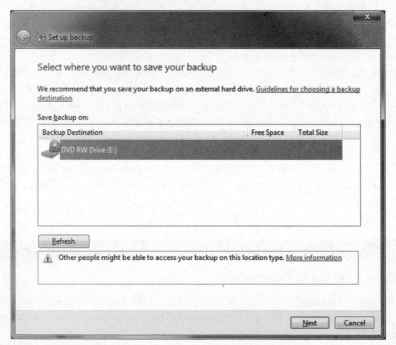

3. Choose the destination and click Next.

4. Select Let Me Choose (the screen was shown in Figure 11.12) and click Next.

5. Check the boxes for types of files you want to back up, as shown in Figure 11.15. The Data Files section lets you select fairly broad areas to back up, such as your documents, music, pictures, and videos libraries. Additional locations contains items such as your contacts, Desktop, and favorites. If you want to get more granular on folders to back up, you can do so in the Computer section. Click Next.

FIGURE 11.15   Reviewing backup settings

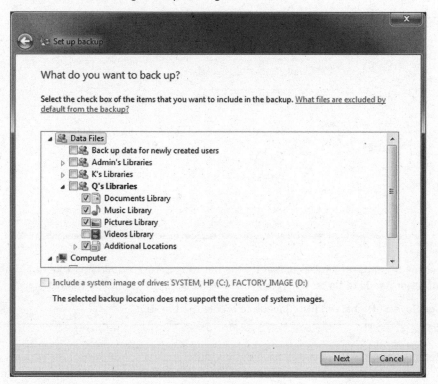

6. Review your backup settings and make sure they are correct. This screen also shows you the backup schedule. Click Change Schedule.

7. Figure 11.16 shows the options for scheduling backups. Configure them as appropriate and click OK.

FIGURE 11.16   Backup scheduling options

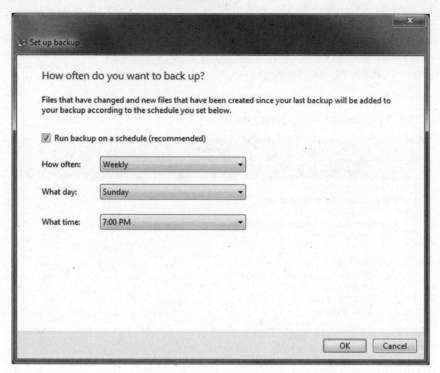

One key thing to remember is that for the backups to run properly as scheduled, the computer needs to be on when the scheduled backup is supposed to take place.

8. Click Save Settings and Run Backup to create the backup.

Different backup programs will have slightly different steps, but overall the process is the same: choose what you want to back up, decide where to back it up to, and set up a schedule. Backup programs will include options to restore folders and files from a backup as well.

Verifying and Testing Backups

Creating a backup should give you a feeling of security. Now if something happens to your system, at least your data is protected. Before feeling too comfortable, though, you need to complete one more step—verifying your backups. This is a step that many people completely forget, but it's critical. To understand why, it's probably best to share a real-world scenario.

🌐 Real World Scenario

Learning Lessons about Backups

People don't back up data enough, plain and simple. Scheduling regular backups is a good protective measure, but just because you are backing up your data doesn't mean you're completely saved if something goes wrong.

Several years ago, one of my former students related a story to me about a server crash at his company. A server had mysteriously died over the weekend, and the technicians were greeted with the problem first thing Monday morning. Not to worry, they thought, because they made regular backups.

After several attempts to restore the backup tape, a second, more serious problem was readily apparent. The backup didn't work. They couldn't read the data from the tape, and it was the only backup tape they had. It wasn't going to be a very good Monday. Ultimately, they ended up losing extensive data from the server because their backup didn't work.

How do you prevent tragedies like this from happening? Test your backups. After you make a backup, ensure that you can read from it. If you've just backed up a small amount of data, restore it to an alternate location and make sure you can read it. If you are backing up entire computers, a good idea is to run a test restore on a separate computer. No matter what your method, test your backup, especially when it's the first one you've made after setting up backups or you have made backup configuration changes. It isn't necessary to fully test each single backup after that, but it is a good idea to spot-check backups on occasion.

Here are two more ideas that will help if you back up locally. One, rotate backup discs. Alternate discs every other backup period, or use a separate disc for each day of the week. This lessens the risk of having a bad disc bring you down. Two, store your backups offsite. If your backup is sitting on top of the server, and you have a fire that destroys the building, then your backup won't do you any good. There are data archiving firms that will, for a small fee, come and pick up your backup tapes and store them in their secure location.

Be vigilant about backing up your data, and in the event of a failure, you'll be back up and running in short order.

Summary

In this chapter, you learned about computer support and backup concepts. First, you learned about troubleshooting theory. Troubleshooting can be a combination of art and science, but if you follow some basic concepts, you can be a very effective troubleshooter even without much experience.

In troubleshooting theory, the first step is to identify the problem. This includes talking to the customer, gathering information, and isolating the issue. After that, establish a theory as to what is causing the problem. Sometimes the theory is very easy to identify. Other times, you need to eliminate possibilities to narrow down the problem or use external resources such as the manufacturer's website, technical community groups, or the Internet to help. Once you have established a theory about what caused the problem, test possible solutions. Start with the simple stuff first, such as loose cables or connections, loss of power, or physical damage. It could also be user error or simply require a reboot.

Establish a plan of action to solve the problem—you might need to fix one computer or one hundred computers with this issue. Then verify functionality, and finally document your work.

Next, you reviewed some common troubleshooting examples. Groupings of problems you read about included the computer not starting, operating system errors and slowdowns, application failures, and device failures.

The final section of the chapter covered backing up computers. Backups are critically important yet often overlooked. Of course, the problem is that users don't always realize how important backups are until it's too late and they have lost data. Backups often work by utilizing the archive bit on a file. When you set up a backup, you need to choose the type of backup, the location (such as local storage, a network server, or the Internet/cloud), and the frequency and schedule. Finally, always verify your backups by testing them, so you don't get a very bad surprise when trying to restore them.

Exam Essentials

When given a scenario, know the right steps to take to identify and solve a problem. The steps include identifying the problem, establishing a theory of probable cause, testing solutions, establishing a plan of action, verifying functionality, and documenting the work.

When given a scenario, know some of the basic external issues to check. Always check the easy stuff first, such as loose cables or connections, if the system has power, and if there is physical damage.

Know the external resources you can use to help troubleshoot a problem. The manufacturer's documentation and website should always be at the top of your list. In addition, you might find help from online technical community groups, Internet searches (Ask Google!), or technical support.

Know the common locations to store backup files. Common locations are local storage (external hard drives or optical drives), network locations, or offsite or in the cloud.

After backing up, know the next step to take. Don't consider a backup complete until it has been tested and verified that it will work if it's needed.

Understand the importance of data backups and how it relates to scheduling and frequency. The more important data is, the more important backups are. The more frequently the data changes, the more frequently it should be backed up. Scheduling backups is a good idea to keep people from forgetting to do them.

Chapter 11 Lab

Chapter 11 covered troubleshooting concepts and computer backups. It's challenging to write a lab about troubleshooting—breaking your computer (or a friend's computer) just for the sake of fixing it can be risky. Instead, this lab will focus on establishing and enacting a good backup plan.

Step 1: Determine the scope of your backup plan.   Are you backing up just one computer? Or do you have a small group of computers to back up? The answers here will determine many of the answers for future steps.

Step 2: Understand the importance of the data.   Does anyone care if the data is lost? Or on the other end of the spectrum, would a business fail or your life be ruined if you were to lose the data?

Step 3: Understand how much data there is to back up and how often the files change. Perhaps there are terabytes of data on the system or systems you need to back up, but only a few hundred megabytes of data change frequently. Or maybe if it's your local computer, there are only a few hundred megabytes you are concerned with.

Step 4: Where do you want to store the backup files?   In general, your choices are local media (such as external hard drive or optical disc), a network server, or in the cloud. The answer will likely depend on how important the data is, how often it changes, and how much there is.

Step 5: Decide on backup software.   If it's just your computer, perhaps the OS backup program is fine. Or you can purchase an external hard drive backup system and use its software. Third-party backup solutions are needed for bigger jobs, or you might find a viable cloud solution online.

Step 6: Configure the backup and run it.   Simple enough, right? Run the backup based on the solution you chose in Step 5. Also note that if the backup is difficult to configure or run, you might want to re-evaluate your choice of backup software.

Step 7: Test and verify the backup.   Don't forget this step! Restore some files from your backup just to make sure that it's working properly.

Step 8: Schedule recurring backups.   How often depends on the needs. If the data is critical and changes daily, then daily backups may be in order. Once a week tends to be a common schedule, as does once per month for less-critical data.

Step 9: Document the backup process and schedule.   If you're just backing up your own computer, this step probably isn't needed. If it's multiple systems, though, and if multiple people are involved, documentation is critical. Write down the software, the settings, and the overall plan so others know what is happening and when. If other administrators are involved, you will also need to share critical security information such as backup passwords so they can perform backup and restoration tasks as needed.

Review Questions

1. When troubleshooting a computer problem, which of the following are steps you can take to identify the problem? (Choose two.)

   A. Use external resources such as the Internet.

   B. Talk to end users.

   C. Isolate the issue.

   D. Attribute it to user error.

2. You are troubleshooting a MacBook Pro. When it turns on, you receive a screen with a flashing question mark. What is the likely cause?

   A. Device driver failure

   B. Video card failure

   C. Memory failure

   D. Hard drive failure

3. When providing computer support and testing solutions, what should you always do first?

   A. Assume user error.

   B. Test the simple stuff.

   C. Check Internet resources for solutions.

   D. Establish a plan of action.

4. Your computer has been running backups for a year. Today, you make a change from backing it up to an external optical drive to backing it up to the cloud. What should you do next?

   A. Secure the cloud backup location.

   B. Schedule regular cloud backups.

   C. Destroy the old optical discs.

   D. Verify that the cloud backup works.

5. You are troubleshooting a computer problem. After testing the solution, what should you do next?

   A. Establish a plan of action.

   B. Verify functionality.

   C. Document the work.

   D. Identify the problem.

6. After installing several new software applications, your friend notices that her computer boots very slowly. Which tool can she use to disable programs from running on startup of Windows?

   A. Recovery Console

   B. System Configuration

   C. System Restore

   D. Safe Mode

7. Raul has just installed an older application on his Windows 8 computer and it will not run. He asks you for advice. What should you tell him to try to make it run?

   A. Delete and reinstall.

   B. Run it as an administrator.

   C. Use Safe Mode.

   D. Use compatibility mode.

8. You are troubleshooting a Windows PC that will not load the operating system. You insert the Windows DVD and reboot. Which utility can you use to repair Windows?

   A. Recovery Environment

   B. MSCONFIG

   C. System Restore

   D. Safe Mode

9. What is the last step in the process of troubleshooting a computer?

   A. Verify Internet functionality.

   B. Document the work.

   C. Clean up the mess.

   D. Retest the solution.

10. You have been asked to design a backup solution for your manager's workstation. Which option will be the fastest?

   A. Cloud storage.

   B. Network storage.

   C. Local storage.

   D. They are all the same speed.

11. What type of computer backup will back up all selected files and then clear the archive bit?

   A. Normal

   B. Differential

   C. Incremental

   D. Copy

12. You have just installed a new printer on your computer, and while it seems to be recognized by the operating system, it will not print. What is the first source to check for information on the problem?

    A. The OS manufacturer's website

    B. The printer manufacturer's website

    C. Google search

    D. Internet technical community groups

13. You need to run an emergency backup of your computer, and you need it to finish as fast as possible. You just backed up about three weeks ago. Which backup option should you use?

    A. Normal

    B. Differential

    C. Incremental

    D. Copy

14. While troubleshooting a Windows computer that may have a bad memory module, the computer freezes and displays a blue screen with white text and a STOP error. What generated that error message?

    A. The memory module

    B. Windows

    C. BIOS

    D. MSCONFIG

15. Ron's computer behaves normally for a time, and then his screen completely freezes up. The mouse and keyboard do not respond. What is the most likely cause of his problem?

    A. Faulty video driver

    B. Faulty mouse or keyboard driver

    C. Failing hard drive

    D. Overheating

16. You are troubleshooting a PC and see a gray text-based message about the boot disk on a black screen. What is the most likely source of this error message?

    A. Windows

    B. CHKDSK

    C. BIOS

    D. POST card

17. David is using a laptop that is about four years old. Recently he installed a few new applications, and the system performance is now very slow. Which components are the most likely ones being overworked?

    A. HDD and RAM

    B. RAM and video card

    C. RAM and CPU

    D. CPU and NIC

18. You are asked to troubleshoot a computer, and your friend recommends you take a POST card with you. What can the POST card help you diagnose?

    A. Application problems

    B. Overheating problems

    C. Startup problems resulting in a BIOS error message

    D. Startup problems where nothing is displayed on the screen

19. What type of backup will make a copy of all files on the computer, including user files and operating system files, to use in the event of a complete failure?

    A. System image

    B. Full backup

    C. Incremental backup

    D. Complete backup

20. You're asked to troubleshoot a PC that's not working properly. You push the power button but don't see anything on the screen or hear any fans spinning. What is the most likely reason?

    A. Defective monitor

    B. Defective power supply

    C. Broken fan

    D. Defective network adapter driver

Chapter 12

Environmental and Safety Concepts

THE FOLLOWING COMPTIA IT FUNDAMENTALS EXAM OBJECTIVES ARE COVERED IN THIS CHAPTER:

✓ **5.5 Describe the importance and impact of various environmental and safety concepts**

- Proper disposal methods
  - RoHS
  - CRT monitors
  - Scanners
  - Batteries
  - Ink/toner
  - Hard drives
- Power
  - Energy efficient devices
  - Power profiles
    - Power options
    - Sleep/hibernation
  - UPS vs. surge protector vs. power strip
    - Power limitations
  - International power differences
  - Device placement
    - Airflow
    - Humidity
    - Temperature
    - Dust accumulation
    - EMI

- Electrostatic discharge concepts
- Ergonomic concepts
  - Proper keyboard and mouse placement
  - Sitting positions
  - Monitor level placement
- Follow manufacturer safety guidelines

The environment and safety might, at first glance, seem like strange topics for a book on IT fundamentals. We're talking about computers here, right? In reality, computers *can* have a big impact on the environment—many of the components contain environmentally unfriendly or toxic materials. The goal is to minimize the negative impact that computers could have on our surroundings.

Safety is also a valid concern and it can take several forms. Granted, it's not like working with computers is as dangerous as being a firefighter or a chef (flames and knives, what could go wrong?) or several other professions, but there are still things to watch out for. Your own personal safety and health can be affected by using poor posture for hours on end while working with a computer. Computers use electricity, and if you're not careful you could get hurt or even possibly killed. (The odds of dying are very small provided that you are careful!) There's also the safety of your components. Treating them the right way extends their lives. Doing things like immersing your laptop in water will result in more frequent hardware purchases.

So even though the environment and safety aren't likely to be the two topics at the top of your mind when you think about computers, they are important factors to be aware of. This chapter will teach you about concepts related to safety—both yours and your hardware's—as well as how to properly dispose of items to not damage the environment.

Safe Interactions with Computers

Working with computers isn't as unsafe as many other jobs out there, but there are still potential ways to hurt yourself or others by using computers. One of the most important things you can do is to always follow the manufacturer's safety guidelines. This is true for all computer components, but it's especially true when working with potentially hazardous materials such as CRT monitors, batteries, and toner. Some safety guidelines are relatively simple and common-sense, while others are critical and prevent serious injuries or death.

Over the next several sections, I will share concepts related to safe interactions with computers. I will start with a discussion on ergonomics, which is about your own personal safety and health. Next, I'll talk about power and electricity—as you know, electricity can kill you if you're not careful! After that, I will cover the safety of your computers and components such as how to clean them properly and where they should be placed for optimal health. Finally, I will talk about environmental safety and how to properly dispose of your old computer equipment.

Using Proper Ergonomics

Ergonomics is the study of people's efficiency in their working environment. Many people have bad posture or typing form when using computers, which can result in headaches, neck problems, back problems, strain on shoulder and arm muscles and joints, and repetitive stress injuries such as carpal tunnel syndrome.

If you work in an office, look around at your co-workers. Who is sitting with proper posture and device positioning like what's shown in Figure 12.1?

FIGURE 12.1   Proper ergonomic positions

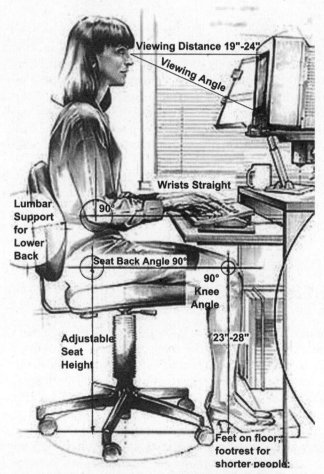

"COMPUTER WORKSTATION VARIABLES CLEANUP" BY YAMAVU - OWN WORK.
LICENSED UNDER CC0 VIA WIKIMEDIA COMMONS - HTTP://COMMONS.WIKIMEDIA
.ORG/WIKI/FILE:COMPUTER_WORKSTATION_VARIABLES_CLEANUP.PNG#/MEDIA/
FILE:COMPUTER_WORKSTATION_VARIABLES_CLEANUP.PNG

It's probably not many. Some people don't know what proper mechanics are, and others might know but have fallen into bad habits. In either case, those people are damaging their bodies by not following a few basic principles. Here are the guidelines to follow:

Sit straight with your feet flat on the floor.   This might sound like what your teachers told you when you were young, but it's good advice. Your upper body should be at a 90–120 degree angle to your thighs, which should be parallel to the floor. Or, your hips can be slightly above your knees. You should have support of your lower back (lumbar) area. Try to distribute the pressure on your seat evenly, make sure the area behind your knee is not touching the chair. Adjust your seat so it's low enough for you to have your feet flat on the floor or on a footrest.

Keep your elbows relaxed at your side and at 90 degrees.   Your keyboard and mouse should be placed in such a way that there is minimal to no bend in your wrists, and your elbows are at a 90 degree angle. Some people find it easier to use an ergonomic keyboard and mouse (covered in Chapter 2, "Peripherals and Connectors"). The keyboard and mouse should be directly between you and your monitor, at or slightly below your elbow height, and close to each other to minimize reaching.

Look straight at your monitor.   The top of your monitor screen should be parallel to or slightly lower than your eyes. Looking up at your monitor will cause undue neck strain. In addition, the screen should be approximately 19 to 24″ from your eyes. (Some resources say up to 28″, or roughly arm's length away.)

And here are a few more tips:

- Use a headset if you are on the phone. Don't cradle the phone between your head and your shoulder.

- Use a document holder to keep paper documents you need to see at eye level, so you don't have to look down at them.

- Take periodic breaks, every 30 minutes or so, to get up and stretch! Even if it's just for 15–30 seconds, it greatly helps your circulation and keeps you more alert.

Many companies offer their employees free ergonomic assessments as part of their benefits packages. An ergonomics expert can come and assess your workplace and make suggestions on how to improve your positioning. Many of the same companies will also pay for ergonomic chairs, desks, or computer accessories for employees who need them. Exercise 12.1 will show you how to assess ergonomics. You can do this on yourself or on a co-worker. Just warn the other person first before doing it!

EXERCISE 12.1

Assessing Ergonomics

1. Assess the sitting position. The ideal position is sitting straight up (or slightly reclined) with lower back support, thighs parallel to the floor, back of the knees not touching the seat, and feet flat on the floor or a footrest.

2. Assess keyboard and mouse placement. Are they situated so that the user's elbows can be relaxed at their side at a 90 degree angle and the user's wrists have minimal to no bend?

3. Assess monitor placement. Is the top of the screen at or slightly below eye level? Is the monitor an appropriate distance from their eyes (at least 18″, up to arm's length)?

4. Does the user have a headset for telephone calls?

5. Does the user take regular breaks to stand up for at least 15–30 seconds to stretch?

Understanding Power and Electricity

Computers need power to operate, and they're actually rather particular about the power they need. Too much or too little and the computer won't work or may sustain permanent damage. Unintended electricity from the wrong sources—the obvious one being electrical storms, but the un-obvious one being people improperly touching components—can also result in fried parts.

The other aspect to understanding power and electricity is to know how your computer, whether it be the hardware or the operating system, can help the computer conserve electricity or power. For a desktop, this can mean monetary energy savings. For a laptop, it can mean the difference between a two-hour battery life and a six-hour one. This section will look at various power and electricity concepts in depth.

International Power Differences

Computer components require direct current (DC) power, whereas the electrical power systems across the world provide alternating current (AC). The computer's power supply is the conduit between the electricity coming from a wall outlet and the system itself, and it converts AC to DC. For laptop computers, the power adapter provides the same functionality. The only difference is that laptops have an attached battery that can store electricity for use when the system is not plugged into the wall. Smaller portable devices rely solely on an internal battery, which gets charged through an adapter that plugs into an electrical outlet as well. As you can see, there's a common theme developing here, and it's that all computer devices plug into an outlet at some point. The question is, what kind of outlet is it? It depends on where you live.

In the United States, the power grid supplies 120 volts AC. In Europe, China, and many other parts of the world, the power grid supplies from 220 to 240 volts AC. The adapter's prongs to plug into the wall outlet are different enough that you can't plug a device intended for one range into an outlet for the other, but if you were able to, it could have disastrous consequences—the very least of which are fried components.

Most computer power supplies have a switch on the back like what you see in the dusty image in Figure 12.2. (Reminder: clean the dust from your power supply fans!) This switch is red, and it might be hard to read, but on the right side it says 115. Options will be 110 and 220, 115 and 230, or 120 and 240. If you're in the United States and you set the switch to the 220–240 range, the power supply will expect more voltage than what it will receive, and it probably won't power up. If you are in a country with higher voltage and you select the 110–120 setting, the power supply will get overloaded. You will surely fry the components, and it's possible the power supply could catch on fire.

FIGURE 12.2   Power supply voltage switch

 If a computer has recently been relocated overseas, always check the power supply switch before trying to turn it on! If you're in the United States and other countries that use 110–120 voltage, check the switch if the computer fails to power up.

Maintaining Power

Most people realize that when a computer is plugged into a wall, having too much power (a power surge) is a bad thing because it can fry electronic components. Having too little power, such as when a *blackout* occurs, can also wreak havoc on electrical circuits.

Power strips come in all shapes and sizes and are convenient for plugging multiple devices into one wall outlet. This solves the problem of having a computer, monitor, printer, speakers, and other peripherals that require a power outlet, but only two plugs in the wall outlet. Most power strips even have an on/off switch so you can turn all of the devices on or off at the same time. A simple British power strip is shown in Figure 12.3. It has switches for each individual outlet as well as a power light.

FIGURE 12.3 A power strip

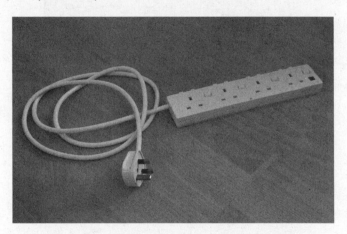

Don't make the mistake of thinking that power strips will protect you from electrical surges, though. Power strips are nothing but glorified extension cords. If you get a strong power surge through one of these devices, the strip and everything plugged into it can be fried. Some people like to call power strips "surge protectors" or "surge suppressors," but power strips do nothing to protect or suppress.

Devices that actually attempt to keep power surges at bay are called *surge protectors*. They often look just like a power strip so it's easy to mistake them for each other, but protectors are more expensive, usually starting in the $25 range. They have a fuse inside them that is designed to blow if it receives too much current and not transfer the current to the devices plugged into it. Surge protectors may also have plug-ins for RJ-11 (phone), RJ-45 (Ethernet), and BNC (coaxial cable) connectors as well. Figure 12.4 shows a surge protector.

FIGURE 12.4   Surge protector

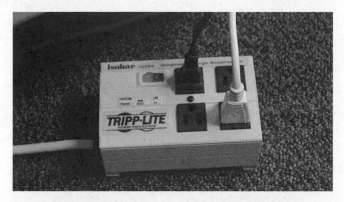

"SURGE SUPPRESSOR" BY ENCRYPTEDRULER - OWN WORK. LICENSED UNDER CC BY-SA

3.0 VIA WIKIMEDIA COMMONS - HTTP://COMMONS.WIKIMEDIA.ORG/WIKI/FILE:SURGE_

SUPPRESSOR.JPG#/MEDIA/FILE:SURGE_SUPPRESSOR.JPG

The best device for power protection is called an *uninterruptible power supply (UPS)*. These devices can be as small as a brick, like the one in Figure 12.5, or as large as an entire server rack. Some just have a few indicator lights, while others have LCD displays that show status and menus and come with their own management software. The back of the UPS will have several power plugs. It might divide the plugs such that a few of them provide surge protection only, whereas others provide surge protection as well as backup power, as shown in Figure 12.6.

FIGURE 12.5   An uninterruptible power supply

FIGURE 12.6   The back of an uninterruptible power supply

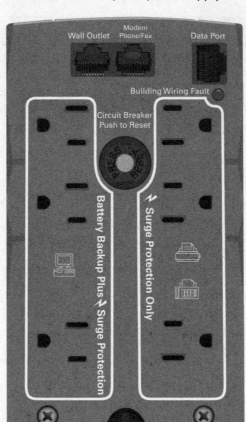

Inside the UPS are one or more batteries and fuses. Much like a surge suppressor, a UPS is designed to protect everything that's plugged into it from power surges. UPSs are also designed to protect against power sags and even power outages. Energy is stored in the batteries, and if the power fails, the batteries can power the computer for a period of time so the administrator can then safely power it down. Many UPSs and operating systems will also work together to automatically (and safely) power down a system that gets switched to UPS power. These types of devices may be overkill for Uncle Bob's machine at home, but they're critically important fixtures in server rooms.

The UPS should be checked periodically to make sure its battery is operational. Most UPSs have a test button you can press to simulate a power outage. You will find that batteries wear out over time, and you should replace the battery in the UPS every couple of years to keep the UPS dependable.

 Power strips, surge protectors, and UPSs all have a limit to how many devices they can handle at once. These power limitations should be strictly observed. If overloaded, power strips and other devices can cause a short, which could potentially result in fire.

Electrostatic Discharge

Electrostatic discharge (ESD) is the most common culprit for ruined PC parts, although many people have never heard of it. ESD is really just static electricity, the same thing that can shock a person on a low-humidity day.

ESD occurs when two items of unequal voltage potential come into contact with one another. The item with the higher charge passes electricity to the one with the lower charge to even out the voltage. As an analogy, picture two bodies of water meeting; if one has a higher level, water will flow quickly into the other one until they're the same. In the case of electricity, the equalization happens so fast that the item of lower charge receives a rush of electricity that feels like a shock. You've experienced ESD firsthand if you've ever scuffed your socks on the carpet and then touched someone, giving the person a shock. You were not shocked yourself because, in that case, *you* were the item of higher charge.

Whereas voltage (measured in volts) is the difference in electrical charge, *current* is the rate at which electrical charge flows and is measured in *amps*. ESD is a high-voltage shock (3,000 volts or so), but it doesn't harm a person because it has very low current. The human body doesn't draw electricity very strongly; it merely draws enough to equalize the charge and then stops. To damage a human body, there must be sufficient amps as well as volts. That is why a 110-volt wall outlet can hurt a person more than a 3,000-volt static electricity shock—the static electricity shock has low amperage.

Electronic equipment, though, is extremely sensitive to damage by high voltage, even when the amperage is very low. Humans notice ESD only when it reaches 3,000 volts or so, but ESD can damage a circuit board with less than 300 volts. (Some experts say as little as one volt is enough to do some damage.) This means that a person could touch a circuit board and destroy it with static electricity without even noticing. The next time they tried to use that circuit board it would be dead, and they would have no idea why. Furthermore, ESD damage doesn't always show up immediately. It may cause the device to malfunction, or it may weaken the device to the point that it fails a week or a month later.

Generally speaking, any exposed circuit boards are targets for ESD damage, especially motherboards. Also at risk are microchips both on and off those boards, particularly RAM and ROM. Devices *not* very susceptible to ESD damage include those in which circuit boards are never exposed, such as keyboards, mice, speakers, monitors, and printers, and those that don't contain circuit boards.

If you never open your computer's case, the risks of harming it via ESD are very low. If you have to work inside a computer for some reason, such as to install a new circuit board or more RAM, here are some tips:

1. Be aware of the clothing you wear when working inside a PC. Synthetic materials such as nylon generate much more ESD than natural fibers like cotton and wool, so dress in natural fabrics. Avoid working in stocking feet—wear rubber-soled shoes.

2. Keeping the humidity high in the work area can also help considerably. The ideal humidity for working on PC hardware is 40 to 80 percent but preferably right around 50 percent.

3. The work surface can also make a difference. Try not to work in a carpeted area; tile or linoleum is preferred. Carpet, especially nylon carpet, tends to generate ESD the same way that nylon clothing does.

4. Grounding both the person and equipment can eliminate ESD risk, because any ESD that builds up can bleed off to the ground harmlessly. To ground yourself, wear an *antistatic wrist strap* as you work (see Figure 12.7). At your end of the strap is a Velcro bracelet containing a diode that fits against your skin. At the other end is an alligator clip that you attach to the grounding pin on an electrical outlet (the round, third hole) or to some other grounding source. If no grounding source is available, attach the clip to the PC's metal frame. For maximum ESD prevention, wear an antistatic wrist strap whenever you're working on a PC with the cover off, especially when handling circuit boards.

FIGURE 12.7   An antistatic wrist strap

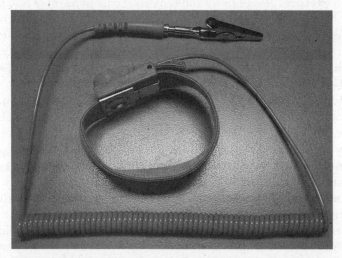

Another way to minimize ESD risks is to touch the metal frame or power supply of the PC frequently as you work. Doing so doesn't ground you, but it does equalize the electrical charge between you and the PC so there is no difference in potential between you and the components you touch. Do this every few minutes to make sure no build-up occurs.

Antistatic mats are also available. These sit on the work surface and perform the same function for the parts on which you're working as the wrist strap does; the mat has a cord that attaches to the ground pin on an outlet.

Whenever transporting components, use an antistatic plastic bag. These bags are usually pink or gray and have a coating that collects static charge on the outside of the bag, keeping it away from what's inside the bag. Expensive circuit boards should always be stored in an antistatic bag when not in use. Computer stores sell extra bags, but most people accumulate a collection of them simply from buying and installing new hardware.

Finally, you can buy antistatic spray that minimizes static charge in your environment. This is usually a colorless, odorless liquid in a pump bottle that you spray on the carpet and on your clothing.

 Real World Scenario

The Downy Solution

In one of the offices I used to work in, we had terrible static electricity problems, especially in the winter. It seemed that no matter how hard we tried, we inevitably fried memory or other components. Sometimes we would even see a little blue lightning bolt between ourselves and the computer components. That stung our fingers a little, but stung our budget worse. Most of the time we wouldn't notice anything, but the computers would start having random memory problems, and we would have to replace parts anyway.

One of the newer technicians introduced us to the Downy solution. He took a spray bottle and mixed equal parts Downy liquid fabric softener and water. He then spritzed down the floors, the chairs, and the work tables. Not only did the room smell springtime fresh but our ESD problems went away.

If you work in a high-static environment (usually one with low humidity), this is an inexpensive solution that can save you from frying your hardware. Don't soak items down, but spritz them with the solution every month or two, and ESD should be less of a worry moving forward.

The flipside of the ESD conversation isn't about how you can hurt computer components, but how they can hurt you. For the most part, working inside a computer case is pretty safe. You have to watch out for sharp metal edges, but as long as the computer is powered off when you are working on it, you should generally be fine. There are two notable exceptions though—the inside of power supplies and CRT monitors.

CRT monitors and power supplies contain capacitors, which store electricity. They can store electricity for years, even when unplugged from a power source. Touching a full capacitor can cause it to release its energy through you at very high amperage, which could kill you. Capacitors need to be drained by a trained professional using a high-voltage probe. The moral of the story is to never open the back of a CRT monitor or the case surrounding a power supply.

Energy-Efficient Personal Computing

Saving energy is not only good for the environment but good for your wallet as well. A computer's operating system can help save energy by powering off devices that are not actively in use or by suspending power to the system or monitor during periods of inactivity. In addition, some hardware devices are specifically designed to consume lower levels of power, which is a good thing. In the following sections, you'll learn how to minimize the amount of power your computers use while impacting your productivity as little as possible.

Power-Management Plans

Most systems have built-in power-management features that enable you to save energy by shutting down the computer or by placing it in a low-power mode after a specified period of inactivity. The operating system typically controls power management, but some systems also have power-management features available via BIOS Setup.

LOW-POWER MODES

Different OSs call the various modes by different names, but here are the basic modes. You can set the OS to put the PC into one of these modes automatically after a specified period of inactivity:

Sleep/Standby   All components of the PC except RAM are powered down so that the computer uses only the tiny amount of power required to keep the RAM's content alive. When you resume, all the devices are powered on again. Because the content of RAM remains, waking up from this mode is nearly instantaneous. In Windows and Mac OS, this is called Sleep mode; in Linux it's called Suspend to RAM.

Hibernate   The content of RAM is copied to a special holding area on the hard disk, and then the system is powered off completely, including the RAM. When you resume, the previous RAM content is copied back into RAM, and all the devices are powered on again. Waking from this mode takes a little longer (up to 1 minute), but that's less time than it would take to start up the computer completely after it's been off. In Windows, this feature is called Hibernate or Hybrid Sleep. On Linux, it's called Suspend to Disk. On a Mac, the Safe Sleep mode copies the contents of RAM to the hard disk before sleeping, so that if the battery runs out and the computer loses RAM power, hibernation automatically is in effect.

In addition, some OSs enable you to specify a time period of inactivity after which the display dims or turns off completely, and the hard disk stops spinning its platters (if it's a mechanical hard disk, rather than solid state). Exercise 12.2 gives you practice putting a computer to sleep.

EXERCISE 12.2

Putting a Computer to Sleep

1. In Windows 7, click Start and click the right-pointing triangle arrow next to the Shut Down command. A menu opens.

2. Choose Sleep. Your computer goes to sleep.

3. Press a key. Some computers may be configured to wake up on a key press. If yours doesn't wake up, press the Power button to wake it up.

4. Click Start, click the triangle next to Shut Down, and choose Hibernate. (This might not be available on your computer—it's a common option for laptops.) Wait for the computer to enter Hibernate mode.

5. Press the Power button to wake up the computer from hibernation.

CHOOSING POWER-MANAGEMENT SETTINGS

Some companies have energy-saving policies, which dictate that employees must place their computers in a low-power mode, or turn them off completely, at the end of a workday. Even if your company doesn't have an official policy, you may want to create one for yourself.

You can do this in your OS by setting up a *power plan*. A power plan tells the computer to shut down or to go into one of the power-saving modes from the previous section after a specified period of inactivity. If it's a notebook computer, you can choose separate settings for when it's on battery power versus when it's plugged in. Windows, Mac OS X, and Linux all have similar power-management features.

In Windows, you can choose a standard power plan that includes settings for the display, the hard disks, and the amount of time before the computer goes to sleep. After choosing a plan, you can then customize that plan in a variety of ways, as you'll see in Exercise 12.3.

Mac OS X has an additional power-management feature: it enables you to set the computer to start up and shut down at a certain time every day (see Figure 12.8). In System Preferences, click the Energy Saver icon, which looks like a light bulb. Then, on the Energy Saver screen, click the Schedule button.

FIGURE 12.8 Configuring a Mac to shut down or start up at a certain time

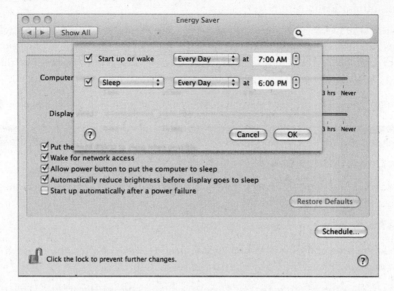

EXERCISE 12.3

Customizing a Power Scheme in Windows 7

1. In Windows 7, open the Power Options app in Control Panel. (It is located under Hardware And Sound if you are viewing categories.) It will look like Figure 12.9.

FIGURE 12.9 Power Options in Windows

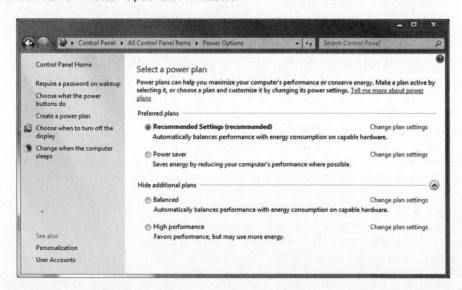

2. Select the Balanced power plan if it isn't already selected.

3. Click the Change Plan Settings hyperlink for the Balanced plan. Additional options appear. If you're using a notebook PC, you'll have separate options for On Battery and Plugged In. Otherwise, you'll have only one option for each line.

4. Open the Turn Off The Display drop-down list (for Plugged In, if you have a choice), and select 20 minutes.

5. Click Change Advanced Power Settings. The Power Options dialog box opens.

6. Click the plus sign next to Hard Disk, opening its category.

7. Under Hard Disk, click the plus sign next to Turn Off Hard Disk After, opening its category.

8. Next to Plugged In, change the value to 30 minutes. (If you're on a desktop PC, there are no separate lines for On Battery and Plugged In.)

9. Click the plus sign next to Power Buttons And Lid to expand that category.

10. Click the plus sign next to Power Button Action to expand that category.

11. Set the value for both On Battery and Plugged In to Sleep. (If you're on a desktop PC, there is only one setting.)

12. Click OK.

13. Click Save Changes.

14. If you want to change the power settings back to the default, click the Balanced option again, and click Change Plan Settings.

15. Click Restore Default Settings for this plan.

16. Click Yes to confirm.

17. Close Control Panel.

Power-Conserving Equipment

In addition to the OS settings for conserving power, some hardware devices also have their own power savings. For example, notebook PCs use less power than desktops, so replacing as many desktops as possible with notebooks can save a company a significant amount of power. The following sections cover some other component savings you can achieve.

MONITORS AND ENERGY SAVINGS

The computer display, whether it's built into your notebook computer or a separate stand-alone monitor connected to a desktop PC, consumes the most power of any component in an average system. CRTs consume more power than LCDs, so one way you can conserve energy is to switch over to LCDs for as many computers as possible.

Another way to conserve power is to decrease the brightness of the monitor. Especially on an LCD, doing this can make a big difference; the brighter the display, the more light it generates, and more light means more power.

You can change screen brightness in several ways. One is via the power plan in the OS. This is configured via the Power Options app in Control Panel. You can also manually adjust a monitor's brightness. On a stand-alone monitor, there are typically buttons that open a menu system onscreen from which you can control brightness along with many other factors. On a notebook display, there is usually a brightness control associated with one or more of the keyboard keys plus the Fn key. Hold down Fn, and press the key that is associated with Increase Brightness or Decrease Brightness.

HARD DRIVES AND ENERGY SAVINGS

Some hard drives are more energy-efficient to operate than others. Solid-state drives, for example, have much lower power needs because there are no mechanical parts. Unless there is a read-write operation, they consume no power. Among mechanical hard disks, drives with lower rotational speeds sometimes use less power than their high-performance counterparts, although the age of the drive is also a factor; newer hard drives use newer technologies that make them more efficient.

ENERGY STAR

Originating in the United States, the Environmental Protection Agency Energy Star rating system for computer technology is now recognized internationally; many other nations use the standard as part of their own power-reduction policies. When you see the Energy Star logo on a PC or a component, as shown in Figure 12.10, you can assume that the device meets certain energy-efficiency standards. For example, an Energy Star monitor puts itself into standby (a low-power mode) when it doesn't detect a signal from the PC, and Energy Star laptops are able to go into Sleep or Hibernate mode when the lid is shut. Energy Star also applies to motherboards, power supplies, and BIOSs that are able to manage power consumption.

FIGURE 12.10   Energy Star logo

PHOTO CREDIT: WWW.ENERGYSTAR.GOV

> ### 🌐 Real World Scenario
>
> #### Laptop Battery Conservation
>
> On a notebook computer, nothing can kill a productive work session like a dead battery. For people who frequently travel where no electrical outlet is available, lack of battery power is a big risk of service loss.
>
> One guard against loss of service via battery power is to carry one or more extra batteries with you. Batteries for notebook computers are available as replacement parts from a variety of vendors and are usually specific to a certain model or narrow range of models. (Some notebooks, mostly Macs, don't have user-replaceable batteries, so you must have the battery replaced by a service center if it fails.)
>
> Another option is to adjust the power settings on your notebook PC to extend the battery life. Windows has a Power Options group in Control Panel that lets you make some adjustments. On a Mac, these settings are found in the Energy Saver preference pane in System Preferences. You can further extend your battery's life by using some of these tips:
>
> - Turn off your wireless network adapter unless you're actively using it.
> - Set the screen display to be less bright.
> - Set the computer to Sleep mode when you aren't actively using it.
> - Set the screen saver to blank the screen after a certain amount of idle time.
> - Mute the sound.
> - Minimize the use of external devices that draw power from the notebook, such as external keyboards and pointing devices.
> - Remove any unused ExpressCards or other peripheral cards.

Practicing Good Device Care and Placement

Preventive maintenance is an important part of computer usage. This can include backing up files, preventing damage from electrical surges and static electricity, and cleaning the computer. Cleaning the computer regularly and placing devices in a good setting to ensure proper performance will extend the life of its components. This helps your budget as well as the environment.

Cleaning a Computer

Computers that are cleaned regularly are not only more pleasant to use but also can last longer. Dirt, clumps of debris, and other accumulation can make components run hotter, shortening their lives. In the following sections, you'll learn about some of the cleaning products available for cleaning a computer inside and out. You'll also study some techniques for cleaning various areas without damaging them.

Cleaning Supplies

Expensive cleaning supplies aren't required to clean a PC, but neither should you use whatever products happen to be lying around. Here is a list of basic supplies to have on hand:

- A spray cleaning product designed for plastics, preferably one designed for computers. The ones designed for computers often have antistatic properties that regular cleaners lack.

- A monitor cleaner, either spray or towelette, designed specifically for cleaning monitors or other electronics screens (like televisions). Don't use a glass-cleaning product that contains ammonia because ammonia can destroy the antiglare coating on some monitors.

- A can of compressed air for blowing dust out of crevices.

- Cotton swabs.

- Denatured isopropyl alcohol (not rubbing alcohol, because that has too much water in it).

- An antistatic spray designed for computer work areas.

- (Optional) A small handheld vacuum cleaner designed for electronics. (Don't use a regular vacuum cleaner because the filter isn't fine enough and because a regular vacuum can generate static electricity that can harm equipment.)

Cleaning a Monitor

Always turn a monitor off before cleaning it. If any liquid gets inside, the monitor can air dry without worries of short-circuiting. It's also much easier to see dirt and spots on the screen when it's dark.

First, clean the outer casing with a spray computer-cleaning solution. Spray the cleaner on the cloth, not directly on the casing, to avoid spraying into vent holes.

Next, clean the glass using a cleaner designed specifically for monitors. This can be in the form of a spray or a towelette. Don't use ordinary cleaning products on monitors because they can leave streaks and sometimes harm the antiglare coating. Don't use regular glass cleaner either, because it contains ammonia, which can also harm the surface. Don't spray the screen directly, because the liquid may drip down below the bottom bezel; spray a cloth and then wipe the screen.

Cleaning External Surfaces

As with monitors, clean the outside casing of PCs, printers, scanners, and similar equipment with a computer-cleaning spray product. Mild general-purpose spray cleaners also work. You can also use mild soapy water and a damp cloth (not soaking wet) to clean external surfaces only—nothing internal or with a vent or crack that leads inside.

Cleaning a Keyboard

Because it's always at the forefront of activity, the keyboard can get very dirty. Although technicians may remind end users to keep their computing areas clean, more often than not people neglect to do so. They may type with unwashed hands or eat, drink, or even play with their pets while they work. All this activity leaves dirt, oil, and other residue on the keyboard.

To clean a keyboard, first turn off the PC. The keyboard need not be unplugged from the PC. Then, turn the keyboard upside down and shake it or tap it (it's called *burping a keyboard*) to remove any loose debris. Or, hold it over a trashcan and spray beneath the keys with compressed air. What falls out—and the amount of it—is often surprising!

Use a cloth dampened with a spray cleaning solution designed for PCs, or a towelette containing a PC cleaning product, to clean all visible surfaces. Get down between the cracks with a cotton swab or a bit of folded paper towel. Removing the keys isn't recommended because it can be difficult to get them back on again. If you have access to one, a small handheld vacuum cleaner designed specifically for working with electronics can be useful in sucking debris out from under the keys.

If liquid is spilled onto a keyboard, turn the keyboard upside down and unplug it immediately from the PC (if possible), or turn off the PC. Turn the keyboard upside down to release as much of the liquid as possible, and then let it dry for at least 48 hours. If the liquid was plain water, the keyboard will probably be fine after it dries; just clean the outside as well as possible. But if the liquid contained sugar, the keyboard may never be completely clean again. Some people have successfully cleaned sticky keyboards (the separate kind, not those found on a notebook PC) in a dishwasher. To try this (there is little to lose with a keyboard that is otherwise on its way to the trash can), place the keyboard on the upper rack, wash it without using the heat-dry feature and with very little or no detergent, remove it after the wash, rinse it, and set it in a dish drainer for several days to dry out.

Cleaning a Mouse

A mouse, like a keyboard, gets very dirty because it's constantly being handled. In addition, older mechanical mice have the added feature of the ball on the bottom, which rolls across the desk picking up dirt and lint and moving it inside the mouse. As a result, the rollers and sensors on a mechanical mouse can become encrusted with dirt rather quickly, causing the mouse to malfunction. An optical mouse has fewer problems with dirt inside, but dust and hair can still accumulate at the opening where the light shines through.

When a mouse is dirty, the pointer on-screen may jump or stutter, or moving the mouse in one direction may result in no action at all. In addition, the mouse may become more difficult to roll.

To clean a mouse, first wipe off the outside with mild soapy water or cleaning product designed for computers. Then turn the mouse on its back. If it's an optical mouse, use a cotton swab dipped in denatured alcohol to clean out the hollow area where the light shines through if there is any debris inside. (Alcohol dries quickly, so it's used instead of water anytime you clean internal areas of electronics.)

If it's a mechanical mouse, rotate the plastic plate that holds the ball in place. Then turn the mouse over again, and the ball and plate should fall into your hand. Clean inside the ball's chamber with alcohol on a cotton swab. Clean the ball itself with mild soapy water, and dry it thoroughly. (Don't use alcohol on a rubber ball because it dries the rubber and makes it brittle.)

Cleaning the Inside of a PC

A desktop PC should be cleaned out regularly—at least once a year. Its cooling and ventilation fans suck in a lot of air, and with that air come pollutants that can build up over time. Even a thin layer of dust on a circuit board can make it run hotter, shortening its life, and clumps of dirt and hair can prevent the free flow of air through the case.

Remove the cover from the case (following the directions that came with it on how to do so). Inside a desktop PC there may be big clumps of hair and dirt; fish these out by hand and throw them away. Then check the motherboard and expansion boards for dust accumulation, and blow it out with compressed air. If it's been a long time since the PC has been cleaned, you may want to take it outside or to an open area so you don't blow dust all over someone's work area. The motherboard doesn't have to be sparkling clean; it just needs to have the major clumps of visible debris removed. A handheld vacuum cleaner designed for electronics can come in handy if available.

Hold your breath as you blast out the dust with compressed air, or you'll be coughing from the dust flying around. It's best to do it outdoors if weather permits. Keep in mind, too, that canned air generates a blast of cold, so don't blow it on yourself or others. Some technicians use this side effect as a tool for cooling off overheated chips on a circuit board when troubleshooting.

To clean anything that involves circuit boards or chips, stay away from liquids, especially water, because of the danger of short-circuiting if the board isn't completely dry when the PC powers up. If some kind of moisture is absolutely necessary, use alcohol on a cotton swab.

Old circuit boards can build up deposits on the metal pins (contacts) along the edge; you can remove these deposits with a pencil eraser or with alcohol and a cotton swab. Avoid touching any of the circuitry, chips, or transistors on a circuit board; it's easy to damage them. Handle circuit boards only by the edges.

Other parts that tend to accumulate dust include the fan on the power supply, the fan on the processor, and the air vents in the case. Wipe off the case's air vents with a damp paper towel. For the power supply, point the compressed air nozzle at an angle to the fan opening rather than blowing straight down into it to avoid driving the dirt even deeper into the power supply box instead of blowing it out. Exercise 12.4 walks you through cleaning a desktop computer.

EXERCISE 12.4

Cleaning a Desktop Computer

1. Turn off the PC, and unplug it.

2. Clean all the externally accessible plastic surfaces with a spray cleaner designed for electronics and paper towels or a soft cloth.

3. Clean the mouse, using whatever techniques are most appropriate for the model.

4. Clean the keyboard, including turning it upside down and shaking it to remove debris under the keys. Clean the individual keys with the spray cleaner and paper towels or cloth.

5. Clean the monitor screen with a spray or towelette cleaner designed for monitors. Don't spray the cleaner directly onto the monitor surface.

6. Remove the cover from the case. Remove any clumps of hair or dirt with your fingers.

7. If there is additional dust inside, vacuum it out with a vacuum designed for electronics, or blow it out with compressed air.

8. Wait for all damp areas to dry, and then plug the computer back in and restart it.

Notebook PCs and all-in-ones also need to be cleaned out periodically, although not as often as desktops because there is less airflow in them and the vents are smaller, so less debris tends to accumulate. Non-desktop models are often harder to get into; you may need to obtain instructions from a service manual to know which screws to remove to open one and access its inner spaces where dust and dirt may have accumulated.

Moisture inside a PC can be a problem in humid environments because water conducts electricity, which can create short-circuiting. Many server rooms have environmental dehumidifiers to control moisture in the atmosphere. You may wish to use a room-based dehumidifier if your region is prone to high summer humidity.

Cleaning a Printer and Replacing Consumables

All types of printers can be cleaned on the outside with a cloth dampened with a spray cleaner for PCs. This won't make the printer perform any better, but it will make for a nicer working environment.

The only parts inside an inkjet printer that need cleaning are the inkjets, and these aren't cleaned by hand—a utility built into the printer cleans them. The ink in an inkjet printer is liquid; if the printer isn't in frequent use, the ink dries out and bits of dried ink remain in the nozzles. The cleaning procedure flushes out any dried-up ink. It uses some ink to do so, so don't clean the inkjets unless the print quality has declined.

On most inkjet printers, there are two ways to activate the cleaning utility: pressing a sequence of buttons on the printer itself or using the cleaning utility in the printer's software. For example, Figure 12.11 shows the Clean Printhead option on an HP inkjet printer; there are also commands for aligning print cartridges and printing test pages.

FIGURE 12.11 Menu options on an HP inkjet printer

Laser printers use toner rather than ink. Because toner is a dry substance (a mixture of plastic resin and iron oxide), it doesn't clog things the way liquid ink does. However, toner is a loose powder that can scatter over clothing and the work area if the cartridges aren't handled with care. Clean up any spilled toner with a vacuum designed for electronics or with a damp paper towel. If it gets on clothing, you can get it out with a magnet, because toner is half iron. Don't use a regular vacuum cleaner: general-use vacuums don't have fine enough filters, so the toner particles can pass through them and get into the air where they become a health hazard to breathe.

Several specific parts of a laser printer can accumulate toner, making them less effective over time. Depending on the age and model of the printer, though, these parts may or may not be reachable. Consult the manual that came with the printer to find out what you can do to clean your laser printer. Always be careful inside a laser printer as there are components hot enough to burn you or give you an electric shock.

Consumables is another name for the ink or toner cartridges in a printer, the paper, and any other parts that regularly must be replaced, such as a felt cleaning pad on some models of laser printers.

When considering what printer to buy, it is prudent to look at the TCO, or total cost of ownership. This includes not only the initial cost of the printer but also the cost of the consumables.

Each printer has a specific procedure for replacing consumables; follow the instructions for your model. Here are some general tips, though:

Inkjet Tips

- On an inkjet printer, the printer will tell you when it's low on ink or completely out. You may also notice degradation in image quality or a missing, faded, or striped color on some printouts.

- The printer may have a sequence of buttons you have to press to bring the ink cartridge into view where it's accessible, or the cartridge may move into an accessible position when you open the lid.

- There is usually a lever or button you press to release the old cartridge. Then it slides out of a groove or socket.

- Unwrap the new cartridge, and remove the piece of tape that is covering the metal contacts on the bottom of the cartridge. Insert it firmly into the socket in the same orientation as the one you removed. Then close the printer.

- The printer may ask you to print a test page or to clean or align the print heads. Do whatever it suggests. Check the manual as needed.

Laser Tips

- On a laser printer, the printer will indicate when it's getting low on toner. At this point, you may be able to get a bit of extra life out of the cartridge by taking it out and shaking it gently from side to side. Don't turn it upside down or tilt it, or toner may fall out. Handle it very gently.

- A new toner cartridge may have multiple pieces of tape or plastic guards on it to prevent toner leakage. Make sure you remove them all before inserting the cartridge.

- The printer may recognize the new toner cartridge immediately, or you may have to use the printer's menu system to let it know that it has new toner.

Both ink and toner cartridges can be recycled. Recycling companies often offer free shipping bags that you can use to send in your used cartridges. Some companies even pay you (a small amount) for empty toner cartridges.

Using refilled ink or toner cartridges can void your printer's warranty. Don't attempt to refill cartridges yourself, as tempting as that may seem. It's messy, and if you do it wrong, you can damage your printer. In addition, some cartridges have print heads or drums built into them, and those parts need replacing as often as you replace the ink or toner. Reusing them results in degraded print quality.

Cleaning Removable Media

Disc drives that read removable media like CDs and DVDs don't usually require any cleaning. The discs themselves, however, can sometimes become dirty or damaged such that they won't play properly without some rehab. To remove fingerprints, buff them off gently with a soft cloth. If the surface is grimy or sticky, use an alcohol-dampened towelette or cloth, and air-dry the disc thoroughly before use.

Is the problem more than just a few fingerprints? Some scratches on a disc can be minimized by using a scratch-remover kit, to the point that the disc is made readable. These kits are available for home use, and you can easily find them for purchase online.

Proper Device Placement

Computers are fairly sturdy, but they are susceptible to a few risks. Some of the more apparent ones are water and electrical shock, but heat, humidity, dust, dirt, and other issues can harm them as well. Some basic common sense can go a long way toward mitigating any risks, and that includes placing computers in an area that allows for optimal performance. In the following sections, you'll learn some placement principles to keep a computer physically safe and healthy.

Checking the Weather Forecast

PCs generate a lot of heat when they operate; cooling fans and heat sinks help channel the heat away. The cooler the room in which the PC sits, the easier it is for those components to stay cool. Don't make the room too cool, though, because at very low temperatures (below freezing), frost build-up can become an issue. The heat from the PC melts the frost, which creates water, and with water comes the possibility of short-circuiting. Ideally, computers will operate in room temperatures or slightly cooler environments.

In the past, computers were more sensitive to temperature than they are today. At one time it was common to find a computer room at a corporate headquarters where a raised floor kept cool air circulating, where the air conditioning was on high, and where employees dressed warmly all year round. Today these huge computers have mostly been replaced by ordinary-looking PCs that don't require any special temperature treatment. The main reason PC cooling requirements are now less stringent is that today's CPUs run at much lower voltages. Still, it pays to remember that PCs like the cold more than people do. If the people are cold, the PC is probably comfortable. If the people are hot, the PC is probably very hot.

Storage temperature for PC components is less of an issue than operating temperature, but extremes still must be avoided. Don't store your PC in an unheated shed in a cold climate all winter, and don't leave it baking in the back seat of a car in the summer months. When you bring a PC inside after it has been very cold or very hot, let it sit until its temperature is the same as that of the room before turning it on. This is especially important when bringing it in from the cold, because condensation can create dampness inside the PC.

Computers subjected to ultra-hot temperatures, such as in building fires, will probably not work anymore because plastic parts will have melted. However, the hard disk might still have recoverable data. Try connecting the hard disk to another computer to see if it is readable. If it contains very important data and can't be read normally, a data-recovery service may be able to help (although not cheaply).

Along with the temperature, remember to mind the humidity. If the humidity is too high, you run the risk of developing condensation. If it's too low, then ESD will be prevalent. The ideal humidity is around 50 percent, but you should be okay in the 40–80 percent range.

Ensuring Proper Airflow

Proper airflow around a computer helps it stay cool. The exhaust fans can expel hot air from inside the case, and the intake vents will bring in cooler air. The ideal location for computers is in an open environment where they can breathe and stay cool. Some computer desks have convenient cubbyholes to put computers in—those are a bad idea. Enclosed or confined spaces don't let air circulate well, which will make the computer run hotter than it should.

There is one necessary evil that comes with placement in an open area, and that is dust accumulation. Dust is almost everywhere, whether you can see it or not. And having the computer constantly suck in air and push it back out through exhaust fans means that dust comes with the territory. If dust accumulates on components, they will trap heat more efficiently (not a good thing) and therefore heat up quicker. Dust is also electrically charged, meaning that dusty areas are more prone to ESD. The solution is to periodically open the case and clean out the dust, as discussed earlier in this chapter.

Avoiding Electromagnetic Interference

Electromagnetic interference (EMI) is caused when electricity passing nearby generates a magnetic field that interferes with the operation of a cable or device. Another name for this is *crosstalk*. It occurs only when the PC is on, and it goes away when the PC is off. It causes no permanent damage (usually) but can cause data loss if the affected cable is transporting data. EMI affects only copper cables, not fiber-optic ones.

The CompTIA IT Fundamentals objectives include the acronym EMP, which stands for electromagnetic pulse, in the Acronyms list. The most common usage of this term pertains to electromagnetic interference caused by nuclear blasts, which has little to do with computers and is hopefully something you never have to deal with. EMP can also come from lightning strikes, electric motors, and switching equipment such as lifts and magnetic door locks. Make sure you know what EMP stands for, but you shouldn't need to know much more about it than that.

EMI can come from unshielded cables, high-voltage power lines, radio transmitters, motors (even those on refrigerator compressors), microwave ovens, cordless phones, fluorescent lights, and other sources. Electricity passing through a wire generates a magnetic field, and magnetic fields generate electricity. Most computer cables move data via electrical pulses, so a changing magnetic field builds up around the cable. When one cable runs next to another, each cable's changing magnetic field can interfere with the data being sent along the other cable. Why? Because changing magnetic fields generate electricity, and the pattern of electricity through the cable is what forms the data being sent. When that pattern is altered, the data can become corrupted.

EMI may be a problem when a data cable isn't carrying its data reliably to its destination. For example, perhaps a printer is printing garbage characters interspersed with the normal characters, or perhaps a network connection keeps timing out due to transmission errors. Power cables can also be susceptible to EMI; this can manifest itself as a power fluctuation. Power fluctuations, in turn, can cause lasting damage to equipment, so in that sense EMI is capable of causing permanent damage.

One way to avoid EMI problems from unshielded cables is simply not to run any cables next to one another and not to allow a cable to be placed near any other cable. This isn't often practical, though, because most computer users have a tangle of cables behind their PCs going in many directions. More specifically, avoid running network cables and power cables next to each other. If you do have EMI issues, troubleshoot them as they occur by selectively moving cables that seem to be having problems.

 The reason that unshielded twisted pair (UTP) cables are twisted is to reduce the interference from EMI.

Another way to minimize EMI is to select the proper cables to begin with. Shorter cables are less prone to EMI than longer ones, so use the shortest cable that will do the job. Many cables sold these days are shielded, which means they have a special wrapping that minimizes EMI interference. Buying shielded cables, although more expensive, can help greatly with EMI problems. EMI problems caused by external sources, such as power lines, can be difficult to solve; sometimes moving the devices to a different area in the room or building can help.

Surveying for Other Dangers

Temperature, humidity, airflow, dust, and EMI can all pose dangers to computers, but there are other threats out there as well. Some of the main categories include liquids, magnets, and physical damage.

LIQUIDS

Water and electronics don't mix. Do whatever you can to keep water away from your computer. This includes not setting beverages near the computer where they can be knocked over into it, not setting cold items on an air vent that may drip water from condensation into the PC, and not spraying liquid cleaning products directly onto the PC, especially anywhere near its air vents.

A computer damaged by flooding or submersion in water may be beyond repair, but to maximize the chances of recovering some of the data, you should disassemble the computer and dry the pieces out thoroughly, and then reassemble it before attempting to turn it on. Any water left in crevices can cause a short circuit, ruining whatever is left of the computer's functionality.

MAGNETS

Magnets and computers don't mix. You learned in the discussion of EMI that changing magnetic fields generate electricity. A magnet can create an electrical charge in a component just by being near it, and that charge can harm the component or cause data corruption in magnetic storage devices such as hard disks. For this reason, you shouldn't use magnetic screwdrivers or other magnetized tools inside a PC. Toolkits designed for use with electronics are non-magnetized.

PHYSICAL TRAUMA

Computers aren't highly susceptible to physical trauma, but it's always best to handle them with reasonable care. Everyday bumps like inadvertently kicking a PC that is sitting on the floor probably won't cause any problems, but knocking a PC off a table while it's running can cause some damage.

There are two reasons why physical trauma is bad for a PC. One is that it causes parts to come loose. If someone drops a bare circuit board and it hits the floor just right, a wire connecting a chip or resistor to the board can come undone, or some solder can be knocked off. Most people don't have the skill to repair a circuit board, so a board with a broken connection is basically ruined. Connectors inside a PC can come loose as well. For example, the cables that connect drives to the motherboard can work loose, as can power supply plugs to drives. Circuit boards can also pop out of expansion slots, and chips can pop out of their sockets.

The other reason to avoid physical trauma pertains specifically to magnetic hard disks. A hard disk has read/write heads that skim just above the surface of the drive. When the drive is subjected to physical trauma, those heads can bounce, scratching the surface of the drive and causing disk errors. The risk of this type of damage is less when the computer is off because the read/write heads move into a parked position away from any data when the drive powers down.

"Be careful" is the best advice to follow for avoiding physical trauma. Examine your work area for hazards such as cords running across a path where people walk or devices sitting too near the edge of a table. Make any corrections you can to ensure a safer work area. If you accidentally jar a PC so that it stops working, remove the cover and check that all the connections are snug. For a notebook computer, invest in a well-padded carrying case for use whenever you transport it. Exercise 12.5 walks you through checking a work area for potential risks.

EXERCISE 12.5

Looking for PC Environment Risks

1. Check to make sure there are no cables stretching across areas where people walk.

2. Check to see where the PC is plugged in. Is there a surge suppressor or UPS? If so, does it have a light on it that indicates whether it's in good operating condition?

3. Check to see whether the PC is near the edge of the desk or whether it's in any danger of being accidentally knocked off the desk.

4. Evaluate the temperature and humidity in the room. Could the room temperature be cooler without making people uncomfortable? The ideal humidity for a computing environment is around 50 percent; would a humidifier or dehumidifier be useful?

5. Check what you're wearing. Are you wearing artificial-fiber clothing that generates static electricity?

6. Look for any food or drink hazards at the workstation. Is there any food or liquid in danger of coming into contact with any part of the computer?

Using Proper Disposal Methods

Certain computer components and consumable supplies can pollute the environment if you dispose of them along with your regular trash. That's why, in some countries, laws or guidelines require special disposal techniques for certain items. The laws vary depending on the country and state in which you reside, so it's important to familiarize yourself with what's required in your region. In addition, even if your region doesn't require a certain environmentally friendly disposal technique, you may wish to go the extra mile to help the environment and practice that disposal method anyway. When in doubt, find a recycling center or other authorized disposal company.

Restriction of Hazardous Substances

In 2003, the European Union passed the *Restriction of Hazardous Substances (RoHS)* Directive, and it took effect in 2006. This directive restricts the use of six hazardous materials in the manufacture of various types of electronic equipment. These six substances are lead, mercury, cadmium, hexavalent chromium, polybrominated biphenyls, and polybrominated diphenyl ether. (The latter two are flame retardants used in some plastics.) RoHS is closely linked to the Waste Electrical and Electronic Equipment (WEEE) Directive, which sets collection, recycling, and recovery targets for electrical goods.

Consumer electronic components that may be affected by RoHS include just about anything with a circuit board in it, including computers, cell phones, routers, and printers.

RoHS is primarily an issue on which device manufacturers focus; consumers aren't required by law to do anything. However, consumers are strongly encouraged to dispose of items that contain one or more of the six restricted substances by recycling electronic components or delivering them to a hazardous-materials facility rather than discarding them in the trash.

RoHS doesn't require specific product labeling, but many manufacturers have adopted their own compliance marks. Visual indicators may include "RoHS Compliant" labels, green leaves, check marks, and "PB-Free" markings. The WEEE trashcan logo with an X through it is also an indicator that the product may be compliant (see Figure 12.12).

FIGURE 12.12 The WEEE Directive logo

Monitor Disposal

As you learned in Chapter 2, "Peripherals and Connectors," CRT stands for cathode ray tube; it's the older, boxy type of monitor. LCD monitors have largely replaced CRTs, but there are still CRTs in service that are now reaching the end of their useful lives. Therefore, CRT disposal is a very timely topic.

Along with the glass that can shatter and cause problems and the potentially lethal capacitors, CRTs contain many environmentally harmful chemicals. Older CRTs contained phosphorous as well. Phosphorous is volatile, and it can explode or start a fire when it combines with the oxygen molecules in water. Therefore, in most regions, it's illegal to dispose of a CRT with your regular trash. You must take it to a community recycling or hazardous-waste disposal facility or pay a recycling company to dispose of it for you.

LCD monitors include circuit boards that contain a small amount of lead, and they're treated similarly to desktop PCs in their disposal.

Scanner Disposal

Scanners aren't quite as bad for the environment as monitors are, but they are still pretty bad. They contain a glass screen, like a monitor does, and also chemicals that are hazardous to the environment. By recycling a scanner, it's possible that the glass and metals can be used for the manufacture of other items. Plus, it's less hazardous material sitting in landfills.

Battery Disposal

All batteries contain toxic substances, such as metals, and can contaminate the environment. Wet-cell (lead-acid) batteries, such as those used in cars and boats, are the most environmentally harmful and have the most stringent disposal guidelines. However, dry-cell batteries, such as those used in PCs and other electronics equipment, are also environmentally hazardous. They contain heavy metals such as mercury, lead, cadmium, and nickel, all of which can contaminate the environment when not disposed of properly, and they can release toxic chemicals into the air when incinerated.

Some of the places where batteries are used in PCs include the following:

- Portable computing devices (laptops, phones, and so on)

- Wireless input devices, such as wireless mice and keyboards

- Motherboards

- Uninterruptible power supplies (UPSs)

Most regions have laws requiring retailers that sell certain types of batteries also to collect them for recycling. The exact rules depend on the battery type and the region. For example, the Battery Directive in the EU (2006) regulates the manufacture and disposal of batteries in the EU. These regulations don't require consumers to recycle; they only require retailers to make that option readily available. The same is true in the United States. Consumers aren't required to recycle most batteries, but vendors are required to take them if consumers want to bring them back.

 One way to reduce the environmental impact of batteries is to use rechargeable ones. The U.S. Environmental Protection Agency estimates that one in five dry-cell batteries purchased in the U.S. today is rechargeable. Over its life, each rechargeable battery may substitute for hundreds of single-use batteries.

Printer Ink and Toner Disposal

The toner used in laser printers and photocopiers is carcinogenic, so proper disposal of toner is a matter of public safety. Toner cartridges should be returned to the manufacturer or another company that reclaims and recycles them. Handle toner cartridges with some respect to keep the toner from spilling on you and to keep it out of the air where it could enter a person's lungs. (That's why you shouldn't use a regular vacuum cleaner to clean up toner spills—the air filter isn't fine enough to catch the toner particles, so they get back into the air.)

Printer ink cartridges contain some of the same heavy metals mentioned before as are in batteries and CRT monitors. Recycling them is the best way to go as well.

Hard Drives and Other Computer Component Disposal

Working personal computers can often be donated to charitable organizations that recover and restore them so they can be reused by others in your hometown or halfway across the world. Even a nonworking computer can often be repaired to working condition. For that reason, and to protect your privacy, you should erase the data on your hard disk before disposing of a computer.

Nonworking computer parts should be discarded at local recycling or hazardous-waste disposal centers rather than thrown in the trash, because they may contain components that can be reclaimed. For example, circuit boards contain lead solder, and some of them have coin-style batteries as well.

Cleaning-Supply Disposal

Some of the cleaning supplies used on IT equipment can be hazardous to the environment. Most of the really nasty stuff is associated more with the manufacturing of electronics than with its everyday use, but it still pays to be careful.

You should be able to find disposal instructions on the container of any cleaning chemical. There are different rules in different regions, so check the label. For example, in the U.K., the Control of Substances, Hazardous to Health (COSHH) regulations describe how hazardous substances are to be used, stored, and disposed.

Rather than put complete disposal and handling instructions on the packaging, some products refer you to a material safety data sheet (MSDS) on their website. The MSDS explains what hazards are present in the item, and it dictates the proper disposal and handling of the item.

Summary

This chapter covered important environmental and safety concepts related to computers. The intent of the chapter was to provide a good foundation in how to safely interact with a computer, so that no personal injury or harm to the environment occurs. Following all manufacturer safety guidelines is required for proper safety.

The first topic was ergonomics, which is related to how people interact with their computers. Most people don't intend to have bad posture or otherwise damage themselves when they interact with a computer, but in fact that's what most people do. By following good ergonomic principles, such as sitting upright with both feet flat on the floor, people can avoid injury or pain from using a computer.

The second topic was power and electricity. Everyone knows that computers need electricity to operate, but the power needs to be controlled—too much or too little is no good. There are differences between countries in how much power is supplied, and the power supply can be switched to an appropriate setting based on the locale the machine is in. Maintaining the right power is also critical, and UPSs can help protect a system from brownouts or power spikes. ESD can damage computers, even when undetected by people. Energy-efficient devices and settings within an operating system can save energy as well as money.

Third was device care and placement. Preventive maintenance might not seem directly related to safety, but improper maintenance to computer equipment can result in personal injury or harm to computers. It's important to know how to clean equipment to avoid having problems later. Placement is important too, in order to ensure that the computer operates in the right temperature and humidity, gets the right airflow, avoids EMI problems, and stays clear of liquids, magnets, and other physical hazards.

The chapter closed with a discussion on proper disposal methods. Many computer components contain materials that are hazardous to people and the environment and should be disposed of via recycling centers.

Exam Essentials

Understand the proper sitting position for working with a computer. Users should be seated upright or slightly reclined, with both feet flat on the floor or a footrest. The chair should provide lower back (lumbar) support. Arms should be at the sides, with elbows bent approximately 90 degrees.

Understand proper keyboard and mouse placement. The keyboard and mouse should be placed so the user's elbows can be at a 90 degree angle, and there is little or no flex needed in the wrists. The devices should also be close together to avoid reaching.

Know what the proper monitor placement is. The top of the monitor should be eye level or slightly lower. The screen should be at least 18″ from the eyes, up to about arm's length away. Users should be able to look straight ahead or slightly downward at their monitor, not upward.

Understand international differences in power sources. You don't need to memorize the power output of national power grids, but do know that it's different in various countries. For example, the United States has 120V power and most of Europe has 240V power. The power supply on computers has a switch to set it for the region it's used in.

Know what device can help protect computers from power surges or brownouts. Surge protectors and UPSs can help protect against power surges. Only a UPS contains batteries to supply computers with power in the event of a low-power or no-power state.

Understand what ESD is and how to avoid it. Electrostatic discharge is static electricity. It gets released when one object touches an object with a different charge, and it can damage computer components at levels undetectable to humans. Avoid it by maintaining proper levels of humidity and using antistatic wrist straps, mats, and bags.

Know how to conserve energy when using computers. Options include using energy efficient hardware, as well as setting power options within an operating system to power down devices that are inactive.

Know how to properly clean computer components. The proper method depends on the component, but good rules of thumb are to avoid water or anything with harsh chemicals in it.

Understand proper device placement. Ensure that the computer has proper airflow, with around 50 percent humidity and low dust, is kept at room temperature or cooler (but not freezing), and is not near any potential sources of EMI.

Understand proper computer disposal techniques. Computer components often have heavy metals or other materials that are hazardous to the environment. Don't throw components in the trash. Take them to an approved recycling center.

Chapter 12 Lab

Properly disposing of used computer parts is a very important topic, yet it's something that most people don't know how to do. Bigger devices such as monitors might be more top of mind for people, because they're not disposed of regularly. Batteries are perhaps the easiest to "forget" to recycle and simply throw in the trash. If you or your family uses quite a few batteries, you should set up a small box or other container next to your trash for their disposal, so you can take them to a recycling place.

For many, it's a behavior change to recycle batteries and other hazardous materials. One of the most common excuses is that they don't know where to take recyclable parts. This lab will remove that barrier. Using the Internet, find three computer recycling places near you. Is there cost for disposing of items? Consider places that will accept working components as well as ones that take anything.

Review Questions

1. You need to purchase an inkjet printer cartridge, and you want to see what chemicals are in it. How do you obtain the MSDS for this product?

   A. You are not legally allowed to have an MSDS for this product.

   B. Visit the website of the printer cartridge manufacturer.

   C. The store is required to give you one at the time of purchase.

   D. It's contained in the packaging of the printer cartridge.

2. When cleaning a monitor, you should not use cleaning solutions that contain what?

   A. Water

   B. Alcohol

   C. Ammonia

   D. All of the above

3. When considering ergonomics, where should the keyboard and mouse be placed?

   A. Level with the user's elbows

   B. Six inches below the user's elbows

   C. Six inches above the user's elbows

   D. On the computer desk where they work

4. What is the approximate minimum level of static charge for humans to feel a shock?

   A. 30 volts

   B. 300 volts

   C. 3,000 volts

   D. 30,000 volts

5. Geri, a user, is complaining of neck pain and thinks it's because of work. What should you check to see if it's a problem?

   A. If her monitor is too high or too low

   B. If her monitor is too far away or too close

   C. If her keyboard and mouse are level with her wrists

   D. If she is not sitting properly with her feet flat on the floor

6. Why does static electricity not kill you, given that it is a high-voltage shock?

   A. Short duration

   B. Low amps

   C. It's DC volts, not AC

   D. Low resistance

7. Which of the following can cause data loss via crosstalk between adjacent cables?

   A. ESD

   B. RFD

   C. EMI

   D. MSDS

8. Which of the following contains a carcinogen and therefore needs to be recycled?

   A. Laser printer toner

   B. Inkjet ink cartridges

   C. Scanners

   D. Batteries

9. In an ergonomic assessment, which of the following is true about the optimal sitting position?

   A. Feet should be flat on the floor or on a footrest.

   B. The hips should be at a 90 degree angle to the top of the legs.

   C. Elbows should be at the sides and at a 90 degree angle.

   D. A and B

   E. A and C

   F. B and C

   G. A, B, and C

10. You are recycling non-working computer parts. Which components contain capacitors and should not be opened? (Choose two.)

    A. CRT monitors

    B. LCD monitors

    C. Power supplies

    D. Spinning hard drives

11. You are configuring an office with new computers. What should you recommend the temperature be set at for optimal desktop computer performance?

    A. Warmer than is comfortable for humans

    B. The same as is comfortable for humans

    C. Colder than is comfortable for humans, but not freezing

    D. Below freezing

12. Which of the following is a more common name for ESD?

    A. Static electricity

    B. Radio frequency interference

    C. Magnetic interference

    D. Battery backup

13. You need to purchase a battery backup system for a desktop PC. What type of device do you need?

    A. API

    B. RFI

    C. UPS

    D. EMI

    E. ESD

14. You have four AA alkaline batteries that you just removed from a remote-control device. What is the recommended way to dispose of these batteries?

    A. Throw them in the trash.

    B. Flush them down the toilet.

    C. Incinerate them.

    D. Take them to a recycling center.

15. What is the optimal humidity level for computer operation?

    A. 30 percent

    B. 50 percent

    C. 70 percent

    D. 90 percent

16. What is the recommended way to get debris out from under the keys of a keyboard?

    A. Dig it out with a screwdriver.

    B. Blow it out with compressed air.

    C. Heat it until the debris burns up.

    D. Use a magnet.

17. Which of the following measures can be implemented to reduce the risk of ESD? (Choose two.)

    A. Antistatic wrist strap

    B. Antistatic bag

    C. Antistatic hair net

    D. Shuffling your feet

18. You are placing computers at users' workstations. What consideration should you make for airflow, if any?

    A. No airflow considerations need to be made.

    B. Place the system to minimize airflow around the computer to reduce dust.

    C. Place the system to maximize airflow around the computer.

    D. Place the system on the edge of the desk to maximize airflow.

19. Your home office experiences frequent power surges. You want to purchase a device to protect your computer equipment. What should you buy? (Choose two.)

    A. UPS

    B. Surge protector

    C. Power strip

    D. Power generator

20. What is the name of the directive that restricts the use of six hazardous materials in the manufacture of various types of electronic equipment?

    A. MSDS

    B. RoHS

    C. ESD

    D. EMI

Appendixes

Appendix A

Answers to Written Labs

Chapter 1: Core Hardware Components

For this lab, there are not necessarily any right answers. The goal was to get you to compare specifications and get more familiar with the language used to describe PCs. As I mentioned, all three of these desktop PCs were the same price on a major electronics retailer's web site. It's almost shocking how much specifications can differ from computer to computer, even at the same price point. It's always best to shop around. Here are my thoughts on answers to this lab:

Based on the system specifications, which one would you recommend and why?   It's between System A and System L. You probably can't go wrong with either. System A is probably a touch quicker, but you might not notice unless you have superhuman abilities. System L is probably better if you are more concerned with future expansion. If it's a tossup, it might come down to product reviews, which brand you like better, or even which case you think looks better.

What specifications made you not choose the others?   System D does not appear to be a good choice due to the small hard drive. You get a lot less SSD space than you do HDD space for the same money. Plus, System D does not have a memory card reader. If this person takes a lot of photos, they might just want to pop the memory card into the computer for easier file transfers. (We haven't talked about external storage yet—we'll do that in Chapter 2. But some of you might have noticed that and called it out as a reason.)

If you were looking for a computer for someone who played a lot of online action games, would you change your recommendation? Why?   System L is probably better for a gamer. More RAM is a plus, as is the ability to expand the RAM. Also, the video card is separate and has its own memory. That's a bonus over System A.

Which computer has the best expansion capabilities?   Probably System D, but System L isn't too bad either. System D has more types of external connectors, and it has USB 3.0. Much like the memory card reader, we haven't talked about that yet either, but that is a nice feature to have. More to come on that in Chapter 2 as well.

Chapter 2: Peripherals and Connectors

This lab could have several different answers. Here I'll provide some principles that I would use to think about the situation.

First, consider Elise's goals. She wants more storage. So that takes you toward external hard drives. She wants it to be easily accessible for multiple people. That steers you toward

NAS, which is basically multiple hard drives. She also would like some sort of fault-tolerance, which, fortunately, many NAS devices can provide.

Second, let's think about technology. Elise has a Mac, so you are probably safe going with Thunderbolt. If she gets a new Mac, or James upgrades to a new Mac, you know that those computers will have Thunderbolt support. That's good, because then they won't have wasted money on peripheral devices that they can't use any longer.

Third, look at potential expansion. If Elise gets the right NAS device, additional users will be able to use it without a problem.

So, you should go looking for a NAS device that supports Thunderbolt. In addition, you should probably start with a NAS with SSDs because they are so much faster than HDDs. They are more expensive, so you might want to consider HDD options as well. Just be sure to let Elise know that they will be a lot slower on data transfers, which she will be doing a lot of.

If NAS is out of her range, she can consider simply purchasing additional external hard drives. Price it out for her, and give her some options! If this was your business, what would you go with?

Chapter 3: Operating Systems

Using Lubuntu will probably feel quite a bit like using Windows. The interfaces have quite a few similarities in terms of navigation. Here are some hints on where you can find the utilities you need to complete the exercises you did in this chapter.

Exercise 3.1: Creating a user account. You can do this by clicking the launcher (it looks like a button with a bird on it, about where you would expect the Start button to be in Windows) and then going to System Tools ➤ Users And Groups. Click the Add button to create a new user.

Exercise 3.2: Managing storage space. Open the launcher and go to Preferences ➤ Disk Utility. This one won't work exactly like the one in Windows since it's on a virtual hard drive.

Exercise 3.3: Manipulating files. Open the launcher and go to Accessories ➤ File Manager. Once that opens, you can right-click files to perform your tasks. Or choose File Manager using the icon to the right of the launcher.

Exercise 3.4: Creating a shortcut. Right-click the desktop, and choose Create New ➤ Shortcut.

Exercise 3.5: Configuring accessibility options in Windows 7. As of now, Lubuntu does not have accessibility options like Windows does. They are committed to accessibility but have not developed it yet. For more information see https://wiki.ubuntu.com/Lubuntu/Developers/Accessibility. Maybe you can help!

Chapter 4: Software Applications

Answers will vary depending on the user.

For the OpenOffice lab, the Apache versions should work similarly to their Microsoft counterparts. If you open basic text or worksheet files, you should be fine as well. Opening more intricately formatted documents or worksheets with fancy graphs could pose some issues.

The security portion of the lab will have different answers as well. The key is to raise awareness of key security concepts so that readers are aware of the best ways to protect their computers versus malicious software.

Chapter 5: Networking Technologies and Wireless Routers

There are no right answers to Part 1 of the lab; the intent is to give you experience properly setting up a wireless router.

For Part 2, answers may vary. Note that if you were to get onto another unsecured network, you would be able to open up the Network and Sharing Center in Control Panel and see other devices on the network. This means that if you were on your neighbor's network, you could probably see the other computers on their network. As a big warning, I do not recommend doing this, because it is illegal to snoop on someone else's network in many places. Just know that if you do not secure your network, unsavory people could get on your network and see your computers and very possibly your files as well. Secure your network!

Chapter 6: Network Sharing and Storage

Answers to the lab questions:

1. Use the Create button in the upper-left corner, and choose Folder, Document, or the corresponding icon for what you want to create.

2. The up-arrow button next to Create lets you upload files.

3. In the upper-right corner, there is a button with a lowercase *i* and a circle around it. That lets you see recent activity.

4. Click the Install Drive For Your Computer link to get Drive for your hard drive and enable synchronization.

5. Click Create and then Connect More Apps to get more apps associated with your Google Drive account.

6. In the lower-left corner, you will see how much space you have used and what percentage of your allotment that is.

7. Use the gear button in the upper-right corner to change your settings such as language and time zone, as well as profile information or to buy more storage.

Chapter 7: Mobile Devices

Here are answers to the nine questions asked in the Chapter 7 lab.

1. From left to right, the three buttons are Back, Home, and Recents (or Recent Apps). Usually these are physical buttons on your Android device. Some Android devices also come with a physical button for Search and have a Menu button instead of Recents.

2. Click Google in the upper-left corner.

3. There are two ways to get to apps. The first is to use the middle icon on the row of apps at the bottom of the home page. The second is to tap the icon of six boxes in the upper-right corner.

4. The seven buttons are, from left to right: Chrome browser, Gmail, ES File Explorer, Apps, Settings, Camera, and Play Store.

5. Tap the Recents button. To close an app, touch it and swipe downward.

6. Open Settings, and scroll down to Accessibility.

7. Open Settings, and scroll down to Security.

8. Hopefully installing the app was easy! It should create an icon for you on the home screen, and you can tap the app to open it. To delete it, double-tap and choose Remove. This will not uninstall the app but just remove the shortcut from the home page.

9. In the Apps app, tap the icon in the upper-right corner that looks like three stacked boxes, and choose Manage Groups. In the Manage Groups window, tap the plus sign above the pencils on the right side. Give the new group a name. To move your app icon there, choose the group, tap the three boxes again, and select Setup Group. Tap the apps you want to be in that group (they will get a check next to them) and then tap the Back button. Those apps should be in the group you moved them to.

Chapter 8: Security Threats

As with many labs, answers can vary. The goal of this lab is to get you familiar with the different types of threats out there and the damage they can do. Education is the best way to help prevent attacks or at least mitigate the damage they do. Hopefully this lab exposed you (safely!) to some common threats so you have a better idea of what to watch out for.

1. The number will vary based on the date you pick. As of this writing, a quick check of Symantec.com showed their most recent update to include 117 new detections. If you get lucky, you might find an update with several thousand.

2. It depends on the day you pick, but most security sites will give you a security indicator from low risk to high risk.

3. According to http://uk.norton.com/top-5-viruses/promo, MyDoom was the worst of the bunch, dealing 38 billion dollars in damage, affecting two million PCs in about two hours. That's pretty impressive and scary.

4. An example of a polymorphic virus is the Virus.Win32 series, including Virus.Win32. Virut and Virus.Win32.Virut.ce. Phoenix, Evil, and Proud are the names of some other polymorphs. Michelangelo, Stone, and Disk Killer are some of the more infamous boot viruses. Multipartite viruses include Invader, Flip, and Tequila.

5. CryptoLocker is probably the most famous, but WinLock gained notoriety as well.

6. Back Orifice is relatively well known, as are the worms Sobig and MyDoom, which contained backdoor components.

7. There are many commercial password crackers, including John the Ripper, Ophcrack, Brutus, and RainbowCrack.

Chapter 9: Security Best Practices

There are no specific answers for the Chapter 9 lab.

Chapter 10: Buying and Configuring a Workstation

There are no specific answers to the Chapter 10 lab.

Chapter 11: Computer Support and Backups

There are no right or wrong answers to the Chapter 11 lab. The answers will vary based on the computer or computers you need to back up. Here's a table that will help you collect your answers:

CHAPTER 11   Lab: Information Gathered

Step	Information/Notes
Scope of backup plan	
Importance of data	
How much data	
How often data changes	
Where to store	
Backup software to use	
Configuring the backup	
Test and verify	
Backup schedule	
Documentation and notes for others	

Chapter 12: Environmental and Safety Concepts

The answers will vary based on your location. Here are some examples of sites that handle computer recycling:

Computer Recycle Center at http://www.recycles.com/

Computer Recycling Center at http://www.crc.org/

RE-PC at http://www.repc.com/

Tech Dump at http://www.techdump.org/

Appendix B

Answers to Review Questions

Chapter 1: Core Hardware Components

1. A, B, E. RAM is memory, which is a temporary data storage area. SSD is a hard drive technology for data storage, and BD-ROM discs store data as well. PCI is an expansion slot type, and PSU is a power supply unit.

2. B. A network interface card (NIC) lets your computer participate on a network, either wired or wireless. Modems require telephone lines. PSU is a power supply unit and PCIe is an expansion slot type.

3. C. PCIe is the fastest expansion slot standard in the market today. PCI is much older and slower. Of the PCIe slots, PCIe x16 is the fastest. There is no PCIe x64 (not yet anyway).

4. D. Blu-ray discs (BD-ROM) store 25 GB per side per layer. That's far more than DVDs or CDs.

5. B. The chipset on the motherboard controls communications between the processor (CPU) and memory (RAM). The motherboard itself just provides connectivity.

6. A. Joe needs to make sure his power supply has a free connector, as well as enough power to supply the drive. Hard drives do not use expansion slots. The CPU and RAM are indifferent to how many hard drives a computer has.

7. B. Many sound cards had 15-pin joystick ports on them, as well as audio input and output jacks.

8. C. A solid-state drive (SSD) will provide faster bootup times than a conventional hard disk drive (HDD). Neither RAM nor CPUs provide storage space.

9. D. Virtual memory is hard drive space used as extra memory, if your system runs low on physical memory. It's slower than physical memory, though.

10. A, B. Parallel ATA (PATA) and Serial ATA (SATA) are two hard drive connection types. PCIe and AGP are expansion slots.

11. A. The BIOS stores configuration information such as time and date but is powered by the CMOS battery when the system is off. If the CMOS battery fails, the system will no longer retain its BIOS configuration.

12. B. Monika will definitely need SODIMMs, which are made for laptops. DIMMs are for desktop computers. SODIMMS come in both DDR2 and DDR3, so without more information you don't know which one she needs.

13. D. The power supply is connected to the motherboard with a 24-pin block connector.

14. A. Cache is temporary memory that is closer to the processor than RAM and is therefore slightly quicker. It usually comes in smaller quantities, though.

15. D. Your neighbor needs RAID 1, also known as disk mirroring. It writes data to both hard drives simultaneously. If one hard drive fails, the other will still be operational.

16. C. If you want to upgrade a BIOS, the best way to do so is to flash it.

17. B. The processor, or CPU, produces the most heat of any internal component. Care must be taken to ensure that the heat is properly dissipated or the processor will fail.

18. B. Dual inline memory modules (DIMMs) use 240-pin connectors. SODIMMS are smaller. SATA and PATA are hard drive connectors that are smaller as well.

19. A, B, C. Solid-state drives (SSDs) are faster, generate less heat, and quieter than conventional HDDs. They are not cheaper per megabyte than HDDs, though.

20. A, B. Network interface cards (NICs) and modems are devices that allow your computer to communicate with other computers and therefore are communications devices.

Chapter 2: Peripherals and Connectors

1. C. Thunderbolt was developed by Apple, in partnership with Intel. eSATA and S-video are industry standards. There is no Mac Video port.

2. C, D. Keyboards can be plugged into either USB or PS/2 ports. Parallel ports were used for printers, and serial ports were used for modems and older mice.

3. B. Twisted-pair network cables are terminated with RJ-45 connectors.

4. A. HDMI is the best video connection standard available today. DVI and component video are older standards. HEMI is not a video connector.

5. A, B, D. Component video is also named RGB, standing for the three colors it uses: red, green, and blue.

6. D. Laser printers use toner, which is an ink-like plastic powder. The toner is held to the paper via weak electrical charges and then melted onto the paper via the printer's fuser.

7. B. A touchpad is a pointing device similar to a mouse. It's located on most laptop keyboards just below the keys.

8. A, E. Network attached storage and smartphones are both input and output devices. Flat screens are output, whereas scanners and webcams are input devices.

9. B. The PS/2 connector is round and used for keyboards and mice. USB is also used for both devices, but it is rectangular.

10. A. The device you are looking for is network attached storage. External hard drives will give you extra storage but do not have built-in fault tolerance such as RAID 1 or RAID 5.

11. C. SuperSpeed is a trade name for USB 3.0, so your friend is talking about USB devices. SSDs are solid state hard drives, and CRTs are monitors. eSATA is an external standard used mostly for hard drives.

12. B. Color inkjet printers use cyan, magenta, yellow, and black ink. Those cartridges are called CMYK.

13. D. A webcam allows you to record or transmit video, which is needed for a video teleconference.

14. A. RJ-11 connectors are used at the ends of phone lines, which are plugged into modems. RJ-45 connectors are used on the ends of twisted-pair network cables.

15. C. Laser printers use a fuser, which heats and melts the toner into the paper.

16. A. CRT monitors used vacuum tubes to show images, which sometimes built up static charges. The Degauss button removed the built-up charges.

17. B, D. Joysticks today typically have USB connections. Older joysticks might have plugged into a game port, which was a 15-pin connector called a DA15.

18. C. DVI connectors are digital in nature, but they are backward-compatible with analog VGA devices.

19. B, C. RJ-45 connectors are at the ends of network cables, so they are a distinct possibility. FireWire can also be used to create a network for Mac OS X or Linux computers.

20. D. Although the answer of "stop typing" might be tempting, it's probably not the best answer if Robert wants to get work done. Disabling the touchpad will keep this problem from happening.

Chapter 3: Operating Systems

1. B. An operating system provides an environment for the software to function but does not coordinate between software applications.

2. D. Linux is the only open-source OS discussed in this book.

3. A. A piece of software written for an OS will work only on that type of OS.

4. C. Chromebooks often have very small hard drives, and they are not used for file storage. By default, all files are stored on Google's cloud.

5. A. When you delete a shortcut, nothing happens to the file the shortcut pointed to. The shortcut is just an easy way to access the file.

6. D. With the FAT and NTFS file systems, you cannot rename a file, or change any of the metadata, while the file is open or in use.

7. A. iPhones come with the iOS operating system.

8. B. Moving a file is analogous to a cut and paste. It takes the file from one folder and places it in another.

9. C. Android versions are currently named after different types of sweets. iOS versions don't have nicknames. OS X was named after big cats and is now named after California locations.

10. D. Chrome OS uses the Windows Switcher key to create a screen capture.

11. C. Linux is a kernel, which is the core of an OS. Linux packages are put together as distributions and marketed as such.

12. A. Accessibility options allow you to configure a computer to be easier for people with disabilities to use.

13. D. When you copy a file, the original file remains intact, and a new version of that file is created elsewhere on the hard drive. The new version is associated with the new folder.

14. A. The answer is it depends on the OS. For example, ext3 allows for 32,000 subdirectories, and ext4 allows for 64,000 subdirectories.

15. A. A Linux-based OS is called a distribution, which is a combination of the kernel, shell, and utilities needed for a fully functional OS.

16. C. File Allocation Table (FAT) does not have built-in security. All of the other OSs listed do.

17. D. Before the hard drive can be used for file storage, it needs at least one partition. Once it's partitioned, you can format the drive, which will install a file system.

18. A. Ctrl+S is usually a hot key to save a file within Word or Excel. It does not open the Start menu.

19. B. Any data or information inside a file is part of the file itself, not the metadata for the file. Metadata is information about the file, such as its name, size, creator, and security.

20. A. Windows 7 uses the Windows NT kernel. Windows 3.11 was created before the NT kernel was. Mac OS X and Chrome OS do not use the NT kernel.

Chapter 4: Software Applications

1. C, D. The .aac and .m4a file formats are designed to replace .mp3. There is no .mp4 format, and .flac is a competing standard.

2. A. If a software product is giving you a limited number of uses, you must activate that software with the manufacturer. This typically requires you to have a software license and a product key.

3. C. Macs use .app files as applications.

4. B. The product key will be required to install or use any licensed software product. The manufacturer will include this on the installation media or email it to you.

5. A. The .iso format is used on optical media, such as CD-ROMs.

6. C. Single-user software licenses typically state that the software can be used on only one computer. John should uninstall it from the second computer unless he purchases a second license.

7.   A. The `.tiff` format produces the best quality images, along with `.png`.

8.   A. Word processing, spreadsheets, and presentation software are three examples of productivity software. Other types are email, PDF viewers, desktop publishing, personal information manager, and remote desktop software.

9.   C. Mac OS X disk image files have a `.dmg` extension.

10.   A. Drivers are designed to let the OS talk to hardware. Each piece of hardware must have a driver to work with the operating system.

11.   B. The `.tar` (tape archive) file extension is listed among the compression file formats, but it doesn't actually use compression. All of the others do.

12.   B, C. The two most important things to consider are if the software was written to work with that operating system and if the computer has enough hardware to run the application.

13.   C. If you're ever missing a driver, go to the manufacturer's website to download it, and then install it.

14.   A. Susan can go into the Software app in Control Panel to install or remove OS features, such as games.

15.   D. Microsoft Excel will use the `.xls` or `.xlsx` file extension. (It uses others too, but not any of the other options listed.)

16.   A. For security software such as antivirus protection, you should update the definition file at least once per week. Better yet, set the software to update automatically.

17.   B. Batch files, or those with a `.bat` extension, are used to execute multiple commands at the same time from the Windows command prompt.

18.   A, B. Software product keys are typically included on the package in which the installation CD-ROM was shipped. If the software was downloaded, then the manufacturer usually sends the software key via email.

19.   D. Microsoft PowerPoint, which creates presentations, uses the `.ppt` and `.pptx` extensions.

20.   A. If you receive emails with executable files from unknown sources, delete them. Some companies require you to report those types of emails to security or the IT department. In any case, do not open that attachment!

Chapter 5: Networking Technologies and Wireless Routers

1.   A, D. For network communications on a TCP/IP network, an IP address and a subnet mask are required. If you want to communicate outside your network, a default gateway is also required. DHCP servers automatically assign clients IP configuration information.

2.   A. Wired networks can provide the highest data throughput rates of any of the connection types.

3.   C. Network Address Translation (NAT) is a service run on a router that translates private IP addresses into a public IP address, so you can get on the Internet.

4.   D. Wireless routers will have a reset button on their bottom or back. Press and hold the button for about 30 seconds and the router will reset to factory specifications. If you never changed the password, then using admin would work, but I am hoping you changed the password!

5.   B. The DHCP server automatically configures clients with TCP/IP information. If the server is not able to provide information, your computer will automatically configure itself with an APIPA address, which starts with 169.254.

6.   C. The network password for clients to use is Tx$pr4y2.

7.   D. Wired connections are more secure than wireless ones, and the only wired connection listed is UTP.

8.   A. Addresses that are in the 192.168.x.x range are private IP addresses, as are those in the 10.x.x.x range and the 172.16.x.x–172.31.x.x range.

9.   C. WPA2 is the most secure wireless security protocol in use today.

10.   A. Cellular networks give you the best mobility, with a range of up to several miles. Even then, unless you go out of the range of a tower completely, you will be handed over to the next cell tower.

11.   B. The 802.11ac standard is the fastest one available on the market today. In this list, 802.11n is the next fastest, followed by 802.11g and then 802.11a.

12.   A, B. Cable Internet and DSL are the two fastest broadband options listed. Both satellite and cellular are slower.

13.   D. Cellular has the longest delay, because the signal needs to travel the farthest distance.

14.   B. Wired connections in general are faster than wireless ones, and fiber-optic cable can provide much faster speeds than copper cable can.

15.   D. If you are in a remote location, it's very possible that satellite is the only option that will work for you.

16.   B, D. Two additional security options are disabling SSID broadcasts and using MAC filtering. Neither is a true security method that will keep determined hackers off your network, but they will keep casual attackers at bay.

17.   A. The ifconfig command is used on Macs and in Linux and UNIX to show your IP address and other TCP/IP configuration information.

18.   A. The Service Set Identifier (SSID) is the wireless network name.

19.   B, C. You should always change the SSID and the administrator password on a wireless router.

20.   B. The guest network password for clients to use is tpg$2015.

Chapter 6: Network Sharing and Storage

1. D. A client-server network is one where servers control security for the network, as well as provide resource sharing and management.

2. B, D. To join a homegroup, the computer must be running Windows 7 or newer. The person who wants to join must also know the password to the homegroup.

3. A. A small network in one geographical location is a local area network (LAN). It could be either peer-to-peer or client-server depending on how you set it up.

4. B. Since all client computers are running Windows 7, you can create a homegroup. A homegroup requires a password to join, and you are able to share files across the network without requiring the users to have individual accounts on all computers.

5. C. Bluetooth devices create personal area networks (PANs) called piconets. Multiple piconets can be connected to form a scatternet.

6. B. Mary should have Modify privileges. If you give her full control, she can take ownership and grant others access. Read will not let her make changes. There is no Edit share permission.

7. D. In this situation, all users will need user accounts on all computers. Five users on five computers means 25 total user accounts.

8. D. If the printer is attached to Martha's local computer, then her system needs to be operational for others to use her printer.

9. D. Client-server networks are also called domains. A server (or multiple servers) manages security and is often called a domain controller.

10. A. Google Drive and Google Docs are examples of Software as a Service, or SaaS.

11. B. Direct attached storage (DAS) is the best choice here for quick and cheap storage. DAS can be as simple as an external hard drive.

12. B. The Secure File Transfer Protocol (SFTP), also called the SSH File Transfer Protocol, uses SSH for security. It also uses port 22.

13. A. The proper context to use when mapping a shared drive is *servername**sharename*.

14. C. A network drive is a mapped logical drive on your computer, pointing to a shared drive on another computer.

15. A. Network attached storage (NAS) is an external hard drive (or multiple hard drives) complete with its own file management and sharing software.

16. B. Cloud computing uses virtualization, which means that multiple servers can be created on one physical server.

17. A, D. There are two options for directly connecting two PCs to each other. The first is a USB direct link cable. The second is a Cat 5 (or Cat 6) crossover cable. It needs to be a crossover cable so that the signals sent from one end are directed to the receive pins at the receiving end.

18. C. Web servers use HTTP, which uses port 80. That was most likely blocked. HTTPS, which is secure, uses port 443. FTP uses ports 20 and 21.

19. B. Since all computers are running Windows 7 or newer, you can configure them as a homegroup to share resources. Homegroups are easier to configure and share resources within than workgroups.

20. B, C. HTTPS can use either TLS or SSL for encryption of its connection.

Chapter 7: Mobile Devices

1. A. To scroll down, you need to "pull" the page up, so swipe up.

2. B. POP3 uses 110, IMAP uses port 143, and SMTP uses 25. HTTPS uses port 443.

3. B and D. To zoom in on a map, you double tap or use reverse pinch.

4. C. SMTP is used to send email. IMAP and POP3 are receiving protocols. SNMP is a network management protocol.

5. D. The gyroscope detects rotational movement within a mobile device.

6. A. IMAP natively uses port 143. IMAP with SSL uses port 993. POP3 uses ports 110 and 945 with SSL.

7. B. Not all apps support rotation, and Settings is one of them. The app needs to be specifically programmed to support rotation.

8. C. To have two Bluetooth devices communicate with each other, they need to be paired.

9. C. With biometrics enabled, she can use either the passcode or her fingerprint to access a locked device.

10. D. Bluesnarfing is stealing data using a Bluetooth connection. Bluejacking is sending a spam message via Bluetooth.

11. B. The Wi-Fi settings are in the Settings app in Android as well as in iOS.

12. A. The Simple Mail Transfer Protocol (SMTP) is used to send email. It uses port 25. Internet Message Access Protocol (IMAP) is used to retrieve email and uses port 110.

13. D. The proper steps in order are to verify wireless capabilities, turn on Wi-Fi, locate SSID, enter the wireless password, and verify the Internet connection.

14. B, C. For syncing and backing up iPhones (and iPads), you can use iCloud to back up to the Internet or use iTunes to back up to a local computer.

15. A, B. The IMAP and POP3 protocols are used to retrieve email. SMTP is for sending email. SNMP is a network management protocol.

16. D. Airplane mode turns off all wireless connections on your mobile device.

17. B. Odds are that your company uses the same email server for incoming and outgoing messages, so using the same server name as the IMAP server will probably work. IMAP is for receiving email and not for sending.

18. D. The Google Play store has apps for Android devices. iTunes is for iOS devices only. Google Drive is the name of Google's cloud-based storage.

19. C. IMAP uses port 143. SMTP uses 25, and POP3 uses 110. HTTPS uses port 443.

20. A. For games and other apps for an iPad, she should use the iTunes store. It's accessed by tapping the App Store icon on the home page.

Chapter 8: Security Threats

1. E. Hackers may have different motivations, but their activities can include stealing usernames and passwords, modifying website content, disrupting network communications, and analyzing network traffic.

2. C. A retrovirus works by directly attacking antivirus software designed to keep it at bay. If the virus can disable the antivirus software, then it can infect the computer.

3. A, D. Examples of physical security risks include hardware damage and theft, software and license theft, shoulder surfing, and dumpster diving.

4. D. A Trojan horse might look like helpful software but will actually do harm to your computer. An example could be a program that looks like a security scanner but actually installs malware. (Ironic, isn't it?)

5. B. Going through the trash to find confidential information is considered dumpster diving, and it's illegal in most areas. Social engineering means trying to get information out of another person. Phishing is social engineering via email.

6. A. A keylogger is a program that tracks a user's keystrokes and then transmits that information back to the attacker. This can be used to gather usernames and passwords.

7. B, D. Social engineering occurs when attackers ask people for information to help them gain access to sensitive information. Examples of this are shoulder surfing and phishing.

8. B. A worm is a piece of self-replicating malware that can either do damage itself or act as a transport for other malware. If acting as a transport, the malware it carries is its payload.

9. D. Phishing is a form of social engineering where an attacker sends an email asking for personal information to use in an attack. This might also be considered spam, but phishing is more specific here.

10. C. Adware will create pop-ups advertising websites, even when you don't want it to. It's possible it was attached to the search engine that Rose downloaded.

11. C. Shoulder surfing is trying to see private information on someone else's computer. This can include information on the computer screen, but also can be something like trying to see a password.

12. B. This is one case where using a password cracker is legal and helpful. Just don't ever use one on a system where you don't have explicit permission to do so!

13. D. All current end-user operating systems are susceptible to viruses and malware.

14. A. A backdoor is an attempt to avoid normal security mechanisms. A backdoor can be as simple as using the default password if it wasn't changed, or it can be a malware program.

15. C. An armored virus covers itself with protective code, like a suit of armor, to make it harder to detect and eliminate.

16. D. Ransomware is malware that demands money or else something bad will happen to your computer.

17. A. Programs such as Microsoft Excel and Word can be modified (for good purposes) by using small programs called macros. Virus programmers can also use macros for bad purposes too.

18. B. Spam is the receipt of unsolicited emails. It can also refer to repeated messages sent by someone, which serve no purpose other than to annoy.

19. B. A multipartite virus can affect multiple areas of your computer, such as the boot sector on the hard drive and the file system.

20. D. In the UNIX world, root is the name of the all-powerful Administrator account. A rootkit will grant an attacker full control over a computer, much like an administrator would have.

Chapter 9: Security Best Practices

1. A, D. All four answers are device-hardening options. If you are worried about local theft, installing a hardware lock is a must. In addition, if your device does get stolen, encryption will prevent thieves from accessing your files unless they know your username and password.

2. D. A screensaver password will require someone to enter your password to gain access to the computer. File encryption won't help if the attacker has access to the computer as you.

3. **B, C.** You should disable Bluetooth and Near Field Communications (NFC) to help prevent attacks. Autofill is a browser setting. There is no FFC in this context.

4. **A.** Secure websites start with HTTPS://. Also tell her to look for the lock symbol nearby.

5. **D.** The only plausible answer is that someone else had your username and password and logged onto the computer as you.

6. **A, B, C.** Adware can give you a barrage of pop-ups as well as cause browser and search engine redirection.

7. **A.** A software firewall protects your computer against malicious network traffic. Antispyware and antivirus software packages are good, but they protect against malicious programs.

8. **D.** Chrome's version of private browsing is called Incognito. Microsoft's version of private browsing is called InPrivate.

9. **A.** Disabling the Guest account is a good security measure to reduce the number of entry points a potential attacker could use. You cannot disable the Administrator account, although renaming it is a good idea.

10. **C.** You should recognize untrusted source warnings and act on them appropriately. Good practices include limiting the use of personally identifiable information (PII), disabling Autofill, and updating plugins, toolbars, and extensions.

11. **B.** Multifactor authentication increases security by requiring users to use more than one method to authenticate. They need to use two or more items among something they know, something they have, and something they are.

12. **D.** Rachel is experiencing Autofill, which is a feature in a browser that automatically populates your information in the right fields when you start entering any of the information. It can be convenient, but it can also be a potential security risk.

13. **B, D.** You should use complex passwords that are still easy for you to remember. Changing default passwords is a good idea, as is not reusing a password on multiple systems or after it has been changed.

14. **E.** Shoulder surfing, keyloggers, and unsecured wireless networks are all potential security risks associated with public workstations.

15. **A, B.** Single sign-on can be a convenience for users, but it does introduce potential security risks. It does not require multifactor authentication, and it will work across different operating systems and software platforms.

16. **A, C.** Strong passwords are long, complex, and use a variety of symbols, numbers, and letters. Passwords should not contain any personally identifiable information (PII), and patterns in passwords make them easier to guess.

17. **C.** Antivirus software programs protect against worms and Trojan horses. Software firewalls can prevent malicious network traffic but do not recognize viruses or worms.

18. D. It's possible that your friend sent you a very cool executable file. It's also possible that her email has been hijacked and you've just been sent a virus or other malware. Don't click it until you talk to her first and verify that it's legitimate.

19. C, D. Two things you can do are upgrade your browser to the newest version (as well as any plugins, toolbars, and extensions) and configure security zones (if you are using IE). Enabling Autofill and accepting all cookies can increase your security risk.

20. A. Web browser plugins, toolbars, and extensions can add functionality to your web browser. To make sure you maintain the best security possible, ensure that they are updated to their most current versions.

Chapter 10: Buying and Configuring a Workstation

1. A. The first thing to determine is what the computer will be used for. Then, you can move on to determine what OS is needed, what type of system they should get, and the budget.

2. D. If the image is distorted, it's most likely due to an aspect ratio that is not correct for the monitor. For example, if you selected a standard resolution for a widescreen monitor, the image would be distorted.

3. D. Macs tend to be a little more expensive than comparable PC counterparts; therefore the correct answer is OS X.

4. D. After setting up and verifying the Internet connection, the next step is to install additional software (if applicable). If the user does not have any additional software to install, then proceed to updating security and other software.

5. A, C. The weight, battery life, and screen size are all important factors that are more relevant to laptops than they are to desktops. Having a car adapter is nice, but it is an accessory that can be purchased separately.

6. A. You probably chose a resolution that is not supported by the monitor, and it can't display it. If you wait for 15 seconds, the system will revert to the previous setting, which you should be able to see. Then choose a different resolution.

7. B, D. Android and iOS dominate the mobile market, including smartphones and tablet computers.

8. B. Widescreen monitors use 16:10 aspect ratios. High definition televisions use 16:9, and standard VGA monitors use 4:3.

9. D. The biggest advantage for Joe is that he can choose his own hardware. He can get the processor, memory, video card, and other hardware he wants without being constrained by preconfigured choices from manufacturers. He will have to buy his own OS, but this is not a major factor. Tech support will be free because he will provide it himself!

10. C. Localization settings are chosen during the initial setup wizard but can easily be changed in Windows Control Panel.

11. A, C. Graphic design workstations should have better processors, memory, and video systems than standard workstations.

12. D. The last step in the workstation setup process is to perform basic cable management tasks, such as moving them out of the way and securing them.

13. A. Home theater systems need upgraded audio and video systems. Therefore, an upgraded GPU (video card) will help the system deliver the quality that's expected.

14. C. The best time to install and configure peripherals is after installing the security software.

15. C, D. Audio/video editing workstations need superior audio and video performance. An enhanced video card with its own GPU is needed. The workstation will also need a large amount of hard drive space for storage of large files.

16. D. After configuring the Internet connection, verify that it works! The next step in the process after configuring and verifying the Internet connection is to install additional software, if applicable.

17. C. The first step in setting up a workstation is to plug in the cables.

18. B. Per the exam objectives, uninstalling unneeded software should occur after plugging in cables, powering on the computer, setting up the OS, installing security software, and configuring peripherals.

19. A. After completing the OS setup wizard, the next step is to install security software. Remember that the security software is the second most important piece of software on the computer, so it should be taken care of immediately after the OS setup.

20. C. Applications can't be deleted during the initial OS setup wizard. Deleting the icons does not properly uninstall programs, and you might still get reminders. Control Panel is the best option to remove software applications.

Chapter 11: Computer Support and Backups

1. B, C. To identify the problem, you can talk to users, gather information, and isolate the issue. Using external resources such as the Internet is part of the process to establish a theory of probable cause.

2. D. If the hard drive is not detected, or if a specific folder needed to load Mac OS X is not detected, the Mac will display a flashing question mark.

3. B. Always test the simple stuff first. Assuming user error is not a good way to endear yourself to your clients.

4. D. Whenever setting up a new backup system or making a change to an existing backup solution, verify that the backup works. Once you have done that, then you can perform other tasks.

5. A. The solution might have worked, and it might not have. Based on if it appeared to or not, you should establish a further plan of action. If it worked, you can move on to verifying full functionality. If not, you may need to go back to trying additional solutions.

6. B. The System Configuration utility, or MSCONFIG, allows users to see which applications are loading at the startup of Windows. If too many programs load on startup, it will slow down the boot process.

7. D. Older applications might not work with current operating systems unless you use compatibility mode.

8. A. The Windows Recovery Environment is a feature of Windows Vista and newer setup programs that lets you repair an installation of Windows when booting to the installation CD. All of the other options require the OS to load before using them.

9. B. The last step in the troubleshooting process, and one that is often overlooked, is to document the work. (Cleaning up is important to do if you made a mess, but it's not specifically a step in the troubleshooting process.)

10. C. Local backup solutions will always be faster than network storage or cloud-based solutions. This is because the transfer rate to a local hard disk or optical disc is faster than network connections.

11. A. A normal (or full) backup will back up all selected files and then clear the archive bit. An incremental backup will clear the archive bit as well, but it will not back up files that have not been changed since the last backup.

12. B. Always check the manufacturer's website first. Since it's hardware, check that manufacturer and not the OS manufacturer.

13. C. Incremental backups will back up only the files that have changed since the last backup. They are the quickest backups to make.

14. B. STOP errors, also known as the Blue Screen of Death (BSOD), are generated by Windows. The faulty memory module may have caused the error, but Windows generated the message.

15. D. The most likely cause of intermittent hard locks like this is an overheating system. Power the system down, give it a chance to cool off, and then inspect for damage or excessive dust in the fans. With the case open, power it back on and ensure that all cooling fans are running.

16. C. A black-screen error usually comes from the BIOS, such as a message indicating that the hard disk is not bootable.

17. C. The most likely culprits of a computer slowdown are the processor and the memory. If he can run fewer applications at once, that might help. Otherwise, he might want to consider a computer upgrade.

18. D. A POST card is a circuit board you insert into an open slot on the motherboard. It displays a two-digit code to tell you where the system is in the booting process. This is useful when nothing is displayed onscreen.

19. A. A system image makes a copy of the entire hard drive, which can be used in the case of a complete system failure. It takes a long time to make and you can't restore individual files from one like you can with a normal backup program.

20. B. The most likely cause is the power supply, since there are no fans spinning. Of course, don't forget to first check that it's plugged in!

Chapter 12: Environmental and Safety Concepts

1. B. The manufacturer of the ink cartridge will have an MSDS on their website.

2. C. Ammonia can ruin the coating on a monitor screen, so it should never be used. Many common glass cleaners contain ammonia, so be careful of them.

3. A. The keyboard and mouse should be approximately level with the user's elbows, so the elbows can be at 90 degrees and there is little to no bend required in the user's wrists. If the desk does not allow for this, then adjustments to the desk or seating arrangement should be made.

4. C. Humans can feel a shock of as little as 3,000 volts. However, computer equipment can be damaged by as little as 300 volts.

5. A. Neck issues can be caused by a monitor being too high or too low, causing the user to strain their neck up or down in order to read it. The top of the screen should be at or slightly below eye level for optimal placement.

6. B. Shocks from static electricity can hurt a bit, but generally they won't kill a person. This is because the amps of an electric shock are low.

7. C. Electromagnetic interference (EMI) can cause loss of data due to crosstalk, which occurs when one electrical signal interferes with another.

8. A. All of the answers (toner cartridge, inkjet cartridges, scanners, and batteries) should be recycled. The only one of the four that is a known carcinogen is laser printer toner.

9. G. All three answers provided are correct. Feet should be flat on the floor or on a footrest. The user should be sitting upright with the hips bent 90 degrees or slightly more. Elbows should be at the sides and at a 90 degree angle. The lower back should have lumbar support from the chair.

10. A, C. CRT monitors and power supplies contain capacitors, which can store energy even after they are powered off and unplugged. Never open either one.

11. C. Computers like it colder than humans do. Below freezing is not good though, because if there is frost, and it's heated by computer components, that can form water, which can cause a short circuit.

12. A. ESD is short for electrostatic discharge, which is static electricity.

13. C. An uninterruptable power supply (UPS) is a device with batteries in it that can power a computer in the event of a power failure.

14. D. Batteries should always be taken to a recycling center to dispose of them properly.

15. B. A good range for humidity for computers is between 40 and 80 percent, but the ideal is around 50 percent.

16. B. There are two ways to remove debris from a keyboard. The first is to blow it out with compressed air. The second is to turn it upside down and shake or tap it.

17. A, B. Antistatic wrist straps and bags are good to use to help reduce the risk of ESD. Antistatic mats to work on computers are useful as well. Shuffling your feet actually increases the risk of ESD.

18. C. Maximizing airflow around a computer is a good thing. You don't want to set the system on the edge of the desk, though, because that introduces a risk of having the computer falling off or getting knocked over.

19. A, B. An uninterruptable power supply (UPS) and surge protector can protect your computer equipment versus power surges. Power strips can accommodate multiple components but do nothing to protect against surges.

20. B. The Restriction of Hazardous Substances (RoHS) Directive, which took effect in 2006, restricts the use of lead, mercury, cadmium, hexavalent chromium, polybrominated biphenyls, and polybrominated diphenyl ether in the manufacture of various types of electronic equipment.

Index

Index

Note to the Reader: Throughout this index **boldfaced** page numbers indicate primary discussions of a topic. *Italicized* page numbers indicate illustrations.

C

T

X

Z

Free Online Learning Environment

Register on Sybex.com to gain access to the free online interactive learning environment and test bank to help you study for your CompTIA IT Fundamentals certification.

The online test bank includes:

- **Assessment Test** to help you focus your study to specific objectives
- **Chapter Tests** to reinforce what you learned
- **Practice Exams** to test your knowledge of the material
- **Electronic Flashcards** to reinforce your learning and provide last-minute test prep before the exam
- **Searchable Glossary** gives you instant access to the key terms you'll need to know for the exam

Go to http://sybextestbanks.wiley.com **to register and gain access to this comprehensive study tool package.**